The Reach of Free Movement

Mads Andenas · Tarjei Bekkedal
Luca Pantaleo
Editors

The Reach of Free Movement

ASSER PRESS

Springer

Editors
Mads Andenas
Faculty of Law
University of Oslo
Oslo
Norway

Tarjei Bekkedal
Faculty of Law
University of Oslo
Oslo
Norway

Luca Pantaleo
Faculty of Public Management, Law and Safety
The Hague University of Applied Sciences
The Hague
The Netherlands

ISBN 978-94-6265-194-4 ISBN 978-94-6265-195-1 (eBook)
DOI 10.1007/978-94-6265-195-1

Published by T.M.C. ASSER PRESS, The Hague, The Netherlands www.asserpress.nl
Produced and distributed for T.M.C. ASSER PRESS by Springer-Verlag Berlin Heidelberg

Library of Congress Control Number: 2017943109

Printed on acid-free paper

This T.M.C. Asser Press imprint is published by Springer Nature
The registered company is Springer-Verlag GmbH Germany
The registered company address is: Heidelberger Platz 3, 14197 Berlin, Germany

Contents

1 **The Reach of Free Movement and the Gradualist Approach of the CJEU: An Introduction** 1
Mads Andenas

Part I The Reach of Free Movement

2 **The Reach of Free Movement. A Defence of Court Discretion** 17
Tarjei Bekkedal

3 **Free Movement of Persons Through the Lenses of 'Discrimination' and 'Restriction'** 57
Alina Tryfonidou

4 **Restrictions on the Use of Goods and Services** 85
Stefan Enchelmaier

5 **To Use or Not to Use—That's the Question. On Article 34 and National Rules Restricting the Use of Lawfully Marketed Products** 109
Niels Fenger

Part II Justifications and Proportionality

6 **Justifications for Restrictions to Free Movement: Towards a Single Normative Framework?** 131
Vassilis Hatzopoulos

7 **The Justification and Proportionality of Certain Administrative, Regulatory and Political Concerns** 157
Pål Wennerås

8 The Guardianship of European Constitutionality: A Structural Critique of European Constitutional Review 173
Agustín José Menéndez

9 The Criterion of "Consistent and Systematic Manner" in Free Movement Law 205
Tor-Inge Harbo

Part III Fundamental Rights

10 Legitimacy and the Charter of Fundamental Rights Post-Lisbon 229
Christoffer C. Eriksen and Jørgen A. Stubberud

11 False Friends and True Cognates: On Fundamental Freedoms, Fundamental Rights and Union Citizenship 253
Francesco De Cecco

12 Fundamental Freedoms, Fundamental Rights, and the Many Faces of Freedom of Contract in the EU 273
Olha O. Cherednychenko

13 The Charter of Fundamental Rights and the Reach of Free Movement Law 293
Filippo Fontanelli and Amedeo Arena

Part IV Looking Abroad

14 Creating a National Market in the United States Through the Dormant Commerce Clause? 315
Eszter Belteki

15 Beyond Parallel Powers. EU Treaty-Making Power Post-Lisbon 367
Mads Andenas and Luca Pantaleo

Table of Cases 399

List of Contributors

Mads Andenas is Professor at the Department of Private Law, University of Oslo. He has held senior academic appointments in the United Kingdom, including Director of the British Institute of International and Comparative Law, London and Director of the Centre of European Law at King's College, University of London. He remains a Visiting Research Fellow of the Institute of European and Comparative Law, University of Oxford and a Senior Research Fellow at the Institute of Advanced Legal Studies, School of Advanced Studies, University of London. He holds the degrees of Cand jur (Oslo), Ph.D. (Cambridge) and MA and DPhil (Oxford).

Dr. Amedeo Arena is Associate Professor of European Union Law at the University of Naples "Federico II" School of Law, where he teaches EU Internal Market law. He co-authored a textbook on EU free movement law (Giappichelli, Turin, 2016) and published several articles on that subject in edited books and peer-review journals, including the Common Market Law Review, the Yearbook of European Law, and the Columbia Journal of European Law.

Tarjei Bekkedal is Professor at the Centre for European Law, University of Oslo and is also the head of the Norwegian Association for European Law. His main interests are European Law, Constitutional Law and Human Rights Law.

Eszter Belteki is currently a Ph.D. candidate in EU and Comparative Constitutional Law at Durham University. After finishing her LL.B. studies in Business Law with First Class Honours from London Metropolitan University, Eszter graduated from Durham University with a Distinction in LL.M. European Trade and Commercial Law. She was also a Michigan Grotius Research Scholar at the University of Michigan Law School and the PGR Co-Convenor and subsequently the PGR Convenor of the Durham European Law Institute.

Francesco De Cecco is Lecturer in Law at Newcastle Law School, Newcastle University (United Kingdom). He is the author of several articles, book chapters and a monograph entitled State Aid and the European Economic Constitution (Hart Publishing, 2013). Together with François-Charles Laprévote and Joanna Gray, he has recently edited the Research Handbook on State Aid in the Banking Sector (Edward Elgar, 2017).

Prof. Dr. Olha O. Cherednychenko holds the Chair in European Private Law and Comparative Law at the University of Groningen. She is also the Founder and Director of the Groningen Centre for European Financial Services Law. She has written extensively on issues relating to the impact of EU primary law and fundamental rights law on private law relationships and the interplay between public regulation of EU origin and national private law systems, in particular in the area of financial services. She has also conducted studies in the area of EU law / financial services law for national and European institutions, in particular the European Parliament.

Stefan Enchelmaier studied law, philosophy and Latin at the Universities of Cologne, Hamburg, and Edinburgh; obtained his doctorate from the University of Bonn with a thesis on European competition law, and his habilitation from the University of Munich with a thesis on comparative Anglo-German property law; following a stint in practice and academic posts in Oxford, Munich, and York, he is now Professor of European and comparative law at the University of Oxford, and a fellow of Lincoln College, Oxford.

Christoffer C. Eriksen is Professor at the Department of Public and International Law, University of Oslo. He is the author of several publications studying the relation between legal orders within and beyond state borders, including The European Constitution, Welfare States and Democracy: The Four Freedoms vs National Administrative Discretion. His current research explores the possibilities of critique of international law and global governance.

Niels Fenger is Judge in the Eastern Court of Appeal and Professor in Administrative Law at Copenhagen University, Dr.jr. (habilitation) 2004 on the relationship between EU law and national administrative law. Fenger is former head of the Legal Service at the EFTA Surveillance Authority and former legal secretary at the Court of Justice. Previously he has also held posts in the Danish Ministry of Justice and the Ministry of the Interior. Fenger is the author of 11 books and more than 90 articles on EU law, administrative law and procedural law.

Dr. Filippo Fontanelli is Lecturer of International Economic Law at the University of Edinburgh. He read Law at the University of Pisa, at the Sant'Anna

School and at NYU. He worked at Cleary, Gottlieb, Steen and Hamilton LLP and at the International Court of Justice. Dr Fontanelli is a fellow of the Higher Education Academy, a member of the Centre for Judicial Cooperation of the European University Institute, a member of the Faculty of the Master in International Law of the Universidad La Sabana (Bogota) and Visiting Lecturer at the University of Stockholm. He is co-rapporteur of the ILA Committee on the Procedure of International Courts and Tribunals.

Tor-Inge Harbo is Professor of Law at the School of Business and Law at the University of Agder, Norway. He has a Ph.D. in Political Science from the Free University in Berlin and a Ph.D. in Law from the European University Institute in Florence. He teaches in and writes on the fields of European law, European integration, international law, constitutional law, human rights law, and legal and political theory. He has held leading positions in the Norwegian public administration.

Vassilis Hatzopoulos is Professor of EU Law and Policies at the Democritus University of Thrace (Greece). He is visiting Professor at the College of Europe, Bruges (Belgium) and honorary Asst. Professor at the University of Nottingham (United Kingdom). His interests cover EU institutional law and governance, the EU internal market with special focus on service liberalisation and the provision of services of general economic interest, state aid and public procurement, as well as EU asylum and immigration law. He has published three monographs, on the principle of mutual recognition in the internal market (in French, Bruylant/Sakkoulas, 1999), on the doctrine of essential facilities under EU competition law (in Greek, Sakkoulas, 2002) and on the regulation of services in the EU (in English, OUP, 2012). He has also published over a hundred articles and case notes, in English, French and Greek, in all the major EU-related reviews and periodicals and in edited volumes. He has a longstanding experience as a lawyer, practicing before the highest national courts and the Court of Justice of the EU. He has consulted i.a. the Greek Government (on the OECD-led regulatory reform), the EU Commission (on the Services Directive) and the European Parliament (on EU patients' rights). Lately his research interests turn around the sharing economy and the EU preferential trade agreements (TTIP, CETA etc.).

Agustín José Menéndez is Lecturer of Political and Legal Philosophy, Universidad de León, Spain and research fellow at ARENA, Universitetet i Oslo. He is currently editor in chief of the European Law Journal. He is the author of Justifying Taxes, and The Constitution's Gift (together with John Erik Fossum).

Dr. Luca Pantaleo obtained a Ph.D. in International and EU Law in 2013 at the University of Macerata (Italy). His Ph.D. thesis focused on EU Member States International Agreements and EU Law. In the course of his academic career,

Pantaleo has been appointed visiting researcher in several institutions, such as the Pontifical Catholic University of San Paulo/PUC SP (Brazil), the Max Planck Institute for Comparative Public Law and International Law, and the Department of Private Law of the University of Oslo under the 'Yggdrasil' Programme. Before joining the Hague University of Applied Sciences in August 2016, he worked at the University of Luxembourg as Senior Researcher (Postdoc) and at the Asser Institute, where he served as both Senior Researcher in EU Law and Academic Coordinator of CLEER.

Jørgen A. Stubberud is advocate, cand.jur and cand.mag. He is currently a practicing lawyer and a Ph.D. student at the Faculty of Law of the University of Oslo. He is also the President of the Norwegian section of the IVR, the Norwegian Association for Legal Philosophy.

Dr. Alina Tryfonidou is Associate Professor in EU Law at the School of Law, University of Reading (United Kingdom). Before joining the University of Reading in 2011, she was a Lecturer in Law at the University of Leicester (2007-2011) and a Visiting Tutor (2005-2007) and Visiting Lecturer (2010-2011) at King's College London. Dr Tryfonidou obtained her LL.B. (2001), LL.M. (2002) and Ph.D. (2008) from King's College London and is an Associate of King's College (AKC) (2008). She is a non-practising member of the Cyprus Bar since 2003, a Fellow of the Centre of European Law at King's College London since 2007, and a Fellow of the Higher Education Academy since 2016.

Dr. Pål Wennerås is advocate, Office of the Attorney General, Norway. He holds the degrees of Cand.jur (Oslo), LL.M. (University of Amsterdam) and Ph.D. (University of Amsterdam). He has written extensively on issues relating to the enforcement of EU law, including the monograph The Enforcement of EC Environmental Law (Oxford 2007). Dr. Wennerås was awarded the IUS Commune Prize (2006).

Chapter 1
The Reach of Free Movement and the Gradualist Approach of the CJEU: An Introduction

Mads Andenas

Abstract The article introduces the topic of this book: the reach of free movement, and the book's focus on what constitutes a *restriction* to free movement. That threshold remains low, for all freedoms. However, the discussion of what constitutes restriction continues. That is not surprising: the restriction concept is the most basic component of free movement. The article sets out the argument for different tests, discrimination, market access or *de minimis* thresholds. It puts forward one explanation for the CJEU's *Keck* line of cases on selling arrangements and use restrictions. It is an incremental approach to forms of restrictions without impact on free movement in the Internal Market. The CJEU cannot replace this jurisprudence with a general test different from 'restriction', which in practice would mean that many forms of restrictions, including new ones, would not be reviewed by the CJEU. This incremental approach is in the nature of court review. Academic scholarship has criticised the *Keck* approach, and those defending it have not provided much in terms of analysis. Scholarship should be a force for coherence and convergence, and assist in the development of general free movement and Internal Market concepts. This chapter also provides an overview of the contributions in the book and explains how they fit into this project.

Keywords Free movement · Restriction · Discrimination · Market access · Selling arrangements · Use restrictions · Internal Market · Unified freedom jurisprudence · Charter of Fundamental Rights · Citizenship · Constitution

---

M. Andenas (✉)
Department of Private Law, University of Oslo, St. Olavs plass,
PO Box 6706, 0130 Oslo, Norway
e-mail: mads.andenas@jus.uio.no

M. Andenas et al. (eds.), *The Reach of Free Movement*,
DOI 10.1007/978-94-6265-195-1_1

Contents

1.1 The Topic of the Book 2
1.2 Explaining the Gradualist Approach of the CJEU 6
1.3 The Long-Term Project on the Reach of Free Movement 7
1.4 Outline of This Book 7
References 14

1.1 The Topic of the Book

The topic of this book is the reach of free movement, and the focus on what constitutes a restriction to free movement.[1]

That threshold remains low, for all freedoms. Anything that makes movement less attractive or more burdensome, which dissuades or discourages, may constitute a restriction. Restrictions require justifications, and they are only justified if they are proportionate. Discriminatory measures can only be justified if they fall into one of the explicit categories that are listed. With such a low threshold, the real review is at the justification stage, and that is a proportionality review.

However, the discussion of what constitutes restriction continues. That is not surprising: the restriction concept is the most basic component of free movement. When does free movement apply? It is fundamental in the Internal Market, both for the economic constitution and more and more for individual rights in a European legal order that provides constitutional guarantees for rights, also beyond free movement. The interaction between fundamental rights and fundamental freedoms to movement sets the EU legal order apart from the national.

Some continue to argue for different forms of discrimination tests, others that the restriction must be on market access or *de minimis* thresholds.

The CJEU has identified certain categories of state measures which only constitute a restriction if they are discriminatory. First out was *Keck*[2] in 1993, on the category of 'certain selling arrangements', as opposed to 'product bound measures' or 'product requirements'. Only if discriminatory did these selling arrangements constitute a restriction under Article 34 TFEU (ex Article 28 EC). Selling arrangements, the CJEU clarified in its subsequent jurisprudence, were certain restrictions on when, where and by whom goods may be sold (such as Sunday trading restrictions), certain restrictions on advertising and certain price controls.

---

[1] This book is one outcome of a long-term project on The Reach of Free Movement, see under Sect. 1.3 below.

[2] Joined Cases C-267/91 and 268/91 *Keck and Mithouard* [1993] ECR I-6097.

Sixteen years later, in 2009, *Commission v. Italy (Trailers)*[3] made clear that a market access criterion had to be added to the discrimination test for the *Keck* category. The same year, the CJEU in *Mickelsson & Roos*[4] kept to the limited boundaries of the *Keck* category, selling arrangements, and restrictions on use did not fall in under the same discrimination/market access or any similar test more lenient to national measures.

There is an intense discussion in the CJEU, the Commission and other EU legislative bodies, and in academic writing. Member States most often argue against wider restrictions concepts which also have consequences for the legal base for EU competences and action, including legislation and the division of powers between the EU and Member States, even in external relations.

The interplay between the fundamental freedoms is a central cross-cutting theme for the book. EU secondary legislation and jurisprudence apply the freedoms as they are set out in the treaties with separate parts for free movement of goods, persons and capital.

Each question and criterion is discussed in relationship to the respective freedom applied. There is little common ground in general freedom case law or jurisprudence. Close reading of the cases and their interpretation in later cases or legislation is required to understand what the main rule is in a particular sector. The cases are a force of fragmentation, and the CJEU seldom make explicit contributions to general freedom jurisprudence or a unified jurisprudence of free movement. The CJEU refers to general principles of the internal market but does not take that down to the level of a general law of free movement, across the different freedoms.

The interaction between scholarship, legislation and jurisprudence has continued to be intense since the 1980s. Community legislation and the jurisprudence of the CJEU move between different concepts of what constitutes a 'restriction' and free movement rights, and always within the boundaries of one of the freedoms. Many of the questions remain the same and unanswered: is discrimination still a core concept or will it be replaced by a more neutral, general and sweeping 'market access' criterion? Does the concept of 'market access' pave the way for another approach where the ambition is to eliminate burdensome and inefficient regulation in a matured internal market? What are the implications for the review of proportionality? Does the market access test confirm a uniform approach towards the fundamental freedoms, and would a uniform approach be desirable?

The reach of free movement is a classical dilemma of EU law. The contributions in this book argue the different sides in the discussion. It still remains unclear whether the right to free movement is exhausted by the right to equal treatment, *de iure* and *de facto*, of EU market operators in the broad sense, or whether the rights conferred by the treaties have a broader scope. A particularly controversial issue is whether the set of rights connected with the freedom of movement reach as far as to converge into a general protection of individual freedom as such.

---

[3] Case C-110/05 *Commission v. Italy (Trailers)* [2009] ECR I-519.

[4] Case C-142/05 *Åklagaren v Percy Mickelsson and Joakim Roos* [2009] I-4273.

There has been a convergence towards the threshold the CJEU set for establishment and then for goods under Article 34 TFEU. Free movement has been applied to sector after sector. An early battle in the 1970 was about the professions where the legal profession provided strong resistance to the right of establishment.[5] In the 1980s patents and immaterial rights more generally was subjected to free movement[6] against opposition from industry and the legal profession servicing it. By the turn of the century the turn came for German company law[7] and in the 2000s the right to collective action.[8]

Just completed, the unified free movement jurisprudence broke up with the *Keck*[9] exception for 'selling arrangements' for goods. Suggestions to extend the *Keck* exception for goods to 'use restrictions' have not been adopted.[10] Neither has the *Keck* exception been received outside goods. What was a narrow majority for an uneasy compromise in *Keck*, was not strong enough to expand further in the field of goods or carry over into the other freedoms. There is no agreement on the impact of *Commission v. Italy (Trailers)*[11] which made clear that a market access criterion had to be added to the discrimination test for the *Keck* category. It may have opened up for a more general criterion and may promote convergence. Restrictions on the *export* of free movement of goods are prohibited in Article 35 TFEU, and there the case law has moved from a more narrow discrimination concept to the same restrictions concept as under Article 34 for the import of goods. That is one move in the direction of a unified free movement jurisprudence, *within* the free movement of goods.

Free movement rights remain primarily a right against the state, or that of a private party against public authorities. The limitation is less important as the law has to be applied to give effect to free movement also between private parties. The duty of the state to give effect to free movement also leads to damages liability when it does not prevent restrictions on free movement rights in the actions of private parties. The convergence between the freedoms seemed to be broken up each time the CJEU advanced free movement rights between private parties, so-called horizontal direct effect. The jurisprudence makes this distinction between

[5] Case 2/74 *Reyners v Belgium* [1974] ECR 631, Case 33/74 *Van Binsbergen v Bestuur van de Bedrijfsvereniging voor de Metaalnijverheid* [1974] ECR 1299 and Case C-71/76 *Jean Thieffry v Conseil de l'ordre des avocats à la cour de Paris* [1977] ECR 765.

[6] Case 192/73 *Van Zuylen v Hag* (Café Hag I), [1974] ECR 731 and Case C-10/89 *CNL-Sucal v Hag* (Café Hag II) [1990] ECR I-3711.

[7] C-212/97 *Centros Ltd v Erhvervs-og Selskabsstyrelsen* [1999] ECR I-01459 and C-208/00 *Überseering BV v Nordic Construction GmbH* [2002] I-9919.

[8] C-438/05 *International Transport Workers Federation v Viking Line ABP* [2007] ECR I-10779, *Laval Un Partneri Ltd v Svenska Byggnadsarbetareforbundet Laval and Partneri* [2007] ECR I-11767.

[9] Joined Cases C-267/91 and 268/91 *Keck and Mithouard* [1993] ECR I-6097.

[10] Case C-142/05 *Åklagaren v Percy Mickelsson and Joakim Roos* [2009] I-4273.

[11] Case C-110/05 *Commission v Italy (Trailers)* [2009] ECR I-519.

horizontal and vertical direct effect less important and also seem to gradually extend horizontal direct effect across the freedoms.[12]

Yet another aspect of the reach of free movement is the relationship between free movement and competition law. The way in which these areas develop makes the traditional dichotomy between state—private party (fundamental freedoms) and private parties/undertakings—less relevant. State aid and public procurement rules add further issues, and in the jurisprudence all sets of rules may possibly be applied to the same restriction or private law relationship.

Legislation and scholarship is more fragmented than jurisprudence: courts move from one field to another and carry with them concepts and insights. From any or all angles discussed above, it is not given that the development of the rules are to take place within jurisdictional limitations and dichotomies such as between 'private parties'/'undertakings' and 'state'/'public authorities'.

The developments in the case law of the CJEU raise important constitutional questions. What are the constitutional foundations for the jurisprudence of the CJEU? What are the implications for the balancing of power between the Union and the Member States, and between legislators and courts? The question of legitimacy is relevant to the determination of the outer limits of what constitutes a restriction. It is clear that the reach of free movement does not only relate to the functioning of the common market in the strict sense. It also gives rise to constitutional concerns, as it affects the balancing of power both between the EU and domestic jurisdictions and between legislators and courts. Much is left to the CJEU, too much, some of the contributors to this book argue. However, it is also possible to consider the CJEU as an enabler. A far-reaching restriction criterion will vest the institutions of the European Union with flexible competences which enable them to pursue the project of European integration. The CJEU itself can apply the principle of proportionality as a filter to show deference towards the democratic processes of the Member States, especially in fields where no secondary legislation exists.

The flexible concept of a "restriction" is dependent upon the objectives of the European Union, but at the same time it plays an important role in confirming, and re-defining, them. One well established objective is to provide those who conduct business access to the European market. Another and more general objective, which also can serve as a source of legitimacy, is to provide the European citizen new opportunities—but possibly at the cost of the protection traditionally provided for by their national states. An important question in this regard is to what extent the concept of European citizenship changes the relationship between the EU and its states, and between the states and its citizens. The citizens' status as Europeans is a catalyst towards an ever more expansive notion of free movement, which could make it appropriate in certain regards to consider free movement as a fundamental right. The increasing interplay between the fundamental freedoms and the EU

[12] Case C-171/11, *Fra.bo*, ECLI:EU:C:2012:453.

Charter of Fundamental Rights constitutes a new dynamism which will further this development.

The aim of the book is to provide the reader with an analysis of such issues, with a view to assessing the constitutional reach of the rights conferred by the Treaties in the framework of the freedom of movement.

1.2 Explaining the Gradualist Approach of the CJEU

The current pressure points are often in the field of the free movement of persons, and stopping so-called benefit tourism has become a political priority. The EU as legislator provides for restrictions in the face of political pressure from some Member States. The CJEU allows restrictions it would not have done only a few years ago. The CJEU not only slows the development towards free movement down but is taking steps backwards. This happens at a time when EU citizenship and the Charter together had started to have joint effect on free movement, speeding up the movement forward towards free movement.

The low threshold remains for all the freedoms. The *Keck* exception for 'selling arrangements' is the one exception, and it applies only for goods. One explanation is that what was a narrow majority for an uneasy compromise in *Keck*, has not been strong enough to expand further in the field of goods or carry over into the other freedoms.

There is one further explanation. The CJEU had a rich jurisprudence on goods and selling arrangements. It was in a position to conclude that most selling arrangements would not constitute any restriction on free movement or have any negative impact on the internal market. The more relaxed test in *Keck* would not threaten the internal market. The same test across free movement of goods or across the freedoms could.

Free movement cases come before the CJEU either as Commission actions against Member States or as references from national courts. National courts would rarely see the need or any duty to refer a question of what constitutes a selling arrangement to the CJEU. The consequence of *Keck* could be that the CJEU would get very few cases about restrictions on selling arrangements before it. That has proved right. In practice, national courts and national authorities apply the *Keck* test without much actual or potential supervision from the CJEU. The same test, or any other test, across free movement of goods or across the freedoms would have dramatic consequences for that supervision of the CJEU on most free movement issues and severely limit the effectiveness of EU law.

Keck provides an alternative route towards a new test. The CJEU approaches the matter in an incremental way, the way in which courts are best suited to operate, without ceding jurisdiction. *Keck* may be a way to try out a test of discrimination for more general application, and perhaps through further categories added to 'selling arrangements.' It may also in the event reject a more general discrimination test.

1.3 The Long-Term Project on the Reach of Free Movement

This book is one outcome of a long-term project on The Reach of Free Movement, of which the 2003 book on *Services and Free Movement in EU Law*[13] was one of the first publications. This was followed up with the major 2007 conference on 'The Direction of Free Movement', organised with the UK Association of European Law, King's College, University of London, the Institute of Advanced Legal Studies, University of London and the British Institute of International and Comparative Law.[14]

The most recent events are several seminars at the University of Oslo, organised with the Norwegian Association of European Law, including 'The Reach of Free Movement' at the Department of Private Law, University of Oslo in 2011[15] and 'The Constitutional Implications of Free Movement' in 2014.[16]

Services of general interest is the subject of one parallel project with the book on *Developments in Services of General Interest*,[17] and the conference on 'Services of General Interest in a Global World' and the work shop 'On SGEIs, The European Social Model and Free Movement', at the Institute of Advanced Legal Studies, London 2009.[18] Another closely related project at the University of Oslo is the project on 'International Financial Market Regulation, Institutions and Efficiency' of which this book is a part.[19]

1.4 Outline of This Book

The book falls into four parts. Part I has the heading 'The Reach of Free Movement', Part II 'Justifications and Proportionality', Part III 'Fundamental Rights' and Part IV 'Looking Abroad'.

Part I 'The Reach of Free Movement'

Chapter 2 has the title 'The Reach of Free Movement. A Defence of Court Discretion'. Professor Tarjei Bekkedal, Oslo, argues that the reach of the

---

[13] Andenas and Roth 2003.

[14] https://www.biicl.org/files/2729_programme_3_28_april.pdf.

[15] http://www.jus.uio.no/ifp/forskning/prosjekter/markedsstaten/arrangementer/2011/free-movement-oslo/.

[16] http://www.jus.uio.no/english/research/networks/european-law-network/events/other-events/06112014.html.

[17] Szyszczak et al. 2011.

[18] http://www.jus.uio.no/ifp/forskning/prosjekter/markedsstaten/arrangementer/2009/vedlegg/programme_government_services_280509.pdf.

[19] http://www.jus.uio.no/ifp/english/research/projects/financial-market-regulation/. See Andenas and Wooldridge 2009, Andenas 2012, Andenas et al. 2012, Andenas 2015, Andenas 2016 and Andenas et al. 2016.

fundamental freedoms and the content of the notion of a "restriction" cannot and should not be expressed in a rule-like manner. To the contrary, the fundamental freedoms function as overarching constitutional principles that both demand and legitimize the execution of court discretion. Public bodies, like courts, are vested with discretion in situations where rules are to be avoided, due to the magnitude of phenomena that are subject to regulation. Because of their stiffness, rules cannot serve the purposes of a legal system that pursues numerous, shifting and colliding objectives, such as the EU legal order. Any attempt to establish tests or categorizations that aim to define and exhaust the reach of the fundamental freedoms in a rule-like manner will obstruct the nature of the principles through which free movement is established, secured and developed, and the nature of the legal order in which they operate. Tarjei Bekkedal explores the legal basis for court discretion, whether discretion is compatible with the principle of legal certainty, how discretion can fit a conception of the right to free movement as a personal individual right and the constitutional limitations to court discretion.

In Chap. 3, Dr. Alina Tryfonidou, Reading, explores 'Free Movement of Persons Through the Lenses of "Discrimination" and "Restriction"'. The notions of 'restriction' and 'discrimination' are the soul and life of EU free movement law. These are the notions that define what is caught within the net of the free movement provisions, as well as the limits that are placed on their scope of application. These concepts are not monolithic but their interpretation is constantly changing and adapting and, together with this, the relationship between them is redefined. Dr. Tryfonidou seeks to consider the reach of the provisions governing the free movement of persons, taking as its point of reference the ECJ's interpretation of the notions of 'discrimination' and 'restriction' in this context. In particular, she analyses how the meaning of the above notions has developed through the years and it will explore how the relationship between the two has evolved from originally being one of interdependence to one that is of (almost) complete independence. Dr. Tryfonidou concludes that the main reason behind these developments is the (gradual) attribution to the free movement of persons provisions of a double status of instrumental freedoms and fundamental (citizenship) rights.

Chapter 4 has the title 'Restrictions on the Use of Goods and Services'. Professor Stefan Enchelmaier, Oxford, picks apart 'market access' as applied by the CJEU for establishing whether the free movement of goods and the freedom to provide services are restricted. So far, Professor Enchelmaier says, the criterion is ill-defined, especially in its application to restrictions of use. Professor Enchelmaier suggests that predictability can be restored to the assessment under both freedoms through a properly understood discrimination test, complemented by a prohibition of universal bans, proceeding in the following steps:

(1) Does the restriction of use apply in law equally to domestic producers and providers as to those from other Member States (i.e. is it 'indistinctly applicable')? If yes,

(2) Does the restriction have the same factual repercussions on imports and domestic products/on services provided by operators established in the same Member State as the recipient, and on services in whose provision a border between Member States is crossed (if there are any domestic goods or services)? If yes,

(3) Does the restriction prohibit the last remaining use in the Member State in question in a situation where either such use remains legal in at least one other Member State, or the importing Member State is the last to allow this use?

If the answer to (1) or (2) is 'no', or if it is 'yes' to (3), Professor Enchelmaier suggests, the measure restricts the free movement of goods or the freedom to provide services, and therefore requires a justification. Otherwise, it does not because it leads to a mere reduction in the volume of trade.

Chapter 5 has the title 'To Use or Not to Use—That's the Question. On Article 34 and National Rules Restricting the Use of Lawfully Marketed Products'. Professor Niels Fenger, Copenhagen, examines the extent to which Article 34 TFEU encompasses national rules that neither prohibit the sale or the use of a product, but merely regulate how, where and when the product may be used. He argues that the CJEU was right not to apply its case law concerning selling arrangements to such kinds of rules. He also discusses whether the Court's approach to use restrictions, and the market access test that the Court applies in such cases, has a spill over effect on other aspects of its case law under Article 34 TFEU. Finally, he provides a suggestion for how to draw the line for when a restriction on the use of a legally marketed product constitutes a measure of equivalent effect.

Part II 'Justifications and Proportionality'

Chapter 6 has the title 'The Justifications for Restrictions to Free Movement: Towards a Single Normative Framework?' Professor Vassilis Hatzopoulos, the Democritus University of Thrace, addresses overriding reasons of general interest, including objective justifications, express exceptions and economic justifications, and explains how they fit into a proportionality analysis. In the vast majority of internal market cases a restriction is readily identified, and it is at the level of justification that the basic judicial choices operate. This is done either by virtue of 'objective justifications' or by the much more limited list of express exceptions foreseen by the Treaty. These two 'systems' of justifications have been developed in partial contradiction with one another in terms of the types of measures upheld and the *ex ante/ex post* application of the justification. Throughout the years, however, the practical differences as well as the normative underpinnings of the two systems have been greatly confused. So much so that, nowadays, it seems more exact from a positivist view and more desirable from a normative point of view to view all the justification grounds as parts of a single normative framework. The proposed framework would be 'single' in two ways, in the sense it should apply both to all the fundamental freedoms alike (material unicity), and to discriminatory and non-discriminatory measures (restriction unicity). Professor Hatzopoulos exposes the incoherencies and inconsistencies of the current situation before he explains why the conditions are now ripe for a new unified approach. He explores how a single justification framework could be affected by other, neighbouring, EU rules.

In Chap. 7, ‘The Justification and Proportionality of Certain Administrative, Regulatory and Political Concerns’, Dr. Pål Wennerås, Oslo, continues the analysis of justification and proportionality. He is critical of the current state of the law where the scope of the four freedoms has become so broad that it is liable to capture a plethora of national acts that, at least originally, would have appeared to lie on the outer fringes of the Court of Justice’s competence. In Dr. Pål Wennerås’ view this situation is exacerbated by the fact that administrative considerations are in principle not capable of justifying restrictions on freedom of movement. Proportionality presents several substantive and procedural hurdles for attaining legitimate regulatory and political concerns. Member States will therefore often find it difficult to justify measures that restrict freedom of movement, irrespective of the fact that they are not intended to regulate freedom of movement and clearly pursue a common good. More recent developments in case law suggest, however, that the Court of Justice has become increasingly aware that such a situation poses not only challenges for Member States, but also for the Court itself and the proper role of the judiciary in an EU of 28 or 27 Member States. Some recent judgments thus seem to temper the concept of restrictions on the freedom of movement, but above all the Court seems more willing to entertain the justification and proportionality of certain administrative, regulatory and political concerns that entail restrictions on the freedom of movement.

Chapter 8 has the title ‘The Guardianship of European Constitutionality: A Structural Critique of European Constitutional Review’. Professor Agustín José Menéndez, Universidad de León, Spain, develops a critical analysis of proportionality which gives economic freedoms above collective goods and socio-economic rights. On his analysis, European courts have radically altered the substance of European law under the cloth of the projection of the national principle of proportionality to Union law. This has been done both to supranational and national constitutional law and by means of redefining its substantive content. European courts have through proportionality assigned an abstract and a concrete constitutional weight to the right to private property and to entrepreneurial freedom through the four economic freedoms and the principle of undistorted competition. That has placed outside the realm of the constitutionally possible key public policies without which some of the fundamental collective goods at the core of the social and democratic *Rechtsstaat* become extremely vulnerable. Professor Menéndez shows how this accentuated bias of the European socio-economic constitution follows from the way in which European courts have defined economic freedoms as the yardstick of European constitutionality. This entails the automatic assignment of the argumentative benefit to economic freedoms, the construction of all other constitutional goods in the semblance of economic freedoms, and the use of asymmetric standards of evidence when having to justify the adequacy and necessity of economic freedoms and other constitutional goods.

Chapter 9 has the title 'The Criterion of "Consistent and Systematic Manner" in Free Movement Law'. It is by Professor Dr. Tor-Inge Harbo, Agder, Norway. His starting point is that the conflict between the four freedoms and national regulation is not merely about colliding interests but also of colliding values and thus has, potentially, constitutional implications. The conflict has often been phrased as one between national sovereignty and European integration, but is far more than this. It is about marked liberalism and market regulation, the latter constituting the very fundament upon which the European welfare states rest.

In settling conflicts between the two constitutional orders—the ordo-liberal and the welfare-state constitutions—the Court of Justice of the European Union (CJEU) applies the proportionality principle. However, the proportionality principle is arguably of such a discretionary character that one could question its legal credentials. The discretionary character of the proportionality principle thus threatens to undermine the legitimacy of the Court and in turn the legitimacy of the European legal order.

In this chapter, the author discusses the invocation of the "consistent and systematic manner" criterion. Has it contributed to the formalization of the proportionality analysis? Does it secure the legitimacy for the Court's proportionality analysis and its corresponding market liberalizing effects? The point of departure is taken in the gambling case saga.

Part III 'Fundamental Rights'

Chapter 10 has the title 'Legitimacy and the Charter of Fundamental Rights Post-Lisbon', and is by Professor Christoffer C. Eriksen and Jørgen A. Stubberud, Oslo. They ask if the incorporation of the Charter of Fundamental Rights into the Lisbon Treaty has strengthened our reasons for accepting the powers entrusted to the European Union. The Charter of Fundamental Rights was adopted and later transformed into primary law in order to enhance the legitimacy of the EU. This echoed a critique of the gradually expanding powers of the EU, including the expanding reach of the right to free movement, more supranational decision-making procedures and new Union powers in novel policy areas such as the area of justice and home affairs. One line of criticism held that the wide powers of the Union were not balanced with sufficient level of democratic control and effective protection against abuse. The Lisbon Treaty sought to enhance legitimacy in three ways: decision-making processes were to some extent democratised; the Member States agreed that the Union shall accede to the ECHR; and the Charter was transformed into primary law. There is a partly competing perspective from which the EU's legitimacy may depend more on its ability to facilitate effective problem-solving to acute problems of public policy including migration and economic crises. In this chapter, we inquire to what extent the transformation of the Charter into primary law has and may succeed in providing better reasons for accepting the powers entrusted to the EU. In this context we provide, first, an analysis of certain questions regarding the interpretation and application of the Charter, questions which are key to assessing what changes to EU law the said transformation has and may lead to, as compared to older epochs of EU law when fundamental rights were based on unwritten law. In the final assessment, we argue that the answer to the legitimacy question depends on the extent to which European courts will allow Member States with flexibility regarding how fundamental rights are protected in different institutional environments. Effective problem-solving may require the ability to adapt different solutions in different locations and to different situations, based upon different weighing of interests.

In Chap. 11, 'False Friends and True Cognates: On Fundamental Freedoms, Fundamental Rights and Union Citizenship', Francesco De Cecco, Newcastle, analyses the relationship between these concepts upon which the EU order builds.

Both the case law on fundamental freedoms, and the selective manner in which these freedoms are incorporated in the Charter of Fundamental Rights of the EU are consistent with an account of fundamental rights that places a non-instrumental focus on the protection of the interests of the right-holder (the Union citizen). According to the account advanced here, those free movement rights that are non-instrumental in nature are treated as fundamental rights, whereas those free movement rights that remain predominantly instrumental are not. Yet, developments in the case law on Union citizenship that have occurred during the current decade present a challenge to this account. On the one hand they appear to draw on the conceptual toolkit of fundamental rights; on the other, they contradict key features of a fundamental rights conception of Union citizenship.

In Chap. 12, 'Fundamental Freedoms, Fundamental Rights, and the Many Faces of Freedom of Contract in the EU', Professor Olha O. Cherednychenko, Groningen, turns to contract law. As a result of the growing involvement of the EU in regulating private conduct and private law relationships, EU law increasingly affects the scope of freedom of contract. In this way, it shapes the European model of freedom of contract based first and foremost on the internal market rationale, sparkling tensions with the concepts of freedom of contract that have evolved in the national contract laws of the Member States.

Whilst EU secondary legislation plays a major role in this context, the understanding of freedom of contract can also be profoundly affected by EU primary law. Professor Olha Cherednychenko seeks to determine the reach of EU free movement law in the contractual sphere, with a particular focus on (financial) services. It explores the conceptualisation of freedom of contract in free movement law in light of the concept of 'formal' freedom of contract and that of 'substantive' freedom of contract in national contract laws, as well as the notion of the freedom of contract regulated in the name of the internal market in EU secondary legislation. Particular attention in this context is given to the interplay between fundamental economic freedoms and fundamental rights.

Chapter 13, 'The Charter of Fundamental Rights and the Reach of Free Movement Law' is written by Dr. Filippo Fontanelli, Edinburgh, and Dr. Amedeo Arena, Naples. They discuss two underrated and connected aspects that determine the applicability of the Charter in the area of the market freedoms.

First, the Charter can be a decisive standard of review for domestic measures only when they are covered by EU law but are not precluded by it. In this respect, the distinction between non-preclusion and non-application of EU law is overlooked in the case law and in the scholarship. Second, because the applications of EU law and the Charter are aligned, the latter suffers from the uncertainties of the former. Dr. Fontanelli and Dr. Arena conclude that the entry into force of the Charter has exposed the blurred contours of the application of EU law, in particular in the area of the market freedoms.

Part IV 'Looking Abroad'

Chapter 14 provides a comparative perspective: 'Creating a national market in the United States through the dormant commerce clause?' Eszter Belteki, Durham, compares the development of the internal market in the EU and the creation of the national market in the United States of America.

The author claims that the US experience provides an excellent starting point for understanding the EU Internal Market. The author demonstrates, through a historical analysis, how such a market could materialise without an express provision about this in the Constitution of the United States of America. She first examines the drafting and early interpretation of the commerce clause in the first part. She then turns to the main decisions of the US Supreme Court, in which the negative or dormant commerce clause developed, focusing on the extent to which limitation placed on the states under this clause assisted in the creation of the national market. The author finally turns to what she sees as a worrying trend. Even though there is a strict scrutiny of state laws under the modern interpretation of the commerce clause, recent Supreme Court decisions allow discriminatory laws to be imposed by the states against other states and their nationals.

Chapter 15 moves on to external relations: 'Beyond Parallel Powers. EU Treaty-Making Power Post-Lisbon'. The authors Mads Andenas, Oslo, and Dr. Luca Pantaleo, The Hague, analyse EU external treaty-making and internal law-making powers. In the codification and development in the Treaty of Lisbon and the developments subsequent case law and practice, there is an emerging trend towards a conceptual and practical separation of EU external and internal powers—that is, EU treaty-making and law-making powers. This trend is reflected in the framework of the Common Commercial Policy. This is natural, as EU trade policy is traditionally the most proactive of EU foreign policies. However, the same dynamics may apply to other EU external powers, such as development cooperation, as showed by the Philippines case.

The authors argue that the principle of parallel powers only works in one direction. The principle requires that EU internal competences be mirrored by corresponding parallel external competences. However, it does not impose a parallel in the other direction. This position may well entail that the EU has the power to conclude an agreement even in areas where the corresponding internal powers belong to the Member States. The competence of the latter would not be infringed or encroached upon by the conclusion of such an agreement to the extent that the Member States retain the power, at the very least, to implement the agreement at the internal level. It is worth noting that this does not imply a breach of the principle of conferral. That principle would be infringed in the case of a so-called reverse ERTA-effect, as codified by Article 216 TFEU, in other words, if the EU could derive implied internal powers from express external powers. This is evidently not the case.

The uncoupling of EU external powers from the internal division of competence would mark the constitutional ripeness of a system that is becoming less and less a common market and more and more an inextricable set of interconnected policies. The development may be slowed down if the full court (plenary) of the CJEU follows the Advocate General's Opinion in Opinion Procedure 2/15 on the Singapore Free Trade Agreement. (The CJEU did not, and the development continues, as explained in the post scriptum to this chapter, written after the CJEU's opinion.)

References

Andenas M (2012) European Monetary Law. In: Wolfrum R (ed) Max Planck Encyclopedia of Public International Law. Oxford University Press, Oxford

Andenas M (2015) Civil Liability of Credit Rating Agencies in the European Union 11 International and Comparative Corporate Law Journal, Special Issue: Civil Liability of Credit Rating Agencies in the European Union

Andenas M (2016) The European Union as a Global Model for Trade and Investment. Social Science Research Network. ISSN 1556–5068

Andenas M et al. (eds) (2012) Theory and Practice of Harmonisation. Edward Elgar Publishing, London

Andenas M et al. (eds) (2016) Regulating and Supervising European Financial Markets. More Risks than Achievements. Kluwer, Heidelberg

Andenas M, Roth WH (eds) (2003) Services and Free Movement in EU Law. Oxford University Press, Oxford

Andenas M, Wooldridge F (2009) European Comparative Company Law. Cambridge University Press, Cambridge

Szyszczak E, Davies J, Andenas M, Bekkedal T (eds) (2011) Developments in Services of General Interest. TMC Asser Press, The Hague

Part I
The Reach of Free Movement

Chapter 2
The Reach of Free Movement. A Defence of Court Discretion

Tarjei Bekkedal

Abstract This chapter argues that the reach of the fundamental freedoms and the content of the notion of a "restriction" cannot and should not be expressed in a rule-like manner. To the contrary, the fundamental freedoms function as overarching constitutional principles that both demand and legitimize the execution of court discretion. Public bodies, like courts, are vested with discretion in situations where rules are to be avoided, due to the magnitude of phenomena that are subject to regulation. Because of their stiffness, rules cannot serve the purposes of a legal system that pursues numerous, shifting and colliding objectives, such as the EU legal order. Any attempt to establish tests or categorizations that aim to define and exhaust the reach of the fundamental freedoms in a rule-like manner will obstruct the nature of the principles through which free movement is established, secured and developed, and the nature of the legal order in which they operate. The chapter explores the legal basis for court discretion, whether discretion is compatible with the principle of legal certainty, how discretion can fit a conception of the right to free movement as a personal individual right and the constitutional limitations to court discretion.

Keywords Charter of Fundamental Rights · Constitution · Discretion · Discrimination · Free movement · Individual rights · Legal certainty · Market access

T. Bekkedal (✉)
University of Oslo, St. Olavs plass, PO Box 6706, 0130 Oslo, Norway
e-mail: tarjei.bekkedal@jus.uio.no

M. Andenas et al. (eds.), *The Reach of Free Movement*,
DOI 10.1007/978-94-6265-195-1_2

Contents

2.1 Introduction—The Fetish for Rules 18
2.2 The Legal Basis for Court Discretion 20
2.2.1 Introduction 20
2.2.2 The Treaty Provisions 20
2.2.3 The Case Law of the Court and the Nature of the European Legal Order 24
2.3 The Objections: Court Discretion Is Arbitrary and Disregards the Principle of Legal Certainty 26
2.3.1 Introduction 26
2.3.2 Court Discretion 27
2.3.3 Legal Certainty 29
2.3.4 Is There Any Alternative? The Broad Concept of "Discrimination" as a Prime Example of Court Discretion 34
2.4 Discretion and the Individual Right to Access the Market 38
2.4.1 From Instrumental to Personal Rights 38
2.4.2 The Structure of the Legal Assessment and the Notion of "Market Access" 40
2.4.3 The Increasing Use of the Term "Market Access" 42
2.4.4 Example: Restrictions on Use—The Constitutional Twist in the Court's Case Law 44
2.4.5 Market Access and the Personal Right to Free Movement 46
2.5 The Constitutional Limits to Court Discretion 51
2.6 Conclusions 53
References 54

2.1 Introduction—The Fetish for Rules

The provision on the free movement of goods (Article 34 TFEU), the provision on the freedom of establishment (Article 49 TFEU), the provision on the freedom to provide services (Article 56 TFEU) and the provision on the free movement of capital (Article 63 TFEU) prohibit restrictions on free movement. Workers (Article 45) and EU-citizens (Article 21) enjoy a personal right to move freely within the territory of the Member States. Superficially, this promises both unity and simplicity. The reach of free movement and, in this respect, the reach of EU law, hinges on the notion of a "restriction".

We all know that things are not as simple as they appear. So much ink has been spilt on the topic that one observer has noted that EU lawyers may be accused of "fetishizing" the case law on the scope of the Treaty rules.[1] One reason is that the reach of free movement is of seminal practical importance; another is the constitutional implications. If a restriction is identified, courts can proceed and subject national legislation to scrutiny, pursuant to the principle of proportionality. Thus, the notion of a restriction has been described as a mechanism for the allocation of competences between the supranational and the national sphere, and between lawmakers and courts. The understanding of the term "restriction", its content and its nature, pose the intriguing question of what EU law is about, and what it is not

[1] Dougan 2010, p. 165.

about—whether we should apply a protectionist reading of the Treaty, an economic freedom reading, or search for a third way.[2]

In spite of all the efforts, no consensus has been established with regard to what a restriction is, and what it should be. The only thing upon which everyone would seem to agree is that not *every* piece of national legislation can be regarded as a restriction without any further qualification and that measures which only incur extra costs or reduce the volume of trade do not as such affect the right to access the market.[3] The opposite position would represent an application of EU law which is too simplistic and it would raise serious concerns about legitimacy if courts were to second-guess every minor decision enacted by national lawmakers. This is where all the problems start. Apart from the negative finding, no one seems to have identified the rule, or the combined set of rules, that define the notion of a restriction in a manner which is generally accepted among other scholars and which is able to account for the practice of the ECJ in the field.[4] To add to the difficulties, this practice is often accused of being inconsistent or unsystematic.[5]

In this chapter, I will argue that the rules are not yet identified because no rules exist, nor should exist. Secondary legislation provides rules. To the contrary, the fundamental freedoms function as overarching constitutional principles that both demand and legitimize the execution of court discretion. Public bodies, like courts, are vested with discretion in situations where rules are to be avoided, due to the magnitude of phenomena that are subject to regulation. Because of their stiffness, rules cannot serve the purposes of a legal system that pursues numerous, shifting and colliding objectives, such as the EU legal order. Any attempt to establish tests or categorizations that aim to define and exhaust the reach of the fundamental freedoms in a rule-like manner will obstruct the nature of the principles through which free movement is established, secured and developed, and the nature of the legal order in which they operate. The one fetish that should be tempered is lawyers' affinity for rules. Instead we will have to explore the legal basis for court discretion (Sect. 2.2), whether discretion is compatible with the principle of legal certainty (Sect. 2.3), how discretion can fit a conception of the right to free movement as a personal individual right (Sect. 2.4) and the constitutional limitations to court discretion (Sect. 2.5).

---

[2] See e.g. Bernard 1996, p. 82; Maduro 1998, pp. 58–60; Snell 2002, pp. 1–4; Oliver and Roth 2004, p. 413; Dougan 2010, p. 165; Snell 2010, p. 469; Nic Shuibhne 2013, p. 189 and the famous opinion of AG Tesauro in Case C-292/92, *Hünermund*, EU:C:1993:863.

[3] Established case law. See e.g. Joined Cases C-267/91, *Keck and Mithouard*, EU:C:1993:905, para 13; Case C-20/03, *Burmanjer*, EU:C:2005:307, paras 30–31; Case C-518/06, *Commission v. Italy*, EU:C:2009:270, paras 62–63; Opinion of AG Poiares Maduro in Case C-446/03, *Marks & Spencer plc v Halsey (Her Majesty's Inspector of Taxes)*, EU:C:2005:201, para 37: Jansson and Kalimo 2014, p. 526.

[4] See e.g. Enchelmaier 2004 and 2016 for a critical assessment of the seminal works of Snell 2002 and Nic Shuibhne 2013. For a convincing critique of Maduro 1998 and the conception of the four freedoms as fundamental political rights, see Roth 2002, p. 22 in particular.

[5] See e.g. Snell 2010, pp. 461–467; Davies 2011, p. 9; 2012b, p. 25; Jansson and Kalimo 2014, p. 530.

2.2 The Legal Basis for Court Discretion

2.2.1 *Introduction*

In Sect. 2.2.2 below, it will be argued that the far-reaching notion of a restriction established by the written treaty provisions on free movement constitutes a textual legal basis for the execution of court discretion. It is submitted that even the proponents of a restrained and rule-based approach to the reach of free movement (normally grounded in a wide notion of discrimination) must accept discretion as a fundamentally important concept within the EU legal order in general, and within free-movement law in particular. In the absence of discretion, the requirement of self-restraint, which is so often argued in favour of, cannot be construed.

Section 2.2.3 proves that discretionary decision-making is foreseen, legitimized and required by Article 19 TEU, which states that the Court "shall ensure that in the interpretation and application of the Treaties the law is observed". A number of constitutionally important examples have shown how the European legal order was construed through the exercise of court discretion; this has become an established and accepted necessity of the European legal system.

2.2.2 *The Treaty Provisions*

The Treaty provisions on free movement establish the competence of the CJEU and of the national courts to assess whether national regulatory measures restrict free movement. The provisions legitimize judicial review, and in this regard, the execution of what we might call court discretion in the "thin" sense. By this, I refer to the considerations which judges cannot avoid taking into account, weigh and assess, whenever they conduct a review of whether the law is observed, except for in cases where the outcome follows mechanically from the wording of the relevant provision.

From a literal point of view one could actually argue that at least some of the provisions on free movement, those that apply the term "restriction", do not allow for court discretion, as the term is clear to the extent that it demands a mechanical application of the law. "Restriction" means anything that restricts those who are subject to regulation, or in short: anything. Article 45 TFEU could be taken to support such an encompassing and literal interpretation as the latter provision; in contrast to its seemingly more all-encompassing cousins, only requests the "abolition of any discrimination based on nationality". Of course, such a broad, unconstrained and utterly naïve application of the restriction criterion is methodologically wrong and would run counter to the far more nuanced practice of the CJEU. Still, it reveals, as I will submit, the dynamic potential that is inherent in the textual law on free movement, a potential that the CJEU has carefully preserved, although not always applied to its fullest extent.[6]

In its case law, the Court tends to present the notion of a restriction in sweeping terms which comes close to the naïve and literal reading of the Treaty which was explained above. According to the famous judgment in Dassonville[7]:

> [a]ll trading rules enacted by Member States which are capable of hindering, directly or indirectly, actually or potentially, intra-Community trade are to be considered as measures having an effect equivalent to quantitative restrictions.

In the field of services, the judgment in *Binsbergen* provided an early confirmation that even if the concept of discrimination is central to the notion of a restriction, it is not exhaustive[8]:

> The restrictions to be abolished pursuant to Articles [56 and 57 TFEU] include all requirements imposed on the person providing the service by reason in particular of his nationality or of the fact that he does not habitually reside in the State where the service is provided, which do not apply to persons established within the national territory *or which may prevent or otherwise obstruct the activities of the person providing the service.*

In the famous *Gebhard* ruling, on the freedom of establishment, the Court stated[9]:

> It follows, however, from the Court's case-law that national measures liable to hinder or make less attractive the exercise of fundamental freedoms guaranteed by the Treaty must fulfil four conditions: they must be applied in a non-discriminatory manner; they must be justified by imperative requirements in the general interest; they must be suitable for securing the attainment of the objective which they pursue; and they must not go beyond what is necessary in order to attain it.

In the latter formula, the open term "hinder or make less attractive" defines the notion of a restriction, while the concept of discrimination fulfils a more limited role: The functioning of the latter is to clarify that unless the national measure is non-discriminatory, the doctrine of mandatory requirements cannot be invoked.[10] The antithesis is that non-discriminatory measures may indeed constitute restrictions.

In accordance with the wording of the Treaty provisions on free movement, the Court has consistently repeated its broad interpretation of what may constitute a

---

[6] See also Nic Shuibhne 2013, p. 191: "It is thus important to note that it is not (just) *the Court* that is pushing for an understanding of restrictions beyond discrimination it is (also) the Treaty."

[7] Case 8/74, *Procureur du Roi v Dassonville*, EU:C:1974:82, para 5, cf. e.g. Case C-320/03, *Commission v. Austria*, EU:C:2005:684, para 67.

[8] Case 33/74, *Van Binsbergen v Bestuur van de Bedrijfsvereniging voor de Metaalnijverheid*, EU:C:1974:131, paras 10–11 (emphasis added).

[9] Case C-55/94, *Gebhard*, EU:C:1995:411, para 37.

[10] Cf. Case C-375/14, *Laezza*, EU:C:2016:60, para 25.

restriction.[11] Legal scholars, however, have been somewhat reluctant to accept these sweeping Court-made re-assertions without any further qualification, for reasons that closely mirror the arguments against a literal reading of the Treaty provisions in the first place. If we accept that additional qualifiers are demanded, they will have to be Court-made. Even if a common understanding exists that at least some limitations must be identified and established, this exercise cannot sensibly be described as discretion in the "thin sense". On the contrary, concerns about democratic legitimacy and Member State autonomy, which are commonly referred to as arguments in favour of judicial deference towards national policy choices, appear to be some of the blurriest deductions that a court can ever make, because they must be abstracted from an uncertain perception of the functioning of the legal system as such. A claim for limitations is thus a claim for the execution of judicial discretion, though it is often framed in terms that are more acceptable to lawyers, like "self-restraint".

Lawyers tend to look for the *rules* on self-restraint in the case law of the Court. Pursuant to a classical legal approach, the ideal of which is to identify rules, emphasis will be put on analysis of the law in its application phase. The classical approach rests on the premise that the application of a rule must necessarily mirror the rule itself; thus the rule can be identified through its application. It does not matter what the Court says, what matters is what the Court does. The status of the generally worded formulas applied by the Court in its introduction of the "rule", are thereby reduced to preliminary remarks, which may appear to be misleading rather than helpful. Bernard's explanation of the judgment of *Vlassopoulou* illustrates this legal approach. The case concerned the mutual recognition of diplomas. According to the Court[12]:

> It must be stated in this regard that, even if applied without any discrimination on the basis of nationality, national requirements concerning qualifications may have the effect of hindering nationals of the other Member States in the exercise of their right of establishment guaranteed to them by Article 52 of the EEC Treaty. That could be the case if the national rules in question took no account of the knowledge and qualifications already acquired by the person concerned in another Member State.

Bernard claims that "[d]espite the wording of this last sentence, *Vlassopoulou* can still be seen as a discrimination case. Insistence on a national diploma will disadvantage nationals of other Member States, since they are less likely to have studied in the host State."[13] On the facts, it is hard to disagree. However, it is also clear that the Court did not approach the restriction criterion as a prohibition on

---

[11] See e.g. Case C-76/90, *Säger*, EU:C:1991:331, para 12, Case C-415/93, *Bosman*, EU:C:1995:463, para 99; Case C-212/06, *Walloon*, EU:C:2008:178, para 48; Case C-442/02, *Caixa Bank*, EU:C:2004:586, para 11; Case C-65/05, *Commission v Greece ('Electronic games')*, EU:C:2006:673, para 27; Case C-142/05, *Mickelsson and Roos*, EU:C:2009:336, para 24; Case C-110/05, *Commission v. Italy* ("*Trailers*"), EU:C:2009:66, para 37; Case C-375/14, *Laezza*, EU:C:2016:60, para 21.

[12] Case C-340/89, *Vlassopoulou*, EU:C:1991:193, para 15.

[13] Bernard 1996, p. 84.

discrimination. In a forward-looking statement about how we should understand and interpret the (case-) law, it is somewhat problematic to disregard what the Court actually says about the potential reach of an overarching principle, and to substitute it for a narrower rule which is construed by reference to some more limited rationale which the Court, operating in full accordance with the wording of the Treaty, did not apply.

Still, it is probably fair to say that in the field of free movement of goods, persons and services, the academic legal debate "focused on more direct forms of discrimination [in the early years], followed by several decades of jurisprudential and legal debate over more indirect kinds of discrimination".[14] "[T]he free movement of persons—workers, establishment and services were generally regarded as an expression of the general principle of non-discrimination".[15] The approach towards the free movement of goods was to some extent understood as more expansive, but also in this field has it been argued that the notion of a "restriction" in the case-law of the CJEU largely coincided with the finding of discrimination, meaning that the existence of different treatment will appear as the guiding rationale if the facts of the cases are taken into consideration.[16] The famous judgment in *Keck* was deemed to confirm that rationale and to literally spell out the rules that a careful analysis of the case law would have proved existed beforehand.[17]

Conceived of as an exercise of discretion, the case law of the Court will present itself in quite another manner. The "rule" will by definition be wider than the concrete assessment, as discretion is exercised within the "rule" but is also guided by a number of different and supplementary objectives, which are of concrete relevance to the case at hand. Accordingly, outcomes will normally be narrower than the potential reach of the "rule", as they reflect the rationale that solves the particular case at a particular time.[18] Its limited use will not affect or change the "rule" itself, however, which is why I do not refer to the fundamental freedoms as "rules", but as principles. Applying Kelsen's notion of discretion, the principle of free movement can be seen as "a legal norm that governs the process whereby another legal norm is created, and also governs—to a different degree—the content of the norm to be created".[19] In other words, there is an important difference between the rational of the overarching principles on free movement and their potential reach, compared to the narrower rules that they produce in the assessment of concrete cases. The fact that the rules defining the concrete outcomes may differ

[14] de Búrca 2002, p. 184.

[15] Oliver and Roth 2004, p. 411.

[16] Opinion of AG Maduro in Joined Cases C-158/04 and C-159/04, *Alfa Vita Vassilopoulus*, EU:C:2006:212, para 46: "It seems to me that a consistent approach emerges from this case-law. These three criteria, as they have been applied by the Court, amount in substance to identifying *discrimination against the exercise of freedom of movement.*"

[17] See in particular the elegant analysis of Enchelmaier 2003.

[18] The dynamic development of the free movement of capital is illumining in this regard, see Flynn 2001.

[19] Kelsen 1998, p. 63.

does not necessarily entail that the practice of the CJEU is inconsistent. Convergence can still exist on the level of principles.

For a long period, the prevailing objective in free movement law was of an instrumental and to some extent narrow character: to establish a common market without internal frontiers.[20] If the objectives that guide the execution of court discretion change, broaden, mature or become more ambitious—as we are about to witness—it is fully legitimate that the written law on free movement produces other outcomes. The Treaty provisions are worded in a broad and sweeping manner, thereby leaving much to the judge's discretion.

2.2.3 The Case Law of the Court and the Nature of the European Legal Order

The Union is based on the rule of law. The Court has never understood this notion as the law of rules, but as an ideal, an objective that must not only be guarded, but also *realized*. Discretion is foreseen by Article 19 TEU, which states that the Court "shall ensure that in the interpretation and application of the Treaties the law is observed." Obviously, this constitutes a competence that is more comprehensive than a mere obligation to interpret and apply the Treaties.

As noted by Federico Mancini in 1989, [if] one were asked to synthesize the direction in which the case-law produced in Luxembourg has moved since 1957, one would have to say that it coincides with the making of a constitution for Europe.[21] The transformation of a multilateral treaty into a legal order could not have taken place in the absence of the "activism" of famous cases such as *Van Gend en Loos*, *Costa v. Enel* and *Commission v. United Kingdom* through which the principles of direct effect, supremacy and pre-emption were established.[22]

Another and better word for "activism" is "discretion", firstly because the findings of the Court were guided by the perceived objectives of the legal system in which it operated and not by the personal preferences of the judges. Secondly, while the term "activism" hints at the unacceptable, described by Hjalte Rasmussen as "revolting judicial behaviour", the discretionary findings of the Court became not only good law, but constitutional axioms, because indeed they were accepted.[23] The latter observation reveals a hidden but extremely important source both for the legitimacy and for the control of Court discretion. A national supreme court can do wrongs, and they will still stand. The CJEU is dependent on the loyalty of national courts. If their judgments do not deserve that loyalty, they will fall. A good

[20] See e.g. Lianos 2010; Case C-112/00 *Schmidberger*, EU:C:2003:333, paras 53–54.

[21] Mancini 1989, p. 595.

[22] Case 26/62, *Van Gend en Loos*, EU:C:1963:1; Case 6/64 *Costa v. Enel*, EU:C:1964:66; Case 804/79 *Commission v. United Kingdom*, EU:C:1981:93.

[23] Rasmussen 1986, p. 12.

illustration is the way in which the threat of non-loyalty has, in the extreme sense, necessitated and guided discretion. On 18 October 1967, the German Constitutional Court declared that the Community legal order had no lawful democratic basis, as it lacked a catalogue of human rights. Thus, its compatibility with basic constitutional requirements had to be examined at the national level. The CJEU responded in *Nold* and declared that "fundamental rights form an integral part of the general principles of law".[24] As Mancini rhetorically asks: "what book would they have to consult for the identification and the protection of such rights?"[25] Not the rulebook at any rate.[26]

Court discretion is at the core of free movement law as well. Below we shall return to the dynamic notion of a restriction, but let us first have a look at the closely related concept of justifications. The seminal judgment in *Cassis* established that "obstacles to movement within the community resulting from disparities between the national laws relating to the marketing of the products in question must be accepted in so far as those provisions may be recognized as being necessary in order to satisfy *mandatory requirements*".[27] This was a brave step. Contrary to the examples set out above, the Treaty did not lack written law in this regard. All the fundamental freedoms are subject to a catalogue of exceptions. As noted by Gormley[28]: "The rule of reason is entirely the creation of the Court of Justice." Still, the discretionary expansion was both principled and legitimate, due to one reason that is of particular importance to us. It anticipated and facilitated a similar expansion of the notion of a restriction, the purpose of which was to refine the functioning of the market.

In *van Duyn*, the Court noted that "the particular circumstances justifying recourse to the concept of public policy may vary from one country to another and from one period to another, and it is therefore necessary in this matter to allow the competent national authorities *an area of discretion within the limits imposed by the Treaty*".[29] This observation affects the understanding of the notion of a restriction as well. It should be remembered that originally, the doctrine on mandatory requirements was not set out as an additional, unwritten and Court-made list of new exceptions, but as an interpretation of the very rules of the Treaty: Measures which can be justified due to some objective policy concern do not constitute restrictions in the first place.[30] The concepts of "restrictions" and justifications are thus

[24] Case 4/73, *Nold*, EU:C:1974:51, para 13.

[25] Mancini 1989, p. 610.

[26] For another example, see the judgment in Case C-159/90 *Grogan*, [1991] I-4685, ingeniously analyzed by Lindahl 2008, pp. 303–313.

[27] Case 120/78, *Cassis de Dijon*, EU:C:1979:42, para 8 (emphasis added).

[28] Gormley 2005, p. 22.

[29] Case 41/74, *van Duyn*, EU:C:1974:133, para 18.

[30] E.g. Case 113/80, *Commission v. Ireland*, EU:C:1981:139, Case 177/83 *KOHL v. Ringelhan*, EU:C:1984:334; Case 207/83, *Commission v. United Kingdom*, EU:C:1985:161. According to Weiler 1999, p. 366 this approach was "no more than formalist sophistry", and as pointed to by Hatzopoulus in another chapter in this volume, we have witnessed a change. The Court frequently applies the term "overriding requirements of general public importance", see e.g. Joined Cases

inextricably linked. To state that discretion must be exercised within the limits imposed by the treaty is the same as saying that the treaty imposes discretion. Court discretion appears as the necessary corollary to the discretion that is vested in the Member States.

The observations above proves how the European legal order in general, and the functioning of the principle of free movement in particular, have been established and developed through the exercise of court discretion, which constitutes an indispensable component of the Courts competence, attributed to it by the open ended provisions in the Treaty, read in conjunction with the basic requirement that the law must both be observed *and realized*. As Halberstam has noted[31]:

> All too frequently, we encounter… a jaundiced view of individual actors' motivations. Some scholars, for example, suggest that judges are simply clever opportunists who appeal to purported legal norms solely as a means to promote "their independence, influence and authority" Others suggest that law is merely a "mask" for the promotion of one particular set of political objectives against contending objectives in the purely political sphere". In general, these critics would seem to imply that granting supranational actors any "strategic zone of discretion" must be a mistake. Decisional autonomy, on this view is simply an invitation to another set of actors to engage in self-promotion. In the case of the ECJ, the suggestion seems to be that the Court's law talk simply has the rest of us fooled…We must recognise, however, that the decisional autonomy of judges (and other individual actors) creates an important space for principled behaviour.

Court discretion is not something we should fear. Although the findings of the CJEU may in some instances be criticized, it is the best institution overall to handle and understand the content and reach of EU law, and its implications on a case-by-case basis. Discretion is controlled by the requirement that the national Courts and the political institutions of the Member States must accept it—and indeed, discretion has been accepted.

2.3 The Objections: Court Discretion Is Arbitrary and Disregards the Principle of Legal Certainty

2.3.1 Introduction

The objections against court discretion are quite predictable. Discretion is seen as being arbitrary or at least as something which does not pay due respect to the principle of legal certainty. In its strongest version, the argument would be that discretion runs contrary to the basic ideal of the "rule of law". Discretion is exactly the evil which the legal order was established to curtail, namely, a "rule of men".

(Footnote 30 continued)

C-34/95, C-35/95 and C-36/95 *de Agostini*, EU:C:1997:344, para 45 or similar expressions, see e.g. Joined Cases C-340/14 and C-341/14 *Trijber* ECLI:EU:C:2015:641.

[31] Halberstam 2005, pp. 781–782.

This part will proceed in three steps. In Sect. 2.3.2, I explain why legal discretion differs from free and personal choice. Far from being arbitrary, discretion is a particular form of legal decision-making subject to normative guidelines and constraints. Section 2.3.3 assesses the principle of legal certainty and the quest for clarity in more detail. Section 2.3.4 turns to the practical questions. It is submitted that a seemingly more rule-like approach to the fundamental freedoms, grounded in a wide concept of discrimination, is actually a prime example of court discretion. When it is realized that discretion cannot be avoided, it becomes clear that the resort to a wide notion of discrimination hides rather than guides.

2.3.2 Court Discretion

Court discretion is a necessary component of every legal system.[32] If we accept that it is (yet) not possible to enter the relevant legal provisions and the facts of a case into a computer and ask it to calculate the outcome mathematically; we will also have to accept legal discretion to some extent.

Court discretion is sometimes referred to as an exercise of intuition informed by subjective preferences.[33] That is to confuse legal discretion and true discretion. True discretion, or discretion in its strongest sense, exists when the decision-maker may simply refer to the existence of discretion as the legitimate reason for the choice being made, and thereby legitimately ignore any rational counter-argument. An example would be the smoker, who, confronted by all the rational arguments that go against smoking, validly defends his personal choice simply by stating that he smokes because he wants to. Generally speaking, the existence of true discretion is the corollary of either private autonomy or unfettered authority. Courts are public organs. They have to provide rational reasons for their findings, and as observed by Schauer: "The act of giving reasons is the antithesis of authority."[34]

It is not possible to provide a full-blown account of how court discretion works within the space constraints of this chapter. Instead, I will point to the practically most important manner of reasoning in discretionary decision-making: the "substantially the same argument". The most common technique, both in law and rhetoric, is to establish a starting point on which everyone will agree, and then to prove that the particular situation which is being assessed is "substantially the same".

The intriguing and well-known judgments of the CJEU on restrictions on use are illuminating (*Mickelsson and Roos* / *Italian trailers*). As a starting point, it is

[32] Dworkin 1963, p. 624.

[33] Snell 2010, p. 469; Jansson and Kalimo 2014, p. 540.

[34] Schauer 1995, pp. 636–637.

common ground that total bans on the sale of a commodity constitutes a restriction.[35] We can agree that restrictions on the use of a product do not constitute an absolute ban, but, so goes the argument, if the restriction on use has "a considerable influence on the behaviour of consumers", the effects are substantially the same as the effects of a total ban.[36] Thus, the legal approach towards severe restrictions on use should be the same as the approach towards total bans. Notably, opponents of this finding would argue in the same manner, but choose a different paradigm as their starting point.[37] In the field of goods, "selling arrangements" do not constitute restrictions as long as both national and foreign products are treated in the same manner, even though the volume of sales is being reduced. Thus, it may be argued that restrictions on use are substantially the same as "selling arrangements".[38] The latter is also a discretionary choice, but the pick between the two solutions is by no means unbound: it is guided by traditional and rational legal arguments. For one thing, restrictions on use *are not* "selling arrangements", and it would be easy to circumvent the prohibition on total bans if severe restrictions on use were not treated in the same manner. Most importantly, the Treaty provision on goods provides solid support to the approach chosen by the Court.[39] "Quantitative restrictions on imports and all measures having equivalent effect shall be prohibited". An effects-based application of the "substantially the same" argument is not demanded by the legal system in the mechanical sense, but it is definitely the execution of discretion which best fits the system.

The findings of the Court in the judgments on restrictions on use can of course be criticized, but they cannot be criticized for being arbitrary. On the contrary, the Court's approach is open to criticism because the judgments are not arbitrary, but based on rational arguments. Our engagement in the discussions on the outcome of the cases rests on the premise that the prevailing arguments should be the best arguments, and with regard to that, opinions will normally differ. The reason why we engage, however, is grounded in the belief that it is possible to have a meaningful discussion about what the better arguments are. If our sense of meaningfulness is true, it must also be true that legal discretion is not unbound, but can be guided by rational considerations.

---

[35] See e.g. case C-34/79 *Henn and Darby*, EU:C:1979:295, para 12: "a prohibition on imports [...] is the most extreme form of restriction".

[36] Case C-142/05 *Mickelsson and Roos*, EU:C:2009:336, para 26; Case C-110/05 *Commission v. Italy* ("*Trailers*"), EU:C:2009:66, para 56, Opinion of AG *Léger* in *Trailers*, C:2006:646, para 40; opinion of AG Bot in *Trailers*, EU:C:2006:646, paras 103–105 and paras 157–159.

[37] See Enchelmaier in Chap. 4 in this volume.

[38] Opinion of AG Kokott in *Mickelsson and Roos*, EU:C:2006:782, paras 47–56.

[39] In the same manner AG Bot in *Trailers*, para 102 of the opinion.

2.3.3 *Legal Certainty*

2.3.3.1 Introduction

Some observers have praised the rule-like approach in the judgment in *Keck* for providing clarity and legal certainty.[40] To assess whether a formalist approach towards the application of the restriction criterion is more favourable than a discretionary case-by-case assessment, we have to ask ourselves: What exactly is meant by references to clarity or legal certainty? Why is it important and what (if anything) do we lose if we choose to pursue these ideals?

2.3.3.2 The Principle of Legal Certainty

In its strongest version, the clarity provided by a rule-like application of the restriction criterion can be understood as a requirement stemming from the principle of legal certainty. That principle however, is not at stake, and will not be challenged by an approach which embraces judicial discretion.

Due to the rule of precedent, the case law of the ECJ will provide paradigmatic guidance on the interpretation of free movement law. Absolute prohibitions constitute restrictions, the same is true for national regulations that create double burdens, have a disparate impact on products and services from other member states, and so on. Because of the dynamic character of the interpretation of free movement law, the hard cases will normally occur when the question is whether to push the reach of free movement further, into new territory, as in the cases on restrictions on use mentioned above. From the perspective of the plaintiffs, it must have appeared as highly unpredictable whether the Court would assert their arguments in favour of a broad reading of the provision on the free movement of goods. That uncertainty however, is of a far more general and practical character than the specific values and interests that are being protected by the principle of legal certainty. The core objective of that principle is to protect the citizen from state *interference* that is not specified in a clear rule. It would appear as a misunderstanding of the principle, which would run contrary to its objective of protecting the citizens, if the plaintiffs in *Mickelsson & Roos* lost the case, by reference to the fact that they tried to break new legal ground.

The rule of law is a way of restraining state power by "rational principles of civic order".[41] The principle of legal certainty is one element of the rule of law. The admission to argue in favour of an expansive interpretation of a right, with recourse to rational arguments is another. There is no conflict between the principle of legal certainty and Court discretion, which should instead be regarded as complementary components of the rule of law, for the protection of the citizen.

---

[40] See in particular Oliver 1999, pp. 793–799.

[41] Selznick 1969, p. 11.

2.3.3.3 Practical Uncertainty

If discretion is introduced, it may be argued that it will be more difficult for national courts to understand and apply EU law and the notion of a "restriction".[42] Obviously, the courts themselves are not protected by the principle of legal certainty, but, from a practical perspective, it may be held that discretion introduces some kind of ambiguity, which in the end threatens the efficiency of EU law.[43] For a number of reasons, this fear seems to be exaggerated.

For a start, it is debatable whether a rule-like approach towards the application of the rules on free movement and the notion of a restriction is able to provide its promised clarity. In his assessment of the Keck-judgment in *Trailers*, AG Bot noted that[44]:

> The distinction made by the Court may therefore be artificial and the demarcation line between those different categories of measures may be uncertain. In some cases, the Court describes rules on product characteristics as 'selling arrangements'. In other cases, it treats measures concerning selling arrangements for goods as rules concerning product characteristics. That applies, in particular, to rules governing advertising where they have an effect on the packaging of the product. Finally, it may happen that the Court abandons that distinction and makes an analysis based only on the effects of the rules. Those examples demonstrate the difficulties which the Court may encounter in classifying certain measures. It is therefore, in my view, difficult to work on the basis of categories when, in practice, national courts and the Community judicature may be confronted with very different rules, which they must assess having regard to the circumstances of each individual case.

In short, the point of AG Bot is that rule-like classifications of national regulatory measures create their own difficulties, and that the resort to a discretionary assessment, case-by-case, is more straight-forward than a rule-like approach.

In any case, difficulties with regard to the interpretation and application of EU law is foreseen and remedied by the preliminary-rulings mechanism enshrined in Article 267 TFEU.[45] Further, it must be emphasized that the application of EU law in national courts has always been a highly discretionary exercise.[46] If a restriction exists, Union objectives and national objectives will have to be reconciled through the application of the principle of proportionality. A complex and case-specific assessment is required. The outcome will be decisive to the efficiency

[42] See e.g. Enchelmaier in Chap. 4 in this volume.

[43] See e.g. Snell 2010, p. 459.

[44] AG Bot in *Trailers*, para 81 of the opinion.

[45] I.e. Case 166/73, *Rheinmühlen*, EU:C:1974:3; Case C-224/01, *Köbler*, EU:C:2003:513.

[46] As Maduro 1998 rhetorically asks at pp. 163–164: "if the court is the more appropriate and legitimate institution, in the second stage, to balance all the interests and values involved, why is this not always the case?"

of EU law. Still, a very basic tenet of free movement law is that the assessment of proportionality is solely a task for the national courts.[47]

Principally, it is submitted that it is mistaken to focus on the possible challenges that a discretionary approach to the restriction criterion may pose when the reach of EU law is being negotiated in the courtroom. The voluminous case law of the CJEU leaves us with the impression that EU law and the application of the fundamental freedoms are primarily being handled by courts.[48] In fact, it is the supranational and national lawmakers who are primarily coping with the provisions on free movement. From the latter perspective, a rule-like definition of where EU law stops and national legal autonomy starts appears to be counterproductive and could actually threaten the efficiency of EU law.

At the outset, it seems evident that a clear defining line between EU objectives and national objectives and between the competence of the Union and the autonomy of the Member States does not exist out-there somewhere, neither as an empirical nor as a legal fact. In *Germany v. Parliament and Council*, the Court clarified the reach of the legislative competence of the Union, and established that[49]:

> While a mere finding of disparities between national rules is not sufficient to justify having recourse to Article [114 TFEU], it is otherwise where there are differences between the laws, regulations or administrative provisions of the Member States which are such as to obstruct the fundamental freedoms and thus have a direct effect on the functioning of the internal market.

As noted by Weatherill, the Court bestows the Union legislature with a competence that is "strikingly broad" and leaves "a significant breadth of discretion".[50] The Court's finding reflects that by nature, the interface between the national legal systems and the EU legal order is of a highly complex nature.

Should the CJEU *introduce* and apply rules that establish and define a more clear-cut interface between EU law and national law in fields where there does not (yet) exist secondary legislation, and where the reach of free movement will thus mark the borderline between national autonomy and Union objectives? Resorting to formalism will of course amount to a mere fiction, introduced for the sake of clarity, addressing the alleged needs of national courts.[51] One problem which will not be further elaborated upon here is the hypothesis that such an artificially construed defining line may negatively affect the reach of the legislative competence of the

---

[47] E.g. Joined Cases C-34/95, C-35/95 and C-36/95, *de Agostini*, EU:C:1997:344, para 45; Case C-438/05, *Viking*, EU:C:2007:772, para 80; Case C-142/05, *Mickelsson and Roos*, EU:C:2009:336, para 26; Joined Cases C-340/14 and C-341/14, *Trijber* EU:C:2015:641, para 75; Davies 2012b.

[48] See e.g. Roth 2002, p. 8: "Control of Member State measures by the ECJ involves a replacement of a decision reached in the national political process through the Community judiciary."

[49] Case C-380/03 *Germany v. Parliament and Council*, EU:C:2006:772, para 37.

[50] Weatherill 2009, pp. 900–991.

[51] On the introduction of a fiction, see Oliver 1999, p. 798.

Union legislature, because the substance of free movement-law constitutes one component of the competences that are conferred to the Union.[52] Instead, I will concentrate on the other side of the problem that relates to the role of national lawmakers in the European project.

AG Maduro has observed that it is not the task of the Court "to review the political choices made by the Member States. Judicial review of measures likely to prohibit, impede or render less attractive the exercise of the freedoms of movement rather seeks to ensure that those choices take account of the impact which they may have on transnational situations."[53] These two axioms are easy to accept, but difficult to reconcile in practice. More or less all national political choices may in some sense affect transnational situations and actors, and may in some sense make it less attractive to exercise the freedom of movement.

From a normative theoretical perspective, it could instead be argued that the rules on free movement should reach further when they address national lawmakers than when applied in the courtroom.[54] For one thing, national parliaments have a greater *political* obligation to consider the European project than do the national courts, and to consider the possibility of harmonization even though it is not strictly demanded. In addition, lawmakers possess greater flexibility than courts. The latter will have to apply or disapply national rules, while the lawmaker has the possibility to consider whether the national rules can be shaped in a manner which is slightly less burdensome ("more proportionate") for international actors. To the national lawmakers, a discretionary and possibly far-reaching right to free movement introduces a general requirement of good governance.[55]

At the practical level however, it seems impossible to establish two different notions of a restriction, one to be applied in court, and one which addresses national lawmakers. Then the latter should prevail. The most important constitutional question when the reach of free movement is defined is not the extent to which courts should be vested with the competence to scrutinize political choices, but the extent to which the national lawmakers should be generally subject to taking the European perspective into account. A fluid conception of the notion of a restriction, clarified through the exercise of discretion on a case-by-case basis, may prove to be overreaching when applied in the courtroom, in the sense that measures which consistently will be "Court-proportionate" will be caught to a greater degree than

[52] On the intimate relationship between the notion of a restriction and the legislative competences of the Union, see e.g. Dougan 2010, pp. 171–179.

[53] Opinion of AG Poiares Maduro in Case C-446/03 *Marks & Spencer plc v Halsey (Her Majesty's Inspector of Taxes)*, EU:C:2005:201, para 37.

[54] On proportionality as a "bridge between courts and legislatures", see in particular Jackson 2015, pp. 3144–3147.

[55] See also Kumm 2010.

pursuant to a rule-based notion of a restriction. It is not necessarily the case that such measures are also "lawmaker-proportionate", in the sense that national law-makers should not be required to consider whether better and less burdensome solutions are possible, *strictu sensu*.

In short therefore, an account of the notion of a restriction which rests on discretion, not rules, is the one that best reflects law-making as an exercise of discretion. If the finding of a restriction hinges on the discretionary identification of some relevant Union objective, all possible Union objectives must be investigated, assessed and accounted for in the national regulatory process. To the contrary, if the notion of a restriction is made dependent on rule-like, fictional categorizations, relevant considerations may be ruled out and ignored in the national law-making process.

2.3.3.4 The Floodgate of Cases?

The risk that a somewhat vague restriction criterion can be used by traders to invoke the "Treaty as a means of challenging any rules whose effect is to limit their commercial freedom", must be taken seriously, and indeed was taken seriously by the Court in its judgment in *Keck*.[56] While the judgment is often being discussed as a constitutional clarification of the objectives and reach of the principle of free movement, the argument provided by the Court was far more pragmatic. Apparently, the claimant would lose the case at the level of proportionality anyway. In practical terms, what the Court stated was that "restrictions" which we foresee that we will *always* judge as being (court-)proportionate are henceforth no longer called "restrictions"—and thus a simplified judicial procedure was established for some specific national measures ("certain selling arrangements"). When it comes to practical arguments about workload, the Court is definitely the best institution to consider their weight, and in this regard, the judgment in *Keck* is a perfect example of legitimate court discretion.

The risk of overload may however be questioned, as the timeliness and costs of legal processes will discourage plaintiffs from challenging national measures which are undoubtedly court-proportionate. In addition, fewer situations are guided solely by the fundamental freedoms today than in 1993, as the amount of secondary legislation has increased. It suffices to say that the Court has not repeated its practical concerns in other fields of free movement law, and though it could be argued that it should, such arguments are not particularly weighty unless the Court itself puts them forward.

[56] Joined Cases C-267/91 *Keck and Mithouard*, EU:C:1993:905, para 14.

2.3.4 Is There Any Alternative? The Broad Concept of "Discrimination" as a Prime Example of Court Discretion

2.3.4.1 Introduction

Those who argue in favour of a rule-based approach to free movement law, and the notion of a restriction, will normally resort to a wide concept of discrimination, to avoid the alleged uncertainty and potential overreach of a discretionary approach. It is submitted that their proposition has three flaws. The first is the lack of a convincing normative theory. The second is that the application of a *wide* concept of discrimination is indeed an exercise of discretion.[57] The third is that the approach is out of line with the approach of the CJEU. As noted by AG Kokott, it is established case law that the notion of a restriction encapsulates both the prohibition of discrimination and indistinctly applicable measures that constitute a hindrance to free movement.[58]

2.3.4.2 The Core Meaning of Discrimination

To substantiate the critical observations set out above, I will make use of a well-known proposition devised by Hart as a starting point. Rules have a core meaning and a penumbra where their meaning is more uncertain.[59] It has been observed that the "more complex and changing the phenomenon being regulated, the wider that penumbra is likely to be; indeed in the most difficult contexts the penumbra of uncertainty swallows up the core".[60] As we shall see, a *wide* notion of discrimination explores the penumbra. For that reason it is encumbered with uncertainty, it lacks a normative foundation, and in the end, it poses a threat to the core concept of discrimination that it is crucial to preserve.

---

[57] Bernard 1996, p. 95.

[58] Opinion of AG Kokott in Case C-222/07, *Unión de Televisiones Comerciales Asociadas (UTECA) v Administración General del Estado*, EU:C:2008:468, para 77 referring to, on free movement for workers: Case C-415/93, *Bosman*, EU:C:1995:463, paras 92, 103 and 104; Case C-190/98, *Graf,* EU:C:2000:49, paras 21–23 and Case C-464/02, *Commission* v Denmark, EU: C:2005:546, para 45; on freedom of establishment: Case C-55/94, *Gebhard*, EU:C:1995:411, para 37, and Case C-442/02, *CaixaBank France*, EU:C:2004:586, para 11; on freedom to provide services: Case C-76/90, *Säger*, EU:C:1991:331, para 12 and Case C-490/04, *Commission* v *Germany*, EU:C:2007:430, para 63; on the free movement of capital: the golden shares judgments Case C-367/98, *Commission* v *Portugal*, EU:C:2002:326, para 44, Case C-483/99, *Commission* v *France*, EU:C:2002:327, para 40 and Joined Cases C-463/04 and C-464/04, *Federconsumatori and Others*, EU:C:2007:752, para 19.

[59] Hart 1961.

[60] Braithwaite 2002, p. 54.

In European Union law, the prohibition against discrimination has a clear legal basis in Article 18 TFEU, which defines its core in very precise words. Discrimination *on grounds of nationality* is prohibited. The rationale is obvious. Considerations about nationality are simply irrelevant in a single market. Discrimination in this core meaning, in academic legal writing often presented as direct or overt discrimination, does not appear very often. Of greater practical importance are the obstacles to free movement stemming from the disparities created by the different laws of the Member States. Measures which create dual burdens or which conserve established trading patterns are well known examples. Such measures are motivated by sensible and legitimate concerns in the general interest, like the protection of health, irrespective of nationality.[61] They differ from discrimination in the true sense—perhaps not always in their practical effects, but definitely from a normative point of view.[62] In many instances, the foreigner's claim is *not* to be treated in the same manner as the national actors.[63] The foreigner wants to be treated *as a foreigner*, and to rely wholly on the regulation in his home state. The foreigner's problem is not discrimination in any direct or personal sense, but that the market is fragmented from a regulatory point of view, something that creates "obstacles to movement".[64]

As part of his critique of Nic Shuibhne, Stefan Enchelmaier, a strong proponent of a rule-like approach grounded in a wide notion of discrimination, has observed that: "The prohibition of *such discrimination* [the wide notion of discrimination] follows not from Article 18, as this is not a case of discrimination based on nationality, but from Article 26."[65] There is definitely some truth in this, but at the same time, the observation may seem to fall on its own sword. "Such discrimination" (e.g. regulation which creates disparate impacts) is actually not "discrimination" according to the definition of the term contained in Article 18 TFEU, but apparently some other kind of discrimination according to Article 26 TFEU. The latter provision does however not apply the term "discrimination" at all. It protects free movement by stating, "The internal market shall comprise an area without internal frontiers in which the free movement of goods, persons, services and capital is ensured in accordance with the provisions of the Treaties."

From the foregoing it is clear that a *wide* application of the concept of discrimination would be the perfect example of the penumbra swallowing the core. The problem with a conceptualization as Enchelmaier's is that it threatens to compromise the basic notion of discrimination, the fundamental right not to be

[61] E.g. Case C-405/98 *Gourmet* [2001] ECR I-1795.

[62] See also Ortino 2002, pp. 161–183.

[63] Case 136/78 *Auer* [1979] ECR 437, para 21.

[64] The expression used in *Cassis de Dijon* Cited *supra* note 27, para 8. For a similar link to "the single market and [...] the achievement of its objectives" in the field of services, see e.g. Case C-522/04 *Commission v. Belgium* [2007] ECR I-5701, para 37.

[65] Enchelmaier 2016 p. 14.

discriminated against.[66] According to the Dworkinian conception, a fundamental right can be rebutted by a clear and major public benefit, but not by a mere reference to the general interest. In the latter situation, the claim of a fundamental right would be pointless, and would show that the term is used in some sense other than the strong sense.[67] On this conception of a right, the prohibition on discrimination is fundamental, as the doctrine of mandatory requirements cannot be invoked to justify direct discrimination; the only available justification will be the written exceptions in the Treaty.[68] This is the narrow conception of discrimination which the Court tried to preserve in its Gebhard-formula, quoted in Sect. 2.2.2 above. The judgment made it clear that the notion of a restriction reaches further than the notion of discrimination, but the latter concept does still have an important role to play. It suspends the possibility of invoking the mandatory requirements doctrine, and conserves the fundamental status of the core-right not to be discriminated against *on the basis of nationality*.

2.3.4.3 The Wide Notion of Discrimination

If the concept of "discrimination" is to be applied outside its core, in an attempt to conserve a rule-like definition of the restriction-criterion, it becomes nothing but an exercise of discretion. For one thing, we (or in the last instance the Court) will have to define how "wide" the notion is. Oliver has argued that the "concept of discrimination should be as wide as possible", but what exactly does that mean?[69] Supposedly, the concept can be construed extremely broadly, as rules do always have a disparate impact, in the sense that those who are subject to regulation feel the effects differently. For a business to have to cope with 28 different legal regimes is in itself burdensome, even though the troublesome rules no not create disparate impacts in a narrow sense. Why not therefore apply the notion of disparate impact in its widest sense? We did so with the notion of discrimination, leaving its normative rationale behind. Why not repeat the manoeuvre and simply state the obvious: that all rules have a disparate impact?[70]

---

[66] While on the other hand the right to free movement is construed too narrowly, see Sect. 2.4.

[67] Dworkin 1977, p. 192.

[68] E.g. Case 120/78 *Cassis de Dijon*, [1979] ECR 649; Case C-55/94 *Gebhard* [1995] ECR I-4165; *Servizi Ausiliari Dottori Commercialisti* [2006] ECR I-2941, para 36; Case C-546/07 *Commission v. Germany* [2010] ECR I-439, paras 39–53; Joined Cases C-344/13 and C-367/13 *Blanco & Fabretti* ECLI:EU:C:2014:2311, para 37; Case C-375/14 *Laezza* EU:C:2016:60, para 25.

[69] Oliver 1999, p. 796.

[70] To paraphrase the Court in the "posted workers" judgment, it may be argued that every national rule "involves an additional administrative and financial burden for undertakings established in another Member State, so that the latter are not on an equal footing". Undertakings established in another Member State must adjust to the peculiarities of the regulation in the host state, to which national undertakings have already adapted. Cf. Case C-319/06, *Commission v. Luxembourg*, EU: C:2008:350, para 85.

The problem with the term "discrimination" is that, outside its core, detached from its normative rationale, it is just a word, a label. It cannot guide us when we try to solve the questions set out above. The answers will not be an exercise of informed and legally constrained discretion, but a matter of personal choice. In this regard, it is quite telling how the notion of "discrimination" has been applied in a notoriously unclear manner in legal scholarship, as famously described by Hilson.[71]

The Court escapes the criticism. Normally it avoids the language of discrimination.[72] This has been explained by reference to the fact that the term is "loaded".[73] A term that is scarcely used can hardly be "loaded" in the linguistic sense. The straightforward explanation is that the term is loaded with normative content, and that its normative content does not fit the penumbra cases. Another explanation is that other terms such as "market access" or simply the "functioning of the internal market", as applied in Article 26.1 TFEU, provide more precise guidance in such situations. Judicial discretion cannot be avoided, but the questions set out above can be answered in a more precise and direct manner than a wide concept of discrimination would entail. The following observation presented by Davies, in a defence of a wide notion of discrimination, can be used to illustrate the point[74]:

> It may be suggested that the picture above does not work in reality. For example, a regulation increasing the costs of market entry, even if applicable to all market participants, may deter businesses in states where it is hard to raise capital, or may deter smaller businesses who may consider it too risky. Even equal-burden rules may therefore, it could be argued, deter entry in the real world. However, this misses the logical point: if the measure actually has the effects described, so that as a result of problems with access to capital or varying firm sizes it discourages market entry, then it will be, as a matter of fact, discriminatory in effect. The identity between inequality and restraints on market access is not a contingent one, but a necessary one.

The argument made by Davies is much the same as to accept that, in the real world, the real effect of regulation on market access and the functioning of the market must be taken into account, but then to reassert that if a restriction on market access exists, it proves that the contested regulation is in fact discriminatory. It is of course possible to argue in this manner, but it would seem to hide rather than to guide. If (at least in some instances) the notion of market access informs the application of the concept of discrimination, then the latter is just a useless and misleading label.

Another illustration is the observation made by Bernard, that[75]:

---

[71] Hilson 1999, pp. 448–451.

[72] According to Davies 2003, p. 58, even though the Court has eliminated the concept of indirect discrimination from its language, it is still relevant and at the core of the restriction criterion. "It is just that the discussion of it is avoided." However, one has to wonder: Can a court announce that it will no longer discuss the only thing that matters?

[73] Snell 2010, pp. 449, 468.

[74] Davies 2011, p. 22.

[75] Bernard 1996, pp. 86–87 (emphasis added).

> It is not that the Treaty cannot be interpreted so as to prohibit discrimination against one's own nationals. While this is an aspect of discrimination that the Founding Fathers *probably did not have in mind, it would not be unreasonable* to argue that the notion of a common market necessarily implies a uniform treatment of all regardless of nationality and therefore prohibits any kind of discrimination, even discrimination by a state against its own nationals.

Even if the suggested approach may lead to correct outcomes in substantial terms, a finding that hinges on the argument that something is "not unreasonable" appears to be highly discretionary. It may also appear to be arbitrary if it is anchored in a wide concept of discrimination. Even if applied in its wide sense, discrimination is by definition confined to the different treatment of actors from other Member States. It is simply not possible for a Member State to discriminate against its own nationals. Again, what we see is an approach where "discrimination" is reduced to an empty slogan, which derives its substance from other considerations, namely that "the notion of a common market necessarily implies a uniform treatment of all regardless of nationality". The Court has been right in addressing this issue from a different angle, the right to access the market.[76]

To artificially force new considerations into old concepts hides rather than guides. Instead, we should let the notion of discrimination perform its basic function according to its normative rational, and focus more directly on the substantial question. What will the notion of a restriction designate if discretion is guided by the objective of creating a truly uniform single market and to protect its "functioning", as required by Article 26 TFEU?[77]

2.4 Discretion and the Individual Right to Access the Market

2.4.1 From Instrumental to Personal Rights

As observed by Ioannis Lianos, until recently the political necessity of completing the internal market led to a somewhat narrow, instrumental application of the fundamental freedoms, the objective of which was to remove existing barriers to economic integration. To some extent, this approach marked a decoupling from other objectives.[78] We may be about to witness a change, as the regulation of the Union is more and more becoming the regulation of a society, a development to which the functioning of the market, and the application of its four freedoms must contribute. A qualified prediction is that the character and the application of the fundamental freedoms will shift. To an increasing extent, the four freedoms will be

---

[76] As in Case C-384/93 *Alpine Investments*, [1995] ECR I-1141, paras 37–38.

[77] In the opposite direction, Snell 2010, p. 449.

[78] Lianos 2010, pp. 705–706.

taken to constitute not only instrumental rights, but also personal rights.[79] As noted by AG Maduro: It would be neither "satisfactory nor true to the development of the case-law to reduce freedom of movement to a mere standard of promotion of trade between Member States. It is important that the freedoms of movement fit into the broader framework of the objectives of the internal market and European citizenship. (…). They represent the cross-border dimension of the economic and social status conferred on European citizens."[80]

The personalization of economic rights that were initially of a purely instrumental character is not an unprecedented process. The judgment in *Lilli Schröder* is both famous and illumining. The case concerned the interpretation of Article 119 of the EC Treaty, now Article 157 TFEU. The Court stated that the original aim of the provision was "to avoid a situation in which undertakings established in States which have actually implemented the principle of equal pay suffer a competitive disadvantage in intra-Community competition as compared with undertakings established in States which have not yet eliminated discrimination against women workers as regards pay".[81] It proceeded by emphasizing that the provision formed a "part of the social objectives of the Community, which is not merely an economic union but is at the same time intended, by common action, to ensure social progress and seek constant improvement of the living and working conditions of the peoples of Europe, as is emphasised in the Preamble to the Treaty".[82] Based on that observation and referring to the developments in the case-law, the conclusion of the Court was that the "economic aim pursued by Article 119 of the Treaty, namely the elimination of distortions of competition between undertakings established in different Member States, is secondary to the social aim pursued by the same provision, which constitutes the expression of a fundamental human right".[83]

Today, there are two main catalysts to the personalization of the right to free movement: The increasing importance of the concept of citizenship analysed in detail in other chapters in this volume and the enactment of the Charter of Fundamental Rights.[84] In *Grzelczyk* the Court stated that "Union citizenship is destined to be the fundamental status of nationals of the Member States".[85] The Charter of Fundamental Rights establishes a similar requirement of fit, as fundamental rights are by definition the overarching guideline for the application of the other provisions contained in a legal system.[86] The enactment of the Charter signals

---

[79] See De Cecco 2014.

[80] Opinion of AG Maduro in Joined Cases C-158/04 and C-159/04, *Alfa Vita Vassilopoulus*, EU:C:2006:212, para 40.

[81] Case C-50/96, *Deutsche Telekom AG* v *Lilli Schröder*, EU:C2000:72, para 54.

[82] *Lilli Schröder*, para 55.

[83] *Lilli Schröder*, para 57.

[84] See the contributions of Tryfonidou, Eriksen and Stubberud, and De Cecco in Chaps. 3, 10 and 12 in this volume.

[85] Case C-184/99, *Grzelczyk*, EU:C:2001:458, para 31.

[86] Petersman 2012, p. 307.

an "individual rights approach" to European Union Law in general, marked by its Article 16, which constitutionalizes the right to conduct a business.[87] Further, the Charter reflects the constitutional conception of the status of Union Citizens. Article 45 establishes that every citizen has the right to move and reside freely within the territory of the Member States while Article 15 protects the freedom to choose an occupation and the right to engage in work. Other provisions, such as Articles 35 and 36 mark the integration between fundamental rights, citizens' rights, market rights and social rights, by recognizing the right to *access* healthcare and services of general economic interest.[88]

Based on the observations above, it seems uncontroversial to state that "the relationship between fundamental freedoms and fundamental rights is characterized by a broad convergence both in terms of *structure and content*".[89] However, how is the basic requirement that the application of the fundamental freedoms must fit into its legal surroundings to be coped with in practice?

The focus in scholarly literature has been on the content of rights. While appreciating the importance of such analyses, the remaining part of this chapter will focus on another question: How does the *structure and character* of rights affect the process of reviewing and interpreting their content? The basic observation is as follows: The application of instrumental rights may legitimately be made dependent on rule-like tests. One breaks some eggs, so to speak, to gain other benefits, such as clarity and procedural economy. The reach and content of individual rights that have status as "fundamental" or "personal" cannot be cut off as easily. They require a thorough, substantive and individual assessment. As we shall see, the personalization of rights seems to demand court discretion.

2.4.2 The Structure of the Legal Assessment and the Notion of "Market Access"

The judgment in *Keck* has been thoroughly analysed in writings on the fundamental freedoms. Mainly, the academic interest stems from the presupposition that the rationale behind the rule-like categorizations established in that judgment may help to define both the objective and the reach of free movement law in general. In other words, *Keck* is very often subject to analysis when the content of the free movement rights is being assessed. However, as pointed to by Niels Fenger in another chapter in this volume, the importance of the judgment stems largely from its *structuring* of the legal assessment[90]:

---

[87] Petersman 2005.

[88] On the integration, see Bekkedal 2011.

[89] Opinion of Trstenjak AG in Case C–271/08 *European Commission v. Federal Republic of Germany*, EU:C:2010:183, para 187 (emphasis added).

[90] See Chap. 5 in this volume, Sect. 5.4.2.

> …one of the main purposes of *Keck* was to avoid the need for (…) concrete assessments by making that evaluation once and for all with regard to the types of rules covered by the judgment, *i.e.*, rules concerning to whom, where and when a product might be sold. Or to put it differently, with the statement that no market access is restricted by non-discriminatory selling arrangements, the Court in *Keck* insisted on a legal fiction in the name of legal certainty and operability.

The position taken by AG Jacobs in his famous opinion in *Leclerc-Siplec* marks a diametrically opposed approach to the question of how the legal assessment is to be *structured*.[91] The AG argued in favour of a "market access" test[92]:

> There is one guiding principle which seems to provide an appropriate test: that principle is that all undertakings which engage in a legitimate economic activity in a Member State should have unfettered access to the whole of the Community market, unless there is a valid reason for denying them full access to a part of that market. In spite of occasional inconsistencies in the reasoning of certain judgments, that seems to be the underlying principle which has inspired the Court's approach from *Dassonville* through "Cassis de Dijon" to *Keck*. Virtually all of the cases are, in their result, consistent with the principle, even though some of them appear to be based on different reasoning.

Notably, the AG did not challenge neither the objective nor the rational on which *Keck* rests. He reasserted that "the central concern of the Treaty provisions on the free movement of goods is to prevent unjustified obstacles to trade between Member States", emphasizing that it was the Court's reasoning in *Keck*, not the result, that he considered to be "unsatisfactory".[93] Subject to the criticism of AG Jacobs was the *structure* of the judgment and its legal reasoning, the rule-like approach to the legal assessment. The AG criticized rule-like categorizations for their rigidity: their fictional boxing in of matters that, to the individual affected by burdensome regulatory measures, are a matter of degree.[94] What the AG acknowledged is that a rule-based approach may be unable to produce outcomes that realize the objectives that justified the rules in the first place. As noted by Fredrick Schauer: "Rule based decision making is … the theory of the second best".[95] "A decision-maker instructed to make decisions according to a set of rules is … instructed not to consider certain facts, certain reasons and certain arguments".[96] Rules conserve the competence of the instructor and deprives the decision-maker of the possibility of making, in the substantive sense, the best decision. A "non-mistaken rule-constrained decision-maker can never do better

---

[91] As noted by Snell 2010, p. 455 the recent developments in the case law of the ECJ may indicate that the Court has finally embraced the approach suggested by AG Jacobs.

[92] Opinion of Jacobs AG in Case C-412/93, *Leclerc-Siplec*, EU:C:1994:393, para 41.

[93] Para 39 of the opinion, cf. para 48.

[94] Para 38 of the opinion.

[95] Schauer 1991, p. 152.

[96] Schauer 1991, p. 158.

than a non-mistaken particularistic decision maker can do under the same substantive theory of decision, but can often do worse".[97]

For obvious reasons, the AG did not suggest another rule. Far more radically, he favoured discretion. He argued that legal fictions and constructions should be eliminated and substituted by concrete assessments on a case-by-case basis.[98] For that reason, in my opinion, to ask what rule the term "market access" is intended to represent is to pose the wrong question.[99] The notion was invented to become the negation of any specific rule, to facilitate a discretionary assessment that ensures the full realization of individual rights in the substantive sense.[100]

Not only will an approach as set out by the AG cope with the under- and over-inclusiveness of rules, compared to their objectives; the open term "market access" is a sponge that makes it possible for the Court to realize the requirement that its assessments must fit into the legal surroundings.[101] It may also tend to change and to widen our perception of what the relevant Union objectives are, as we have to actively start and search for them. Rules cages in specific objectives. Since it is difficult to make rules for every thinkable situation, rules will tend to focus on the *main* objective(s) only. Guided by rules, we will not bother with the thinkable, but resort to what has already been thought. Discretion on the other hand, will allow us to produce new rules when needed, and will demand that we elaborate upon whether a Union objective exists that can legitimize a particular construction of the restriction criterion in the particular case.

2.4.3 The Increasing Use of the Term "Market Access"

The sections above provide some explanation as to why the term "market access" is increasingly being used by the CJEU in its assessment of whether national regulation constitutes a restriction on free movement. The notion provides flexibility and in that regard it vests the Court with discretion. Its introduction may be seen as a necessary step to enable the Court to manage the personalization of the right to free movement. This point will be further elaborated upon in the sections below. First, I shall present some additional basic reasons for the Court's adherence to the notion.

As a start, the term "market access" expresses a self-explanatory objective that provides a neutral guideline for the execution of discretion. While the term "discrimination" is loaded with specific normative content and should be reserved for

---

[97] Schauer 1991, p. 157.

[98] Para 42 of the opinion.

[99] Snell 2010.

[100] Thus, as noted by Snell 2010, p. 468 "the notion of market access has in practice had several different usages"—but that in itself is not a valid criticism of the use of the concept.

[101] As noted by Enchelmaier in Chap. 4 in this volume, Sect. 4.4.2: "Market access is not a test but an objective".

discrimination in its true sense, the term "market access" advances a realistic approach to the "penumbra-cases".[102] The judgment in *Gourmet* can serve as an example. The case concerned the Swedish general ban on commercial advertising of alcoholic beverages in periodicals. According to the Court, the ban affected "the marketing of products from other Member States more heavily than the marketing of domestic products". Thus, it constituted "an obstacle to trade between Member States", as advertising is an indispensable tool when entering new markets.[103] Even though the regulation created disparate impacts, it would seem strained to characterize the Swedish rules as discriminatory.[104]

Many other examples can be mentioned. One is the approach of the Court to national regimes that require registration or licensing prior to the exercise of an economic activity. Such regimes *may* be used to discriminate against foreign actors. They *may* be compared to absolute bans, as the activity will normally be forbidden until a licence has been issued. In any case, it is both realistic and straightforward to state that the proportionality and necessity of a system of prior approval should always be assessed. Systems of prior approval are set up to control access to the market and thus, by definition, affect market access.[105] The conclusion that they constitute restrictions can be reached without further ado. The more general point is that quite often it appears construed to handle the wide notion of discrimination and the notion of market access as "two distinctly relevant and distinctly applied devices" or to present the discrimination theory as the "initial framework for case analysis" while the "market access theory fulfils an ancillary role".[106] "Covert discrimination" or "discrimination in fact" should rather be conceived of as a specific (but not exhaustive) instance of hindrances to market access, as regulation which creates disparate impacts obviously impedes free movement.

A second reason explaining the increasing use of the term 'market access' is that many direct obstacles to trade and free movement exist that do not constitute discrimination even in its widest sense, but which still have to be dealt with, like absolute bans, restrictions on use, or the closure of important roads and transit routes.[107] The inevitable logic of the argument of AG Jacobs in his opinion in *Leclerc Siplec*, that if "an obstacle to inter-State trade exists, it cannot cease to exist simply because an identical obstacle affects domestic trade" was adhered to by the

[102] See Sect. 2.3.4.2.

[103] Case C-405/98, *Gourmet*, EU:C:2001:135, para 25.

[104] Case C-442/02, *CaixaBank France*, EU:C:2004:586, para 11 provides a similar example.

[105] E.g. Case C-473/98 *Toolex*, EU:C:2000:379, para 35; Case C-205/99 *Analir*, EU:C:2001:107, para 22; Case C-483/99 *Commission* v. *France*, EU:C:2002:327, para 41; Case C-372/04 *Watts*, EU:C:2006:325, paras 95–98; Case C-400/08 *Commission* v. *Spain*, EU:C:2011:172, paras 66–70; Case C-472/14, *Canadian Oil Company Sweden and Rantén*, EU:C:2016:171, para 44.

[106] Nic Shuibhne 2013, p. 206; Meulman and de Waele 2006, p. 218.

[107] Case 34/79 *Henn and Darby*, EU:C:1979:295; Case C-275/92 *Schindler*, EU:C:1994:119; Case C-42/07 *Liga Portoguesa*, EU:C:2009:519; Case C-142/05 *Mickelsson and Roos*, EU:C:2009:336; Case C-110/05 *Commission v. Italy* ("*Trailers*"), EU:C:2009:66; Case C-112/00 *Schmidberger*, EU:C:2003:333; Case C-320/03 *Commission v. Austria*, EU:C:2005:684.

Court in *Bosman*.[108] It has been restated in later cases, like *Commission v. Cyprus* where the Court held that:[109]

> As regards the Republic of Cyprus's argument that the legislation at issue in the present case does not treat migrant workers less favourably on the ground that it applies indiscriminately to all workers choosing to leave the Cypriot civil service in order to work in their Member State of origin or in another Member State, it should be recalled that for a measure to restrict freedom of movement, it is not necessary for it to be based on the nationality of the persons concerned or even for it to have the effect of bestowing an advantage on all national workers or of operating to the detriment solely of nationals of other Member States, but not of nationals of the State in question. It is enough that the measure should benefit certain categories of persons pursuing occupational activity in the Member State in question.

The third and most intriguing reason that can explain the increasing use of the notion of market access is that it gives the fundamental freedom teeth, which realize the protection of the individual right to free movement fully. This particular feature will be assessed below.

2.4.4 Example: Restrictions on Use—The Constitutional Twist in the Court's Case Law

The hypothesis of Sect. 2.4, as set out above, is that the personalization of rights seems to require individual and substantive assessments that demand court discretion. To make the hypothesis less abstract, this section will present a concrete example, before we return to the general issues in Sect. 2.4.5 below. First we shall study how the judgments on restrictions on use, as introduced above, may reveal the links between the personalisation of rights, the introduction and application of a market access test and the resort to court discretion.[110]

It has been argued that goods are not persons, and for that reason, the right to free movement of goods should continue to be treated as instrumental rather than fundamental or personal.[111] Still, "[f]ree movement of goods concerns not only traders but also individuals"; namely buyers.[112] If persons are missing, it does not require much creativity to introduce them. It is submitted that the Court did so in its judgments on restrictions on use by referring to the demand of citizens. The main catalyst for the dynamic interpretation of Article 34 in *Trailers* and *Mickelsson &*

[108] Opinion of Jacobs AG in Case C-412/93 *Leclerc-Siplec*, EU:C:1994:393, para 39; Case C-415/93 *Bosman*, EU:C:1995:463.

[109] Case C-515/14 *Commission v. Cyprus*, EU:C:2016:30, para 46. Cf. e.g. Case C-370/05 *Festersen*, EU:C:2007:59, para 25.

[110] *Mickelsson & Roos*, para 28; *Trailers* para 58.

[111] Oliver and Roth 2004, p. 441; De Cecco 2014, pp. 384, 390.

[112] Case C-362/88 *GB-INNO*, EU:C:1990:102, para 8. Cf. opinion of AG Trstenjak in case C-445/07, *Danske Slagterier*, EU:C:2008:464, para 83.

Roos was the observation that the restrictions on use had a "considerable influence on the behaviour of consumers".[113] This may at first glance look as pragmatic reasoning, but in fact, it is a constitutional observation, pointing to the most fundamental consideration of them all. Why bother to establish a market if not for the fulfilment of public demand?

The doctrine of "demand limitation" originated in *Höfner*, which concerned the application of the competition rules to Members States. According to the doctrine, a restriction is said to exist if the actors on a market, due to excessive regulation, are "manifestly not in a position to satisfy demand".[114] A few decades ago, the constitutional rational of the doctrine on demand limitation provided the necessary force to pave the way for EU law into fields of the economy which were formerly monopolized or highly regulated as they were considered by the Member States to be of general economic interest. In its modernized version, considerations about demand limitation have been central to the reasoning of the Court when the fundamental freedoms have been applied in the health-sector.[115]

The demand limitation test appears as a natural source of inspiration when the difficult question of when limitations on use should count as restrictions on the right to free movement is being solved. In the end, that will require a concrete assessment. If we accept that fulfilment of demand is an individual right of basic constitutional importance, we will also have to accept that discretion is being executed in the assessment of whether the traders' right to access the market, to the benefit of consumers, is being affected by national regulatory measures. No rule can define once and for all, and in a precise manner, when the citizen's interest in the market is duly respected. The court clothed its assessment in the language of "market access".

The judgments in *Trailers* and *Mickelsson & Roos* provide another feature of an individual, rights-based approach to free movement law as well. Contrary to a classical rule-based approach, analogous to the handling of "certain selling arrangements", the assessment of the Court did not attribute any weight to concerns about democracy or Member State autonomy. If rights are seen as instrumental, their reach may be subject to limitations grounded in considerations about the nature of the international cooperation to which they belong. Substantive, individual rights cannot be cut-off in the same manner. To the contrary, the reach of an individual right must be considered to pursue the interests of the individual until the right, interpreted on its own terms, is exhausted. Broader considerations that are of no relevance to the concerned individual, who is protected in his own right, cannot inform the interpretation of the scope of a personal right. The relevancy and weight of concerns about democracy and Member State autonomy are accounted for

[113] *Mickelsson & Roos*, para 26; *Trailers* para 56.

[114] Case C-41/90 *Höfner*, EU:C:1991:161, paras 25 and 31. For a presentation of the doctrine on demand limitation, see Buendia Sierra 1999, pp. 163 et seq.

[115] Case C-475/99 *Ambulanz Glöckner*, EU:C:2001:577; Case C-157/99 *Smits & Peerbooms*, C:2001:404, para 103; Case C-385/99 *Müller-Fauré*, EU:C:2003:270, para 91; Case C-372/04 *Watts*, EU:C:2006:325, paras 73–74.

through the construction of the principle of proportionality, and will only appear at the later stage of the proportionality review.

2.4.5 Market Access and the Personal Right to Free Movement

2.4.5.1 Diversification or Unification?

Section 2.4.4 above proved how an individual-rights account of the right to free movement might explain the intriguing judgments on restrictions on use. Let us now address the bigger picture. How can the personalization of the right to free movement be explained in general, and what are the consequences?

A preliminary observation would be that it is a mere (instrumental) fiction to submit that the elimination of any kind of discrimination will mark the full realization of an internal market. Such a timid achievement will provide for the formal right to move between 28 different national markets, but it will not contribute to the establishment of a single, uniform market. It is one thing to say that it is as easy to travel to Stockholm as to Rome; it is quite another thing to claim that the two cities are identical.

The Swedish tourist would probably appreciate that the secrets and pitfalls of Rome are other than those of Stockholm. The pleasure is more doubtful from the perspective of a European business, struggling with the peculiarities of the massive amounts of rules in the different Member States.[116] The judgment of the Court's grand chamber in *Commission v. Italy* provides a good illustration. The case concerned Italian regulation, which imposed an obligation to contract upon on all insurance undertakings operating in the field of third-party liability motor insurance, and in relation to all vehicle owners. The Court found that the Italian system restricted both the freedom to provide services and the freedom of establishment as it dissuaded insurance undertakings established in other Member States from establishing themselves or offering services in Italy. The system was said to constitute a substantial interference in the freedom to contract which rendered the right to access the market less attractive.[117]

> Inasmuch as it obliges insurance undertakings which enter the Italian market to accept every potential customer, that obligation to contract is likely to lead, in terms of organisation and investment, to significant additional costs for such undertakings. If they wish to enter the Italian market under conditions which comply with Italian legislation, such undertakings will be required to re-think their business policy and strategy, inter alia, by considerably expanding the range of insurance services offered.

---

[116] Cf. opinion of AG Alber in case C-176/96 *Lehtonen*, EU:C:1999:321, para 48.

[117] Case C-518/06, *Commission v. Italy*, EU:C:2009:270, paras 69–70.

The reasoning is realistic from an individual rights-based perspective. Substantial differences among the regulatory regimes of the Member States may in many instances discourage free movement to a greater extent than e.g. regulation that creates disparate impacts in the narrow sense. As argued in Sect. 2.3.2 above, the "substantially the same argument" is central to the notion of dynamic rights, and then the answer begs the question. Why should the bigger hindrance not be considered to constitute a restriction?

Some would argue that the bigger hindrance is simply irrelevant, as it is something you experience after you have exercised (exhausted) your right to free movement, i.e. after you have accessed the market, as the Treaty provisions only require the elimination of obstacles *to move between the Member States*. On such grounds, Oliver has criticized the more visionary ambition set out by the judgment in *Gaston Schul*, where the Court stated:[118]

> The concept of a common market as defined by the Court in a consistent line of decisions involves the elimination of all obstacles to intra-Community trade in order to *merge the national markets into a single market bringing about conditions as close as possible to those of a genuine internal market*. It is important that not only commerce as such but also private persons who happen to be conducting an economic transaction across national frontiers should be able to enjoy the benefits of that market.

According to Oliver, "it is scarcely open to the Court to ignore the clear wording of the Treaty", while Davies has asserted that the "clear intention of the text of Article 34 is to capture measures which *specifically* affect cross-border movement".[119] Let us assess these submissions in more detail.

As a preliminary observation, it would seem rather formal to disregard the regulatory problems that may be experienced by a business only after the exercise of its right to access a new market. Rational actors do not shut their eyes, move and hope for the best. Problems which—in theory—will appear only after the exercise of the right to free movement, are—realistically speaking—impediments to free movement in the first place. The question is therefore whether the wording of the Treaty rules may exclude an interpretation that from the individual point of view would appear both realistic and efficiency-oriented.

Contrary to the observations referred to above, it is submitted that terms such as "between Member States" are notoriously unclear. The wording of Article 34 is open to interpretation. There is nothing in that specific Article, or similar provisions, which requires that a measure cannot be caught unless it *specifically* affects cross border-movement. To the opposite, the words "having equivalent effect" legitimize the gradual development of the law—a discretionary exercise that must be guided by the judge's vision of what a single market in the true sense should

118 Case 15/81, *Gaston Schul*, EU:C:1982:135, para 33 (emphasis added).

119 Oliver 1999, p. 785; Davies 2012a, b, p. 27 (emphasis added).

entail.[120] With regard to the latter, there is no objective answer and opinions will vary. Still a choice will have to be made.

Bernard has observed that the "most obvious consequence of a theory of free movement based on discrimination is that it promotes regulatory diversity: (…) It is therefore a very different picture from that of a single market characterised by uniform rules apparently implied in some dicta of the Court".[121] Two points can be deducted from this important observation, the first being that it is the vision of what the internal market should entail which informs the interpretation and understanding of the wording of the Treaty, not the other way around. The second point is that it is far from obvious that "regulatory diversity" would fit a conception of a genuinely internal market, construed upon a set of individual rights: the fundamental freedoms. It suffices to say that at the least it appears as a legitimate act of discretion if the Court chooses a more ambitious approach, aiming for unification rather than diversification.

2.4.5.2 The Protection of Substantive Individual Rights

Nic Shuibhne presents another possible objection to a substantive, rights-based reading of the fundamental freedoms[122]:

> Even taking the particular plight of new market entrants into account, is the obligation to 'rethink business policy and strategy' really that objectionable a burden to place on an economic operator seeking—choosing—to exploit a new market? Or, put another way, why is it so objectionable a burden that the EU should intervene and assess it?

It is tempting simply to counter-assert that a burden does exist which, from the individual point of view, may make it less attractive to exercise the right to free movement. That is enough to legitimize the way in which the Court executed its discretion. Its chosen approach fits both the objective of establishing a genuine internal market, and the personalization of the right to free movement as described in Sect. 2.4.1 above. To ask whether the obligation to rethink business policy and strategy is "really that objectionable" is much the same as asking, "is an elephant really that heavy?" The question is impossible to answer in the absence of a proportionality review, the prerequisite of which is that the national measure qualifies as a restriction in the first place.

Davies presents a seemingly more principled objection: "Litigants who challenge non-protectionist regulation are not in fact claiming that they are denied

[120] Similarly Weiler 1999, p. 353: "the prohibition in the Treaty on (…) measures having an equivalent effect to quantitative restrictions seems (…) opaque and (…) open-textured. [T]he text seems to invite a teleological interpretation conditioned by an overarching vision of the Community as a single market place (…)".

[121] Bernard 1996, p. 103.

[122] Nic Shuibhne 2013, p. 243.

market access. They are claiming that a different market should exist."[123] Indeed. That is the claim of the right to free movement as well, the aim of which is to merge 28 national markets into one. One may of course argue that the rules on free movement *should* be interpreted and construed in a manner which is not too intrusive, and that their focus *should* be on restrictions that appear at the border and which thereby affect free movement in a direct sense. Such reasoning will necessitate a distinction between access to the market and the exercise of an activity, as suggested by AG Lenz in his opinion in *Bosman*.[124] The Court, however, has not endorsed that view, for reasons spelled out in *Commission v. Denmark*:

> The manner in which an activity is pursued is liable also to affect access to that activity. Consequently, legislation which relates to the conditions in which an economic activity is pursued may constitute an obstacle to freedom of movement within the meaning of that case-law.[125]

Notably, the approach of the Court is not in any way legally demanded. A choice has to be made, but the way in which the Court has executed its discretion is legitimate if the comprehensive legal framework is taken into consideration: it makes sense from a personal, rights-based perspective. The stage on which the restriction appears is simply irrelevant. What matters is that the burdens created by national regulation are substantial enough to make free movement less attractive. It must be emphasized that his does not entail that the interpretation of the Treaty collapses into an "economic freedom reading", protecting individual freedom as such.[126] As proven by several judgments, e.g. the judgment in *Graf*, it is not enough that individual freedom is touched upon; the national rules must affect free movement.[127] The approach taken by the Court marks a third way, one that mediates between a protectionist reading and an economic freedom reading of the Treaty. Or, as Roth and Oliver have put it: "the Court of Justice has moved into the role of arbiter between the demand of the internal market on the one hand and the effectiveness of a decentralized decision making process on the level of the Member states on the other."[128]

2.4.5.3 "As Union Law Now Stands"... The Indispensable Notion of Discretion

The mediation between "the demand of the internal market on the one hand and the effectiveness of a decentralized decision making process on the level of the Member states on the other" requires legal discretion. The existence of discretion in law may

---

[123] Davies 2012b, p. 29.

[124] Opinion of AG Lenz in Case C-415/93 *Hünermund*, EU:C:1995:293.

[125] Case C-464/02, *Commission v. Denmark*, EU:C:2005:546, para 37.

[126] Snell 2010, p. 438.

[127] Case C-190/98, *Graf*, EU:C:2000:49, paras 24–25.

[128] Oliver and Roth 2004, p. 413.

in turn affect the conception of what the law is. To illustrate the point, I will briefly discuss Enchelmaier's claim that the problems which non-discriminatory regulation causes to individual traders are of a "factual" nature only: "We can look at the economic realities as much as we want, we will not find the legal principle. The question is not empirical, it is normative".[129]

While the latter is true, the question of what a restriction connotes to is normative, it would also be true that the answer to the question "what counts as normative?" depends, at least to some extent, on how the principle of free movement is being interpreted by the Court.

One *could* assert that the right to access the market is unlawfully restricted *only* if Member States "either discriminate (treat differently without justification) or impose unjustified bans".[130] Apparently, one would then be wrong, empirically speaking, as a descriptive account of the case law proves that the Court has opted for a more far-reaching notion of the right to free movement. Still, if the assertion is true in the normative sense, one could of course try and claim the victory of being correct normatively speaking, implying that the Court is correct in the descriptive sense only (which a court of last instance is by definition). Moreover, an important role of scholarly literature is indeed to present a normative corrective to existing practice.

However, if we accept that legal discretion both exist as a part of legitimate legal reasoning, and does mark that a specific creative (constitutional) competence is attributed to the courts, the sharp distinction between the normative and the descriptive evaporates. As long as the discretion exercised by the Court is at the least *legitimate*, one will be wrong not only in the descriptive sense but also in the normative sense, if one not only criticizes the choices made by the Court, but also argues that some other solution is actually, not to say continuously or eternally, the one and only normatively correct solution. It is important to note in this regard that one is wrong in the practical *normative* sense even if one's criticism of the Court, on some abstract philosophical, normative level, is correct. Why?

Court discretion is not about finding the one answer that is objectively correct, i.e. to distinguish between the lawful and the unlawful in the strict metaphysical sense. Court discretion entails a practical competence to choose between *possibly* lawful alternatives, implying that even though one solution may, on some abstract level, be proven to be the best in objective terms, the inferior solution will still be binding and valid in the normative sense as long as it can legitimately be argued in favour of, *and* has actually been chosen by the authority which possesses the *creative constitutional competence* to do so: the Court. To draw a comparison: A law which is enacted according to the correct procedures is still good law, even if one may successfully argue, on some normative, philosophical level, that it is not a terribly good law, but only a terrible one.

[129] Enchelmaier 2016, p. 17.

[130] Enchelmaier 2016, p. 23.

For such reasons alone, Enchelmaier overstates the point when he argues that the burdens created by the different legal systems in the Member States are merely a factual problem. Through the exercise of its discretion, vested to it by the Treaties, the Court has turned such burdens into a normative problem. In his defence, Enchelmaier, who is a strong proponent of a rule-like approach would probably not approve the notion of discretion that this chapter argues in favour of. His critique does, however, show the importance of such a notion. Without it, there will only be rights and wrongs. In practical law, the concept of discretion represents an indispensable intermediate level which does not provide us with the truth, but more modestly and thus more importantly, establishes the prevailing norms at the time. Without it, EU law would lose its ability to respond dynamically to relevant and changing concerns. If that was the case, EU law would also lose itself.

2.5 The Constitutional Limits to Court Discretion

In his famous opinion in *Hünermund*, AG Tesauro asked whether the right to free movement is intended to liberalize intra-Community trade, or, more generally, to encourage the unhindered pursuit of commerce in individual Member States.[131] In scholarly literature, this dichotomy has been presented as the choice between two interpretative paradigms: a protectionist reading of the Treaty and an economic-freedom reading of the Treaty.[132] As it has become clear that the Court understands the notion of a restriction to include more than discrimination, it could appear that it has opted for the latter reading of the Treaty, i.e. the economic freedom reading. Spaventa's claim is that[133]:

> A new layer of protection to personal freedom is added, and the very claim which traditionally pertains to the realm of national constitutional law, the right not to be constrained without a good reason, becomes a Community right, albeit restricted mainly to the economic dimension.

However, there are constitutional limits to court discretion. An economic freedom reading of the Treaty would mark that the Court overstepped its competences. Why?

Admittedly, freedom or liberty is the basic constitutive value of both the national and the supranational legal order. Nevertheless, (constitutional) courts never can or

---

[131] Opinion of AG Tesauro in Case C-292/92, *Hünermund*, EU:C:1993:863, para 1.

[132] See in particular Maduro 1998, pp. 58–60; Snell 2002, pp. 1–4; 2010, p. 471.

[133] Spaventa 2004, p. 765. According to Spaventa, this would not amount to a neo-liberal reading of the Treaty, as long as the proportionality test is flexible and not hostile to regulation as such, just measures that are unnecessary. However, there is a thin wall between the two, and one could very well argue that the hallmark of the neo-liberal approach would be that the necessity of every piece of legislation is questioned (in this regard, see also paras 62–63 of the opinion of AG Tizzano in *CaixaBank*).

will protect freedom or liberty as such, i.e. in the broad and unqualified sense. According to every national constitution, that belongs exclusively to the elected. We live in the era of rights, but let us not forget that regulation is not the juxtaposition of freedom, but its expression. Throughout history, when the People have reclaimed their liberty, when blood has flowed in the streets like champagne, the People have achieved the freedom to govern themselves: liberty. There is a basic and conceptual difference between the political freedom/liberty to rule one-self on the one hand and civil rights/liberties on the other.

Constitutions and Courts protect the right to freedom/liberty in the thick albeit unqualified sense, in a formal manner only (the formal notion of the rule of law). The simplest example is the procedural requirement that democratic will must be enacted through laws. Of great practical importance is the requirement, adopted by the ECJ, that statutes that vest the national administration with powers must be sufficiently clear and precise.[134] In the substantive, material sense, courts confine themselves to protect liberties. Liberties are characterized by being (far) more specific and qualified than liberty, and thus the different constitutional systems include a catalogue of them. The difference between liberty and liberties mirrors the difference between freedom and freedoms—like in the four freedoms.

Provisions that establish liberties or freedoms need to be interpreted. In international law generally, and in EU law in particular, a dynamic interpretation is legitimate. Nevertheless, even if a legal question is highly unclear and leaves considerable room for judicial discretion, there is one limitation of fundamental constitutional importance: The judge cannot legitimately choose a certain interpretation of specific liberties/freedoms, only because it will enhance freedom in the general sense. A collapse of everything into a broad protection of freedom would ignore the institutional differences between lawmakers and courts. It would be unconstitutional and lack any historical parallel in the legal traditions of the Member States.

Of course AG Tesauro knew all this, when the opinion in *Hünermund* was written. He had made his point some months before, in the opinion in *Meng*, where he emphasized that "the progressive development of the case law should not lose sight of the ever necessary normative aspect, which underlies and shapes the strict interpretative approach which must be adopted in reading the Treaty".[135] The Court adhered to his arguments.[136] The conception of the Treaty as an "economic constitution" which could be used as a liberalizing tool turned out to be nothing more than "political wishful thinking"—it always was and still is.[137] The question posed by the AG in his opinion in *Hünermund* was highly rhetorical, as the dichotomy is false.

---

[134] E.g. Case 124/81 *Commission v. United Kingdom*, EU:C:1983:30; Joined Cases C-358/93 and C-416/93 *Bordessa*, EU:C:1995:54; Case C-157/99 *Smits and Peerbooms*, EU:C:2001:404; Case C-250/06 *UPC*, EU:C:2007:783. Cf. Eriksen 2011.

[135] Opinion of AG Tesauro in Case C-2/91 *Meng*, EU:C:1993:308, para 29 of the opinion.

[136] See Reich 1994.

[137] Neergaard 1998, pp. 225–226.

Obviously, the right to free movement cannot be cut off to mimic one of the alternatives in some presupposed dichotomy which in fact does not exist. A protectionist reading of the Treaty is illegitimate simply because individual rights must be interpreted in their own terms. On the other hand, the minimal requirement which can be deducted from there being a catalogue of liberties/freedoms, is that the judge must qualify what, in the particular case, which touches upon an objective that is *more specific* than freedom in the general sense, and thus defines the content of the freedoms which the judge administers. That the execution of the judge's discretion can never collapse into the protection of freedom as such marks the basic constitutional limitation to the discretionary competence which an *individual rights reading of the Treaty* vests in courts.

2.6 Conclusions

In areas that are not exhausted by secondary legislation, cases that concern free movement must be assessed based on the principles of the Treaty. Where no rules exist, the execution of court discretion is required. In the field of free movement, legal theory should not try to rationalize the practice of the ECJ in a rule-like manner. That would re-introduce the problem of generalizations which discretion by definition is meant to avoid.

The notion of market access should be accepted as the main guideline and qualifier when the reach of the right to free movement is being assessed. The concept provides a link to the objectives of the Treaty, which can guide the execution of discretion in every instance, on the facts, without formal rules, categorizations or tests as an intermediary. At the same time, the market access criterion underscores that there must be a link between the national measure and the functioning of the market if the national measure is to count as a restriction.

Constitutional and institutional considerations establish further limits to the legitimate execution of court discretion. It would be unconstitutional if national measures were taken to constitute restrictions only because that finding will enhance freedom/liberty in the general and broad sense. The minimal requirement that can be deducted from there being a catalogue of free movement rights is that the judge must qualify what, in the particular case, touches upon an objective that is *more specific* than freedom in the general sense, and thus defines the content of the freedoms that the judge administers.

A protectionist reading of the Treaty is too narrow. An economic-freedom reading of the Treaty is too broad. The construed dichotomy has turned parts of the academic discussion in the field of free movement into a hypothetic exercise of which of the alternatives to choose if one was forced to.[138] In his famous opinion in *Hünermund*, AG Tesauro did not state any reasons that explain where the

[138] Snell 2010, p. 471 insists that a choice has to be made.

dichotomy is rooted. His point was mainly rhetorical, and a normative explanation would have been impossible to provide. The right to free movement, and the project of European integration, cannot be reduced to a simple question of which of the two theoretically construed alternatives one should pick. Instead, an individual rights reading of the Treaty makes it possible to concentrate on the multitude of objectives and concerns that lie between them. That will require court discretion.

References

Bekkedal T (2011) Article 106 TFEU is Dead. Long Live Article 106 TFEU! In: Szyszczack E, Davies J, Andenæs M, Bekkedal T (eds) Developments in Services of General Interest. TMC Asser Press, The Hague, pp. 61–102

Bernard N (1996) Discrimination and Free Movement in EC Law. The International and Comparative Law Quarterly 45:82–108

Braithwaite J (2002) Rules and principles. A Theory of Legal Certainty. Australian Journal of Legal Philosophy, 27:47–82

Buendia Sierra JL (1999) Exclusive Rights and State Monopolies under EC Law. Oxford University Press, Oxford

Davies G (2003) Nationality Discrimination in the European Internal Market. Kluwer Law International, The Hague

Davies G (2011) Discrimination and beyond in European economic and social law. Maastricht Journal of European and Comparative Law 18:7–28

Davies G (2012a) Activism relocated. The self-restraint of the European Court of Justice in its national context. Journal of European public policy 19:76–91

Davies G (2012b) The court's jurisprudence on free movement of goods: Pragmatic presumptions, not philosophical principles. European Journal of Consumer Law 2:25–38

de Búrca G (2002) Unpacking the Concept of Discrimination in EC and International Trade Law. In: Barnard C, Scott J (eds) The Law of the Single European Market. Hart, Oxford/ Portland, pp 181–196

De Cecco F (2014) Fundamental Freedoms, Fundamental Rights, and the Scope of Free Movement Law. German Law Journal 15:383–406

Dougan M (2010) Legal Developments. Journal of Common Market Studies 48:163–181

Dworkin R (1963) Judicial Discretion. The Journal of Philosophy, 60:624–638

Dworkin R (1977) Taking Rights Seriously. Harvard University Press, Cambridge, Massachusetts

Enchelmaier S (2003) The awkward selling of a good idea, or a traditionalist interpretation of Keck. Yearbook of European Law 22:249–322

Enchelmaier S (2004) Four Freedoms, how many principles. Oxford Journal of Legal Studies 24:155–172

Enchelmaier S (2016) Four Freedoms, Ever More Principles? Oxford Journal of Legal Studies 36:1–26

Eriksen CC (2011) The European Constitution, Welfare States and Democracy: The Four Freedoms vs National Administrative Discretion. Routledge

Flynn L (2001) Coming of age: The free movement of capital case law 1993–2002. Common Market Law Review 38:773–805

Gormley LW (2005) The Genesis of the Rule of Reason in the Free Movement of Goods. In: Schrauwen A (ed) Rule of reason. Europa Law Publishing, Groningen, 19–34

Halberstam D (2005) The Bride of Messina: Constitutionalism and Democracy in Europe. European Law Review, 30:775–801

Hart HLA (1961) The Concept of Law. Oxford University Press, Oxford

Hilson C (1999) Discrimination in Community Free Movement Law. European Law Review 24:445–462
Jackson V (2015) Constitutional Law in an Age of Proportionality. The Yale Law Journal 124:3094–3196
Jansson MS, Kalimo H (2014) *De minimis* meets "market access": Transformations in the substance – and the syntax – of EU free movement law? Common Market Law Review, 51:523–558
Kelsen H (1998) Introduction to the Problems of Legal Theory. Paulson BL, Paulson SL (translation). Oxford University Press, Oxford
Kumm M (2010) The Idea of Socratic Contestation and the Right to Justification: The Point of Rights-Based Proportionality Review. Law & Ethics of Human Rights 4:140–175
Lianos I (2010) Shifting Narratives in the European Internal Market: Efficient restrictions of Trade and the Nature of "Economic" Integration. European Business Law Review 21:705–760
Lindahl H (2008) Discretion and Public Policy: Timing the Unity and Divergence of Legal Orders. In: Prechal S, van Roermund B (eds) The Coherence of EU Law. Oxford University Press, Oxford, pp 291–313
Maduro M P (1998) We, the Court. Hart, Oxford
Mancini F (1989) The making of a constitution for Europe. Common Market Law Review 26: 595–614
Meulman J, de Waele H (2006) A retreat from Säger? Legal issues of Economic Integration 33:207–228
Neergaard U (1998) Competition & Competences. DJØF
Nic Shuibhne N (2013) The Coherence of EU Free Movement Law. Oxford University Press, Oxford
Oliver P (1999) Some further reflections on the scope of Articles 28–30 (ex 30–36) EC. Common Market Law Review 36:783–806
Oliver P, Roth W-H (2004) The internal market and the four freedoms. Common Market Law Review 41:407–441
Ortino F (2002) Basic Legal Instruments for the Liberalisation of Trade. Hart, Oxford
Petersman E-U (2005) International Trade Law, Human Rights and Theories of Justice. In: Charnovitz S, Steger D P, Van den Bossche P (eds) Law in the Service of Human Dignity. Cambridge University Press, Cambridge, pp 44–57
Petersman E-U (2012) International Economic Law in the 21st Century. Hart, Oxford
Rasmussen H (1986) On Law and Policy in the European Court of Justice: A Comparative Study in Judicial Policymaking. Martinus Nijhoff, Dordrecht
Reich N (1994) The "November Revolution" of the European Court of Justice: *Keck, Meng and Audi* revisited. Common Market Law Review, 31:459–492
Roth W-H (2002) The European Court of Justice's Case Law on Freedom to Provide Services: Is Keck Relevant? In: Andenas M, Roth W-H (eds) Services and Free Movement in EU Law. Oxford University Press, Oxford, pp 1–24
Schauer F (1991) Playing by the Rules. Oxford University Press, Oxford
Schauer F (1995) Giving Reasons. Stanford Law Review 47:633–659
Selznick P (1969) Law Society and Industrial Justice. Russell Sage Foundation, New York
Snell J (2002) Goods and Services in EC Law. Oxford University Press, Oxford
Snell J (2010) The notion of market access: A concept or a slogan? Common Market Law Review 47: 437–472
Spaventa E (2004) From Gebhard to Carpenter: Towards a (non-)economic European Constitution. Common Market Law Review, 41:743–773
Weatherill S (2009) Free Movement of Goods. The International and Comparative Law Quarterly 58: 985–993.
Weiler J H H (1999) The Constitution of the Common Market Place: Text and Context in the Evolution of the Free Movement of Goods. In: Craig P, de Búrca G (eds) The Evolution of EU Law. Oxford University Press, Oxford, pp 349–376

Chapter 3
Free Movement of Persons Through the Lenses of 'Discrimination' and 'Restriction'

Alina Tryfonidou

Abstract The notions of 'restriction' and 'discrimination' are the soul and life of EU free movement law. These are the notions that define what is caught within the net of the free movement provisions, as well as the limits that are placed on their scope of application. These concepts are not monolithic but their interpretation is constantly changing and adapting and, together with this, the relationship between them is redefined. This chapter will seek to consider the reach of the provisions governing the free movement of persons, taking as its point of reference the ECJ's interpretation of the notions of 'discrimination' and 'restriction' in this context. In particular, it will analyse how the meaning of the above notions has developed through the years and it will explore how the relationship between the two has evolved from originally being one of interdependence to one that is of (almost) complete independence. The chapter will conclude that the main reason behind these developments is the (gradual) attribution to the free movement of persons provisions of a double status of instrumental freedoms and fundamental (citizenship) rights.

Keywords EU law · Union citizenship · Free movement of persons · Restriction · Non-discrimination · Fundamental (citizenship) rights · Instrumental freedoms

Contents

3.1 Introduction 58
3.2 'Discrimination' and 'Restriction': The Original Approach 59
3.3 'Discrimination' and 'Restriction': The Current Approach 63
3.3.1 'Restriction': The Current Approach 63

A. Tryfonidou (✉)
School of Law, University of Reading, Whiteknights Road, Earley, Reading
RG6 7BA, UK
e-mail: a.tryfonidou@reading.ac.uk

M. Andenas et al. (eds.), *The Reach of Free Movement*,
DOI 10.1007/978-94-6265-195-1_3

3.3.2 'Discrimination': The Current Approach 71
3.4 The Rationale Behind the Court's Current Approach: The Free Movement of Persons Provisions as Fundamental (Citizenship) Rights 75
3.5 Conclusion 80
References 81

3.1 Introduction

The notions of 'restriction' and 'discrimination' are the soul and life of EU free movement law. These are the notions that define what is caught within the net of the free movement provisions, as well as the limits that are placed on their scope of application. These concepts are not monolithic, but their interpretation is constantly changing and adapting, making it hard for EU lawyers to reach a consensus as to their true meaning,[1] and even harder to agree on the exact relationship between the two.[2] The confusion regarding the meaning of these terms is further compounded by the different approaches to their interpretation that have been followed in the context of the various freedoms: in the 1980s and early 1990s, the scope of the free movement of goods provisions was drawn more broadly than that of the free movement of persons provisions, a situation that was, nonetheless, reversed by the mid-1990s.[3] Yet, in recent years, a tendency to adopt a common interpretation across the freedoms can be discerned, this arguably implying a determination to embrace a position of convergence in their scope of application.[4]

This chapter will seek to consider the reach of the EU free movement of persons provisions,[5] taking as its point of reference the ECJ's interpretation of the notions of

[1] Chris Hilson, for instance, has bemoaned the lack of a commonly agreed interpretation of the term 'discrimination' (Hilson 1999, pp. 448–451); and Jukka Snell has noted that the definition of the notion of 'restriction' has 'varied both in time and among the freedoms' (Snell 2011, p. 554). Morano-Foadi and de Vries have noted that 'The "scope of application" of the Treaties, mentioned in Article 18 TFEU, has not been explicitly defined and contracts or expands depending on the interpretation provided by the CJEU' (Morano-Foadi and de Vries 2012, p. 22).

[2] de Búrca 2002, p. 195.

[3] Roth 2002; Poiares Maduro 2002.

[4] See Barnard 2001; Enchelmaier 2007, pp. 146–156; Tryfonidou 2010. Snell, however, is of the view that convergence between the free movement of goods and persons is not desirable—see Snell 2004.

[5] The free movement of persons provisions are Articles 45, 49, and 56 TFEU, which govern the (cross-border) rights of economic actors and which, together with the free movement of goods and the free movement of capital provisions, will be referred to as 'the market freedoms'; and Article 21 TFEU, which is one of the citizenship provisions of the Treaty, and has always been considered *lex generalis* in relation to the other free movement of persons provisions. Articles 45, 49 and 56 TFEU will, also, be referred to in this chapter as 'the economic free movement of persons provisions', when there is a need to distinguish them from Article 21 TFEU. Finally, the general phrase 'free movement provisions' will be used to refer to the market freedoms plus Article 21 TFEU; whilst 'EU free movement law' should be taken to refer to the law governing the interpretation of the free movement provisions.

'discrimination' and 'restriction' in this context. In particular, it will analyse how the meaning of the above notions has developed through the years and it will explore how the relationship between the two has evolved, from originally being one of interdependence to one that is of (almost) complete independence. The chapter will be divided into three main sections. Section 3.2 will present the Court's original approach to the interpretation of the notions of 'discrimination' and 'restriction' and to the relationship between them, in the context of the provisions governing the free movement of persons. It should be noted that the section will seek to provide only a brief explanation of this approach, as the focus of the chapter will be to demonstrate *the Court's current approach* to these terms and to the relationship between them, which will be analysed in Sect. 3.3. Section 3.4 will, then, explore the rationale that appears to lie behind the developments analysed in Sect. 3.3, whilst Sect. 3.5 will form the conclusion.

3.2 'Discrimination' and 'Restriction': The Original Approach

The market freedoms have always been read as making reference to two concepts when defining what type of national measures can be caught within their scope —'restriction' and 'discrimination'—and the interpretation of these terms has been the bread and butter of the Court in its free movement jurisprudence. Some of the market freedoms refer to only one of these terms,[6] whereas the others make reference—or allude—to both.[7] On the other hand, the more recently added Article 21 TFEU—one of the citizenship provisions—only includes the term 'right' (to move and reside freely in the territory of the Member States), this possibly demonstrating a desire on the part of the Treaty drafters to indicate that the citizenship provisions attach primary importance to the bestowal of individual rights on Union citizens, and that the latter are, therefore, no longer 'only by repercussion that they benefit from the favourable consequences of the direct application of a rule of Community law and, more generally, of the implementation of the economic objectives of the Community legal order'.[8]

Nonetheless, leaving the semantics aside, what is important for our purposes is that the Court in its case-law has read all the free movement of persons provisions as containing a prohibition on 'restrictions' and 'discrimination'. It is the

[6] See, for instance, Articles 34, 35, and 63 TFEU referring to 'restrictions', and Article 45 TFEU referring to 'discrimination'.

[7] Article 49 TFEU explicitly mentions 'restrictions' on the freedom of establishment but it also makes reference to 'discrimination', albeit without using the exact term; Article 56 TFEU refers to 'restrictions', whilst Article 57 TFEU places the emphasis on discrimination on the grounds of nationality.

[8] Opinion of AG Cosmas in Case C-378/97, *Wijsenbeek*, ECLI:EU:C:1999:144, para 82.

interpretation of these terms that constitutes the main focus of this chapter and in this section the Court's original approach to this issue will be examined.

In the EU's internal market policy, the principle of equality traditionally had a merely market-unifying role since it underpinned 'the creation of the unified market and [was] applied to facilitate equality of access for products, services, and persons regardless of their EU national origin'.[9] More specifically, the prohibition of discrimination in this context had originally been viewed as 'an adjunct to the right to free movement' and as an indicator that national measures which are capable of hampering free movement because they discriminate should be removed, unless they are justified on a non-economic ground.[10]

Hence, (direct and indirect)[11] discrimination on the ground of nationality (and, in the field of services, also residence/establishment),[12] has always been prohibited by the free movement of persons provisions, since it is obvious that it can deter the exercise of cross-border movement. In particular, the economic free movement of persons provisions expressly prohibit discrimination on the ground of nationality with regards to certain issues such as employment or the taking-up of a self-employed activity in the territory of another Member State, *since such discrimination is clearly capable of leading to a restriction on free movement.* However, it has, also, been established that nationality discrimination in relation to other issues *not expressly mentioned* in these provisions and which, nonetheless, can lead to a restriction on free movement can, also, amount to a violation of the economic free movement of persons provisions (e.g. nationality discrimination as regards the grant of social advantages unrelated to employment).[13] Moreover, the Court (relatively) early on accepted that discrimination against free movers or, more broadly, cross-border situations (i.e. discrimination against the exercise of free movement rights), can also create a restriction on free movement and, thus, should also be caught by these provisions.[14] The same (free movement) rationale has been

---

[9] More 1999, p. 518.

[10] Chalmers 1994, p. 397.

[11] For a discussion as to how direct discrimination should be distinguished from indirect discrimination see the Opinion of AG Sharpston in Case C-73/08, *Bressol*, ECLI:EU:C:2009:396, paras 43–57.

[12] Case 33/74, *Van Binsbergen*, ECLI:EU:C:1974:131; Case C-288/89, *Gouda*, ECLI:EU:C:1991:323. For comments see Roth 2002, p. 5.

[13] See, for instance, the case-law interpreting Article 7(2) of Council Regulation (EEC) No. 1612/68 *on freedom of movement for workers within the Community*, O.J. L 257/2 (1968) (which has, now, been replaced by (the identical) Article 7(2) of Council and Parliament Regulation (EU) No. 492/2011 *on freedom of movement for workers within the Union*, O.J. L 41/1 (2011)): Case 32/75, *Cristini*, ECLI:EU:C:1975:120; Case 63/76, *Inzirillo*, ECLI:EU:C:1976:192; Case 94/84, *Deak*, ECLI:EU:C:1985:264; Case 152/82, *Forcheri*, ECLI:EU:C:1983:205; Case 261/83, *Castelli*, ECLI:EU:C:1984:280; Case 157/84, *Frascogna*, ECLI:EU:C:1985:243. For an authoritative analysis of this case law see O'Keeffe 1985.

[14] See, for instance, Case C-109/04, *Kranemann*, ECLI:EU:C:2005:187; Case C-18/95, *Terhoeve*, ECLI:EU:C:1999:22; Case C-76/05, *Schwarz*, ECLI:EU:C:2007:492. For an interesting discussion see Bernard 1996, pp. 85–89; Szydlo 2010, pp. 760–762; Wollenschläger 2011, p. 26.

adopted for Article 21 TFEU and, thus, any form of differential treatment that gives rise to a restriction on free movement is prohibited by this provision, even though its text does not make reference to discrimination.[15] It is not surprising, therefore, that discrimination against persons who have *not* exercised free movement rights—known as 'reverse discrimination'—has always been held by the Court to fall outside the scope of the free movement of persons provisions, *exactly because it is incapable of impeding the achievement of their free movement aims.*[16]

However, it is interesting to note that, despite the fact that the Court had originally regarded the prohibition of discrimination in EU free movement law in a purely instrumental manner, as simply aiming to ensure that restrictions on free movement do not emerge, it has, nonetheless, never required actual proof that the discrimination complained of in a case is, indeed, capable of leading to such a restriction.[17]

'Restriction', on the other hand, has been more loosely defined by the Court. In common parlance, a 'restriction' is something that limits one's freedom to act (or not to act) in a particular way, or to enjoy a certain right. In the context of EU free movement law, the interpretation of this term has, naturally, been informed by the aims that this policy area seeks to achieve, at any particular time. Accordingly, and since the market freedoms had traditionally been viewed as—simply—the tools that would be used to liberalise inter-State movement for the purpose of establishing an internal market in labour, this term had originally been read as referring to a restriction on inter-State movement exercised for an economic purpose.[18] This free *movement* rationale was transposed, also, into the Article 21 TFEU context, whereby it was traditionally considered that that provision was targeted at removing restrictions on free inter-State movement.[19]

Hence, the main question traditionally posed in free movement case-law has been whether the measure in question is capable of leading to a restriction on inter-State *movement*; and it has traditionally been accepted that this can be the result of a restriction on the exercise of inter-State movement as such, or of a restriction on the exercise of the other rights explicitly mentioned in the text of the free movement provisions (i.e. primary rights), or—more broadly—of other rights

---

[15] See, for instance, Case C-224/98, *D'Hoop*, ECLI:EU:C:2002:432; Case C-224/02, *Pusa*, ECLI:EU:C:2004:273; Case C-221/07, *Zablocka-Weyhermüller*, ECLI:EU:C:2008:681.

[16] Case 98/86, *Mathot*, ECLI:EU:C:1987:89; Case 44/84, *Hurd v Jones*, ECLI:EU:C:1986:2; Joined Cases C-29-35/94, *Aubertin and Others*, ECLI:EU:C:1995:39. For an analysis of reverse discrimination see Tryfonidou 2009a.

[17] See Opinion of AG Fennelly in Case C-190/98, *Graf*, ECLI:EU:C:1999:423, para 23. For commentary see Sibony 2012, especially pp. 340–341.

[18] This has been made clear in a long line of case-law, most prominently in Case 175/78, *Saunders* ECLI:EU:C:1979:88, and has recently been confirmed in Case C-212/06, *Walloon (Flemish care insurance scheme)*, ECLI:EU:C:2008:178. For an analysis of these requirements see Tryfonidou 2009b, pp. 1592–1595.

[19] See, for instance, the submissions of the UK and Irish governments in Case C-200/02, *Zhu and Chen*, ECLI:EU:C:2004:639. Moreover, it has recently been confirmed by the Court in its judgment in Case C-434/09, *McCarthy*, ECLI:EU:C:2011:277.

related, in some way, to the exercise of free movement and the refusal of which is capable of impeding free movement (i.e. secondary rights e.g. family reunification rights).

This can explain the Court's original focus on 'movement', *both as a jurisdictional and as a substantive requirement*: traditionally, in order for a situation to fall within the scope of the free movement provisions, free movement should have been exercised on the facts of the case (jurisdictional requirement) *and* the contested measure should be capable of impeding that movement (substantive requirement).[20] This meant that the other prohibitions (or entitlements) explicitly mentioned in the text of these provisions, were originally merely viewed as instrumental to the free movement aims of these provisions and, hence, only measures which were contrary to these prohibitions (or which refused those entitlements) *and* which would lead to a restriction on free movement, could amount to a breach of the free movement of persons provisions.

Although, as will be seen in the next section, it was made clear relatively early on in the Court's jurisprudence that the free movement of persons provisions catch within their scope both discriminatory and non-discriminatory restrictions on free movement, this chapter will consider that under the Court's original approach, the notion of 'restriction' was defined and limited by the concept of 'discrimination' and, accordingly, only *discriminatory* restrictions on free movement could, originally, amount to a violation of the relevant provisions.[21] This may not have been so much a conscious and intentional choice on the part of the Court, but may have rather been the result of a confluence of factors, such as the discrimination-centred wording of (some of) the free movement of persons provisions; the types of cases that were referred to the Court at the time, which could easily be resolved by the application of a discrimination-based analysis;[22] and, of course, the fact that discriminatory restrictions are, obviously, opposed to the aim of establishing an internal market and thus it is clear that they must be prohibited.

Accordingly, under the Court's original approach, the notions of 'discrimination' and 'restriction' were closely intertwined and interdependent: the only form of restriction that was clearly caught by the free movement of persons provisions was a discriminatory restriction on free movement; and only discriminatory treatment that was either expressly prohibited by these provisions or that led to restrictions on free movement, was traditionally caught by the above provisions.

[20] For an analysis of this see Tryfonidou 2009a, Chapter 2.

[21] This was stated explicitly by the Court as late as in 1987 in Case C-221/85, *Commission v Belgium*, ECLI:EU:C:1987:81.

[22] Opinion of AG Lenz in Case C-415/93, *Bosman*, ECLI:EU:C:1995:293, para 192.

3.3 'Discrimination' and 'Restriction': The Current Approach

Having provided an explanation of the Court's original approach to the interpretation of the concepts of 'restriction' and 'discrimination' and to the relationship between them, the chapter will now proceed to an examination of the Court's current approach to these issues.

Before proceeding to do so, however, a few preliminary points must be made.

First, the reader should keep in mind that—what I call—the 'original' and 'current' approaches to the interpretation of the notions of 'restriction' and 'discrimination' and to the relationship between them, do not fall into neatly packaged periods of time. This, together with the fact that the various developments that are considered to fall within the current approach have occurred at different times, make it impossible to set a specific chronological point which forms the beginning of this approach.

Second, the two approaches that are examined in this chapter are academic categorisations that I have devised in order to provide a logical taxonomy, separating the Court's original approach to the issues under consideration from all the developments that followed; the reader should, therefore, approach these categories with this predisposition in mind. In particular, it should be borne in mind that what is labelled as the 'current approach' is not an approach that has been adopted only recently, but, as will be seen, the roots of certain developments that are considered to fall within this approach can be traced back as early as the 1970s.

Finally, and most importantly, there are many cases which are currently resolved in the same way as they would have been under the Court's original approach (e.g. discriminatory restrictions on free movement). This illustrates that the two approaches analysed in this piece are not mutually exclusive but, rather, the current approach appears to be a continuation and development of the original approach. Hence, measures that would amount to restrictions under the original approach and instances involving discriminatory treatment that fell within the scope of the free movement provisions under that approach, continue to be caught by these provisions under the current approach. However, at the same time, under the latter, the notion of 'restriction' has acquired a broader meaning, and the instances in which discriminatory treatment can fall within the scope of EU free movement law have, gradually, increased.

3.3.1 'Restriction': The Current Approach

3.3.1.1 The Non-Discriminatory Restriction

As seen in the previous section, the notions of 'discrimination' and 'restriction' seemed, originally, to have coincided in the Court's free movement of persons jurisprudence, and, more specifically, the notion of 'restriction' was limited and defined by the notion of 'discrimination'. This was because, until the 1990s, it was widely believed that it is only measures that are discriminatory on the grounds of nationality (or against free movers) and lead to a restriction on inter-State movement, that are caught by the free movement of persons provisions.[23] There had, of course, been cases in the 1970s and 1980s, where the Court's analysis did not focus on the fact that the measure involved was discriminatory but, rather, focused on that it created a restriction on the exercise of free movement rights. Yet, these cases could not constitute conclusive evidence that the free movement of persons provisions covered non-discriminatory obstacles to free movement, since the impugned measures were, in reality, discriminatory.[24]

The Court could not, however, perpetually avoid a direct confrontation with the question of whether these provisions could catch within their scope genuinely non-discriminatory restrictions on free movement. The first signs of a move towards this direction can be seen in the early 1990s. In *Säger*, the Court pointed out that (what is now) Article 56 TFEU 'requires not only the elimination of all discrimination against a person providing services on the ground of his nationality but also the abolition of any restriction, even if it applies without distinction to national providers of services and to those of other Member States, when it is liable to prohibit or otherwise impede the activities of a provider of services established in another Member State where he lawfully provides similar services'.[25] This, however, could not, again, conclusively be taken as evidence that genuinely non-discriminatory restrictions on free movement are caught by the free movement of persons provisions, given that the contested measure on the facts of the case was a measure that imposed a dual-burden on services provided across borders, in that services which were lawfully provided in the territory of the home Member State had, in addition, to comply with the requirements of the host State: in the context of the free movement of goods, such rules have been considered to amount to indirect discrimination on the ground of origin, rather than to constitute non-discriminatory restrictions on free movement.[26]

It was, rather, in 1994, in the services case of *Schindler*,[27] however, that the Court found for the first time that a provision governing the free movement of persons (and services)—Article 56 TFEU—can catch within its scope a genuinely non-discriminatory measure.[28] In that case, the Court held that the UK prohibition

[23] See, for instance, the Opinion of AG Lenz in Case C-221/85, *Commission v Belgium*, ECLI:EU:C:1986:456.

[24] See, for instance, Case C-205/84, *Commission v Germany*, ECLI:EU:C:1986:463. For an analysis of these cases see the Opinion of AG Lenz in Case C-415/93, *Bosman*, ECLI:EU:C:1995:293, paras 166–192.

[25] Case C-76/90, *Säger*, ECLI:EU:C:1991:331, para 12.

[26] Toner 2004, p. 277.

[27] Case C-275/92, *Schindler*, ECLI:EU:C:1994:119.

[28] Though, it should be noted that on the facts of the case the prohibition was applied in a situation which involved the free movement of services as such, instead of the free movement of persons.

on the holding of lotteries—clearly a non-discriminatory measure—amounted to a restriction on the free movement of services, albeit one which was justified and, thus, not contrary to the above provision.[29]

The following year, the Court made it clear that the provisions governing the free movement of workers (*Bosman*)[30] and the freedom of establishment (*Gebhard*),[31] also prohibit *both* discriminatory and genuinely non-discriminatory restrictions on free movement which are not justified. In the above cases, the contested national measures could in no way fit within a discrimination analysis: they were genuinely non-discriminatory and were capable of having exactly the same restrictive impact on access to the market, in cross-border and purely internal situations; in other words, they did not have 'cross-border specificity'.[32]

A few years afterwards, the Court also made it clear that genuinely non-discriminatory restrictions which cannot be justified are, also, prohibited by Article 21 TFEU.[33]

Accordingly, it is clear from the Court's case-law that the free movement of persons provisions prohibit both discriminatory and non-discriminatory restrictions.

The Court has used the terms 'obstacle' or 'impediment to free movement' as synonyms for the notion of 'restriction' in this context, and has, since the mid-1990s, taken a very broad approach to the interpretation of these terms, which have been read to include measures which are 'liable to hinder or make less attractive the exercise of fundamental freedoms guaranteed by the Treaty',[34] or which affect access to the market[35] of another Member State.[36] Yet, the Court has been wary of the danger of an over-extension of the scope of the free movement provisions, akin to that experienced in the context of the free movement of goods prior to *Keck*.[37] Hence, together with the purely internal rule, the application of which is continuously affirmed in the Court's case-law to the present day, the Court has applied another filtering mechanism—the principle of remoteness—in order to

---

[29] This was confirmed in Case C-384/93, *Alpine Investments*, ECLI:EU:C:1995:126 which, again, involved the free movement of services as such, and in Case C-60/00, *Carpenter*, ECLI:EU:C:2002:434, which involved the free movement of a service-provider.

[30] Case C-415/93, *Bosman*, ECLI:EU:C:1995:463.

[31] Case C-55/94, *Gebhard*, ECLI:EU:C:1995:411.

[32] For a more detailed analysis of the notion of cross-border specificity and, more specifically, for its (non-)application in these (and other) cases see Tryfonidou 2016, pp. 15–17 and 91–109, respectively.

[33] See, for instance, Case C-378/97, *Wijsenbeek*, ECLI:EU:C:1999:439.

[34] Case C-55/94, *Gebhard*, ECLI:EU:C:1995:411, para 37; Case C-285/01, *Burbaud*, ECLI:EU:C:2003:432, para 95; Case C-442/02, *CaixaBank*, ECLI:EU:C:2004:586, para 11.

[35] Case C-384/93, *Alpine Investments*, ECLI:EU:C:1995:126, para 38; Case C-415/93, *Bosman*, ECLI:EU:C:1995:463, para 103. For more on the notion of market access see Snell 2010; Davies 2010; and Sibony 2012.

[36] In this chapter, the broader notion of 'restriction' will be used, which should be taken to include all these synonyms.

[37] Joined Cases C-267 & 268/91, *Keck and Mithouard*, ECLI:EU:C:1993:905.

exclude from the scope of the free movement of persons provisions, restrictions which are 'too uncertain and indirect' a consequence of the application of the contested measure.[38]

An approach which includes within the scope of the free movement provisions genuinely non-discriminatory restrictions does, clearly, appear more apt in a mature internal market. As Advocate General Jacobs noted in his Opinion in *Alpine Investments*, 'Whether a rule of the Member State of origin constitutes a restriction on the freedom to provide services should be determined by reference to a functional criterion, that is to say, whether it substantially impedes the ability of persons established in its territory to provide intra-Community services. It seems to me that that criterion is consonant with the notion of an internal market and more appropriate than the criterion of discrimination'.[39] Similar considerations apply, of course, by analogy, in relation to the other market freedoms, and, even more so, in situations concerning measures imposed by the host Member State. Hence, the inclusion of non-discriminatory restrictions within the scope of the free movement of persons provisions has been a step which has been in line with the renewed determination of the EU institutions in the late 1980s—bolstered by the Single European Act—to establish (and maintain) a genuine internal market where, inter alia, factors of production can move freely between Member States, without any unjustified restrictions on such movement being imposed.

Moreover, as will be explained in more detail in the last main section of the chapter, the move of expanding the notion of 'restriction' to encompass non-discriminatory restrictions on free movement is, also, in line with the introduction of the status of Union citizenship in 1993 by the Treaty of Maastricht, which was a codification of the incipient form of European citizenship, which had been (implicitly) developed in the Court's case-law from the 1970s onwards.[40] As will be explained in more detail in Sect. 3.4 of the chapter, if the free movement provisions were now to be considered rights granted to all Union citizens—as the wording of Article 20 TFEU may be taken to suggest[41]—it goes without saying that a mere prohibition of discriminatory restrictions would clearly no longer suffice.

[38] It should be noted that although the Court has in a number of cases employed what academics call the notion of remoteness, a *precise* remoteness test has never been articulated by the Court. However, this appears to be, in essence, a question of causation which seeks to exclude from the ambit of the free movement of persons provisions measures which do not appear to be a cause of the contested restriction. The most widely-cited example of a case in this context where the Court found that the situation was too remote is Case C-190/98, *Graf*, ECLI:EU:C:2000:49. For an analysis of the various filtering mechanisms employed by the Court in its free movement case-law see Horsley 2012 (focusing on the free movement of goods); Tryfonidou 2016, pp. 173–192.

[39] Opinion of AG Jacobs in Case C-384/93, *Alpine Investments*, ECLI:EU:C:1995:15, para 47. See, also, in the same vein, the Opinion of the same AG in Case C-412/93, *Leclerc-Siplec*, ECLI:EU:C:1994:393, in relation to the delimitation of the scope of Article 34 TFEU.

[40] Kochenov and Plender 2012, p. 370.

[41] Article 20(2) TFEU provides, inter alia, that 'Citizens of the Union shall enjoy the rights and be subject to the duties provided for in the Treaties'. For an analysis of this argument see Tryfonidou 2010.

The subsequent part of this section will be devoted to the question of what, under the current approach, is a (discriminatory or non-discriminatory) restriction that is contrary to the free movement of persons provisions. As we have seen, under the original approach, this was taken to mean 'a restriction on free movement'. Is this still the case?

3.3.1.2 Restriction on What?

In the past couple of decades, it appears to have been made clear that the scope of the free movement of persons provisions does not merely encompass restrictions on free movement, but also restrictions on the exercise of the (other) rights bestowed by these provisions. In particular, this subsection will illustrate that the free movement of persons provisions do not merely bestow a right to (*physically*) *move* across borders, the violation of which is required in order for a breach to be established, but they also grant a number of other—*independent*—rights, which have to be respected in their own right and not simply in order to ensure that free movement is secured. This extension to the scope of the notion of 'restriction' has become particularly obvious from case-law which did not involve the exercise of physical movement between two Member States, but rather, a national of one Member State seeking to exercise the (other) rights bestowed by the free movement provisions in the territory of another.

For instance, in *Collins*,[42] the eponymous applicant was a dual Irish-US citizen who had never lived in the EU (bar a short period in the UK twenty years before, which, thus, did not count) and moved to the UK directly from the USA to look for work. The Court found that the situation fell within the scope of, inter alia, Article 45 TFEU, due to the fact that Collins was an Irish national looking for work in the UK. Similarly, in the citizenship case of *Zhu and Chen*,[43] it sufficed that the baby involved was the holder of a passport of a Member State (Ireland) other than that where she was seeking to permanently reside (UK), in order for Article 21 TFEU (and the relevant secondary legislation at the time)[44] to apply; the fact that the child was born in one part of the UK (Northern Ireland) and was relying on EU law in order to reside in another part of the *same* Member State (Wales), and thus the (physical) movement that was going to be exercised would be within one and the same Member State, did not lead to a ruling that the situation was purely internal to the UK.

The acceptance by the Court that such situations fall within the scope of the free movement of persons provisions is important, in that it shows that the notion of

---

[42] Case C-138/02, *Collins*, ECLI:EU:C:2004:172.

[43] Case C-200/02, *Zhu and Chen*, ECLI:EU:C:2004:639.

[44] Council Directive (EEC) No. 90/364 *on the right of residence*, O.J. L 180/26 (1990); repealed and replaced by Parliament and Council Directive (EC) No. 2004/38 *on the right of citizens of the Union and their family members to move and reside freely within the territory of the Member States*, O.J. L 158/77 (2004).

'restriction' is, now, broader than the original 'restriction on (physical) movement', this illustrating that free movement rights are only part of the parcel of rights that are bestowed on Union citizens by these provisions. In this way, the scope of these provisions is extended to cover restrictions on the exercise of *all* the rights expressly provided by them (i.e. primary rights), which are, nonetheless, rights of an inherently cross-border nature. More specifically, in the above cases the Court appears to have interpreted Articles 45 and 21 TFEU, respectively, as bestowing, inter alia, a right to seek work and not to be discriminated against with regards to that right *in a Member State other than that of nationality* or a right to reside *in such a Member State*, as opposed to solely, a right to work and not be discriminated against *after moving* or a right to reside in a Member State *after exercising free movement*.

Despite the fact that the above extension to the meaning of the notion of 'restriction'—as a restriction on the primary rights bestowed by the free movement of persons provisions and not, solely, as a restriction on (physical) free movement—is a welcome and logical interpretation of these provisions, the Court should nonetheless place some limits to the ambit of this notion. In fact, an indication as to how the scope of this (broader) notion of 'restriction' can be limited, can be gathered from a comparison of the Court's approach in *Zhu and Chen* and *Collins*, on the one hand, with that in *Garcia Avello*,[45] on the other.

In the two former cases, the Court examined whether there was a restriction on the right of residence (*Zhu and Chen*) or whether the right not to be discriminated against on grounds of nationality with regards to access to employment was violated (*Collins*), these both being restrictions on the enjoyment of rights which are *expressly* provided by the free movement of persons provisions (i.e. they are primary rights): Article 21 TFEU expressly grants a right to move and a right to reside in the territory of another Member State, whilst Article 45 TFEU provides, inter alia, for the right to have access to the employment market of the host State and not to be discriminated against on grounds of nationality with regards to this right. In these two cases, the Court was right in using the free movement provisions to find a violation of EU law, given that there was a restriction on the exercise of the primary rights bestowed (expressly) by these provisions.

Conversely, in *Garcia Avello*,[46] where at issue was a right which is not expressly granted by the free movement provisions (the right to have your surname registered in accordance with the rules of your (other) Member State of nationality), the Court did not hold that there was a breach of the free movement provisions. Rather, it concluded that there was a violation of Article 18 TFEU (when read together with Article 20 TFEU) after finding that Belgium's laws in relation to this right were discriminatory against Union citizens who held dual Belgian and Spanish, as

[45] Case C-148/02, *Garcia Avello*, ECLI:EU:C:2003:539.

[46] Which concerned two dual Member State nationals who, likewise, had not *moved* between Member States.

opposed to only Belgian, nationality.[47] The aim of the applicants in this case was not to exercise one of the rights expressly bestowed by the free movement provisions (i.e. a primary right)—they had neither moved to another Member State, nor worked and/or resided in a Member State other than that of their nationality. Nor were there any *concrete* plans for the exercise of such rights in the future. Moreover, a restriction on the exercise of the right claimed on the facts of the case was incapable of impeding the exercise of one of the primary rights granted by the free movement provisions and, hence, the said right could not even qualify as a secondary right deriving from the free movement provisions. This is probably the reason why the Court in its judgment did not make reference at all to Article 21 TFEU—which is one of the free movement provisions—but, rather, employed Article 20 TFEU for establishing that the Garcia Avello children fell within the personal scope of EU law and, by virtue of that, they could rely on the prohibition of discrimination on the ground of nationality laid down in Article 18 TFEU. Hence, the aim of the Court in this case had not been to protect the exercise of the rights derived from the free movement provisions by the Garcia Avello children but, rather, to outlaw discrimination on the ground of dual (as opposed to single) Member State nationality—a form of discrimination which is entirely unrelated to the rights granted by the free movement provisions and, as such, (rightly) escapes their ambit.[48]

One could, therefore, say that the notion of 'restriction' in the context of the free movement of persons provisions now entails: (a) the classic restriction on free (physical) movement between Member States; as well as (b) restrictions on the exercise of the other (primary) rights bestowed by the free movement of persons provisions. In particular, both of the above types of restriction can emerge as a result of restrictions on any of the primary rights bestowed by the free movement provisions (e.g. a refusal to allow the migrant to move or to access the employment market of the host State) *or* as a result of restrictions on the exercise of secondary rights, which, in their turn, lead to restrictions on the exercise of the primary rights bestowed by these provisions.

Before proceeding to the next part of the chapter, it is worth mentioning another line of case-law which appears to be supporting the above reading for the notion of 'restriction': the *Ritter-Coulais* saga.[49]

It was originally considered that in order for a situation to fall within the scope of the economic free movement of persons provisions, the exercise of inter-State

---

[47] Case C-148/02, *Garcia Avello*, ECLI:EU:C:2003:539, paras 37–38.

[48] The Court provided a somewhat different reading of *Garcia Avello* in Case C-434/09, *McCarthy*, ECLI:EU:C:2011:277, noting that the reason for finding a breach of Articles 18 and 20 TFEU was that the discriminatory treatment suffered on the facts of the case could lead to potential restrictions on free movement. However, as I argued elsewhere, this does not appear to be a correct reading of the case—see Tryfonidou 2012, pp. 516–518.

[49] See, inter alia, Case C-152/03, *Ritter-Coulais*, ECLI:EU:C:2006:123; Case C-470/04, *N*, ECLI:EU:C:2006:525; Case C-527/06, *Renneberg*, ECLI:EU:C:2008:566; Case C-379/11, *Caves Krier Frères*, ECLI:EU:C:2012:798; Case C-87/13, *X*, ECLI:EU:C:2014:2459.

movement *for an economic purpose and the possibility of an impediment to that movement* on the facts, should be established. This requirement was evident in a long line of (older) cases, but was exemplified most clearly in *Werner*, where the Court held that a German national who was pursuing a self-employed economic activity in his State of nationality and had merely moved to the territory of another Member State for the purpose of taking-up residence there, fell outside the scope of Article 49 TFEU.[50] His situation was considered to be purely internal to Germany: the fact that his movement to another Member State for the purpose of taking-up residence could be impeded as a result of the contested measure, could not amount to a breach of that provision, since that movement lacked a sufficient link with its *economic* objectives.

In the second half of the previous decade, nonetheless, the Court departed from its strict adherence to the above approach and dispensed with the requirement that the movement that has been exercised and is hampered as a result of the application of the contested measure, has to have an economic aim. In a group of cases (the *Ritter-Coulais* saga), Union citizens who *continued* exercising an economic activity in their home State and merely moved their residence to another Member State, were held to fall within the scope of the *economic* free movement of persons provisions, even though the movement that was going to be impeded as a result of the measure that was complained of in the facts, had been exercised for a non-economic purpose (i.e. for the purpose of taking-up residence in another Member State).

The key question for our purposes is, admittedly, what is the link that the Court found in these cases with the economic free movement of persons provisions? Obviously, the scope of these provisions could not, simply, be stretched to cover any situations involving an impediment to inter-State movement that was exercised for a non-economic purpose; after all, this is the 'job' of Article 21 TFEU. Moreover, in all the cases under examination, the Union citizens that were involved were economically active (albeit in their home State) and, thus, this must have served to bring them within the scope of the economic free movement of persons provisions.[51] Therefore, the most plausible underlying rationale for this line of case-law is a desire on the part of the Court to ensure that Union citizens can begin pursuing an economic activity in a cross-border context which is the case when the economic actor pursues an economic activity in one Member State whilst he resides in the territory of another.[52]

Accordingly, the *Ritter-Coulais* saga appears to have made it clear that the economic free movement of persons provisions are not, anymore, merely regarded

---

[50] Case C-112/91, *Werner*, ECLI:EU:C:1993:27.

[51] This is obvious from Case C-544/07, *Rüffler*, ECLI:EU:C:2009:258, where the facts were quite similar to those in the *Ritter-Coulais* group of cases but because the applicant was not economically active *at the time that the movement was exercised*, the situation did not fall within the scope of the economic free movement of persons provisions.

[52] For a more detailed analysis of this case-law and—especially—the rationale behind it see Tryfonidou 2016, pp. 88–91, 111–112, 159, 166–173.

as provisions which enable Union citizens to move to another Member State *in order to pursue an economic activity* there but, rather, they are now viewed as provisions which provide a bundle of independent rights—including the right to reside in one Member State whilst working in the territory of another—to economically active Union citizens, irrespective of whether the economic activity is taken-up in the territory of another Member State or continues to be exercised in their State of nationality or origin.[53]

These cases, therefore, appear to confirm the character of the economic free movement of persons provisions as fundamental rights which have to be respected for their own sake, as opposed to merely as freedoms allowed to Member State nationals in order to enable them to further the economic aims of the Treaty.[54] This is because these cases demonstrate that the economic free movement of persons provisions are no longer merely viewed as provisions which aim to enable Member State nationals to move to another Member State *for the purpose of taking-up and/or pursuing an economic activity there*, but rather, as provisions which bestow certain (primary) rights—which are independent of each other—on Union citizens who are economically active. Similarly, as seen in preceding parts of this section, Article 21 TFEU is no longer considered to be a provision which solely enables Union citizens to move to another Member State or to move and reside in the territory of another Member State but, rather, it is a provision which also enables Union citizens to simply reside in the territory of a Member State other than that of their nationality.

Accordingly, it is now clear that (discriminatory or non-discriminatory) restrictions on the exercise of *any* of the primary rights granted by the free movement of persons provisions are capable of amounting to a violation of the latter; and this is so even when the violation of the relevant right does not give rise to a restriction on (physical) free movement.

3.3.2 'Discrimination': The Current Approach

The starting point of the analysis in this part of the chapter is that, despite the fact that a broader meaning is currently attributed to the notion of 'restriction' and that this notion has been detached from that of 'discrimination', the latter continues to be read as covering only discrimination on the grounds of nationality or migration. Moreover—and more importantly—the notion of 'discrimination' continues to be

[53] As explained elsewhere, however, a literal and/or teleological approach to the interpretation of the economic free movement of persons provisions does not justify such a reading and, hence, this right can only stem from these provisions if they are read together with Article 21 TFEU—see Tryfonidou 2016, pp. 171–172.

[54] For a discussion of the issue of whether the free movement provisions can be seen as sources of 'fundamental rights' see Spaventa 2007; Krenn 2012, p. 191; Wollenschläger 2011, p. 16; De Vries 2013, pp. 83–86; De Cecco 2014; Tryfonidou 2016.

dependent on that of 'restriction' for the purposes of finding a violation of these provisions. In other words, in order for discrimination to be found to amount to discrimination *contrary to the free movement of persons provisions*, it must be such as to be capable of leading to a restriction that amounts to a violation of these provisions: this has been the Court's original approach, and it continues to be its current approach to this issue.

However, the Court's current approach has also seen the inclusion within the scope of EU free movement law of discrimination that does not lead to restrictions that are contrary to the free movement of persons provisions. In particular, since the 1970s, the Court has devised new ways of bringing such instances of discrimination within the scope of EU free movement law (albeit *not* within the scope of the free movement provisions). This has been done through—what Jo Shaw has called—the Court's 'proto-citizenship' case-law,[55] in which the prohibition of nationality discrimination was read in a way which appeared to be separated from any requirement of a link between the discrimination suffered and a restriction contrary to the free movement of persons provisions.

The classic examples of this case-law are cases concerning the interpretation of Article 7(2) of Regulation 1612/68,[56] the free movement of students case-law,[57] as well as cases involving migrants who were discriminated against in the territory of the host State, such as the famous *Cowan* ruling.[58] In these groups of cases, the Court appears to have tentatively decoupled the notion of 'discrimination' from that of 'restriction', recognising that migrant Member State nationals are first and foremost human beings who should be treated equally with the nationals of the host State in all situations that fall within the material scope of EU law.[59]

Take the *Cristini* case,[60] for example. There, the Court held that Article 7(2) of Regulation 1612/68 was breached as a result of the French authorities' refusal to grant reduced rail fares to the family members of a deceased migrant worker, since such fares were given to the family members of French workers. It is immediately apparent that the differential treatment in this instance was quite far removed from the (deceased) migrant's exercise of free movement as a worker, and the exercise of the latter movement would by no stretch of the imagination be deterred as a direct result of the contested differential treatment.

[55] Shaw 2011, p. 584.

[56] (n. 13) above.

[57] Case 293/83, *Gravier*, ECLI:EU:C:1985:69; Case 24/86, *Blaizot*, ECLI:EU:C:1988:43.

[58] Case 186/87, *Cowan*, ECLI:EU:C:1989:47.

[59] Eeckhout 2002, p. 961; Prechal and de Vries 2009, pp. 16–17. As explained by Wilsher, in this line of case-law the Court appears to have embraced 'status equivalence' as its basis for a finding of discrimination, which is based on the assumption that migrant Union citizens and, in particular, their status as 'denizens' entitles them to be treated as of equivalent status to nationals of the host State—see Wilsher 2008, pp. 8–9.

[60] Case 32/75, *Cristini*, ECLI:EU:C:1975:120.

The paradigmatic case in this context, nonetheless, is *Cowan*.[61] The judgment—delivered in 1989—is particularly significant because it put the first building blocks of what would, within a decade, form the basic mode of reasoning in the Court's citizenship jurisprudence.[62] The Court in that case resorted to the use of a combination of Treaty provisions (a market freedom plus Article 18 TFEU), in order to bring discrimination that did not lead to a restriction caught by the free movement provisions, within the scope of EU free movement law.[63] More specifically, the nationality discrimination that was suffered on the facts in relation to the receipt of a benefit (damages for victims of a crime the assailant of which remained unidentified), was held to be contrary to EU law and, in particular, Article 18 TFEU, because it was suffered by a Member State national who has a migrant service-recipient and, as such, fell within the personal scope of EU free movement law via Article 56 TFEU.[64] Given the lack of a link between the discrimination complained of and a restriction contrary to the free movement provisions, the Court was right in not finding a violation of Article 56 TFEU. However, because the claimant had exercised free movement rights, his situation fell within the scope of EU law and, hence, he could rely on the prohibition laid down in Article 18 TFEU. The same 'technique' was followed by the Court when applying the citizenship free movement provision (Article 21 TFEU), almost a decade later, in the case of *Bickel and Franz*,[65] and was later followed in a long line of citizenship cases.[66]

Accordingly, in the context of the free movement of persons provisions, the notion of 'discrimination' has never been entirely decoupled from that of 'restriction'; in other words, it is still only instances of discrimination that lead to restrictions, that can be caught by the free movement provisions, *when the latter are employed alone*. Despite the fact that in cases like *Cowan*, the free movement of persons provisions were used in order to bring the applicants within the scope of EU law and allow them to rely on Article 18 TFEU, it should be underlined that the scope of the former has—rightly—not been extended to cover instances of discrimination that *do not* lead to restrictions that are contrary to those provisions. Rather, such instances of differential treatment have been held to be prohibited, either by secondary legislation (i.e. Regulation 1612/68 which has, now, been

[61] Case 186/87, *Cowan*, ECLI:EU:C:1989:47. For a more recent case where exactly the same approach was followed see Case C-164/07, *Wood*, ECLI:EU:C:2008:321.

[62] O'Leary 2009, note 47; Schrauwen 2000, p. 782; Reich and Harbacevica 2009, p. 616.

[63] According to Tridimas, 'The rationale which underlies *Cowan* is that the prohibition of discrimination on grounds of nationality extends to situations which are not related to the exercise of economic rights strictly understood'—Tridimas 2006, p. 124.

[64] See, also, the comments in Weatherill 1989, pp. 565–568.

[65] Case C-274/96, *Bickel and Franz*, ECLI:EU:C:1998:563.

[66] See, inter alia, Case C-209/03, *Bidar*, ECLI:EU:C:2005:169; Case C-524/06, *Huber*, ECLI:EU:C:2008:724; Case C-103/08, *Gottwald*, ECLI:EU:C:2009:597. Note that in cases where the applicant had not exercised any of the rights stemming from Article 21 TFEU, the Court read Article 18 TFEU *together with Article 20 TFEU*, in order to find a violation of EU law—see, for instance, Case 186/87, *Cowan*, ECLI:EU:C:1989:47.

replaced by Regulation 492/2011), which appears to be aiming at outlawing unjustifiable nationality discrimination *in addition to* removing restrictions on the rights granted by the free movement provisions,[67] or by (the directly effective)[68] Article 18 TFEU.[69]

Hence, recognising the importance of respecting the principle of non-discrimination in a Citizens' Europe, the Court has employed other ways for bringing within the scope of EU free movement law, instances of differential treatment that do not lead to a restriction that is contrary to the free movement provisions.[70] In cases like *Cowan*, where the free movement of persons provisions are solely used in order to bring a Union citizen within the personal scope of EU law (as opposed to deciding, also, the outcome of the case), the only requirement which appears to have to be satisfied for a situation to fall within the scope of EU law is the exercise of the primary rights stemming from the free movement provisions. As Advocate General Jacobs pointed out in his Opinion in *Bickel and Franz*, 'In *Cowan* the only connection with Community law was that the facts occurred while Mr Cowan was in France as a recipient of services. By holding that that was sufficient to trigger the prohibition of discrimination the Court effectively brought any person exercising his right to enter another Member State within the protection offered by Article 6 [now Article 18 TFEU]'.[71]

Accordingly, the mere exercise of the primary rights stemming from the free movement of persons provisions—a jurisdictional requirement in this context—appears to suffice to bring a situation within the scope of EU law via the medium of the free movement provisions, and in order to enable the EU to require the host Member State to extend the treatment it affords to its own nationals, to nationals of other Member States, by applying the Article 18 TFEU prohibition. Therefore, in cases like *Cowan* where discriminatory treatment was held to be contrary to Article 18 TFEU, the requirement of the exercise of the rights stemming from the free movement of persons provisions (including of the right to free movement) has been

---

[67] See the preamble to both of these Regulations.

[68] Joined Cases C-92 & 326/92, *Phil Collins*, ECLI:EU:C:1993:847, para 34.

[69] In another group of cases where the contested measure did not relate to the exercise of free movement but rather gave rise to nationality discrimination against economic actors who were exercising an economic activity across borders, the Court merely used Article 18 TFEU in its judgment and noted explicitly that it was not necessary to connect it with any of the (economic) free movement provisions. See, inter alia, Joined Cases C-92 & 326/92, *Phil Collins*, ECLI:EU:C:1993:847, para 27; Case C-43/95, *Data-Delecta*, ECLI:EU:C:1996:357, para 14.

[70] As AG Jacobs pointed out in para 24 of his Opinion in Case C-168/91, *Konstantinidis*, ECLI:EU:C:1992:504, 'Community law does not regard the migrant worker (or the self-employed migrant) purely as an economic agent and a factor of production entitled to the same salary and working conditions as nationals of the host State; it regards him as a human being who is entitled to live in that State "in freedom and dignity" … *and to be spared any difference in treatment that would render his life less comfortable, physically or psychologically, than the lives of the native population*'. Emphasis added.

[71] AG Opinion in Case C-274/96, *Bickel and Franz*, ECLI:EU:C:1998:115, para 19.

downgraded to a merely jurisdictional requirement: it must be proven that these rights have been exercised, but it is not necessary to show, in addition, that they are going to be impeded as a result of the discrimination that is complained of.

3.4 The Rationale Behind the Court's Current Approach: The Free Movement of Persons Provisions as Fundamental (Citizenship) Rights

The main aim of this last section is to explore, and provide some insights into, the rationale that lies behind the developments analysed in the preceding section. As already noted in Sect. 3.1, my argument is that the main reason behind these developments is the attribution to the free movement of persons provisions of a double status of (instrumental) 'freedoms' *and* (fundamental) 'rights'. In other words, although in the early days of European integration these provisions were simply viewed as sources of instrumental freedoms afforded to Member State nationals for enabling them to further the economic aims of the Treaty, they have, since the 1970s, begun to be read also as sources of fundamental rights which have to be respected and protected for their own sake.[72] This has obviously affected the interpretation of these provisions and, in particular, of the main notions used for establishing their violation. The analysis of this argument will therefore be the focus of this section.

As explained by Judge Skouris while writing extra-judicially, 'In the early stages of the European Community, fundamental freedoms were not considered as having such a strong central position. They were regarded rather like being no more than abstract objectives to be achieved by the means of Community legislation, programs and other measures. Accordingly, the three Founding Treaties did not present them as enforceable rights but as a mandate to the Community Institutions'.[73]

It did not take long, however, for the metamorphosis of the economic free movement of persons provisions into sources of rights. It began in the early 1970s, with the Court's attribution of direct effect to them,[74] and has ever since been reflected in the Court's rulings. For instance, in the *Konstantinidis* judgment, the Court made reference to the 'right of establishment',[75] whilst in *Bosman* it spoke of the 'right to freedom of movement' for the purpose of taking-up an economic

[72] For a similar view see Krenn 2012, p. 185. For an argument that a rights-based paradigm of EU citizenship is only now emerging (in particular, from 2010 onwards, following the Court's judgment in Case C-135/08, *Rottmann*, ECLI:EU:C:2010:104), see Kochenov and Plender 2012.

[73] Skouris 2006, p. 227.

[74] Case 48/75, *Royer*, ECLI:EU:C:1976:57 (workers); Case 2/74, *Reyners*, ECLI:EU:C: 1974:68 (establishment); Case 33/74, *Van Binsbergen*, ECLI:EU:C:1974:131 (services).

[75] Case C-168/91, *Konstantinidis*, ECLI:EU:C:1993:115, para 12. See to the same effect Case 197/84, *Steinhauser*, ECLI:EU:C:1985:260, para 14.

activity in the territory of another Member State.[76] On a number of occasions, the Court went even further and noted that the market freedoms are 'fundamental provisions'[77] of the Treaty and, even more significantly, in some of its rulings it bestowed on them the full status of a 'fundamental right'.[78] In particular, in *Heylens* and *Bosman* the Court stressed that free access to employment is a 'fundamental right which the Treaty confers individually on each worker in the Community'.[79] This latter terminology has also been employed in pieces of secondary legislation that complement the free movement provisions: Regulation 492/2011[80]—in the same way as its predecessor—provides in its fourth Recital that 'Freedom of movement constitutes a fundamental right of workers and their families'.

Although the economic free movement of persons provisions had begun to be reconceptualised as individual and enforceable rights long before the Maastricht Treaty, the introduction of the status of Union citizenship with the coming into force of the latter, enabled their further transformation into sources of fundamental (citizenship) rights; i.e. rights which are granted to Union citizens *because they are Union citizens* and which are granted for their own sake, that is, without having an ulterior aim.[81] In other words, and transplanting into this context what Advocate General Cosmas pointed out referring to Article 21 TFEU, each of the free movement of persons provisions is now 'a right, in the true meaning of the word, which exists with a view to the autonomous pursuit of a goal, to the benefit of the holder of that right and not to the benefit of the Community and the attainment of its objectives'.[82] This appears to be a necessary step in a Citizens' Europe since 'A "true European citizenship" is only possible when an appeal to the legal status of itself creates rights for the bearer and obligations for the public authority vis-à-vis the bearer of the status'.[83] Accordingly, the rights provided by the free movement of persons provisions are now bestowed on Union citizens, without any ulterior motive (such as the creation of an EU-wide labour market); they are simply granted to them *because* they are Union citizens and, hence, these rights can now be characterised as *fundamental (citizenship) rights*.[84]

The important question for our purposes is, of course, what connection can be drawn between the reconceptualisation of the free movement of persons provisions

---

[76] Case C-415/93, *Bosman*, ECLI:EU:C:1995:463, paras 95–96.

[77] See, inter alia, Case C-49/89, *Corsica Ferries*, ECLI:EU:C:1989:649, para 8; Case C-169/98, *Commission v France*, ECLI:EU:C:2000:85, para 46.

[78] See, inter alia, Case 152/82, *Forcheri*, ECLI:EU:C:1983:205, para 11.

[79] Case 222/86, *Heylens*, ECLI:EU:C:1987:442, para 14; Case C-415/93, *Bosman*, ECLI:EU:C:1995:463, para 129.

[80] Council and Parliament Regulation (EU) No. 492/2011 *on freedom of movement for workers within the Union*, O.J. L 41/1 (2011).

[81] For a similar view see AG Cosmas in Case C-378/97, *Wijsenbeek*, ECLI:EU:C:1999:144, para 82. See, also, Johnson and O'Keeffe 1994, p. 1314.

[82] AG Cosmas in Case C-378/97, *Wijsenbeek*, ECLI:EU:C:1999:144, para 84.

[83] Kochenov 2011, p. 13.

[84] For a fuller analysis of this argument see Tryfonidou 2016.

as sources of fundamental citizenship rights, on the one hand, and the developments that were analysed in the previous section, on the other.

Beginning with the Court's decision to include within the scope of the free movement of persons provisions *non-discriminatory* restrictions on the exercise of the rights stemming from these provisions, this is clearly a necessary step in the process of reconceptualising these provisions as sources of fundamental (citizenship) rights for Union citizens. As Advocate General Lenz noted in his Opinion in *Bosman*, 'Any restriction of the right to freedom of movement infringes a fundamental right of the person concerned and therefore requires justification. Since it is a fundamental right which is being infringed, I cannot see, any more than Advocate General Jacobs in his Opinion in the *Konstantinidis* case, how the non-discriminatory character of the measure could mean that it did not fall within the scope of [Article 45 TFEU]. For that reason too, I am therefore of the opinion that [Article 45 TFEU] must also apply to non-discriminatory restrictions on freedom of movement'.[85]

If the free movement of persons provisions were read as only prohibiting discriminatory restrictions on the rights provided by them, this would mean that the said rights would only come into existence if and when the host Member State provided them to its own nationals; in other words, their existence would become conditional. But this is a reading which is, clearly, incongruous with their fundamental rights character. Just as it sounds utterly absurd to say that a person visiting a country which is a signatory to the European Convention on Human Rights has the right to freedom of expression there only if this same right is granted to the nationals of that State, it is equally illogical to say that a Union citizen has the (EU) right to have access to employment in the territory of the host Member State only if this same right is given by the latter to its own nationals.

The impact of the reconceptualisation of the free movement of persons provisions as sources of fundamental (citizenship) rights, nonetheless, becomes even more obvious from the developments analysed in Sect. 3.3.1.2, whereby it was explained that the notion of 'restriction' has been extended to encompass not only (discriminatory or non-discriminatory) restrictions on *free movement*, but, also, restrictions on the exercise of the (other) primary rights provided by the free movement of persons provisions. This development illustrates that we have now moved away from the traditional 'obsession' with movement in EU free movement

[85] Opinion of AG Lenz in Case C-415/93, *Bosman*, ECLI:EU:C:1995:293, para 203. For a similar view see Snell 2004, p. 49: 'When a fundamental right has been impaired, it is of no consequence that rights of home state nationals have also been encroached upon'. To borrow terminology used by de Vries, by expanding the scope of application of the free movement of persons provisions to cover genuinely non-discriminatory rules, the Court appears to have signified that the free movement provisions no longer 'primarily serve transnational integration' but, rather, 'supranational legitimisation'. As de Vries has explained, 'Supranational legitimisation entails that the four freedoms intend "to complement the national and supranational protection of the individual by fundamental rights and service the purpose of general liberalisation", whereas transnational integration implies that the four freedoms merely serve gaps of protection in cross-border transactions'—de Vries 2013, p. 85.

law, and towards a situation whereby the central focus is placed on the protection of the (by nature cross-border) rights that the Union citizen derives from EU law and, in particular, from the free movement provisions.

The important question that follows, therefore, is: what are the rights that Union citizens now derive from the free movement of persons provisions? Advocate General Tesauro in his Opinion in *Brasserie du Pêcheur/Factortame*, noted that it is easy to identify the exact right(s) bestowed by certain Treaty provisions, such as Article 18 TFEU, whereas the same does not hold true for certain other provisions, such as Article 34 TFEU, 'in view of the variety of fact situations conceivable in that area'.[86]

Indeed, it is not overly easy to determine what are the exact rights that are provided by the free movement of persons provisions either, but it is possible to establish a taxonomy which can be used to decide what are the basic rights that are provided by these provisions, and which can also be employed for deciding on a case-by-case basis what further rights can be derived from them. At the core of this taxonomy lies the distinction between primary and secondary rights, briefly touched upon in previous parts of the chapter.

As explained by Goudappel, 'Primary rights are the rights which are laid down in the Treaty texts'.[87] Accordingly, a quick perusal of the free movement provisions, immediately reveals the list of primary rights bestowed on Union citizens by the free movement of persons provisions. If we take Article 45 TFEU as an example, it is clear that the primary rights provided are, inter alia, the right to accept offers of employment in the territory of another Member State, to move freely (and to reside) in the Member State where employment has been taken-up, and the right not to be discriminated against on the grounds of nationality as regards employment, remuneration and other conditions of work and employment.

Whenever any of the primary rights stemming from the free movement provisions is breached this, *automatically* (i.e. without needing to prove anything else) means that there is a violation of the relevant provision from which the right is stemming. Hence, as we saw in the previous section, Union citizens no longer derive merely the right to free movement from the free movement of persons provisions; they can, for example, also rely on the latter to claim the right not to be discriminated against on the ground of their nationality when it comes to access to employment in the host State (a right that is expressly mentioned in the text of Article 45 TFEU), and this is so even if they have not moved between Member States, which is (simply) a(nother)—but no longer the only—primary right stemming from these provisions.

On the other hand, 'Secondary rights are derived rights like the right to bring your family members when you move to another Member State, whether this family member is an EU citizen or a third-country national. Such rights are not laid down

[86] Opinion of AG Tesauro in Joined Cases C-46 & 48/93, *Brasserie du Pêcheur and Factortame*, ECLI:EU:C:1995:407, para 79.

[87] Goudappel 2010, p. 55.

in the Treaty texts but follow from the rights laid down in there'.[88] Secondary rights are, therefore, rights which are *not* found in the text of the relevant Treaty provision but they derive from it if, *on the particular facts of the case*, their violation will lead to a violation of the primary right that has been (or was intended to be) exercised on the facts of the case. An obvious example of a secondary right derived from (all) the free movement of persons provisions is the right not to be discriminated against on the ground of the exercise of the rights stemming from these provisions. This is a right which is not mentioned in the Treaty text (and, hence, it is not a primary right) and, yet, because its breach is obviously capable of impeding the exercise of the rights stemming from the free movement of persons provisions, its breach amounts to a breach of these provisions.

The above distinction between primary and secondary rights helps us to better understand the Court's current approach to the interpretation of the notions of 'restriction' and 'discrimination' in this context. This is because under this approach, each of the primary rights provided by the free movement of persons provisions appears to be an *independent* right granted to Union citizens who fall within the personal scope of those provisions and, hence, the right to free movement is not the *only* right on which the existence of all other rights is dependent. For instance, as can be gathered from *Collins*,[89] in order for a Union citizen to enjoy the right (provided in Article 45(3) TFEU) 'to stay in a Member State for the purpose of employment in accordance with the provisions governing the employment of nationals of that State', he does not have to have previously 'moved freely within the territory of Member States for this purpose'.

Similarly, the above-described dichotomy between primary/secondary rights and its application to the free movement of persons provisions can, also, provide a solid explanation for the Court's approach to the notion of 'discrimination' in EU free movement law. When we read the Treaty text, we can see that Article 21 TFEU does not make reference to non-discrimination (and, thus, this is not a primary right in this context), whereas the economic free movement of persons provisions *do* make reference to a prohibition of nationality discrimination (and, as such, it is a primary right in this context), *albeit* that—as is obvious from the text of these provisions—this is strictly confined to issues relating to the pursuit of an economic activity in the territory of the host State. Accordingly, in order for nationality discrimination to be prohibited by the free movement of persons provisions, it has to be proven either that the discrimination complained of is of a type that is expressly prohibited by these provisions (i.e. its prohibition is one of the primary rights laid down in them) or that it leads to a restriction on the exercise of one of the primary rights provided by these provisions (i.e. it is a secondary right which emerges because of its connection with one of the primary rights stemming from these provisions). The Court has, therefore, been right in not detaching 'discrimination', in the context of the free movement provisions, from the notion of

[88] Goudappel 2010, p. 55.

[89] Case C-138/02, *Collins*, ECLI:EU:C:2004:172.

‘restriction’; in other words, although the notion of ‘restriction’ has been detached from the notion of ‘discrimination’ (in that a restriction does not need to be discriminatory in order to be caught by the free movement of persons provisions), the converse has not happened: if the discrimination complained of is not in relation to one of the matters expressly mentioned in the free movement of persons provisions, it has to be such as to lead to a restriction on the exercise of the primary rights bestowed by them, in order to be caught (i.e. it is only then that it is established as a secondary right granted by these provisions). Conversely, Article 18 TFEU grants to all Union citizens the primary right to be free from discrimination on the grounds of nationality, in all situations that fall within the scope of the Treaties and, hence, the Court, when employing this provision, does not need to find any link between this right and any of the aims of the Treaty: as long as a situation falls within the personal scope of EU law, Union citizens can rely on Article 18 TFEU in order to claim their primary right not to be discriminated against on the grounds of nationality (the *Cowan* scenario).

3.5 Conclusion

This chapter had as its aim to explore the development of the meaning of the notions of ‘discrimination’ and ‘restriction’, when employed for the purpose of finding a violation of the free movement of persons provisions, and to consider how the relationship between them has evolved.

A number of conclusions have been reached.

First, as regards the notion of ‘restriction’, it is clear that this is, now, completely detached from ‘discrimination’, meaning that the free movement of persons provisions prohibit not only discriminatory restrictions but, also, genuinely non-discriminatory ones. Moreover, despite the fact that traditionally the notion of ‘restriction’ was thought to be referring exclusively to ‘restrictions on free movement’, it is now clear that it has a broader meaning and that it also covers restrictions on the exercise of (any of) the (primary) rights provided by the free movement of persons provisions. In particular, it has been seen that since the free movement of persons provisions are no longer viewed purely instrumentally, as provisions allowing Member State nationals the freedom to move across borders in order to further the economic aims of the EU, they can no longer merely be envisaged as prohibitions on restrictions to free movement. Rather, as metamorphosed Union citizenship rights, they attach to the Union citizen a number of (primary) fundamental (citizenship) rights—the right to free, inter-State, movement being only *one* of these rights—which are independent of each other and which have to be respected and protected for their own sake.

Secondly, the notion of ‘discrimination’ is still dependent on that of ‘restriction’, when a violation of the free movement of persons provisions is sought to be established. In other words, discriminatory treatment is taken to amount to a violation of these provisions only if it appears capable of leading to a restriction that is contrary to them (i.e. it is a secondary right (implicitly) prohibited by these provisions) or if it is exercised in relation to matters that are explicitly mentioned in the text of these provisions (and is, thus, a primary right bestowed by them). One might consider this quite disappointing in a Citizens' Europe and, perhaps, as a sign that the EU does not take the principle of equality seriously. However, this chapter has demonstrated that this is not the case and that the Court's case-law from the 1970s onwards illustrates that the EU does take the principle of equality and non-discrimination seriously, since in quite a long line of cases nationality discrimination that did not lead to a restriction contrary to the free movement provisions *was* found to amount to a violation of EU law. Accordingly, Union citizens *are* entitled to a general, primary, right not to be discriminated against on the grounds of nationality in the territory of another Member State or, simply, when they move—without this having to be linked to the enjoyment of any other right—albeit that this right is not granted by the free movement provisions.

Finally, it has been explained that the rationale behind the developments analysed in this chapter is the reconceptualization of the free movement of persons provisions as Union citizenship rights: these provisions are now viewed also (if not primarily) as provisions which bestow certain fundamental rights on Union citizens (simply) because they are Union citizens, and not merely in order to enable them to take part in the circulation process in furtherance of the economic objectives of the EU. Accordingly, the meaning of the terms under examination (and, correspondingly, the relationship between them) has had to adapt accordingly, in order to reflect the rights-based character of these provisions.

Acknowledgements This is an abridged and updated version of Tryfonidou A (2014) The Notions of 'Restriction' and 'Discrimination' in the Context of the Free Movement of Persons Provisions: From a Relationship of Interdependence to One of (Almost Complete) Independence. Yearbook of European Law 33: 385–416. I would like to thank Tarjei Bekkedal and Luca Pantaleo for their comments on an earlier draft of this chapter.

References

Barnard C (2001) Fitting the Remaining Pieces into the Goods and Persons Jigsaw? European Law Review 26: 35–59

Bernard N (1996) Discrimination and Free Movement in EC Law. International and Comparative Law Quarterly 45: 82–108

Chalmers D (1994) Repackaging the Internal Market – The Ramifications of the Keck Judgment. European Law Review 19: 385–403

Davies G (2010) Understanding Market Access: Exploring the Economic Rationality of Different Conceptions of Free Movement law. German Law Journal 11: 671–704

de Búrca G (2002) Unpacking the Concept of Discrimination in EC and International Trade Law. In: Barnard C, Scott J (eds) The Law of the Single European Market: Unpacking the Premises. Hart, Oxford, pp 181–195

De Cecco F (2014) Fundamental Freedoms, Fundamental Rights and the Scope of Free Movement Law. German Law Journal 15: 383–406

De Vries S (2013) The Protection of Fundamental Rights within Europe's Internal Market after Lisbon – an Endeavour for More Harmony. In: De Vries S, Bernitz U, Weatherill S (eds) The Protection of Fundamental Rights in the EU After Lisbon. Hart, Oxford, pp 59–94

Eeckhout P (2002) The EU Charter of Fundamental Rights and the Federal Question. Common Market Law Review 39: 945–994

Enchelmaier S (2007) The ECJ's Recent Case Law on the Free Movement of Goods: Movement in All Sorts of Directions. Yearbook of European Law 26: 115–156

Goudappel F (2010) The Effects of EU Citizenship: Economic, Social and Political Rights in a Time of Constitutional Change. TMC Asser Press, The Hague

Hilson C (1999) Discrimination in Community free movement law. European Law Review 24: 445–462

Horsley T (2012) Unearthing Buried Treasure: Art. 34 TFEU and the Exclusionary Rules. European Law Review 37: 734–757

Johnson E, O'Keeffe D (1994) From Discrimination to Obstacles to Free Movement: Recent Developments Concerning the Free Movement of Workers 1989–1994. Common Market Law Review 31: 1313–1346

Kochenov D (2011) New European Citizenship: A Move Beyond the Market Bias. In: Bellamy R, Staiger U (eds) EU Citizenship and the Market. UCL, London, pp 11–15

Kochenov D, Plender R (2012) EU Citizenship: From an Incipient Form to an Incipient Substance? The Discovery of the Treaty Text. European Law Review 37: 369–396

Krenn C (2012) A Missing Piece in the Horizontal Effect 'Jigsaw': Horizontal Direct Effect and the Free Movement of Goods. Common Market Law Review 49: 177–215

Morano-Foadi S, de Vries K (2012) The equality clauses in the EU directives on non-discrimination and migration/asylum. In: Morano-Foadi S, Malena M (eds) Integration for third-country nationals in the European Union: The Equality Challenge. Edward Elgar, Cheltenham, pp 16–44

More G (1999) The Principle of Equal Treatment: From Market Unifier to Fundamental Rights? In: Craig P, de Búrca G (eds) The Evolution of EU Law. Oxford University Press, Oxford, pp 517–553

O'Keeffe D (1985) Equal Rights for Migrants: The Concept of Social Advantages in Article 7(2), Regulation 1612/68. Yearbook of European Law 5: 93–123

O'Leary S (2009) The Past, Present and Future of the Purely Internal Rule in EU Law. Irish Jurist 44: 13–46

Poiares Maduro M (2002) Harmony and Dissonance in Free Movement. In: Andenas M, Roth W-H (eds) Services and Free Movement in EU Law. Oxford University Press, Oxford, pp 41–68

Prechal S, De Vries S (2009) Seamless Web of Judicial Protection in the Internal Market? European Law Review 34: 5–24

Reich N, Harbacevica S (2009) Citizenship and Family on Trial: A Fairly Optimistic Overview of Recent Court Practice with Regard to the Free Movement of Persons. Common Market Law Review 40: 615–638

Roth W-H (2002) The European Court of Justice's Case Law on Freedom to Provide Services: Is Keck Relevant? In: Andenas M, Roth W-H (eds) Services and Free Movement in EU Law. Oxford University Press, Oxford, pp 1–24

Schrauwen A (2000) Sink or swim together? Developments in European Citizenship. Fordham International Law Journal 23: 778–794

Shaw J (2011) Citizenship: Contrasting Dynamics at the Interface of Integration and Constitutionalism. In: Craig P, de Búrca G (eds) The Evolution of EU Law. Oxford University Press, Oxford, pp 575–609

Sibony A-L (2012) Can Market Access be Taken Seriously? Revue européenne de droit de la consommation 2: 323–342

Skouris V (2006) Fundamental Rights and Fundamental Freedoms: The Challenge of Striking a Delicate Balance. European Business Law Review 17: 225–239

Snell J (2004) And Then There Were Two: Products and Citizens in Community Law. In: Tridimas T, Nebbia P (eds) European Union Law for the Twenty-First Century. Hart, Oxford, pp 49–72

Snell J (2010) The Notion of Market Access: A Concept or a Slogan? Common Market Law Review 47: 437–472

Snell J (2011) Free Movement of Capital: Evolution as a Non-Linear Process. In: Craig P, de Búrca G (eds) The Evolution of EU Law. Oxford University Press, Oxford, pp 547–574

Spaventa E (2007) Free Movement of Persons in the European Union: Barriers to Movement in their Constitutional Context. Kluwer, The Hague

Szydlo M (2010) Export restrictions within the structure of free movement of goods. Reconsideration of an old paradigm. Common Market Law Review 47: 753–789

Toner H (2004) Non-Discriminatory Obstacles to the Exercise of Treaty Rights – Articles 39, 43, 49, and 18 EC. Yearbook of European Law 23: 275–302

Tridimas T (2006) The General Principles of EU Law. Oxford University Press, Oxford

Tryfonidou A (2009a) Reverse Discrimination in EC Law. Kluwer, Dordrecht

Tryfonidou A (2009b) In search of the aim of the EC free movement of persons provisions: Has the Court of Justice missed the point? Common Market Law Review 46: 1591–1620

Tryfonidou A (2010) Further steps on the road to convergence among the market freedoms. European Law Review 35: 36–56

Tryfonidou A (2012) Redefining the Outer Boundaries of EU Law: The Zambrano, McCarthy and Dereci Trilogy. European Public Law 18: 493–526

Tryfonidou A (2014) The Notions of 'Restriction' and 'Discrimination' in the Context of the Free Movement of Persons Provisions: From a Relationship of Interdependence to One of (Almost Complete) Independence. Yearbook of European Law 33: 385–416

Tryfonidou A (2016) The Impact of Union Citizenship on the EU's Market Freedoms. Hart, Oxford

Weatherill S (1989) Annotation of Cowan. Common Market Law Review 26: 563–581

Wilsher D (2008) Does Keck Discrimination Make Any Sense? An Assessment of the Non-Discrimination Principle within the European Single Market. European Law Review 33: 3–22

Wollenschläger F (2011) A New Fundamental Freedom beyond Market Integration: Union Citizenship and its Dynamics for Shifting the Economic Paradigm of European Integration. European Law Journal 17: 1–34

Chapter 4
Restrictions on the Use of Goods and Services

Stefan Enchelmaier

Abstract 'Market access' is the latest of the Court's formulae for establishing whether the free movement of goods and the freedom to provide services are restricted. So far, the criterion is ill-defined, especially in its application to restrictions of use. Nevertheless, predictability can be restored to the assessment under both freedoms through a properly understood discrimination test, complemented by a prohibition of universal bans, proceeding in the following steps:

(1) Does the restriction of use apply in law equally to domestic producers and providers as to those from other Member States (i.e. is it 'indistinctly applicable')? If yes,
(2) Does the restriction have the same factual repercussions on imports and domestic products/on services provided by operators established in the same Member State as the recipient, and on services in whose provision a border between Member States is crossed (if there are any domestic goods or services)? If yes,
(3) Does the restriction prohibit the last remaining use in the Member State in question in a situation where either such use remains legal in at least one other Member State, or the importing Member State is the last to allow this use?

If the answer to (1) or (2) is 'no', or if it is 'yes' to (3), the measure restricts the free movement of goods or the freedom to provide services, and therefore requires a justification. Otherwise, it does not because it leads to a mere reduction in the volume of economic activity.

Keywords Internal market · Free movement of goods · Freedom to provide services · Market access · Discrimination · Trade restrictions · Restrictions of use · Trailers · Jet skis · Court of Justice of the European Union

---

S. Enchelmaier (✉)
Lincoln College, University of Oxford, Oxford OX1 3DR, UK
e-mail: stefan.enchelmaier@law.ox.ac.uk

M. Andenas et al. (eds.), *The Reach of Free Movement*,
DOI 10.1007/978-94-6265-195-1_4

Contents

4.1 Introduction 86
4.2 *Moped Trailers:* Grand Chamber, Small Progress 87
4.2.1 The Court's 'Preliminary Observations' 87
4.2.2 The Application of the Court's Principles 90
4.3 *Mickelsson & Roos*: Principles Written in Water 92
4.4 Parallel Developments in the Case Law on the Freedom to Provide Services 96
4.4.1 The Beginnings: *Alpine Investments* and Other Cases 96
4.4.2 More Recent Judgments: 'Restriction of Market Access/of the Opportunity to Compete More Effectively' 98
4.4.3 Discrimination *Versus* Market Access? 102
4.5 Restrictions on the Use of Services 103
4.6 Conclusion 107
References 107

4.1 Introduction

The case law of the European Court of Justice ('the Court') on the free movement of goods and on the freedom to provide services began in the first half of the 1970s with the judgments in *Dassonville* and *van Binsbergen.*[1] It reached another milestone later that decade in *Cassis de Dijon*, which had a precursor a few weeks earlier in the services case *van Wesemael.*[2] The jurisprudence on the free movement of goods since *Cassis* has been described as the 'pacemaker' for the four freedoms.[3] By the beginning of the 1990s, however, as a consequence of the 'Sunday trading' line of cases,[4] it became clear that the case law had taken a wrong turn. The judgment in *Keck*[5] was supposed to correct this, but it soon became clear that it raised as many questions as it answered. These arose mainly in connection with the nebulous concept of '(rules relating to) selling arrangements'.

Restrictions on use are a paradigm that was not entirely new, but that has received the Court's specific attention (to say no more) only at the end of the 2000s, in *Moped trailers* and in *Mickelsson & Roos.*[6] One of the questions that received a good deal of attention during the proceedings (if not in the judgment in *Moped*

[1] Case 8/74, *Dassonville*, ECLI:EU:C:1974:82; Case 33/74, *van Binsbergen*, ECLI:EU:C:1974:131.

[2] Case 120/78, *Rewe-Zentral AG v Bundesmonopolverwaltung für Branntwein*, ECLI:EU:C:1979:42; Joined Cases 110/78 and 111/78, *van Wesemael*, ECLI:EU:C:1979:8.

[3] Steindorff 1986, p. 692.

[4] One of several examples is Case 145/88, *Torfaen Borough Council v. B&Q*, ECLI:EU:C:1989:593.

[5] Joined Cases C-267/91 and C-268/91, *Criminal Proceedings against Bernard Keck and Daniel Mithouard*, ECLI:EU:C:1993:905.

[6] Case C-110/05, *Commission v. Italy ('Moped trailers')*, ECLI:EU:C:2009:66; Case C-142/05, *Åklagaren v. Percy Mickelsson and Joakim Roos*, ECLI:EU:C:2009:336.

trailers itself) was the question whether and how the idea of 'selling arrangements' could be applied to restrictions of use.

The development of the case law on the freedom to provide services was less spectacular, but it roughly describes a similar trajectory of the Court grappling with the legality under European law of indistinctly applicable measures. In both areas, goods and services, the Court has recently emphasised the idea of 'market access'. Beyond this, in the jurisprudence we find a bewildering array of formulae for the assessment whether a national measure constitutes an obstacle to the freedom to provide services.[7] We shall here consider how restrictions on the use of services might be dealt with, preferably avoiding the shortcomings of the approach suggested by the Court for the free movement of goods.

4.2 *Moped Trailers:* Grand Chamber, Small Progress

4.2.1 The Court's 'Preliminary Observations'

Moped Trailers has been discussed in detail elsewhere.[8] The case arose from an action brought by the European Commission against Italy, where it was allowed to tow trailers only by car, by certain types of bus, and by tractor. In particular, it was not permissible to pull a trailer behind a moped. Before the Court, the Member States debated extensively whether and how *Keck* should apply to restrictions of use. The Grand Chamber ignored their arguments entirely. Instead, it invoked *Sandoz, Cassis de Dijon*, and *Keck* for its finding that 'Article [34 TFEU] reflects the obligation to respect the principles of non-discrimination and of mutual recognition of products lawfully manufactured and marketed in other Member States, as well as the principle of ensuring free access of Community products to national markets'.[9] Then follows a passage that is lifted almost verbatim from paras 16 and 17 of *Keck*, contrasting 'product requirements' with 'rules relating to selling arrangements'. From all this, the Court concluded that:

> … measures adopted by a Member State the object or effect of which is to treat products coming from other Member States less favourably are to be regarded as measures having equivalent effect to quantitative restrictions on imports within the meaning of Article [34 TFEU], as are ['product requirements']. Any other measure which hinders access of products originating in other Member States to the market of a Member State is also covered by that concept.[10]

---

[7] See the inventory in Enchelmaier 2011, pp. 618–633.

[8] Enchelmaier 2010, *passim*, with references to the literature up to that point. See also Fenger, Chap. 5 in this volume.

[9] Case C-110/05 (above n. 6), para 34; the references in the original are omitted.

[10] Case C-110/05 (above n. 6), para 37.

So there appear to be three sorts of measures which, according to the Court, fall foul of the prohibition in Article 34: first, those whose object or effect is to treat imports less favourably than domestic products; secondly, those which impose adaptation costs of whatever sort on imports; and, thirdly, any other measures that hinder market access of imports.

The wording used by the Court to describe the first sort of rules is transferred to the interpretation of Article 34 from the case law on Article 35. That provision, according to the established *Groenveld* formula, 'concerns national measures which have as their specific object or effect the restriction of patterns of exports'.[11] 'Object or effect' encompasses both distinctly and indistinctly applicable measures. Distinctly applicable measures have as their 'object' an impediment to imports. In this context, 'object' does not imply 'intention'. The same concept is used under Article 101, where the 'object' of an agreement means its objectively foreseeable consequences under the circumstances on a given market, regardless of the intentions of the parties.[12] Distinctly applicable measures catch imports only, and impose on them burdens that domestic products do not have to bear. Such rules will of necessity affect market access of imports negatively, whether or not that is what the Member State set out specifically to achieve beyond the other aims it (purportedly) pursued.

Indistinctly applicable measures, on the other hand, will not necessarily have such an 'effect', but might in conjunction with other circumstances. This will be the case if abiding by the national rules imposes burdens on imports that domestic products do not have to shoulder: the latter will always have been made in conformity with national regulations (or would in all likelihood be so made in case there is presently no domestic competition). Imports, made in accordance with a different set of rules in another Member State, might have to be adapted to the standards of the Member State of importation. In other words, even though the rule applies to all, not everyone finds it equally easy to comply with. Member States may only insist on such adaptation, however, if it would be proportional to enforce the national rules.

If not, 'mutual recognition' will have to take place as mentioned by the Court in its 'preamble' in *Moped Trailers*, and as exemplified in *Cassis de Dijon*. This means that the importing Member State has to accept as complying with its own legislation such products made in other Member States as offer essentially equivalent guarantees of safety, wholesomeness, commercial fairness or whatever other policy aim the legislation in the importing Member State seeks to realise.[13]

It is not quite clear what sort of rules the Court had in mind that make up the second category ('product requirements'). More specifically, it is difficult to fathom

---

[11] Case 15/79, *PB Groenveld BV v Produktschap voor Vee en Vlees*, ECLI:EU:C:1979:253, para 7; see more recently Case C-12/02, *Grilli*, ECLI:EU:C:2003:538, para 42, and Case C-137/00, *Milk Marque and National Farmers' Union*, ECLI:EU:C:2003:429, paras 118, 119; Case C-205/07, *Gysbrechts and Santurel*, ECLI:EU:C:2008:730, para 40 (Grand Chamber).

[12] See e.g. Case T-175/95, *BASF Coatings v. Commission*, ECLI:EU:T:1999:99, paras 82–9, with further references.

[13] Armstrong 2002, *passim*. Wilsher 2008, pp. 6 et seq., in this context speaks of 'regulatory equivalence'.

the relation between these and the 'effect' joint of the preceding group. The Court here, by contrast with its description of the first group, does not mention competing domestic products. The presence of any domestic competition is, however, not necessary for a finding that a measure has equivalent effect to a quantitative restriction on imports. The Member State will have to justify its measures whenever any adaptation is required of imports (and if products of a sort lawful in other Member States are universally banned in the importing country, see below). It seems, therefore, that the second group is already included in the first.

The third group of measures according to the Court's formula comprises 'any other hindrances to market access'. Given that the first and second groups cover unequal treatment in law and in fact, the third must contain measures that do not entail unequal treatment (and if there is no justification, discrimination) of any description (direct/indirect, formal/material, overt/covert). Also, mere reductions in trade between Member States are not enough to qualify a measure as one having equivalent effect to a quantitative restriction.[14] The third group must, therefore, be made up of rules that prohibit all sales of the product, or that allow none of its 'normally intended' uses. In other words, the third group consists of universal bans of sales or use.[15] Such bans do not have to be definitive. On the contrary, they are widespread but can normally be overcome by obtaining a licence or an approval, by

[14] *Keck* (above n. 5), para 13: '[A prohibition of resale at a loss] may, admittedly, restrict the volume of sales, and hence the volume of sales of products from other Member States, in so far as it deprives traders of a method of sales promotion. But the question remains whether such a possibility is sufficient to characterise the legislation in question as a measure having equivalent effect to a quantitative restriction on imports.' In the same sense, see Case C-71/02, *Karner v. Trostwijk*, ECLI:EU:C:2004:181, para 42: '[…] Although such a prohibition is, in principle, likely to limit the total volume of sales in that Member State and, consequently, also to reduce the volume of sales of goods from other Member States, it nevertheless does not affect the marketing of products originating from other Member States more than it affects the marketing of products from the Member State in question. […]'; Case C-20/03, *Burmanjer*, ECLI:EU:C:2005:307, paras 30–31: 'It is common ground that a national system such as the rules on itinerant sales is, in principle, likely to limit the total volume of sales of the goods in question in the Member State concerned and, consequently, also to reduce the volume of sales of goods from other Member States. […] However, the information available to the Court does not enable it to establish with certainty whether the national rules on itinerant sales affect the marketing of products from Member States other than the Kingdom of Belgium to any greater degree than that of products from that State. […]'.

[15] *Contra* Fenger (n. 8), Chap. 5, Sect. 5.4.2, who interprets para 17 of *Keck* as a factual statement ('the consequence of fulfilling the test laid down in that judgment') or rather, as a 'legal fiction in the name of legal certainty and operability', with the result that '[f]or non-discriminatory measures, the market test was applied only in the negative sense that as long as the two conditions laid down in Keck were fulfilled no market access problem would by definition arise' (by footnote. 38). This seems due to the absence throughout his text of a reflection on what 'market access' might mean in legal terms (for which ultimately the Court is to blame, not its commentators). If one understands it to mean universal bans, numerous judgments can be found which turn on the assessment of such measures (see next footnote). If one understands as a reduction of turnover, a number of unanswered questions arise.

opening suitable trading premises or hiring qualified personnel, by appointing a local representative etc.[16]

Just as much as the Court's explanation of the principles underlying *Keck* was sparse (to put it mildly), so is its elaboration of the present position. A meagre 'consequently' is all the Grand Chamber offers by way of deriving from, essentially, *Dassonville*, *Cassis de Dijon* and *Keck* its new definition (if it is one) of what amounts to a measure having equivalent effect to a quantitative restriction. The Court offers less a deduction than a vague association, or even only an allusion to the sources of its formula. There is no hint in the judgment as to how the three types of measures translate (as presumably they are meant to do) the principles of non-discrimination, mutual recognition and free market access that the Court invoked in the paragraph immediately preceding.

Even taken on their own, the three categories of measures receive no definition, although some understanding can be gleaned from elsewhere. It is equally unclear how the three types relate to one another, whether they are complementary or alternative and, if the latter, whether there is any order of assessment. The first two overlap in substance: the denial of mutual recognition can render indirectly discriminatory an indistinctly applicable measure that imposes additional burdens on imports. Moreover, the Court gives the apparently 'catch-all'[17] category of 'any other measures' no contours whatsoever. The Court's failure to do so came back to haunt it shortly thereafter, in the *Mickelsson & Roos* judgment discussed below.

4.2.2 The Application of the Court's Principles

The Grand Chamber went on as it had started: the application of the above rules generated yet more uncertainty. The Court distinguished between trailers that were specifically designed for towing behind motorcycles, and those that were of general use. Access to the market of general-use trailers was not hindered by the prohibition of their being towed behind a motorcycle. This was different with regard to motorcycle-only trailers. The Court found that although it was not inconceivable that these trailers could, in certain circumstances, be towed by other vehicles, in

[16] For a temporary ban, see Joined Cases 60/84 and 61/84, *Cinéthèque*, ECLI:EU:C:1985:329 (prohibition of selling or hiring video cassettes of a movie within a certain time of its first showing in cinemas—Prete 2008, p. 145, correctly derives from that judgment that discrimination is not a necessary element of a breach of Article 34, but has only 'market access' to offer (at 151) as to what else is caught, while coming close to the position here advocated at 150; see on this in and by above n. 48); for registration requirements see e.g. Case C-150/00, *Commission v. Austria ('Vitamins')*, ECLI:EU:C:2004:237, paras 83–7 (registration requirement for consumables containing vitamins and minerals); Case C-55/94, *Gebhard*, ECLI:EU:C:1995:411 (establishment); Case C-58/98, *Corsten*, ECLI:EU:C:2000:527 (services); as an example of a requirement of type approval, see Joined Cases C-388/00 and C-429/00, *Radiosistemi Srl v. Prefetto di Genova*, ECLI:EU:C:2002:390, para 43 (granting of a national mark of conformity).

[17] Thus Barnard 2009, p. 289.

particular by automobiles, such use was 'inappropriate' and remained at least 'insignificant', if not 'hypothetical'. The Court pointed out that 'a prohibition on the use of a product in the territory of a Member State has a considerable influence on the behaviour of consumers, which, in its turn, affected the access of that product to the market of that Member State'. From this, the Court concluded that the prohibition prevented a demand from existing in the Italian market for trailers lawfully produced and marketed in other Member States. The Italian provisions therefore, in contravention of Article 34, hindered the importation of these trailers.[18]

This solution appears to be derived from an application of the third category of rules as described in the Court's 'preliminary observations': the prohibition applied to all trailers specifically designed to be towed by motorcycles, no matter where these trailers came from. Also, it did not make the marketing of trailers imported from other Member States any more difficult than the marketing of Italian-made trailers. Demand would evenly dry up for all trailers of that design. The ban, therefore, passed muster under the first two categories. Since, however, such trailers were legally made and used in other Member States, Italy had by that prohibition denied its market from being part of a market in such trailers common to all Member States which had no similar restrictions in force. This can be read to confirm that the third group comprises universal (indistinctly applicable) bans imposed by Member States, whether by means of restrictions of sale or of use of the products. Such bans go against the aim of Article 26 TFEU to create an internal market between all Member States.[19]

The judgment also gives clues as to when the Court thinks restrictions of use will amount to a bar to market access. This will be the case where the remaining uses of the products in issue are 'inappropriate'. For all we can tell, what is a product's 'proprium' is a question of its *qualities*: it depends on the 'specific technical characteristics' of the product. It is these that determine the product's 'normal intended use' (both expressions are from Bot AG's opinion), or its 'specific and inherent purposes' (thus the Court in *Mickelsson & Roos*, discussed below).

While the characteristics of the product will be reasonably clear and thus 'specific', its purposes may not so be: these are essentially left to the imagination of the user. They are not, in this sense, 'inherent' to the product. Quite often, the product's characteristics will allow several appropriate uses. The Court did not expand on this in any way. From the context of the judgment it would appear that a use is 'inappropriate' if the product as designed cannot, or at least not without danger to the user or others, be put to that use. The problem with this understanding is that 'dangerous' and 'safe' at least partly are normative concepts, that is, they take their meaning from legislation as much as from intuition. If, however, the law determines what is 'appropriate' and 'inappropriate', the Court would have to second-guess the legislature's risk assessment and declare remaining lawful uses 'inappropriate', only to find out whether the restriction of use falls under Article 34.

---

[18] Case C-110/05 (above n. 6), paras 49–58; the quotation is from para 56.

[19] This proposition is explained in more detail in Enchelmaier 2003, pp. 298–300.

The few innocent words in the Court's judgment, therefore, raise more questions than they answer. It remains to be seen, of course, whether they are meant to have any lasting significance, or whether they were tailored to the specific circumstances and can be ignored when they appear less suitable on another occasion.[20] Needless to say, the latter would be the opposite of the principled guidelines that national courts need, and are entitled to expect, under Article 267 TFEU. Neither would it make life easier for the Commission as the 'guardian of the Treaty' under Article 258 TFEU.

4.3 *Mickelsson & Roos*: Principles Written in Water

Mickelsson & Roos concerned Swedish rules prohibiting the use of, among others, 'jet-skis' on all public waters and waterways (other than general navigable waterways), except where such use was specifically allowed. Local authorities had to allow the use of these craft under certain conditions on waters to be designated. The conditions were, essentially, that the additional noise and disturbance as a consequence of the use of the craft did not significantly add to the burdens on the public and on the environment imposed by pre-existing human uses; or that the waters were of little value in the protection of the natural and cultural environment and other named public goods; or that there was no nuisance to the public nor a significant risk to fauna and flora. If these conditions were not fulfilled, local authorities were merely allowed (not compelled) to lift the prohibition of the use of jet-skis. Contraventions, such as those perpetrated by Messrs Mickelsson and Roos, were subject to a fine.[21] The two defendants before the referring Swedish court, and the Commission, argued that these restrictions (and hence any fine) were in breach of Article 34. The judgment in *Mickelsson & Roos* followed *Moped Trailers* within a few months. For the assessment under Article 34, the Court's Second Chamber took its cues from the Grand Chamber's judgment in *Moped Trailers*.

---

[20] Shortly after *Moped Trailers*, for instance, the Court reverted to a traditional discrimination analysis in Case C-531/07, *Fachverband der Buch- und Medienwirtschaft v. LIBRO Handelsgesellschaft*, ECLI:EU:C:2009:276, paras 18–22; see also Case C-100/08, *Commission v. Belgium ('Wild Birds')*, ECLI:EU:C:2009:537, paras 81, 82, where the Court first cites para 34 of *Moped Trailers*, then para 35 for the *Cassis* formula which decides the matter; the *Dassonville* formula without a trace of *Moped Trailers* was decisive in Case C-333/08, *Commission v. France ('Positive List')*, ECLI:EU:C:2010:44, para 74 ff; the same (Third) Chamber as in the last-mentioned judgment had already decided on the same basis a case on restrictions of use, namely Case C-265/06, *Commission v. Portugal ('Tinted Film')*, ECLI:EU:C:2008:210, para 31 ff, even after Kokott AG's opinion in *Mickelsson* had led to the reopening of the proceedings in *Moped Trailers*. All these may be taken as reasons for not getting too excited prematurely about the Court's new approach and its longevity.

[21] The exact wording of the Swedish provisions is reproduced in para 12 of the Court's judgment, the Court's own summary is at para 22.

The Court's starting point was again the *Cassis* formula, as before modified in its wording with snippets from *Groenveld* and *Keck*: '[M]easures taken by a Member State, the aim or effect of which is to treat goods coming from other Member States less favourably and, in the absence of harmonisation of national legislation, obstacles to the free movement of goods which are the consequence of applying, to goods coming from other Member States where they are lawfully manufactured and marketed, rules that lay down requirements to be met by such goods, even if those rules apply to all products alike, must be regarded as "measures having equivalent effect to quantitative restrictions on imports" for the purposes of Article [34 TFEU].'[22] The Court cited *Cassis*,[23] *Familiapress*[24] and *DocMorris*[25] as sources of this formula, but not *Keck*. It then added that 'any other measure which hinders access of products originating in other Member States to the market of a Member State is also covered by [the] concept [of a measure having equivalent effect to a quantitative restriction]'.[26]

At the material time, no waterways had been designated for use by jet-skis in accordance with the rules set out earlier. Given the heavy commercial traffic on the general navigable waterways (which anyway made up only a minor portion of all navigable waters in Sweden), using jet-skis there was dangerous. The Court therefore found that the 'actual possibilities' for the use of personal watercraft in Sweden were 'merely marginal'.[27] As in *Moped Trailers*, the Court pointed out that depending on their scope, restrictions of use had a considerable influence on the behaviour of consumers. Consequently, this might affect access of the product to the market in that Member State. This was because consumers, knowing that the use permitted was 'very limited', had only a limited interest in buying that product.[28]

From all this, the Court concluded that where the national regulations for the designation of navigable waters and waterways had the effect of *preventing* users of personal watercraft from using them for the 'specific and inherent purposes for which they were intended', such regulations had the effect of hindering the access to the domestic market in question for those goods. This was also the case where the regulations 'greatly restricted' these uses. In view, however, of the division of functions, under the preliminary reference procedure pursuant to Article 267, between the Court and the national courts, it was for the national court to ascertain

[22] Case C-142/05 (above n. 6), para 24.

[23] Above n. 2.

[24] Case C-368/95, *Vereinigte Familiapress Zeitungsverlags- und -vertriebsGmbH v. Heinrich Bauer Verlag*, ECLI:EU:C:1997:325.

[25] Case C-322/01, *Deutscher Apothekerverband v. 0800 DocMorris and Waterval*, ECLI:EU:C:2003:664.

[26] Case C-142/05, para 24, referring to *Moped Trailers* (both above n. 6), para 37.

[27] Case C-142/05 (above n. 6), para 25.

[28] Case C-142/05 (above n. 6), paras 26–7.

this. If that court found the said effect, the regulation constituted a measure having equivalent effect to a quantitative restriction prohibited by Article 34.[29]

As in *Moped Trailers*, the assessment here plays out under the category of 'other measures'. The Court does not mention the fact that there were no Swedish-made jet-skis. Presumably, therefore, it did not consider it the 'aim' of the prohibition specifically to put imports at a disadvantage: there was no domestic production to protect. The question of the 'effects' of a rule (such as the one in issue) that 'applies to all products alike' is not pursued, either. This may be because the Court in its variation on *Cassis* refers to 'requirements to be met by such goods'. Possibly this is meant to capture (only?) the burdens occasioned by any necessary adaptation of the product itself to the regulations in the importing Member State, as discussed in *Cassis*. Prohibitions of use, by definition, do not require, nor could they here be overcome by, any adaptations of the jet-skis. All this, however, is ultimately left open, and passed on to the national court to contemplate.[30]

In this way, the Court avoids any comparisons: between the rules in different Member States; between the impact of the rules on jet-skis to be imported and on those already in the country;[31] between the effects on jet-skis and on other types of craft etc. In other words, the Court does not inquire whether any discrimination might have occurred. The express invocation of *Cassis*, then, if it makes any sense at all, might be meant to signify that this is indeed a test that is meant to be relevant beyond the present case. Nonetheless, of the whole formula the Court uses only the 'access' limb. The wording of the latter—'any other measure'—would lead one to expect that it is of residual application, only to be drawn on when no unequal treatment (and, for want of a justification: discrimination) has come to light under the first two limbs.

These could of course be two different tests: discrimination on the one hand, and market access on the other.[32] Alternatively, the long first sentence ('aim or effect' etc.) could be mere verbiage. Both hypotheses are unconvincing. If the tests were independent of each other, it would be misleading (to say the least) to mention them in the same breath, and expressly to refer and to subordinate one to the other ('any *other* measure'). As to the second hypothesis, there was no reason to jettison *Cassis*, certainly not by first citing and then ignoring it. If anything can be concluded from this passage, it is that the Court is either not sure about, or oblivious to, a systematic exposition of how to assess cases under Article 34. Despite the lengthy discussion in

[29] Ibid., para 28.

[30] See the opening words in Case C-142/05 (above n. 6), para 26: 'Even if the national regulations at issue do not have the aim or effect of treating goods coming from other Member States less favourably, which is for the national court to ascertain, …'.

[31] The Court uses this comparison under Article 110 in the absence of domestic competition for the imported product allegedly discriminated against (*in casu*, cars): Case C-383/01, *Den Danske Bilimportører*, ECLI:EU:C:2003:352, para 35; see also the summaries on this point in Case C-387/01, *Weigel*, ECLI:EU:C:2004:256, paras 67–75 and in Case C-101/00, *Tulliasiamies*, ECLI: EU:C:2002:505, paras 50–8, 74–9, 85–8.

[32] As suggested by Barnard and Deakin 2002, p. 284 n. 185.

two Advocates General's opinions, 'restrictions of use' do not appear as any kind of special category, nor is their relationship with 'selling arrangements' in any way expounded, or *Keck* even mentioned after the initial reference. One can only wonder why it should have taken the Court four years to come up with so little.[33]

The judgment raises yet more questions. For a start, the 'other measures' are merely defined by their 'hindering access of products originating in other Member States to the market of a Member State'. This aspect, however, appears already covered by the 'obstacles to the free movement of goods' in the preceding quotation from *Cassis:* it is hard to see what 'obstacles' and 'hindrances' are if not synonymous. Maybe 'obstacles' are relevant, under *Cassis*, only in so far as they are 'the consequence of applying to goods from other Member States … rules that lay down requirements to be met by such goods'. If they result from, say, shop opening hours, minimum profit margins or restrictions of use, they might come under the category of 'any other measures'.

The Court does not spell out any of this. Even if it did, the next question would be whether or to what extent these differences should be mirrored in different tests. If the test is meant to identify 'measures of equivalent *effect*', and if untrammelled 'market access' is the concern that underlies the prohibition of such measures, then it cannot matter how exactly the obstacle or hindrance came about, what the precise causation was that lead to the obstacle.[34]

As far as the category of 'other measures' is concerned, this means that it can (and need) only catch national measures that remain permissible under the traditional *Cassis* test, i.e. those that 'apply to all products alike' and do not have as their 'consequence' obstacles specifically for goods from other Member States. For reasons explained above, this leaves only universal bans. If this context is lost, the 'other measures' lose their definition. In this way, we end up with the formula from the *Sunday Trading* cases, according to which a reduction of the volume of trade equals a restriction in the sense of Article 34.

---

[33] Oliver 2010, para 6.88, speaks of a 'disappointment'.

[34] See on this emphatically Gormley 2009, p. 191: 'It has been clear from the very beginning of the attempts to define the notion of measures having equivalent effect that it should be viewed as an effects doctrine rather than dependent upon the nature or contents—or even purpose—of the measure'. *Contra* Fenger, Chap. 5, Sect. 5.5, who argues that, 'no individual assessment under the market access criterion needs to be made in relation to those categories of national measures for which the Court has already made that assessment. Indeed, if a market access test were to be carried out in all cases concerning selling arrangements in the same manner as in other cases concerning Article 34, what would then be the substance of the distinction between selling arrangements and other measures' (paragraph following footnote 50). This adheres to the traditional if little reflected reading of 'selling arrangements' as part of the test in paras 15 and 16 of *Keck.* The relevant questions (the test) are contained in the two phrases beginning with 'so long as'. It is the same (Cassis) test as for 'product requirements' (para 15), only that retail at a loss *did* have the same factual repercussions for all coffees, whereas the minimum alcohol content *did not* for all fruit liqueurs, the rules in both cases being indistinctly applicable. 'Selling arrangements' is, therefore, not part of the test but a laxly worded summary of the outcome before the test is articulated. In this context, the significance of 'certain' was never properly explained by the Court or in the literature—see, e.g., Fenger, Chap. 5, Sect. 5.4.3.

This is, arguably, what happened in *Mickelsson & Roos*. The Court breaks down the 'hindrance' brought about by the 'other measures' into either 'preventing users of personal watercraft from using them … or … greatly restricting their use', so as to leave 'merely marginal' possibilities of actual use for their specific and inherent purposes.[35] This adopts, in essence, the last part of Kokott AG's proposal, but without getting drawn into the discussion about the transferability of the concept of 'selling arrangements'. As the Advocate General had proposed, the Court here uses an absolute measure: establishing that a piece of national legislation is caught by Article 34 does not depend on any comparison. The threshold beyond which it is so caught, however, is indeterminate. One answer is as good as another when it comes to the question whether the remaining possibilities of use are 'significant' or 'merely marginal', or whether the uses are 'greatly' restricted or only slightly.[36]

To reiterate: Member States should have to justify themselves before the Court, and thus ultimately to the other Member States and all economic operators established there, only if they treat imports differently in law or in fact, or ban products altogether that are lawful elsewhere or were lawfully imported in the past. If short of this a Member State merely depresses economic activity on its home market across the board, it can be left to national law and the national electorate to judge those responsible for the legislation.[37] The four freedoms have no position on such autonomous choices of economic policy by each Member State in accordance with local preferences. Seen in this light, the legislation in issue in *Moped trailers* and *Mickelsson and Roos*, respectively, did not fall under the prohibition in Article 34.

4.4 Parallel Developments in the Case Law on the Freedom to Provide Services

4.4.1 The Beginnings: **Alpine Investments** *and Other Cases*

In *Alpine Investments*,[38] the Court discussed the issue of the transferability of the *Keck* criteria expressly. The Dutch and British governments had argued that a prohibition in the Netherlands of financial firms' contacting, unannounced, potential

[35] Case C-142/05 (above n. 6), para 28 read jointly with para 25, last sentence.

[36] Fenger (n. 8), Chap. 5, Sect. 5.6 suggests that 'national measures which merely limit to some extent the general usefulness of a product, and thereby have some potential effect on imports, should not be caught by Article 34. Rather, the threshold should be placed fairly high: Article 34 should apply only where all, or nearly all, normal uses of the good in question are excluded, and imports are therefore likely to be quite severely affected'. The weakness of this test is that with 'fairly', 'some', 'nearly', and 'quite', it hinges on non-justiciable and ultimately arbitrary criteria.

[37] Similarly Fenger (n. 8), Chap. 5, Sect. 5.2, argues that 'when the principle of equality of chances is respected, the Member States should be allowed to freely regulate their respective territories, even when that indirectly affects the total volume of sales of a given product'.

[38] Case C-384/93, *Alpine Investments BV v. Minister van Financiën*, ECLI:EU:C:1995:126.

customers (so-called 'cold calling') for commodities futures contracts, was tantamount to a rule governing selling arrangements. The prohibition therefore, according to the governments, escaped Article 56 altogether (para 33).

For an understanding of the Court's response it is important to underline that the case concerned advertising *for* a service, not advertising *as* a service. A ban on 'cold calling' was at issue, not on the conclusion or execution of commodities futures contracts as such. Alpine Investments' telephone calls to potential clients, made by the firm itself, were not services in the sense of the first subparagraph of Article 57, as they were not provided against remuneration.[39] Their only purpose was to lead to transactions—namely, commodities futures contracts—which would, in their turn, have involved services in the sense of the Treaty.[40] The ban required, in effect, a switch by Alpine Investments to advertising in print or broadcast media, with the attendant expenditure and inconvenience.

The ban thus prohibited the technique that Alpine Investments had traditionally used in order to gain access to clients in other Member States (para 28). It made the provision of a lawful service across the borders—from the Netherlands into Belgium—more difficult than it would have been within Belgium alone, where cold calling remained lawful. Comparison with Dutch providers operating in the Netherlands does not yield this result.

In the perspective of a common market, however, the comparison must comprise the situation in *any* Member State where Alpine Investments' services were provided. Under Article 56, the provider may move from one Member State to another, where the recipient is established, or *vice versa*, or the service may move between them. Either Member State must, therefore, justify its legislation if it makes more difficult the meeting of provider and recipient, no matter where it takes place, or the passing of the service between them. The Court takes this perspective in paras 29 and 30 of the judgment. There, it held that the application of Article 56 was not excluded by the fact that the Member State of establishment regulated services provided in another Member State.

The Court cited para 16 of *Keck*, and continued that the ban 'directly affects access to the market in services in the other Member States' (para 38). This wording is somewhat unfortunate. The reason why *Keck* did not apply was that the Dutch rule imposed an additional burden on those, such as Alpine Investments, who wanted to provide services across the border into another Member State[41]: it denied Dutch firms an easy if dubious means of approaching clients which their Belgian competitors were still allowed to use. That is, the condition in para 16 of *Keck* was

[39] This is overlooked by Torgersen, [1999] 10 EBLR 371, at p. 383, left col., who therefore sees a parallel with Cases C-76/90, *Säger v. Dennemeyer*, ECLI:EU:C:1991:331, and Case C-275/92, *Schindler*, ECLI:EU:C:1994:119, both involving bans, and by Nic Shuibhne 2013, pp. 239, 240, 245, 248.

[40] *Alpine Investments* managed portfolios for its clients, gave them investment advice, and transmitted their orders to brokers operating on commodities futures markets, para 4 of the judgment.

[41] Same result in Davies 2003, pp. 82–83.

not fulfilled. Market access as such was, and remained, possible for Alpine Investments, but, as a consequence of the Dutch rule, not on equal terms with its Belgian competitors. Instead, the company had to overcome an obstacle its competitors were spared, namely the prohibition on using its habitual and convenient method of marketing over the telephone.

Because 'cold calling' was the very means by which Alpine Investments had hitherto acquired customers in other Member States, the prohibition 'directly' affected its market access. Paragraph 54 of the judgment in *Alpine Investments* makes it plain that the Court distinguishes between the issues of market access, and of additional burdens. In this paragraph, the Court emphasised that other techniques for making contact are still available, and that existing clients can always give written consent to further calls. Thus, Alpine Investments was not excluded from the Belgian market altogether.

Clarification on this point comes from a later judgment, *TK-Heimdienst Sass*,[42] where the Court quoted *Alpine Investments.* An Austrian provision required that all bakers and butchers selling their wares on rounds have a fixed establishment in an Austrian administrative district adjacent to the area of the rounds. This requirement was indistinctly applicable, but indirectly discriminatory as it put operators from other Member States at a disadvantage without objective justification. The Court held that the provision 'in fact *impedes access* to the market of the Member State of importation for products from other Member States *more than* it impedes access for domestic products' (para 29 with reference to *Alpine Investments*, emphasis added). The same situation prevailed in *Alpine Investments* which, hence, also hinges on the notion of discrimination (paras 15, 16 of *Keck*), not market access in the sense of a universal ban (para 17 of *Keck*). The Court's recently increased invocation of the market access criterion does not, therefore, mean that the traditional discrimination assessment has been superseded.

4.4.2 More Recent Judgments: 'Restriction of Market Access/of the Opportunity to Compete More Effectively'

In some recent judgments on Article 56 TFEU (ex-Article 49 EC), we find an approach to what amounts to a restriction on the freedom to provide services that is similar to the approach the Court adopted in *Moped Trailers* and *Mickelsson & Roos*. The Court here takes the perspective of the market and of the competition that takes place between service providers on that market. It will be remembered that the creation of the Internal Market is meant to throw the hitherto isolated national

[42] Case C-254/98, *Schutzverband gegen unlauteren Wettbewerb v. TK Heimdienst Sass*, ECLI:EU: C:2000:12.

markets open to competition, that is, to the activities of competitors, from other Member States.

We thus read in the Court's judgment in an action brought by the Commission against Luxembourg that the obligation that providers of building services from other Member States designate an *ad hoc* agent residing in Luxembourg to retain the documents necessary for monitoring by the competent national authorities 'involves an *additional administrative and financial burden* for undertakings established in another Member State, so that the latter are *not on an equal footing, from the point of view of competition*, with employers established in the host Member State, and they may be dissuaded from providing services in the latter Member State.'[43] Similarly, the Court found that compulsory minimum rates in Italy deprived economic operators established in other Member States of the 'opportunity to compete more effectively', by offering charges lower than those in the scale of charges imposed, with the economic operators traditionally established in Italy.[44]

There can be no doubt that every additional burden imposed on would-be providers from other Member State puts them at a disadvantage vis-à-vis their domestic competitors; for some, this might tip the scales against expanding their activities into the other Member State at all. It must be said, however, that this test —if it is one—would add unnecessary complexity to the assessment. Under the previous formulae, it was enough to find that national regulations imposed adaptation costs on providers from other Member States. Now, it seems, we have to take a wider perspective, and consider the competitive position of domestic providers also. The judgment could be read to mean that there will be a restriction only if on balance (as the net result, so to say), providers from other Member States are at a competitive disadvantage. We are not told which factors ought to go into the equation. Nevertheless, it would seem that all other regulatory burdens that domestic providers are subject to would also have to be taken into consideration.

An alternative and more plausible interpretation of this passage, however, is that the Court here does no more than openly articulate the *reason why* no additional burdens should be heaped on providers from other Member States, and tells us the expected outcome ('so that …'). Foreign providers normally have complied with one set of regulations already, namely that of their home Member State. To comply

[43] Case C-319/06, *Commission v. Luxembourg ('Posted workers')*, ECLI:EU:C:2008:350, para 85, emphasis added; similarly, the Court found in Case C-565/08, *Commission v. Italy ('Lawyers' fees')*, ECLI:EU:C:2011:188, para 51 that a restriction would exist if lawyers were 'deprived of the opportunity of gaining access to the market of the host Member State under conditions of normal and effective competition'.

[44] Case C-134/05, *Commission v Italy ('Extrajudicial debt recovery')*, ECLI:EU:C:2007:435, paras 71–2; Joined Cases C-94/04 and C-202/04, *Cipolla*, ECLI:EU:C:2006:758, para 70; the Court said the same in Joined Cases C-147/06 and C-148/06, *SECAP and Santorso v. Comune di Torino*, ECLI:EU:C:2008:277, para 28, about a rule requiring the automatic exclusion of abnormally low tenders to contracts of certain cross-border interest. This argument about the restrictive effects of minimum price-legislation has a long tradition in the case law on goods, see Oliver 2010, paras 7.87–104.

with the host Member State's set on top of that can be costly, and these costs must be recouped. Domestic competitors have already paid this entry price, as it were, to the market of that state, their home Member State. They can, therefore, offer their services more cheaply.

For this reason, it is enough to consider the position of providers from other Member States alone. Any wider perspective would be boundless: beyond the regulation immediately in issue, shall we (and how?) also quantify the impact the host Member State's tax, environmental, planning, transport, and employment legislation, to name but a few? It is impossible to reach any justiciable conclusions in this respect. For this reason, the Court rightly turned its face against such balancing exercises in the field of taxes and charges having equivalent effect to customs duties.[45]

It is a truism to say that competition takes place on markets. Hence, the provision of services in one Member State by a provider established in another means the extension of that provider's activity into a new market (at least in the typical paradigm of a provider who is active on his home market as well). To put it differently, in this situation the provider seeks access to the market in the other Member State. From the finding of competitive disadvantages imposed on foreign providers of services it is, therefore, only a small step to say that their market access is negatively affected, that is, restricted. Again, this is no surprise: the entire project of creating the Internal Market is about guaranteeing economic operators established in *any* Member State the legal possibility of access to the markets *everywhere* in the Union; it is then for other policies to make actual entry into foreign markets a commercially attractive proposition.

Notice, however, that we are again speaking of motivations. The aim of creating, as between Member States, conditions that come close to a single market on a continental scale is in the Treaty translated into specific provisions, among them Article 56. This and the other freedoms are all about market access: the 'restrictions' they seek to remove are restrictions to market access.[46] Market access is nothing but free movement *between* Member States. It adds nothing to our understanding, therefore, to say that we are in the presence of a restriction when market acccss is made more difficult—we already knew that. Market access is, so to say, about the 'why', not the 'how' of creating the Internal Market through addressing prohibitions at Member States. Market access is not a test but an objective. The crucial question is, what specifically must Member States not do that restricts market access?

The Court, therefore, turns in circles when it says that 'the concept of restriction covers measures taken by a Member State which, although applicable without distinction, affect access to the market for undertakings from other Member States

[45] Case 132/78, *Denkavit Loire*, ECLI:EU:C:1979:139, para 8: taxes on imported lard that were meant to offset the slaughter fees borne by domestic pork producers.

[46] Concurring, Fenger (n. 8), Chap. 5, Sect. 5.5, argues that '[o]n closer reflection, the market access test, however, may be rather less novel and practically significant. Ensuring market access for foreign products was always a major preoccupation of the Court even though it has used different terms to express that concern'.

and thereby hinder intra-Community trade.'[47] The Court does not, however, allow itself to be distracted by this. In the same judgment, it goes on to say that the obligation imposed by Italian law on insurers to accept anyone as a customer for certain types of insurance is likely to lead, in terms of organisation and investment, to significant additional costs for providers from other Member States. These might be required to re-think their business policy and strategy by, inter alia, considerably expanding the range of insurance services offered. 'Inasmuch as it involves changes and costs on such a scale for those undertakings,' the Court continues, 'the obligation to contract renders access to the Italian market less attractive and, if they obtain access to that market, reduces the ability of the undertakings concerned to compete effectively, from the outset, against undertakings traditionally established in Italy.'[48] This brings together a number of the elements already discussed above. The result is certainly correct, but the way the Court gets there is not exactly straightforward.

The whole array of more or less helpful descriptions or illustrations of what are 'restrictions' in the sense of Article 56[49] accompany, as a kind of mood music, what really matters, namely the examination of the burdens imposed on domestic providers and those from other Member States, respectively. So much verbiage is apt to confuse the national courts and others called upon to interpret and apply Union law. It can also obfuscate the Court's reasoning or, more worryingly, tempt it to substitute intuition for reasoning.

---

47 Case C-518/06, *Commission v. Italy ('Third party liability motor insurance')*, ECLI:EU:C:2009:270, para 64; also in Case C-565/08, *Commission v. Italy ('Lawyers' fees')*, ECLI:EU:C:2011:188, para 46. Equally critical of the Court's case law on this point is Snell 2010, pp. 468 et seq.: 'Ultimately, the notion of market conceals rather than clarifies. The very ambiguity of the term may explain its use by and usefulness for the Court. … Market access may simply provide a sophisticated-sounding garb that conceals decisions based on intuition.' See also Davies 2010, *passim.*

48 Case C-518/06 (n. 47), paras 66–70. The Court reasoned in a similar manner in Case C-465/05, *Commission v. Italy ('Private security services')*, ECLI:EU:C:2007:781, para 125, with regard to administrative control of the fees providers were allowed to charge, and in Joined Cases C-147/06 and C-148/06 (n. 44), para 28, concerning a rule requiring the automatic exclusion of abnormally low tenders which 'could *deprive* economic operators from other Member States *of the opportunity of competing more effectively* with operators located in the Member State in question *and thereby affect their access to the market in that State*, thus impeding the exercise of freedom of establishment and freedom to provide services' (emphasis added).

49 See also the doubts entertained by Edward and Nic Shuibhne 2009, p. 256: 'If market access is ultimately the best criterion, applicable across the range of internal market law, there must nevertheless be some way of delimiting the scope of the freedom in relation to non-discriminatory obstacles. Otherwise, there is a danger of setting off again down the *fausse piste* that ended with *Keck*'—too right, but in what sense, then, is market access 'the best criterion'?

4.4.3 *Discrimination* Versus *Market Access?*

To make sense of the Court's jurisprudence, the distinction has been suggested between a (mere) 'discrimination test', applicable to 'rules relating to selling arrangements', and a (more stringent) 'market access test' for 'product requirements'.[50] There are hints to that effect in the wording of some of the Court's judgments but overall, the Court's jurisprudence hardly tallies with it. In *Morellato*, for example, both terms appear side by side. On the one hand, the Court held that the wrapping requirement was 'in principle such as to fall outside the scope of Article [34 TFEU], provided that it does not in reality constitute discrimination against imported products.'[51] 'Rules relating to selling arrangements' hence seem to be subject to a discrimination test.

On the other hand, the Court goes on to say that in the absence of domestic competition, the wrapping requirement 'discourages [imports] or makes them less attractive to the final consumer.'[52] This could be read as a 'market access' test. The quoted passage is preceded, however, by the words, 'such a requirement, although it applies without distinction, disadvantages imported products only'—the traditional test for indirect discrimination known since *Cassis de Dijon*. The language of 'market access' is also used in the advertising and distribution cases discussed above, but it always appears in the context of a comparison between domestic and imported products.

This points to the fundamental problem with the suggested scheme: discrimination hampers market access; conversely, when market access is hindered one can (often) describe the obstacle in terms of discrimination. Article 34 certainly prohibits hindrances to market access—this is but a negative way of saying that the provision aims at promoting the creation of the internal market.[53] At the same time, discrimination is no doubt one way of frustrating the aims of Article 34. Market access, however, is an aim and as such uncontroversial; to prohibit discrimination is a means to that end, if perhaps not the only one. To declare each of them a 'test' and to contrast them with one another yields no clear-cut results: they are not opposed to each other but correlated. 'Discrimination' and 'hindrances to market access' are not separate species of the same overarching *genus* of 'hindrances to market access'. Instead, we have to look for subdivisions within the means of achieving market access. The search is really for a means to guarantee market access for imports that consists in prohibiting something other than discrimination.

If one were to extract some general statement from the Court's case law on discrimination, one could safely say that the concept is a wide one. It encompasses both *direct* discrimination as a consequence of *distinctly* applicable national measures without a justification, and *indirect* discrimination ensuing from unjustified

---

[50] See Oliver and Roth 2004, pp. 412, 413.

[51] Case C-416/00, *Morellato v. Commune di Padova*, ECLI:EU:C:2003:475, para 36.

[52] *Morellato* (above n. 51), para 37.

[53] Case C-65/05, *Commission v. Greece ('Electronic games')*, ECLI:EU:C:2006:673, para 25.

indistinctly applicable provisions in Member States.[54] The missing subdivision of 'hindrances to market access' would, hence, have to be a non-discriminatory measure, that is, one with the same repercussions in law and in fact on imports and on domestic products. It must, furthermore, not merely depress the overall level of an otherwise continuing trade between Member States.[55] This has been the fallacy underlying the "Sunday trading" cases. The only remaining hindrance to market access to answer this description is a universal (indistinctly applicable) ban.[56] Once the unnecessary confusion surrounding (rules relating to) 'selling arrangements' is overcome, a unified approach to the free movement of goods and the freedom to provide services becomes possible.

4.5 Restrictions on the Use of Services

Restrictions on the use of services have not yet, as far as one can see, been the subject of any judgment by the Court. Nevertheless, it is not difficult to imagine a situation in which the question would become relevant, modelled on the facts of *Mickelsson & Roos*. As an example, we can take the prohibition in Member State A of using mobile phones while driving a vehicle on public roads. To make this into a problem for European law, let us presume that the police in one Member State have fined a driver whose provider of mobile telephony services is established in another Member State. For simplicity's sake, let us further presume that this driver is a national of the first Member State who has never lived or worked in another Member State and has no intentions of doing so. That driver will raise the usual 'Euro defence' against the fine, namely that the prohibition cannot be enforced against him or her because it puts an unjustified obstacle in the way of the freedom to provide services (or here rather, to receive services). For a solution to this, we must return to the two judgments on the free movement of goods. The Court's solution has been criticised above. Here is an alternative suggestion for a test that can also be applied to restrictions on the use of services.

When restrictions of use of goods are under scrutiny, we can compare outright the legal regimes that govern the use of a given product in various Member States. It is true that one Member State's rules do not apply in another, as much as one and the same tangible object cannot normally be used in two different Member States at the same time. Nevertheless, this was no obstacle in the paradigm case, *Cassis*, either. The French rules in accordance with which the blackcurrant liqueur was made were relevant in that case not because they *applied* in Germany. Instead, they remained the point of reference for the finding that the German authorities'

---

[54] For a detailed discussion of the concept of discrimination in the context of the free movement of goods and of the other freedoms, see Enchelmaier 2003, pp. 252–272, with references to various alternative proposals.

[55] See in and by n. 14.

[56] Concurring, Oliver and Roth 2004, pp. 414, 415; see already above in and by n. 16.

insistence on compliance with the German rules would have imposed *additional* costs on importers and others marketing the French product in Germany.

In the end, the importers etc. did not have to bear the additional costs of a separate production run for the German market since the German rules could not be enforced against Cassis: a declaration of the alcohol content on the label of the bottle afforded German consumers adequate safeguards. This declaration, in turn, made the French rules on alcohol content visible to the German consumer. The liqueur, or more precisely, the French rules in accordance with which it was made, thus benefitted from 'mutual recognition'.[57] Seen in this light, the comparison is ultimately of the rules in force in the different Member States.

Moreover, the additional costs (had they arisen) of reformulating the liqueur so as to contain more alcohol would have reduced the benefit that consumers hoped to derive from obtaining the product as it was. It is this benefit from products coming from other Member States, be it an economic or any other benefit, that the creation of the internal market is meant to afford anyone anywhere in the Community. The reduction of this benefit, therefore, calls for a justification. In this respect, it does not matter whether the loss results from additional costs or missed opportunities of use: in both cases, what is legal *anywhere* in the Community must in principle be legal *everywhere*, except where concerns of public policy, as found in Article 36 and beyond mandatory requirements,[58] allow the importing Member State to deny 'mutual recognition'.

Because the whole of the internal market is the perspective of Articles 18, 26, and 34 TFEU, the reference uses are not only those legal in the Member State of *exportation*. In principle, i.e. justified denials notwithstanding, a product that can lawfully be marketed and used in any one Member State must be so marketable and usable in every other. This is again the principle of mutual recognition that the Court invoked in its 'preliminary observations' in *Moped trailers*. It follows from these same observations that the principle is applicable not only to national rules affecting the composition, presentation or marketing of a product, but also its uses. In other words, even though a particular use may be illegal in both the Member State of manufacture or export, and in the Member State of import, Article 34 will still apply if the use is legal in a third Member State.[59]

The application of this standard is straightforward if a given product has only one 'appropriate' use, such as motorcycle trailers. As these can lawfully be used on (most) public roads in other Member States, the Italian prohibition required a justification. For this, it would be irrelevant whether, say, a French-made trailer may in France be used on all or any roads, as long as such use is legal in, for instance, Denmark: if anyone may use the trailer in this way, a justification is required why people in Italy should be denied this use, and vice versa. This is because no one would foreseeably buy such a 'use-less' product. Likewise, no one would draw on

[57] See Armstrong 2002 and Wilsher 2008.

[58] On the Court's methodology in this respect, see Enchelmaier 2003, pp. 276–8.

[59] For a detailed discussion of this, see Enchelmaier 2003, pp. 300–6.

services whose result (such as a telephonic connection or internet access) has no lawful use.

Matters are more complicated where a product has several uses, such as chemical compounds used as raw materials or in another capacity in a number of different production methods for a whole host of intermediate or end products.[60] As far as mobile telephones are concerned, we could think of their use as traditional telephones on the one hand, and as satellite navigation terminals on the other. One could either require a justification whenever a Member State bans or restricts a (single) use that is more lightly regulated in another Member State. Such a restriction of individual uses will reduce demand from those consumers who sought that specific use, but not from others. Total demand will, therefore, be abated. Mere reductions in the volume of trade do not, however, qualify as restrictions of either the free movement of goods, or of the freedom to provide services.

The restriction of a single use would, in other words, reduce overall turnover. Nevertheless, the market would remain open as consumers with different needs would still demand the product and could lawfully use it. It is irrelevant whether it would be an attractive proposition for importers to continue to meet the (reduced) demand. Article 34, as much as Article 56, seeks to keep markets open, not to guarantee the precise balance of supply and demand found on the market at any one time. These articles are meant to ensure the *legal possibility*, not the *economic viability*, of economic exchanges between Member States. In the same vein, 'the market' is the place (a real or virtual location) where supply and demand can meet. The market as a legal concept (as envisaged in Article 26 and the four freedoms) is not equivalent to the present, real suppliers and consumers. For this reason, it is not open to an individual who is only interested in one, now illegal, use to argue that 'their' market is closed as a consequence of the restriction. As the product or service has, *ex hypothesi*, several appropriate uses, the market continues to exist, if on a smaller scale.

Following the restriction, however, there may be no use permissible anymore in the importing Member State (the Member State of the recipient of the service). That Member State, moreover, may be the only (or last) to permit any use of the product. By prohibiting that remaining use the importing Member State would close down the market for any existing foreign suppliers of goods or services. These would until then have enjoyed market access protected by Articles 34 and 56 because legal use of the product in the suppliers' home Member State is not a precondition for their right to market the product in the Member State that now proposes to ban the product's use. The restriction would, therefore, be tantamount to a universal ban on the marketing of the product or service. Metaphorically speaking, with respect to the particular product the Member State has, as a consequence of the ban, ceased to be part of an 'internal' market, that is, one that is common to all the Member States.

---

[60] For an example, see Case C-473/98, *Kemikalieinspektionen v. Toolex Alpha*, ECLI:EU: C:2000:379.

This is contrary to Article 26 TFEU. The restriction would hence require a justification.

This requirement would, however, only apply to the last restriction that the Member State imposed. The ones that went before were outside the scope of Articles 34 and 56, even though they may individually have shrunk the market more than the last. This may at first sight appear arbitrary. It is unavoidable, however, if one accepts the Court's starting point in *Keck* that not every limitation of traders' commercial freedom (and *pace Moped Trailers*, likewise not every conceivable restriction of consumers' use of a product) can lay national regulations open to scrutiny under Article 34. For such scrutiny to take place, imports must be subject to further-reaching restrictions in law or in fact, or the restriction must amount to a ban on the marketing of domestic and imported products alike.
To sum up, the test would be as follows:

(1) Does the restriction of use apply in law equally to domestic producers and providers as to those from other Member States (i.e. is it 'indistinctly applicable')? If yes,
(2) Does the restriction have the same factual repercussions on imports and domestic products (if there are any)? If yes,
(3) Does the restriction prohibit the last remaining use in the Member State in question in a situation where either such use remains legal in at least one other Member State, or the importing Member State is the last to allow this use?

If the answer to (1) or (2) is 'no', or if it is 'yes' to (3), the measure restricts the free movement of goods or the freedom to provide services, and therefore requires a justification. Otherwise, it does not because it leads to a mere reduction in the volume of trade. Because the use in Sweden of jet-skis remained permissible at least on private waters and on general navigable waterways (however unattractive, unless 'inappropriate'), the restrictions were not in breach of Article 34.

To return to the example of the prohibition of using mobile telephones while driving a vehicle on public roads:

- Firstly, the rule applies regardless of where the provider is established, in the Member State prohibiting this use, or in another Member State.
- Secondly, there is no indication that the prohibition would affect providers from other Member States more gravely than those established in the prohibiting Member State. The choice made by residents of that Member State of a domestic or a foreign provider will not be affected by the prohibition: they would not be allowed to draw on the telephony services offered by either. (For the same reason, existing customers in other Member States will not abandon their home-state providers if they go on holiday in the prohibiting Member State, and switch to providers established there.)
- Thirdly, the prohibition in issue does not prohibit the last remaining use. Away from the vehicle, or even inside it while not participating in traffic on public roads, customers remain as free as ever to receive telephony services from other

Member States. They can also continue to use any available satellite navigation services. In all, therefore, the prohibition does not require a justification.

The Court, finally, would probably reach the same conclusion, as the remaining uses for mobile telephones using the services of providers established in other Member States could with some conviction be described as both 'appropriate' and 'significant'. Trouble is, the Court might as well decide otherwise: these criteria are incapable of even a roughly foreseeable quantification.

4.6 Conclusion

The Court's jurisprudence on the reach of the free movement of goods and of the freedom to provide services is again in flux, and following *Moped trailers* and *Mickelsson & Roos*, its direction is not entirely clear, nor are the results entirely satisfactory. 'Market access' is no panacea for defining which measures amount to restrictions of the respective freedom, nor has the Court developed a convincing methodology for dealing with restrictions of use. These problems can, however, be solved with some traditional tools that the Court has developed earlier, before it got into experimenting with ill-defined concepts over ones that were reasonably established and predictable in their application. Satisfactory results are perfectly possible, under both the provisions on the free movement of goods and on the freedom to provide services, through a properly understood discrimination test (shorn of the confusion surrounding 'selling arrangements'), complemented by a prohibition of universal bans.

References

Armstrong K (2002) Mutual Recognition. In: Barnard C, Scott J (eds) The Law of the Single European Market. Unpacking the Premises. Hart, Oxford/Portland, Oregon, pp 225–267

Barnard C (2009) Case Comment: Trailing a new approach to free movement of goods. CLJ 68:288–295

Barnard C, Deakin S (2002) Market Access and Regulatory competition. In: Barnard C, Scott J (eds) The Law of the Single European Market. Unpacking the Premises. Hart, Oxford/Portland, Oregon, pp 197–224

Davies G (2003) Nationality Discrimination in the European Internal Market. Kluwer Academic Publishers, The Hague/ London/New York

Davies G (2010) Understanding market access: exploring the economic rationality of different conceptions of free movement law. German Law Journal 11:469–501

Edward D, Nic Shuibhne N (2009) Continuity and change in the law relating to services. In: Arnull A, Eeckhout P, Tridimas T (eds) Continuity and Change in EU Law. Essays in Honour of Sir Francis Jacobs. Oxford University Press, Oxford, pp 243–261

Enchelmaier S (2003) The Awkward Selling of a Good Idea, or a Traditionalist Interpretation of Keck. YEL 22:249–325

Enchelmaier S (2010) Moped Trailers, Mickelsson & Roos, Gysbrechts: The Court's Case Law on Goods Keeps on Moving. YEL 29:190–223
Enchelmaier S (2011) Always at your service – within limits. EL Rev. 36:615–650
Fenger N (2017) To use or not to use – that's the question. On Article 34 and national rules restricting the use of lawfully marketed products. In: Andenas M, Bekkedal T, Pantaleo L (eds) The Reach of Free Movement. TMC Asser Press, The Hague
Gormley L (2009) The Definition of Measures Having Equivalent Effect. In: Arnull A, Eeckhout P, Tridimas T (eds) Continuity and Change in EU Law. Essays in Honour of Sir Francis Jacobs. Oxford University Press, Oxford, pp 189–215
Nic Shuibhne N (2013) The Coherence of EU Free Movement Law. Oxford University Press, Oxford
Oliver P (2010) Free Movement of Goods in the European Union, 5th edn. Hart, Oxford/Portland, Oregon
Oliver P, Roth W-H (2004) The Internal Market and the Four Freedoms. CML Rev. 41:407–441
Prete L (2008) Of Motorcycle Trailers and Personal Watercrafts: the Battle over Keck. LIEI 35 (2):133–155
Snell J (2010) The notion of market access: a concept or a slogan? CML Rev. 47:437–472
Steindorff E (1986) Gemeinsamer Markt als Binnenmarkt. Zeitschrift für Handelsrecht 150:687–692
Wilsher D (2008) Does Keck discrimination make any sense? An assessment of the non-discrimination principle with the European Single Market. EL Rev 33:3–20

Chapter 5
To Use or Not to Use—That's the Question. On Article 34 and National Rules Restricting the Use of Lawfully Marketed Products

Niels Fenger

Abstract This chapter examines the extent to which Article 34 TFEU encompasses national rules that neither prohibit the sale or the use of a product, but merely regulate how, where and when the product may be used. It argues that the Court of Justice was right not to apply the Court's case law concerning selling arrangements to such kinds of rules. Moreover, it discusses whether the Court's approach to use restrictions, and the market access test that the Court applies in such cases, has a spillover effect on other aspects of its case law under Article 34 TFEU. Finally, it provides a suggestion for how to draw the line for when a restriction on the use of a legally marketed product constitutes a measure of equivalent effect.

Keywords Internal market · Free movement of goods · Freedom to provide services · Market access · Discrimination · Trade restrictions · Restrictions of use · Trailers · Jet skis · Court of Justice of the European Union

Contents

5.1 The Definition of 'Measures Having Equivalent Effect' Under Article 34 110
5.2 Use Restrictions as Measures of Equivalent Effect 112
5.3 The Court's Case Law on Use Restrictions 115
5.4 Understanding and Evaluating the Court's Approach 118
  5.4.1 The Wish to Maintain Judicial Control 118
  5.4.2 *Keck* Does Not Encompass a Case-by-Case Market Access Test 119
  5.4.3 *Keck* Does Not Cover All Non-Product Related Measures 120
  5.4.4 A Desire to Avoid Rigid Categorisation 121
  5.4.5 Alignment with the Other Freedoms 121
5.5 A Unified Market Access Test for All National Measures? 122
5.6 Finding the Suitable Threshold 125
References 127

N. Fenger (✉)
University of Copenhagen, Copenhagen, Denmark
e-mail: NielsFenger@OestreLandsret.dk

M. Andenas et al. (eds.), *The Reach of Free Movement*,
DOI 10.1007/978-94-6265-195-1_5

5.1 The Definition of 'Measures Having Equivalent Effect' Under Article 34

The purpose of this chapter is to analyse the relationship between Article 34 TFEU and national rules regulating when, where, how and by whom a lawfully imported and marketed product may be used.

According to that provision, '[q]uantitative restrictions on imports and all measures having equivalent effect shall be prohibited between Member States.' The Treaty is silent on how one should understand the words 'all measures having equivalent effect'. In *Dassonville*, the Court held that these words cover '*all trading rules enacted by member states which are capable of hindering, directly or indirectly, actually or potentially, intra-community trade are to be considered as measures having an effect equivalent to quantitative restrictions*.' This definition is far from being as operational as is sometimes presumed, since it begs at least two questions. First, what measures constitute 'trading rules' and, second, how serious an impact must a measure have before it is 'hindering' intra-community trade.

In its practice, the Court has attached very little, if any, importance to whether national rules aim to regulate trade in goods or whether they pursue other aims. Indeed, in the case law it uses interchangeably the phrases 'trading rules', 'all commercial rules', 'all measures', 'all rules' and 'all legislation', thereby ruling out any limitation relating to the regulatory subject matter of the national rule in question.[1] The Court's focus is thus on the effects, not the aim or purpose or the subject matter, of the measure in question.

[1] The expression 'trading rules' is used in e.g. Case C-481/12, *UAB Juvelta*, ECLI:EU:C:2014:11; Case C-385/10, *Elenca Srl*, ECLI:EU:C:2012:634; Case C-456/10, *ANETT*, ECLI:EU:C:2012:241; Case C-484/10, *Ascafor*, ECLI:EU:C:2012:113; Case C-108/09, *Ker-Optika*, ECLI:EU:C:2010:725; Case C-531/07, *Fachverband*, ECLI:EU:C:2009:276; Case C-244/06, *Dynamic Medien*, ECLI:EU:C:2008:85; Case C-434/04, *Ahokainen and Leppik*, ECLI:EU:C:2006:609. The expression 'all commercial rules' is used in e.g. Case C-333/08, *Commission v France*, ECLI:EU:C:2010:44; Case C-254/05, *Commission v Belgium*, ECLI:EU:C:2007:319; and Case C-192/01, *Commission v Denmark*, ECLI:EU:C:2003:492. The expression 'all measures' is used in e.g. Case C-333/14, *Scotch Whisky Association*, ECLI:EU:C:2015:845; Case C-354/14, *SC Capoda Import-Export*, ECLI:EU:C:2015:658; Case C-573/12, *Ålands Vindkraft*, ECLI:EU:C:2014:2037 (any measure); Case C-150/11, *Commission v Belgium*, ECLI:EU:C:2012:539 (any measure); Case C-88/07, *Commission v Spain*, ECLI:EU:C:2009:123; Case C-319/05, *Commission v Germany*, ECLI:EU:C:2007:678; Case C-158/04, *Alfa Vita Vassilopoulos*, ECLI:EU:C:2006:562; and Case C-366/04, *Schwarz*, ECLI:EU:C:2005:719. The expression 'all rules' is used in e.g. Case C-171/11 *Fra.bo SpA*, ECLI:EU:C:2012:453; and Case C-265/06, *Commission v Portugal*, ECLI:EU:C:2008:210. The expression 'all legislation' is used in e.g. Case C-443/10, *Bonnarde*, ECLI:EU:C:2011:641; Case C-421/09, *Humanplasma*, ECLI:EU:C:2010:760; Case C-141/07, *Commission v Germany*, ECLI:EU:C:2008:492; Case C-143/06, *Ludwigs-Apotheke*, ECLI:EU:C:2007:656; and Case C-170/04, *Rosengren and Others*, ECLI:EU:C:2007:313.

Similarly, regarding the second condition that the national measure must be capable of 'hindering' intra-community trade, the Court has consistently refused in principle to apply any *de minimis* test under Article 34.[2] Measures which affect trade only indirectly or potentially therefore fall within the definition of a trade restriction.[3] Indeed, the Court in several cases has disregarded statistical evidence showing that imports have increased after a measure was introduced, on the basis that imports might have increased even more in the absence of such a measure.[4]

Consequently, the definition of a trade restriction has become almost all-encompassing, and the legality of huge swaths of national rules therefore depend on the proportionality and justification-test enshrined in Articles 34 and 36 (ex Article 30). This in turn reduces legal certainty for both Member States and traders, and implies a significant risk of judicial overload for the Court itself. As the Sunday-trading saga illustrates, the Court is well aware of these concerns.[5] Its ruling in *Keck*, in relation to a particular group of national rules (i.e., selling arrangements), can be seen as an attempt to meet them.[6] Moreover, in another line of cases, the Court in reality has come close to introducing a *de minimis* test (albeit at a very low threshold level) by holding that the restrictive effects which a national measure has on the free movement of goods may be too uncertain and too indirect for it to be regarded as capable of hindering trade between Member States (hereafter called the *Krantz* case law).[7]

The difficulty of establishing the appropriate scope of Article 34 of the Treaty is illustrated by the fact that while the *Keck* jurisprudence has been criticised for being too inflexible and unable to catch all genuine barriers to trade, it has been argued that the *Krantz* case law is too difficult to apply and therefore generates legal uncertainty.[8]

---

[2] Case C-67/97, *Bluhme*, ECLI:EU:C:1998:584; Case C-184/96, *Commission v France*, ECLI:EU:C:1998:495; and Case 177/82, *Van de Haar*, ECLI:EU:C:1984:144.

[3] Case C-184/96, *Commission v France* ('foie gras'), ECLI:EU:C:1998:495.

[4] Case C-463/01, *Commission v Germany* ('mineral water'), ECLI:EU:C:2004:797, para 65; Case C-405/98, *Gourmet International Products*, ECLI:EU:C:2001:135, para 22; and Case 249/81, *Commission v Ireland* ('Buy Irish'), ECLI:EU:C:1982:402, paras 22 and 25.

[5] Case C-169/91, *Stoke-on-Trent*, ECLI:EU:C:1992:519; and Case C-145/88, *Torfaen Borough Council*, ECLI:EU:C:1989:593.

[6] Joined Cases C-267/91 and C-268/91, *Keck and Mithouard*, ECLI:EU:C:1993:905.

[7] Case C-291/09, *Guarnieri & Cie*, ECLI:EU:C:2011:217; Case C-412/97, *ED*, ECLI:EU:C:1999:324; and C-44/98, *BASF*, ECLI:EU:C:1999:440; Case C-266/96, *Corsica Ferries France*, ECLI:EU:C:1998:306; Case C-140/94, *DIP*, ECLI:EU:C:1995:330; Case C-134/94, *Esso Española*, ECLI:EU:C:1995:414; Case C-379/92, *Peralta*, ECLI:EU:C:1994:296; and Case C-69/88, *Krantz*, ECLI:EU:C:1994:296. See similarly Case C-112/00, *Schmidberger*, ECLI:EU:C:2002:437, Opinion of AG Jacobs, para 65 ff.

[8] Case C-142/05, *Mickelsson and Roos*, ECLI:EU:C:2006:782, Opinion of AG Kokott, paras 57–63.

5.2 Use Restrictions as Measures of Equivalent Effect

Against this background, let us turn to the relationship between Article 34 and national measures which allow the importation and marketing of a given product, but restrict when, where, how or by whom it may be used (hereafter 'use restrictions'). Such rules are very common in national legislation. As an example, one could mention a requirement for persons to have attained a particular age before acquiring or using the product, such as a rule preventing minors from purchasing and/or drinking alcohol. The notion also covers rules prohibiting the use of the product in certain places or at certain times, like a ban on the use mobile phones in airplanes or a prohibition on the use of fireworks save for a few days of the year. Other examples would be local planning rules prohibiting the use of a given kind of brick or tile for the construction of houses in a particular area or a ban of certain activities for which a good is normally used, for example a ban on hunting with dogs and horses.[9] Even a prohibition on wearing a particular type of clothing, such as a burka, in public places is arguably covered by this concept.

Considering the vast number of such rules, it is important to consider whether use restrictions should be regarded as trade restrictions at all, and if so, how intrusive they must be to be caught by Article 34.

On the one hand, the aim of such rules is normally not to regulate trade. Moreover, they generally do not affect the sale of imported goods more than they affect the sale of domestic goods. Finally, with a literal reading of Article 34 of the Treaty and the Court's own ruling in *Dassonville*, it may be questioned how rules which do not limit the importation and marketing of the relevant product, but merely regulate how it may be used after its sale, can be said to constitute 'trading rules'.

On the other hand, it is clear that *some* limitations on how a product may be used can negatively affect sales and import to a very significant extent. Indeed, whereas a prohibition on using mobile phones in airplanes hardly has any such effect, a ban on using fireworks all year except on 31 December is likely to (greatly) reduce demand for, and thus sales and import of, that good. Similarly, one may imagine that a ban on the use of SUVs in congested urban zones would constitute an efficient means for diminishing sales and import of such cars to the benefit of more environmentally friendly vehicles.

---

[9] In *Countryside Alliance and others v HM Attorney General* [2006] EWCA Civ 817, the English Court of Appeal denied that a hunting ban constituted a restriction for the purposes of Article 34, since it was not aimed at products from other Member States and did not have a discriminatory effect on imported products. In a judgment on appeal of 27 November 2007, the House of Lords found it questionable whether the ban was caught by Article 34, but found that issue to be of little importance, as any restriction clearly was justified, see House of Lords Session 2007–08 [2007] UKHL 52.

Still, while it may be relatively easy to accept that rules completely banning the use of a given product constitute measures with equivalent effect to a quantitative restriction, it may be questioned whether rules merely limiting its lawful use need to be subject to a common European judicial control as to their legitimacy, suitability and necessity.

To answer this question, it is, in my view, necessary to consider the practical and economic effect on trade of rules restricting the lawful use of goods. An argument can be made that, with the exception of (virtually) complete bans on use, the effects of use restrictions differ fundamentally from the effects of product related rules, and that use restrictions should rather be compared to selling arrangements.[10] In a seminal article, White argued that:

> The different legal and economic environment of the Member State of origin finds its expression in the different characteristics of an imported product compared with the national product. Consequently, as the judgment of the Court in Cassis de Dijon clearly shows, Member States are not entitled to require that imported products have the same characteristics as are required of, or are traditional in, domestic products unless this is strictly necessary for the protection of some legitimate interest. There is not, however, the same need to require the rules relating to the circumstances in which certain goods may be sold or used in the importing Member State to be overridden for this purpose as long as imported products enjoy equal access to the market of the importing Member State. In such a case the imported product is not deprived of any advantage it derives from the different legal and economic environment prevailing in the place of production. In fact, any reduction of total sales (and therefore imports) which may result from restrictions on the circumstances in which they may be sold does not arise out of disparities between national rules but rather out of the existence of the rules in the importing Member State.[11]

On that basis, White suggested that state measures which are entirely neutral in their effect on foreign and domestic goods—because they merely regulate the circumstances in which all goods of the same kind may be sold or used—should not fall under Article 34. This should only be different when the restrictions on the circumstances in which the goods may be used depend on their characteristics (in which case they should be judged according to *Cassis de Dijon*) or are so severe that they amount to a virtual prohibition of the product (in which case they should be assimilated to prohibitions).[12] The judgment in *Keck*, in my view, is based on the same logic: national measures must ensure '*equality of chances*' for domestic and imported goods. The Court will interfere and assess the legitimacy of state measures only when they potentially affect imported goods relatively more than domestic goods. However, when the principle of equality of chances is respected, the Member States should be allowed to freely regulate their respective

---

[10] Spaventa 2009, pp. 922–923. Compare Oliver 2011, p. 1456.

[11] White 1989, p. 246, underlined by White.

[12] White 1989, pp. 247, 253–254 and 258.

territories, even when that indirectly affects the total volume of sales of a given product.[13]

Going further, Horsley has argued that requiring use restrictions to be justified under Article 34 would turn that provision into a tool to increase the domestic market for the relevant product or even to create a market for that product where none existed previously. He objects to this on the basis that, in his view, Article 34 seeks only to prevent distortion of competition; it does not carry an obligation to allow for a market place where competition can take place.[14]

In my view, White's analysis strikes the appropriate balance. On the one hand, Article 34 can indeed, according to its own wording ('quantitative restrictions') and the Court's case law, entail an obligation for a Member State to justify provisions which exclude *any* market whatsoever for a given product.[15] On the other hand, there is little basis in the Treaty for the proposition that Article 34 encourages a general deregulation of national economies.[16] Although some liberalising effects are bound to flow from Article 34, its fundamental objective is to ensure that producers are put in a position to fully benefit from the right to carry out their activity at a cross-border level, while consumers are put in a position to access products from other Member States *in the same conditions* as domestic products.[17]

---

[13] Case C-441/04, *A-Punkt Schmuckhandel*, ECLI:EU:C:2006:141; Case C-20/03, *Burmanjer and Others*, ECLI:EU:C:2005:307; Case C-71/02, *Karner*, ECLI:EU:C:2004:181; and Case C-418/93, *Semeraro Casa Uno*, ECLI:EU:C:1996:242.

[14] Horsley 2009, pp. 2012, 2014 and 2017–8. See also Enchelmaier 2007, pp. 130–132. Indeed, this was the very reasoning that led the UK Court of Appeal in the above-mentioned *Countryside Alliance* case to hold that English law did not constitute a trade restriction. For the Court of Appeal it did not matter that the rule had the practical effect of taking products off the market, as '*the implication of the argument is that a member state can be under an obligation to keep intact, or even possibly to create, a market for the benefit of importers from other member states. That cannot be so, at least where the state is equally depriving its own citizens of that benefit*'.

[15] Case C-192/01, *Commission v Denmark*, ECLI:EU:C:2003:492.

[16] See similarly Joined Cases C-158/04 and 159/04, *Alfa Vita Vassilopoulos*, ECLI:EU:C:2006:212, Opinion of AG Maduro, paras 37–40; and Case C-442/02 *CaixaBank France*, ECLI:EU:C:2004:187, Opinion of AG Tizzano, para 63, arguing that such an interpretation '*would be tantamount to bending the Treaty to a purpose for which it was not intended: that is to say, not in order to create an internal market in which conditions are similar to those of a single market and where operators can move freely, but in order to establish a market without rules. Or rather, a market in which rules are prohibited as a matter of principle, except for those necessary and proportionate to meeting imperative requirements in the public interest*'. See somewhat similar Davies 2014, p. 29, according to whom '*litigants who challenge non-protectionist regulation are in fact not claiming that they are denied market access. They are claiming that a different market should exist.*'

[17] For a broader view of the purpose of Article 34, see Case 412/93, *Leclerc-Siplec*, ECLI:EU:C:1994:393, Opinion of AG Jacobs, and Spaventa 2009, pp. 925 and 929.

5.3 The Court's Case Law on Use Restrictions

Traditionally, however, the Court has not distinguished between national rules which ban *any* use of the product concerned and rules *limiting* its lawful use. In a series of cases concerned with relatively severe use restrictions, it applied the classic *Dassonville* test and found such rules to be measures of equivalent effect without discussing the applicability of either the *Keck* reasoning or the *Krantz* case law. For example, in *Commission v Portugal*, the question was whether a Portuguese prohibition on the affixing of tinted film to the windows of passenger or goods vehicles fell foul of Article 34.[18] Noting that the only exception to the Portuguese ban concerned the affixing of tinted film to the goods compartments of goods vehicles and to non-wheeled vehicles, the Court held that '*potential customers, traders or individuals have practically no interest in buying them in the knowledge that affixing such film to the windscreen and windows alongside passenger seats in motor vehicles is prohibited*'.[19]

Further, the Community legislator seems to have viewed restrictions on use as being capable of constituting trade restrictions: some such rules are covered by the obligation to notify draft technical regulations under Directive 98/34 on the laying down of a procedure for the provision of information in the field of technical standards and regulations. According to the Court, that notification obligation applies not only with regard to full-fledged prohibitions on use, but also with regard to '*national measures which leave no room for any use which can reasonably be made of the product concerned other than a purely marginal one*'.[20]

In 2009, two cases offered the Court an opportunity to reconsider this case law. The first one, *Commission v Italy* (hereafter *Trailers*), concerned an Italian prohibition on attaching trailers to motorcycles.[21] In his Opinion, AG Léger found that the Italian rule in question did constitute a trade restriction (and, moreover, could not be justified). Following that Opinion, the Court referred the case to the Grand Chamber, re-opened the oral procedure and invited the parties and Member States to comment on whether national use restrictions are to be regarded as measures having equivalent effect to quantitative restrictions. Of those Member States

---

[18] Case C-265/06, *Commission v Portugal*, ECLI:EU:C:2008:210.

[19] Paras 33–34 of the judgment. See also Case C-65/05, *Commission v Greece*, ECLI:EU:C:2006:673; Case C-473/98, *Toolex*, ECLI:EU:C:2000:379; Case C-67/97, *Bluhme*, ECLI:EU:C:1998:584; and Case 60/84, *Cinéthèque*, ECLI:EU:C:1985:329. For a different kind of use restriction related to transit-transport see Case C-28/09, *Commission v Austria*, ECLI:EU:C:2011:854.

[20] Case C-267/03, *Lindberg*, ECLI:EU:C:2005:246. As will be shown later, this formulation is strikingly close to that adopted by the Court in the judgments discussed below concerning Case C-142/05, *Mickelsson and Roos*, ECLI:EU:C:2009:336; and Case C-110/05, *Commission v Italy*, ECLI:EU:C:2009:66. Already directive 66/683 eliminating all differences between the treatment of national products required Member States to abolish measures which partially or totally prohibited the use of an imported product.

[21] Case C-110/05, *Commission v Italy*, ECLI:EU:C:2009:66.

presenting observations, nearly all argued that use restrictions should be assessed in the same way as selling arrangements and thus be excluded from the scope of Article 34 altogether, provided that the conditions laid down by the Court in the *Keck*-judgment were met. In his Opinion on the reopened case, AG Bot strongly opposed those arguments, and warned against extending *Keck* to cover use restrictions. In his view, to exclude such rules from the scope of Article 34 would undermine its *effet utile* and the Court's review of measures, which, in fact, may constitute serious obstacles to intra-Community trade. It was therefore, Bot submitted, preferable to continue to examine measures of that kind under the classic test in *Dassonville* and *Cassis de Dijon*, rather than to exclude them from the scope of the Treaty.[22]

The second case, *Mickelsson*, concerned a Swedish law that defined (and restricted) the waters in which lawfully imported and sold personal watercraft (sometimes referred to as jet-skis) could be used.[23] These rules imposed a general ban on sailing with personal watercraft in all Swedish waters except in so-called general navigable waterways. Whereas there were about 300 such general navigable waterways, it also appeared that general navigable waterways did not exist in large portions of the country, they were not interconnected, they were difficult to reach, and for safety reasons they were often unsuitable for the use of a personal watercraft. In a criminal case concerning a violation of the prohibition against sailing outside such general navigable waterways, the defendants, Mickelsson and Roos, argued that Swedish law was contrary to Article (now) 34, as the prohibition greatly reduced potential consumers' interest in buying personal watercrafts. The Swedish Government disputed that the rules constituted a measure of equivalent effect (and argued that in any event they were justified) since the situation was not different from when a Member State regulates where land-based vehicles are allowed to drive. And who would ever argue that a prohibition for a 4WD vehicle to drive off the road in forests and mountains should be viewed as a trade restriction?

AG Kokott basically agreed with the approach of the Swedish Government. Drawing implicitly on the above-cited reasoning of White, she suggested that national rules regulating the use of a good should be dealt with in the same way as selling arrangements and thus be excluded from the scope of Article 34 altogether, provided that the conditions laid down by the Court in the *Keck* judgment were met. Otherwise, individuals would be able to invoke Article 34 to challenge national rules, the effect of which is merely to limit their general freedom of action. Moreover, arrangements for use and selling arrangements in her opinion were comparable in terms of the nature and the intensity of their effects on trade in goods. In her view, it followed from this analogy with *Keck* that such rules however will fall within the scope of Article 34 when in reality they prevent access to the market

---

[22] Case 120/78, *Rewe-Zentral*, ECLI:EU:C:1979:42.

[23] Case C-142/05, *Mickelsson and Roos*, ECLI:EU:C:2009:336. See on the same matter, Case C-433/05, *Sandström*, ECLI:EU:C:2010:184; and the judgment of the Danish Supreme Court in Ugeskrift for Retsvæsen 2011.539 H.

for the product in question. That would be the case not only for rules which result in complete exclusion, such as a general prohibition on using a certain product, but also when only a marginal possibility for using a product remains.[24]

In both cases, the Court started out by restating its classic case law that obstacles to the free movement of goods, which are the consequence of applying (to goods coming from other Member States where they are lawfully manufactured and marketed) rules that lay down requirements to be met by such goods, must be regarded as measures having equivalent effect to quantitative restrictions on imports for the purposes of Article 34. It then added that the same applies to '*any other measure which hinders access of products originating in other Member States to the market of a Member State*'.[25]

Tacitly refusing to apply an analogy of its case law concerning selling arrangements, as suggested by AG Kokott, the Court then approached the Italian and Swedish rules by looking at their likely effect on the behaviour of potential buyers of a trailer or a watercraft. According to the Court, it was not decisive that national regulations concerning where and how a product may be used normally do not have the aim or effect of treating goods coming from other Member States less favourably. What mattered was rather that a rule which restricts the use of a product might, depending on its scope, have a considerable influence on the behaviour of consumers, which may, in turn, affect the access of that product to the national market.

In *Trailers*, for some products the national rule prohibited the only relevant use of the relevant good (the towing of a trailer).[26] It was thus no big surprise that the Court, in line with its above-mentioned older case law, found such a rule to constitute a trade restriction. In comparison, in *Mickelsson* the Court went further by holding that Article 34 also encompasses certain national rules that merely regulate how, where and when a product may be used. In this respect, the Court found that the Swedish rules had the effect of preventing owners of personal watercrafts from using them for the specific and inherent purposes for which they were intended or, at least, greatly restricted their legal use. Thus, in economic terms such regulations had the effect of hindering access to the domestic market in question for those goods and therefore constituted measures having equivalent effect to quantitative restrictions on imports prohibited by Article 34.

The Court has confirmed this approach in *Commission v Spain* (hereafter '*Trucks*').[27] The case concerned a Spanish regulation for the licensing of companies providing road transport services according to which the age of the first vehicle of more than 3.5 tons in the fleet of a newly licensed company should not exceed five months from the date of its first registration. Referring to *Trailers*, the Court found

[24] For a critique of the Kokott's reasoning, see Oliver 2010, pp. 127–128.

[25] Case C-110/05, *Commission v Italy*, ECLI:EU:C:2009:66, para 37, and Case C-142/05, *Mickelsson and Roos*, ECLI:EU:C:2009:336, para 24.

[26] As to dual use see Sect. 5.6.

[27] Case C-428/12, *Commission v Spain*, ECLI:EU:C:2014:218.

that this age-limit on the truck could have a considerable influence on the behavior of firms wishing to use a vehicle of this nature for complementary private transport as the firms concerned would only have a limited interest in buying a truck for their complementary private transportation activities. In other words, restricting the use of a vehicle whose registration exceeds five months, as the first heavy vehicle of a fleet of heavy trucks, had the effect of limiting the possibility for firms to make a normal use of the vehicle, whose inherent function is to be used, hence hindering its market access in Spain.

5.4 Understanding and Evaluating the Court's Approach

If there are, as argued above in Sect. 5.2, clear parallels between the effects on trade of selling arrangements and use restrictions, why did the Court reject the suggestions of AG Kokott in *Mickelsson* to extend the *Keck* case law to use restrictions?

5.4.1 The Wish to Maintain Judicial Control

The first likely reason is that the Court found it appropriate to maintain its judicial control over rules regulating the use of lawfully marketed products. At the same time, the Court may have taken into account that, in contrast to what was the case concerning selling arrangements before *Keck*, there have not been many cases concerning restrictions on use.

These considerations concerning the Court's own powers and its workload however hardly provide the full picture. As discussed in more detail below in Sect. 5.6, in *Mickelsson* the Court found it decisive whether the Swedish rules had '*the effect of hindering the access to the domestic market*' and in that connection put emphasis on the fact that the actual possibilities for the use of personal watercraft were '*marginal*' such that the restriction of its legal use was liable to have '*a considerable influence on the behaviour of consumers*'. In practical effects, although not in its theoretical approach, the Court's test thereby comes close to the *Keck*-based approach suggested by AG Kokott. As will be recalled, she suggested that a non-discriminatory measure restricting certain types of use should be classified as a measure of equivalent effect if it '*prevents access to the market for the product in question*'. According to Kokott, this would be the case not only for rules that contain a general prohibition on using a certain product, but also for '*a situation where only a marginal possibility for using a product remains*'.[28] There must

[28] Para 67 of the Opinion.

therefore be additional reasons why the Court decided not to follow AG Kokott's suggestion to extend its practice concerning selling arrangements to cover also use restrictions.

5.4.2 Keck *Does Not Encompass a Case-by-Case Market Access Test*

A second possible reason for why the Court refused to extend its case law concerning selling arrangements is that, contrary to what AG Kokott suggested, *Keck* actually does not contain a market access test for non-discriminatory measures. An application of the *Keck* principle could therefore not be used to reserve the desired judicial control for the Court that would make it possible for it to strike down use restrictions that come close to a genuine ban.

It is of course correct that in *Keck* the Court held that when national selling arrangements satisfy the two conditions laid down in that judgment, such arrangements are not '*by nature such as to prevent their access to the market*' and consequently fall outside the scope of Article 34.[29] Moreover, by distinguishing various categories of measures, the Court evidently endeavoured to identify the conditions under which each of those categories may affect access to the market.

However, the Court's just-cited statement only showed that it took the view that no access problem arises in situations where the two *Keck* conditions are fulfilled. In contrast, the Court has been much less willing to make the reverse finding suggested by AG Kokott that it is part of the *Keck* test to examine *on a case-by-case basis* whether the national rule in question actually restricts market access although it fulfils those two conditions. In fact, one of the main purposes of *Keck* was to avoid the need for such concrete assessments by making that evaluation once and for all with regard to the types of rules covered by the judgment, i.e., rules concerning to whom, where and when a product might be sold. Or to put it differently, with the statement that no market access is restricted by non-discriminatory selling arrangements, the Court in *Keck* insisted on a legal fiction in the name of legal certainty and operability.[30] Somewhat sharply phrased, it could be argued that the reading of *Keck* suggested by AG Kokott introduces a third condition into a judgment that only has two and that her approach thus confuses what the Court saw as the consequence of fulfilling the test laid down in that judgment with the actual test itself.

It is true that, already before *Mickelsson* and *Trailers*, many commentators had seen a trend in the Court's case law towards the recognition of a broader market

[29] Paras 16–17 in *Keck*.

[30] Oliver 1999a, pp. 797–799, who commends the Court for this approach and warns against an economic assessment on a case-by-case basis. See also Case C-98/01, *Commission v UK*, ECLI:EU:C:2003:273.

access test akin to that suggested by AG Kokott.[31] In this respect, reference was usually made to *Gourmet*, where the Court held that in order to escape Article 34, national selling arrangements '*must not be of such a kind as to prevent access to the market by products from another Member State or to impede access any more than they impede the access of domestic products*'.[32] However, this statement was not decisive for the Court's conclusion in the case, and in its later case law the Court never referred to that part of the *Gourmet* judgment. Nor did the Court actually apply a market access criterion in relation to national selling arrangements that genuinely affected domestic and imported goods in the same way. Rather, the market test was applied in order to show that rules which protected the status quo of the national market could make it more difficult for foreign operators to penetrate the national market. In other words, the market test was not seen as a third condition to be applied case by case. Instead, it was used as a means to apply the second condition relating to factual equality between domestic and imported goods.[33] For non-discriminatory measures, the market access test was applied only in the negative sense that as long as the two conditions laid down in *Keck* were fulfilled no market access problem would by definition arise.[34]

5.4.3 **Keck** ***Does Not Cover All Non-Product Related Measures***

A third reason the Court chose not to follow the approach suggested by White and Kokott is that it would have given *Keck* a substantially wider scope of application than so far accepted in the Court's case law. Whereas White and Kokott seem to advocate that the relevant distinction is between product-related requirements and other national measures able to affect trade, the Court's case law tends to make a distinction between selling arrangements and all other measures, be that product-related measures or other types of measures.[35] Indeed, when a measure is

[31] On this issue, see Weatherill 1996, pp. 887, 894 and 896–898; Straetmans 2002, pp. 1407, 1415.

[32] Case C-405/98, *Gourmet International Products*, ECLI:EU:C:2001:135.

[33] Case C-239/02, *Douwe Egberts*, ECLI:EU:C:2004:445 (but compare paras 71–75 of the Opinion of AG Geelhoed); Case C-322/01, *Deutscher Apothekerverband*, ECLI:EU:C:2003:664 (but compare paras 74–96 of the Opinion of AG Stix-Hackl); Case C-254/98, *TK-Heimdienst*, ECLI:EU:C:2000:12; and Case C-34/95, *De Agostini*, ECLI:EU:C:1997:344.

[34] C-141/07, *Commission v Germany*, ECLI:EU:C:2008:492; Case C-244/06, *Dynamic Medien*, ECLI:EU:C:2008:85; Case C-158/04, *Alfa Vita Vassilopoulos*, ECLI:EU:C:2006:562, and Case C-71/02, *Karner*, ECLI:EU:C:2004:181. As will be explained in Sect. 5.5, this remains the legal position.

[35] See also Wennerås and Moen 2010, pp. 389, 393 and 399. Somewhat surprisingly the two authors read *Trailers* and *Mickelsson* as confirming their view that the test in *Keck* is not restricted to selling arrangements, but rather of general application and that the delimitation of 'certain selling arrangements' therefore is redundant as it is only necessary to distinguish between products requirements and other types of possible restrictions.

neither a selling arrangement nor regulating product characteristics, the Court has traditionally subjected them either to the traditional *Dassonville* and *Cassis* test or applied the *Krantz* case law to find their effects on the free movement of goods too uncertain and indirect to be caught by Article 34.[36] As shown above in Sect. 5.3, this has also been true for cases concerning restrictions on use.

5.4.4 A Desire to Avoid Rigid Categorisation

A fourth possible explanation may be that the Court did not wish to face fierce academic criticism, of the kind levelled at the ruling in *Keck*, for relying on overly 'rigid' categorisation of different types of national measures to delimit the scope of Article 34.[37] The Court is likely to have weighed that concern against the risk of criticism that the market access approach is inherently vague and will give rise to legal uncertainty for operators and Member States alike.[38] For example, as further developed under Sect. 5.6, it is far from evident how one would assess under the market access test a national rule that allocates 10 or 20% of all waters suitable for sailing with a personal watercraft as open for such use or a rule allowing the use of a personal watercraft, but restricting the speed limit to 10 knots per hour. However, the Court may have concluded, correctly in my view, that the legal uncertainty inherent in the market access test is in any event no greater, and possibly even lesser, than the uncertainty inherent in the general criteria laid down in *Dassonville* combined with the *Krantz* case law.

5.4.5 Alignment with the Other Freedoms

A fifth and final possible reason the Court chose not to apply the *Keck* approach in *Trailers*, *Mickelsson* and *Trucks* is that it wished to align to some extent its practice in the field of free movement of goods with its case law concerning the other

[36] For example, Cases C-434/04, *Ahokainen and Leppik*, ECLI:EU:C:2006:609; Case C-320/03, *Commission v Austria*, ECLI:EU:C:2005:684; and Case C-323/93, *Crespelle*, ECLI:EU:C:1994:368. The Court has continued taking this approach after the judgments in *Trailers* and *Mickelsson*, cf. e.g. Case C-456/10, *ANETT*, ECLI:EU:C:2012:241; and Case C-333/14, *Scotch Whisky Association*, ECLI:EU:C:2015:845.

[37] See, for example, Moore 1994, p. 195; Reich 1994, p. 459; Gormley 2007, p. 189, and Gormley 2008, p. 1637.

[38] For such criticism, see Oliver 2011, p. 1456, and Spaventa 2009, pp. 922–924.

fundamental freedoms.[39] In relation to these other freedoms, the Court has never adopted the 'selling arrangement' classification, but rather views as restrictions on freedom of movement all measures which prohibit, impede or render less attractive the exercise of the relevant freedom.[40] Indeed, in its more recent case law concerning the right of establishment, the Court has referred to the market access test in Trailers and thereby made an analogy between Articles 34 and 49.[41] Hence, by combining a market access test with a refusal to apply an expanded *Keck* test, the Court has increased the unity and consistency of its case law concerning the different freedoms.[42] This is especially so as the case law concerning the other provisions on free movement also draws a distinction between, on the one hand, impediments to the market and, on the other hand, rules that merely limit the exercise of a given activity.[43] Similarly, the principle that a restriction may be too remote and uncertain has been applied in the case law concerning the other freedoms.[44]

5.5 A Unified Market Access Test for All National Measures?

Based on para 37 of the judgment in *Trailers*, where the Court stated that Article 34 not only covers product rules, but '*any other measure which hinders access of products originating in other Member States to the market of a Member State*', it might be tempting to conclude that the Court has introduced market access as a new overarching test to be applied, on a case-by-case basis, to all national measures to

[39] Such an alignment of the different freedoms was proposed by AG Maduro in paras 37–40 of his Opinion in Case C-158/04, *Alfa Vita Vassilopoulos*, ECLI:EU:C:2006:212. See also Oliver 1999a, b, p. 1377; O'Keeffe and Bavasso 2000, p. 541; Barnard 2001, p. 35; Straetmans 2002, p. 1407; and Snell 2002.

[40] Case C-212/09, *Commission v. Portugal*, ECLI:EU:C:2011:717; Case C-169/07, *Hartlauer*, ECLI:EU:C:2009:141; Case C-500/06, *Corporación Dermoestética*, ECLI:EU:C:2008:421; Case C-452/04, *Fidium Finanz*, ECLI:EU:C:2006:631; Case C-451/03, *Servizi Ausiliari Dottori Commercialisti*, ECLI:EU:C:2006:208; Case C-442/02, *CaixaBank France*, ECLI:EU:C:2004:586; and Case C-384/93, *Alpine Investments*, ECLI:EU:C:1995:126.

[41] Case C-400/08, *Commission v Spain*, ECLI:EU:C:2011:172.

[42] Pecho 2009, p. 264.

[43] Case 544/03, *Mobistar*, ECLI:EU:C:2005:518; Case C-442/02, *CaixaBank France*, ECLI:EU:C:2004:187, Opinion of AG Tizzano, para 66; and Case C-415/93, *Bosman*, ECLI:EU:C:1995:463.

[44] Concerning Article 39 EC, see Case C-190/98, *Graf*, ECLI:EU:C:2000:49. With regard to Article 49 EC, see Case C-134/03, *Viacom Outdoor*, ECLI:EU:C:2004:676, Opinion of AG Lenz, para 205.

determine whether they fall within the scope of Article 34. Several authors seem to believe that this is the case.[45]

On closer reflection, the market access test, however, may be rather less novel and practically significant. Ensuring market access for foreign products was always a major preoccupation of the Court even though it has used different terms to express that concern. Moreover, as already discussed above under Sect. 5.4.4, the market access test does not provide precise operative criteria for how to assess whether a given national rule impedes market access sufficiently to be caught by Article 34. Indeed, until now the test has not lead to significant changes in terms of outcomes compared to previous case law. The novelty of the market access test has thus, ultimately, been more terminological than substantive.

This point is neatly illustrated by the position of selling arrangements under the post-*Trailers* case law. Based on para 37 of the judgment, it has been argued that *Trailers* prescribes a case-by-case assessment of whether a non-discriminatory selling arrangement actually impedes market access—or to put it differently, that AG Kokott's reading of *Keck* has now been confirmed.[46]

However, *Trailers* should not read in that manner. Indeed, immediately before stating that a market access criterion has now become the relevant yardstick, the Court restates *Keck* and maintains that a selling-arrangement fulfilling the two conditions on factual and legal equality '*is not by nature such as to prevent their access to the market*'. Therefore, it is more plausible to read *Trailers* as meaning that no individual assessment under the market access criterion needs to be made in relation to those categories of national measures for which the Court has already made that assessment. Indeed, if a market access test were to be carried out in all cases concerning selling arrangements in the same manner as in other cases concerning Article 34, what would then be the substance of the distinction between selling arrangements and other measures? And why would the Court in that case have chosen to restate that fully non-discriminatory selling arrangements do not by nature pose problems under a market access test?

This interpretation, according to which non-discriminatory selling arrangements are not subject to a case-by-case market access test, is corroborated by the Court's case law after *Trailers* and *Mickelsson*. Indeed, in *Fachverband*, the Court continued to apply classic *Keck* reasoning and even referred to *Trailers* to support the

[45] See, for example, Lianos 2014, p. 24, according to whom '*the broad market access concept seems to indicate a tectonic shift in the governance of the EU Internal Market and, in particular the law on the free movement of goods*'. See also Pecho 2009, p. 262. In Case C-61/12, *Commission v Lithuania*, ECLI:EU:C:2014:172; Case C-639/11, *Commission v Poland*, ECLI:EU:C:2014:173; and Case C-385/10, *Elenca Srl*, ECLI:EU:C:2012:634, the Court used the 'market access' terminology to product related national legislations. See also Case C-443/10, *Bonnarde*, ECLI:EU:C:2011:641, where the market access test was applied to a national rule requiring, for the award of the subsidy to imported demonstration motor vehicles, that the first registration document of those vehicles bear the words 'demonstration vehicle'. In Case C-456/10, *ANETT*, ECLI:EU:C:2012:241, the market access test implied that a national legislation prohibiting tobacco retailers from importing tobacco products was caught by Article 34.

[46] Ibid.

proposition that selling arrangements do not need to be assessed under a new case-by-case market access test.[47] Similarly, in *Ker-Optika* concerning a national legislation authorising the selling of contact lenses only in shops which specialise in medical devices, the Court first restated the general market access in *Trailers*, but then referred to *Keck* and held that it was *'necessary to examine whether the national legislation at issue in the main proceedings.. applies to all relevant traders operating within the national territory and whether it affects in the same manner, in law and in fact, the selling of domestic products and the selling of those from other Member States*', in other words, the classic *Keck* test.[48] Finally, also in the most recent judgment concerning selling arrangements, *Visnapuu*, the Court applied the normal *Keck* reasoning.[49]

Thus, the better reading of *Trailers* and *Mickelsson* would seem to be that they introduce an overall market access test, the consequences of which the Court already spelled out in *Keck* with respect to selling arrangements so that no case-by-case analysis is required for such measures.[50]

Similarly, it is far from clear that the market access test will in practice affect the outcomes of for example cases concerning formalities to be respected in connection with the passing of a frontier. Hitherto, the Court has viewed such formalities as trade restrictions even where they are minor and not a precondition for the lawful import and marketing of the product.[51] It seems very likely that, as for selling arrangements, the Court will take the view that the consequences of the market access test for border formalities have already been spelled out by the existing case law.[52] It also telling that the *Krantz* case law has been maintained after *Trailers* without the Court even mentioning the broader market access test and explaining how the *Krantz* case law relates more precisely to that test.[53]

In other words, while market access appears to have been established as the unifying test under Article 34, the application of that test varies significantly depending on the type of national measure at issue.

---

[47] Case C-531/07, *Fachverband*, ECLI:EU:C:2009:276.

[48] Case C-108/09, *Ker-Optika*, ECLI:EU:C:2010:725.

[49] Case C-198/14, *Visnapuu*, ECLI:EU:C:2015:751.

[50] Oliver 2010, p. 130, and Snell 2010, p. 456.

[51] Joined Cases 51-54/71, *International Fruit Company*, ECLI:EU:C:1971:128.

[52] See also Case C-421/09, *Humanplasma*, ECLI:EU:C:2010:760 concerning a rule prohibiting the importation of blood products derived from donations which were not entirely unpaid. Although the national legislation in question was neither a selling arrangement nor a product requirement, the Court did not refer to the market access test in *Trailers*, but cited instead the old *Dasonville* test. Another issue is whether these so-to-speak pre-decided subgroups correctly reflect the restrictive effects that they generally have. As noted by Spaventa 2009, p. 922, one might question, e.g., whether an obligation to provide statistics (which has been and probably continues to be assessed under the *Dassonville* test, cf. Case C-114/96, *Kieffer and Thill*, ECLI:EU:C:1997:316) really hampers market access more than certain types of non-discriminatory advertising restrictions that, according to *Keck*, fall outside the scope of Article 34 altogether.

[53] Case C-291/09, *Guarnieri & Cie*, ECLI:EU:C:2011:217.

5.6 Finding the Suitable Threshold

To understand the implications of the new case law on use restrictions, I will examine two questions. First, should a national court faced with a case regarding a use restriction seek information as to the degree to which that restriction actually reduces import volumes or rather examine the content of the contested rule and assess the extent to which it prevents normal use of the good in question? Second, how much must either import volumes be reduced, or normal use be restricted, before the national measure is caught by Article 34?

Regarding the first question, it is submitted that the national court does not have to engage in a sophisticated economic analysis of trade volumes, but may limit itself to examining the extent to which the national measure restricts—temporally, geographically, substantively and/or personally—the use of the good. Indeed, both in *Mickelson*, in *Trailers* and in *Trucks*, the Court focused on the fact that the rules in question prevented the products from being used '*for the specific and inherent purposes for which they were intended or of greatly restricting their use*'.[54] It noted that consumers on the whole therefore had '*practically no interest in buying*' or only '*a limited interest in buying that product*'.[55] In contrast, the Court did not invite the parties or the referring court to seek statistical information on the actual effects of the contested national rules. Hence, it was this limitation—inherent in the scheme of the measures themselves—rather than an economic analysis of their actual impact on imports that led the Court to consider them as measures of equivalent effect.

As for the second question, according to the classic *Dassonville* formula, Article 34 covers national measures that merely have the potential to hinder trade and hitherto the Court has refused to apply a *de minimis* test.[56] This has led Oliver to assert that all use restrictions should be caught by Article 34 unless their effects on trade are too indirect within the meaning of the *Krantz* case law. At the same time Oliver argues that it follows from *Krantz* that minor restrictions on use such as speed limits for cars; a ban on commercial flights at night; a prohibition on using hand-held mobile phones when driving and using ultraviolet sun-beds would fall outside Article 34 altogether.[57] In a broadly similar manner, Gormley rejects any suggestion that the Court introduced a *de minimis* exception for use restrictions, but agrees that use restrictions similar to those mentioned by Oliver would not be caught by Article 34 because of the *Krantz* case law.[58]

In my opinion, AG Kokott in *Mickelsson* was right to argue that a literal application of the *Dassonville* formula, however, risks entailing an unreasonably

[54] Para 28 in *Mickelsson* and broadly similarly para 32 in *Trucks*.

[55] Para 57 in *Trailers*, para 27 in *Mickelsson*, and para 31 in *Trucks* respectively. See similarly Case C-265/06, *Commission v Portugal*, ECLI:EU:C:2008:210.

[56] See Sect. 5.1.

[57] Oliver 2011, pp. 1456–1457 and 1467.

[58] Gormley 2010, pp. 1599 and 1624–1626.

broad delimitation of what restrictions on use constitute measures of equivalent effect.[59] On that basis, it is suggested that national measures which merely limit to some extent the general usefulness of a product, and thereby have some potential effect on imports, should not be caught by Article 34. Rather, the threshold should be placed fairly high: Article 34 should apply only where all, or nearly all, normal uses of the good in question are excluded, and imports are therefore likely to be quite severely affected.[60]

Support for this suggestion can be found in the Court's own approach to national rules restricting some, but not all, of several purposes for which a good may be used: in *Trailers*, the Court refused to accept the existence of a trade restriction with regard to an Italian rule that prohibited motorcycles from towing trailers not specially designed for towing behind motorcycles, but equally intended to be towed by automobiles or other types of vehicles. Admittedly, the Court did not exclude explicitly that a restriction could persist even if there was still room for some legal use. It merely noted that the Commission had adduced no proof that the Italian rules hindered access to the market for that type of trailer. It is thus not clear how the Court would have reacted if the Commission had shown that the great majority of such trailers were in fact, on other markets, bought with a view to being towed by motorcycles.

Finally, some indications can be found in the above-mentioned case in *Commission v. Portugal* concerning tinted film on car windows, where the Court held that a minor exception to a general rule prohibiting the use of a product for the purpose for which it has been designed was not sufficient to remove the prohibition from the ambit of Article 28.[61] Similarly, in *Commission v Greece*, concerning a prohibition on the installation and operation of certain games of chance on all public or private premises apart from casinos, the Court indicated that it will not be enough to escape Article 28 EC that the product is allowed for a very restricted group of potential buyers.[62] Although both those ruling predate *Trailers* and *Mickelsson*, it is submitted that they are still good law as to the threshold they lay down.

---

[59] Similarly Prete 2008, p. 141.

[60] See also Weatherill 2012, p. 542, according to whom the restriction should be 'considerable'.

[61] Case C-265/06, *Commission v Portugal*, ECLI:EU:C:2008:210.

[62] Case C-65/05, *Commission v Greece*, ECLI:EU:C:2006:673. Case C-142/09, *Lahousse*, ECLI:EU:C:2010:694, concerned a general prohibition on the sale or use of equipment designed to increase the power and/or speed of mopeds and, therefore, obviously constituted a measure of equivalent effect. In Case C-443/10, *Bonnarde*, ECLI:EU:C:2011:641 the Court seems to imply that Article 34 TFEU may encompass rules that 'may influence the behaviour of consumers and, consequently, affect the access of those [products] … to the market' of the regulating State'. The case did not, however, concern use restrictions and should probably not be read to imply that any use restriction having a slight impact on consumer behaviour constituted a trade restriction.

References

Barnard C (2001) Fitting the remaining pieces in the goods and persons jigsaw. 26 ELRev: 35
Davies G (2014) The Court's jurisprudence on free movement of goods: Pragmatic presumptions, not philosophical principles. European Journal of Consumer Law 2: 25
Enchelmaier S (2007) The ECJ's Recent Case Law on the Free Movement of Goods: Movement in All Sorts of Directions. 26 YEL: 115
Gormley L (2007) The Definition of Measures Having Equivalent Effect. In: Arnull A et al (eds) Continuity and EU Law: Essays in Honour of Sir Francis Jacobs. Oxford University Press, Oxford, p 189
Gormley L (2008) Silver Threads Among the Gold ... 50 Years of the Free Movement of Goods. 31 Fordham Int'l L.J: 1637
Gormley L (2010) Free Movement of Goods and their Use – What is the Use of it? 33 Fordham Int'l L.J:.1589
Horsley T (2009) Anyone for Keck? 46 CMLRev: 2001
Lianos I (2014) In Memoriam Keck, The Reformation of the EU Law on the Free Movement of Goods. CLES Research Paper Series, 5: 24
Moore S (1994) Quantitative restrictions and measures having equivalent effect: Re-visiting the limits of Article 30 EEC. 19 ELRev: 195
O'Keeffe D, Bavasso A (2000) Four Freedoms, One Market and National Competence. In: Andenas M, Fairgrieve D (eds) In Search of a Dividing Line. Liber Amicorum in Honour of Lord Slynn of Hadley, vol. 1. Kluwer Law International, Alphen aan den Rijn/New York, p 541
Oliver P (1999a) Some Further Reflections on the Scope of Articles 28–30 (ex. 30-36) EC. 36 CMLRev: 783
Oliver P (1999b) Goods and Services: Two Freedoms Compared. In: Dony M, de Walsche A (eds) Mélanges en l'honneur de Michel Waelbroeck, Vol. 2. Bruylant, Brussels, p 1377
Oliver P (2010) Oliver on Free Movement of Goods in the European Union, 5th edn. Hart, Oxford/Portland, Oregon.
Oliver P (2011) Of Trailers and Jet-Skis: Is the Case Law on Article 34 TFEU Hurtling in a New Direction? 33 Fordham Int'l L.J.: 1423
Pecho P (2009) Good-Bye Keck? A Comment on the Remarkable Judgment in Commission v Italy, C-110/05. 36 LIEI: 257
Prete L (2008) Of Motorcycle Trailers and Personal Watercrafts: The Battle over Keck. 35 LIEI: 133
Reich N (1994) The November Revolution of the European Court of Justice: Keck, Meng and Audi Revisited. 31 CMLRev: 459
Snell J (2002) Goods and Services in EC Law: A Study of the Relationship between the Freedoms. Oxford University Press, Oxford
Snell J (2010) The notion of market access: A concept or a slogan? 47 CMLRev 437
Spaventa E (2009) Leaving Keck Behind? The Free Movement of Goods after the Rulings in Commission v Italy and Mickelsson and Roos. 34 ELRev: 914
Straetmans G (2002) Case C-405/98 Konsumentombudsmannen (KO) v Gourmet International Products AB (GIP). 39 CMLRev: 1407
Weatherill S (1996) After Keck: Some Thoughts on How to Clarify the Clarification. 33 CMLRev: 885
Weatherill S (2012) Free Movement of Goods. ICLQ vol. 61, p 541
Wennerås P, Moen K (2010) Selling Arrangements, Keeping Keck. 35 ELRev 387
White E (1989) In Search of the limits to Article 30 of the EEC Treaty. 26 CMLRev: 235

Part II
Justifications and Proportionality

Chapter 6
Justifications for Restrictions to Free Movement: Towards a Single Normative Framework?

Vassilis Hatzopoulos

Abstract In the vast majority of internal market cases a restriction is readily identified, and it is at the level of justification that the basic judicial choices operate. This is done either by virtue of 'objective justifications' or by the much more limited list of express exceptions foreseen by the Treaty. These two 'systems' of justifications have been developed in partial contradiction with one another in terms of the types of measures upheld and the *ex ante/ex post* application of the justification. Throughout the years, however, the practical differences as well as the normative underpinnings of the two systems have been greatly confused. So much so that, nowadays, it seems more exact from a positivist view and more desirable from a normative point of view to view all the justification grounds as parts of a single normative framework. The proposed framework would be 'single' in two ways, i.e. in the sense it would/should apply (a) to all the fundamental freedoms alike (material unicity) and (b) to both discriminatory and non-discriminatory measures (restriction unicity). The present chapter exposes the incoherencies and inconsistencies of the current situation, then explains why the conditions are now ripe for a new unified approach, and finally speculates on the ways such a single justification framework could be affected by other, neighbouring, EU rules.

Keywords Overriding reasons of general interest · Objective justifications · Express exceptions · Free movement · Economic justifications · Proportionality

V. Hatzopoulos (✉)
Democritus University of Thrace, Komotini, Greece
e-mail: vasshatz@socadm.duth.gr

V. Hatzopoulos
College of Europe, Bruges, Belgium

V. Hatzopoulos
University of Nottingham, Nottingham, UK

V. Hatzopoulos
Lykavittou 39-41, 106 72 Athens, Greece

M. Andenas et al. (eds.), *The Reach of Free Movement*,
DOI 10.1007/978-94-6265-195-1_6

Contents

6.1 Introduction 132
6.2 Deconstruction 133
6.2.1 Confusion Between Express Exceptions and Objective Justifications 133
6.2.2 Inconsistency as to the Legal Effects of Express Exceptions and Objective Justifications 136
6.3 Reconstruction 139
6.3.1 A Category Necessary for the Development of a Coherent Framework for the Internal Market 139
6.3.2 A Category Applicable on Non-Economic and (Macro) Economic Measures 141
6.3.3 A Single Category Moderated by a Variable Proportionality Control 142
6.4 In Perspective 146
6.4.1 Categorisation of Interests Pursued Through ORPIs 146
6.4.2 Ongoing EU Measures and/or Policies Affecting ORPIs 148
6.4.3 Alternative Theories and Means for Allowing Member States to Pursue ORPIs 150
6.5 Conclusion 153
References 155

6.1 Introduction

There is a great paradox with legal doctrine relating to the internal market: while in the cases decided by the Court of Justice of the EU (CJEU) a restriction to the fundamental freedoms is almost immediately identified[1] and the question then revolves around its possible justification, the few tens of pages of scholarly comment dedicated to the latter hardly compare with the thousands of pages analysing the former! This discrepancy between judicial reality and doctrinal approach holds as much true in English[2] as in French literature.[3] The ambition of the present chapter is to bring to the surface the various elements, both positivist and normative, of the different justification techniques followed by the Court, try to identify the coherences and inconsistencies thereto and put forward a single normative framework underpinning all means of justifying national measures which restrict free movement. The proposed framework would be 'single' in two ways, i.e. in the sense it would/should apply (a) to all the fundamental freedoms alike (material unicity) and (b) to both discriminatory and non-discriminatory measures (restriction unicity).

---

[1] Indeed in a quantitative study I conducted few years ago on the Court's case law in the field of services for the period from 1958 to (June 2009) I found that out of 466 measures which had been brought before the CJEU, only 19 had been cleared as being completely innocuous, while all the remaining have been examined under the spectre of their justification; see Hatzopoulos 2012a, Chapter 4.

[2] Fernandez Martin and O'Leary 2002, pp. 163–95.

[3] Hatzopoulos 1998, pp. 191–236; Martin 1998, pp. 261–318; and more recently Bertrand 2012, pp. 6–12; Hatzopoulos 2013, pp. 205–229.

From a positivist point of view the existence of 'material unicity' in relation to *justifications* supposes that some kind of unicity has beforehand been established in relation to *restrictions* to all freedoms; a debate still open.[4] From an analytical and normative point of view, however, the two issues correspond to distinct concepts and raise different questions.

A note on terminology may be useful at this point. There are two series of justifications for restrictions to the fundamental freedoms. On the one hand there are the exceptions foreseen by the Treaty, also called 'express exceptions'. On the other hand there is a long series of judge-made justifications. These have been called different names, but in the most recent years the terms mostly used are 'overriding reasons of public interest' (or ORPIs),[5] or 'objective justifications'; the two will be used here interchangeably.

In order to expose my thesis, i.e. the need for a single justification framework for all freedoms and all measures, I will first try to expose all the problems and inconsistencies of the current situation (Sect. 6.2), then explain why the conditions are now ripe for a new unified approach (Sect. 6.3), and finally project on the ways such a single justification framework could be affected by other, neighbouring, EU rules (Sect. 6.4). Hence, this chapter will be presented in terms of 'Deconstruction' of the current situation, 'Reconstruction' of a new framework and 'In Perspective' of the ways this framework could work.

6.2 Deconstruction

The current situation, whereby different grounds justify supposedly different kinds of restrictions, need not be actively 'deconstructed'; it is enough that its confused state and the inconsistencies associated thereto be put into perspective. Such inconsistencies are recurrent both at the level of distinguishing the grounds which serve as express exceptions and as objective justifications, respectively (Sect. 6.2.1), and at the level of their legal effects (Sect. 6.2.2).

6.2.1 Confusion Between Express Exceptions and Objective Justifications

Objective justifications have been recognised by the Court, starting with *Cassis de Dijon* and (before it) *Van Binsbergen*, in order to offer Member States flexibility in

---

[4] See, among many, the various contributions in the volume edited by Dubout and de la Motte 2013; see also Tryfonidou 2010, pp. 36–56; and Caro de Suza 2014, pp. 499–519.

[5] A term 'consecrated' by the EP and Council Directive 2006/123 on the free provision of services [2006] OJ L 376/36, Article 4(8).

protecting legitimate interests not foreseen by the Treaty. The relatively short list of express exceptions has been complemented by a much longer—and open-ended—list of objective justifications. A summary list of the recognised objective justifications (in the field of services) may be found in Article 4 of the Services Directive; more recent justifications with references to the relevant case law (not restricted to services case law) are proposed by the various textbooks and commentaries.[6] Given the fact that objective justifications greatly outnumber express exceptions and that they have been developed by the Court itself, it comes as no surprise that the Court systematically prefers judge-made to treaty-based justifications.[7] This finding, however, needs to be relativised in view of the way the two categories are being brought together by the Court, the legislator and even the EU Treaties.

6.2.1.1 In the Case Law

The Court has been blurring the distinction between the two categories of justifications in several ways. For one thing, the Court has recognised as ORPIs those express exceptions which are available in the free movement of goods but unavailable in the other freedoms. Hence, public morality has been recognised as an autonomous judge-made justification (rather than as an extension of public order) in *Schindler*.[8] Similarly, the protection of health and life of humans has been given the status of an ORPI in the patient mobility cases.[9] The protection of cultural heritage also has been recognised as an objective reason in the Tourist Guides saga.[10] Last but not least the protection of intellectual property rights has also been given the status of an ORPI in *Coditel v Cine Vog*.[11] In this way, while it is true that all the interests enumerated in Article 36 TFEU are also protected in the other freedoms, it is also true that they are given a different legal status (as ORPIs instead of express exceptions): a difference which does blur the supposed distinction between the two categories.

---

[6] See e.g. Barnard 2011, pp. 149–192 and 479–518; Hatzopoulos 2012a, pp. 146–178.

[7] In a survey of all the services cases between 1958 and July 2009, I was able to identify 283 cases concerning some 447 restrictive measures, half of which had been held to be justified. From the 220 justified measures only 47 had been upheld on the basis of some treaty-based express exception, while the remaining was justified by some objective justification; see Hatzopoulos 2012a, pp. 146–178.

[8] Case C-275/92, *H.M. Customs and Excise v Schindler*, ECLI:EU:C:1994:119.

[9] See for instance Case C-157/99, *Smits and Peerbooms*, ECLI:EU:C:2001:404; Case C-372/04, *Watts*, ECLI:EU:C:2006:325. For the Court's ambivalent approach in respect of the justifications used in these cases see below the text accompanying n. 14.

[10] See for the first of a series of cases, Case C-154/89, *Commission v France*, ECLI:EU:C:1991:76, Case C-180/89, *Commission v Italy*, ECLI:EU:C:1991:78 and Case C-198/89, *Commission v Greece*, ECLI:EU:C:1991:79 etc.

[11] Case C-62/79, *Coditel v Ciné Vog Films*, ECLI:EU:C:1980:84.

Further, the Court occasionally blurs the distinction between express exceptions and ORPIs without any apparent reason. Hence, in the Greek Online Games case, the Court held that the protection of public morality, public order and public security 'considerations, which must be taken together, concern the protection of the recipients of the service and, more generally, of consumers, as well as the maintenance of order in society, and those objectives are amongst those which may be regarded as overriding reasons relating to the public interest'.[12]

A third ground of confusion arises in relation to public health which, although expressly foreseen in the Treaty, has occasionally been qualified as an ORPI.[13] More confusingly still, in the patients' rights cases, health protection has been used interchangeably with the ORPI of securing the financial equilibrium of social security systems.[14]

Funding social security systems and public services in general is a recognised ORPI which, however, is very close in logic to Article 106(2) TFEU and the relevant case law of the Court, notably in cases *Corbeau, Almelo* and *Glöckner*.[15]

Last but not least the protection of vital state interests (e.g. the continuous supply of oil), as well as the provision of basic public services (e.g. planning for health facilities, securing the viability of social security systems) which are recognized as ORPIs, may also qualify as the pure exercise of official authority and be altogether excluded from the Treaty's scope of application;[16] another fine line need be drawn between these two legal qualifications.

In view of all the above it becomes clear that there is very little certainty as regards the precise content and scope of application of ORPIs and their relationship with other Treaty rules having the same or similar effect, i.e. to give Member States leeway to deviate from the fundamental freedoms.

6.2.1.2 In Secondary Legislation—The Services Directive

The fact that the Services Directive has been the object of fierce negotiations between the co-legislators has clearly marked its content and stands for the several

[12] Case C-65/05, *Commission v Greece (online games)*, ECLI:EU:C:2006:673, para 33.

[13] See case C-788/79, *Gilli and Andres*, ECLI:EU:C:1980:171; Case C-130/80, *Kelderman*, ECLI:EU:C:1981:49; confusion dissipated already in joined cases C-1/90 and 176/90, *Aragonesa de Publicidad Exterior SA and Publivía SAE v Departamento de Sanidad y Seguridad Social de la Generalitat de Cataluña*, ECLI:EU:C:1991:327, paras 12–13.

[14] Case C-158/96, *Köhll*, ECLI:EU:C:1998:171; *Smits and Peerbooms,* above n. 9; Case C-385/99, *Müller-Fauré and E.E.M. van Riet*, ECLI:EU:C:2003:270; *Watts*, above n. 9; See also Case C-262/02, *Commission v France (alcoholic beverages advertisement)*, ECLI:EU:C:2004:431.

[15] Case C-320/91, *Corbeau*, ECLI:EU:C:1993:198; Case C-393/92, *Gemeente Almelo ea v Energiebedrijf IJsselmij*, ECLI:EU:C:1994:171; Case C-475/99, *Ambulanz Glöckner*, ECLI:EU:C:2001:577.

[16] Case C-70/95, *Sodemare SA ea*, ECLI:EU:C:1997:301; Case C-355/00, *Freskot AE*, ECLI:EU:C:2003:298.

inconsistencies and contradictions it contains. The definition and function of ORPIs is one of those. First, in Article 4 the Directive defines ORPIs as 'reasons recognised as such in the case law of the Court of Justice, including the following grounds: public policy; public security; public safety; public health; preserving the financial equilibrium of the social security system; the protection of consumers [etc.]'. Hence, the Directive starts its definition of ORPIs by listing the express exceptions foreseen by the Treaty! Further, Article 16 of the Directive foresees that Member States may justify restrictions to the free provision of services for four reasons: the three express exceptions (i.e. public order, public security and public health) and the protection of the environment. Therefore, both at the level of the definitions and at the level of their actual function within the Directive the legislature seems oblivious to the distinction between treaty-based and judge-made justifications.

6.2.1.3 In the Treaties: The Uncertain Effect of the 'Mainstreaming' of Various ORPIs

Since the entry into force of the Lisbon Treaty several ORPIs have made their way into primary law, in particular in the horizontal clauses of the TFEU 'having general application' (Articles 7–17). Henceforth the promotion of employment, social protection, education, training and human health (Article 9), the protection of the environment (Article 11) and of consumers (Article 12), animal welfare (Article 13), the funding of public services (Article 14) and the protection of personal data are supposed to constitute guiding principles in all EU policies. While it is unlikely that these 'horizontal' Treaty provisions produce any direct effect, it is unclear how the selective 'constitutionalisation' of these ORPIs is going to impact on the consistency of this legal category; in other words are these to become a first class category of ORPIs, are they to be assimilated to the other express exceptions or are they to acquire a status of their own.

6.2.2 Inconsistency as to the Legal Effects of Express Exceptions and Objective Justifications

6.2.2.1 Exclude or Justify

The 'invention' of ORPIs by the Court in *Van Binsbergen* and, more explicitly, in *Cassis de Dijon* has immediately raised the question of their precise legal function: were they to be considered as an extension of the list of Treaty-based exceptions, thereby operating as *ex post* justifications of national measures previously qualified as restrictive? Or were they to apply *ex ante* as part of the very definition of 'restriction', hence taking the measure concerned outside the scope of the Treaty freedoms altogether? The latter option seemed to find support in the early case law of the Court relayed by the dominant legal doctrine of the time.[17] The Commission itself in its *Cassis de Dijon Communication* made reference to 'national provisions which are *admissible* under the criteria set by the Court'.[18] Indeed, this approach seems justified on two grounds, one more formalistic and one more substantial. From a formalistic point of view, it would be inappropriate to admit an open-ended list of exceptions to be added to the few ones expressly foreseen by the Treaty. From a substantial point of view it has been convincingly argued that measures which genuinely pursue some objective interest are not protectionist and should not be qualified as restrictions at all.[19]

This early case law, however, is not pursued in a systematic way. In several of the patient's rights cases the Court treats ORPIs together and interchangeably with express exceptions, as *ex post* justifications.[20] In the ongoing gambling saga, however, the Court seems to be embracing the precise opposite view from the one followed in its early case law. In these more recent cases the Court states that 'it is necessary to consider to what extent the restriction at issue in the main proceedings may be *allowed* as a *derogation expressly provided* for by Articles 45 EC and 46 EC, applicable in this area by virtue of Article 55 EC, or *justified,* in accordance with the case-law of the Court, by *overriding reasons* in the public interest'.[21] But one may not talk of a systematic reversal of the Court's previous position since at the same time the Court still admits that 'a restriction on the freedom of establishment and the freedom to provide services may be *justified* where it serves *overriding requirements relating to the public interest*'.[22] More alarmingly, it occurs that the Court in one and the same judgment makes one statement and its precise opposite. Hence in *Dickinger and Ömer* the Court starts by stating that 'such a restriction of the freedom to provide services may be *allowed* as a *derogation expressly* provided for in Articles 45 and 46 … or *justified* in accordance with the case-law of the Court *by overriding reasons in the public interest*'; before admitting that the requirement in question is 'a discriminatory restriction which can therefore be *justified* only on one of the grounds set out in Article 46 EC [i.e. *express exception*]!'[23]

---

[17] Mattera 1990, pp. 274–5.

[18] Communication from the Commission concerning the consequences of the judgment given by the Court of Justice on 20 February 1979 in case C-120/78 ('Cassis de Dijon') [1980] OJ C 256/2, emphasis added.

[19] See, among many, Regan 2001, pp. 1853–902; 2006, pp. 951–88.

[20] See e.g. *Müller-Fauré*, above n. 14, para 68 where the Court reasons that '*justification* is based on an exception laid down by the Treaty *or* indeed on an overriding general-interest reason', emphasis added.

[21] See e.g. Case C-42/07, *Liga Portuguesa*, ECLI:EU:C:2008:560, para 55.

[22] Case C-518/06, *Commission v Italy (car insurance)*, ECLI:EU:C:2008:477, para 72, emphasis added.

[23] Case C-347/09, *Dickinger and Ömer*, ECLI:EU:C:2011:582, paras 42 and 79, respectively, emphasis added.

In view of all the above it may securely be assumed that the Court is rather agnostic as to the doctrinal debate concerning the legal effects of ORPIs, hence denying the importance of the distinction between them and the Treaty-based exceptions.

6.2.2.2 Discriminatory or Just Non-Discriminatory Measures

If the discussion about the *ex ante/ex post* application of ORPIs presents limited practical interest, the same is not true for the other unclear point stemming from the Court's case law, i.e. the question whether ORPIs can serve to uphold only non-discriminatory, or also discriminatory measures. On this question also the Court has not been consistent.

In many cases the Court treats together express exceptions and ORPIs without distinguishing whether the measure concerned is discriminatory or not.[24] In other cases, the Court applies ORPIs alone without ever asking the question of the discriminatory nature of the measures concerned.[25] In some cases, the Court disguises discriminatory measures into non-discriminatory in order to uphold them with some ORPI.[26] Last but not least, there are cases where ORPIs are used to uphold openly discriminatory measures.[27]

The orthodox approach, however, inaugurated with *Van Binsbergen* and *Cassis de Dijon*, and reinstated in recent case law allows only non-discriminatory measures to be saved by ORPIs.[28] Such approach seems justified for at least two reasons, one historic and one of substance. Given that ORPIs have been 'invented' in the above mentioned cases in order to make it up for the risk that non-discriminatory national measures may be struck down, it would be logic that only non-discriminatory measures be upheld by virtue of ORPIs. Substance-wise, given that discriminatory measures are, by nature and by principle, against the idea of an internal market, they should only be upheld by virtue of the few express exceptions foreseen in the Treaty.

---

[24] See e.g. health cases more representatively in *Köhll*, above n. 14; *Smits and Peerbooms*, above n. 9; *Müller-Fauré*, above n. 14; *Watts*, above n. 9; See also *Commission v France (alcoholic beverages advertisement)*, above n. 14.

[25] Case C-250/95, *Futura Participations SA & Singer v Administration des Contributions*, ECLI:EU:C:1997:239; Case C-118/96, *Safir v Skattemyndigheten i Dalarnas Län*, ECLI:EU:C:1998:170; see also *Köhll*, above n. 14.

[26] Case C-2/90, *Commission v Belgium (Walloon waste)*, ECLI:EU:C:1992:310.

[27] Case C-204/90, *Bachmann v Belgian State*, ECLI:EU:C:1992:35.

[28] Case C-33/74, *van Binsbergen*, ECLI:EU:C:1974:131; Case C-120/78, *Rewe-Zentral AG v Bundesmonopolverwaltung für Branntwein (Cassis de Dijon)*, ECLI:EU:C:1979:42; and more recently Case C-341/05, *Laval un Partneri Ltd*, ECLI:EU:C:2007:809, para 117; Case C-219/08, *Commission v Belgium (posted workers)*, ECLI:EU:C:2009:599; Case C-153/08, *Commission v Spain (gambling tax)*, ECLI:EU:C:2009:618.

The above orthodoxy, however, should be relativized in at least four ways. First, as already explained, the distinction between discriminatory and non-discriminatory measures is not systematically pursued by the Court. Second, the experience of over 50 years of internal market has shown that there are some legitimate interests that may only be pursued by discriminatory measures. In such circumstances the Court either neglects the existence of discrimination,[29] or, in a more sophisticated manner, plays with the principle that discrimination ceases to exist where there are objective differences between the situations caught by the different rules.[30] Third, the fact that the concept of discrimination is itself open-ended and that there are as many definitions thereof as there are authors writing about it, does not help clarify the situation. Last but not least, it has been explained above that the very distinction between express exceptions and ORPIs is not crystal clear either.

Summing up, it may be said that even if, as the most recent case law seems to suggest, the Court did insist on the principle that ORPIs may only justify non-discriminatory measures, the fluidity of the concept of discrimination itself would prevent the emergence of a clear and systematic framework.

6.3 Reconstruction

Above in Sect. 6.2, it has been shown that the current situation is pregnant with inconsistencies and uncertainties. This, however, does not mean that the existence of objective justifications should be dropped altogether. On the contrary, this legal category is, nowadays, as necessary as ever. Indeed, it is hereby argued that the conditions are ripe for a single justification framework to emerge, embracing both express exceptions and judge-made ORPIs.

6.3.1 A Category Necessary for the Development of a Coherent Framework for the Internal Market

ORPIs have been recognised in the very same judgments in which the Court introduced the principle of mutual recognition—and as compensation thereto: on the one hand the Court establishes that non-discriminatory national measures are liable to be struck down merely for restricting the internal market, but on the other hand it acknowledges that Member States have the right to protect ORPIs by means of restrictive measures. Hence the principle of mutual recognition, designed to

[29] As e.g. in the case of *Walloon waste*, above n. 26.

[30] See e.g. joined Cases C-197/11 and 203/11, *Libertao v Flemish Government*, ECLI:EU:C:2013:288.

make it up for the absence of any harmonisation,[31] may be set aside if the same ORPIs are not protected—or are not protected in some comparable way—by the home State.[32] Hence, the lack of harmonisation may, depending on the circumstances (i.e. the level of ORPI protection), serve either as the trigger or as the tombstone of the principle of mutual recognition. Conversely, Member States cannot invoke the protection of ORPIs when such interests are already protected at the EU level; ORPIs are subject to the principle of pre-emption, in the sense that Member States lose the right to pursue interests which are already protected by some harmonised EU rule.[33] This idea, already clearly expressed in the founding cases (*Van Binsbergen* and *Cassis de Dijon*) has been repeatedly confirmed ever since.[34]

Today, there is no doubt that the rules on the fundamental freedoms may be infringed by non-discriminatory measures. This idea, already expressed in the founding cases and constantly confirmed by the Court[35] has not been easily embraced by legal scholarship. Next to the authors who, on the face of wording to the opposite, tried to show that all the case law was in fact based on some kind of discrimination,[36] others questioned the legitimacy of the EU to censor non protectionist national measures.[37] These voices have been echoed by the violent reversal by the Court in *Keck and Mithouard* and,[38] in a more thoughtful way, by Advocate General Jacobs in his famous Opinion in *Leclerc-Siplec* where he proposed a *de minimis* test.[39] These same preoccupations have nourished other alternative ways of limiting the reach of the freedoms, such as the 'remoteness test';[40] nurtured by the evaporation of mutual trust under the ongoing crisis conjecture,[41] they have ended up in the brutal rejection of the principle of mutual recognition in the recent gambling saga.[42]

---

[31] For a more thorough analysis on the role of the principle of mutual recognition in services see Hatzopoulos 1999; and more recently see Hatzopoulos 2010, pp. 48–93.

[32] For a clear expression of this idea see *Dickinger and Ömer*, above n. 23, paras 96–98.

[33] Cross 1992, p. 447.

[34] For example in regard to goods see Case C-216/84, *Commission v France (milk substitutes)*, ECLI:EU:C:1988:81, para 6; in regard to establishment see Case C-71/76, *Thieffry*, ECLI:EU:C:1977:65, para 16; in regard to services see Case C-14/96, *Paul Denuit*, ECLI:EU:C:1997:260.

[35] See for the most prominent expressions of this idea: Case C-76/90, *Säger*, ECLI:EU:C:1991:331; Case C-415/93, *Bosman*, ECLI:EU:C:1995:463; Case C-55/94, *Gebhard*, ECLI:EU:C:1995:411.

[36] Marenco 1984, pp. 291–364.

[37] White 1989, pp. 235–80.

[38] Joined cases C-267 and 268/91, *Keck and Mithouard*, ECLI:EU:C:1993:905.

[39] See Opinion of AG Jacobs in Case C-412/93, *Leclerc-Siplec v TF1 and M6*, ECLI:EU:C:1994:393.

[40] See e.g. Case C-379/92, *Peralta*, ECLI:EU:C:1994:296; Case C-134/03, *Viacom II*, ECLI:EU:C:2005:94 and Case C-293/10 *Stark v DAS*, ECLI:EU:C:2011:355.

[41] Barnard 2009a, pp. 575–606 and Snell 2010, pp. 437–72.

[42] *Dickinger and Ömer*, above n. 23.

This notwithstanding, the idea that non-discriminatory measures may violate the freedoms, still holds good. Especially so, in view of the attachment recently displayed by the Court to the 'market access' criterion, both in the field of goods[43] and services.[44] Although the actual content of this principle is not all that clear,[45] what is clear is that it needs be tempered by a coherent framework allowing Member States to protect/promote their vital interests. Such framework should apply to all national measures, discriminatory and non-discriminatory alike. Under this perspective the emergence of a single justification framework would allow for a coherent and unitary definition of 'market access' without the need for other, unpredictable, mitigating theories.

6.3.2 A Category Applicable on Non-Economic and (Macro) Economic Measures

Such a category would serve to uphold measures of both economic and non-economic nature. The current situation shows towards this direction, but, again, is pregnant with uncertainty. The formal position of the Court is that ORPIs may not justify measures of pursuing an economic objective. Reality, however, is much more nuanced. In fact the Court follows three courses whereby it allows Member States the pursuance of economic aims[46]: (a) it interprets restrictions restrictively in order to avoid altogether the question of justification,[47] (b) it associates the economic objective with some express exception (such as e.g., public health),[48] (c) it applies ORPIs to economic measures without admitting it.[49] In some circumstances, on the other hand, the Court puts much more weight on the economic objectives of some measures and ignores other, as legitimate, objectives thus leaving them without any protection.[50]

The case law, however, may be coherently accounted for in the following way. Objectives of a macro-economic nature, having structural effects on the market, are accepted as ORPIs; examples would constitute the provision of basic goods and/or

---

[43] Case C-110/05, *Commission v Italy (trailers)*, ECLI:EU:C:2009:66; Case C-142/05, *Mickelsson and Roos*, ECLI:EU:C:2009:336, para 28; as well as case C-265/06, *Commission v Portugal (tinted windows)*, ECLI:EU:C:2008:210.

[44] *Commission v Italy (car insurance)* above n. 22.

[45] On this recent case law see Derlén and Lindholm 2010, pp. 191–231; Barnard 2009b, pp. 288–90; Spaventa 2009, pp. 914–32; Gormley 2010, pp. 1589–628; Oliver 2010, pp. 1423–71; Davies 2010, pp. 671–704; Sibony 2012, pp. 323–342; Fromont and Verdure 2011, pp. 717–48.

[46] In regard to the three trends described, for further exploration see Snell 2005, p. 37; for an updated and different view of the issue, see Oliver 2016, pp. 147–75.

[47] *Sodemare SA ea*, above n. 16.

[48] *Smits and Peerbooms* above n. 9.

[49] *Köhll* above n. 14 and 24.

[50] Case C-398/95, *SETTG v Ypourgos Erasias,* ECLI:EU:C:1997:282.

services,[51] the coherence of a fiscal system[52] and the protection of social security systems.[53] On the opposite end are not-accepted, micro-economic, conjectural objectives, such as the satisfaction of the demands of a certain profession.[54]

Express exceptions also follow the same logic: they primarily concern non-economic objectives, but when economic concerns may be connected with public order, public security and public health, these will typically be of a macro, rather than a micro, nature.

Hence, also under this perspective the two justification pathways seem to converge into one single framework.

6.3.3 A Single Category Moderated by a Variable Proportionality Control

Inherent to the application of any exception to a general rule, is the principle of proportionality. For objective justifications this stems directly from the logic of the Treaty. 'if it is accepted that free movement goes beyond equal treatment and requires freedom of access to the market, then […] proportionality is elevated to the principal criterion for determining the dividing line between lawful and unlawful barriers to trade'.[55]

6.3.3.1 Standard Proportionality Control

The precise content of the proportionality test is still hotly debated in EU scholarship. What is certain is that it contains two prongs, of the *appropriateness* of the measure for attaining the set objective and of the *necessity* of the level of restriction imposed.[56] Under this two-tier proportionality control, solemnly expressed in *Gebhard* and repetitively thereafter,[57] the Court does not question the pursued objective itself, but merely checks that the measures adopted are

[51] Case C-72/83, *Campus Oil*, ECLI:EU:C:1984:256.

[52] Case C-204/90, *Bachmann v Belgian State*, ECLI:EU:C:1992:35.

[53] Case C-422/01, *Skandia*, EU: C:2003:380.

[54] *SETTG v Ypourgos Ergasias*, above n. 50.

[55] Tridimas 2006, p. 196.

[56] Ibid., p. 139, where reference is made to further jurisprudence.

[57] Case C-55/94, *Gebhard v Consiglio dell'Ordine degli Avvocati e Procuratori di Milano*, ECLI: EU:C:1995:411, para 37.

appropriate for its attainment. It is a control 'internal' to the legal order concerned, whereby national measures are accounted against national regulatory objectives.

What is disputed is whether a third prong, that of the *stricto sensu* proportionality, should also be performed by the Court.[58] This third branch would allow the Court to weigh the objective of the national measure against the corresponding/antagonistic EU objective; it is an 'external' control, whereby national regulatory objectives are counted against EU objectives. Such test has been carried out by the Court in few occasions: in *Säger* the Court held that the protection of patent holders (pursued by the German rule) could not overtake the internal market objective;[59] in *Mazzoleni* and *Portugaia Construçoes* the Court held that the objective of equal pay for posted and domestic workers should be measured against the administrative and economic burden that this would represent for the employers (service providers under Article 56 TFEU);[60] and in *Viking and Laval* the Court directly measured the value of collective action against that of free movement.[61] If such an external proportionality control were to be generalized, it would systematically frustrate national interests which do not square well with EU policies. It would also lead to regulatory competition as it would favour EU-compatible national regulations over other, less compatible ones. By the same token the role of the judiciary, national and EU, would be significantly increased over that of national legislatures.

Conscious of the above dangers the CJEU (a) typically avoids this part of the proportionality test[62] and (b) tries to alleviate the relevant fears by stating that "the need for and proportionality of the relevant provisions … must be assessed solely by reference to the objectives pursued by the competent authorities of the Member State concerned and the level of protection which they seek to ensure".[63] Most importantly (c) the Court systematically uses the 'coherence and systematicity' test, often a substitute to the true proportionality test. The question whether a national restrictive measure pursues the stated objective in a 'coherent and systematic' manner allows the Court to appreciate the way in which the measure at stake creates synergies or, in the contrary, collides, with other relevant national measures; in the former case a genuine policy pattern will be assumed, while in the latter the isolated measure will be seen as inappropriate to attain the stated objective and, thus, disproportionate. This test introduced by the Court in *Gambelli* in order to dismiss Italy's allegation that it was not delivering any new authorisations in an effort to

---

[58] See, among many, Snell 2000, pp. 50–7.

[59] Above n. 35.

[60] Case C-165/98, *Mazzoleni and ISA*, ECLI:EU:C:2001:162; Case C-164/99, *Portugaia Construçoes Lda*, ECLI:EU:C:2002:40.

[61] Case C-438/05, *The International Transport Workers' Federation and the Finnish Seamen's Union*, ECLI:EU:C:2007:772; Case C-341/05, *Laval un Partneri Ltd*, ECLI:EU:C:2007:809.

[62] Except in cases putting at stake fundamental rights, for which see Sect. 6.2.2.2.

[63] *Dickinger and Ömer*, above n. 23, para 97.

limit gambling, while at the same time the monopoly was pursuing an aggressively expansive policy.[64] The 'coherence' part of the test seems to be 'internal' into the very contested regulation (or group of regulations). In this sense it has been applied in *Hartlauer* in relation to an Austrian measure which prohibited the establishment of dental clinics while allowing new group practices having very similar characteristics;[65] and in *Dermoestetica* in relation to a Spanish regulation which prohibited the publicity of aesthetic surgery in the national press while allowing it in the local press.[66] The 'systematicity' test looks at the wider image, i.e. is external to the contested measure, and examines how this measure combines (or does not combine) with other national legislation affecting the same activity. It is this part of the test which failed the Italian legislation on gambling authorisations in *Gambelli* and its progeny.[67]

This coherence and systematicity test, either as a third prong of the wider proportionality test, or a part of the appropriateness test (i.e. the first prong of the traditional proportionality test), being internal to the national legal order concerned (a) avoids regulatory competition, (b) serves as a 'hypocrisy test' for national measures, thus uncovering protectionism[68] or at least (c) brings up regulatory deficiencies of the national regulatory systems, thus pushing forward the agenda of 'better regulation'.

6.3.3.2 Special Cases

Morality, an express exception in the field of goods and an ORPI in all other freedoms, has been invoked in cases concerning pornographic goods, prostitution, gaming and other games putting at stake human dignity.[69] In all these circumstances the Court shows extreme leniency towards national choices and its proportionality control is limited to the coherence of the measures concerned: these are held to be disproportionate only where the immoral activity is tolerated,[70] openly practiced or even encouraged[71] when practiced by nationals of the State concerned.

---

[64] Case C-243/01, *Gambelli*, ECLI:EU:C:2003:597. For this test see Mathisen 2010, pp. 1021–48.

[65] Case C-169/07, *Hartlauer*, ECLI:EU:C:2009:141.

[66] Case C-500/06, *Corporación Dermoestética SA*, ECLI:EU:C:2008:421.

[67] See *Gambelli* above n. 64; joined cases C-338, 359 and 360/04, *Placanica* e.a., ECLI:EU:C:2007:133; and more recently joined cases C-72 and 77/10, *Costa and Cifone*, ECLI:EU:C:2012:80.

[68] The term 'hypocrisy test' was introduced by AG Mengozzi in his Opinion in joined cases C-316/07, C-409–410/07 & C-358-360/07, *Stoß*, ECLI:EU:C:2010:504, para 50.

[69] For the role of public morality in the jurisprudence of the Court concerning the free movement see Catchpole and Barav 1980, pp. 1–21; Hetsch 1982, pp. 511–25; and more recently de Witte 2013, pp. 1545–78.

[70] Joined Cases C-115 and 116/81, *Adoui and Cornuaille v Belgian State*, ECLI:EU:C:1982:183.

[71] Element raised in all the judgments concerning the Italian legislation on games of chance, cited above n. 67.

Similarly, solidarity, an argument typically invoked in relation to the organisation, delivery and funding of public services, is widely admitted by the Court; rightly so, it is submitted, given that it is connected to specific economic and societal choices of each Member State. In the Court's case law solidarity has a double function, depending on how strong it is. Activities which are fundamentally impregnated by solidarity, such as compulsory insurance funds for pensions,[72] for work accidents,[73] and for agricultural risks,[74] as well as the organisation of nursing homes[75] have been held to constitute non-economic activities, thus falling altogether outside the scope of the TFEU. On the other hand, activities which do encompass solidarity but are closer to the market, such as e.g. complimentary pension funds,[76] constitute economic activities; solidarity, in these cases operates as an ORPI either in its own right or as a trigger for the application of Article 106(2) TFEU.

Thirdly, there is the question of fundamental rights; an issue of ever increasing importance in view of the binding force accorded to the EU Charter of Fundamental Rights[77] and of the intensifying dialogue between the Luxembourg and Strasbourg Courts.[78] The fact that fundamental rights may serve to block the fundamental freedoms has been recognised for the first time in *Schmidberger*, where the freedom of expression was opposed to the free movement of goods;[79] after an extensive proportionality control the Court tilted in favour of the former. It was again in favour of the fundamental right, but without carrying out any proportionality control, that the Court decided in Omega, where human dignity was opposing the free provision of services.[80] In *Viking and Laval* on the other hand, where the freedom of collective action was counted against the free provision of services, the Court carried out an extensive proportionality control but gave preference to the latter.

The above inconsistency as to the final result is made even worse by the legal qualification the Court awards to fundamental rights: while in *Omega* the fundamental right (human dignity) was held to be part of public order, in *Laval* the right at stake (collective action) was qualified as an ORPI and in *Schmidberger* the freedom of expression was treated as an exception of its own. The qualification

---

[72] Joined Cases C-159/91 and C-160/91 *Poucet and Pistre*, ECLI:EU:C:1993:63.

[73] Case C-218/00, *Cisal*, ECLI:EU:C:2002:36; Case C-350/07, *Kattner Stahlbau GmbH*, ECLI:EU:C:2009:127.

[74] *Freskot AE*, above n. 16.

[75] *Sodemare SA ea*, n. 16.

[76] Cases C-67/96, *Albany*, ECLI:EU:C:1999:430, C-115-117/97, *Brentjens*, ECLI:EU:C:1999:434, and C-219/97, *Drijvende*, ECLI:EU:C:1999:437; on these cases see Idot 1999, pp. 4–8.

[77] See *inter alia*, Von Bogdandy 2000, pp. 1307–38; Lenaerts 2000, pp. 1–25; Weuwahl and Rosas (eds) 1995; Tridimas 2006, especially Chapter 7 where further references can be found.

[78] See e.g. Douglas-Scott 2006, pp. 629–65; on a more critical tone on relations between the two legal systems and two jurisdictions see Greer and Williams 2009, pp. 462–81.

[79] Case C-112/00, *Schmidberger,* ECLI:EU:C:2003:333.

[80] Case C-36/02, *Omega*, ECLI:EU:C:2004:614.

chosen is not without incidence since in *Laval* the fact that the fundamental right was treated as an ORPI prevented it from justifying a measure held to be discriminatory. In view of the above, while it is clear that fundamental rights may be invoked to 'save' restrictive national measures, it is much less clear (a) whether they qualify as ORPIs, as express exceptions or as a special category, (b) what kind of proportionality control they are subject to and (c) whether they may serve to uphold discriminatory measures.

The above special categories notwithstanding, the proportionality test applied by the Court is increasingly clarified and well-defined—and it clearly applies indistinctively to all fundamental freedoms.

6.4 In Perspective

In order to make some projections on the way ORPIs may evolve in the coming years, it is worth identifying the basic interests pursued through this legal category (a); on the basis of this enumeration we shall then examine other EU measures or policies (b) and other EU theories (c) which may serve to pursue these same interests.

6.4.1 Categorisation of Interests Pursued Through ORPIs

There are many ways in which the various ORPIs recognised by the CJEU may be accounted for. In a quantitative study pursued some years ago, concerning the Court's case law on services during the period 1958 to mid-2009, I examined 288 cases corresponding to 466 measures, out of which 447 were held to constitute prima facie restrictions to Article 56. From these only 47 were justified on the basis of some express exception, while the vast majority of the others were justified on the basis of some ORPI. All these objective justifications may be brought together under the following headings: (1) environment, (2) social (security, dumping, health etc.), (3) morality, (4) fairness of transactions/fraud, (5) protection (of service recipients and consumers, creditors etc.), (6) quality, (7) intellectual property, (8) heritage/culture and pluralism, (9) education, (10) justice, (11) public service (other), (12) fundamental rights, (13) tax. See Table 6.1.

Table 6.1 ORPIs accepted by the CJEU in the field of services (*Source* Hatzopoulos 2012a, pp. 153–154)

	Broad categories	ORPIs Sub-categories	No. of cases	Total
1.	Environment	Natural	4	5
		Urban	1	
2.	Social	Social order	5	48
		Financial equilibrium of social services system	10	
		Respect of the essential characteristics of the social services system	1	
		Protection of workers/employment conditions	22	
		Regulate the access of third country nationals on the 1 all our market	5	
		Prevent social dumping	2	
		Prevent undeclared labour	1	
		Social policy objectives (other than the protection of workers)	1	
		Social protection of the victims of road accidents	1	
3.	Morality/Public morals	(Mostly used as a reason to allow member state greater flexibility—not as an ORPI; *but as in Commission v Greece (online games)*)	1	1
4.	Fairness of transactions/fraud	Fairness of commercial transactions	4	16
		Prevention of fraud/Protection of reputation/credibility	12	
5.	Protection	Of service recipients	13	51
		Of consumers	23	
		From the propensity of spending	9	
		Of citizens/the public in general (including from terrorism)	2	
		Of creditors	2	
		Navigation security	1	
		Of confidential information	1	
6.	Quality	Of craftsmen work	2	16
		Of providers qualifications	3	
		Professional/disciplinary rules, etc.	10	
		Ease of communication between providers/recipients (patients)/authorities	1	
7.	Intellectual property		1	1
8.		Protection of historic/cultural heritage	3	19
		Cultural policy	9	

(continued)

Table 6.1 (continued)

	Broad categories	ORPIs Sub-categories	No. of cases	Total
	Historic and cultural heritage/Cultural policy/Pluralism	Protection of ethnic-cultural minority	1	
		Pluralism	6	
9.	Organization of educational system	Promotion of research, education, etc.	3	4
		Guarantee a high level of higher education	1	
10.	Operation of justice	Smoothness of procedures	5	7
		Determination of competent jurisdiction if claims raised	1	
		Protection of rights stemming from EU law	1	
11.	Public service mission	Without reference to Article 106(2)	2	6
		With reference to Article 106(2)	4	
12.	Fundamental rights		8	8
13.	Tax ORPIs	Fiscal balance (impossibility to tax non-residents)	3	46
		Tight against tax evasion/fraud	6	
		Efficiency of fiscal control	13	
		Coherence of fiscal system	14	
		Smooth operation of the system of imposition at the source	4	
		Balanced distribution of the power to raise tax	1	
		Territoriality principle	5	

6.4.2 *Ongoing EU Measures and/or Policies Affecting ORPIs*

Several from the above mentioned interests are being increasingly taken care by the EU itself. Given that ORPIs are subject to the principle of pre-emption,[81] this would affect the way in which regulatory activity at the EU level may impact the relevant ORPIs.

Consumer protection, already protected by a series of Directives dating back to 1985, has been subject to a major reshuffle by Directive 2011/83.[82] This Directive

[81] See above under Sect. 6.4.1.

[82] EP and Council Directive on consumer rights amending Directives 93/13/EEC and 1999/44/EC and repealing Directive 85/577/EEC and Directive 97/7/EC [2011] OJ L304/64.

was supposed to be transposed into national law by the end of 2013 but the measures thereby adopted should become effective by June 2014. Hence, it remains to be seen how these new rules will actually impact consumer protection in the Member States and what kind of interests will remain for the Member States to protect individually. In the meanwhile, the 'European Civil Code' is work in progress and advances in this field could further restrict Member States' ability to unilaterally protect specific interests. Soft harmonisation by means of self-regulation, promoted *inter alia* by the Services Directive,[83] is likely to further circumscribe the discretion of Member States; although the extent to which the existence of self-regulation may be used in order to counter national hard-law initiatives is unclear.

Soft rules, the development of nation-wise or EU-wise codes of conduct and the development of national or EU technical standards are also likely to negatively impact on Member States' capacity to invoke the 'protection' category of ORPIs.

Fundamental rights initially recognised by the Court as general principles of EU law are now systematically protected by the EU Charter of Fundamental Rights. The scope of application of the Charter has been extensively interpreted by the Court to cover all national measures directly stemming from, or indirectly connected to, the application of EU law.[84] Hence, interests protected under the Charter are likely to be more largely accepted by the CJEU as restrictions to the fundamental freedoms but, at the same time, they are likely to be interpreted (as to their actual content and the proportionality control attached thereto) in an increasingly 'European' manner fashioned by the very CJEU and hence, distancing themselves from the national legal orders. Put in another way, the laconic hands-off judgment of the Court in *Omega* is not likely to repeat itself in the future.

Last but not least, tax-related ORPIs are likely to lose in importance as the 'economic' pillar of the EMU is being progressively strengthened. While tax harmonisation is in the pipeline, the Fiscal Compact and, more importantly, the European Semester,[85] have the potential of bringing into line the manner national taxes are being imposed, calculated and perceived.

[83] EP and Council Directive 2006/123 on the free provision of services [2006] OJ L 376/36; see in particular Articles 26 and 37.

[84] Case C-617/10, *Åklagaren v Hans Åkerberg Fransson*, ECLI:EU:C:2013:105.

[85] For a brief presentation of these new EU fiscal governance measures see the official Commission ECFIN page at http://ec.europa.eu/economy_finance/articles/governance/2012-03-14_six_pack_en.htm.

6.4.3 Alternative Theories and Means for Allowing Member States to Pursue ORPIs

6.4.3.1 Non-Economic Activities

It has already been discussed that ORPIs are supposed to pursue non-economic objectives of general interest.[86] In their vast majority these non-economic objectives are connected to some economic activity, but some of them concern activities which are altogether outside the market. It is common knowledge that the TEU rules on the internal market suppose a 'market' and do not apply to non-economic activities.[87] The criteria for determining what constitutes an economic activity have been lengthily discussed elsewhere.[88] In brief it may be said that there are two basic characteristics which render an activity non-economic: the exercise of public authority, involving what may be termed as 'strategic services'; and the expression of social solidarity, involving social services. Examples in the first category may be cited in relation to communal funeral services,[89] mooring services in ports,[90] air traffic control,[91] anti-pollution surveillance.[92] Private security services, however, are not, according to the Court strategic services and are fully subject to the Treaty rules,[93] the same as the labelling and the control of ecological products.[94] The confines of the second category are even less clear, as it is very difficult to know when any given activity embodies 'enough' solidarity for it not to qualify as economic.[95] According to the Court, the organisation of primary pension schemes

---

[86] See above Sect. 6.1.3.2.

[87] See e.g. Odudu 2009, pp. 225–43.

[88] See Hatzopoulos 2012b, pp. 973–1007; the examples in the following lines are taken from this earlier article.

[89] Case 30/87, *Corinne Bodson v SA Pompes funèbres des régions libérées*, ECLI:EU:C:1988:225.

[90] Case C-49/89, *Corsica Ferries France*, ECLI:EU:C:1989:649.

[91] Case C-364/92, *SAT Fluggesellschaft mbH v Eurocontrol*, ECLI:EU:C:1994:7; Case C-481/07 P, *Selex Sistemi Integrati SpA. v Commission*, ECLI:EU:C:2009:461.

[92] Case C-343/95, *Diego Calì & Figli Srl v Servizi ecologici porto di Genova SpA (SEPG)*, ECLI:EU:C:1997:160.

[93] See e.g. Case C-114/97, *Commission v Spain (private security)*, ECLI:EU:C:1998:519; Case C-355/98, *Commission v Belgium (private security)*, ECLI:EU:C:2000:113; Case C-283/99, *Commission v Italy (private security)*, ECLI:EU:C:2001:307; Case C-171/02, *Commission v Portugal (private securities)*, ECLI:EU:C:2004:270; Case C-189/03, *Commission v Netherlands (private security firms)*, ECLI:EU:C:2004:597; Case C-514/03, *Commission v Spain (private security)*, ECLI:EU:C:2006:63.

[94] Case C-393/05, *Commission v Austria (ecological labelling)*, ECLI:EU:C:2007:722; Case C-404/05, *Commission v Germany (ecological labelling)*, ECLI:EU:C:2007:723.

[95] See Hervey 2000, pp. 31–47; see also Dougan 2009, pp. 119–65; generally on the issue of solidarity, see also Houtepen and Ter Meulen 2000, pp. 329–40; White 2003, pp. 40–57; and on a more philosophical tone, see Karagiannis (ed) 2007.

is outside the market,[96] the same as statutory insurance against work accidents,[97] mandatory indemnity systems for farmers[98] and running homes for the elderly.[99] The same is not true, however, for the organisation of second and third pillar (complementary and voluntary) pension schemes,[100] or the operation of ambulance services.[101] Thus, in all the above sectors Member States are free to regulate as they see it fit unrestricted by the Internal Market rules. Similarly, non-economic activities also evade the application of the EU competition rules.[102]

6.4.3.2 'Very Objective' of National Regulation

In addition to looking at the nature of the *activity*, in some occasions the Court accommodates Member States' discretion by looking at the content of the *measure* concerned. Thus, in few cases the Court has held the EU measures to be inapplicable to national measures because the main object or, to use the Court's language, 'the very objective' of such measures was not to regulate or else affect economic activity, but to set the rules for some activity of a different kind. Hence, in two sporting cases, the Court held that the anti-doping rules and the selection rules for the national representative team 'do not constitute restrictions on freedom of movement because they concern questions of purely sporting interest and, as such, have nothing to do with economic activity'.[103] Similarly, in the more specific area of public procurement national measures which do not set a public market but are limited to organising the 'in house' arrangements for providing specific services, are by their object outside the scope of the relevant rules and principles.[104]

The same logic, but with different wording has been also followed in the area of competition law. Hence, in the 'trilogy' cases concerning supplementary pension

---

[96] *Poucet and Pistre*, above n. 72.

[97] *Cisal*, above n. 73; *Kattner Stahlbau GmbH*, above n. 73.

[98] *Freskot AE*, above n. 16.

[99] *Sodemare SA ea*, above n. 16.

[100] *Albany*, *Brentjens*, *Drijvende*, above n. 76.

[101] *Firma Ambulanz Glöckner*, above n. 15; Case C-160/08, *Commission v Germany (ambulance services)*, ECLI:EU:C:2010:230.

[102] *Poucet and Pistre*, above n. 72; *SAT FluggesellschaftmbH v. Eurocontrol*, above n. 91; *Selex Sistemi Integrati SpA. v Commission*, above n. 91.

[103] Case C-519/04 P, *Meca-Medina and Majcen v. Commission*, ECLI:EU:C:2006:492, para 31; along the same lines see joined Cases C-51/96 and C-191/97, *Deliège*, ECLI:EU:C:2000:199, para 43.

[104] See e.g. Case C-26/03, *Stadt Halle and RPL Lochau*, ECLI:EU:C:2005:5; Case C-458/03, *Parking Brixen*, ECLI:EU:C:2005:605; Case C-410/04, *ANAV*, ECLI:EU:C:2006:237; Case C-295/05, *Asociación Nacional de Empresas Forestales (Asemfo)*, ECLI:EU:C:2007:227; Case C-324/07, *Coditel Brabant*, ECLI:EU:C:2008:621; for a recent account of all the relevant case law, see Frenz and Schleissing 2009, pp. 171–87; Kaarresalo 2008, pp. 242–54; see also the various contributions in Comba and Treumer (eds) 2010.

funds,[105] the Court accepted that the agreements concluded between employers and employees, making affiliation compulsory lied outside the scope of Article 101 TFEU by holding that 'certain restrictions of competition are inherent in collective agreements between organisations representing employers and workers [and that] the social policy objectives pursued by such agreements would be seriously undermined if management and labour were subject to Article 85(1) [now 101(1) TFEU]'.[106] In a similar fashion (although in a more circumscribed manner) the Court held the state aid rules to be inapplicable where the aim of the national measure is genuinely to fund the provision of some service of general economic interest, rather than to confer an advantage to some undertaking.[107]

6.4.3.3 Article 106(2) TFEU

Close to the *Altmark* logic but directly grounded in the TFEU is Article 106(2) which allows for derogations to all the Treaty rules whenever this is necessary for the provision of some service of general economic interest. This Treaty provision is also very closely related to the Court's case law in the *Corbeau, Almelo* and *Glöckner* case law,[108] whereby the Court has held the competition rules may remain without application, hence allowing for the award of special or exclusive rights whenever this is justified by the need to fund non-profitable activities in the general interest.[109]

While it is true that this provision is included in the Treaty Chapter on Competition Law, there is no doubt that it also covers the Internal Market rules.[110] Hence, Article 106(2) TFEU offers yet another ground for Member States to by-pass EU imposed constraints in order to pursue legitimate interests. The measures which may be justified under Article 106(2), just as under the *Corbeau* case law, are essentially of an economic nature: they are aimed at securing the financial equilibrium of services of general economic interest. In that they are difficult to distinguish from those measures which come under the ORPI pertaining to the maintenance of the financial equilibrium of a healthcare or of a social security system.[111]

---

[105] *Albany, Brentjens, Drijvende*, respectively, above n. 76. On these three cases, see Idot 1999, pp. 4–8.

[106] Ibid., para 46.

[107] Case C-280/00, *Altmark*, ECLI:EU:C:2003:415.

[108] Above n. 15.

[109] Indeed, Article 106(2) is so closely intertwined with the case law mentioned above that some commentators suggest that it has henceforth become obsolete, see Davies 2009, pp. 51–67.

[110] See e.g. Case C-266/96, *Corsica Ferries v La Spezia*, ECLI:EU:C:1998:306.

[111] See e.g. for healthcare *Smits and Peerbooms*, above n. 9; and for social security Case C-136/00, *Danner*, ECLI:EU:C:2002:558.

6.4.3.4 Relationship with Justifications Under Competition Law

This last point clearly shows that the distinction between economic and non-economic measures which may/may not be justified by ORPIs is a tenuous, if not artificial, one. Indeed, if it is clear that ORPIs are not there to serve short-term sector specific interests (which arguably would not qualify as being of 'general' interest), any other legitimate economic objective pursued by Member States (typically connected to some service of general economic interest), will enjoy different bases for being exempted by the Treaty rules.

Taken with the previous points about activities which qualify as non-economic and about national measures which have as their 'main object' a non-economic objective, the above point also shows that the logic for admitting Member States' measures is equally valid in the area of internal market and of competition law. This finding puts into question the traditional view that exceptions to the Internal Market are essentially of a non-economic nature while exceptions to competition law are essentially economic. By the same token it raises the question of the existence of a catch-all horizontal 'rule of reason' fashioned on the basis of ORPIs applicable in both fields of law. Indeed, in *Wouters*,[112] confirmed by *Meca Medina*,[113] the Court held that the very same ORPIs liable to justify restrictions to the free movement rules may also serve to justify anti-competitive conduct. This finding, although repeated only twice, squares well with the Court's finding in *Consten and Grundig*, according to which 'an agreement between producer and distributor which might tend to restore the national divisions in trade between Member States might be such as to frustrate the most fundamental objections (sic) of the Community';[114] and with the fact that in *Metro I*, the Court exempted the selective distribution put into place by SABA because it constituted 'a stabilizing factor with regard to the provision of employment'.[115] Indeed, the case that ORPIs may serve to justify agreements restrictive of competition, at least where such agreements are restrictive by effect and not by object, has been convincingly made in legal doctrine.[116]

6.5 Conclusion

A number of points has been made in the preceding analysis. Namely that

(a) the actual distinction between ORPIs and express exceptions is less clear from what legal doctrine teaches us, both with regards the interests protected and the legal effects attached to each category;

---

[112] Case C-309/99, *Wouters*, ECLI:EU:C:2002:98.

[113] *Meca-Medina and Majcen v. Commission*, above n. 103.

[114] Case C-56/64, *Consten and Grundig v Commission*, ECLI:EU:C:1966:19.

[115] Case C-26/76, *Metro SB Grossmarkte v Commission*, ECLI:EU:C:1977:167, para 43 *in fine*.

[116] Enchelmaier 2012, pp. 182–199.

(b) the inconsistencies, both in terms of definition and of effects, of the exceptions to the fundamental freedoms are cross-cutting, in the sense that they are to be found in all the freedoms;
(c) the need for a justification theory is common to all fundamental freedoms; to a large extent also for the competition rules;
(d) the external boundaries to the application of justifications, express and judge-made, are being increasingly well-designed, both in terms of the applicable proportionality test and of the interests (economic vs. non-economic) pursued;
(e) the scope and effect of justifications, express and judge-made, is being affected by recent and/or ongoing developments, relevant for all freedoms;
(f) justifications, express and judge-made, are complemented in practice by other means and theories allowing for the exercise of Member State discretion and applicable in all freedoms—and even in the field of competition.

In view of all the above, it is submitted, it is high time that the distinction between express and judge-made justifications be altogether abandoned. If it finds a historic explanation, nowadays it corresponds to nothing tangible and coherent in positive law. Rather, it is a source of inconsistency in the Court's case law, occasionally leading to undesirable solutions. It is true that putting in the same plane Treaty-based and judge-made exceptions would lead to a *de facto* revision of the Treaty. But such revision is there already, hypocritically hidden behind ill-chosen terms and nonsensical doctrinal debates, finding support on the occasional incongruence of the Court's case law.

This single justification theory would be tempered by a scalable proportionality control allowing for more leniency towards non-discriminatory measures (nowadays essentially justified through ORPIs) but would be much more demanding towards discriminatory ones (nowadays essentially justified through express exceptions); in this way express exceptions would be still given a better treatment than judge-made justifications. Fundamental rights would be assimilated to the express exceptions and would be subject to a variable proportionality control, depending on the very content of each right and its interpretation by the CJEU. Such theory would apply in the same manner to all the fundamental freedoms and would occasionally spill-over to competition law. But this requires a different essay…

Acknowledgements I would like to thank Ms. Sofia Roma for her valuable help in updating and editing the present chapter; any errors are mine.

References

Barnard C (2009) Restricting Restrictions: Lessons for the EU from the US? Cambridge LJ 68:575–606

Barnard C (2009) Trailing a New Approach to Free Movement of Goods? Cambridge LJ 68:288–290

Barnard C (2011) The Substantive Law of the EU. Oxford University Press, Oxford

Bertrand B (2012) Que reste-t-il des exigences impératives d'intérêt général? Europe 1:6–12

Caro de Suza P (2014) Quest for the Holy Grail – Is a Unified Approach to the Market Freedoms and European Citizenship Justified? ELJ 4:499–519

Catchpole L, Barav A (1980) The Public Morality Exception and the Free Movement of Goods: Justification of a Dual Standard in National Legislation? LIEI 7:1–21

Comba M, Treumer S (eds) (2010) The In-House Providing in European Law. DJØF Publishing, Copenhagen

Cross V E (1992) Preemption of Member States in EEC: A framework for analysis. CMLRev 29:447

Davies G (2009) What does Article 86 actually do? In: Krajewski M, Neergard U, Van de Gronden J (eds) The Changing Legal Framework for Services of General Interest. TMC Asser Press, The Hague, pp 51–67

Davies G (2010) Understanding Market Access: Exploring the Economic Rationality of Different Conceptions of Free Movement Law. German Law Journal 7–8:671–704

De Witte F (2013) Sex, Drugs and EU Law: The Recognition of Moral and Ethical Diversity in EU Law. CML Rev 50:1545–78.

Derlén M, Lindholm J (2010) Article 28 EC and rules on use: A step towards a workable doctrine on measures having equivalent effect to quantitative restrictions. Columbia J of Eur L 16:191–231

Dougan M (2009) Expanding the Frontiers of EU Citizenship by Dismantling the Territorial Boundaries of the National Welfare States? In: Barnard C, Odudu O (eds) The Outer Limits of EU Law. Hart Publishing, Oxford/Portland, Oregon, pp 119–65

Douglas-Scott S (2006) A Tale of Two Courts: Luxembourg, Strasbourg and the Growing European Human Rights Acquis. CML Rev 43:629–665

Enchelmaier S (2012) "Mandatory Requirements" under Art 101(3) TFEU? The Complementary Relationship between EU Competition and Free Movement Law. Comp Law 3:182–199

Fernandez Martin J M, O'Leary S (2002) Judicial exceptions to the free provision of services. In: Andenas M, Roth W H (eds) Services and Free Movement in EU Law. Oxford University Press, Oxford, pp 163–95

Frenz W, Schleissing P (2009) The Never Ending Story of "In-house" Procurement. In: Krajewski M, Neergard U, Van de Gronden J (eds) The Changing Legal Framework for Services of General Interest. TMC Asser Press, The Hague, pp 171–87

Fromont A, Verdure Ch (2011) La consécration du critère de l'accès au marché" en matière de libre circulation des marchandises: mythe ou réalité? RTDEur 4:717–48

Gormley L (2010) Free movement of goods and their use – What is the use of it? Fordham Int'l L J 33:1589–628

Greer S, Williams A (2009) Human Rights in the Council of Europe and the EU: Towards "Individual", "Constitutional" or "Institutional" Justice? ELRev 15:462–481

Hatzopoulos V (1998) Exigences essentielles, impératives ou impérieuses: une théorie, des théories ou pas de théorie du tout? RTDEur 2:191–236

Hatzopoulos V (1999) Le principe communautaire d'équivalence et de reconnaissance mutuelle dans la libre prestation de services. Sakkoulas/Bruylant, Athens/Brussels

Hatzopoulos V (2010) Le principe de la reconnaissance mutuelle dans la libre prestation de services. CDE 45:48–93

Hatzopoulos V (2012a) Regulating Services in the EU. Oxford University Press, Oxford

Hatzopoulos V (2012b) The Economic Constitution of the EU Treaty and the Limits between Economic and Non-economic Activities. EBLR 23:973–1007
Hatzopoulos V (2013) La justification des atteintes aux libertés de circulation: cadre méthodologique et spécificités matérielles. In: Dubout E, de la Motte A (eds) L'unité des libertés de circulation. Bruylant/Larcier, Brussels, pp 205–229
Hervey T (2000) "Social Solidarity": A Buttress against Internal Market Law? In: Shaw J (ed) Social Law and Policy in an Evolving EU. Hart Publishing, Oxford/Portland, Oregon, 31–47
Hetsch P (1982) Émergence de valeurs morales dans la jurisprudence de la CJUE. RTDEur 18:511–525
Houtepen R, Ter Meulen R (2000) New Types of Solidarity in the European Welfare State. Health Care Analysis 8:329–340
Idot L (1999) Droit social et droit de la concurrence: confrontation ou cohabitation: A propos de quelques développements récents. Europe 11:4–8
Kaarresalo T (2008) Procuring in-house: The impact of the EC procurement regime. Public Procurement L Rev 17:242–254
Karagiannis N (2007) European Solidarity. Liverpool University Press, Liverpool
Lenaerts K (2000) Respect for Fundamental Rights as a Constitutional Principle of the European Union. Columbia J of Eur L 6:1–25
Marenco G (1984) Pour une interprétation traditionnelle de la notion de mesure d'effet équivalent à une restriction quantitative. CDE 19:291–364
Martin D (1998) "Discriminations", "entraves" et "raisons impérieuses" dans le traité CE: Trois concepts en quête d'identité, (partie 1e). CDE 34:261–318
Mathisen G (2010) Consistency and Coherence as Conditions for Justification of Member State Measures Restricting Free Movement. CML Rev 47:1021–1048
Mattera A (1990) Le Marché Unique Européen: Ses règles, son fonctionnement. Jupiter, Paris
Odudu O (2009) Economic Activity as a Limit to Community Law. In: Barnard C, Odudu O (eds) The Outer Limits of EU Law. Hart Publishing, Oxford/ Portland, Oregon, pp 225–43
Oliver P (2010) Of Trailers and Jet-Skis: Is the Case Law on Article 34 TFEU Hurtling in a New Direction? Fordham Int'l LJ 33:1423–1471
Oliver P (2016) When, If Ever, Can Restrictions on Free Movement Be Justified on Economic Grounds? ELRev 2:147-75
Regan D (2001) Judicial Review of Member-State Regulation of Trade within a Federal or Quasi-federal system: Protectionism and Balancing, Da Capo. Michigan L Rev 99:1853–1902
Regan D (2006) What Are Trade Agreements For? Two Conflicting Stories Told by Economists, with a Lesson for Lawyers. J Int Economic L 9:951–88
Sibony A L (2012) Can market access be taken seriously? Revue européenne de droit de la consommation 2:323–342
Snell J (2000) True Proportionality and Free Movement of Goods and Services. EBL Rev 11:50–7.
Snell J (2005) Economic aims as justifications for restrictions to free movement. In: Schrauwen A (ed) Rule of Reason: Rethinking Another Classic of European Legal Doctrine. Europa Law Publishing, Groningen, pp 37–56
Snell J (2010) The Notion of Market Access: A Concept or a Slogan? CML Rev 47:437–472
Spaventa E (2009) Leaving Keck behind? The free movement of goods after the rulings in Commission v Italy and Mickelsson and Roos. EL Rev 15:914–932
Tridimas T (2006) The General Principles of EU Law. Oxford University Press, Oxford
Tryfonidou A (2010) Further Steps on the Road to Convergence Among the Market Freedoms. ELRev 1:36–56
Von Bogdandy A (2000) The European Union as a human rights organisation? Human rights and the core of the European Union. CML Rev 37:1307–1338
Weuwahl N, Rosas A (eds) (1995) The EU and Human Rights. Martinus Nijhoff, The Hague
White E L (1989) In Search of the Limits to Article 30 of the EEC Treaty. CML Rev 26:235–280
White J (2003) Rethinking Transnational Solidarity in the EU. Perspectives 20:40–57

Chapter 7
The Justification and Proportionality of Certain Administrative, Regulatory and Political Concerns

Pål Wennerås

Abstract The scope of the four freedoms has become so broad that it is liable to capture a plethora of national acts that, at least originally, would have appeared to lie on the outer fringes of the Court of Justice's competence to arbiter. This situation is exacerbated by the fact that administrative considerations are in principle not capable of justifying restrictions on freedom of movement, while the proportionality principle presents several substantive and procedural hurdles for attaining legitimate regulatory and political concerns. Member States will therefore often find it difficult to justify measures that restrict freedom of movement, irrespective of the fact that they are not intended to regulate freedom of movement and clearly pursue a common good. More recent developments in case law suggest, however, that the Court of Justice has become increasingly aware that such a situation poses not only challenges for the Member States, but also for the Court itself and the proper role of the judiciary in an EU of 28 Member States. Some recent judgments thus seem to temper the concept of restrictions on the freedom of movement, but above all the Court seems more willing to entertain the justification and proportionality of certain administrative, regulatory and political concerns that entail restrictions on the freedom of movement.

Keywords Administrative · Burden of proof · Consistent and systematic · Imperative requirements · Integration · Justification · Market access · Public interests · Proportionality

---

The views expressed are personal and do not necessarily reflect those of the Office of the Attorney General.

P. Wennerås (✉)
Office of the Attorney General, PO Box 8012 DEP, 0030 Oslo, Norway
e-mail: pw@radv.no

M. Andenas et al. (eds.), *The Reach of Free Movement*,
DOI 10.1007/978-94-6265-195-1_7

Contents

7.1 Introduction 158
7.2 The Orthodox Case Law Concerning Justification of Restrictions on Freedom of Movement 159
7.3 Modifications in Recent Case Law 162
7.3.1 The Type of Regulation Employed—Use Restrictions and Other Restrictions on Consumer Behaviour 162
7.3.2 The Sensitivity of the Policy Area and the Objectives Pursued 164
7.3.3 Areas in Which Administrative Considerations Are Legitimate 167
7.4 Drawing the Lines Together 170
References 171

7.1 Introduction

Considerations of an administrative nature play a significant part in most legal systems and influence the drafting of regulation in at least two ways. In the first place, substantive provisions must of course be coupled with a set of rules allowing for the management, control and enforcement of the scheme. Administrative considerations also impact the design of substantive rules. The extent to which the material rules are apt to ensure effective application and enforcement is often a decisive factor for the ultimate attainment of the underlying policy objectives. Most Member States therefore acknowledge the benefits of general and simple rules. Such regulations can be easily understood and applied by the persons who are subject to them, while allowing for expedient management and supervision by the competent authorities. National courts will accordingly often favour a broad interpretation of the main rules and strictly interpret any exceptions since such a judicial approach promotes the objectives of the scheme, ensures legal certainty and enhances enforcement.

The EU institutions largely adhere to the same principles with regard to their own acts, but take a markedly different stance in relation to domestic acts falling within EU law, and in particular the four freedoms.[1] Although recognising, in principle, that restrictions posed by administrative provisions can be justified in the same vein as material rules, the Court of Justice has been sceptical of administrative regulations involving significant restrictions on freedom of movement.[2] The same applies to substantive rules whose scope and design have been influenced by

[1] See, to this effect, e.g. judgments in C-319/06, *Commission v Luxembourg*, ECLI:EU:C:2008:350, para 49, and C-374/14, *Attikis*, ECLI:EU:C:2015:582, para 50.

[2] For instance prior authorization schemes, see e.g. the judgment in C-390/99, *Canal Satélite Digital*, ECLI:EU:C:2002:394, paras 35–41.

considerations of an administrative nature.[3] This is presumably because general and simple rules often correspond with significant and unreserved restrictions on freedom of movement.[4]

While stopping short of introducing an assessment of proportionality *sensu stricto* of such measures, case law contains various means of censoring the justification and proportionality of general measures that directly or indirectly restrict freedom of movement (Sect. 7.2). This includes application of the doctrine that considerations of an administrative nature cannot justify derogation from the rules of EU law, thus putting general and simple rules at risk already at the justification stage.

Recent case law suggests, however, that the Court of Justice has found it opportune to modify this jurisprudence (Sect. 7.3). This seemingly stems from the realisation that the scope of the four freedoms has become so broad that it is liable to capture a plethora of national acts that lie on the outer fringes of EU competence to regulate, and the Court of Justice to adjudicate. This involves common national measures that are not intended to regulate trade, but which indirectly affect the volume of sales of products from other Member States, e.g. regulations on the use of products and other restrictions on consumer behaviour (Sect. 7.3.1). Other categories include acts involving distinctly political balancing acts in sensitive areas (Sect. 7.3.2) and, at the other end of the spectrum, mundane regulations concerning the proper organisation of administrative systems (Sect. 7.3.3). Although Luxembourg is still unwilling to let go of competence in respect of such measures, and the concept of restrictions on freedom of movement will capture most of them, case law suggests a more lenient approach when reviewing their proportionality. The Court has modified the principle that administrative considerations cannot justify derogations from the freedom of movement and even found that promotion of such concerns may bolster the proportionality of the national measures (Sect. 7.4).

7.2 The Orthodox Case Law Concerning Justification of Restrictions on Freedom of Movement

It may be appropriate at the outset to recall the basic tenets of the jurisprudence concerning the justification of measures restricting freedom of movement. Such measures are compatible with the Treaty provisions in so far as they fulfil three material conditions.[5] In the first place, restrictions on the freedom of movement must be justified by public interests grounds set out in the Treaty, or imperative

---

[3] E.g. the judgment in C-265/06, *Commission v Portugal*, ECLI:EU:C:2008:2010, paras 42-47. See also Sect. 7.2 and the case law cited.

[4] See, to this effect, Opinion in C-110/05, *Commission v Italy*, ECLI:EU:C:2006:646, para 60.

[5] See e.g. the judgment in C-198/14, *Visnapuu*, ECLI:EU:C:2015:751, para 110 and the case law cited.

requirements of public interest.[6] Overriding reasons of public interest that justify substantive provisions may also justify control and enforcement measures needed to ensure compliance with them.[7] However, considerations of an administrative nature cannot justify derogation by a Member State from the rules of EU law.[8] The Court of Justice is particularly sceptical of administrative considerations that influence the scope and content of *substantive* provisions, even if this would enhance the effectiveness of the public interests pursued.[9]

In addition, the national measures must comply with the two limbs of the proportionality principle, that is to say that they must be suitable to attain their objectives and do not go beyond what is necessary in order to attain them.[10] The suitability requirement may also, according to more recent developments in the case law, involve an assessment of whether the national measures attain the objectives in a consistent and systematic manner.[11] The necessity requirement entails a functional test of whether the objectives may be achieved in an equally effective manner by measures that are less restrictive of trade.[12] The Member States thus retain the right to set their level of protection and the proportionality principle does not involve an assessment of its expediency (proportionality *sensu stricto*).[13]

As for procedural requirements, it is for the national authorities to demonstrate that the contested measures are justified and proportionate.[14] The reasons invoked by a Member State must be accompanied by an analysis of the appropriateness and proportionality of the restrictive measure.[15] On occasion the Court also requires the Member State to provide precise evidence enabling its arguments to be substantiated.[16]

---

[6] Ibid.

[7] E.g. judgments in C-113/89, *Rush Portuguesa*, ECLI:EU:C:1990:142, para 18, and C-369/96 and C-376/96, *Arblade and Others*, ECLI:EU:C:1999:575, para 38.

[8] E.g. judgments in C-18/95, *Terhoeve*, ECLI:EU:C:1999:22, para 45; C-369/96 and C-376/96, *Arblade and Others*, ECLI:EU:C:1999:575, para 37; C-530/13, *Schmitzer*, ECLI:EU:C:2014:2359, para 41, and C-417/13, *Öbb Personenverkehr and Others*, ECLI:EU:C:2015:38, para 36.

[9] See, to this effect, e.g. the judgment in C-265/06, *Commission v Portugal*, ECLI:EU:C:2008:210, paras 42–47.

[10] See e.g. judgments in C-55/94, *Gebhard*, ECLI:EU:C:1995:411, para 37, and C-110/05, *Commission v Italy*, ECLI:EU:C:2009:660, para 59.

[11] E.g. the judgment in C-375/14, *Laezza*, EU.C:2016:60, para 36 and the case law cited. See also Mathisen 2010, p. 1021.

[12] E.g. the judgment in C-456/10, *Anett*, ECLI:EU:C:2012:241, para 45.

[13] See, to this effect, e.g. judgments in C-61/12, *Commission v Lithuania*, ECLI:EU:C:2014:172, para 60, and C-333/14, *Scotch Whisky Association*, ECLI:EU:C:2015:845, para 35.

[14] E.g. judgments in C-297/05, *Commission v Netherlands*, ECLI:EU:C:2007:531, para 76, and C-110/05, *Commission v Italy*, ECLI:EU:C:2009:660, para 62.

[15] E.g. the judgment in C-42/02, *Lindman*, ECLI:EU:C:2003:613, para 25.

[16] E.g. judgments in C-254/05, *Commission v Belgium*, ECLI:EU:C:2007:319, para 36, and C-319/06, *Commission v Luxembourg*, ECLI:EU:C:2008:350, para 51.

The cumulative effect of these material and procedural requirements is that the Member State may often find it difficult to justify restrictions on freedom of movement, even where the regulation is not intended to regulate freedom of movement and clearly pursues a common good. Consider for instance *Commission v Portugal*, concerning a mundane regulation banning the fixing of tinted film on car windows in order to allow visual inspection by traffic authorities and thus enforce the obligation to wear seat belts.[17] The Court agreed that the ban facilitated inspection and that it was an appropriate manner of ensuring road safety, yet deemed the measure excessive and disproportionate. It emphasized that the contested measures on the one hand allowed the marketing of vehicles fitted at the outset with tinted windows in accordance with Directive 92/22 and, on the other hand, that the ban covered some tinted film that apparently was sufficiently transparent to allow for visual inspection.[18] One can only imagine the perplexity of the national legislature when learning that the ban was set aside for being too narrow and too broad at the same time. The Member State might also have struggled to understand why it was faulted for not extending the scope of the act in conflict with the harmonization measures laid down in Directive 92/22. Or why the Court did not recognise that all tinted film necessarily makes visual inspection more difficult and that a general prohibition accordingly ensures road safety more effectively than a partial ban and accommodates easier management and supervision. Above all, the national authorities might have questioned why, in the absence of harmonization, the Court of Justice took it upon itself to essentially censor the degree of protection chosen by the Member States in the field of road safety and the way in which that degree of protection was to be achieved.

A few years later, the Court of Justice got another opportunity to grapple with two cases that resembled *Commission v Portugal* in many respects. The tenor of these judgments and subsequent cases is quite different, however, and indicates a more nuanced approach. While some caution should of course be exercised in attempting to identify the factors influencing the assessment of proportionality,[19] it is nevertheless possible to discern some factors that seem to influence the intensity with which the Court applies the proportionality principle.

[17] Judgment in C-265/06, *Commission v Portugal*, ECLI:EU:C:2008:210.

[18] Ibid., paras 43–46.

[19] As recently observed by the UK Supreme Court in R (on the application of Lumsdon and Others) v Legal Services Board, [2015] UKSC 41.

7.3 Modifications in Recent Case Law

7.3.1 The Type of Regulation Employed—Use Restrictions and Other Restrictions on Consumer Behaviour

The difference in temperament found in *Italian Trailers* compared with *Commission v Portugal* is striking. It is illumining to juxtapose the orthodox view presented by the opinion and the modifications introduced by the judgment. Advocate General Legér held that a measure "as radical as a general and absolute prohibition" on the use of trailers by motorcycles required strict review of necessity.[20] Seemingly not too worried about the comparative effectiveness of the ban in relation to less restrictive measures, he briefly opined that it would have sufficed to employ localized prohibitions on particularly dangerous road stretches, such as alpine crossings or particularly heavily used public highways.[21]

Acknowledging at the outset that it is for the Member States to demonstrate the justification and proportionality of restrictions on freedom of movement, the Court quickly set a different tone. It underscored that the burden of proof cannot be so extensive as to require the Member States to positively prove that no other conceivable measure could enable the relevant objectives to be attained under the same conditions.[22] Although alternative measures indeed could achieve a *certain* level of protection of road safety, Member States could not be denied the possibility of attaining such an objective by general and simple rules which can be easily managed and supervised by the competent authorities.[23] Nor could an alternative measure such as a partial prohibition be *presumed* to ensure the same level of protection as a general prohibition.[24]

The cumulative effect of these three modifying steps in the Court's reasoning comes close to acknowledging that general and simple rules may be presumed to ensure a higher level of protection than measures of lesser scope, which is reinforced by the fact that such rules afford more effective enforcement and control. This reasoning was subsequently repeated in *Mickelsson and Roos*, concerning a prohibition on the use of jet-skis on waters other than general navigable waterways.[25] While recognizing that alternative measures could ensure a certain level of protection, the Court once again found that the Member States could not be denied the possibility of attaining environmental protection by general rules which are easily managed and supervised by the national authorities.[26]

---

[20] Opinion in C-110/05, *Commission v Italy*, ECLI:EU:C:2006:646, para 60.

[21] Ibid., paras 59–60.

[22] Judgment in C-110/05, *Commission v Italy*, ECLI:EU:C:2009:660, para 66.

[23] Ibid., para 67.

[24] Ibid., para 68.

[25] Judgment in C-142/05, *Mickelsson and Roos*, ECLI:EU:C:2009:336.

[26] Ibid., para 36.

So why, then, did the Court of Justice assess proportionality so differently in these cases compared to the review carried out in *Commission v Portugal*? There are, after all, many commonalties. All three cases concerned restrictions on the use of products, they were of similar scope, and both *Italian Trailers* and *Commission v Portugal* concerned road safety. There is one important difference, however. In the first case, *Commission v Portugal*, the Court of Justice did not acknowledge the possible ramifications of treating restrictions on consumer behaviour in the same way as measures directly regulating patterns of trade and the commercial freedom of traders. Instead, it went ahead applying *Dassonville* and a strict assessment of proportionality.[27] When the Court shortly thereafter heard another two cases concerning use restrictions, however, a divergence of opinion arose concerning the proper judicial approach to such types of regulations. The first Opinion in *Italian Trailers*, by Advocate General Legér, approached the matter by reciting the *Dassonville* formula and concluded swiftly that the regulation amounted to a restriction.[28] In contrast, Advocate General Kokott opined in *Mickelsson and Roos* that it was necessary to take into account the specific nature of use regulations and suggested analogous application of the *Keck* doctrine.[29] The Court decided against this background to reassign the first case—*Italian Trailers*—to the Grand Chamber, to reopen oral proceedings and to invite the Member States to give submissions concerning the principles applicable to use regulations. This resulted in a second Opinion in *Italian Trailers*, in which Advocate General Bot proposed a third approach, namely a strict market access test analogous to that which the Court had rejected as concerned selling arrangements.[30] In the end, the Court essentially opted for non-discrimination as the primary criterion for whether such measures fall within Article 34 TFEU, coupled with a proviso for indistinctly applicable measures which hinder market access.[31] Furthermore, the subsequent ruling in *Mickelsson and Roos* indicated a high threshold in order to meet the subsidiary test of market access hindrance. The national regulations must have the effect of preventing consumers from using the products for the specific and inherent purposes for which they were intended, or of greatly restricting their use.[32]

---

[27] Judgment in C-265/06, *Commission v Portugal*, ECLI:EU:C:2008:210, paras 31 et seq.

[28] Opinion of A.G. Legér, delivered October 5, 2006, in C-110/05, *Italian Trailers*, ECLI:EU:C:2006:646, paras 32–33.

[29] Opinion of A.G. Kokott, delivered December 14, 2006, in C-142/05, *Mickelsson and Roos*, ECLI:EU:C:2006:782, para 56.

[30] Opinion of A.G. Bot, delivered July 8, 2008, in C-110/05, *Italian Trailers*, ECLI:EU:C:2006:646, para 107. Cf. e.g. judgments in C-412/93, *Leclerc Siplec*, ECLI:EU:C:1995:26, paras 21–22, and C-322/01, *DocMorris*, ECLI:EU:C:2003:664, para 68. For a comprehensive presentation of the three Opinions, see Spaventa 2009, pp. 915–917.

[31] Judgment in C-110/05, *Commission v Italy*, ECLI:EU:C:2009:660, para 37. See also in this regard Wennerås and Boe Moen 2010, p. 387 and a similar, but critical, analysis by Enchelmaier in Chap. 4 in this volume. For a different view, see Fenger in Chap. 5 in this volume.

[32] Judgment in C-142/05, *Mickelsson and Roos*, ECLI:EU:C:2009:336, para 28.

Leaving aside the intricacies of the test laid down by the Court, the emphasis on non-discrimination and the high threshold for the market access test indicate that the Court was wary of opening the flood-gates for litigation on regulation of consumer behaviour.[33] What is particularly interesting is that this prudent approach also influenced the proportionality assessment. There is in fact a distinct symmetry to the Court's reasoning. Non-discriminatory restrictions on the use of products are not regarded as MEEQs unless they prevent or greatly restrict their use, while the Member States can justify general rules with reference to the fact that they can be easily managed and supervised by the competent authorities.

Conversely, the Court's tempered approach to use restrictions and other restrictions on consumer freedom appears contingent on the national measures being indistinctly applicable. The justification for the soft touch diminishes where the domestic regulation falls within the first limb of the test laid down in *Italian Trailers*, that is to say, measures adopted by a Member State the object or effect of which is to treat products coming from other Member States less favourably than domestic ones.[34] This also follows from the orthodox case law. Directly discriminatory measures may not be justified on grounds of imperative requirements.[35] Indirectly discriminatory measures risk falling foul of the requirement of a consistent and systematic regulation.[36] Concerns over discrimination may nevertheless, to some extent, be balanced out by having regard to the area of regulation and the objectives pursued, which brings us to the next factor of interest.

7.3.2 The Sensitivity of the Policy Area and the Objectives Pursued

The deferential approach in *Italian Trailers* and *Mickelsson and Roos* was likely also influenced by the fact that the national measures intended to ensure road safety

---

[33] Enchelmaier Chap. 4 and Fenger Chap. 5. For a cautious view, see e.g. Weatherill 2009, p. 987, and Wennerås and Boe Moen 2010, p. 387. For a different and more expansive view, see e.g. Spaventa 2009, p. 914; Pecho 2009, p. 257; Horsley 2009, p. 2001; and Barnard 2009, p. 288.

Compare the judgments in C-267/91 and C-268/91, *Keck and Mithouard*, ECLI:EU:C:1993:905, para 14: "In view of the increasing tendency of traders to invoke Article 30 of the Treaty [Article 34 TFEU] as a means of challenging any rules whose effect is to limit their commercial freedom even where such rules are not aimed at products from other Member States, the Court considers it necessary to re-examine and clarify its case law on this matter [regulation of certain selling arrangements]."

[34] Judgment in C-110/05, *Commission v Italy*, ECLI:EU:C:2009:660, para 37.

[35] Judgments in C-110/05, *Commission v Italy*, ECLI:EU:C:2009:660, paras 60–65, and C-142/05, *Mickelsson and Roos*, ECLI:EU:C:2009:336, paras 30–36.

[36] E.g. the judgment in C-375/14, *Laezza*, ECLI:EU:C:2016:60, para 36 and the case law cited.

and environmental protection.[37] These are areas in which the Court often—but not always, as illustrated by *Commission v Portugal*—displays a less intense scrutiny of proportionality. An even clearer example of this approach may be found in *Josemans*, concerning a prohibition on admitting non-residents to Dutch coffee (cannabis) shops.[38] Since the measure was discriminatory and in any event appeared inconsistent with an aim of combatting drugs, one might have thought that the Dutch rules would not fare well. The Court had previously slammed down on similar measures regulating prostitution in *Adoui and Cornuaille*, which is another sensitive policy area.[39] Carving a way out, the Court held at the outset that the discriminatory nature of a national measure does not mean that it pursues its intended objective in an inconsistent manner.[40] Although *Adoui and Cornuaille* held that a Member State cannot invoke public policy with regard to the behaviour of non-nationals without extending repressive measures to its own nationals, the Court found that judgment "part of a different legal context", since international law and EU law prohibited the marketing of narcotic drugs.[41] That still did not rid the Court of the problem that the regulation was hardly a consistent and systematic manner of combatting drugs. This objection was subtly eliminated by accepting the legitimacy of the narrower (and seemingly inherently discriminatory) objective of combatting drug *tourism*.[42] Finally, in response to the fact that it was possible to conceive of less restrictive measures, e.g. allowing non-residents access into coffee-shops without selling cannabis to them, the Court reiterated that the Member States could not be denied general rules which are easily managed and supervised.[43] Furthermore, in the same vein as in *Italian Trailers*,[44] the Court essentially shifted the burden of proof and held that it could not be *assumed* that less restrictive measures could attain the same level of protection.[45]

The sensitivity of the area in question and the objectives pursued are primarily of relevance to substantive rules and the political balancing which they express. A similar margin of appreciation is less often extended to administrative regulations. In the field of games of chance, for instance, the Court has thus emphasized the distinction between the detrimental effects of competition in the market of betting, which may justify restrictions, and the effects of regulating that activity in

---

[37] See also the judgment in C-400/08, *Commission v Spain*, ECLI:EU:C:2011:172, para 124.

[38] Judgment in C-137/09, *Josemans*, ECLI:EU:C:2010:744.

[39] Judgment in C-115/81 and C-116/81, *Adoui and Cornuaille*, ECLI:EU:C:1982:183.

[40] Judgment in C-137/09, *Josemans*, ECLI:EU:C:2010:744, para 76.

[41] Ibid.

[42] Ibid., paras 70–75.

[43] Ibid., paras 80–82.

[44] Judgment in C-110/05, *Commission v Italy*, ECLI:EU:C:2009:660, para 68.

[45] Judgment in C-137/09, *Josemans*, ECLI:EU:C:2010:744, para 82.

so far as it permitted.[46] Recent case law nevertheless suggests that the Member States' margin of appreciation in this field may also include measures of an administrative nature. *Stanley Betting International* concerned whether a shorter period of validity of new betting licenses could be justified for reasons of reorganising the licensing system.[47] The Court recalled at the outset that considerations of an administrative nature cannot justify derogations by a Member State from the one of the fundamental freedoms of EU law.[48] However, the Court continued, the specific nature of legislation on betting and gambling must also be appreciated in this context.[49] National authorities enjoy a wide measure of discretion to determine what is required in that field, including the appropriateness of reorganizing the licensing system.[50]

It is perhaps not surprising that the Member States have been granted a margin of appreciation in fields such as drugs and gambling, but the Court often employs a reasoning of general application when justifying that the national authorities enjoy certain discretionary competence. The stepping stone in *Italian Trailers* and *Stanley Betting International* was the dictum that, in the absence of harmonisation at EU level, it is for the Member States to decide upon the level of protection which they wish to ensure as regards legitimate objectives in their territory.[51] The Member States may also determine the way in which that degree of protection is to be achieved.[52]

These statements serve primarily to explain the content of the proportionality principle, however, and not the intensity of its application. It is true that absence of harmonisation entails that the Member States retain the right to determine their level of protection. This is why the proportionality principle is limited to a functional assessment of whether less restrictive measures exist that can attain the objectives as effectively, as opposed to an assessment of proportionality *sensu stricto*.[53] But the absence of harmonisation and the corresponding prerogative of Member States to set their level of protection do not explain why national authorities *also* should have a margin of appreciation to determine the way in which that degree of protection is to be achieved, i.e. the functional test of necessity. This becomes even more perplexing when recalling that the prerequisite for an assessment of

---

[46] See, to this effect, the judgment in C-203/08, *Sporting Exchange*, ECLI:EU:C:2010:307, para 58.

[47] C-463/13, *Stanley International Betting and Others*, ECLI:EU:C:2015:25.

[48] Ibid., para 50.

[49] Ibid., para 51.

[50] Ibid., paras 52–53.

[51] Judgments in C-110/05, *Commission v Italy*, ECLI:EU:C:2009:660, para 61, and C-463/13, *Stanley International Betting and Others*, ECLI:EU:C:2015:25, para 51.

[52] Judgments in C-110/05, *Commission v Italy*, ECLI:EU:C:2009:660, para 65, and C-463/13, *Stanley International Betting and Others*, ECLI:EU:C:2015:25, para 52.

[53] See Sect. 7.2 and the case law cited.

proportionality under the Treaty provisions is that the question is not harmonised.[54] The Court's statements would thus, if taken literally, in practice mean that the Member States always enjoy a margin of appreciation with regard to the necessity test. That is certainly not the case. The absence of harmonisation can thus not explain why the Court employs varying degrees of intensity of review in certain areas of law.

It is only in some sectors, such as public health, the environment (the health and life of animals), road safety and gambling, that the Court regularly states that the Member States are free to set their level of protection in the absence of harmonisation.[55] But the same logically holds true for all areas in which the EU legislature has not yet enacted total harmonisation.[56] Nor can any explanation be found in a hierarchy of norms based on a distinction between Treaty provisions expressly allowing for derogations from EU law for certain public interests and the imperative requirements of public interests acknowledged in the case law. Several of the cases above involved restrictions justified by imperative requirements, i.e. road safety, environmental protection, combatting drugs tourism as well as consumer protection. Nevertheless, it would seem that some areas of law are more equal than others. With regard to public health measures, for instance, the Court often initiates its assessment of proportionality by stating that account must be taken of the fact that the health and life of humans rank foremost among the assets and interests protected by the Treaty.[57]

7.3.3 *Areas in Which Administrative Considerations Are Legitimate*

Several of the foregoing judgments may at first sight sit uneasily with the doctrine that considerations of administrative nature may not justify derogations from the freedom of movement. Closer inspection reveals that there is not necessarily any

---

[54] See, to this effect, e.g. judgments in C-324/99, *DaimlerChrysler*, ECLI:EU:C:2001:682, para 32, and C-423/13, *Vilniaus energija*, ECLI:EU:C:2014:2186, para 39 and the case law cited.

[55] On public health see e.g. the judgment in C-198/14, *Visnapuu*, ECLI:EU:C:2015:751, para 110 and the case law cited. On environment see e.g. the judgment in C-131/93, *Commission v Germany*, ECLI:EU:C:1994:290, para 16. In the field of the environment, there are even examples where the Court essentially dispenses of the proportionality assessment after having ascertained that the national measure is suitable to attain its objectives, see e.g. the judgment in C-67/97, *Bluhme*, ECLI:EU:C:1998:584, paras 37–38. On road safety see e.g. the judgment in C-110/05, *Commission v Italy*, ECLI:EU:C:2009:660, para 61 and the case law cited. On gambling see e.g. the judgment in C-98/14, *Berlington Hungary and Others*, EU:2015:386, para 56 and the case law cited.

[56] See, to this effect, e.g. judgments in C-318/98, *Fornasar and Others*, ECLI:EU:C:2000:337, paras 46–48, and C-49/98, C-50/98, C-52/98, C-54/98, and C-68 to C-71/98, *Finalarte and Others*, ECLI:EU:C:2001:564, paras 57–58.

[57] E.g. the judgment in C-198/14, *Visnapuu*, ECLI:EU:C:2015:751, para 118 and the case law cited.

conflict. In none of the judgments did the Court find that administrative considerations constituted legitimate objectives in themselves. The reason why the Member States could not be denied general rules which are easily managed and supervised was that such administrative benefits bolstered the effectiveness of the ultimate objectives pursued, be they environmental protection, road safety, combatting public nuisance, or consumer protection.[58]

Another matter is that this logic holds true for most national measures that are easily managed and supervised. One might therefore question what is left of the doctrine that administrative considerations are illegitimate. However, in so far as the administrative simplifications are incidental beneficial consequences, it seems entirely appropriate that the Member States should not be prevented from adopting rules that lend themselves to effective management and supervision, in particular where this also bolsters other objectives.[59] In fact, in some areas it would seem prudent to acknowledge that administrative considerations may be legitimate in themselves. In two recent cases the Court has come close to doing just that.

Commission v Spain concerned a regulation imposing restrictions on the establishment of shopping centres with a view to promoting environmental protection, town and country planning, and consumer protection.[60] One of these restrictions related to a retail licensing procedure involving a "negative silence" rule. According to this provision, a failure to act by the national authorities within the requisite time period amounted to a rejection of the application and the burden shifted on the applicant to bring that implied decision before the courts.[61] Such a regime is evidently motivated by administrative considerations. It was also difficult to see that the rule indirectly promoted environmental protection or town and country planning in any significant way. Seemingly recognising this aspect of the case and the challenges posed by the orthodox case law, the Court took the further step of acknowledging rules which the competent authority can easily manage and supervise when it occurs in the *context* of a licensing procedure, the objectives of which are environmental protection and town and country planning.[62]

The tacit approval of administrative considerations was also apparent in *Sopora*.[63] This case concerned tax exemption for the reimbursement of expenses incurred by workers in connection with employment in the Netherlands. The system allowed for tax exemption on the basis of actually incurred expenses or, for the benefit of workers resident more than 150 km from the Dutch borders, a flat rate

---

[58] See, to this effect, judgments in C-110/05, *Commission v Italy*, ECLI:EU:C:2009:660, paras 67–68; C-142/05, *Mickelsson and Roos*, ECLI:EU:C:2009:336, para 36; C-137/09, *Josemans*, ECLI:EU:C:2010:744, paras 81–82; and C-463/13, *Stanley International Betting and Others*, ECLI:EU:C:2015:25, paras 50–53.

[59] See, to this effect, e.g. judgments in C-118/96, *Nertsvoederfabriek*, ECLI:EU:C:1987:424, paras 14–15, and C-67/98, *Zenatti*, ECLI:EU:C:1999:514, para 36.

[60] Judgment in C-400/08, *Commission v Spain*, ECLI:EU:C:2011:172.

[61] Ibid., para 120.

[62] Ibid., paras 124–125.

[63] Judgment in C-512/13, *Sopora*, ECLI:EU:C:2015:108.

exemption irrespective of the expenses actually incurred.[64] The general objective behind the scheme was to facilitate free movement of workers residing in other Member States, but the specific purpose of the flat-rate exemption, and its absolute conditions, was administrative simplification.[65] Furthermore, the distance requirement was liable to discriminate in fact. Most Belgian workers and some German, French, Luxembourgish and United Kingdom workers were thus excluded from the benefits of the flat-rate exemption.[66] Recalling that considerations of an administrative nature cannot justify a derogation from the rules of EU law, the Court this time found it opportune to state that it is *also* clear from recent case law that Member States cannot be prevented from attaining legitimate objectives by virtue of rules which are easily managed and supervised.[67] Moreover, the Court remarked that rules of this kind are necessarily approximate in nature and *therefore* cannot amount to indirect discrimination.[68] This essentially amounts to a reversal of the logic employed in the past, according to which the Court would have been expected to say that administrative simplification cannot justify rules that are approximate in nature and *therefore* lead to indirect discrimination.

This is not to say that the Court of Justice got it wrong in these judgments. These developments rather indicate a greater appreciation of the fact that in some areas of law administrative considerations are legitimate and necessary in order to ensure a well-functioning system. This applies in particular to areas which are characterised by a significant amount of administration. It is hardly a coincidence that these judgments involved areas such as town and country planning and taxation. Even though it may be a stretch to claim that the rules at issue in these judgments benefit environmental protection or mobility of workers, they nevertheless do so indirectly where the scheme of which they are part promotes such objectives and the administrative rules are necessary cogs in the system.[69] Who knows, for instance, whether the Netherlands would have bothered to have in place a generous tax regime for certain migrant workers if the competent authorities had to carry out individual assessments of each and every application?

---

[64] Ibid., paras 19–20.

[65] Ibid., para 30.

[66] Ibid., para 31.

[67] Ibid., para 33.

[68] Ibid., para 34.

[69] See, to this effect, e.g. the judgment in C-118/96, *Nertsvoederfabriek*, ECLI:EU:C:1987:424, para 14.

7.4 Drawing the Lines Together

It appears from these recent strands in the case law that the Court of Justice has become more accommodating of certain regulatory, political and administrative concerns than before. In the first place, it has acknowledged the legitimacy of general rules which are easily managed and supervised by the national authorities.[70] This creates some tension to case law dictating that considerations of administrative nature do not constitute legitimate objectives. The Court has also softened the requirement that it is for the Member States to demonstrate the proportionality of the national measures. Hence, the burden of proof cannot be so extensive as to require the Member State to prove, positively, that no other conceivable measure could enable the objectives to be attained as effectively.[71] Furthermore, case law has acknowledged that general and simple rules which are easily managed and supervised often will attain the objectives pursued more effectively than measures of lesser scope and greater complexity.[72] In some judgments the Court has in fact come close to shifting the burden of proof, stating that it may be not be *assumed* that such alternative measures can attain the objectives as effectively.[73]

The logic employed in this jurisprudence is flawless and sound. But it means at the same time that the Member States may actually have incentives to opt for regulation which is more restrictive of trade when pursuing legitimate objectives, which in turn lessen the effectiveness of the project of negative integration. This could nevertheless be explained by a greater faith on the part of the Court of Justice in positive integration through enactment of harmonizing measures and the proper division of competence between the judiciary and the legislature.[74] This constitutes a natural progression in a maturing legal system and represents a sensible use of scarce judicial resources. It would nevertheless be a hasty conclusion to infer that Luxembourg has slackened the reins in general. There are still only some categories of regulation in respect of which the Court of Justice grants the Member States

---

[70] Judgments in C-110/05, *Commission v Italy*, ECLI:EU:C:2009:660, para 67; C-142/05, *Mickelsson and Roos*, ECLI:EU:C:2009:336, para 36; C-137/09, *Josemans*, ECLI:EU:C:2010:744, para 82; C-400/08, *Commission v Spain*, ECLI:EU:C:2011:172, para 124; and C-512/13, *Sopora*, ECLI:EU:C:2015:108, para 33.

[71] Judgments in C-110/05, *Commission v Italy*, ECLI:EU:C:2009:660, para 66, and C-400/08, *Commission v Spain*, ECLI:EU:C:2011:172, para 123.

[72] See, to this effect, judgments in C-110/05, *Commission v Italy*, ECLI:EU:C:2009:660, paras 67–68; C-142/05, *Mickelsson and Roos*, ECLI:EU:C:2009:336, para 36; C-137/09, *Josemans*, ECLI:EU:C:2010:744, paras 81–82; C-400/08, *Commission v Spain*, ECLI:EU:C:2011:172, paras 123–125; C-463/13, *Stanley International Betting and Others*, ECLI:EU:C:2015:25, paras 50–53; and C-512/13, *Sopora*, ECLI:EU:C:2015:108, paras 33–34.

[73] Judgments in C-110/05, *Commission v Italy*, ECLI:EU:C:2009:660, para 68, and C-137/09, *Josemans*, ECLI:EU:C:2010:744, para 82.

[74] On the merits of negative and positive integration respectively, see e.g. Craig and de Búrca 2011, Chapter 6 and references cited. See also Wennerås and Boe Moen 2010, p. 400.

some deference and thereby bridges the gap between the proportionality assessment of EU acts pursuing legitimate objectives and national acts doing the same.

References

Barnard C (2009) Trailing a new approach to free movement of goods. 68 C.L.J. 288
Craig P, de Búrca G (2011) EU Law, 5th edn. Oxford University Press, Oxford
Horsley T (2009) Anyone for Keck? 46 C.M.L. Rev. 2001
Mathisen G (2010) Consistency and coherence as conditions for justification of Member State measures restricting free movement. 47 C.M.L. Rev. 1021
Pecho P (2009) Good-Bye Keck? A Comment on the Remarkable Judgment in Commission v. Italy, C-110/05. 36 L.I.E.I. 257
Spaventa E (2009) Leaving Keck behind? The free movement of goods after the rulings in Commission v Italy and Mickelsson and Roos. 34 E.L. Rev. 914
Weatherill S (2009) Current Developments. (58) I.C.L.Q. 985
Wennerås P, Boe Moen K (2010) Selling Arrangements, Keeping Keck. 35 E.L. Rev. 387.

Chapter 8
The Guardianship of European Constitutionality: A Structural Critique of European Constitutional Review

Agustín José Menéndez

Abstract Under the cloak of the projection of the national principle of proportionality to Union law, European courts have radically altered the substance of European law. This has been done both to supranational and national constitutional law and by means of redefining its substantive content. European courts have through proportionality assigned an abstract and a concrete constitutional weight to the right to private property and to entrepreneurial freedom through the four economic freedoms and the principle of undistorted competition. That has placed outside the realm of the constitutionally possible key public policies without which some of the fundamental collective goods at the core of the social and democratic Rechtsstaat become extremely vulnerable. This chapter shows how this accentuated bias of the European socio-economic constitution follows from the way in which European courts have defined economic freedoms as the yardstick of European constitutionality. This entails the automatic assignment of the argumentative benefit to economic freedoms, the construction of all other constitutional goods in the semblance of economic freedoms, and the use of asymmetric standards of evidence when having to justify the adequacy and necessity of economic freedoms and other constitutional goods.

Keywords Proportionality · Constitutional Review · Economic Freedoms · Collective goods · Socio-economic rights · Judicial Dialogue

---

A.J. Menéndez (✉)
Departamento de Derecho Público, Facultad de Derecho, Área de Filosofía del Derecho, Universidad de León, Campus de la Vegazana s/n, 24071 León, Spain
e-mail: agustin.menendez@unileon.es

A.J. Menéndez
ARENA, Centre for European Studies, University of Oslo, Oslo, Norway

M. Andenas et al. (eds.), *The Reach of Free Movement*,
DOI 10.1007/978-94-6265-195-1_8

Contents

8.1 Introduction 174
8.2 What Proportionality Is and What It Is Not 177
8.2.1 Proportionality as One of the Characteristic Syntaxes of Constitutional Reasoning in Democratic Constitutional States, Not a Positive Constitutional Principle 177
8.2.2 What Is Proportionality About: Legitimising Device or Critical Reconstructive Device? 179
8.3 Sharpening Proportionality as a Critical Reconstructive Tool of the Case Law of European Courts 180
8.3.1 The Lack of a Common European Constitutional Vocabulary and the Way European Courts Go About Proportionality 180
8.3.2 The Five Steps of the European Proportionality Review 182
8.3.3 Five Steps in Proportionality as an Indicator of European Constitutional Law Being Sui Generis? 184
8.4 Review of European Constitutionality: From Proportionality CJEU Style to the Structural Bias in European Constitutional Law 185
8.4.1 (Mis)translating the Conflict: A Too Wide Understanding of a Far Too Narrow Yardstick of Constitutionality 185
8.4.2 Automatic Assignment of the Argumentative Burden 192
8.4.3 Adequacy and Necessity Distorted (1): Redefining and Distorting Fundamental Legal Positions in Conflict with the Narrow Yardstick of European Constitutionality 195
8.4.4 Adequacy and Necessity Distorted (2): Proof Burdens 197
8.5 Conclusions 199
References 202

8.1 Introduction

The European Union Treaties require the European Court of Justice and the General Court of the European Union (hereafter, the European courts) to ensure that the 'law is observed' (Article 19.1 TEU).[1]

On the basis of such a mandate, European Courts have not only been key promoters of the interpretation and application of European law in a constitutional key, but have turned themselves into constitutional courts to all effects and purposes.[2] This is despite their constant pretence of doing nothing else but applying the law.[3]

[1] Article 19.1 TEU reads: "The Court of Justice of the European Union shall include the Court of Justice, the General Court and specialised courts. It shall ensure that in the interpretation and application of the Treaties the law is observed." There is also a third European Court, the Civil Service Tribunal, which basically decides controversies between the institutions of the Union and the supranational civil service. This entails that such a Court rarely decides questions with a constitutional dimension. For that reason I do not pay attention to it in this chapter.

[2] See Stein 1981; Mancini 1989; Weiler 1991 and Rasmussen and Boerger 2014.

[3] With the key difference that European Courts remain, contrary to national constitutional courts, free to make the lack of a formal mandate to review the constitutionality of norms to bear.

A key cause of the wide acceptance of this radical (self-) transformation of the role of European courts is to be found in the fact that European courts are regarded as having gone about the business of constitutional review in roughly the same fashion as national constitutional courts. European courts have defined the European canon of constitutionality by reference to a set of fundamental constitutional positions, as is the case with national canons of constitutionality. The European canon of constitutionality is, it is said, made up of fundamental rights, originally derived from the constitutional traditions common to Member States, as enshrined in the Charter of Fundamental Rights. This canon is said to be specifically defined by the relevance of the 'four' economic freedoms and the principle of undistorted competition, as affirmed in the founding Treaties of the European Communities. These may be (and regularly are) depicted as fundamental rights. It is frequently added that economic freedoms are the operationalisation of the right to private property and entrepreneurial freedom. By the same token, the key method used by European courts to determine the European constitutionality of supranational and national laws has been proportionality review, the working tool *par excellence* of post-war European constitutional courts. Both choices have contributed to render plausible the assumption that the role that European Courts play as guardians of the European constitutional law is but the projection to the supranational level of the role that national constitutional courts play as guardians of national constitutions. Indeed, such affinity and homogeneity is at core of the ever more fashionable understanding of the relationship between the European courts and national constitutional courts as a matter of "judicial dialogue".[4]

In this chapter, I claim that the similarities between the original model of constitutional review in national constitutional review and its alleged reflection or extension in supranational constitutional review are more apparent than real. Under the cloth of a supranational version of the national principle of proportionality, European courts have radically altered the substance of European constitutional law (both supranational and national) by redefining its substantive content. Key in this regard is the extent to which under the form of proportionality review, the abstract and concrete force of the right of private property and of entrepreneurial freedom has been altered. From *Cassis de Dijon* and onwards, the substantive content of the four economic freedoms and of undistorted competition has been emancipated from substantive national constitutional law; the European Court of Justice, quite frequently relying on the arguments of the European Commission, has put forward an *autonomous, self-standing* substantive content of the said economic freedoms by reference to a maximalistic understanding of the right to private property and of entrepreneurial freedom. This is tantamount to a form of constitutional revisionism that relativises the key post-war constitutional choices that cut the sharpest corners of private property and entrepreneurial freedom to create the political space in which different socio-economic policies were possible. The 'new' understanding of the four economic freedoms and of undistorted competition closes this political

[4] See, among others, Claes et al. 2012 and Rosas 2007.

space, and in the process, renders some of the fundamental collective goods at the core of the Social and Democratic Rechtsstaat extremely vulnerable. The consequences for European proportionality review is to take it away from the weighing and balancing of competing fundamental rights positions in full attention to the specific circumstances, place and time in which they enter into conflict (as is the case at the national level). European proportionality review becomes the conduit through which the resolution of conflicts between economic freedoms and any other constitutional good is biased in favour of the former over the latter. To put it differently, the review of European constitutionality has become a means of reaffirming the primacy of the rights to private property and freedom of enterprise, repacked as the subjective fundamental economic freedoms and the collective good of enhanced competitiveness. Thus, economic freedoms and undistorted competition prevail over all other fundamental rights positions and, very particularly, socio-economic rights. As a result, the normative foundations (fundamental rights) and the argumentative syntax (proportionality) of post-war democratic constitutional law have been turned upside down and used to justify fundamental decisions that collide with the substantive content of the post-war European constitutions.[5]

The argument is structured in three parts. In Sect. 8.2, I challenge the standard characterisation of the principle of proportionality in mainstream European legal studies and propose using proportionality as a critical reconstructive yardstick. In Sect. 8.3, I reconstruct the structure of the principle of proportionality as applied by European courts. I show in particular why we need to consider two more steps in addition to the 'canonical' three (adequacy, necessity and proportionality in a strict sense) by reference to which proportionality is usually reconstructed, namely the translation of the underlying social conflict into constitutional language, and the assignment of the argumentative burden and benefit. In Sect. 8.4, I approach the proportionality of European courts equipped with proportionality as a critical reconstructive yardstick. I show that the biasing of European constitutional law resulting from the way in which European courts do proportionality stems from (1) a very problematic definition of the breadth, scope and substance of economic freedoms as the yardstick of the constitutionality of national laws, (2) the automatic granting of the argumentative benefit to the parties advocating the resolution of conflicts in favour of economic freedoms, (3) the constant re-characterisation of collective goods and in general all constitutional norms in the image of economic freedoms, and (4) an asymmetric assignment of the burdens of proof.

[5] This is so because the national constitutions of the Member States (as, I would argue, the founding Treaties of the Communities) are underpinned by the characterization of the state as a Social and Democratic Rechtsstaat, aimed at the simultaneous realization of the civic, political and socio-economic rights of its citizens, something which required playing down and circumscribing the protection afforded to the right to private property.

8.2 What Proportionality Is and What It Is Not

Mainstream European legal scholarship revolves around three wrong assumptions regarding what proportionality is. The first one concerns the status of proportionality: It tends to be assumed that it is a principle of positive law. The second concerns the function of proportionality: Proportionality is characterised as a legitimising template, to the extent that if a decision has been written following the three 'canonical' steps by reference to which proportionality is reconstructed, then the resulting decision will be legitimate. In Sect. 8.2.1, I demonstrate that proportionality is not a principle of positive law, but a reasoning structure of general practical reasoning which is used and applied in legal reasoning. In Sect. 8.2.2, I argue that the legitimacy that results from the mechanical application of the proportionality template is purely procedural, and thus rather limited. We can use proportionality differently, as a critical reconstructive device, with the help of which to render explicit the implicit substantive choices with which courts, institutional actors or interpreters of the law at large 'fill in' the formal structure of proportionality.

8.2.1 Proportionality as One of the Characteristic Syntaxes of Constitutional Reasoning in Democratic Constitutional States, Not a Positive Constitutional Principle

It tends to be assumed in European studies that the principle of proportionality is a 'legal transplant'. Originating in German administrative law, the principle of proportionality would have been imported into European law by the European Court of Justice. The "incoming tide" of European law would then have resulted in its being projected into all national constitutional orders.[6]

This reconstruction not only confounds a pattern of influence (that of German administrative law on the reasoning of the European Court of Justice) with the genealogy of the principle of proportionality; but also, and fundamentally, obscures what proportionality actually is, namely, a syntactic pattern of legal reasoning borrowed from general practical reasoning.

Proportionality is a structural principle of general practical reason which is put to use in legal argumentation.[7] Use of proportionality is especially intense in legal systems characterised, as modern democratic constitutional systems, by commitment to a pluralistic set of values. Once law is expected to be the main tool of societal integration not only by means of solving specific conflicts but also by

[6] Among others, Jacobs 1999.

[7] Alexy 1989, pp. 212–22; 2002, pp. 66–69.

means of coordinating action with a view to achieve collective goals, law tends to be written by reference first and foremost to legal principles, not to narrow legal rules. To put it differently, once law becomes an empowering device, and not a restraining device of state action, the democratic discipline of state power is carried through legal principles that are established to *programme* state action.[8] As state action unavoidably collides with other legal principles, we need a structural framework with the help of which to analyse these problems. That framework is proportionality as a structural principle. Indeed, as Alexy reminds us in *The Theory of Constitutional Rights*:

> [T]here is a connection between the theory of principles and the principle of proportionality. This connection is as close as it could possibly be. The nature of principles implies the principle of proportionality and vice versa. That the nature of principles implies the principle of proportionality means that the principle of proportionality with its three sub-principles of suitability, necessity (use of the least intrusive means) and proportionality in its narrow sense (that is, the balancing requirement) logically follows from the nature of principles.[9]

Proportionality seems promising in terms of doing what is the core point of the Social and Democratic Rechtsstaat:[10] combining a commitment to both a plural set of principles which are far from obviously open to be easily reconciled (starting from the reconciliation of the regulatory ideals of the Rechtsstaat, the Democratic State and the Social State) and to being capable of acting, so always capable of determining what the reconciliation of such principles entails in each concrete instance or case. Proportionality imposes the consideration of *all relevant* interests at stake: the pondering of both the abstract and the concrete importance of the principles in conflict. Nonetheless, proportionality leads to a considered judgment which settles the conflict, because "[proportionality] makes it possible to compare and evaluate interests and ideas, values and facts that are radically different in a way that is both rational and fair."[11]

---

[8] García Pelayo 1977.

[9] Alexy 2002, p. 66.

[10] See Heller 1929, later enlarged and published as a book Heller 1930; English translation Heller 1987. I have read the Spanish translation, Heller 1985.

[11] Beatty 2004, p. 169. Both Alexy and Beatty would further add that a constitution cannot exist without reference to proportionality as an optimizing principle (of the realization of constitutional principles) (Beatty 2004, p. 163). But perhaps we can suspend our disbelief on this regard, as it may well be, as Habermas claims, that such understanding of principles fails to give proper due to some specific norms in modern legal systems, such as the prohibition of torture, which *should not* be regarded as being subject to being *optimized*. But that is not of essence in our previous discussion. What matters is that proportionality is not a positive principle, but a structural principle of legal reasoning.

8.2.2 *What Is Proportionality About: Legitimising Device or Critical Reconstructive Device?*

Most EU legal scholarship regards proportionality as a *legitimising* template. Or what is the same, the very fact that a court reaches a decision after having followed the 'canonical' three steps in which proportionality is usually disaggregated (adequacy, necessity, proportionality in a narrow sense) constitutes a guarantee of the *correctness* of the ruling at hand.[12]

Such an understanding is to be criticised on two accounts.

Firstly, it overestimates the legitimacy that can be drawn from deciding a conflict by reference to proportionality. A *formal reasoning structure*, such as proportionality (or for that matter, syllogisms) can only produce *formal legitimacy*. Proportionality guarantees, if the three steps are correctly followed, that all relevant aspects of the case have been taken into account before taking a decision. At most, proportionality guarantees a very thin substantive legitimacy; the same as indeed the classical *Wednesbury* review in British administrative law (which could be regarded as a variant of proportionality). Proportionality review ensures that the decision is not foolish in the sense that its aim makes sense and that no obvious alternative solution that could reconcile the colliding principles at stake was available. But proportionality cannot guarantee the *substantive correctness* of the decision in full. Substantive correctness depends on the correctness of the substantive choices with which the *formal syntactic structure* (proportionality) is filled in.[13]

Secondly, proportionality can still be useful when it comes to substantive choices, but not as a legitimising template, but as a critical reconstructive device.

Instead of considering legal reasoning from the standpoint of institutional actors interpreting and applying the law, we should consider legal reasoning from the perspective of *citizens* aiming at determining whether the law has been interpreted and applied *correctly*. Proportionality provides the critical lenses with which to render explicit all substantive choices made by judges. Proportionality as a critical reconstructive device allows us to move from the surface structure of the argument to the deep structure of the argument, and in the process, make explicit the complete supporting arguments which fill in the structure of proportionality (including empirical arguments about how the world is or how it will be, interpretative arguments, precedents, dogmatic arguments, and, critically, general practical reasons). This is but a necessary step to assess the substantive correctness of the decision by reference to the coherence between the substantive choices underlying the ruling and the substantive choices that a systematic reconstruction of the legal order would have required. To put it briefly, proportionality can be turned upside down. What makes a ruling legitimate is to a very minimal extent the fact that the

---

[12] Tridimas 2006.

[13] Alexy 1989, p. 230.

court conducts an assessment of proportionality, and to a much larger extent that it makes *justified* substantive choices *when making proportionality*.[14]

8.3 Sharpening Proportionality as a Critical Reconstructive Tool of the Case Law of European Courts

In this section, I argue that the reconstruction of the way in which European courts go about proportionality should take into account the structural differences between European and national constitutional law, as a yardstick of constitutionality. While in the latter case a wide and thick agreement on the constitutional vocabulary can be taken for granted, this is not the case regarding European constitutional law (Sect. 8.3.1). This accounts for the reconstruction of proportionality review as a five-pronged, not a three-pronged, test, adding to the 'canonical' adequacy, necessity and proportionality in a strict sense (1) the translation of social conflicts into constitutional language and (2) the assignment of the argumentative burden (Sect. 8.3.2). This specific reconstruction of proportionality does not result from the idiosyncratic character of European constitutional law, but from the fact that the essentially contested character of the European constitutional vocabulary renders problematic what national constitutional courts tend to do in a rather routine fashion (Sect. 8.3.3).

8.3.1 The Lack of a Common European Constitutional Vocabulary and the Way European Courts Go About Proportionality

The key thesis I put forward in this section is that the way in which European Courts apply proportionality is better reconstructed by means of a five-pronged, not

[14] Proper attention to the *structural* nature of the principle of proportionality as a syntactic structure of general practical reasoning should lead us to distinguish very clearly between the *formal* requirements of practical reasoning and the *substantive* elements with which we fill in the syntactic structure, and to which I have just referred. The correctness of a legal argument depends not only on following the structure of proportionality, but in getting the substance right. Indeed, in that distinction, in rendering us capable of making that distinction, resides the key analytical value of the principle of proportionality. It allows us to distinguish what parts of the decision are required by the very structure of legal reasoning (as a special case of general practical reasoning), which parts of the decision are dependent on substantive assumptions made in a rather uncontroversial way in previous legal decisions (essentially, through acts of constitutional significance and importance) and which parts depend on substantive assumptions made by the decision-maker. In particular, attention should be paid to the actual foundation of assumptions on the argumentative and proof burdens, the specific conceptions of each legal principle and the abstract weight assigned to each of them.

a three-pronged, proportionality test. In practical terms, this entails adding to the 'canonical' steps of adequacy, necessity and proportionality *stricto sensu*, two extra steps: (a) that of translating the underlying social conflict into constitutional language and (b) that of assigning the argumentative burden (and consequently, benefit).

These two additional steps are to be taken very seriously because, contrary to what is taken to be the case at the national constitutional level, European courts enjoy a very considerable discretion when doing both things. The lack of a strong consensus on the proper constitutional vocabulary by reference to which to translate social conflicts into constitutional conflicts adds a normative dimension to the institutional pluralism characteristic of European constitutional law. Under such circumstances, European Courts not only enjoy a considerable margin of discretion, but can also implicitly and explicitly justify their making use of it on purely functional reasons.

National constitutional courts (and in general all institutional actors and all individuals) can rely on a very dense web of previous authoritative constitutional decisions which contribute to the detailed conceptualisation of the principles involved and to the determination of the constitutional weight the principles are assigned in general, abstract terms and also in specific contexts. In particular, national constitutional vocabulary is shaped by both the constitutional debates preceding key constitutional decisions and by the political debates triggered by the passing of new legislation, in which the relationship between the new norms and constitutional norms is revisited.[15]

A European common constitutional vocabulary does not stem in an unproblematic fashion neither from authoritative decisions on the identity, shape and breadth of constitutional principles nor from a wide-ranging and vibrant political debate revolving around a common constitutional language. Indeed, the peculiar way in which legislation proceeds at the European level restrains the authoritative guidance to be derived from legislative debates, even from such debates in the European Parliament. By the same token, it certainly makes full sense to speak of the common constitutional law (i.e. the collective of national constitutions) as the deep constitution of the European Union. However, while the normative commonality underpinning the common constitutional law is very marked, it does not extend to a wide and deep background agreement on a common constitutional vocabulary. The peculiar constitutional path through which the European Union has evolved entails that contestation over the proper conceptualisation of basic constitutional principles is rendered endemic by the structural fact that Union law is the constitutional framework in which a (growing) number of constitutional legal

[15] Explicit constitution-making processes in "revolutionary" constitutional traditions—such as the French, Italian or to a rather large extent, Spanish one—and key constitutional moments in "evolutionary" constitutional traditions—such as the British or to a rather large extent, German one.

orders integrate. Thus, while the constitutional principles are largely the same in all legal orders, the way in which such principles are fleshed out is far from homogeneous.

Indeed, it is far from implausible to conclude that the ubiquity of proportionality in the reasoning of European courts is largely the result of European Courts operating in a far more pluralistic constitutional setting than national constitutional courts.

8.3.2 The Five Steps of the European Proportionality Review

The review of the European constitutionality of a legal norm is triggered by a *prima facie* or *apparent* conflict between a supranational or national legal norm and a European constitutional law norm. E.g. in *Cassis de Dijon*, the conflict was between on the one hand the national German law prohibiting the sale as "cassis" of liquors having less than 25 degree and on the other hand the right to free movement of goods (Article 30 TEC). *Avoir Fiscal* concerned a conflict between a particular French norm included in the French tax code (regulating the assessment of the tax debt in the corporate income tax) and article the freedom of establishment of companies (ex Article 52 TEC).

8.3.2.1 Figuring Out the Fundamental Norms in Conflict

The first step in the assessment of proportionality consists in determining what is the principle which underpins the EU constitutional norm *allegedly* infringed, and which principle underpins the *allegedly infringing* supranational or national legal norm. To put it differently, the first step consists in the translation of the underlying social conflict into constitutional language, i.e. into a conflict between the constitutional principles underlying each of the social positions at stake.

This translation tends to be largely taken for granted in conflicts before national constitutional courts. If it reappears it does so as one of the dimensions of the adequacy test, in the not so frequent cases in which the conflict is solved in a rather straightforward manner because the norm breaching one of the constitutional interests at stake is found not to be capable of realising the constitutional principle which is supposed to justify it. In most cases, however, the disagreement between the parties does not extend to the 'translation' of the conflict into constitutional language, but rather focuses on the way in which the conflict has to be resolved. This is largely due to the strength of the underlying consensus on the vocabulary of constitutional law and politics, or what is the same, on the consensus on the categories by reference to which to characterize constitutional conflicts.

8.3.2.2 Assignment of the Argumentative Burden

Once the two principles underlying the norms in apparent conflict are identified, the next step is to determine which is the prima facie normative centre of gravity of the case, or what is the same, which is the principle to be regarded as *prima facie* being infringed and which is the principle considered as prima facie *infringing* the other. This depends on which of the conflicting principles is regarded as being normatively more salient in the concrete factual and normative setting of the case.

The determination of the centre of gravity of the case is of great practical importance, because it determines which party bears the argumentative burden and which party enjoys the argumentative benefit. It is important to notice that the commutative principle does clearly not apply to legal argumentation. Whether we start considering whether it is justified to breach freedom of movement of goods to realize the collective goods of consumer protection or protection of human health, or, alternatively, whether instead we consider if it is justified to breach the collective good of consumer protection or the protection of human health to realize the subjective right to free movement of goods may be far from irrelevant. The party which bears the argumentative burden may still prevail, but has to make a bigger argumentative effort. How we allocate the argumentative burden makes a big difference. It may indeed mark the difference at the end of the day.

8.3.2.3 Adequacy

The third argumentative step requires us to assess the adequacy of the *allegedly infringing* norm to realise the principle which underlies it. Or what is the same, we have to test whether, as a matter of factual possibility and not merely legal possibility, the action that infringes one principle actually realises the other.

8.3.2.4 Necessity

The fourth step consists in the determination of the *necessity* of the allegedly infringing norm, or what is the same, whether there is no other normative alternative which would also realize the principle underlying the allegedly infringing norm while not affecting the allegedly infringed principle (or infringing it to a significant lesser extent).

Necessity calls for the consideration of factual possibilities, but contrary to what is the case in the adequacy step, such possibilities tend to be largely hypothetical. The court may be provided with actual empirical evidence of the consequences of the allegedly breaching norm, but can only speculate on the consequences of an *alternative* derivate rule that would solve the conflict in a different fashion.

8.3.2.5 Proportionality in a Narrow Sense

Finally, we have to weigh and balance the conflicting principles, so as to decide which should carry more weight in this concrete case. The weight to be assigned to each of the competing principles depends on two variables: the *abstract weight* of the principle (resulting from the "place" the principle has in the constitutional system) and the *concrete weight* of the principle (which results from the degree of infringement of the principle in the case at hand). The very facts that render visible the steps of translating the conflict into constitutional vocabulary and assigning the argumentative burden render the discretion enjoyed by European Courts wider when undertaking proportionality review in a strict sense.

8.3.3 Five Steps in Proportionality as an Indicator of European Constitutional Law Being Sui Generis?

Should we conclude from the observation that the way European Courts do proportionality requires a more nuanced reconstruction of proportionality review: that European constitutional law is *structurally different* from national constitutional law? Does this finding give comfort to the *sui generis* characterisation of the European Union and of European Union law? My view is that it does not. The very distinction of the two additional steps is the result of the perception, lacking at the national constitutional level, that European Courts are exercising massive and very relevant discretion when translating into constitutional language the underlying social conflicts, and when assigning the argumentative burden. The point is not that national courts do not translate conflicts into the constitutional language, or that they do not assign the argumentative benefit and the argumentative burden. The point is that while the background consensus on the constitutional vocabulary largely predetermines how national constitutional courts go about these two steps, so there is no decision in a meaningful sense being taken, the same is clearly not the case regarding European courts.[16]

To put it differently, it is not so much that European law is radically different, but that there are good reasons why some steps, taken for granted and largely unproblematic at the national constitutional level, become highly problematic at the supranational level.

---

[16] It should be added that the lack of a common constitutional vocabulary is a contingent feature. It is the result not of what European is a strong sense (in a deep ontological sense, if such pedantic expression is necessary), but of how it has become to be what it is. Similarly, the in-built bias in favour of economic freedoms, implicit in the automatic assignment of the argumentative burden to economic freedoms, is not intrinsic to what European Union is, but the result of a discretionary choice taken by European Courts that can be reversed.

As we will see *infra*, these two first steps in the way European courts do proportionality are indeed at the core of the tension between European and national constitutional law.

8.4 Review of European Constitutionality: From Proportionality CJEU Style to the Structural Bias in European Constitutional Law

In this section I apply proportionality as a critical reconstructive yardstick with a view to make explicit the implicit decisions taken by European Courts when reviewing the European constitutionality of national laws. I show that European Courts distort the meaning, salience and constitutional force of fundamental legal positions in both national and European constitutional law when 'filling in' the structural principle of proportionality with highly problematic substantive choices. This distortion follows in particular from (1) the peculiar definition of the yardstick of European constitutionality by exclusive reference to a highly contestable conception of economic freedoms; (2) the automatic assignment of the argumentative burden to plaintiffs defending a national law that constitutes an obstacle to the realisation of an economic freedom; (3) the re-characterisation of all constitutional positions in conflict with economic freedoms by reference to the political philosophy which the Court claims underpins economic freedoms; and (4) the application of standards of proof depending on whether evidence is being gathered regarding the adequacy and necessity of economic freedoms or of constitutional positions in conflict with economic freedoms. The European way of doing proportionality, far from being the projection to the supranational level of the understanding of proportionality characteristic of national constitutional courts, is actually at odds, both in procedural and substantive terms, with national constitutional understandings of proportionality.

8.4.1 (Mis)translating the Conflict: A Too Wide Understanding of a Far Too Narrow Yardstick of Constitutionality

The first question that I claim we need to focus on is the way in which European Courts translate underlying social conflicts into constitutional conflicts, and in particular, the way in which European Courts characterise economic freedoms as the yardstick of European constitutionality (especially when reviewing the validity of national laws).

European legal scholarship takes for granted and as almost obvious that European constitutionality should be determined by reference to a yardstick of constitutionality made of two key components, namely, economic freedoms and fundamental rights.

The first thing to be observed is that this definition of the yardstick of European constitutionality is far from obvious, being itself the outcome of the acceptance of the case law of European Courts themselves. The European Union was not constituted through a formal constitution defining a 'canon of constitutionality' or a 'constitutional yardstick'. The European Union was instead established by a set of international Treaties that came to be construed in a constitutional key by the European Court of Justice (with such a reading being progressively accepted, more tacitly than expressly, by national institutional actors). European Union law is based on the regulatory ideal of a common constitutional law, only partially fleshed out in the founding Treaties plus national constitutions.[17] As a result, the yardstick of European constitutionality is not formally established in a single authoritative constitutional document. Instead, the European Courts have played and keep on playing a key role in defining the implicit constitutional yardstick. This role is at the core of the process of *transformative constitutionalisation*, the internalization by constitutional actors (especially, national constitutional actors) of the constitutional character of European Union law.[18] The process was rather belated. While the Court had enunciated the core structural principles governing the relationship between Community law and national constitutional law in the early 1960s (*Costa*, jointly with *Van Gend*, laying the ground for both the reading in a constitutional key of the Treaties and for the primacy of Community over national law, the two foundational blocks of European constitutionality review), it was only in the 1970s that structural principles were filled in with constitutional substance, or what is the same, that the yardstick of European constitutionality was defined.[19] The leading case on the protection of fundamental rights, *Internationale Handelsgesellschaft,* was decided in 1970, a year after the first tentative affirmation of the unwritten principle of protection of fundamental rights in *Stauder*.[20] The leading case on the direct effect of economic freedoms was *Dassonville*, decided in 1974.[21] The Court turned the Treaty provisions enshrining the different fundamental freedoms into key components of the yardstick of European Constitutionality by means of affirming that the articles in which they were established were to be acknowledged direct effect.[22]

---

[17] Fossum and Menéndez 2011.

[18] Ibid.

[19] Case C-26/62, *Van Gend en Loos*, ECLI:EU:C:1963:1; Case C-6/64, *Costa v E.N.E.L.*, ECLI: EU:C:1964:66.

[20] Case C-11/70, *Internationale Handelsgesellschaft*, ECLI:EU:C:1970:114; Case C-29/69, *Stauder*, ECLI:EU:C:1969:57.

[21] Case C-8/74, *Dassonville*, ECLI:EU:C:1974:82.

[22] In formal terms, thus, the role played on national constitutional texts by the norms affirming a "constitutional core" (as the eternity clause in the German constitution, the norms distinguishing different review procedures and making more onerous to amend certain provisions of the

A second observation is that the canon of European constitutionality may seem *prima facie* as largely equivalent in both functional and normative terms to national canons of constitutionality; however, the two canons are substantially different once we analyse them in more detail. There is no doubt that fundamental rights are a key component of the canon of national constitutionality, while economic freedoms can be regarded as the operationalisation of the right to private property and entrepreneurial freedom, and consequently, as part of the yardstick of constitutionality *as* fundamental rights. However, the emphasis on economic freedoms is clearly *particular* and *peculiar* of European Union law. In national constitutional vocabularies, the fundamental status of the right to private property and of entrepreneurial freedom is highly contestable. Indeed, in some, if not in most Member States, they are not regarded as *fundamental rights*, but as *ordinary rights*, with an abstract and relative constitutional weight lower than that of fundamental rights. It could be counter-argued that the Treaties themselves stress the importance of economic freedoms as a key means of achieving the very socio-economic and legal integration that the European Union aims at, and that this justifies the decision of the European Court of Justice to consider them as part and parcel of the canon of European constitutionality. However, the practice of the European Court of Justice has not resulted in the integration of economic freedoms as an *instrumental* component of the canon of European constitutionality, but in the implicit affirmation of economic freedoms as *the* yardstick of the European constitutionality of national laws. This is the result of the deeply asymmetric way in which European constitutional review has proceeded, which has prevented an *integrated construction of the two components of the yardstick* of European constitutionality. On the one hand, the European Court has tended to review the European constitutionality of supranational law (regulations and directives) more nominally than substantially by reference to economic freedoms, and in very deferential ways by reference to fundamental rights. Review by reference to economic freedoms has been more nominal than actual because courts have tended to search in the very regulations and directives operationalising economic freedoms for the substantive criteria by

(Footnote 22 continued)

Constitution in other constitutional traditions; or the norms defining the set of fundamental rights whose protection citizens can directly seek from the constitutional court) is played in Community law by the criteria which make of a Treaty provision one with direct effect. The "economic" side of the substantive constitutional yardstick was only very preliminary developed in the early case law of the ECJ on customs (as in *Van Gend en Loos*) and in the old Article 95. But it was fleshed out in earnest from mid-1968 onwards, that is, once the fourth stage towards the common market was completed. From that date onwards, the ECJ considered that three of the four economic freedoms (and the principle of undistorted competition) were so defined in the Treaties as to merit to be acknowledged direct effect once the transitory phases were over. The fourth freedom (the free movement of capital) was so circumscribed and limited in the original drafting of the Treaties as to be considered as not having direct effect. That would remain being the case until the 1988 Directive (ad intra) and the Maastricht Treaty (1991) radically changed the Community legal discipline and consequently the status of this freedom, which within a decade moved from Cinderella to über-freedom.

reference to which the review of those same regulations and directives take place.[23] Review by reference to fundamental rights has been very deferential, with courts finding in favour of the validity of the contested norms. On the other hand, European Courts have (rightly) defined review of national laws by reference to supranational fundamental rights standards as beyond their competence. As a result, not only the exclusive yardstick by reference to which national laws have been reviewed has been economic freedoms, but the way in which economic freedoms has been defined has been totally autonomous and emancipated from the substantive requirements of fundamental rights. Indeed, as we will see, fundamental rights are regarded not as defining the very way in which we understand economic freedoms as canons of European constitutionality, but merely as reasons that may justify the breach of an economic freedom.

Thirdly, at the very same time that European Courts have affirmed economic freedoms as the yardstick of European constitutionality of national laws, they have radically expanded the breadth and depth of the said economic freedoms. This transformation has been the result of a double process.

Firstly, European courts have assimilated all economic freedoms to the right to free movement of goods: to a rather large extent overcoming the literal tenor of the Treaties, which strongly suggests a differentiated analysis of on the one hand the right to free movement of goods and on the other hand the other three economic freedoms. The Treaties, now as when they were written, do not contain a single chapter enshrining all economic freedoms and clearly assigning them a fundamental status. To start with the 'physical location' of economic freedoms, there is no single chapter dealing with all economic freedoms; rather, we find that there is one chapter which deals with the right to free movement of goods, and there is another chapter where the other three economic freedoms are enshrined. Interestingly, between these two chapters we find a chapter consecrated to common agricultural policy. It is very important to notice that the *means* of achieving the goals are very different in each case. In the original Treaties there was a detailed calendar aiming at the realisation of free movement of goods largely by means of reducing and then eliminating customs duties, quantitative restrictions and measures having an equivalent effect. A common market on agricultural products was envisaged, but this was expected to result from public intervention in both structures of production

[23] This is the lasting legacy of the fact that under the traditional Community Method, the Council of Member States was required to unanimously support a given legislative proposal for its becoming Community law in force. Even if procedurally speaking a decision of the Council (even if unanimous) was rather different from a decision taken in an Intergovernmental Conference, the fact of the matter was that a unanimous decision of the Council came close to a decision supported by a constitutional will. So in fact the ECJ tended to look for inspiration to construct Treaty provisions on secondary legislation and not the reverse. Even if qualified majority making and co-decision have changed things, the fact still is that the degree of legitimacy which a regulation or directive carries with it makes the ECJ very cautious when undertaking review on the basis of economic freedoms. Very different considerations apply when it comes to the protection of fundamental rights. Here it is not only the case that the main reference point cannot be the decisions of the Council of Ministers (a body of an open executive nature), but the substantive contents of national constitutions.

and on the very prices at which agricultural products were sold. Finally, the other three economic freedoms were to be realised *after* positive re-regulation of the key background conditions of each of the economic freedoms (indeed, the Treaties explicitly aimed at guaranteeing not free movement of capital *tout court*, but freedom of payments). This structure of the Treaties is not casual or random, but reflects the socio-economic vision underlying the post-war democratic constitutions (even if, less so originally, the socio-economic policy implemented under the referred constitutions). The common market aimed at liberalising movement of goods, while creating the conditions for national autonomous regulation of socio-economic policies, something which was regarded as requiring regulation of labour and capital. In other words, external trade in goods was to be turned into an engine of economic growth, while the regulation of labour and capital (whether national or supranational) was to ensure the autonomy and actual capacity of Member States to pursue economic policies aiming at realising the key objectives of the Social and Democratic Rechtsstaat.

This structure calls for a differentiated construction of on the one hand the right to free movement of goods and on the other hand the other three economic freedoms, which was largely corresponding to the case law of European Courts until the eighties.

What we find from the eighties is a progressive construction of all economic freedoms (and the principle of undistorted competition) *as if the Treaty* did not contain significant literal elements pointing to the need of pursuing a differentiated interpretation. In practical terms, what the European Court of Justice did was to reconstruct the right to free movement of workers (later persons), the right to freedom of establishment, and the right to free movement of capital, and the principle of undistorted competition *in the semblance* of the right to free movement of goods, setting aside not only the Treaty literal basis for a differentiated interpretation, but also the very different constitutional implications of each of the economic freedoms.

Secondly, European courts have reconceptualised all four economic freedoms. If on the basis of the literal tenor of the Treaties European courts originally characterised economic freedoms as operationalisations of the principle of non-discrimination, from the mid-eighties European courts have favoured a new understanding of economic freedoms as self-standing constitutional standards.

Under the common market conception of the Treaties, economic freedoms aimed at operationalising the right of a resident, and the right of economically active non-nationals, to be treated in the same way as nationals were dealt with: Non-nationals are denied the right to vote in national elections, and as a consequence, lack in most cases direct means to influence the actual content of legislation.[24]

---

[24] Their right not to be discriminated through the enjoyment of Community fundamental rights and economic liberties compensates the democratic pathology stemming from the mismatch between the circle of those affected by national laws and those entitled to participate in the deliberation and

In the late seventies economic freedoms were transformed into self-standing constitutional norms, the substantive content of which is to be determined by reference to a transcendental ideal of freedom. The right-holders of economic freedoms are no longer non-nationals, but actually all European citizens, including nationals, as the very aim of the single market is to get rid of all borders and distinctions, including reverse discrimination and purely internal situations. Any *obstacle* to the exercise of *any* economic freedom of *anybody*, was now regarded as breaching Community law. Breaches of economic freedoms are thus no longer limited to discriminatory normative patterns (which implied the anchoring of the European yardstick of constitutionality to the national one, because non-discrimination is a formal, not a substantive, principle) but are now extended to cover any "obstacle" to the realisation of the economic freedoms (something which by definition could not be determined by reference to national constitutional standards).

The shift from the common to the single market conception of economic freedoms is to be traced back to Cassis de Dijon. In that judgment, the ECJ established a derivative constitutional rule according to which goods in compliance with any national regulatory standard should be allowed unhindered access to all national markets, as all national regulatory standards would realize a functionally equivalent regulatory function. Indeed, the Commission drew the conclusion that the derivate constitutional rule affirmed in the *Cassis* could be generalised into the wider paradigm of the mutual recognition of laws. Mutual recognition, the Commission claimed, rendered unnecessary positive European regulation before incorporating specific goods or sectors to the *common market*.[25] This jurisprudential move was fully confirmed when the line of jurisprudence in *Cassis* was extended to the other three economic freedoms, a further step in the remaking of all economic freedoms in the semblance of free movement of goods.[26] The shift was normatively crowned in the ruling in *Martínez Sala*, as the European Court of Justice started to refer to citizenship as the new fundamental principle.[27] In *Martínez Sala* economic freedoms were operationalised under this new paradigm. In the process, the Court identified European citizenship with a set of economically based, even if not

(Footnote 24 continued)

decision-making over national laws. This is perhaps the core implication of Weiler's principle of constitutional tolerance. See Weiler 2002.

[25] Cf. 'Declaration of the Commission concerning the consequences of the judgment given by the European Court of Justice on 20 February 1979 ("Cassis de Dijon"), OJ C 256, of 30.10.1980, pp. 2 and 3.

[26] Key leading cases were Case C-76/90, *Säger*, ECLI:EU:C:1991:331; Case C-55/94, *Gebhard*, ECLI:EU:C:1995:411; Case C-415/93, *Bosman*, ECLI:EU:C:1995:463; and after the entry into force of Directive 88/361 on free movement of capital, Case C-163/94, C-165/94 & C-250/94, *Sanz de Lera*, ECLI:EU:C:1995:451. On the literature, see Castro Oliveira 2002; Hatzopoulos and Uyen 2006; Wymeersch 2002; Mohamed 1999; Landsmeer and Flynn 2002; Andenas et al. 2005. An overall interpretation congenial to the one hinted at here can be found in Somek 2008.

[27] Case C-85/96, *Martínez Sala*, ECLI:EU:C:1998:217.

economically conditioned, faculties.[28] Later judgments such as *Viking* and *Laval* are but concrete applications of this new understanding of economic freedoms.

At this point, it is necessary to take stock of what the 'obstacle' conception entails from a constitutional perspective.

The obstacle conception implies a yardstick of European constitutionality, emancipated from national constitutional law, and derived by the Court from the rather dry and concise literal tenor of the Treaties.

Firstly, European constitutional law emancipates itself from national constitutional law. The substantive content of economic freedoms while understood as operationalisation of non-discrimination was still determined by reference to national constitutional law. It did not require this or that specific treatment, but that non-nationals were treated in the same way as nationals. But once there is an autonomous substantive content of economic freedoms, what economic freedoms require is more than equal treatment. They require their holders being treated in line with what the autonomous substantive content of economic freedoms demands, whether or not such treatment is the one required by national law, or whether it enters into conflict with what national law requires. This emancipation is especially momentous and transcendental because European courts, as was pointed to above, expanded at the same time the width and breadth of economic freedoms, disconnecting it from the legislative competence of the European Union. The result is the expansion of the normative force of European constitutional law, which now reaches in its revamped form (economic freedoms as self-standing constitutional standards) all four corners of national legal systems. The re-calibration of economic freedoms has resulted in a massive growth of the horizontal effect of European constitutional principles. Areas of national law which had not been much Europeanised through supranational law-making (such as personal tax law) or which seemed clearly outside the scope of the Treaties (such as non-contributory pensions) were *absorbed* into European constitutional law, with national policy decisions being progressively subject to a review of their European constitutionality. This is why we are confronted with vertical conflicts proper, in which the collision between supranational and national law is not the result of a horizontal conflict among national constitutional norms competing to define the common, collective standard, but rather results from a conflict between an autonomously defined supranational constitutional standard and national ones (even most or even all national constitutional standards, viz the kind of situation underlying Viking or Mangold). Indeed, *Cassis* implies doing away with the idea of a constitutional space in which economic freedoms do not mediate the constitutional validity of any national legal norm. The idea of a *diagonal* conflict (as in Joerges' theory of constitutional conflicts) is either quaint or obsolete if one embraces *Cassis*, or else it constitutes an implicit vindication of the old understanding of economic freedoms as principles of non-discrimination.

Secondly, control over the substantive shape of integration shifts from the law-making process (precisely at the time at which that was becoming potentially

[28] See Somek 2008 and Menéndez 2010.

democratic with the direct election of the Members of the European Parliament) to the constitutional adjudication process into which preliminary requests have been turned into processes of review of the European constitutionality of national statutes. To put it differently, if one endorses *Cassis de Dijon* and *Centros*, one is endorsing not a process of juridification (as these are matters which are within the realm of the law anyway) but a process of judicialisation.[29] As the shape of economic freedoms as constitutional standards became progressively specific, the negative move in mutual recognition was harder to combine with the positive move of re-regulation, because the combined effect of European constitutional decisions by the European Court of Justice was to foreclose the realm of national legislative autonomy. *Centros* is, indeed, a poignant case. The best illustration of how far the judgment re-inforced the structural power of capitalists and weakened the taxing and regulatory grip of the state as *longa manus* of the public interest is provided by the 400% increase of the number of "shell" companies constituted in England after *Centros*, most of which were German.[30] It should be added that the more the Court has developed its jurisprudence, the more it has foreclosed the actual realm of re-regulatory discretion on the side of the Member States. This is, in my view, fully illustrated by the tragic case law of the Court on personal taxation, where the much maligned harmonisation has, to a large extent, progressed thanks to the iron fist of market adaptation accelerated by the ECJ.[31] The decoupling of the breadth and width of European constitutional review from the legislative competence of the European Union leads indeed to the judicial empowerment of big market actors, equipped now with legal tools to subvert political integration. The price of substituting politically-led harmonisation by market-led harmonisation is always paid in the hard currency of (a lesser modicum) of distributive justice, in flat contradiction with the basic principles of the Social and Democratic Rechtsstaat.

8.4.2 Automatic Assignment of the Argumentative Burden

The development of a jurisprudential bill of rights entails not only defining which rights are *fundamental* (something on which there is far from being complete agreement among the Member States) but also how different fundamental rights are to relate to each other (as indeed, the Social and Democratic Rechtsstaat is based on the full convergence, of the ideals of the rule of law, the democratic state, and the social/welfare state). The solemn proclamation of the Charter of Fundamental Rights and its later formal incorporation into the primary law of the Union should be regarded by the European Courts as authoritative decisions relieving them of

[29] Case 120/78, *Rewe-Zentral (Cassis de Dijon)*, ECLI:EU:C:1979:42; Case C-212/97, *Centros*, ECLI:EU:C:1999:126.

[30] The figures are taken from Becht et al. 2008.

[31] Menéndez 2011.

many of these discretionary choices. However, as I will argue in the coming paragraphs, the Charter renders even more visible the problematic character of the assignment of the argumentative benefit to economic freedoms and the criteria which the European Courts follow when assigning specific weight to European constitutional principles.

A fundamental feature of the review of European constitutionality of national norms is that European Courts always assign the argumentative burden to the party that argues in favour of solving the underlying conflict *against* the narrow yardstick of European constitutionality. The actual consequences of the automatic assignment of the argumentative burden are multiplied by the fact that European Courts have developed a very wide conception of what constitutes an infringement of economic freedoms.

As a result, the review of European constitutionality does not really consist in the weighing and balancing of conflicting fundamental legal positions, as in the determination of whether there are good reasons that justify *the infringement* of an economic freedom or of the collective good to undistorted competition.[32] This in itself implies that the review of European constitutionality is seriously biased in favour of economic freedoms as understood by European Courts.[33]

It is no longer the case that the argumentative preference granted to the narrow yardstick of constitutionality can be justified on the basis that economic freedoms and the collective good of undistorted competition were positively enshrined in the Treaties while the principle of protection of fundamental rights was not. Since the affirmation of the principle of protection of fundamental rights in *Stauder* and *Internationale*, even more so since the solemn proclamation of the Charter of Fundamental Rights in 2000, and definitely so since the full incorporation of the Charter into the primary law of the Union, such a premise is simply wrong. At any rate, it cannot be sustained by claiming that the literal tenor of the Treaties limits the *yardstick* of constitutionality of Union law to the narrow yardstick of European constitutionality.

---

[32] Or eventually, with the principle of non-discrimination on the basis of sex by reference to Article 157 TFEU or to citizenship to the extent that it gives rise to autonomous rights.

[33] The argumentative benefit granted to economic freedoms was rather inconsequential as long as economic freedoms were understood as operationalisations of the principle of equality, and thus were substantially defined by national standards. This was so because the national standards of protection of economic freedoms were the result of weighing and balancing economic freedoms with other constitutional principles, so that the *renvoi* to national constitutional standards implies that the argumentative benefit is based on a previous balancing undertaken at the national constitutional level. Indeed, when national norms enter into conflict with economic freedoms as operationalisations of the principle of non-discrimination, what is put into question is exclusively the personal scope of application of the national norms, not their inner normative logic. Things change considerably once we conceptualise economic freedoms as self-standing, transcendental standards defined at the end of the day by the European Courts. This is so because the Community conception of economic freedom replaces the national standard, and as such, does away with the crafted balance reached at the national level. But if that is so, there is no obvious reason why we should assign an argumentative favour to economic freedoms.

The coupling of the automatic granting of the favour of the argumentative burden to the party that favours the narrow yardstick of European constitutionality and the very wide understanding of what constitutes a breach of an economic freedom are contrary to the characterisation of European Union law as a constitutional order. If European Union law is to be understood as the means through which constitutional states integrate by reference to constitutional norms, there is a very good case to follow the consistent practice of national constitutional courts. Such a practice, far from being automatic, is based on the case by case consideration of several relevant variables, including the different abstract constitutional weight of the fundamental legal positions in conflict (something determined by reference to the literal tenor and systematic structure of the fundamental law itself, the constitutional debates the interpretation consolidated in statutes and previous judicial decisions) and the specific weight of the fundamental legal positions in conflict in the case at hand (and in cases which may resemble the case at hand). It is on such a basis that the normative centre of gravity of each case is determined, leading to the assignment of the argumentative favour to the party advocating the resolution of the conflict in favour of the fundamental legal position that constitutes the said centre of gravity.

Indeed, the full acknowledgment of the constitutional nature of the Treaties *after the formal incorporation of the Charter* would require a deep reconsideration of the assignment of the argumentative burden.

This is something which was hinted at in the opinion of the late AG Geelhoed in *American Tobacco*.[34] Geelhoed revisited in his opinion the relationship between economic freedoms and social goals in Community law. He argued that at the stage of development at which it was a decade ago (following the solemn proclamation of the Charter in 2000), Community law did not aim exclusively at the creation of a single market, but also at other fundamental legitimate goals of Community action, such as the protection of public health. The basis of the competence of the Union might still be grounded on the realization of the basic economic freedoms, but this did not entail that the *actual* exercise of Community competences was to be exclusively aimed at market-making.[35] Indeed, some of the social goals constitute basic preconditions for a single market. This prompts the late AG to hint at a radical change in the structure of the review of European constitutionality. Instead of focusing in a first step on whether a given national provision distorts the common

[34] Case C-491/01, *British American Tobacco*, ECLI:EU:C:2002:741.

[35] Case C-112/00, *Schmidberger*, ECLI:EU:C:2002:437, Opinion delivered on July 11, 2002, para 100: "The issue boils down to the following: if a (potential) barrier to trade arises, the Community must be in a position to act. Such action must, as I construe the biotechnology judgment, consist in the removal of those barriers. Article 95 EC creates the power to do so". Cf. para 106: "In other words, the realisation of the internal market may mean that a particular public interest—such as here public health—is dealt with at the level of the European Union. In this, the interest of the internal market is not yet the principal objective of a Community measure. The realisation of the internal market simply determines the level at which another public interest is safeguarded" (my emphasis).

market, and only in a second step on whether such a measure can be justified by reference to some legitimate public goal, some paragraphs of the opinion invite a shift of the argumentative burden.[36]

The opinion of Advocate General Cruz in *Santos Palhota and Others* might be hinting at something similar.[37] The AG considers in particular the impact that the changes introduced by the Lisbon Treaty, and paramount, the incorporation of the Charter of Fundamental Rights, must have in the solving of conflicts between freedom of establishment and fundamental collective goods. Cruz argues explicitly for recalibrating the specific weight to be assigned to the principle allegedly infringing a Community freedom in the fifth step of the proportionality argument (when considering proportionality *strict sensu*), but seems to be favouring implicitly a thorough reconsideration of the way in which proportionality is applied in line with the new literal tenor of the Treaties. It is worth quoting at length:

> As a result of the entry into force of the Treaty of Lisbon, when working conditions constitute an overriding reason relating to the public interest justifying a derogation from the freedom to provide services, they must no longer be interpreted strictly. In so far as the protection of workers is a matter which warrants protection under the Treaties themselves, it is not a simple derogation from a freedom, still less an unwritten exception inferred from case-law. To the extent that the new primary law framework provides for a mandatory high level of social protection, it authorises the Member States, for the purpose of safeguarding a certain level of social protection, to restrict a freedom, and to do so without European Union law's regarding it as something exceptional and, therefore, as warranting a strict interpretation. That view, which is founded on the new provisions of the Treaties cited above, is expressed in practical terms by applying the principle of proportionality.[38]

8.4.3 Adequacy and Necessity Distorted (1): Redefining and Distorting Fundamental Legal Positions in Conflict with the Narrow Yardstick of European Constitutionality

The third set of problems concerns the fact that the European Courts systematically distort the meaning and implications of fundamental legal positions in conflict with the narrow yardstick of European constitutionality. The European Courts appraise and de facto redefine the fundamental legal positions in conflict with the narrow yardstick of European constitutionality by reference to the goal of the realisation of the single market.

---

[36] Para 229: "The value of this public interest [public health] is so great that, in the legislature's assessment other matters of interest, such as the freedom of market participants, must be made subsidiary to it."

[37] Case C-515/08, *dos Santos Palhota*, ECLI:EU:C:2010:245, Opinion of 5 May 2010.

[38] Para 53.

When confronted in *Viking* with a conflict between the right to strike and the right to freedom of establishment, the CJEU opted for not solving the conflict between the right to freedom of establishment as understood in its case law and the right to strike as understood in the constitutional traditions common to the Member States which constitute the constitutional law of the European Union, and consequently, the ground on which Article 28 of the Charter stands, but between the right to freedom of establishment as understood in the case law of the CJEU and a peculiar conception of the right to strike, in particular, the right to strike that would be *functional* to the full realization of the single market as the CJEU understands it.[39]

Similarly, when the Court of Justice is confronted with a conflict between the right to freedom of establishment or the right to free movement of capital and the collective good of a progressive and coherent tax system (in the jargon of the CJEU the principle of coherence of the tax system), the Court does not resolve the underlying conflict so much as it redefines coherence of the tax system as the kind of coherence that would further the realization of the single market.

By de facto redefining all conflicting fundamental legal positions by reference to the normative vision of the "single market" underpinning the CJEU's current understanding of economic freedoms, the European Courts "do" proportionality in a very different manner than national constitutional courts. In fact, one can actually doubt whether it is proper to speak of a proportionality review at all.[40] The national constitutional practice of proportionality takes the pluralism of constitutional principles, seriously. One of the key social tasks of constitutional law is indeed that of resolving conflicts, including conflicts involving constitutional principles. The solving of all conflicts entails that the principles at stake are far from fully realized in the case at hand. However, the principles retain their normative identity after the conflict is solved. This is certainly not the case in the case law of the CJEU. The right to strike was not only left aside in Viking. The way in which the Court *redefined* the right to strike implied that it was basically *defined away*. The collective good of a progressive and coherent tax system was not only defeated in the saga of cases above referred, but redefined not as a collective good at all, but as a subjective right of individual citizens.

The systematic recharacterisation of fundamental constitutional positions in conflict with economic freedoms entails a structural bias in the European review of constitutionality. Instead of taking seriously the *normative point* and *underlying philosophy* of both subjective rights and collective goods, of the narrow yardstick of European constitutionality and the whole set of relevant constitutional positions, the European Courts assume that the *meta-constitutional* standard in European law are the rights to private property and entrepreneurial freedom.

[39] Case C-438/05, *Viking*, ECLI:EU:C:2007:772.

[40] Niglia 2016.

In addition, European Courts assign a much higher abstract weight to economic freedoms than to fundamental rights when the two "arms" of the yardstick of constitutionality come into conflict. While this conflict was present all through the process of European integration, the case law of the European Courts remained rather unproblematic until the late seventies. Indeed, the European Courts solved this conflict in line with the basic constitutional choices of post-war national constitutions. It is worth keeping in mind that the first cases on the protection of fundamental rights concerned in many occasions the conflict between the right to private property and the collective goals pursued through common agricultural policy. By means of giving preference to the latter, the European Courts may have been furthering European integration; but in doing that, they were solving the conflicts in a way congenial to the characterization of private property in the social and democratic Rechtsstaat. In fact, the key leading cases concerned conflicts in which Community law fostered collective goods and interests, and plaintiffs claimed that it was in breach of their right to private property.[41] However, once the European Courts affirmed an autonomous and self-standing conception of economic freedoms, once they favoured a different conceptualization of economic freedoms, the tension at the core of the yardstick of European constitutionality could only mount over time. This is a typical, almost millenarian conflict at the core of fundamental rights protection.[42] *Viking* and *Laval* are but late chapters in a long saga from this perspective.

8.4.4 Adequacy and Necessity Distorted (2): Proof Burdens

European courts apply different evidence standards to the parties arguing in favour of the prevalence of the narrow yardstick of European constitutionality and those arguing in favour of the prevalence of other fundamental legal positions. Such asymmetry affects both the adequacy and necessity steps of the review of proportionality, but very especially the latter.

Whether a measure is adequate or not to achieve a certain objective, and, very especially, whether there is a feasible alternative rule which reconciles better the two fundamental principles in conflict, depends to a rather large extent on the assumptions we make about the external (empirical) world. Such assumptions do

---

[41] Typically, Case 4/73, *Nold*, ECLI:EU:C:1974:51 and Case 44/79, *Hauer*, ECLI:EU:C:1979:290, where the right to private property was invoked against regulatory powers on coal retailing and on use of agricultural land.

[42] What is revealing is that it is substantively identical to the ones which have been at the heart of public debate in the last years, with the revealing difference that what conflicted with collective goods was a Community protected economic freedom, and that the Court solved the conflicts according to a different normative logic.

not follow from the principle of proportionality, but depend on substantive decisions on how we pass judgment on the probability that a future event will come to happen.

The European Courts should apply the same criteria to consider the likelihood of events whether they support the adequacy and necessity of the infringing norm or they work on the opposite direction. However, that is not always the case. The European Courts tend to lower the threshold to proof the probability of a fact happening in the future when that fact contradicts the adequacy or necessity of the infringing principle; and do the opposite (raising the threshold of proof) when the fact supports the adequacy and necessity of the infringing norm.

The "effectiveness of fiscal supervision" was one of the first "rules of reason" or "overriding interests" to be acknowledged by the ECJ as justifying the infringement of an economic freedom even if not explicitly stated in the Treaties.[43] The Court has turned the principle almost ineffective by applying unrealistic proof standards to Member States invoking the principle. Firstly, the ECJ has systematically rejected that the curtailment of economic freedoms can be justified by any evidence of a revenue loss. Secondly, the ECJ once and again has rejected the argument that the monitoring of tax compliance is hampered by "informative" deficits concerning economic transactions on other Member States, and thus restricting economic freedoms *ex ante* was justified. Member States have once and again stumbled on the rock of Directive 77/799, despite the fact that the Commission itself has recognised once and again the limited effectiveness of cross-border tax administrative cooperation, and that indeed the Community seems now to be heading to automatic exchanges of tax information.[44]

Similarly, a very peculiar set of (highly artificial) factual assumptions concerns the rationale which moves tax lawyers to create complex corporate structures and incorporate companies in a multitude of jurisdictions where they have no observable business.

The ECJ has claimed that a breach of an economic freedom is justified if it is intended to avoid that "*wholly* artificial arrangements" (my italics) are employed to reduce the tax bill.[45] This has been confirmed in *Lankhorst*, *Marks and Spencer,*

[43] Indeed even before that personal taxation was subject to review of European constitutionality in *Avoir Fiscal*. It was in the leading judgment on *Cassis de Dijon*, precisely in the ruling in which "rule of reason" exceptions were first referred to, that the ECJ coined the justification (see para 8 of the ruling).

[44] See for example the Commission Communication (2006) 254 on a European strategy to combat tax fraud.

[45] Case C-264/96, *ICI v United Kingdom*, ECLI:EU:C:1998:370, para 26: "As regards the justification based on the risk of tax avoidance, suffice it to note that the legislation at issue in the main proceedings does not have the specific purpose of preventing wholly artificial arrangements, set up to circumvent United Kingdom tax legislation, from attracting tax benefits, but applies generally to all situations in which the majority of a group's subsidiaries are established, for whatever reason, outside the United Kingdom. However, the establishment of a company outside the United Kingdom does not, of itself, necessarily entail tax avoidance, since that company will in any event be subject to the tax legislation of the State of establishment".

Halifax and *Cadbury Schweppes*.[46] Still, the residual justification is not only limited, but the phrase "wholly artificial arrangements" is indicative of a rather peculiar understanding of economic and legal realities. In line with the structural implications of *Centros* and *Inspire Art*[47] on freedom of establishment, the ECJ has said that "the fact that the company was established in a Member State for the purpose of benefiting from more favourable legislation [my note: thus including tax legislation] does not in itself suffice to constitute abuse of that freedom".[48] It is only an abuse when what is being used is a mere "letter box corporation". Only that seems to qualify as a "wholly artificial" institutional structure.[49] *A contrario*, partially artificial structures, or for that purpose, any structure that is not "wholly artificial" should be considered as the exercise of economic freedoms, and consequently the justification could not be invoked. Can this be regarded as *factually* accurate?

8.5 Conclusions

In this chapter, I claim that European Courts have come to play a key role as guardians of European constitutionality. In discharging such a task, European Courts have made use of the working tools par excellence of national constitutional courts, a yardstick made up of fundamental rights and the argumentative syntax of the principle of proportionality. This has contributed to the acceptance of the self-assigned role played by European courts as guardians of European constitutionality.

Making use of the critical potential of proportionality I approach the case law of the European Court of Justice on economic freedoms. This leads me to four key problems in the fleshing out of European constitutional law in the jurisprudence. Firstly, I find that while the affirmation that economic freedoms constitute a key part of the canon of European constitutionality is well-grounded, the European Court of Justice has shifted its characterization of economic freedoms from operationalisations of the principle of non-discrimination on the basis of nationality and building blocks of a common market to concretizations of a self-standing and transcendental economic freedom and vanguard of the single market. Such a shift may seem to have been endorsed (even if, *ex post casu*) by the Treaty amendments introduced by the Single European Market and the Treaty of Maastricht. However, I claim that it remains hard to reconcile with the synthetic constitutional identity of the European Union and impossible to square with the constitutional identity of the Member

[46] C-324/00, *Lankhorst-Hohorst*, ECLI:EU:C:2002:749; C-446/03, *Marks & Spencer*, ECLI:EU:C:2005:763; C-255/02, *Halifax*, ECLI:EU:C:2006:121; C-196/04, *Cadbury Schweppes*, ECLI:EU:C:2006:544.

[47] C-167/01, *Inspire Art*, ECLI:EU:C:2003:512.

[48] C-167/01, *Inspire Art*, ECLI:EU:C:2003:512.

[49] Opinion of AG Mengozzi in C-298/05, *Columbus Container Services*, ECLI:EU:C:2007:197, paras 182 and 183: actual physical existence plus financial activity are enough to pass the test.

States as social and democratic *Rechtsstaten*. Indeed, it seems to me much more plausible to conclude that the jurisprudence of the European Courts took a *wrong turn* when it shifted from one conception of economic freedoms to the other, or what is the same, that *Cassis de Dijon* and the later jurisprudence expanding the "obstacles" conception of breaches to economic freedoms are properly characterized as part of a "constitutional dérapage" in the development of Community law. Secondly, I find extremely problematic the tendency of the European Court of Justice to invariably assign the argumentative benefit to the economic freedoms and the argumentative burden to the principle underlying the colliding norm. That is difficult to reconcile with the fact that fundamental rights have long been acknowledged to be part of the yardstick of European constitutionality, and become formally and undeniably so after the formal incorporation of the Charter of Fundamental Rights to the primary law of the Union. The opinions of AG Geelhoed in *American Tobacco* and of AG Cruz Villalón in *Santos Coelho* could be so constructed as to become precedents of a more flexible and balanced approach. Thirdly, I have serious objections to the standards which the European Court of Justice employs to determine the probability of events when assessing the adequacy and necessity of the norms colliding with an economic freedom. While the ECJ assumes without paying much attention to any evidence that all breaches of economic freedoms would result in a *grave infringement*, it eventually sets a too high threshold to prove the adequacy and necessity of infringing norms. This was exemplified by the fully unrealistic assumptions the ECJ makes on the alternative means on the hands of Member States to ensure the effectiveness of fiscal supervision (flatly contradicted by the several legislative initiatives of the Commission, only partially successful, to increase the degree of tax assistance, especially in the form of automatic exchange of tax data). Fourthly, the European Court of Justice tends to fail to approach on its own terms the principles underpinning the norms colliding with economic freedoms. The breadth and scope of these principles is not only defined in the most restrictive manner, but the inner normative logic of these principles tends to be neglected. This was exemplified by considering the peculiar characterization of the overriding national interest in the coherence of the national tax system. Such a conception should be reconsidered and revised in the case law of the European Court of Justice. It does not only severe a basic source of legitimacy of Community law (the transfer of legitimacy through the key role played by the common constitutional law as the deep constitution of the European Union) but runs the risk of placing Union law at constitutional odds with national constitutional law, to the extent that the latter keeps on being inspired by the normative goal of reconciling the rule of law with the democratic and the social state. The Court should indeed take seriously the pluralistic basis of Community law, and keep in mind that its role as guardian of European constitutionality is one in which it has to be especially attentive to the substantive content of the constitutional law common to the Member States, and which it shares with national constitutional courts. Where the European Courts to persist in putting forward this peculiar understanding of economic freedoms, it is more than likely that national constitutional courts would act on the basis of their legitimate role as part of the collective of guardians of European constitutional law.[50]

Having argued all that, it might not be completely improper to make in the conclusions a plea for the recalibration of the case law of the European Courts. There is a very good case for the European Courts playing a key role in the guardianship of European constitutionality. The European Court of Justice was reasonably successful in the way it discharged this task in the first decades of European integration. Not only were the rulings very attentive and indeed deeply informed by the pluralistic nature and institutional setup of the European Union, but the Court avoided pushing its autonomous characterization of the norms of Community law too far. The paradigmatic shift which followed from *Cassis de Dijon* led not only to a major structural change in the conception of economic freedoms, but also to paying much lesser attention to the pluralistic nature of European integration. The argumentative benefit assigned to economic freedoms, coupled with a tendency to distort the understanding of other colliding principles when assigning concrete weight to them and resort to biased criteria to determine the probability of future events have stressed if not severed the fundamental link between national and European constitutional law. The price of the wider autonomy in the short run may be a loss of legitimacy in the long run. The Court runs a double risk in that regard. As a supranational institution, it is not in a position to search for cover in the direct legitimacy of European decision-making processes, as that direct legitimacy is still very thin. As a judicial institution, it is in a position to limit the realm of what is politically possible, but not of taking constructive political decisions, not even when the cumulative effect of its case law is the full disempowerment of all levels of government.

Finally, let me add that the characterisation of the relationship between European and national courts as a 'judicial dialogue' is premised on the two parties speaking a common language, or what is the same: in all courts applying legal systems premised on the same normative principles through methods of reasoning and argumentation that are basically equivalent. Leaving aside whether the concept of 'dialogue' is really fit for purpose when describing the relationship between courts, the arguments I have put forward in this chapter should lead us to the conclusion that there can be no real dialogue between European and national courts because the courts have radically different understandings both of what is the substantive content of the yardstick of European constitutionality and about the key methods of constitutional reasoning. Formal similarities (a yardstick of constitutionality pitched to fundamental rights, proportionality as the key working tool of the courts) cloak in plain sight fundamental disagreements. The growing number of constitutional conflicts pitting the European Court of Justice against national constitutional courts is a symptom of both the judicialisation of politics in Europe and of the tensions

[50] A most benign manifestation of such a role would follow the path of the German Constitutional Court in several of its "European" judgments, including the Lisbon judgment. A rather less benign result would ensue if national constitutional courts would limit themselves to act as guardians of the national constitutional law.

that have been explored in this chapter. For a period, conflicts were largely confined to matters of competence between courts, even if expressed through different understandings of how specific fundamental rights were to be constructed. By now, as the recent rulings of the Italian and the German Constitutional Court seem to indicate, the conflict has become a fully substantive one. If European integration continues to unfold in the way in which it has been unfolding in the last years, it is just a matter of time that constitutional conflicts with courts are but a herald of political constitutional resistance.[51]

References

Alexy A (1989) A Theory of Legal Argumentation. Oxford University Press, Oxford

Alexy A (2002) A Theory of Constitutional Rights. Oxford University Press, Oxford

Andenas M, Gütt T, Pannier M (2005) Free Movement of Capital and National Company Law. European Business Law Review 16: 757–86

Beatty D (2004) The Ultimate Rule of Law. Oxford University Press, Oxford

Becht M, Mayer C, Wagner HF (2008) Where do Firms Incorporate? Deregulation and the Cost of Entry. Journal of Corporate Finance, 14: 241–56

Castro Oliveira A (2002) Workers and Other Persons: Step-by-Step from Movement to Citizenship. Common Market Law Review, 39: 77–127

Claes M, de Visser M, Popelier P, van den Heyning C (eds) (2012) Constitutional Conversations in Europe. Intersentia, Cambridge

Flynn L (2002) Coming of Age: The Free Movement of Capital Case Law. Common Market Law Review, 39:773–805

Fossum JE, Menéndez A J (2011) The Constitution's Gift. Rowman and Littlefield, Lanham

García Pelayo M (1977) Las Transformaciones del Estado Contemporáneo. Alianza, Madrid

Hatzopoulos V, Uyen Do T (2006) The Case Law of the ECJ concerning the free provision of services: 2000–2005. Common Market Law Review, 43: 923–91

Heller H (1929) Rechtsstaat oder Diktatur? Die Neue Rundschau 40: 721–735

Heller H (1930) Rechtsstaat oder Diktatur? In: Gesammelte Schriften II. J.C.B. Mohr, Berlin, pp 443–462

Heller H (1985) Estado de Derecho o Dictadura? In: Heller H, Escritos Políticos. Alianza, Madrid, 283–301.

Heller H (1987) Rechtsstaat or Dictatorship. Translated by Kennedy E. Economy and Society, 16:127–142

Jacobs F (1999) Recent Developments in the Principle of Proportionality in Community law. In: Ellis E (ed) The Principle of Proportionality in the Laws of Europe. Hart, Oxford/Portland, Oregon, pp 1–22

Landsmeer A (2001) Movement of Capital and other Freedoms. Legal Issues of Economic Integration 28: 57–69

Mancini GF (1989) The Making of a Constitution for Europe. Common Market Law 26:595–614

Menéndez AJ (2010) More Humane, Less Social. In: Poiares M, Azoulay L (eds) The Past and Future of EU Law: The Classics of EU Law Revisited on the 50th Anniversary of the Rome Treaty. Hart, Oxford/Portland, Oregon, 363–393

[51] As I argue in Menéndez 2017.

Menéndez AJ (2011) The Unencumbered European Taxpayer as the Product of the Transformation of Personal Taxes by the Judicial Empowerment of 'Market Forces'. In: Letelier R, Menéndez AJ (eds) The Sinews of Peace. ARENA, Oslo, RECON Report 10/2011, 157–268
Menéndez AJ (2017) From constitutional crisis to constitutional resistance. In: Innerarity D (ed) Blazing the trail of a new narrative for a new Europe. Forthcoming.
Mohamed S (1999) European Community Law on the Free Movement of Capital. Kluwer Law International, The Hague
Niglia L (2016) Eclipse of the Constitution {Europe Nouveau Siècle}. European Law Journal, 22:132–156
Rasmussen M, Boerger A (2014) Transforming European Law: The Establishment of the Constitutional Discourse from 1950 to 1993. European Constitutional Law Review 10: 199–225
Rosas A (2007) The European Court of Justice in Context: Forms and Patterns of Judicial Dialogue. European Journal of Legal Studies, http://www.ejls.eu/2/24UK.htm
Somek A (2008) Individualism. Oxford University Press, Oxford
Stein E (1981) Lawyers, Judges, and the Making of a Transnational Constitution. American Journal of International Law 75: 1–27
Tridimas T (2006) General Principles of EU Law. Oxford University Press, Oxford
Weiler JHH (1991) The Transformation of Europe. Yale Law Journal 100: 2403–83
Weiler JHH (2002) Federalism and Constitutionalism: Europe's Sonderweg. In: Howse R, Nicolaidis K (eds) The Federal Vision. Oxford University Press, Oxford, pp 54–70
Wymeersch E (2002) The Transfer of the Company's Seat in EEC Law. Common Market Law Review 40: 661–95

Chapter 9
The Criterion of "Consistent and Systematic Manner" in Free Movement Law

Tor-Inge Harbo

Abstract The conflict between the four freedoms and national regulation is not merely about colliding interests but also of colliding values and thus has, potentially, constitutional implications. The conflict has often been phrased as one between national sovereignty and European integration, but is far more than this. It is about marked liberalism and market regulation, the latter constituting the very fundament upon which the European welfare states rest. In settling conflicts between the two constitutional orders—the ordo-liberal and the welfare-state constitutions—the Court of Justice of the European Union (CJEU) applies the proportionality principle. However, the proportionality principle is arguably of such a discretionary character that one could question its legal credentials. The discretionary character of the proportionality principle thus threatens to undermine the legitimacy of the Court and, in turn, the legitimacy of the European legal order. In this chapter, the author discusses the invocation of the "consistent and systematic manner" criterion. Has it contributed to the formalization of the proportionality analysis, and thus decreased its discretionary character? Does it secure the legitimacy for the Court's proportionality analysis and its corresponding market liberalizing effects? In answering these questions, the point of departure is taken in the gambling case saga.

Keywords EU law · Free movement · Infringement · Proportionality principle · Consistency · Coherence · Gambling cases · Legal argumentation · Legitimacy · Constitution · Hard cases

T.-I. Harbo (✉)
University of Agder, PO Box 422, 4608 Kristiansand, Norway
e-mail: tor-inge.harbo@uia.no

M. Andenas et al. (eds.), *The Reach of Free Movement*,
DOI 10.1007/978-94-6265-195-1_9

Contents

9.1 Introduction 206
9.2 The Proportionality Principle and "Hard Cases" 207
9.3 The Establishment of the Consistent and Systematic Manner Criterion in the Case Law of the Court of Justice 210
9.4 Doctrinal Inductions from the Case Law 215
9.5 The Consistent and Systematic Manner Criterion as a Vehicle of Legitimacy 219
9.6 The Quest for Legitimacy Undermined? 222
9.7 Conclusions 224
References 225

9.1 Introduction

The conflict between the four freedoms and national regulation is not merely about colliding interests but colliding values and thus has potential constitutional implications. The conflict has often been phrased as one between national sovereignty and European integration, but it is far more than this. It is also about market liberalism and (sound) market regulation, the latter constituting the very fundament upon which the European welfare states rest.

The conflict between these two basic orders of values has been the object of numerous challenges before the Court of Justice of the European Union. Many may recall the *Posted workers* cases and the controversy they created:[1] May one interpret the provisions on free movement and secondary legislation in a way which challenges established workers' rights and benefits and introduce a wage-race to the bottom? Alternatively, must the four freedoms thus interpreted be perceived as an act of true European solidarity with the nationals of Eastern Europe? According to the marked liberal template pursued by the Court, competition on wages provide important incentives for long due adjustments to the overburdened and inefficient European welfare states. Thus interpreted, wage competition is a vehicle to revitalize the European economy, which will secure Europe's long-term survival in an ever more competitive world market.[2]

In settling conflicts between the two constitutional orders—the European ordo-liberal and the welfare-state constitution—the Court of Justice applies the proportionality analysis.[3] However, the proportionality principle is arguably of such a discretionary character that one could question its legal credentials.[4] The discretionary character of the proportionality principle may in turn undermine the

[1] Case C-438/05, *Viking*, ECLI:EU:C:2007:772; Case C-341/05, *Laval un Partneri*, ECLI:EU:C:2007:809; Case C-346/06, *Rüffert*, ECLI:EU:C:2008:189.

[2] For the academic debate see, Joerges 2009.

[3] On the establishment and application of the proportionality principle in EU law, see for example Tridimas 2006. On the ordo-liberal constitution, see Joerges 2004.

[4] Harbo 2010, 2015.

legitimacy of the Court and, subsequently, the legitimacy of the European legal order.

Around the turn of the century, the Court introduced the "consistent and systematic manner" criterion as a sub-element of the suitability test of the proportionality analysis in a number of cases concerning the lawfulness of national regulation restricting gambling activities. Accordingly, the Court stated in the *Gambelli* case, which concerned Italian regulations on sports and horse race betting preventing a British betting company to establish, that national measures restrictive of free movement had attaining the purported objective "in a consistent and systematic manner."[5]

The object of this study is to reveal the function of the mentioned criterion on the proportionality assessment of the Court of Justice, the underlying question being whether the criterion diminishes the discretionary character of the proportionality analysis. In the following, I will first elaborate on the function of the proportionality principle in EU law as a tool to solve so-called "hard cases" (Sect. 9.2). Secondly, I will analyse the Court's establishment and development of the consistent and systematic manner criterion in its case law and discuss what may be deduced from this (Sects. 9.3 and 9.4). Thirdly, I will attempt to find out why the Court decided to invoke the criterion in its case law, the underlying question for the discussion being concerned with its legitimizing function (Sect. 9.5). Fourthly and finally, I will examine how recent case law threatens to undermine the criterion's legitimacy quest (Sect. 9.6).

9.2 The Proportionality Principle and "Hard Cases"

The four freedoms as laid down in the European constitution are not absolute "rights," meaning that they always overrule competing interests and considerations. National measures infringing one or more of the four freedoms may be lawful. However, this requires firstly the absence of harmonised secondary EU legislation; secondly, that a legitimate ground is provided under derogations laid down in the TFEU or, for indistinctly applicable measures, mandatory requirements as recognised in the case law; and finally, that the measure is proportionate. The latter requirement means, in brief, that: the measure must be *suitable* to reach its aim; that it must not go beyond what is considered *necessary* to achieve that aim; and, not impose an *excessive burden* on the individual affected by the measure.[6]

Regardless what sub-test the Court applies to solve a concrete case at hand—the suitability, the necessity, or the *stricto sensu* test—it is difficult to escape the fact that the proportionality assessment leaves wide scope for judicial discretion.

[5] Case C-243/01, *Gambelli*, ECLI:EU:C:2003:597, para 67.

[6] There are a number of cases, which may illustrate the Court's application of the various sub-tests of the proportionality principle. In the literature case C-331/88, *Fedesa and Others*, ECLI:EU:C:1990:391 (suitability test and *strictu sensu* test); Case 104/75, *de Peijper*, ECLI:EU:C:1976:67 (necessity) are often mentioned, see for example Tridimas 2006, Chapters 3–5; Craig 2006, pp. 655–715; de Búrca 1993, pp. 105–150.

A strong judicial branch facilitating integration through adjudication, has been a crucial drive for European integration in times of empty chairs and political stalemate. However, although the Court's role in securing integration has been necessary, it has not been uncontroversial. In the introduction, I mentioned the political and academic controversy over the *posted workers* cases. The reasons for the controversy were at least twofold. Firstly, the conflicting interests at stake were of a constitutional nature, i.e. they concerned core values of two constitutional regimes: the ordo-liberal EU constitution and the respective country's welfare state constitution. Secondly, the outcomes were difficult to predict since they were "hard cases," i.e. cases that could not be solved according to a clear rule of law, laid down by some institution in advance.[7]

In the *Laval* judgment, for example, the Court favoured its classic market template in a horizontal situation of trade unions against the individual building companies and workers. It was a "hard case" because, on the one hand, the Court had to ensure that free movement was complied with and to make sure that national protectionism was avoided at all costs. On the other hand, there were sensitive labour law and social protection issues at stake. The Court chose to uphold free movement law.[8]

True, the Court operated fully within the established methodology of law when it carefully balanced the conflicting interests. The critique of the judgment, thus, reaches beyond legal doctrines. Clearly, this is also a question of EU constitutional law and the EU concept of law, raising questions such as: did the Court, as a point of departure, perceive the two conflicting interests as having the same weight?[9] In that case, were the judges free to decide the hard case at hand "either way?" Alternatively, were the judges bound to decide the case in favour of the four freedoms?

According to normative (constructive) legal theory, the judge must in hard cases decide according to "arguments of principle," i.e. by arguing that the decision respects or secures some individual or group right to justify what may appear to be a political decision.[10] According to normative legal theory, a decision is within the frames of law when it is decided according to a liberal theory of justice.[11] Applied

[7] Dworkin 1977, Chapter 4; Hart 1994, p. 136 ff. The so-called Hart-Dworkin debate concerns the question as to how the judges should go about when deciding a case where there is no rule of law, which may be applied to solve a case at hand. According to Hart, the judges must in these cases act as "deputy legislators" and fill the "legal gap" in the way he believes the legislator would. According to Dworkin there really are no "legal gaps" since judges are bound to solve these cases according to the non-positivist concept of "arguments of principle."

[8] One could argue that most of the early cases in which the Court established the autonomous EU legal system as in case 26/62, *Van Gend en Loos*, ECLI:EU:C:1963:1 and case 6/64 *Costa v ENEL*, ECLI:EU:C:1964:66, etc., where all so-called hard cases.

[9] Ref. the principle of *practical concordance* in Schwarze 2006, p. 690.

[10] Dworkin 1977, Chapter 4.

[11] The connection between the liberal political theory of John Rawls, as for example elaborated on in his "A theory of Justice" and "Political liberalism" Dworkin's liberal theory of law, as elaborated on in his "Taking rights seriously" is obvious.

in EU law, and provided that we applaud the claim that the four freedoms may somehow be perceived as individual economic rights in the ordo-liberal constitution of the EU, normative theory may legitimize the Court's priority of the four freedoms over national measures when balancing these conflicting interests and values within the frame of the proportionality analysis. The Court of Justice' application of a strict necessity norm when reviewing the proportionality of national measures reflects this perception.[12]

If the proportionality analysis is connected to a normative conceptualization of law, which grants the four freedoms *a priori* priority over national consideration and interests, the scope of judicial discretion decreases as the predictability of the analysis increases. However, as displayed in the political and academic debates subsequent to the *posted workers* cases, this normative conceptualization of EU law is highly contested. If judges cannot rely on the political aim of "an ever closer union" normatively promoted by the four freedoms, they have to find other ways to secure legitimacy for their judgments in hard cases.

According to a pragmatic conception of law, judges are not bound by the "rights thesis" when deciding hard cases, but may decide the particular lawsuit at hand "either way."[13] However, although they are not bound by any individual rights promoting imperative, this does not mean that judges are unconstrained when making their decision. According to this conception of the law, judges are bound to act within the frames of the legal argumentation. Moreover, judges proceed by analogy to ensure that the new law they make is in accordance with principles or underpinning reasons recognized as already having footing in the existing law:

> (…) judges do not just push away their law books and start to legislate without further guidance from the law. Very often, in deciding such cases, they cite some general principle or some general aim or purpose which some considerable relevant area of the existing law can be understood as exemplifying or advancing and which points towards a determinate answer for the instant hard case.[14]

The questions, which are of concern in our context, are firstly, whether the introduction of the consistent and systematic manner criterion in the proportionality analysis has narrowed down the discretionary character of the proportionality analysis. Secondly, whether this "gap-filling" requires that the judges pursue a normative approach with basis in a liberal normative conceptualization of EU law, whether it implies that judges act as "deputy legislators" i.e. whether the criterion may be framed by a pragmatic legal methodology. In the following, I will proceed first by analysing the legal doctrinal qualities of the criterion as applied in the gambling cases, and secondly, attempt to explain its function.

---

[12] Harbo 2015.

[13] With a pragmatic concept of law, I mean legal positivism, legal institutionalism, legal realism, although clearly there are some major differences between the three. The better tag for them would probably be non-normative.

[14] Hart 1994, 274.

9.3 The Establishment of the Consistent and Systematic Manner Criterion in the Case Law of the Court of Justice

The aim of this study is, as mentioned in the introduction, to reveal the nature of the consistent and systematic manner criterion in the case law of the Court of Justice or, to be more precise, its functioning as a legal requirement determining the lawfulness of measures infringing the four freedoms. In order to reveal this, I will assess how the Court of Justice has developed the consistent and systematic manner criteria in its case law, with a point of departure taken in cases concerning gambling.

The *Gambelli* case, mentioned above, constitutes a milestone to this effect. In the case, the Court for the first time explicitly introduced what has also been termed "the hypocrisy test," stating that a national measure restrictive of free movement has to serve its function and attain the purported objective "in a consistent and systematic manner."[15]

The case concerned the Italian licensing requirement for betting on sports events. More precisely, the case concerned Italian agencies, Gambelli among them, accused of having unlawfully collaborated with a foreign bookmaker in collecting bets. In its assessment as to whether the licensing system, which in effect restricted the establishment of non-state betting agencies and thus infringed the freedom of services and establishment, could be justified, the Court stated:

> (…) that restrictions on gaming activities may be justified by imperative requirements in the general interest, such as consumer protection and the prevention of both fraud and incitement to squander on gaming, restrictions based on such grounds and on the need to preserve public order must also be suitable for achieving those objectives, inasmuch as they must serve to limit betting activities in a consistent and systematic manner.[16]

The Court's introduction of the consistent and systematic manner criterion was provoked by the fact that the Italian authorities pursued two apparently contradictory aims. At the same time as the authorities restricted the establishment of foreign providers of gaming activities in order to preserve public order, it pursued a policy of substantially expanding betting and gaming with a view to obtaining funds financially benefiting the public purse, as noted by the Court:

> In so far as the Authorities of a Member State incite and encourage consumers to participate in lotteries, games of chance and betting to the financial benefit of the public purse, the authorities of that State cannot invoke public order concerns relating to the need to reduce opportunities for betting in order to justify measures such as those at issue in the main proceedings.[17]

[15] Op cit. C-243/01, *Gambelli*, ECLI:EU:C:2003:597, para 6.

[16] Ibid. (my italics).

[17] Ibid., para 69 (my italics).

The Court left it to the referring national court to decide whether this was the case.

As noted above, the consistent and systematic manner criterion constitutes an element of the suitability test of the proportionality analysis. The suitability requirement implies that a measure must be appropriate to achieve the aim, which serves as justification to adopt the measure. On the face of it, one could claim that the suitability test as applied by the Court is not a very strict test. Thus, a legislative or administrative measure adopted in order to accommodate a particular political goal is seldom outright unsuitable, although it is clear that a bottom line must be drawn as, for example, suggested by AG La Pergola in *Centros*: "the supposed causal connection between that need and the contested measure appears to be too tenuous and indirect to be regarded as relevant for the purposes of Community law."[18]

It is difficult to pin-point how suitable a means must be in order to fulfil the requirement reflected in the suitability test. From an etymological point of view, "suitable" as in the suitability test seems to imply a closer relationship than the word "useful" would imply, while at the same time not as close as "indispensable." Furthermore, suitability in the context cannot be understood in absolute terms. Thus, it makes sense to refer to suitability as *a matter of degrees*.

The Court has also upheld Community measures where the measure under scrutiny was said to be "a choice of economic policy which [was] in certain respects regrettable," or were found to be outright "ineffective."[19] If the measure is unsuitable, one would assume that it has been passed by mistake: the legislator or an administrative body was, for example, not properly informed about how a particular political challenge should best be handled; or, it mistakenly believed that a particular measure would secure a desired aim. In these cases, the suitability test functions as a safety valve for erroneous administrative and legislative decision-making.

Apparently, the Court has been reluctant to hold measures downright unsuitable. In most cases, this may be avoided if the measure does not pass the necessity-test of the proportionality assessment. However, there are examples in the case law of the Court of Justice where the suitability of a measure has been decisive for the outcome. The Court's *British poultry* case concerned an import ban on poultry aimed at countries which adopted a policy of vaccination rather than slaughter in response to the Newcastle disease.[20] The Court found that the measure reached beyond what was deemed necessary to achieve the proposed aim, was thus disproportionate and therefore unlawful. However, the Court did not leave it with that. In addition, it stated that the measure "did not form part of a seriously considered health policy" and suggested that the real aim of the ban was to block, for commercial and

---

[18] C-212/97, *Centros*, ECLI:EU:C:1999:126, para 22.

[19] Case 138/78, *Stoelting v. Hauptzollamt Hamburg-Jonas*, ECLI:EU:C:1979:46, para 7 of the Advocate General's opinion; Case C-133/93, *Crispoltoni II*, ECLI:EU:C:1994:364.

[20] Case 40/82, *Commission v. UK*, ECLI:EU:C:1984:33.

economic reasons, imports of poultry products from other Member States. Clearly, if a measure does not form part of a seriously considered health policy, there is a presumption that it is unsuitable to reach this aim.

The Court in *Läärä* arguably also takes this broader approach. *Läärä* concerned the lawfulness of a Finnish betting monopoly.[21] The question raised was whether the Finnish government imposed an unlawful restriction on the free movement of betting services, since it did not outright ban gambling activities but actually allowed them, on condition that they were monopolized by the state. Addressing this claim, the Court of Justice stated: "the fact that the games in issue are not totally prohibited is not enough to show that the national legislation is not in reality intended to achieve the public interest objectives at which it is purportedly aimed, which must be *considered as a whole*."[22] The Court entrusted the referring national court to undertake this consideration.[23]

The key requirement is that the policy must be "considered as a whole." If the monopoly regime is "considered as a whole," there may still be room for inconsistencies. Allowing gambling activities while simultaneously fighting gambling addiction is apparently inconsistent. However, as the Court noted, fighting gambling addiction does not mean that all gambling has to be banned. One could assume that banning legal gambling would create a black market for these types of activities. Taking into account the limited law enforcement resources and the weaknesses of human nature, a balance between the two aims is found by channelling gambling through controllable institutions, something which establishing a gambling monopoly could ensure.

In *Zenatti,* the question discussed was whether a restrictive gambling regime could be justified despite the Italian authorities raising a levy on the proceeds of authorized games to the benefit of various social activities. Whereas the Court had no reason to believe that the Italian government did not pursue a seriously considered policy, it is clear that in effect the taxation policy undermined the aim of restricting gambling opportunities. Thus, the Court stated that such restriction could only be accepted if, from the outset, it reflected a concern to bring about a *genuine diminution* in gambling opportunities and if the financing of social activities

[21] Case C-124/97, *Läärä*, ECLI:EU:C:1999:435.

[22] Ibid., para 37 (my italics). The paragraph continues: "Limited authorisation of such games on an exclusive basis, which has the advantage of confining the desire to gamble and the exploitation of gambling within controlled channels, of preventing the risk of fraud or crime in the context of such exploitation, and of using the resulting profits for public interest purposes, likewise falls within the ambit of those objectives." In later cases the Court has reviewed the consistency of gambling monopolies, see case C-42/07, *Liga Portuguesa*, ECLI:EU:C:2009:519, which concerned the granting of an exclusive rights to operate games of chance via the internet to the operator, Santa Casa, the Court while upholding the restrictive measure referred explicitly to the consistency and systematic manner-criterion, paras 59–61 (norm) para 67 (application of the norm on the facts).

[23] For a similar deferent approach see Case C-275/92, *Schindler*, ECLI:EU:C:1994:119, para 61: "In those circumstances, it is for [the Member States] to assess not only whether it is necessary to restrict the activities of lotteries but also whether they should be prohibited, provided that those restrictions are not discriminatory."

constituted only an incidental beneficial consequence, and not the real justification for the restrictive policy adopted.[24]

The conflicting aims are clearly more apparent in *Gambelli*. In that case, Italian authorities had *incited* and *encouraged* consumers to participate in lotteries, games of chance, and betting to increase tax revenues at the same time as they had invoked public order concerns relating to the need to reduce opportunities for betting in order to justify measures such as those at issue in the main proceedings.[25] What separates *Gambelli* from *Zenatti* is the way in which the Italian government consciously promoted the public participation in gambling in the latter (which one could suspect was motivated by a desire to increase tax revenues). In order to be consistent, the Court held, the government may not at the same time endorse measures, such as extensive marketing, which could lead to an increase of gambling opportunities.

The consistent and systematic manner formula, introduced in *Gambelli*, has been applied in later gambling cases. In *Placanica,* an Italian legislative act which sought to expand activities in the betting and gaming sector in order to attract more players was challenged, since it was perceived as inconsistent with the stated aim fighting gambling addiction.[26] However, the Italian government had stated another aim of the measure, namely that of drawing players away from clandestine betting and gaming.[27] Whereas expanding gambling possibilities was inconsistent with the aim of fighting gambling addiction, it was consistent with the aim of fighting fraud. Moreover, since legal gambling was presumably expanded at the expense of clandestine gambling, one could argue that overall gambling activities would not increase.

The invocation of the consistent and systematic manner criterion has not been limited to cases concerning gambling. A German company, Hartlauer, wished to open private outpatient dental clinics in Vienna. The Länder concerned refused to grant it authorization, since there was no need to set up such institutions. Hartlauer brought proceedings against the decision. The Austrian court referred the case to the Court of Justice, questioning the compatibility of the Austrian legislation with Community law rules on freedom of establishment. Regarding the question as to whether the infringing measure could be justified, the Court referred to the consistent and systematic manner criterion: "First, it must be recalled that national legislation is appropriate for ensuring attainment of the objective pursued only if it

[24] Case C-67/98, *Zenatti*, ECLI:EU:C:1999:514, para 36.

[25] Op. cit. *Gambelli*, para 69.

[26] Joined cases C-338/04, C-359/04 and C-360/04, *Placanica and others*, ECLI:EU:C:2007:133.

[27] Ibid., para 55: "(…) viewed from that perspective, it is possible that a policy of controlled expansion in the betting and gaming sector may be entirely consistent with the objective of drawing players away from clandestine betting and gaming—and, as such, activities which are prohibited—to activities which are authorized and regulated (…) authorized operators must represent a reliable, but at the same time attractive, alternative to a prohibited activity" and that "[T]his may as such necessitate the offer of an extensive range of games, advertising on a certain scale and the use of new distribution techniques."

genuinely reflects a concern to attain it in *a consistent and systematic manner*."[28] The Court found that the legislation in question was inconsistent as far as prior authorization was only applied for new independent outpatient clinics, and not for new group practices. This amounted to an "inconsistency" which also affected the attainment of the objective to prevent a risk of serious harm to the financial balance of the national social security system.[29]

Corporación Dermoestética concerned the prohibition of advertisements on national television networks for medical and surgical treatments carried out in private health care establishments for reasons of public health. The Court held that introducing a measure prohibiting on advertisements for medical and surgical treatments on national television networks, while at the same time making it possible to broadcast such advertisements on local television networks, exhibited "an *inconsistency*" which the Italian Government had not attempted to justify. Consequently, the national legislation could not be regarded "as being *appropriate* for the purpose of securing the attainment of the objective of public health."[30]

Apothekerkammer des Saarlandes et al. concerned a German law requiring that pharmacies may be owned and operated by pharmacists alone.[31] A Dutch company whose business included the selling of medicinal products by mail order challenged the national law on the grounds that it infringed the freedom of establishment. The Court agreed that the Member State was allowed to take the view that the operation of a pharmacy by a non-pharmacist may present a risk to public health, because the non-pharmacist's pursuit of profit would not be "tempered by his training, by his professional experience and by the responsibility which he owes," unlike professional pharmacists.[32]

The national legislation did not exclude the operation of pharmacies by non-pharmacists absolutely. Thus, the question of the legislation's consistency was raised. The Court noted, with reference to its aforementioned case law that "national legislation is appropriate for securing attainment of the objective relied upon only if it *genuinely* reflects a concern to attain that objective in a *consistent and systematic manner*."[33] Assessing for example the Member State's *justification* for accepting heirs of a pharmacist who do not themselves have the status of pharmacist to operate a pharmacy for 12 months, the Court noted that this exception could not be regarded as *inconsistent* since the law required that a qualified pharmacist must be responsible for operating the inherited pharmacy in this period.[34] The Court

[28] Case C-169/07, *Hartlauer*, ECLI:EU:C:2009:141, para 55 (my italics).

[29] Ibid., para 61.

[30] Case C-500/06, *Corporación Dermoestética*, ECLI:EU:C:2008:421, paras 39 and 40 (my italics).

[31] Joined cases C-171/07 and C-171/07, *Apothekerkammer des Saarlandes et al.*, ECLI:EU: C:2009:316.

[32] Ibid., para 37.

[33] Ibid., para 42.

[34] Ibid., paras 43–50.

concluded that the law was *appropriate* for ensuring that the provision of medicinal products to the public is reliable and of good quality, and it did not go beyond what was necessary for attaining its public health objective.[35]

9.4 Doctrinal Inductions from the Case Law

The next question is what we may infer from these observations concerning the application of the consistent and systematic manner criterion by the Court. Firstly, it might be asked whether invoking this criterion implies the establishment of a new principle of EU law, with which national legislation restricting free movement must comply in order to be justifiable. What is clear is that the criterion in the previously mentioned cases does constitute an important element in the assessment as to whether a measure is *suitable* to reach a proposed aim. As such, it forms part of the proportionality analysis, which is acknowledged as a principle of EU law. Whether the criterion is framed as an independent principle of EU law or not, it is nevertheless important to determine the legal content of the criterion. This will be attempted in the following.

When seen in context, together with the explanation the Court provides, one could claim that the meaning of the criterion is somewhat self-explanatory: It may appear obvious in the case that national authorities' policy to fight gambling addiction by means of expanding gambling possibilities is inconsistent, in the meaning of *contradictory* to that policy. However, this is not as straightforward as it may appear. One could, for example, argue that if the aim of a restrictive gambling policy is to fight fraud and clandestine gambling, an expansive policy aiming to attract gamblers to authorized gambling activities may also be non-contradictory with the aim of fighting gambling addiction, if it leads to a decrease in the overall gambling activities offered, and if the activities provided are less addictive.

Furthermore, if the authorities have prohibited the advertisement of medical treatment on national television, as was the issue in *Corporación Dermoestética*, allowing such advertisement on local television will clearly *undermine* the effect of this prohibition. In other words, if the aim of the prohibition is to shield the consumer from this kind of advertisement, the lack of a prohibition on local television clearly is inconsistent with this objective.[36] One could construct the policy for local advertisement as an *exemption* from the prohibition on advertisement at the national level, by arguing that it is the very nature of an exemption to contradict the main rule. However, if the local advertisement policy were to be perceived as an exemption, the Member State would, firstly, have to argue that this is how the local

[35] Ibid., para 58.

[36] The phrase "run counter to" is applied synonymously with inconsistency in the EFTA-Courts case E-3/06 *Ladbrokes*, para 51.

policy is to be perceived; and, secondly, have to provide plausible justifications for invoking such an exemption.

In this chapter, I am concerned with the consistent and systematic manner criterion applied as a requirement by the Court, when it reviews the lawfulness of measures infringing one or more of the EU's four freedoms. As noted above, the criterion is a court-created phenomenon. Nevertheless, there is a presumption that the term consistency, as in the consistent and systematic manner, bears the same meaning as the term consistency in other parts of EU law.

A requirement of consistency appears in a number of EU treaty provisions. Article 13(1) TEU reads: "The Union shall[...]ensure the *consistency*, effectiveness and continuity of its policies and actions."[37] Article 7 of the TFEU states that: "The Union shall ensure *consistency* between its policies and activities, taking all of its objectives into account and in accordance with the principle of conferral of powers."[38] The consistency requirement mentioned covers a variety of different situations, horizontal as well as vertical. The requirement thus plays an important role in determining the relationship between EU and Member State law, and between the various EU policies.[39] A number of scholars have elaborated on the term consistency in the field of EU external relations.[40] A point of departure is taken in Article 21(3) in the chapter on the EU external relations which reads: "The Union shall ensure *consistency* between the different areas of its external action and between these and its other policies."[41] After the Treaty of Lisbon, it has been claimed that this "duty of consistency", now more than ever features dominantly in the Union's constitutional texts.[42] It could be seen as a general principle of EU law applicable to all fields of EU external relations.[43]

In the academic discourse, the term consistent is often defined by comparing, or contrasting, it with/to the term *coherence*. Some have argued that the two terms—consistence and coherence—are more or less interchangeable, not at least due to the way the terms are applied in the different languages of the EU. Whereas consistency and coherency appear to be distinct terms with differing meanings in the English

---

[37] The German version reads: "die Kohärenz," and the Danish version: "sammenheng," the latter closer to the notion of coherence, in the meaning of connection, context or unity, than contradiction.

[38] The German version reads: "Kohärenz, and the Danish version: "sammenheng."

[39] E.g. Herlin-Karnell and Konstadinides 2013; Mathisen 2010; Gralf-Peter Calliess 2003.

[40] E.g. Hertog and Stross 2013; Cremona 2011; Hillion 2008. The Council has recognized the "importance of consistency between internal and external aspects of human rights protection and promotion in the Union framework in terms of enhancing the Union's credibility in its external relations and leading by example in the area of human rights." Council of the EU conclusions of May 2014, http://data.consilium.europa.eu/doc/document/ST-6256-2016-INIT/en/pdf (accessed 30 May 2016).

[41] In the German version the word "die Kohärenz" is applied, and in the Danish version once again "sammenheng."

[42] Op. cit. Hertog and Stross 2013, p. 378 citing Elsuwege and Merket 2012.

[43] Ibid., citing Casolari 2012.

language, the term consistency is, in both German and French, translated to a word with greater etymological similarity to the English term coherency ("Kohärenz" in German and "cohérence" in French).[44] It could be noted that the word "konsistent" as well as "inkonsistent" does exist in the German language. Although it is difficult for a non-German mother tongue to determine the exact meaning of the German word "konsistent", the English term "consistent" is nevertheless translated into "konsistent" in various dictionaries. Thus, there are reasons to believe that "Kohärent" also has a meaning substantially different from "konsistent" in the German language.

This distinction is important to our discussion, since the term "systematic manner", as in the criterion "consistent and systematic manner", has been interpreted as to mean coherence by, for example, AG Maduro. Accordingly, the requirement could be rephrased "consistent and coherent manner". However, when taking into account the different linguistic versions of the relevant Opinion by AG Maduro, the meaning of the term may not appear that clear after all.[45] In the German-language version, consistency is mostly referred to as "Kohärenz", whereas "systematic" is referred to as "systematisch" in some parts, and "Einheitlichkeit" in other parts. In French, the word "cohèrent" and, at some point, the word "constance", which is conventionally translated into constancy, is applied for consistency. It is of interest to note that, when the word "inconsistent" is applied in the English-language version of the Opinion, the French version refers to "contradiction" and the German to "Widersprüchlichkeit". The French word "contradiction" has at least great etymological similarities with the word "contradiction", which constitutes the narrow interpretation of the term consistent, as we noted above. The German word "widersprüchlich" is also mostly translated to the English word contradictory.

Although a dive into the different language versions of AG Maduro's Opinion does not provide us with absolute certainty regarding the meaning of the relationship between the terms consistent and systematic, there are plausible reasons to conclude that consistency in this context must be defined narrowly, since it featured next to the term "systematic", which may be understood as "coherence".

The dominant line of thinking in the academic literature is that coherency and consistency do not carry the same meaning. According to this opinion, consistency is defined narrowly as being the "absence of contradiction"; as "avoiding contradictions among different[…]policy areas"; as "ensuring that individual policies are not internally contradictory"; and as "avoiding policies that conflict with reaching

[44] The Oxford English Dictionary defines coherence as the "action of fact of sticking together" or a "harmonious connection to the several parts of a discourse, system etc., so that the whole hangs together." Consistency is "the quality, state or fact of being consistent."

[45] AG Maduro's Opinion in joined cases C-570/07 and C-571/07, *Blanco Pérez and Chao Gómez*, ECLI:EU:C:2010:300, para 21: "The coherence and consistency requirement lays down that the national legislation is appropriate for securing attainment of the objective relied upon only if it genuinely reflects a concern to attain that objective in a consistent and systematic manner."

for a given policy objective".[46] In contrast, coherence refers to a more positive state in which different policy fields actively work together to achieve common overarching goals. Accordingly, policy coherence is defined as an "achievement of a synergy between [...] policies"; a "desirable plus" that "implies positive connections [and is] more about synergy and adding value"; or a "united whole".[47] Furthermore, "coherence in law is a matter of degree, whereas consistency is a static concept".[48] The latter may appear obvious: there can be no degree of contradiction, as there is no degree of nuance. Either you are, or you are not. It must be understood in an all or nothing fashion.[49]

This distinction may also be found in legal theory. Neil MacCormick perceives consistency as part of the more general demand of coherency in law, and suggests that the requirement of "consistency as being satisfied by non-contradiction."[50] Coherency of law finds its expression, according to MacCormick, in the contention that the law should "make sense" or "hang together" if considered *as a whole*: "A lack of coherence in what is said involves a failure to make sense."[51] This means that "mere consistency of a set of propositions is no guarantee of their coherence as a story."[52] Coherence demands that one takes into account the purpose of the measure, by asking, "does a measure 'make sense?'" In our context, does it "fit," or is it "intelligible" as a means to attain its purported public objective?

Dworkin's idea of coherency is, not surprisingly, informed by his liberal normative understanding of law. Accordingly, coherency in law is more than bare consistency, which he means agreement and compatibility between a set of rules. In addition, coherency represents "a single vision of justice," what he refers to as "law as integrity": "Law as integrity asks judges to assume, so far as this is possible, that the law is structured by a coherent set of principles about justice and fairness and procedural due process, and it asks them to enforce these in the fresh cases that come before then, so that each person's situation is fair and just according to the same standards."[53] In Dworkin's principled view of the law, the legal writer, the advocate, and the judge should assume that the statutes and case law rest on a coherent conception of justice. More precisely, in expounding the law, they should assume a normativity promoting individual rights.

[46] See references in Hertog and Stross 2013, p. 376.

[47] Koutrakos 2001, pp. 39–44; Wessels 1999, p. 297.

[48] Hillion 2008, p. 14, citing Velden 1992.

[49] The distinction gives associations to Robert Alexy's distinction between legal principles and rules, Alexy 2002, although I will not elaborate on these here.

[50] MacCormick 2005, p. 190.

[51] Ibid., p. 189.

[52] Ibid., p. 190.

[53] Dworkin 1998, 243.

9.5 The Consistent and Systematic Manner Criterion as a Vehicle of Legitimacy

Above I have discussed how the Court of Justice applies the consistent and systematic manner criterion when it reviews the proportionality of measures infringing the provisions governing the four freedoms. The discussion is certainly not exhaustive, but it captures some important aspects of the criterion from which valid conclusions may be drawn in a discussion about the criterion's function.

The instrumental function of the consistent and systematic manner criterion is to broaden the factual scope of the suitability assessment. Accordingly, the measure pursued in a policy area—for example, the regulation of gambling activities with the purpose of reducing gambling addiction—must not only be suitable to reach the aim of the provision in question, it must also be suitable to reach aims pursued in connected policy areas. If the Member State is sincere about the argument it makes to justify a measure, there is an assumption that it would pursue this approach in all areas of law affecting the subject matter. Under no circumstances should it undermine this goal by enacting measures which provide conflicting incentives, or are outright contradictory. This latter interpretation is the essence of the consistency criterion, as expressed in *Gambelli*.

The broadening of the scope of the suitability test by requiring that the regulatory regime of a Member State is consistent and systematic in light of the aim of the relevant legislative or administrative measure clearly implies that the threshold as to what constitutes a lawful infringement is set higher than where a narrower approach is taken. The "broader approach" thus means that it takes more to hold a national measure proportionate than when a narrow approach is applied. The intensified proportionality analysis is in this case a consequence of the broadening of the factual basis and not the application of a stricter norm.

Above, I have attempted to explain the invocation of the consistent and systematic criterion within legal doctrinal frames. However, this does not answer all the questions we may have concerning its function. As I have noted above, the requirement of consistency has been an implicit element in the assessment of the lawfulness of measures infringing the four freedoms for decades, albeit in different shapes and contexts.

In the well-known *German Beer* case,[54] the German health authorities argued that beer which was not brewed according to the German Beer purity law could not be marketed as beer. They argued that it would mislead German beer drinkers to consume a drink which could potentially jeopardise their health, since the long term effects of additives were unknown. The Court of Justice ruled that the law could not be justified. According to the existing scientific material, additives posed no risk to public health. In addition, the Court found that Germany permitted additives in

[54] Case 178/84, *Commission v. Germany*, ECLI:EU:C:1987:126.

drinks other than beer, so its policy was *inconsistent*, although it did not state this explicitly.

In its *Kelloggs* case, the EFTA Court even framed consistency as an independent requirement for determining the lawfulness of an infringing measure, i.e. not as a part of, but in addition to the proportionality requirement: "Measures taken by a Contracting Party must be based on scientific evidence; they must be proportionate, non-discriminatory, transparent, and *consistent* with similar measures already taken."[55] In the case, the Court found that the fact that the Norwegian government prohibited an imported fortified product access to the Norwegian market, at the same time as it allowed domestic fortified products to be sold on the same market, was inconsistent.

Both cases were argued as indirect discrimination cases, as quantitative restriction on imports regulated by Article 11 EEA. However, it could be argued that they come close to constituting direct discrimination cases, as it appears that the respective governments had one additive policy for domestic products and one for imported products.[56]

The introduction of the consistent and systematic manner criterion in *Gambelli* must be viewed in light of the Court of Justice's rather deferential approach in earlier cases concerning gambling activities. Gambling is a highly sensitive policy area in most Member States, and there is a general acceptance throughout Europe that these activities must be controlled in one way or another. The Court has explicitly agreed with Member States when they argue that it is not possible to disregard the moral, religious, or cultural aspects of gambling, and even referred to it as "exploitation of a social evil or the weakness of players and their misfortunes."[57]

Accordingly, the Court has taken a deferential approach when reviewing these cases and has been willing to grant the Member State a large margin of appreciation. In *Läära* and *Liga Portuguesa* the Court held that even severely restrictive measures, such as state monopolies, may be justified.[58] If the Court nevertheless found it necessary to strike down a national measure, it would have to provide convincing justification for doing so. This may partly explain the introduction, or rather the clarification, of the consistent and systematic manner criterion.

In the introduction, I suggested that the proportionality principle is applied by the Court of Justice to solve so-called "hard cases." Hard cases are cases which cannot be solved according to a clear rule of law, laid down by some institution in advance. I referred to the Court of Justice's *posted workers* cases as examples of

---

[55] In E-3/00—*EFTA Surveillance Authority v. The Kingdom of Norway*, para 26 (my italics).

[56] The application of the proportionality principle in the Kellogg case is deemed to be problematic due to the invocation of the precautionary principle. Invoking the precautionary principle undermines the proportionality assessment since it allows for the substitution of a fact with an assumption. In these cases, it is difficult to assess whether a measure is suitable or necessary to reach the purported aim.

[57] Joined cases C-447/08 and C- 448/08, *Sjøberg and Gerdin*, ECLI:EU:C:2010:415, para 43.

[58] Op. cit. Case C-124/97 *Läärä*; C-42/07, *Liga Portuguesa*, ECLI:EU:C:2009:519.

such a hard case. In Sect. 9.2, I proposed that there are several ways in which hard cases may be solved. According to normative legal theory, hard cases are solved by binding judicial discretion to arguments of principles.

The existence of hard cases as a concept depends on the conceptualization of law. There is a long European tradition, and a doctrine of the division of powers, which dramatises the distinction between the legislative and judicative branches, and insists that the judge is the mere "mouthpiece" of the law when the existing law is clear. To be sure, very few judges would ever admit that hard cases exist, in the meaning that legal gaps exist, which they in turn would have to fill.

In the EU context, the legitimacy of the normative conception of law, which implies securing the priority of four freedoms over colliding interests, is being questioned. The proportionality principle is a "conflict of laws" norm, which proposes how hard cases, for instance certain conflicts between the four freedoms and national measures, should be solved. In the gambling cases, as in the *posted workers* cases, this conflict may also be conceptualised as a constitutional conflict, namely between that of the EU ordo-liberal constitution and the welfare constitutions of Member States. Taking into account the debates following the Court of Justice's decisions in the *posted workers* cases noted above, one could clearly question the legitimacy of the Court's balancing of the two conflicting constitutional provisions.[59]

Apparently, the proportionality principle in its application to solve hard cases has been interpreted in a way that prioritises, if we stick to Dworkin's terminology, arguments of principles in the shape of the four freedoms.[60] The criticism raised against the *posted workers* decisions suggest that the proportionality principle has to be either reinterpreted and applied more neutrally, take on a different morality, be interpreted more leniently, or be interpreted in a purely procedural manner.[61]

If the Court of Justice, as a response to this criticism, takes on a more pragmatic conception of law, the political dimension of judicial discretion may be more difficult to conceal. As noted above, the consistent and systematic manner criterion does not only figure as a sub-criterion of the suitability test of the proportionality principle. It also constitutes, in different shapes and contexts, an element inherent in the very institution of law. A legal regime or system must, with reference both to legal pragmatists and legal constructivists, be internally coherent. It must "make sense" or "hang together." The legal system must be inherently logical and rationale, one aspect of which is that it must be consistent or non-contradictory. Consistency and coherence, being such a central element in the very institution of law, thus constitutes powerful legal arguments when applied by the Court in the gambling cases. Applied as an element of the proportionality analysis, the

---

[59] Op. cit., Case C-438/05 *Viking*; Case C-341/05 *Laval un Partneri*; Case C-346/06 *Rüffert*.

[60] The four freedoms may also be conceptualised as Dworkian arguments of policy, in so much as they securing the political (some would even say moral) aim of European integration.

[61] Schwarze 2006. See also, perhaps somewhat surprisingly, the presumed legal realists Nielsen 2013 and Eckes 2013. Harbo 2016.

consistency test has the effect of formalizing the proportionality analysis, as well as reducing its discretionary scope. If EU law is conceptualized according to legal pragmatism, the consistent and systematic manner criterion may be perceived as a way in which the discretionary character of the proportionality analysis is formalised.

This legal pragmatic approach could be illustrated with the following example: When the Court of Justice established the principles of supremacy and direct effect, one could argue that the Court was called upon to fill legal gaps by reference to a freedom promoting normativity, in an effort to develop the supranational legal regime of the EU. However, again this depends on the perception. One could hold that the two principles could be logically deduced from the existing treaty regime by applying pragmatic (international) legal methodology. Accordingly, it is not even necessary to refer to the overarching goal of the EU, namely to apply a teleological methodological approach to secure an "ever closer union of the peoples of Europe," to establish the principles. It suffices to refer to the logic of causality: If Community law is binding for the Member States, as they agreed upon when becoming members, it must have supremacy over national law; if Community law is a fact, it has to have direct effect *vis-à-vis* the Member States' citizens.

9.6 The Quest for Legitimacy Undermined?

In a more recent case, *Ladbrokes and Betfair,* the Court deviated from the understanding of the consistent and systematic manner criterion established in *Gambelli.*[62] In the case, the Court of Justice was called upon to consider a Dutch measure which had the dual goal of both curbing gambling addiction and fighting fraud, while allowing economic operators, who had exclusive rights to organize games of chance, to offer new games and to use advertising to make the games more attractive. The Court applauded the right of the Dutch gambling monopolist to exclude the betting companies Ladbrokes and Betfair from Dutch territory, since their exclusion formed part of a broader range of legislation designed both to curb addiction to games of chance and to combat fraud.

Having first stated that the measure did constitute a restriction to the freedom of establishment, the Court noted that the restriction could nevertheless be justified, provided that a legitimate ground existed and the proportionality requirement was satisfied. According to the latter, the restriction "must be suitable for achieving those objectives, inasmuch as they must serve to limit betting activities in a *consistent and systematic manner*."[63]

Apparently focusing only on the consistency of the policy, the Court held that "it is possible that a policy of controlled expansion in the betting and gaming sector

---

[62] Case C-258/08, *Ladbrokes Betting & Gaming*, ECLI:EU:C:2010:308.

[63] Ibid., para 21 (my italics).

may be *entirely consistent* with the objective of drawing players away from clandestine betting and gaming."[64] This framing of the judicial reasoning reveals what is to come: Firstly, the Court merely applied the term consistent in the quotation and not (together with) the term systematic. Secondly, it applied the adverb "entirely" to describe the adjective "consistent," as in "entirely consistent", which grants the term consistent a relative, rather than an absolute, character.

Regarding the dual aims of the Dutch legislation, the Court held that "[W]hile it is true that the grounds of the judgment in *Placanica and others* refer solely to the objective of crime prevention in the betting and gaming sector, whereas, in the present case, the Netherlands legislation is also designed to curb gambling addiction, the fact remains that those two objectives must be considered together, since they relate both to consumer protection and to the preservation of public order."[65]

Apparently, then, in order to reconcile the two objectives of the Dutch regulation, the Court reminds us that these are both legitimate grounds for infringing the provisions related to free movement. To reconcile these aims, the consistency criterion cannot be applied in its absolute sense—in the meaning of non-contradictory—but has to be interpreted in relative terms. Accordingly, the Court formulates the criterion as *a matter of degrees*: "Since the objective of protecting consumers from gambling addiction is, in principle, difficult to reconcile with a policy of expanding games of chance characterized, inter alia, by the creation of new games and by the advertising of such games, such a policy cannot be regarded as being consistent unless *the scale of unlawful activity* is significant and the measures adopted are aimed at channelling consumers' propensity to gamble into activities that are lawful."[66]

Decisive for whether a measure expanding games of chance aiming at fighting crime and fraud connected with gambling services is consistent with fighting gambling addiction is thus the "scale of unlawful activity." How much unlawful activity has to exist before a measure may be considered inconsistent must be determined in the concrete case. However, it was a "fact" that the demand for games of chance in the Netherlands had, at the time it adopted the measure excluding Ladbrokes betting-services from the Dutch market, increased noticeable, particularly at a clandestine level.[67] The Court handed this to the referring Dutch court to decide.[68]

The Member State cannot be expected to accept the development of unlawful gambling activities to develop on its territory without interfering in order to be able to adopt a regulatory regime similar to that imposed by the Dutch government. Thus, making the consistency of the dual aim policy dependent on the "scale of

---

[64] Ibid., para 25 (my italics).

[65] Ibid., para 26 (my italics).

[66] Ibid., para 30 (my italics).

[67] Ibid., para 31.

[68] A similar approach is taken in a later judgment, C-375/14, *Laezzia*, ECLI:EU:C:2016:60, paras 36–38.

unlawful activity" cannot be taken at face value. This understanding is, in my opinion, underpinned by the subsequent invocation of the "fair balance"—norm. According to the Court "a fair balance has to be drawn between" the aim of making the games attractive (which implies the controlled expansion of authorized games of chance) and the need to reduce addiction.[69] The introduction of the fair balance-norm in the case implies that the consistency-criterion is side-stepped. In practical terms, this means that the decisions will be of a more discretionary nature, a discretion that in turn will be granted to the Member States.

Rather than consistency in the meaning of non-contradiction, the broader concept of coherency constitutes the touchstone of the lawfulness of Dutch betting-regime in the *Ladbrokes*-case. Thus, we are back to where it all started before the introduction of the consistent and systematic manner criterion in *Gambelli*: The Member States' regulation in this field is lawful as long as it pursues the (multiple) aim of securing social, economic and political governmental control of gambling activities in a *coherent* way.

The way in which the consistent and systematic manner criterion fared in the gambling cases clearly reveals the dynamism of European law. Having first established the criterion in an attempt to formalize and thus to legitimize its decisions to strike down on national measure restricting the free movement of betting activities, the Court undermines this very function of the criterion in the subsequent case concerning the Dutch betting regime. With the relativisation of the consistency criterion, one could argue that it is more difficult for the Court to rely on this element of the criterion *per se* as a way to legitimize future decisions.

Clearly, there are limits as to how far the dynamic EU law may be formalized. Inconsistencies in law frequently have to be accepted and do not necessarily thwart the integrity of law. Although consistency, in the meaning of non-contradiction, was replaced by consistency, in the meaning of coherency, in the Dutch gambling case, this does not have to mean that a strict consistency criterion cannot be applied in *Gambelli* type cases in the future. The principle of equality (and consistency) in the meaning that like cases should be treated equally suggests that the Court according to conventional legal methodology may refer to *Gambelli* as a *precedent*.

9.7 Conclusions

In this chapter, I have discussed how the Court of Justice has applied the consistent and systematic manner criterion in order to secure legitimation for its proportionality analysis. The point of departure was taken in conflicts, which arise between the free movement of the European constitution and the national welfare state constitutions. Conflicts of this nature may, I propose, be characterized as hard cases. In order to solve these cases, the Court of Justice applies the proportionality principle.

---

[69] Ibid., para 32.

However, the proportionality principle is of a discretionary character and thus needs further legal framing to secure its legal credentials. One way of framing the proportionality analysis is to tie it up to Dworkian arguments of principle. Accordingly, the Courts apparent bias to the four freedoms in cases where it is set to balance national values against the four freedoms may be explained with reference to a particular normative conception of law.

In the gambling cases, the *prima facia* priority of the four freedoms over national gambling regimes relying on Dworkian arguments of principle does not suffice to secure the legitimacy of EU law. If, however, the Court in hard cases are not bound by any normative arguments of principle, but may decide "either way," this does not mean that their decisions are not informed by legal principles and reasoning. Thus, the introduction of the consistency and systematic manner criterion in the suitability test of the proportionality-analysis may be perceived as a way of reducing the discretionary character of the proportionality principle by tying it to established normative concepts/principles.

As the doctrinal discussion revealed, however, the application of the consistent and systematic manner criterion is not as consistent as one would expect. With the relativisation of the consistency criterion in the Court of Justice's *Ladbrokes* case, the criterion's function as a way of formalizing the proportionality analysis is undermined. True, this does not mean that the consistency criterion as applied in *Gambelli* may not be applied in future cases. However, in that case it will be applied as a precedent rather than as an independent element of legal reasoning.

On a more fundamental level, my investigation reveals the difficulties connected to the attempt to framing EU law by introducing quasi-principles of law. Establishing principles of law may, one could hold, be very tempting in an attempt to frame a developing and dynamic legal order as the European. The flipside of this endeavour is that the principles may have to be abandoned at the next crossroad.

The fate of the consistent and systematic manner criterion may provoke the question as to whether the high days of Court of Justice's activism are over. As EU law develops into a mature legal regime, the concept of law and the role of the judiciary would necessarily have to be transformed. Accordingly, rather than creating ever new "legal principles"—which it at the next crossroad has to abandon—the Court should to a greater extent focus on solving the concrete cases at hand whilst connecting them in a consistent and coherent body of law by the institution of precedence.

References

Alexy R (2002) A theory of constitutional rights. Oxford University Press, Oxford

Calliess G-P (2003) Coherence and Consistency in European Consumer Contract Law: A Progress Report. German Law Journal, Vol. 4, No. 4

Casolari F (2012) The Principle of Loyal Co-operation: A "master key" for EU External Representation? In: Blockmans S, Wessel RA (eds) Principles and Practice of EU External Representation. 5 CLEER Working Papers

Craig P (2006) EU Administrative Law. Oxford University Press, Oxford
Cremona M (2011) Coherence in European Union foreign relations law. In: Panos K (ed) European Foreign Policy: Legal and Political Perspectives. Edward Elgar, Cheltenham, pp. 55–92
de Búrca G (1993) The Principle of Proportionality and Its Application in EC Law. Yearbook of European Law, vol. 13
den Hertog L, Stross S (2013) Coherence in EU External Relations: Concepts and Legal Rooting of an Ambiguous Term. European Foreign Affairs Review 18, no. 3, pp. 373–388
Dworkin R (1977) Taking rights seriously. Harvard University Press, Cambridge MA
Dworkin R (1998) Law's Empire. Hart Publishing, Oxford
Eckes C (2013) European Union Legal Methods – Moving Away from Integration. In: Neergaard U, Nielsen R (eds) European Legal Method – Towards a New European Legal realism? DJØF Publishing, Copenhagen, pp. 163–188
Harbo T-I (2010) The Function of the Proportionality Principle in EU law. European Law Journal, Vol. 16. No. 2, March, pp. 158–185.
Harbo T-I (2015) The Function of the Proportionality Analysis in European Law. Brill, Boston
Harbo T-I (2016) Introducing procedural proportionality review in European law. Leiden Journal of International Law (forthcoming)
Hart H (1994) The concept of law, 2nd edn. Oxford University Press, Oxford
Herlin-Karnell E, Konstadinides T (2013) The Rise and Expressions of Consistency in EU Law: Legal and Strategic Implications for European Integration. Cambridge Yearbook of European Legal Studies, p. 139
Hillion C (2008) Tous pour un, un pour tous! Coherence in the external relations of the European Union. In: Cremona M (ed) Developments in EU External Relations Law. Oxford University Press, Oxford
Joerges C (2004) What is left of the European Economic Constitution? EUI Working Paper Law No. 2004/13
Joerges C (2009) Integration through conflicts law. On the defence of the European project by means of alternative conceptualisation of legal constitutionalisation. In: Nickel R (ed) Conflicts of laws and laws of conflict in Europe and beyond: Patterns of supranational and transnational juridification. ARENA Report No 1/09
Koutrakos P (2001) Trade, Foreign Policy and Defence in EU Constitutional Law. Hart, Oxford
MacCormick N (2005) Rhetoric and the rule of law: A theory of legal reasoning. Oxford University Press, Oxford
Mathisen G (2010) Consistency and coherency as conditions for justification of Member State measures restricting free movement. Common Market Law review 47, pp. 1021–1048
Nielsen R (2013) New European Legal Realism – New Problems, New Solutions? In: Neergaard U, Nielsen R (eds) European Legal Method – Towards a New European Legal Realism? DJØF Publishing, Copenhagen, pp. 75–124
Rawls J (1971) A theory of justice. Oxford University Press, Oxford
Rawls J (1993) Political Liberalism. Colombia University Press, New York
Schwarze J (2006) European Administrative Law. Sweet and Maxwell, London
Tridimas T (2006) The General Principles of EU Law, 2nd edn. Oxford University Press, Oxford
van Elsuweg P, Merket H (2012) The role of the Court of Justice in Ensuring the Unity of the EU's External Representation. In: Blockmans S, Wessel RA (eds) Principles and Practice of EU External Representation. 5 CLEER Working Papers
van der Velden W (1992) Coherence in Law: A Deductive and Semantic Explanation of Coherence. In: Brouwer B et al (eds) Coherence and Conflict in Law. Kluwer, The Hague
Wessel RA (1999) The European Union's Foreign and Security Policy – A Legal Institutional Perspective. Kluwer, The Hague

Part III
Fundamental Rights

Chapter 10
Legitimacy and the Charter of Fundamental Rights Post-Lisbon

Christoffer C. Eriksen and Jørgen A. Stubberud

Abstract Has the incorporation of the Charter of Fundamental Rights into the Lisbon Treaty strengthened our reasons for accepting the powers entrusted to the European Union?—The Charter of Fundamental Rights was adopted and later transformed into primary law in order to enhance the legitimacy of the EU. This echoed a critique of the gradually expanding powers of the EU, including the expanding reach of the right to free movement, more supranational decision-making procedures, and new Union powers in novel policy areas such as the area of justice and home affairs. One line of criticism held that the wide powers of the Union were not balanced with a sufficient level of democratic control and effective protection against abuse. The Lisbon Treaty sought to enhance legitimacy in three ways: Decision-making processes were to some extent democratised; the Member States agreed that the Union shall accede to the ECHR; and the Charter was transformed into primary law. There is a partly competing perspective that posits that the EU's legitimacy may depend more on its ability to facilitate effective problem-solving of acute public policy issues, including migration, terror, and economic crises. In this chapter, we analyse to what extent the transformation of the Charter into primary law has already succeeded, and may continue to succeed, in providing better reasons for accepting the powers entrusted to the EU. In this context, we provide, first, an analysis of certain questions regarding the interpretation and application of the Charter, questions which are key to assessing what changes to EU law the said transformation has led to and may lead to, as compared to older epochs of EU law, when fundamental rights were based on unwritten law. In the final assessment, we argue that the answer to the legitimacy question depends on the extent to which European courts will allow Member States flexibility regarding how fundamental

C.C. Eriksen
Department of Public and International Law, Faculty of Law, University of Oslo,
Karl Johans gate 47, St. Olavs plass, PO Box 6706, N-0130 Oslo, Norway
e-mail: c.c.eriksen@jus.uio.no.no

J.A. Stubberud (✉)
Law firm Advokat Jørgen A. Stubberud, Stasjonsveien 109, N-1746 Skjeberg, Norway
e-mail: jorgen.stubberud@ius.no

M. Andenas et al. (eds.), *The Reach of Free Movement*,
DOI 10.1007/978-94-6265-195-1_10

rights are protected in different institutional environments. Effective problem-solving may require the ability to adapt different solutions to various locations and to different situations, based upon the weighing of diverse interests.

Keywords Fundamental rights · Legitimacy · Charter of Fundamental Rights · Natural law · Lisbon Treaty · Human rights · Principles

Contents

10.1 Introduction 230
10.2 Background: Five Historical Epochs in the Development of EU Fundamental Rights Protection 233
10.3 The Fourth Epoch of EU Fundamental Rights Protection: What's New After Lisbon? 237
10.3.1 Introduction 237
10.3.2 The Charter—Also a Shield Against the Member States? 238
10.3.3 The Charter's Impact: Rights Versus Principles 242
10.3.4 Effects on Other Parts of EU Law: Charter-Consistent Interpretation? 245
10.3.5 Summing Up 246
10.4 A Binding Charter—An Additional Argument for Accepting the Powers Entrusted to the EU? 247
10.4.1 Legitimacy—Two Normative Perspectives 247
10.4.2 Rights-Based Legitimacy 248
10.4.3 Charter Legitimacy Assessed on the Basis of the Problem-Solving Capacity of the EU 248
10.5 The Charter of Fundamental Rights, Legitimacy of the EU—Challenges for Future Practice 250
References 250

10.1 Introduction

Today's European Union has a great number of tasks and objectives. Essentially, its ultimate political end has been *peace in Europe*, to be secured through trade. The main means has been the creation of an internal market through the upholding of four freedoms. Securing these freedoms has necessitated integration by means of law, and this has made EU institutions powerful.

With power comes a need for legitimacy. In academic discourses since the late eighteenth century, such legitimacy has been dependent on the possibility of justifying why it is acceptable for free people, and for free peoples, to let any authority exercise power that imposes restrictions on their freedom.[1] According to one

[1] This has been a central concern for modern political philosophy, particularly since the European Enlightenment, and is reflected in the positions of Locke, Rousseau and Kant. Despite their

leading tradition of normative political theory, articulated for example by Jürgen Habermas, power is only legitimate if it is established and exercised in a way that deserves recognition.[2] The possibility of providing justification for why power deserves recognition may have implications for the stability of political regimes and the obedience of citizens to legal and political authority. It would certainly be difficult to explain the stability of authority, and the (more or less) voluntary compliance with authority, if it did not, in some way, *deserve* recognition. Why should people otherwise accept restrictions on their freedom? Why this *servitude volontaire*?

When, during its first decades, the EU was a less notable creature of public international law, the EU's need for legitimacy did not feel so acute. Its power seemed to receive sufficient legitimacy from the fact that the EU was instituted through treaties willingly entered into by authorized representatives of its Founders, and that EU decisions were adopted within the powers so conferred and through appropriate procedures (legitimacy in the juridical sense). However, following the transformation of several European Communities into one Union entrusted with new powers over more policy areas, increased supranationalisation through judicial activism, extended scope of the four freedoms and new legislative processes, there came a need for additional sources of legitimacy. The new and more powerful EU emerging through the 1990s could no longer claim to deserve recognition solely based on relatively thin legitimacy in the juridical sense, derived from the founding treaties. Without a strengthened legitimacy in a normative sense, the EU could risk more criticism, stronger opposition and possibly new desires to withdraw from the Union.

The EU's need for increasing and more compelling forms of legitimacy has occasioned a number of political initiatives. Consistently ongoing reform processes have entailed a constant renewal of juridical legitimacy, in that the EU's powers have been repeatedly re-confirmed (novated) through the signing of renewed founding documents (new versions of the treaties, and amendments to them). In addition there have been efforts to strengthen the protection of fundamental rights, such as the decision adopted by the European Council in Cologne in 1999 to

(Footnote 1 continued)

divergent theoretical stance, they all claimed that the only public authorities that deserved recognition were those based upon principles under which subordination did not violate freedom. The claim is, perhaps, most clearly articulated by Rousseau: "*MAN is born free; and everywhere he is in chains. One thinks himself the master of others, and still remains a greater slave than they. How did this change come about? I do not know. What can make it legitimate? That question I think I can answer.*" Rousseau 1992 [1762], p. 914.

[2] Habermas 2001, p. 113. For application of this understanding of legitimacy to studies of the European integration project, see, for example, Joerges 2006. Habermas' conception of legitimacy has been articulated slightly differently by others. For example, Joseph Raz claims that the question of normative legitimacy is about the moral reasons for obeying governing techniques; see Raz 1979. Another formulation is provided by John Rawls, who focuses on the rational reasons for accepting the institutional framework in which governing techniques are exercised; see Rawls 1999. However, for the purposes of this chapter, there is no need to distinguish between these various articulations.

establish the Charter of Fundamental Rights (the "Charter").[3] This measure in and by itself seemed insufficient since the Charter's status as soft law prevented it from having real impact. The last reform, set out by the Lisbon Treaty (in force since 1 December 2009) contains a mixed bag of initiatives aimed at ensuring legitimacy for the EU. First, decision-making processes have to some extent been democratised. Second, the Lisbon Treaty laid down that the Union shall accede to the ECHR, thereby attempting to provide individuals with a stronger shield against potential abuse of the powers entrusted to the Union.[4] This latter initiative has, however, been struck down by the Court of Justice (the "ECJ") and it is unclear whether and under what conditions the Union may accede to the ECHR.[5] The third Lisbon measure aimed at securing legitimacy for the EU, and the topic of this chapter, was the incorporation of the Charter of Fundamental Rights into the treaties, thus making the Charter primary EU law.

The overarching idea of this chapter is to explore what significance it may have for the peoples of Europe, for EU law and for its legitimacy, that the Treaty of Lisbon has transformed the Charter into a legal instrument with the same legal value as the treaties. Does it currently, and will it continue to, provide the intended legitimacy?[6] Does the incorporation of the Charter of Fundamental Rights into the treaties provide better reasons for accepting the powers entrusted to the EU?

The new status of the Charter may, of course, be seen as having significance to the peoples of Europe in a number of ways. At one level, the transformation of the Charter may be seen as one of a series of initiatives aimed at restricting the powers of the EU through stronger democratic control and more effective rights against possible abuse of power. After a period in which the powers of the European institutions had grown significantly, efforts were made in the 1990s to reform the founding treaties of the EU to increase the protection of the political and individual freedom of European citizens. Arguably, such reforms could provide better reasons for accepting the powers entrusted to the EU, i.e. to increase its legitimacy. In effect, the extent to which the new legal status of the Charter has in fact strengthened fundamental rights protection could also enhance the legitimacy of the EU.

However, inquiries into how the new legal status of the Charter affects the legitimacy of the EU cannot be seen in isolation from the failure to win popular

---

[3] See the Cologne European Council, 3–4 June 1999, The Presidency Conclusions, Annex IV, see http://www.europarl.europa.eu/summits/kol2_en.htm#an4.

[4] The European Convention for protection of Human Rights and Fundamental Freedoms, which is within the jurisdiction of the European Court of Human Rights (the ECtHR).

[5] See TEU Article 6(2) and Opinion 2/13.

[6] In this chapter we focus on legitimacy in a normative sense, not on juridical, psychological or sociological concepts of legitimacy. Legitimacy in the normative sense differs from *actual approval* of authority (psychological conceptions of legitimacy), from legitimacy as (actual) obedience to authority (sociological conceptions of legitimacy), and from legitimacy established by reference to higher-order norms (juridical conceptions of legitimacy). This is not to deny that such other aspects of legitimacy may have normative relevance too. For a general analysis of interrelations between normative, legal and social aspects of legitimacy, see Beetham 1991.

acceptance for other initiatives to reform the European Union's founding treaties. Although the Charter was formally adopted in 2001, it took almost a decade to establish its legal value. The governments of the Member States suggested transforming the Charter into primary law as a part of the Constitutional Treaty. Since the Constitutional Treaty was rejected by referenda in 2006, the transformation of the Charter also failed. As the Treaty of Lisbon succeeded in transforming the Charter into primary law, the peoples of Europe ended up having a *bill of rights without a written constitution*. This legal predicament, and the process out of which it emerged may in itself justify inquiring into the extent to which the new legal status of the Charter affects the reasons for accepting EU power.

From the perspective of political philosophy, we see at least two different potential answers to the question of how the transformation of the Charter affects the legitimacy of the EU. Together they create a particular dilemma. First, the incorporation of the Charter into the treaties can be seen as continuing the celebrated work of constructing European rights. Secondly, it may, however, also be seen as a threat to the vision of Europe as a laboratory for policy experimentation and effective problem-solving, organized under a subsidiarity principle. From the perspective that the legitimacy of the EU is dependent on its capacity to protect individual rights, the incorporation of the Charter into the treaties would seem an appropriate means for increasing legitimacy. On the other hand, from the perspective that the EU is less a protector of rights and more a facilitator of policy experimentation and effective problem-solving, the transformation of the Charter into primary law could also be seen as weakening the legitimacy of the EU, at least to the extent that Charter rights are, in effect, an obstacle to efficient problem-solving.

Our argument is structured as follows: In Sect. 10.2, we provide an account of five historical epochs of fundamental rights protection in the EU. Against this background, in Sect. 10.3, we inquire as to what changes the new legal status of the Charter is bringing about with regard to fundamental rights protection in the EU. Upon this basis, in Sect. 10.4, we will be asking what consequences the findings from Sect. 10.3 may have for the legitimacy of the EU.

10.2 Background: Five Historical Epochs in the Development of EU Fundamental Rights Protection

Fundamental rights protection in EC and EU law can be divided into five distinct historical periods, one of which is still to come in the future.

The First Epoch (1957 to approx. 1970): This period starts from the birth of the European Communities until the ECJ started recognising the existence of fundamental rights in the EC legal order, around the year 1970. Standard accounts of fundamental rights in the EU (EC) legal order typically start at 1970, implying, or even explicitly stating, that there is no basis for speaking of EU fundamental rights before they were recognised in the case law of the ECJ.[7] Such a view, however, depends on a particular theory of law and on a corresponding (non-trivial) choice of criteria for acknowledging the existence of fundamental rights.

Clearly, Europeans could not rely on any positive catalogue of rights derived from explicit treaty provisions or a solid body of case law during this First Epoch. But the reasons that ultimately led the ECJ to recognise fundamental rights as part of EU law must nonetheless have been there all the time (or at least some time prior to the ECJ's recognition of them). Consequently, even before the initial ECJ cases, there must have been certain inalienable rights, the respect for which Europeans were entitled to demand, even if those rights had not yet been explicitly acknowledged either in positive sources of EU law or by the Court. There is no basis for considering the case law of the ECJ to be the sole criterion for the existence of legal norms.

It turns out that answering the question of precisely *when* fundamental rights came into existence within the EU legal order is difficult. It depends on what we mean by "law." Which in turn depends upon our theory of law, upon the concept of law that we choose to apply. At the level of legal theory, there are no courts to direct us.

The Second Epoch (1970s to 2000): This epoch is characterised by a gradual recognition and development, in ECJ case law, of general principles, including the *principle of protection of fundamental rights*, starting with cases such as *Stauder, Internationale Handelsgesellschaft*, *Nold*, etc., in the early 1970s.[8] In this Second Epoch, the Court based its reasoning particularly upon the "common constitutional traditions of the Member States," and upon the international treaties to which all the Member States were party. This comprised, first and foremost, the ECHR, but also some other treaties, such as the European Social Charter and certain ILO conventions. It gradually became clear that EU fundamental rights can be invoked not only *vis-à-vis* the EU, but also *vis-à-vis* the Member States.[9]

In this Second Epoch, the ECJ employed the ECHR as a privileged source. Without seeing itself as being formally bound by the European Convention (from a public international law perspective, or otherwise), the ECJ still acknowledged it as a source of "special significance" for the content of EU fundamental rights.[10] The Court imposed upon itself an obligation to "take into account" ECtHR case law when interpreting rights which were also guaranteed under the ECHR.[11]

---

[7] See e.g. Craig and de Búrca 2008, Chapter 11.

[8] Case 29/69, *Stauder*, ECLI:EU:C:1969:57; Case 11/70, *Internationale Handelsgesellschaft*, ECLI:EU:C:1970:114; Case 4/73, *Nold*, ECLI:EU:C:1974:51.

[9] Case 5/88, *Wachauf*, ECLI:EU:C:1989:321, and C-260/89, *ERT*, ECLI:EU:C:1991:254.

[10] ECJ Opinion 2/94 on the Accession of the Community to the ECHR, ECLI:EU:C:1996:140, para 33.

[11] See, for example, Case C-310/04, Kingdom of Spain v. Council of the European Union, ECLI: EU:C:2006:521 and C-465/07, Meki Elgafaji and Noor Elgafaji v. Staatssecretaris van Justitie, ECLI:EU:C:2009:94.

The status of fundamental rights as general principles of law was formally recognised by the Treaty of Maastricht in 1993.[12] Since this did not go beyond what already followed from established case law, we do not regard this event as epoch-making.[13]

The Third Epoch (2000 to 1 Dec 2009): In Nice, on 7 December 2000, the Presidents of the European Parliament, the Council, and the Commission signed and proclaimed the Charter of Fundamental Rights on behalf of their respective institutions. The Charter contains (and contained before the amendments in 2007) 54 articles distributed into seven chapters. The first six chapters bear titles that reflect the different types of rights the Charter protects, namely, *Dignity*, *Freedom*, *Equality*, *Solidarity*, *Citizens' rights*, and *Justice*. The seventh chapter contains general provisions regarding the interpretation and the application of the Charter.

The rights set out in the Charter have four main sources: EU treaties; general principles of law recognised by the EU courts; the ECHR; and, the common constitutional traditions of the Member States. This means that the Charter both protects transnational economic rights, traditional civil rights, *and* certain social and political rights.

The Charter mainly codified case law. Did it also add new rights and principles? To answer this question with any degree of certainty is conspicuously hard. It is difficult both to provide an account of which fundamental rights were protected as general principles before the adoption of the Charter, and to determine how the Charter is to be interpreted and applied today. Some argue that the Charter was not intended to create any new rights in addition to the rights already in force by virtue of general principles.[14] But whatever the intention might have been, there nevertheless appear to be at least *some* new norms (rights and/or principles) set out in the Charter. One example is the prohibition of reproductive cloning of human beings (Article 3). Another is the right to protection of personal data (Article 8). There is also Article 26 on the "Integration of Persons with Disabilities." Additionally, there seem to be developments concerning family life and children's rights (Article 24).[15] Since the entry into force of the Treaty of Lisbon, these new rights and principles form part of EU law, with the status of primary law.

---

[12] See Article 6 TEU.

[13] The same goes for the Joint Declaration by the European Parliament, the Council and the Commission adopted in 1977, OJ 1977, C 103/1.

[14] Thus, for example, Jacobs 2002, p. 275. Klausen 2001 is among those who see new rights in the Charter.

[15] This is argued by McGlynn 2001, pp. 582–598, who also presents a more general argument for there being new rights in the Charter (*op.cit.* p. 583).

Previously, the Charter was considered merely a political declaration (soft law), and it had limited impact on case law. Until the Treaty of Lisbon entered into force, one could question whether the Charter was a source of law at all. In practice, both the Court of First Instance (CFI) and the ECJ referred to the Charter in their reasoning.[16] Arguably, however, these references to the Charter functioned only, or at least primarily, as support arguments that were not ultimately necessary for the Court's conclusions, since the rights in question were already assumed to be founded in general principles of EU law.[17]

Fourth Epoch (1 Dec 2009 to…?): The Fourth Epoch, which is the current epoch, began on 1 December 2009 when the Treaty of Lisbon entered into force and the Charter acquired the status of primary law. This epoch comprises EU law as it stands today, and will be our topic for the rest of this chapter. This Fourth Epoch will end when (and if) the EU becomes a party to the ECHR, thus marking the advent of the Fifth and last of the epochs that can be foreseen as of today.

The Fifth Epoch: This epoch will only start when the EU becomes a party to the ECHR. The Treaty of Lisbon brought two major changes with regard to fundamental rights. The first is that the Charter became primary law. The second, as set out in TEU Article 6(2), is that the EU "shall accede" to the ECHR. The EU's accession agreement to the ECHR had to become an attempt at answering many difficult, albeit extremely interesting, questions: Which of the two courts, the ECJ or the ECtHR, shall be the court of last resort in various situations? In EU law theory, the expression a "Constitution for Europe" is used in various senses. We may eventually come to see one of them used with regard to this accession agreement.[18] However, after the ECJ found that parts of the draft accession agreement was incompatible with EU law, it is unclear on what terms an accession agreement could be compatible with EU law, and whether it will enter into force at all.[19]

[16] The ECJ referred to the Charter *inter alia* in the following cases: Case C-540/03, *European Parliament* v. *Council of the European Union*, ECLI:EU:C:2006:429, para 38; Case C-432/05, *Unibet* v. *Justitiekanslern*, ECLI:EU:C:2007:163, para 37; Case C-244/06, *Dynamic Medien Vertriebs GmbH* v. *Avides Media AG*, ECLI:EU:C:2008:85, para 41. Prior to this, the Charter was referred to by a number of Advocates General (see, for example, AG Jacobs' Opinion in Case C-50/00, *Unión de Pequeños Agricultores* v. *Council of the European Union*, ECLI:EU:C:2002:197; AG Geelhoed's Opinion in Case C-224/98, *D'Hoop* v. *Office National d'Emploi*, ECLI:EU:C:2002:103, as well as by the Court of First Instance (see, for example, Case T-177/01, *Jégo Quéré et Cie SA* v. *European Commission*, ECLI:EU:T:2002:112), the European Court of Human Rights (see, for example, *Goodwin* v. *UK* [2002] 35 EHRR 18) and national courts (see, for example, *R (on the application of Robertson)* v. *Wakefield MDC* [2002] QB 1052, 170)).

[17] See Rosas and Armati 2010, p. 154.

[18] For further analysis, see, for example, Lock 2010, pp. 777–798.

[19] See Opinion 2/13.

10.3 The Fourth Epoch of EU Fundamental Rights Protection: What's New After Lisbon?

10.3.1 Introduction

We are now in the Fourth Epoch, and the analysis that follows will be limited to that. Except for those changes which ECHR membership may entail, what follows will, however, continue to be relevant for the Fifth Epoch as well, since the Charter will continue to govern EU fundamental rights law after that point in time as well.

The characteristic news of the Fourth Epoch is that the Charter has acquired the status of primary law alongside the treaties and general principles.[20] The new Article 6(1) of the TEU sets out that "*the Union recognises the rights, freedoms and principles set out in the Charter of Fundamental Rights*" and that "*the Charter of Fundamental Rights [...] shall have the same legal value as the Treaties*". What new developments will this bring about?

A catalogue of rights, freedoms and principles with the same legal value as the treaties, subject to the jurisdiction of a court that is famous for its teleological and dynamic treaty interpretation, could spawn a new line of case law with predictable and unpredictable consequences for private parties and Member States. Mirroring what has been referred to as an integrationist or "unionist" judicial activism of the past, we could thus be facing a period of *rights activism* in the future jurisprudence of the ECJ.[21] Possible areas where some would see a real need for rights development within EU law would not only include social and economic rights, but also classical first-generation human rights questions such as *standing*, and individual rights relating to Police and Judicial Co-operation in Criminal matters (former Third Pillar).

There are, however, also significant reasons for not believing in any drastic new rights activism on the part of the Court. First, one could argue that there is not that much which is really *new* after Lisbon, anyway. The Charter was principally a summary of rights that were already in force in EU law by virtue of general principles. And the Charter itself sets out that the different rights protected by the Charter are to be exercised in accordance with their legal background, i.e., more or less "as before".

In what follows, we will discuss certain questions related to the effects of the Charter's new legal status, thus far and into the future. In particular, we focus on three questions that are relevant for interpreting and applying the Charter. They share a common trait, in that they are all relevant to an assessment of the legitimacy of the EU, and concern the effects of the Charter having become primary law.

---

[20] There are some other significant news, too, such as the extended jurisdiction of the ECJ to the former Third Pillar. We do not undertake to map all the changes that the Treaty of Lisbon has created with regard to fundamental rights protection, only those connected to the Charter's new status as primary law.

[21] This is argued by Curzon 2011, in particular at p. 158. See also Rasmussen 2008.

First, we will discuss the extent to which individuals may rely on the Charter when challenging Member State measures. This concerns the Charter's scope of application (Sect. 10.3.2). Secondly, we will discuss the Charter's distinction between rights and principles, which is of significance to fundamental rights protection both at an EU and a Member State level (Sect. 10.3.3). Thirdly, we will discuss the Charter as an instrument for interpretation of other parts of EU law (Sect. 10.3.4). As the discussion will show, the new legal status of the Charter seems to be having noticeable effects for fundamental rights protection in the EU. In Sect. 10.4, we inquire how those effects contribute to (or detract from) the legitimacy of the EU.

10.3.2 The Charter—Also a Shield Against the Member States?

Even though the Charter has become primary law, fundamental rights will also continue to be protected under EU law as unwritten law with the status of "general principles."[22] According to well-known ECJ case law, unwritten fundamental rights may be invoked against acts, omissions and decisions of both the EU's own institutions and those of the Member States.[23] They may be invoked by individuals, both natural and legal persons, and in some cases they may even be invoked by *Member States* against EU measures (for example, as a defence against an alleged breach of treaty obligations, e.g. in state aid cases). The latter category is an interesting and somewhat paradoxical legal creature: *human rights for states*.

According to the ECJ's case law prior to the new legal status of the Charter, there are two situations in which fundamental rights (then considered as general principles) may be invoked against Member States: the first is the so-called "agency-situation." This situation arises when Member States implement EU law in their internal legal orders, whether by adopting legislation or other forms of general regulation, or by adopting individual decisions. This is only natural, since, in the agency-situation, the Member States (or individual Member State authorities) can be seen as acting as Union bodies.[24] The second situation in which fundamental rights and other general principles may be invoked against Member States is the so-called "derogation-situation".

---

[22] See, for example, Article 6(3) TEU, which states that "Fundamental rights … shall constitute general principles of the Union's law".

[23] In Case 4/73, *Nold*, ECLI:EU:C:1974:51, the ECJ declared that it could not uphold community measures that are incompatible with fundamental rights. In Case C-256/90, *Mignini*, ECLI:EU:C:1992:173, a regulation was set aside upon the basis of incompatibility with fundamental rights. The principle that the limitations which fundamental rights place on the EU institutions also apply to Member States when they implement EU law is expressed, for example, in Case 5/88, *Wachauf*, ECLI:EU:C:1989:321 and in C-292/97, *Karlsson*, ECLI:EU:C:2000:202.

[24] See Weiler 1995, p. 68.

This is when Member States derogate from EU law, for example when they adopt measures which fall within the scope of free movement but which are, nevertheless, justifiable on objective grounds.[25] This means that in addition to being proportionate and consistent with other general principles of EU law, such derogative measures must not violate fundamental rights.[26]

There has been some discussion regarding whether fundamental rights set out in the Charter apply both to the agency-situation and the derogation-situation. This question is first and foremost of interest with regard to "new" rights and principles, namely norms that are not already part of EU law by virtue of general principles.[27] For one, Catherine Barnard argued that fundamental rights that are based upon the Charter "*apply to states only when implementing Community law [...] and not when they are derogating from it.*"[28] Barnard based this upon an interpretation of Article 51(1) of the Charter, which contains the wording that "*[t]he provisions of this Charter are addressed to the Member States only when they are implementing Union law.*" However, subsequent case law seems to show that this reading was too literal.[29] In *Pfleger*, the court clarified its position in a case concerning Austrian regulation of gaming machines. Austrian law required authorisation for operating such machines.[30] During inspection, Austrian authorities found and confiscated several unauthorised machines. In the national court proceedings following the confiscation, it was submitted that Austrian rules violated several provisions of EU law, including the provisions in the Charter protecting the freedom to choose an occupation, the freedom to conduct a business and the right to property (Articles 15–17 of the Charter). However, it was also evident that there were no harmonized rules for the operation of gaming machines at the European level. Against this background, the national court requested a preliminary ruling on several questions from the European Court, among them the question of the applicability of the Charter. Against the objections of several Member States, the Court concluded that the Charter was applicable also in the derogation-situation:

> As follows from that case-law, where it is apparent that national legislation is such as to obstruct the exercise of one or more fundamental freedoms guaranteed by the Treaty, it may benefit from the exceptions provided for by EU law in order to justify that fact only in so far as that complies with the fundamental rights enforced by the Court. That obligation to comply with fundamental rights manifestly comes within the scope of EU law and, consequently, within that of the Charter. The use by a Member State of exceptions provided for

[25] See, for example, de Búrca 2001, p. 137.

[26] See C-260/89, *ERT*, ECLI:EU:C:1991:254 an early case showing that Member States must respect fundamental rights when derogating from EU law (in this case, from the four freedoms), and see subsequently C-368/95, *Familiapress*, ECLI:EU:C:1997:325; Case C-459/99, *MRAX*, ECLI:EU:C:2002:461; Case C-60/00, *Carpenter*, ECLI:EU:C:2002:434.

[27] The reason is that "old" norms, i.e., those that already exist by virtue of general principles, clearly continue to apply both in the agency-situation and in the derogation-situation.

[28] Barnard 2008, p. 263.

[29] This is also suggested by Di Federico 2011, in particular at 39–40.

[30] See Case C-390/12, *Pfleger*, ECLI:EU:C:2014:281.

> by EU law in order to justify an obstruction of a fundamental freedom guaranteed by the Treaty must, therefore, be regarded, as the Advocate General states in point 46 of her Opinion, as 'implementing Union law' within the meaning of Article 51(1) of the Charter.[31]

In our opinion, the result in *Pfleger* was a natural one.[32] It was in line with the Court's previous fundamental rights practice. If the Court were to treat fundamental rights set out in the Charter differently from those that have the status of general principles, the result would have been a parallel development of two differing bodies of case law concerning parallel rights. That would have caused a number of practical concerns. The result in *Pfleger* was also in line with the official Explanations to the Charter, which point to a broader understanding of the term "implementing" (Article 51(1)). The Explanations refer to "the scope of Union law", which is used by the Court as a reference also to situations in which the Member States adopt measures which fall within the scope of free movement but which are justified on objective grounds (derogation).[33] The Explanations even make explicit reference to the court's judgment in *ERT*, the first case in which the ECJ determined that Member States are also obliged to respect fundamental rights when derogating from EU law.

True, from the perspective of the Member States, the four freedoms may be seen purely as prohibitions against the Member States introducing restrictions on free movement. But from the perspective of European citizens, the four freedoms are fundamental freedoms that have been granted to them by law. No one, including Member States, can encroach upon fundamental rights and freedoms without possessing the necessary competence to do so. Since the freedoms in question are based upon norms of EU law, the competence to place limitations on those freedoms must necessarily also be based upon norms of EU law. Member States clearly cannot derogate from EU law on the basis of national law. Hence, a Member State that is lawfully derogating from the four freedoms is also exercising EU competences. This creates a normative justification for seeing derogation as a case of "implementing" EU law in the sense of the Charter.

Moreover, the ruling in *Pfleger* was also building on case law from the post-Lisbon era in which the Court had opened up for not only applying the Charter to the agency-situation (implementation in the strict sense), but also to all matters falling within the scope of EU law. Most notably, in *Fransson*, a case that concerned the applicability of the Charter to charges made under Swedish sanction rules for fraud of VAT, the Court held that "*the fundamental rights guaranteed in the legal order of the European Union are applicable in all situations governed by European Union law, but not outside such situations*".[34] Furthermore, the court held that although it has "*no power to examine the compatibility with the Charter of national legislation lying outside the scope of European Union law*", this is not the

[31] C-390/12, *Pfleger*, ECLI:EU:C:2014:281, para 36.

[32] See for the opposite opinion Snell 2015.

[33] See, for example, de Búrca 2001.

[34] See Case C-617/10, *Fransson*, ECLI:EU:C:2013:105, para 19.

case when national legislation is within the scope of EU law.[35] When national legislation "*falls within the scope of European Union law*" and a national court requests a preliminary ruling, the court found that it must "*provide all the guidance as to interpretation needed in order for the national court to determine whether that legislation is compatible with the fundamental rights the observance of which the Court ensures*".[36]

Determining *when* national legislation falls within the scope of EU law opens up several new questions, in respect of which the Court has not yet clarified its own position. So far, the Court has not applied one consistent formula in this regard, but there is no shortage of suggestions.[37] Here we limit ourselves to commenting on one suggestion with the potential to create a particular challenge for the legitimacy of the EU and its legal order, namely the suggestion put forward by Advocate General Sharpston in the advisory opinion in *Zambrano*. According to Sharpston, the clearest rule for identifying whether national measures fall within the scope of EU law would be one that makes the availability of EU fundamental rights protection dependent on the existence and scope of a material EU competence, not on whether a Treaty provision was directly applicable, or on whether secondary legislation has been enacted.[38] In Sharpston's words, "*the rule would be that, provided that the EU had competence (whether exclusive or shared) in a particular area of law, EU fundamental rights should protect the citizen of the EU even if such competence has not yet been exercised*".[39]

While this suggestion would provide both transparency and clarity, it could extend the Charter rights so far that it would generate a vast number of conflicts over numerous policy questions. Given the current range of EU competencies, not only on economic policy but also in areas such as environmental, migration and monetary policy, the result could be too many conflicts over too many policy questions, obstruction and delay of other court cases, and the production of a body of case law which in sum could impose too strict limitations on the Member States' possibility to experiment with different policies, even in policy areas where the EU has not yet exercised its competence.[40] In such areas, fundamental rights may be equally, or perhaps better, protected by national constitutions and other international instruments such as in particular the ECHR.

---

[35] Ibid.

[36] Ibid.

[37] For a discussion, see Snell 2015 and Dougan 2015.

[38] See Opinion of GA Sharpston in Case C 34/09, *Zambrano*, ECLI:EU:C:2010:560.

[39] *Op.cit.* para 163.

[40] For further discussions of such concerns, see below in Sect. 10.4.

10.3.3 The Charter's Impact: Rights Versus Principles

The Charter establishes a distinction between *rights* and *principles*, which is central to an assessment of the impact that the transformation of the Charter into primary EU law is likely to have. According to Article 51 of the Charter, rights are to be "respected," while principles, in contrast, only need to be "observed." Before the entry into force of the Treaty of Lisbon, this distinction was not so important, since the Charter was considered soft law anyway. Now that the Charter has become primary law, however, the distinction between rights and principles is likely to become important for the Charter's impact, and hence, for its importance to European citizens.

The Charter provides courts with a mandate to review the extent to which derogations from rights are sufficiently justified. This is so because the Charter sets out that derogations from Charter rights are permissible only if they are provided for by law, are proportionate to objectives recognised by Union law, and do not encroach upon the essence of the right in question.[41] This gives the courts powers to review the legality and proportionality of measures that violate the rights in question. The courts do not have this mandate with regards to *principles*.

According to the Charter and its Explanations, principles are to be "judicially cognisable" only in the interpretation of legislative and executive acts of Union or Member State bodies, which implement Charter principles. Hence it seems that courts are only allowed to take Charter principles into account in two situations: firstly, when *interpreting* acts which implement such principles. This is natural, and probably unavoidable. Secondly, when courts are called upon to *review the legality* of legislative and executive acts that implement Charter principles. A typical example would be when Member States invoke Charter principles as a justification for restrictions on free movement (the *Omega* and *Schmidberger* situation).[42] Court rulings on the legality of the restriction in question would then have to take Charter principles into account when determining the proportionality of the restriction, as compared to the relevant Charter principle. Finally, the Explanations make it clear that principles do not give individuals the right to claim positive action by Union or Member State authorities, requiring the latter to perform specific acts concerning implementation of Charter principles.

It is important to know how to distinguish between rights and principles, but in this respect, the Charter is not clear. There is, of course, a long-standing tradition in juristic literature by which it distinguishes between "rights" and "principles." Various authors such as Dworkin, Alexy, and others, distinguish in different ways.[43] It cannot be taken for granted that the use of the words "right" and

[41] See Article 52(1).

[42] Case C-112/00, *Schmidberger*, ECLI:EU:C:2003:333; Case C-36/02, *Omega*, ECLI:EU:C:2004:614.

[43] For some "classics" on the distinction between rules and principles, see Esser 1974; Dworkin 1967–68; 1977, Chapters 2 and 3; Alexy 1994, pp. 71 *et seq.*; Alexy 2000.

"principle" in the Charter corresponds to any specific use of these terms in other contexts. Given that the distinction between rights and principles cannot be defined on the basis of any specific external standard, the distinction must be regarded as Charter-autonomous. The Explanations to the Charter do attempt to clarify the distinction by reference to two types of external contexts, namely, to the notion of "principle" as applied in the jurisprudence of the ECJ and the CFI (the General Court), and to "the approach of the Member States' constitutional systems to 'principles.'" Clearly, there is no such thing as "*the*" approach (in the singular) to the distinction between rights and principles in the constitutional systems of the Member States. Nor does the ECJ and CFI case law referenced in the Explanations settle the question.

All in all, the distinction between rights and principles is far from clearly set out in the Charter and its accompanying Explanations.[44] So then how are we to know which Charter provisions contain rights, and which provisions express principles?[45]

The legal-historical background of the provision in question may provide clues: according to Article 52(2) of the Charter, Charter rights which are based on the Treaty on the Functioning of the European Union (TFEU) or the TEU are to be interpreted in accordance with the corresponding treaty provisions. Article 52(3) sets out that Charter rights which correspond to rights that are guaranteed by the ECHR are to be of the same meaning and scope as the corresponding ECHR rights. The same line of thinking has been applied to those fundamental rights that are based on the common constitutional traditions of the Member States: they are to be interpreted in harmony with those traditions.[46] Hence, as concerns Charter provisions which give expression to norms based on the ECHR (and on the common constitutional traditions of the Member States), the question of whether these provisions contain *rights* or *principles* must, as a point of departure, be answered on the basis of whether the corresponding norms of ECHR law (and of Member State constitutional traditions) are rights or principles themselves. Exceptions will be conceivable in instances in which, for whatever reason, EU law should be seen as providing *stronger* protection than the ECHR.[47]

Seeking recourse to ECHR law and the common traditions of the Member States will not, however, always be helpful in determining whether a Charter provision contains a right or a principle. And it will be of no help at all with regard to rights and principles which have no clear equivalent in the ECHR or in the common traditions. So what should the test be? We do not know the answer, but we will now try briefly to sketch some additional ways of thinking about how to distinguish between rights and principles in the Charter.

---

[44] See, concurring, Fredman 2006, p. 57, and Di Federico 2011, p. 41.

[45] Saying that a legal instrument "contains" rights and principles is somewhat misleading. It would be more accurate to say, for example, that it contains provisions and wordings that *give expression to* rights and principles. But this is the language used in Article 52(3) and (5) of the Charter, and we have therefore chosen to use the same language.

[46] Article 52(4) of the Charter.

[47] Article 52(3) of the Charter.

Article 6 TEU states that the Charter is to have the same legal value as the treaties. This could be taken to mean that the Charter is also, as a point of departure, to be *interpreted* according to the same standards as the treaties. In this manner, one could argue that the test for distinguishing Charter rights from Charter principles could be found in the criteria that determine whether treaty provisions are justiciable or not. This would mean that Charter provisions should be read as establishing rights when they intend to confer rights on individuals and are sufficiently clear, precise, and unconditional.[48] The result would be that only those Charter norms that satisfy these criteria are *rights*. The rest would be principles.

One could also ask whether the criteria for justiciability will necessarily be the same for Charter provisions as for treaty provisions. After all, the Charter is a *rights charter*. That could point in the direction of a more lenient test than the test for justiciability of treaty provisions.

Angela Ward has suggested a possible criterion for determining whether a Charter provision establishes a right, or only a principle, based on whether the EU has the competence to legislate in that field or not.[49] This criterion is problematic for two reasons. First, this criterion is very far from the literal sense of the words "right" and "principle," and from how lawyers normally distinguish between rights and principles. Second, it is the same criterion that is being used for determining whether the Charter applies to Member States.

Another factor which could be relevant is whether the norm in question is suitable for adjudication by courts (it would then be a right), or whether it is a norm whose content should, instead, be determined by popular assemblies or administrative bodies (and consequently a principle). This could be the true answer; however, it is a very general statement that provides little guidance.

In addition, in distinguishing between rights and principles, it could also help keeping in mind that second and third generation human rights, as opposed to first generation human rights, do not seem to lend themselves as easily to natural law-based justifications.[50] In the introduction to this section, we stated that the distinction between rights and principles is key to an assessment of the consequences that the transformation of the Charter into primary EU law is likely to have. It is, in this sense, "key" from a particular perspective. This is the traditional juristic perspective that norms must, in order to deserve the name of "fundamental rights", set limits to the acts, omissions and decisions of legislative and (at the very least) executive authorities, limits which can be upheld in a court of law. At the outset,

[48] The exact way of wording these criteria can be discussed. We have used the same wording here as the one used by Craig and de Búrca 2008, p. 277, for formulating the criteria for direct effect of treaty provisions. The ECJ has, in an extensive number of judgments, confirmed that the treaties provide private parties with rights that are enforceable before national courts, provided that the treaty provisions in question are articulated in a precise, unconditional and independent way.

[49] See Ward 2009.

[50] See, also, the line of thinking set out in Protocol 30 to the Treaty of Lisbon, which sets out that Title IV of the Charter (which contains provisions for socio-economic rights and principles), does not create justiciable rights applicable to Poland or the United Kingdom.

only Charter *rights* (as opposed to principles) are able to perform this task. In other words, Charter provisions that set out *principles* alone, can be said to not actually establish norms worthy of the name "fundamental rights."

10.3.4 Effects on Other Parts of EU Law: Charter-Consistent Interpretation?

The Charter has become primary law. If the expression "primary law" is to have any meaning, it must include a sense that primary law is, in some perceived hierarchy of norms, "higher" than other law. In order for primary law to be conceived as *higher* than other forms of law, it must possess an ability to serve as a ground for setting aside other law, and as a basis for interpreting other law (at least to some extent) in conformity with primary law. To the extent that the Charter has not brought into existence new rights in the stricter sense of this word, the latter of the two effects may become the most important one. We will be referring to the effect which the Charter may have on other parts of EU law, not as a ground for invalidation of EU law, but as a basis for preferring one interpretation of it to another, as "Charter-consistent interpretation."

The most clean-cut case of Charter-consistent interpretation will be when *new* rights and principles affect the interpretation of other EU law. The ECJ is under a duty to ensure that in the interpretation and application of the Treaties, the law is observed (Article 19 TEU). Since fundamental rights are protected as general principles of EU law, it follows that the ECJ also has to observe these rights when interpreting and applying EU law.[51] Therefore, even before the Charter became primary law, the ECJ was, based upon its own case law, bound to interpret EU law in conformity with those Charter rights that correspond to rights that are already in force as general principles. The fact that the ECJ continues to interpret and apply EU law in conformity with those fundamental rights that are already recognised as general principles is not the same thing as Charter-consistent interpretation. It is rather interpretation in the light of unwritten general principles, principles that existed and continue to exist independently of the Charter.

Old rights and principles have also acquired enhanced visibility when the Charter became primary law. Depending on whether courts will prefer to refer to the Charter or to general principles, Charter-consistent interpretation may become important outside the context of "new" rights and principles, as well.

There is another distinction to be made between two categories of Charter-consistent interpretation. Firstly, to the extent that the Charter contains new rights not previously recognised as (part of) general principles, the incorporation of

---

[51] See Case 11/70, *Internationale Handelsgesellschaft*, ECLI:EU:C:1970:114. More generally, see Sect. 10.2 and the Second Epoch of Fundamental Rights Protection in the EU.

the Charter into the treaties means that other parts of EU law will also have to be interpreted in conformity with these new rights.

Secondly, even though Charter *principles* may lack direct enforceability, this does not mean that they will be without significance. As Article 52(5) sets out, such principles are to be taken into account by political and administrative authorities. Moreover, such principles will be significant to the interpretation of relevant Member State and Union measures. If two interpretations of such measures are competing, the existence of a Charter principle may be a reason to prefer the interpretation that best accords with such a principle. This is a category of Charter-consistent interpretation that may become important in future practice.

10.3.5 Summing Up

The fact that individuals may now rely on the Charter when challenging certain Member State measures falling within the scope of EU law; the fact that there are Charter rights which are justiciable; and, the possibilities for charter-consistent interpretation all make the Charter a significant resource for legal arguments. The number of cases in which the Charter is invoked has risen. Between 2000 and 1 December 2009, arguments explicitly derived from the Charter appeared in 19 of ECJ's preliminary rulings. From 1 December 2009 to 1 May 2016, arguments derived explicitly from the Charter appeared in 247 preliminary rulings. These rulings form the start of a new body of case law connected to the Charter. Experience from EU law as well as from other legal systems shows that the emergence of such a new body of case law will cause changes to the law in force, both regarding the scope of the law and in detail.

Even if one were to argue that there are no "new rights" in the Charter, the Charter may still be used by the ECJ and other courts as a basis for launching new *interpretations* of existing rights. An emerging body of new case law would increase the ability of lawyers and litigants to foresee the outcome of future cases, which may itself reinforce the propensity for litigation, since the cost would decrease, while the foreseeability of results would increase. Until 2009 there have been doubts about the legal value of the Charter. For litigants, this has meant having to hire lawyers for complicated inquiries into a developing body of case law. Today, litigants *know* that the Charter is an expression of law in force.

Even if the objective behind the adoption of the Charter was not to create new rights but only to make existing rights *visible*, this visibility may still end up creating new law. Cementing general and vague terms into codified law typically drives both litigation and legal development.

If the Charter's way of giving expression to fundamental rights is correct, one could also take the perspective that this will mean that more Europeans will finally get their rights taken seriously.

10.4 A Binding Charter—An Additional Argument for Accepting the Powers Entrusted to the EU?

10.4.1 Legitimacy—Two Normative Perspectives

There remain many open questions regarding interpretation and application of EU fundamental rights law. However, it is clear, to some extent at least, that the Treaty of Lisbon strengthens the protection of fundamental rights and also helps citizens to identify these rights. The Charter's new status provides the Court with a reinforced legal basis for exercising authority over other Union institutions and institutions at Member State level.

In addition, the incorporation of the Charter into the treaties also seems to mean that certain *new* rights and principles have acquired the status of primary law, that some of these new norms may be, or develop to become, rights in the stricter sense of the word, and that other parts of EU law will have to be interpreted in conformity with the new rights and principles set out in the Charter. Finally, the new rights and principles introduced by the Charter could also be used by private parties against the Member States when they implement EU law, including in those situations when they derogate from Union law, for example, by introducing *prima facie* legitimate restrictions on the right to free movement of goods, persons, services, or capital. This also may be viewed as extending the space for policy considerations by the ECJ at the expense of the powers of Member State authorities.

From the perspective of political philosophy, this situation prompts questions concerning the effects of the new legal status of the Charter on the legitimacy of the EU. The new legal status may certainly affect people's lives, but will the new status and the interpretation and application of the Charter necessarily provide better reasons for accepting the powers entrusted to the EU? If the answer is negative, a major part of the very motive for establishing a Charter will have failed. Should it even turn out that the new legal status of Charter has effects which *reduce* the legitimacy of the EU, this could not only lead to more criticism and stronger opposition against the EU, but it could also fuel new desires for Member States to withdraw from the Union. It is therefore important to inquire critically into the extent to which the new legal status of the Charter affects the normative legitimacy of the EU.

The normative legitimacy of the new status of the Charter can be discussed from a number of perspectives. As explained in Sect. 10.1, in this chapter we will restrict ourselves to two of them. First, we will examine the Charter and its new status from the perspective that the EU and its legal order acquire legitimacy through their capacity to protect individual rights. Secondly, we will examine the Charter and its new status from the perspective that the EU and its legal order acquire legitimacy through their capacity to facilitate policy experimentation and effective problem-solving.

Given the motive for adopting the Charter in the first place, the first perspective is obviously important. It is also the dominant perspective in academic commentaries on the Charter. The second perspective is important because it represents a vision of the EU which has been a central aim of the European integration process, but which is often neglected in academic and juristic literature regarding rights within the EU legal order, including the literature on the Charter and its new status.

10.4.2 Rights-Based Legitimacy

The Charter is likely to contribute to a more effective protection of fundamental rights in the Union, empowering individuals not only *vis-à-vis* states, but also *vis-à-vis* increasingly powerful EU institutions.

But the effectiveness of this protection will depend on a number of factors. It is already clear from recent case law that fundamental rights have become more visible for private parties in the period since Lisbon entered into force. The number of cases has risen. But it also remains to be seen to what extent the ECJ is ready to take responsibility for increasing the protection of private parties when answering the many questions relating to the interpretation of the Charter, questions referred to the ECJ by preliminary rulings from national courts.

From this rights-based perspective, the Court's choice in *Pfleger* to interpret the Charter as applicable to all Member States measures falling within the scope of Union law was an important choice, and it contributes to providing reasons for accepting EU power. Moreover, if the scope of Union law is expanded, for example by activist interpretations of the reach of free movement, the Charter could also function as an additional safeguard for individuals against strong market interests. Conversely, the Charter could also function as an instrument for market interests, depending on the selection of Charter provisions given real legal effect as justiciable rights.

10.4.3 Charter Legitimacy Assessed on the Basis of the Problem-Solving Capacity of the EU

In addition to the legitimacy that the EU may acquire through the consent of Member States, and its capacity to protect individual rights, there is potential to legitimise the EU through its capacity to solve policy problems. This is the central aspect of the so-called "output-oriented" theories of legitimacy.[52] Arguably, this requires some level of expert-rule and technocratic governance, rather than processes in which politicians strive for the support of the majority in individual cases. Therefore, the problem-solving capacity of the EU may also affect its legitimacy.

[52] See, generally, Scharpf 1999 and also Majone 2005.

Furthermore, in order to solve policy problems efficiently, it has been argued that the EU, as a system that encapsulates a range of different nationals, cultures, languages and identities, should be seen as a laboratory for experimenting with centralised rule-making, in which miscellaneous authorities have a chance to explore and test solutions to problems of public policy. Arguably, such an institutional architecture, which Charles Sabel and Joshua Cohen have labelled a "deliberative polyarchy," could facilitate a structure in which lower-level actors furnish higher-level units with information regarding their progress in solving policy problems.[53] It would encourage a periodic pooling of results and the "*elaboration of standards for comparing local achievements, exposing poor performers to criticism from within and without, and making good ones (temporary) models for emulation.*"[54]

This vision of the EU as a mechanism for problem-solving and experimentation that allows local variations can generate conflicts with the effective protection of rights by EU institutions.[55] The language of rights seems to allude to a state of affairs in which formal analysis of the content of a right could determine whether collective decision-making based upon broad considerations is to be accepted or not. Therefore, protection of rights can be seen as one of several strategies to conceal conflict of interests in decision-making processes.[56] In contrast, effective problem-solving may require the ability to adapt different solutions in different locations and situations, based upon the weighing of various interests. To the extent that conflicts of interest are concealed and their outcome pre-determined, rights may obstruct effective problem-solving. In as much as EU fundamental rights are addressed both to EU and Member State authorities, such rights may obstruct problem-solving at both of these levels. Consider the example of the rights to social security and social assistance, health care, and services of general economic interest (Articles 34–36 of the Charter). To the extent that such rights become enforceable and courts use them as a means for imposing obligations on Member States to deliver these types of services, this would lead to an increase in public spending. Thus, the freedom of the Member States to efficiently deliver other desirable outcomes could be negatively affected.

From this perspective, the vesting of the Charter with the same legal value as the treaties could have negative effects on the possibility for efficient solving of policy problems within the EU.

There are also some sides to fundamental rights protection that could entail enhanced problem-solving capacity; namely, when Charter rights and principles push EU and Member State bodies towards solving real problems. Some would see

---

[53] See Sabel and Cohen 2004.

[54] *Op.cit.*, p. 168.

[55] See Eriksen 2011.

[56] For this point, see Kennedy 1978–1979.

the obligation to respect the principle of sustainable development (Article 3(3) TEU, and Article 37 of the Charter) as an example.

10.5 The Charter of Fundamental Rights, Legitimacy of the EU—Challenges for Future Practice

In sum, how the Charter's new legal status may affect the legitimacy of the EU is, from both of the aforementioned perspectives, partly dependent upon the future practice of the courts. If the ECJ and other bodies that apply EU law use the Charter as a basis for making fundamental rights more effective, and if they apply a principle of Charter-consistent interpretation to other kinds of EU law, they may thereby also end up undermining the possibilities for effective problem-solving. As discussed, this could in effect diminish the legitimacy of the EU, as it could obstruct the possibilities for the expression of diverse opinions and interests in the European societies, possibilities which could facilitate processes of argumentation involving those affected by a decision.

Similarly, allowing individuals to use the Charter as a shield against Member States in policy areas where the EU has not yet exercised its competence could undermine the possibilities for effective problem-solving. For example, the Charter could be interpreted as imposing so-called positive rights, such as obligations for Member States to provide certain services to its citizens, like education (Article 14) and health care (Article 35). If individuals are allowed to use the Charter against Member States on areas where the EU has not yet exercised its competence, this could perhaps pave the way for court rulings obliging the Member States to allocate more money to education and health care than they would otherwise have agreed to. In turn, that could take money from other policy areas, reducing the capacity to solve other policy problems.

Werc the Charter to inspire the courts to provide stronger protection of rights, and especially of second- and third-generation rights, it would place itself in an inevitable dilemma: stronger protection of rights might both enhance *and* weaken the Union's legitimacy at the same time. This appears to be one of the central challenges in the future work of interpreting and applying the EU's Charter of Fundamental Rights.

Acknowledgements We would like to thank Professor Mads Andenæs and Professor Tarjei Bekkedal, both of the University of Oslo, for their comments on this chapter.

References

Alexy R (1994) Theorie der Grundrechte. Suhrkamp Verlag, Frankfurt am Main

Alexy R (2000) On the Structure of Legal Principles. Ratio Juris 13:294–304

Barnard C (2008) The 'Opt-Out' for the UK and Poland from the Charter of Fundamental Rights: Triumph of Rhetoric over Reality? In: Griller S, Ziller J (eds) The Lisbon Treaty - EU Constitutionalism without a Constitutional Treaty? Springer, Vienna, pp 257–283

Beetham D (1991) The Legitimation of Power. Palgrave Macmillan, London

Craig P, de Búrca G (2008) EU Law, 4th edn. Oxford University Press, Oxford

Curzon S (2011) Internal Market Derogations in Light of the Newly Binding Character of the EU Charter of Fundamental Rights. In: Di Federico G (ed) The EU Charter of Fundamental Rights - From Declaration to Binding Instrument. Springer, Dordrecht, pp 145–159

de Búrca G (2001) The Drafting of the European Union Charter of Fundamental Rights. ELR 26:126–138

Di Federico G (2011) Fundamental Rights in the EU: Legal Pluralism and Multi-Level Protection After the Lisbon Treaty. In: Di Federico G (ed) The EU Charter of Fundamental Rights - From Declaration to Binding Instrument. Springer, Dordrecht, pp 15–54

Dougan M (2015) Judicial Review of Member State Action under the General Principles and the Charter: Defining the "Scope of Union Law". CMLR 52(5):1201–1246

Dworkin R (1967–68) The Model of Rules. University of Chicago Law Review 35:14-46

Dworkin R (1977) Taking Rights Seriously. Harvard University Press, Boston MA

Eriksen C (2011) The European Constitution, Welfare States and Democracy. Routledge, New York

Esser J (1974) Grundsatz und Norm in der richterlichen Fortbildung des Privatrechts, 3rd edn. Mohr, Tübingen

Fredman S (2006) Transformation or Dilution: Fundamental Rights in the EU Social Space. ELJ 12:41–60

Habermas J (2001) Remarks on Legitimation through Human Rights. In: Habermas J (ed) The Postnational Constellation. Political Essays. MIT Press, Cambridge MA

Jacobs F (2002) The EU Charter of Fundamental Rights. In: Arnull A, Wincott D (eds) Accountability and Legitimacy in the European Union. Oxford University Press, Oxford, pp 275–290

Joerges C (2006) 'Deliberative Political Processes' Revisited: What Have We Learnt About the Legitimacy of Supranational Decision-Making? In: J Common Market Stud 4:779–802

Kennedy D (1978–1979) Structure of Blackstone's Commentaries. Buffalo Law Review 28:205-382

Klausen J (2001) Rights Constitutionalism and European Integration: The Charter of Fundamental Rights of the European Union. Paper prepared for the 2001 European Community Studies Association, Madison, Wisconsin, 31 May - 2 June. Available online

Lock T (2010) EU accession to the ECHR: implications for the judicial review in Strasbourg. ELR 35:777–798

Majone G (2005) Dilemmas of European Integration: The Ambiguities and Pitfalls of Integration by Stealth. Oxford University Press, Oxford

McGlynn C (2001) Families and the European Union Charter of Fundamental Rights: Progressive change or entrenching the status quo? ELR 26:582–598

Rasmussen H (2008) EF-domstolen i det 21. århundrede – en mindre dynamisk rolleutførelse. Juristen 2

Rawls J (1999) A Theory of Justice. Harvard University Press, Boston MA

Raz J (1979) The Authority of Law: Essays on Law and Morality. Oxford University Press, Oxford

Rosas A, Armati L (2010) EU Constitutional Law - An Introduction. Hart Publishing, Oxford

Rousseau JJ (1992 [1762]) On the Social Contract Or Principles of Political Right (translation Cress DA). In: Morgan M (ed) Classics of Moral and Political Theory. Hackett Publishing Company, Indianapolis IN

Sabel C, Cohen J (2004) Sovereignty and Solidarity: EU and US. In: Ladeur K-H (ed) Public Governance in the Age of Globalisation. Ashgate Publishing, Aldershot

Scharpf F (1999) Governing Europe: Effective and Democratic? Oxford University Press, Oxford

Snell J (2015) Fundamental Rights Review of National Measures: Nothing New under the Charter. EPL 21: 285–308

Ward A (2009) Fundamental Rights Protection Post Lisbon: The Impact of Incorporation of the EU Charter of Fundamental Rights. Available at http://icel.ie/userfiles/file/conferences/lisbon/Ward.doc

Weiler J (1995) Fundamental Rights and Fundamental Boundaries: On Standards and Values in the Protection of Human Rights. In: Neuwahl N, Rosas A (eds) The European Union and Human Rights. Kluwer, The Hague, pp 51–76

Chapter 11
False Friends and True Cognates: On Fundamental Freedoms, Fundamental Rights and Union Citizenship

Francesco De Cecco

Abstract Both the case law on fundamental freedoms, and the selective manner in which these freedoms are incorporated in the Charter of Fundamental Rights of the EU are consistent with an account of fundamental rights that places a non-instrumental focus on the protection of the interests of the right-holder (the Union citizen). According to the account advanced here, those free movement rights that are non-instrumental in nature are treated as fundamental rights, whereas those free movement rights that remain predominantly instrumental are not. Yet, developments in the case law on Union citizenship that have occurred during the current decade present a challenge to this account. On the one hand, they appear to draw on the conceptual toolkit of fundamental rights; on the other, they contradict key features of a fundamental rights conception of Union citizenship.

Keywords Charter of Fundamental Rights · Citizenship · Constitution · Discrimination · Free movement · Individual rights · Internal market · Market access

Contents

11.1 Introduction 254
11.2 The Dichotomy 254
11.2.1 What Makes Rights Fundamental? 255
11.2.2 The Enduring Instrumentalism in Free Movement Law 258
11.3 The Substantive Implications 259
11.3.1 The Scope of the Internal Market Freedoms 259
11.3.2 EU Citizenship and the Internal Market 262

F. De Cecco (✉)
Newcastle Law School, Newcastle University, 21-24 Windsor Terrace, Newcastle upon Tyne, UK
e-mail: Francesco.de-Cecco@ncl.ac.uk

M. Andenas et al. (eds.), *The Reach of Free Movement*,
DOI 10.1007/978-94-6265-195-1_11

11.3.3 The 'Substance' of Union Citizenship Rights and the 'Essence' of Fundamental Rights ... 264
11.3.4 *Dano* and the Grammar of Rights ... 269
11.4 Conclusion ... 270
References ... 271

11.1 Introduction

This chapter assesses the relationship between free movement rights (the so-called "fundamental freedoms"), Union citizenship and fundamental rights. In doing so, it revisits an earlier publication, which tried to make sense of the linguistic ambivalence of the term "fundamental freedoms" in the internal market case law.[1] That article argued that while the provisions on free movement of goods and free movement of capital cannot be characterised as sources of fundamental rights because of their instrumental nature (they are a means to the internal market end), other free movement provisions (free movement of persons and of services) are sources of individual fundamental rights of Union citizens. This chapter explores the implications of this theoretical framework for the internal market and, in particular, for the rights stemming from the "fundamental status" of EU citizenship. It first sets out, and explains, the rationale of the dichotomy between those internal market freedoms that are regarded as fundamental rights and those that are not. It then goes on to explore the substantive implications of this dichotomy and of its (hypothetical) disappearance. The final section considers the interpretative possibilities arising from the link between Union citizenship and fundamental rights.

11.2 The Dichotomy

The term "fundamental freedoms" is a label which, in the free movement case law, captures all the four internal market freedoms. Although the use of this term may suggest that all free movement rights are fundamental rights,[2] the Charter of Fundamental Rights of the EU makes clear that *only certain* fundamental freedoms are fundamental rights. In particular, Article 15 of the Charter covers free movement of persons and services, while Article 45 of the Charter covers the rights of freedom of movement and residence arising from EU citizenship. There is no mention of the

[1] De Cecco 2014.

[2] In fact, in the language of human rights, "fundamental *freedoms*" and "fundamental *rights*" are used interchangeably.

free movement of goods, nor of the free movement of capital.[3] Unsurprisingly, this dichotomy was present in the case law pre-dating the Charter, though its rationale was never explicitly articulated by the Court. This leads one to wonder whether the case law is consistent with a particular conception of fundamental rights—an embryonic theoretical framework that may elucidate this dichotomy.

11.2.1 What Makes Rights Fundamental?

Although the Court has never explained what characteristics make a particular right "fundamental", its case law offers a number of insights in this respect. In *Lilli Schröder*,[4] the Court recalled that while the initial approach in the case law to (what is now) Article 157 TFEU was aimed at avoiding distortions of competition between undertakings, the right not to be discriminated against on grounds of sex was subsequently recognised as a *fundamental human right*.[5] Crucially, as the Court explained, the economic aim pursued by Article 157 TFEU had become a *secondary* aim of that provision which was now primarily the expression of a fundamental human right.

The Court's explanation seems to be consistent with the view that a right is fundamental if the right-holder's interest is considered to be 'of ultimate value', that is, if it 'does not derive from some other interest of the right-holder or of other persons'.[6] On this account, the values protected by fundamental rights are those that 'need not be explained or be justified by (their contribution to) other values'.[7] The implication is that rights that are protected *primarily* because of their instrumental role in advancing a common purpose, such as the internal market, should not be regarded as fundamental.

This account of fundamental rights seems also capable of explaining the association between certain free movement rights and fundamental rights, which has a long pedigree in the case law. Consider the preamble to Regulation 1612/68, which

---

[3] Apart from a negligible reference in the Preamble which simply states that securing the four freedoms is an objective of the Union.

[4] Case C-50/96, *Schröder*, ECLI:EU:C:2000:72, paras 55–59.

[5] Note that the Court in *Lilli Schröder* refers to fundamental *human* rights. Its approach, however, also applies to those rights that are not human rights, but simply fundamental rights. The key difference between human rights and fundamental rights is that while the former are universal, the latter are grounded in a specific political and legal context. This explains the variation in the substantive interests that are regarded as fundamental among different political and legal systems. As far as the EU context is concerned, there are rights that are peculiar to the EU and are not (in any meaningful way) expression of human rights. Of course, this is true only of a minority of EU fundamental rights, the majority being derived either from the ECHR or from domestic constitutions.

[6] Raz 1986, p. 192. Note that the account of fundamental rights proposed here does not seek to do justice to Raz's theory of rights, but to offer a basic rationale for the partial equivalence between free movement rights and fundamental rights that can be found in the case law.

[7] Ibid., p. 200.

stated in its third recital: "Freedom of movement constitutes a fundamental right of workers and their families".[8] That language was seized upon by the Court, which placed significant emphasis on the characterisation of free movement of workers as a fundamental right.[9] As Advocate General Jacobs explained in *Bettray*: "[t]he recital makes it clear that labour is not, in Community law, to be regarded as a commodity and notably gives precedence to the fundamental rights of workers over satisfying the requirements of the economies of the Member States".[10] For this reason, the Court has, on a number of occasions, expressly recognised that (what is now) Article 45 TFEU confers a fundamental right on individual workers.[11]

A similar understanding of the concept of fundamental right is expressed by several Advocates Generals' explanations of the rationale of the case law on citizenship. This meaning was captured by Advocate General Cosmas in *Wijsenbeek*.[12] The effect of the introduction of the EU citizenship provisions, he argued, was that EU citizens became "holders of a specific right… *irrespective of whether the enjoyment of this right is accompanied by the promotion of other Community aspirations or objectives*".[13] He went on to contrast the "functional"

[8] Regulation (EEC) No. 1612/68 of the Council of 15 October 1968 on freedom of movement for workers within the Community, O.J. 1968, L 257/2 now replaced by Regulation (EU) No. 492/2011 of the European Parliament and of the Council of 5 April 2011 on freedom of movement for workers within the Union, O.J. 2011, L 141/1.

[9] The preamble was repeatedly relied on by the Commission in its submissions before the Court, and was eventually adopted by the Court itself. In *Levin*, both the Commission and the Advocate General emphasised the characterization by Regulation 1612/68 of free movement of workers as a fundamental right, and later, in *Forcheri*, the Court itself adopted that terminology. Opinion of Advocate General Slynn in Case 53/81, *Levin*, ECLI:EU:C:1982:10, para 1057; Case 152/82, *Forcheri*, ECLI:EU:C:1983:205, para 11. In *Heylens*, the Court held that access to employment was a fundamental right conferred by the Treaty: "Since free access to employment is a fundamental right which the Treaty confers individually on each worker in the Community, the existence of a remedy of a judicial nature against any decision of a national authority refusing the benefit of that right is essential in order to secure for the individual effective protection for his right". Case 222/86, *UNCTEF* v. *Heylens*, ECLI:EU:C:1987:442, para 14.

[10] Opinion of Advocate General Jacobs in Case C-344/87, *Bettray*, ECLI:EU:C:1989:113, para 29.

[11] This approach starkly contrasts with the original blueprint offered by the Spaak Report. In line with the neo-functionalist logic that prevailed in the early stages of economic integration, the Report treated labour in instrumental terms, as a "factor of production" that would move across borders to meet demand. Rapport des Chefs de Délégations aux Ministres des Affaires Etrangères (Brussels 1956). On the limitations of this blueprint see O'Leary 2011. In light of this evolution, it is plain that the right to free movement of workers protects even those workers that move from countries with low unemployment to countries with high unemployment levels, in the same way that sex discrimination breaches Article 157 TFEU even where no distortion of competition can be discerned. Of course, this is not to say that Member States will seek to curtail free movement of workers in view of difficulties faced by their economies or by perceived difficulties faced by their welfare systems. None of the fundamental rights discussed in this chapter are absolute—all may be limited in their exercise.

[12] Case C-378/97, *Wijsenbeek*, ECLI:EU:C:1999:439.

[13] Opinion of Advocate General Cosmas, Case C-378/97, *Wijsenbeek*, ECLI:EU:C:1999:144, para 83 (with added emphasis).

nature of the free movement provisions enshrined in the Treaty of Rome with the "substantive" nature of the right to free movement stemming from EU citizenship, the latter being "a right, in the true meaning of the word, which exists with a view to the autonomous pursuit of a goal, *to the benefit of the holder of that right and not to the benefit of the Community and the attainment of its objectives*".[14]

The words of Advocate General Colomer in his Opinion in *Baldinger* characterised the impact of EU citizenship in similar terms:

> … [T]he creation of citizenship of the Union, with the corollary of freedom of movement for citizens throughout the territory of the Member States, represents a considerable qualitative step forward in that it *separates that freedom from its functional or instrumental elements* (the link with an economic activity or attainment of the internal market) and raises it to the level of a genuinely independent right inherent in the political status of the citizens of the Union. Evidence of that qualitative development lies in the fact that freedom of movement and of residence, as an independent right, has been enshrined in Article 45(1) of the Charter of Fundamental Rights of the European Union.[15]

Other areas of free movement witnessed a similar departure from the logic of pure market instrumentalism: already from the 1980s, when the case law recognised that tourists were protected by the Treaty as service recipients it was clear that persons could not be considered as mere agents of economic integration.[16] By the time that EU citizenship had come to fruition, the Court had already stated that persons (not just workers) were holders of a "fundamental right to move freely" within the EU.[17] The advent of EU citizenship meant that the rights to free movement and residence, shorn of any economic purpose, were characterised as fundamental rights stemming from the status of Union citizenship. This happened, first, in the case law, then in Directive 2004/38, and, finally, in Article 45 of the Charter.[18] While differences between economic free movement and non-economic free movement remain significant, as the latter comes with substantial strings attached, much cross-fertilization has occurred between economic free movement and EU citizenship.[19] Article 15 of the Charter re-emphasises the link by stating, "*every citizen of the Union* has the freedom to seek employment, to work, to exercise the rights of establishment and to provide services in any Member State".[20]

---

[14] Para 84 (with added emphasis).

[15] Opinion of Advocate General Ruiz-Jarabo Colomer in Case C-386/02, *Baldinger*, ECLI:EU:C:2003:671, para 25 (with added emphasis).

[16] Case 186/87, *Cowan* v *Trésor Public*, ECLI:EU:C:1989:47.

[17] Case C-416/96, *Eddline El-Yassini*, ECLI:EU:C:1999:107, para 45.

[18] See Case C-200/02, *Zhu and Chen*, ECLI:EU:C:2004:639; Recital 11 of the Preamble to Directive 2004/38 O.J. 2004, L 158/77.

[19] On which see O' Leary 2011.

[20] This does not mean that citizenship is the foundation of all fundamental rights. Citizenship is a status, and not a right. As a status, citizenship gives rise to certain rights (e.g. the right to move and to reside throughout the territory of the EU) and, to a certain extent, colours the interpretation of pre-existing *free movement* rights.

11.2.2 The Enduring Instrumentalism in Free Movement Law

Despite the increasing centrality of individual rights in the case law, the common/internal market project has always been, and continues to be, characterised by a certain degree of instrumentalism. The free movement provisions are, to a greater or lesser extent, a means to an end, the end being market integration (which, in turn, was and remains a means to an end). As Mertens de Wilmars (then a judge at the European Court of Justice) wrote in the 1970s, the Treaty rules did not seek to impose economic liberalism on the national economies, but expressed an "instrumentalist" conception of economic liberalism.[21] The free movement rules were not seen as a means of achieving the emancipation of the individual from the State, but as a means of achieving integration between States. This view was echoed two decades later in Advocate General Tesauro's rhetorical question as to whether Article 34 TFEU was "a provision intended to liberalise intra-Community trade" or "to encourage the unhindered pursuit of commerce in individual Member States".[22] In *Keck*, the Court chose the former alternative, and premised its ruling with the remark that a redefinition of the scope of Article 34 TFEU was necessary in view of the increasing tendency of traders to invoke that provision "as a means challenging any rules whose effect is to limit their commercial freedom even where such rules are not aimed at products from other Member States".[23] Even in *Schmidberger*, a case which is often taken to signify a fundamental rights turn in free movement of goods (given that the Court referred to free movement of goods as a "fundamental principle") the Court did not abandon its instrumental conception of free movement of goods. According to the Court, the provisions on free movement of goods were to be "understood as being intended to eliminate all barriers, whether direct or indirect, actual or potential, *to trade flows* in intra-Community trade", and that Article 34 TFEU was "an *indispensable instrument* for the realisation of a market without internal frontiers".[24]

The Charter's silence in respect of free movement of goods and free movement of capital confirms what was already implicit in the case law: those free movement provisions that cannot be readily linked to a person do not lend themselves to being treated as fundamental rights.[25]

---

[21] 'Les conceptions économiques qu'expriment nombre de règles du traité correspondent à une conception instrumentaliste du libéralisme économique et non à l'idée qu'il est l'*Ordnungsprinzip* des économies intégrées'. Mertens de Wilmars 1976.

[22] Opinion of Advocate General Tesauro in Case C-292/92, *Hünermund and Others*, ECLI:EU:C:1993:863. See also Opinion of Advocate General Tizzano in Case C-442/02, *CaixaBank France*, ECLI:EU:C:2004:187, paras 68–78.

[23] Joined Cases C-267/91 and C-268/91, *Keck and Mithouard*, ECLI:EU:C:1993:905, para 16.

[24] Case C-112/00, *Schmidberger*, ECLI:EU:C:2003:333 (with added emphasis).

[25] Snell 2004.

11.3 The Substantive Implications

At this juncture, one may object that the matter being discussed here, whether or not fundamental freedoms are labelled as fundamental rights, is a matter of pure taxonomy without practical application, since, in the absence of a constitutional hierarchy, fundamental rights and internal market freedoms enjoy the same formal legal status as primary law.[26] What is more, one may add, Article 52(2) CFR provides that rights recognised by the Charter for which provision is made in the treaties are to be exercised under the conditions and within the limits defined therein. Thus, inclusion of certain free movement rights in the Charter should not make a difference in terms of their scope. However, it is worth noting that inclusion (and non-inclusion) in the Charter confirms jurisprudential developments that pre-date the Charter. Furthermore, as the following sections attempt to show, the special emphasis that the language of fundamental rights places on the individual right-holder colours the Court's interpretation of the *substantive scope* of the free movement provisions both in relation to the internal market freedoms, and in relation to the rights stemming from Union citizenship.[27] Moreover, as will be seen below, the classification of certain rights as fundamental may influence the extent to which restrictions on such rights may be tolerated. If rights are fundamental, restrictions on them cannot lead to denying their very essence.

11.3.1 The Scope of the Internal Market Freedoms

There are significant differences in scope between fundamental freedoms. On the one hand, limiting the commercial freedom of traders by restricting the outlets in which a product can be sold is said to be, prima facie, irrelevant as far as Article 34 TFEU is concerned.[28] On the other, any limit on the exercise of a commercial activity exercised by a self-employed person falls within the scope of Article 49 TFEU and requires a justification. In *Commission* v *Greece*, in which the question was whether a Greek regulation that required baby formula to be sold exclusively in pharmacies amounted to an obstacle to the free movement of goods, the Court, applying the *Keck* doctrine, found that the measure did not obstruct trade between Member States.[29] It held that "rules which restrict the marketing of products to

---

[26] Opinion of Advocate General Trstenjak in Case C-271/08, *Commission v Germany*, ECLI:EU:C:2010:183, paras 183–199. Opinion of Advocate General Mengozzi in Case C-341/05, *Laval un Partneri*, 2007 E.C.R. I-11767, para 84.

[27] The view is shared by Tryfonidou 2016, who draws far-reaching substantive implications from a systematic categorisation of free movement rights as fundamental rights.

[28] That is, unless the case can be made that the measure impedes foreign products' access to the market more than it impedes the access of domestic products.

[29] Case C-391/92, *Commission* v *Greece*, ECLI:EU:C:1995:199.

certain points of sale, and which have the effect of *limiting the commercial freedom of economic operators*, without affecting the actual characteristics of the products referred to" were selling arrangement that fell outside the scope of Article 34.[30] Yet, in *Blanco Pérez*, Spanish rules that laid down planning criteria for the licensing of pharmacies—a minimum population threshold to be served by each pharmacy, and a requirement of a minimum distance between pharmacies—were considered to be (justified) restrictions on freedom of establishment. Their effect was "to hinder and render less attractive the exercise by pharmacists from other Member States of their activities on Spanish territory through a fixed place of business".[31]

Even if the case law on free movement of goods has cemented a market access test, which appears to focus more closely on individual traders, this jurisprudential development does not contradict the instrumental nature of the free movement of goods provisions. Market access continues to be relevant only in relation to the impact on products that *originate from other Member States*. Indeed, if the impact of these restrictions is viewed from the macro-level perspective of the internal market this jurisprudential development is far less radical than may appear at first blush.[32] Such restrictions are caught by Article 34 TFEU not purely because of their capacity to restrict the individual traders' commercial opportunities, but ultimately because of their potential to introduce fragmentation in the internal market by effectively cordoning-off the domestic market from the rest of the internal market.

These differences, however, would be substantially less pronounced if *all* free movement provisions were treated as fundamental rights. The case law on the free movement of goods as it currently stands considers the impact on individuals in so far as it is evidence of a restriction on the flow of goods, whereas fundamental rights discourse demands that close attention be paid to the impact of regulation on *individuals as such*.[33] A fundamental rights re-reading of Article 34 TFEU would thus affect both the Court's legal reasoning and national regulatory autonomy, as the existence of an obstacle to free movement would no longer turn on the impact on the free flow of goods between Member States, but on traders' opportunities to market their products. The emphasis would therefore move away from the internal market and would be placed firmly on the individual.

This would transform the Court's role in shaping the Treaty provisions in such a way as to define from the outset the balance between integration and national regulatory autonomy. That balance is normally associated with questions of derogation or justification. Yet, each redefinition of the scope of the free movement provisions entails a reassessment of that balance. In the traditional free movement

---

[30] *Id.*, para 31 (with added emphasis).

[31] *Id.*, para 59.

[32] The restrictions on use case law includes "any other measure which hinders access of products originating in other Member States to the market of a Member State is also covered by that concept" see Case C-110/05, *Commission v Italy (Italian Trailers)*, ECLI:EU:C:2009:66, para 37; Case C-142/05, *Mickelsson and Roos*, ECLI:EU:C:2009:336, para 24.

[33] Granted, the distinction between the impact on individual traders and the impact on trade flows is often an artificial one, as measures that affect trade will necessarily affect individuals.

case law, the public interest in market integration informs the scope of the individual provisions. By contrast, fundamental rights reasoning examines public interest considerations only at a separate stage—that is, the stage at which justifications for a restriction on an individual right are examined.[34] Thus, under a fundamental rights approach, the interest in market integration would no longer determine the scope of free movement of goods and free movement of capital.[35] Such a shift would, in other words, pre-empt the operation of what Horsley has called "exclusionary rules", which are "judicial devices that the Court has developed and applied in order to manage the scope" of the free movement provisions "and, ultimately, draw a line between Union and Member State competence for the regulation of the internal market as a shared regulatory space".[36]

Yet, market integration is a process, not an event; a process marked by different priorities and distinct shifts in emphasis, by phases of increased urgency of certain areas as opposed to other areas. Consider, for instance, the evolution of the case law on free movement of capital. The Treaty of Rome cautiously provided that restrictions on the free movement of capital were to be abolished "to the extent necessary to ensure the proper functioning of the common market". The reason for this limited liberalisation of capital movements was due, among other things, to the need for Member States to maintain capital controls and monetary policy autonomy. The assumption, backed by economic theory, was that it would be impossible for Member States to liberalise capital movements, maintain fixed exchange rates and, at the same time, retain an autonomous monetary policy.[37] These concerns were alluded to in *Casati*, a judgment in which the Court made clear that free movement of capital had a narrower scope than the other fundamental freedoms.[38] As the Court explained, complete free movement was premature at that moment in time, as it could undermine the economic policy of one of the Member States or create an imbalance in its balance of payments, thereby impairing the proper functioning of the common market. However, in subsequent decades, as technological and economic changes made capital controls increasingly ineffective, and the prevailing political and ideological climate became favourable to capital liberalization, capital

[34] See Spaventa 2009, p. 343.

[35] One may object that the adoption by the Court of a restrictions test across most of free movement law has already relegated the interest in market integration to a secondary consideration. There are two responses to this objection. First, free movement of goods does not follow the restrictions approach adopted in the other areas of free movement law. Second, as will be argued in the following pages, while free movement of capital does follow a broadly-formulated restrictions test, at a normative level, it should be open to the Court, to the extent that it may be necessary to do so in light of the evolution of the internal market, to adopt a different interpretation of this fundamental freedom and distinguish more markedly the scope of free movement of capital from that of the free movement of people provisions. Arguably, a fundamental rights approach may inhibit this possibility.

[36] Horsley 2012.

[37] The so-called 'impossible trinity' theorem (severally) attributed to Fleming 1962 and Mundell 1963.

[38] Case 203/80, *Casati*, ECLI:EU:C:1981:261.

controls were gradually loosened and eventually abolished by the Member States. By the time of the Maastricht Treaty, capital liberalization had become an imperative both for the single market and for monetary union, and the EC Treaty was amended to reflect this and to extend the liberalization of capital movements to movements between third countries and the Member States. These developments created the space for the Court to realign free movement of capital with the other freedoms.[39] At the same time, however, free movement of capital has come to occupy a peculiar place in that the Treaty extends its benefits to non-EU nationals and beyond the territory of the EU; this is an instrumental choice based, as the Court has explained, on the need "to ensure the credibility of the single currency on global financial markets and on maintaining financial centres with a world-wide dimension within the Member States".[40]

11.3.2 EU Citizenship and the Internal Market

Given the recognition of the fundamental status of Union citizenship, the loss of an instrumentalist perspective on the internal market may seem warranted. Indeed, as far as free movement of persons is concerned, this is relatively uncontroversial. However, the (more radical) view that *all* free movement provisions should now be considered as fundamental economic rights of Union citizens runs into several difficulties. There are key differences in terms of respective personal and geographical scope between free movement of goods and free movement of capital, on the one hand, and free movement of persons and services, on the other. Once third country products are imported into the EU, they enter into free circulation, which means that they enjoy exactly the same protection under Article 34 TFEU as EU products; naturally, third country nationals are able to invoke Article 34 in the same circumstances as nationals of an EU Member State. As to free movement of capital, Article 63 TFEU can be invoked by non-EU nationals and applies to movements originating from outside the territory of the EU. To treat these provisions as fundamental rights *of EU citizens* would introduce fragmentation in the internal market, as the same right would lose its fundamental status when relied on by Third Country Nationals.

Moreover, the view that EU citizenship is the glue that holds the fundamental freedoms together fails to deliver on its promise to address the inconsistencies and

[39] Alongside direct and indirect discrimination, the Court now applies a broad "restrictions" test. E. g. Case C-302/97, *Konle*, ECLI:EU:C:1999:271; Case C-112/05, *Commission v Germany*, ECLI: EU:C:2007:623; Case C-194/06, *Orange European Smallcap Fund*, ECLI:EU:C:2008:289. See Snell 2011.

[40] Case C-101/05, *A*, ECLI:EU:C:2007:804, para 31. However, the Court has also pointed out that, even allowing for this difference in purpose, the Member States have chosen to enshrine free movement of capital in the Treaty 'in the same terms for movements of capital taking place within the Community and those relating to relations with third countries' (ibid.). But see O'Brien 2008.

iniquities that arise from reverse discrimination—that is, the state of affairs which arises where Member States fail to extend to their own 'static' nationals the treatment that EU law requires them to afford to those who find themselves in cross-border situations. While, over the years, many have argued that Union citizenship should put an end to reverse discrimination,[41] optimism on the Court's willingness to take stock of the full implications of its repeated commitment to Union citizenship as a fundamental status was first fuelled and then dampened by the evolution of a new strand of case law that began with the ruling in *Ruiz Zambrano*.[42] There, the Court held that Article 20 TFEU could be relied on by minors who were nationals of a Member State in which they lived, but who had never exercised their free movement rights, if their father, a third country national, was to be denied residence and a work permit by that same Member State. That provision precluded national measures which had the effect of 'depriving citizens of the Union of the genuine enjoyment of the substance of the rights conferred by virtue of their status as citizens of the Union'.[43] If the father was forced to leave the EU, the children would have to follow suit, thus becoming 'unable to exercise the substance of the rights conferred on them by virtue of their status as citizens of the Union'. Yet, subsequent case law, namely, *McCarthy*, *Dereci*, *Iida*, *Ymeraga*, and *Alokpa,* have made clear that this approach only applies to very specific set of circumstances, in which the application of a national measure would 'undermine the effectiveness' of the fundamental rights that a national derives from her citizenship status.[44] Crucially, it appears that the 'substance of the rights' is undermined only where a national of a Member State is forced to leave the territory of the Union as a whole.

The approach that has ultimately emerged from this case law chimes with the constitutional orthodoxy of EU law, which reflects the Member States' anxieties with regard to the expansive potential of the citizenship provisions. These anxieties emerge from the wording introduced by the Treaty of Amsterdam (in what was then Article 17(2) EC), to the effect that Union citizenship *complements but does not replace national citizenship*, which the Lisbon Treaty turned into 'shall be *additional to* and not replace national citizenship'.[45] However, the logic of complementarity or additionality, while dominant in the Union citizenship case law, is absent in certain areas of internal market law in which there is no domestic

[41] See Nic Shuibhne 2002; Spaventa 2008; Kochenov 2011. See also the Opinion of Advocate General Sharpston in Case C-212/06, *Walloon (Flemish Care Insurance Scheme)*, ECLI:EU:C:2008:178; and Opinion of Advocate General Sharpston in Case C-34/09, *Ruiz Zambrano*, ECLI:EU:C:2010:560.

[42] Case C-34/09, *Ruiz Zambrano*, ECLI:EU:C:2011:124.

[43] Ibid., para 42.

[44] Case C-434/09, *McCarthy*, ECLI:EU:C:2011:277; Case C-256/11, *Dereci and Others*, ECLI:EU:C:2011:734; Case C-40/11, *Iida*, ECLI:EU:C:2012:691; Case C-87/12, *Ymeraga and Ymeraga-Tafarshiku*, ECLI:EU:C:2013:291; Case C-86/12, *Alokpa and Moudoulou*, ECLI:EU:C:2013:645.

[45] Shaw 2010.

equivalent of EU law which EU law can complement or add to. This can be seen in *Carbonati*, in which the Court found that a tax imposed by the municipality of Carrara on marble that was transported across the boundaries of that municipality to the exclusion of marble that remained within that territory was a charge having effect equivalent to a customs duty on exports.[46] The Court found that Article 28 TFEU applied to an *internal* border. The situation was not wholly internal as the marble tax was imposed on all marble from Carrara that crossed that municipality's territorial boundaries, without drawing a distinction between marble destined for Italy and marble destined for export. This is because, in the presence of a customs union, which—in practice—included regional borders, and given the EU's exclusive competence on the customs union, the logic of complementarity could not operate as the State's power to manage its internal frontiers had been made redundant.[47]

A similar approach was suggested by Advocate General Geelhoed in relation to free movement of capital. In *Reischl*, drawing a parallel with the customs union, he argued that 'the unity of the capital market that has emerged within the completed Economic and Monetary Union means that a wholly internal situation can no longer be said to exist in respect of the free movement of capital'.[48] Thus, in some areas of the internal market, the wholly internal rule may be gradually losing its grip; yet, where physical persons are involved, and where the anxieties of the Masters of Treaties are at their most acute, the logic of complementarity/additionality continues to hold sway.

11.3.3 The 'Substance' of Union Citizenship Rights and the 'Essence' of Fundamental Rights

So far we have argued that there are serious obstacles towards a complete convergence of the internal market freedoms towards a citizenship-based model of fundamental rights. In this section, we go on to consider the implications of regarding Union citizenship rights as sources of fundamental rights. The equivalence between citizenship rights and fundamental rights raises some intriguing interpretative questions, which appear to challenge the analytical viability of the post-*Zambrano* case law and may even lead to re-evaluating the meaning of the *Zambrano* ruling itself. In particular, while post-*Zambrano*, the Court may have sought to contain the expansionary potential of that ruling, the logic of the test it

[46] Case C-72/03, *Carbonati Apuani*, ECLI:EU:C:2004:506. The Court's approach was partly based on the one adopted in Joined Cases C-363/93, C-407/93 to C-411/93, *Lancry*, ECLI:EU:C:1994:315.

[47] That is, because internal borders undermine in practice the integrity of the customs union.

[48] Opinion of Advocate General Geelhoed in Joined Cases C-515/99, C-519/99 to C-524/99 and C-526/99 to C-540/99, *Reisch and Others*, ECLI:EU:C:2001:618, para 104.

enshrined remains, even after subsequent rulings, open to different interpretations, some of which draw explicit links with the conceptual toolkit of fundamental rights.

The Opinion of Advocate General Szpunar in *Rendón Marín* and *CS* throw light on an under-explored aspect of the *Zambrano* test.[49] Both *Rendón Marín* and *CS* involve decisions (respectively, the refusal of a residence permit and an expulsion order) by Member States against third-country nationals, which may result in children, who are nationals of the respective Member State, being deprived of the genuine enjoyment of their rights as citizens of the Union; in both cases, the parents are solely responsible for their children's care.

The Opinion of Advocate General Szpunar explores the conceptual relation between, on the one hand, the "substance" of EU citizenship rights, which was fleshed out in *Ruiz Zambrano*, and, on the other, the "essence" of fundamental rights.[50] The latter concept, a familiar doctrine in European constitutional theory and practice, is found in Article 52(1) of the Charter, which states that "any limitation on the exercise of the rights and freedoms laid down by the Charter must be provided for by law, *respect their essence* and, subject to the principle of proportionality…". Article 52(1) CFR thus recognises the existence of an unassailable core of a fundamental right, which represents an absolute limit on interferences with that right; it is a "limit on limits".

The explanations to the Charter make clear that Article 52(1) CFR refers to a long line of case law which holds that restrictions on fundamental rights should not constitute a "disproportionate and unreasonable interference undermining the very *substance* of those rights".[51] The analogy between the "substance" test in *Zambrano* and the language employed in the case law on which Article 52 CFR is based may not be purely coincidental. Given that Article 45 of the Charter asserts that the rights contained in Article 20(2)(a) TFEU and Article 21 TFEU *are* fundamental rights, it follows that any restriction placed on them should be subject to the principles set out in Article 52 of the Charter, including the 'essence' test. If this is true, a number of questions come to the fore. What is the relation between the essence/substance test and proportionality? If there is a link, how can it explain the absence of a reference to proportionality in *Zambrano* and in the rulings that applied the substance of rights test? And, finally: does the substance/essence of rights test presuppose the existence of an interference with the exercise of a right?

The fundamental rights case law displays a number of possible interactions between the essence doctrine and proportionality. There are judgments in which the Court finds that a limitation of a right negates its essence, but in which no mention is made of proportionality.[52] There are also cases in which the Court, first, applies

[49] Opinion of Advocate General Szpunar in Case C-165/14, *Rendón Marín*, ECLI:EU:C:2016:75. The Court has decided that the two cases should be heard jointly before the Grand Chamber.

[50] For an earlier recognition of this equivalence see Schütze 2012 at 419.

[51] Case C-292/97, *Karlsson*, ECLI:EU:C:2000:202, para 45 (with added emphasis).

[52] E.g. Case C-426/11, *Alemo-Herron*, ECLI:EU:C:2013:521; Case C-362/14, *Schrems*, ECLI:EU:C:2015:650.

the essence doctrine, then, after finding that the right's essence is not compromised, goes on to state whether the measure/decision at issue does,[53] or does not,[54] violate the principle of proportionality. While it may appear from this case law that the Court considers the two tests as self-standing, there is (arguably) a connection between the essence doctrine and proportionality. Plainly, it seems illogical for a measure to fail the essence test but to pass the proportionality test. When the first test is sufficient to decide the matter (i.e. because the measure fails the essence test) the second test becomes redundant—it would be superfluous to engage with proportionality analysis when the level of interference with the fundamental right is clearly beyond what the EU's legal system is prepared to tolerate. This is why the Court follows an order which consists in applying the essence test first, and then (eventually) the proportionality test. Moreover, the fact that a measure may pass the essence test and fail the proportionality test does not negate the existence of a connection between the two tests. It simply means that the essence test represents the outer limit of proportionality: a measure/decision that does not go as far as to negate the core content of a right may nonetheless go beyond what is necessary to protect the public interest.

The equivalence between the essence doctrine and the substance of citizenship test may explain the Court's silence in *Zambrano* on the issue of proportionality: there the Court did not need to examine the proportionality of the Belgian decisions, not only because it had not been asked to do so,[55] but (arguably) also because it had already concluded that these decisions constituted an intolerable interference with the rights laid down in Article 20 TFEU. This is consistent with the fundamental rights case law, in which, as we have seen, a finding that a measure undermines the essence of a right seems to make an assessment of its proportionality redundant.[56]

It is less clear, however, why the Court did not engage with proportionality post-*Zambrano*, in cases in which the Court found that the substance of the right was not under threat. There is some scope for the view that even where the substance/essence of citizenship rights is not affected, a (proportionate) interference with these rights is nonetheless present. In other words, the substance test in the post-*Zambrano* case law is simply a light-touch proportionality review, which, however, presupposes that the situation falls within the scope of EU law.[57] The *Dereci* ruling may be relied on to substantiate the point. There, the Court never

---

[53] Joined Cases C-293/12 and C-594/12, *Digital Rights Ireland*, ECLI:EU:C:2014:238.

[54] Case C-283/11, *Sky Österreich*, ECLI:EU:C:2013:28; Case C-547/14, *Philip Morris Brands and Others*, ECLI:EU:C:2016:325.

[55] See Lenaerts 2011 at 15 and Opinion of Advocate General Szpunar in Case *Rendón Marín* (n. 49 above), para 132.

[56] See footnote 52 above.

[57] This would be a review that allows interference with the right to the extent that interference does not negate the very essence of that right. In ECHR parlance, it is an expression of the margin of appreciation that Member States are afforded. For an example in the ECtHR case law of a review that confined itself to finding that the interference with the right did not negate the essence of the right see *Rees v United Kingdom* (1987) 9 EHRR 56, at [50].

stated that the situations at issue were purely internal. Nor did the Court find, as it had done in *Kremzow*, that the situations raised the "purely hypothetical prospect" of the exercise of free movement. Moreover, the Court did not rule out in principle the possibility that the referring court should have regard to the right to respect for private and family life provided for in Article 7 of the Charter.[58] The fact that the Court referred to being able to reside as a family "in the territory of the Union" may also be taken to be significant, as it indicates that there was a link with Union citizenship. In other words, the Court did not deny the possibility that an impact on residence within the Union (i.e. beyond Austria) was present, but it found that the impact was not such as to negate the essence of the Union citizens' rights.

When a national measure interferes with an EU citizen's potential exercise of her (non-economic) citizenship rights, the intensity of judicial review is loosened. In such cases, the scrutiny is limited to verifying whether the measure at issue amounts to a denial of the substance the right, that is, a situation in which it is practically impossible to exercise those rights. The fundamental implication of this construction is that static situations, such as those at issue in *Dereci*, in principle *do* fall within the scope of EU law. If it were otherwise, the Court would not need to examine the question whether the essence of the right is impaired, as that question presupposes a limitation on the exercise of the right to move and reside in the territory of the Member States. As Advocate General Wathelet recently put it: 'if a Treaty provision does not preclude a Member State from refusing a right of residence subject to compliance with certain conditions, it follows by definition that the situation in question falls within the scope of that provision'.[59]

However, the ruling in *Ymeraga* seems to tell against this interpretation of the "substance" of rights. That preliminary ruling concerned the compatibility with EU law of the denial of residence for a third-country family member of a European Union citizen who resided in his Member State of nationality and had never exercised his free movement rights. Asked to rule on the applicability of fundamental rights to the situation at hand, the Court made clear that the exercise of free movement rights engages the Charter rights, as "the law on freedom of movement is indeed intended to implement European Union law".[60] However, it added, the situation at hand was not governed by European Union law, as the refusal to confer a right of residence on the Union citizen's family members did not have the effect of denying him the genuine enjoyment of the substance of the rights conferred by virtue

[58] But see Lenaerts 2012 at p. 387 who interprets this ruling differently. Since the contested decision 'did not fall within the scope of the Treaty provisions on EU citizenship' and Austria was not 'implementing EU law', the ECJ lacked jurisdiction to examine whether such refusal was compatible with the Charter. However, as the same author has later acknowledged, whether or not the Union citizen would have to leave the territory of the Union 'is clearly a factual question for the national court to determine', which suggests the possibility that the situation may indeed fall within the scope of EU law. See Lenaerts 2013, p. 575 footnote 32.

[59] Opinion of Advocate General Wathelet in Case C-115/15, *NA*, ECLI:EU:C:2016:259, para 122.

[60] *Ymeraga and Ymeraga-Tafarshiku* (supra n. 44), para 42.

of his status as citizen of the Union.[61] This finding appears to confirm a reading of the "substance of rights" that yields a significantly different meaning from that associated with the "essence of rights" terminology used in the fundamental rights context. In the latter case law, the application of the substance/essence test always presupposes that a situation falls within the scope of a given fundamental right, even where the essence threshold is not crossed. Instead, *Ymeraga* offers a clear-cut, all-or-nothing alternative: if the threshold is crossed, the material scope of the Treaty is triggered; if not, the situation falls outside the scope of EU law.

If that is so, it is hard to see how proportionality may come into play. Yet, ruling out proportionality would not only work against the Union citizen but also against the Member States. It would work against the citizen because there would only be one trigger for the application of EU law—a forced departure from the territory of the Union as a whole. Yet, at the same time, such an automatic trigger would preclude the possibility of striking a balance between the public interest of the Member States and the rights of the Union citizen. In the absence of proportionality analysis, the Member States would, for instance, be precluded from regarding a *temporary* absence as a proportionate interference with Union citizenship rights.

To avoid being hamstrung in this manner, the Court may therefore decide to follow Advocate General Szpunar's position in *Rendón Marín* and *CS*, which combines the substance and proportionality tests. More specifically, in relation to the *CS* case, the Advocate General considered that a Member State's decision to expel from its territory (and from the territory of the Union) a third-country national, who is the parent and sole carer of a child (a national of that Member State), would deprive the child of the enjoyment of the substance of her/his rights as a citizen of the Union. Nonetheless, he added, in exceptional circumstances, a Member State may take such a measure, provided that it observes the principle of proportionality and is based on the personal conduct of the foreign national, which must constitute a genuine, present and sufficiently serious threat affecting one of the fundamental interests of society.

This solution may seem to conflict with the idea that the essence/substance test represents the outer limit of proportionality, which makes an examination of proportionality not only unnecessary, but also logically impossible. On close inspection, however, the conflict is only superficial. The finding that, in principle, a measure negates the essence of a right may not be incompatible with proportionality if that finding is accompanied by the qualification that, provided that certain safeguards are observed, the measure may be deemed to constitute a proportionate interference with the exercise of the right. In other words, the solution offered by Advocate General Szpunar is that the substance of citizenship is compromised, unless the Member State is able to rebut that presumption. It is only where the Member State is unable to rebut the presumption that the decision negates the substance of citizenship rights. Thus, a blanket policy to deport the parent of a

---

[61] There are some key factual differences between the situation at issue in *Ymeraga* and some of the situations at issue in *Dereci*, the most important being the fact that in *Ymeraga* the Union citizen was not a minor and did not depend on his parents (nor did his parents depend on him).

Union citizen who is a minor would, as such, amount to negating the substance of Union citizenship, but a decision in a specific case would not be so regarded if it complied with the principle of proportionality and the other safeguards outlined in the Advocate General's conclusions. In the context of a preliminary ruling, it is only natural for the Advocate General to consider two alternative solutions whose application turns on the legislative and factual context of the case at hand.[62]

11.3.4 Dano *and the Grammar of Rights*

If the Court's silence on the issue of proportionality in *Zambrano* is not as such incompatible with an interpretation of this case law that allows for the possibility of an (implicit) light-touch review, the same cannot be said of the *Dano* ruling.[63] Academic commentary has (rightly) stigmatised the strident change in approach in the Court's case law.[64] A case law that grounded a narrow reading of limitations and conditions on the exercise of the rights of EU citizens in the fundamental nature of the status of Union citizenship seems to have given way to a radically different position, which downplays these constitutional premises, while at the same time coining new duties that commit the Union citizen to the "values" of the host society.[65] As the literature has amply demonstrated, this dramatic shift in approach rests on frail legal ground, an impression which is only strengthened if Union citizenship rights are analysed under the lens of fundamental rights.

A feature of *Dano*, in particular, appears to be incompatible with a fundamental rights account of Union citizenship rights. The jurisprudential application of fundamental rights, as mentioned before, displays a sharp distinction between the scope of the individual right and the public interest considerations that justify its limitation. Thus, public interest considerations do not feature in the definition of the scope of a right but come into play when considering the extent to which the right may be limited. Instead, such a separation is absent from the traditional approach to the economic free movement provisions. Indeed, the classic example of *Keck*, with its reference to the policy rationale of responding to the "increasing tendency" of traders

[62] Indeed, this reading of the Advocate General's Opinion seems to reflect the Court's statement in *Rottmann* to the effect that a decision entailing the loss of citizenship should be assessed against the principle of proportionality. Case C-135/08, *Rottmann*, ECLI:EU:C:2010:104. It is worth noting that the Advocate General's opinion in *CS* does not articulate in full detail the upshot of the essence test in the case at hand. Were the essence test to represent an absolute limit, and if the deportation decision amounted to an impossibility for the child to exercise her citizenship rights *for an indefinite period*, it would be difficult to see how such decision could ever be found not to be disproportionate and to negate the essence of citizenship.

[63] Case C-333/13, *Dano*, ECLI:EU:C:2014:2358.

[64] See Thym 2015 and Nic Shuibhne 2015.

[65] Case C-378/12, *Onuekwere*, ECLI:EU:C:2014:13; and Case C-400/12, *M.G.*, ECLI:EU:C:2014:9. See Loïc Azoulai 2014.

to rely on Article 34 TFEU as a means of reducing their regulatory burden offers an example of that thin dividing line. In *Dano*, however, the Court's approach to the definition of the scope of the fundamental right to reside in the host state seems to have taken a similar approach to the one displayed in *Keck*. This is evident from the close link drawn between the conditions that, according to the Court, define the citizen's right to reside under the Directive (sufficient resources and comprehensive medical insurance), and the policy purpose of curbing (to use the politically-charged language of Advocate General Wathelet) "benefit tourism".[66] Thus, it seems that the perceived threat of benefit tourism is to the rights of Union citizens what the increasing tendency of traders to rely on Article 34 was to free movement of goods. If this reading of *Dano* is correct, the viability of the theoretical framework advanced here is called into question. If the existence of a right depends on public interest considerations, this right cannot, according to this framework, be fundamental.[67]

11.4 Conclusion

While the terminology of fundamental (internal market) freedoms echoes the terminology of fundamental rights, the resemblance does not always amount to an exact equivalence analogous to that between "true cognates" (those words in different languages that are not only identical in spelling, but also in meaning). The equivalence is partial, as it applies only to those fundamental (economic) freedoms that can be clearly linked to EU citizenship. The other fundamental freedoms are "false friends" to fundamental rights (the relationship occurring between words in different languages with identical spelling, but different meaning). As far as the fundamental (non-economic) freedoms of EU citizens are concerned, the conceptual toolkit of fundamental rights is also fruitful as it allows to make some sense of the puzzles that have emerged from the line of case law that began with *Zambrano*; in particular, the possibility that the "substance" test may be an expression of the "essence" doctrine employed in the fundamental rights case law offers intriguing insights into this case law. Yet, the extent to which the Court is prepared to align the case law on citizenship with the case law on fundamental rights in this respect is a matter that remains to be seen. It also remains to be seen whether the essence doctrine applies to the economic fundamental freedoms of EU citizens as well, and whether free movement of goods and free movement of capital are excluded from its application (as would follow from the account advanced here). It seems regrettably clear, nonetheless, that the *Dano* ruling constitutes a stumbling block towards the development of citizenship rights as fundamental rights.

---

[66] Opinion of Advocate General Wathelet in Case C-333/13, *Dano*, ECLI:EU:C:2014:341, para 131.

[67] See Thym 2015 and Nic Shuibhne 2015 who point out that, in *Dano*, the Court has set aside the distinction between the existence of a right and its exercise.

Acknowledgements I am grateful to Eleanor Spaventa for her comments. The usual disclaimer applies.

References

Azoulai L (2014) The (mis)construction of the European individual: Two essays on Union citizenship law. EUI Working Paper LAW 2014/14

De Cecco F (2014) Fundamental Freedoms, Fundamental Rights and the Scope of Free Movement Law. German Law Journal 15:383

Fleming M (1962) Domestic financial policies under fixed and floating exchange rates. IMF Staff Papers Vol. 9, 369

Horsley T (2012) Unearthing buried treasure: Art. 34 TFEU and the exclusionary rules. European Law Review 37:734

Kochenov D (2011) A Real European Citizenship: A New Jurisdiction Test: A Novel Chapter in the Development of the Union in Europe. Columbia Journal of European Law 18:55

Lenaerts K (2011) 'Civis europaeus sum': From the cross-border link to the status of citizen of the Union. Online Journal on Free Movement of Workers within the European Union 3:6

Lenaerts K (2012) Exploring the Limits of the EU Charter of Fundamental Rights. European Constitutional Law Review 8:375

Lenaerts K (2013) The concept of EU citizenship in the case law of the European Court of Justice. ERA Forum 13:569

Mertens de Wilmars J (1976) La Jurisprudence de la Cour de Justice comme Instrument de l'Intégration Communautaire. Cahiers de Droit Européen 1:135

Mundell R (1963) Capital mobility and stabilization policy under fixed and flexible exchange rates. Canadian Journal of Economics and Political Science 29:475

Nic Shuibhne N (2002) Free Movement of Persons and Wholly Internal Rule: Time to Move On? Common Market Law Review 39:731

Nic Shuibhne N (2015) Limits rising, duties ascending: The changing legal shape of Union citizenship. Common Market Law Review 52:889

O'Brien M (2008) Taxation and the Third Country Dimension of Free Movement of Capital in EU Law: The ECJ's Rulings and Unresolved Issues. British Tax Review 6:628

O'Leary S (2011) Free Movement of Persons and Services. In: Craig P, de Búrca G (eds) The Evolution of EU Law. Oxford University Press, Oxford, p. 503

Raz J (1986) The Morality of Freedom. Oxford University Press, Oxford

Schütze R (2012) European Constitutional Law. Cambridge University Press, Cambridge

Shaw J (2010) Citizenship: Contrasting Dynamics at the Interface of Integration and Constitutionalism. University of Edinburgh School of Law Working Paper No. 2010/14. Available at https://papers.ssrn.com/sol3/papers.cfm?abstract_id=1585938

Snell J (2004) And Then There Were Two: Products and Citizens in Community Law. In: Tridimas T, Nebbia P (eds) European Union Law for the Twenty-First Century, vol. 1. Rethinking the New Legal Order. Hart Publishing, Oxford/Portland, p. 49

Snell J (2011) Free Movement of Capital: Evolution as a Non-Linear Process. In: Craig P, de Búrca G (eds) The Evolution of EU Law. Oxford University Press, Oxford, p. 547

Spaventa E (2008) Seeing the Wood Despite the Trees? On the Scope of Union Citizenship and Its Constitutional Effects. Common Market Law Review 45:13

Spaventa E (2009) Federalisation versus centralisation: Tensions in fundamental rights discourse in the EU. In: Dougan M, Currie S (eds) 50 Years of the European Treaties. Hart Publishing, Oxford

Thym D (2015) When Union citizens turn into illegal migrants: The Dano case. EL Rev. 40:249

Tryfonidou A (2016) The Impact of Union Citizenship on the EU's Market Freedoms. Bloomsbury, Oxford

Chapter 12
Fundamental Freedoms, Fundamental Rights, and the Many Faces of Freedom of Contract in the EU

Olha O. Cherednychenko

Abstract As a result of the growing involvement of the EU in regulating private conduct and private law relationships, EU law increasingly affects the scope of freedom of contract. In this way, it shapes the European model of freedom of contract based first and foremost on the internal market rationale, sparkling tensions with the concepts of freedom of contract that have evolved in the national contract laws of the Member States. Whilst EU secondary legislation plays a major role in this context, the understanding of freedom of contract can also be profoundly affected by EU primary law. This contribution seeks to determine the reach of EU free movement law in the contractual sphere, with a particular focus on (financial) services. It explores the conceptualisation of freedom of contract in free movement law in light of the concept of 'formal' freedom of contract and that of 'substantive' freedom of contract in national contract laws, as well as the notion of the freedom of contract regulated in the name of the internal market in EU secondary legislation. Particular attention in this context is given to the interplay between fundamental economic freedoms and fundamental rights.

Keywords EU free movement law · EU fundamental rights · National contract laws · Freedom of contract · Private law relationships · Services · Financial services

Contents

12.1 Introduction 274
12.2 Freedom of Contract in European Contract Law 276
12.2.1 National Legal Systems: From Formal to Substantive Freedom of Contract... 276

O.O. Cherednychenko (✉)
University of Groningen, Groningen, The Netherlands
e-mail: o.o.cherednychenko@rug.nl

M. Andenas et al. (eds.), *The Reach of Free Movement*,
DOI 10.1007/978-94-6265-195-1_12

12.2.2 EU Contract Law: Freedom of Contract Regulated in the Name of the Internal Market ... 278
12.3 Freedom of Contract in EU Free Movement Law ... 282
12.3.1 The Effect of Fundamental Freedoms in Private Law Relationships ... 282
12.3.2 Fundamental Freedoms: Protecting Unregulated Freedom of Contract with an Interstate Element ... 283
12.3.3 Fundamental Rights: A Different Dimension to the Concept of Freedom of Contract in Free Movement Law? ... 286
12.4 Concluding Remarks ... 290
References ... 291

12.1 Introduction

Freedom of contract has been widely regarded as the cornerstone of European contract law.[1] Conventional wisdom holds that, as a manifestation of private autonomy, freedom of contract allows private parties to freely make their choices as to who they contract with, what they contract for and on what terms. As such it is of particular importance not only for national market economies but also in the context of market integration in the EU.

However, this traditional understanding of freedom of contract does not imply that contractual freedom is a static or unitary concept. The complex and changing nature of freedom of contract does not sustain such a simplistic view. In particular, in the second half of the 20th century the national legal systems witnessed what Max Weber referred to as the 'materialisation of law'.[2] This development is reflected in a major shift from 'formal' freedom of contract between parties (without regard to bargaining power) towards 'substantive' freedom of contract for *both* parties (with regard to bargaining power).[3] Moreover, one may even wonder to what extent major European legal systems share a common understanding of freedom of contract.[4]

In addition, as a result of the growing involvement of the EU in regulating private conduct and relationships between private parties, EU law increasingly affects the scope of freedom of contract.[5] In this way, it shapes the European model of freedom of contract based first and foremost on the internal market rationale,

[1] For the purposes of this contribution, the concept of European contract law is understood in a broad sense, namely as the law governing economic transactions in Europe. As such it comprises both the EU measures in the field of contract law, i.e. EU contract law, and the national contract laws of the Member States.

[2] Weber 1992, p. 886. See also Kennedy 2006, p. 19.

[3] On this development, see, for example, Cherednychenko 2007, pp. 4 et seq. and Grundmann 2011, pp. 504 et seq., both with further references.

[4] Micklitz 2015a.

[5] See, for example, Leczykiewicz and Weatherill 2013.

sparkling tensions with the concepts of freedom of contract that have evolved in national private law systems.

While EU secondary legislation plays a major role in this context, the understanding of freedom of contract can also be profoundly affected by EU primary law, in particular the fundamental economic freedoms enshrined in the Treaty on the Functioning of the EU (TFEU)—the free movement of goods, persons, services, and capital.[6] In fact, these economic freedoms can have far-reaching implications for the relationships between private parties and hence the sphere of freedom of contract, as strikingly illustrated by the judgements of the Court of Justice of the EU (CJEU) in *Viking* and *Laval*.[7]

What is more, private law relationships are also increasingly influenced by EU fundamental rights.[8] Whilst the founding EC Treaties signed in the 1950s contained no express provisions on fundamental rights, Article 6 of the Treaty on European Union (TEU) as amended by the 2007 Lisbon Treaty gives explicit recognition to the three sources of EU fundamental rights: (1) the Nice Charter of Fundamental Rights of the EU (EUCFR), (2) the European Convention on Human Rights, and (3) the constitutional traditions common to the Member States. The EU fundamental rights may pose limits on the exercise of the free movement rights, as shown, for example, by the judgments of the CJEU in *Schmidberger* and *Omega*,[9] affecting in turn the domain of freedom of contract.

Against this background, in this contribution I will explore the reach of the EU free movement law in the sphere of freedom of contract, with a particular focus on (financial) services. I will first take a closer look at the notions of freedom of contract that have developed in the national contract laws of the Member States, on the one hand, and in EU secondary legislation, on the other (Sect. 12.2). Building upon these concepts, I will then proceed to examine an uneasy relationship between fundamental freedoms and freedom of contract and the implications of the interplay between fundamental freedoms and fundamental rights for the conceptualisation of freedom of contract in EU free movement law (Sect. 12.3). This investigation does not aim to provide an exhaustive overview of the case law on the topic but rather to explore the concept of freedom of contract at different levels of the EU multi-level governance system, using some examples from the CJEU's jurisprudence. This analysis will notably focus on the issue of whether recourse to fundamental rights could promote a different notion of freedom of contract from that supported by fundamental economic freedoms. The contribution will conclude with some final

---

[6] See, for example, Cherednychenko 2006; Rutgers 2009; Hartkamp 2010; Schepel 2012; Davies 2012, 2013; Weatherill 2013, pp. 10 et seq.; Schepel 2013; Mak 2016.

[7] Case C-438/05, *Viking*, ECLI:EU:C:2007:772; Case C-341/05, *Laval*, ECLI:EU:C:2007:809.

[8] On this development, see Cherednychenko and Reich 2015, with further references.

[9] Case C-112/00, *Schmidberger*, ECLI:EU:C:2003:333; Case C-36/02, *Omega*, ECLI:EU:C:2004:614.

observations concerning the way in which fundamental freedoms and fundamental rights may shape the concept of freedom of contract in European contract law (Sect. 12.4).

12.2 Freedom of Contract in European Contract Law

12.2.1 National Legal Systems: From Formal to Substantive Freedom of Contract

While freedom of contract across the EU may not necessarily be perceived in the same way,[10] all major European legal systems, to a greater or lesser degree, witnessed a major transformation of this notion in the second half of the 20th century —the shift from form to substance. In fact, as will be shown below, the concept of 'formal' freedom of contract in traditional contract law and that of 'substantive' freedom of contract in modern contract law are key to our understanding of the tension between EU law and the private law systems of the Member States.

Being pervaded by the maxim *caveat emptor*, the traditional general law of contract was predominantly adversary, seeing the contract as a combination of the wills of two free and equal parties protecting their own interests. It generally disregarded the relevant personal qualities and circumstances of the contracting parties and imposed no obligation on the parties to look after each other's interests. Under traditional contract law, an individual was considered to be the best judge of his or her interests, regardless of the actual bargaining power on his or her side, and that person who entered into a contract was considered to have done so at his or her risk. Freedom of contract was thus understood in a purely *formal* sense as the juridical freedom of the two, in theory free and equal, agents to enter into a contract and to decide upon its content.

By contrast, the modern law of contract has clearly moved towards a more society-oriented understanding of the contract which places more emphasis, if not on co-operation between the parties, then at least on conduct which takes account of the justified interests of the other party to the contract. Modern contract law tends to recognize that where there is, as is frequently the case, a significant degree of imbalance in bargaining power between the parties, *real* freedom of contract on the part of the weaker party is absent. In response, sector-specific areas, such as employment law, landlord and tenant law, and consumer law, have emerged that de-formalised freedom of contract by placing mandatory constraints on bargaining processes and outcomes in the terms of contract. Contract-related public regulation in these fields was adopted with a view to achieving more socially just outcomes for the weaker parties, such as employees, tenants, and consumers, compared to those that could be achieved within traditional general contract law.

---

[10] Micklitz 2015a, b.

Moreover, the move away from form to substance also took place within general contract law, with national civil courts increasingly resorting to the general clauses of private law, such as good faith or good morals, in order to restore contractual balance between the parties in individual cases. As a result of this development, modern contract law tends to take a harder look at the all-important predicate that the agreement has been freely made. Certainly, parties should be held to their agreements; contracts should be enforced; no one doubts the wisdom of *pacta sunt servanda*—but only where the parties have come to terms on a free *and informed* basis. To some extent, this development within general contract law was prompted by the presence of social justice-oriented public regulation of relevance to contracts,[11] as well as the impact of fundamental rights.[12] In many cases, however, it was the materialisation of freedom of contract within the general contract itself that led to the adoption of protective regulation.[13]

The scale of the development towards a more society-oriented contract law that took place in the national legal systems has led many scholars to question to what extent the principle of freedom of contract still remains the starting point in modern contract law and what it actually means. Some argued that contract law today is no longer only based on the principle of freedom of contract but also on the principle of the protection of the weaker party or the 'principle of regard and fairness'.[14] However, it can equally be argued that it is not so much the principle of freedom of contract as the starting point in contract law which has been challenged in modern contract law, but rather the formal understanding of freedom of contract prevailing in traditional contract law. The development of a more society-oriented contract law thus did not entail a decline of freedom of contract but rather resulted in the *materialisation* of this concept. In contrast to formal freedom or contract, *substantive* freedom of contract focuses on the existence of true freedom of contract for *both* contractual parties. What is at issue in modern contract law is to what extent the weaker party must be protected in order to be able to enjoy real freedom of contract, or, in other words, where the freedom of one party ends and the freedom of the other party begins. Thus, '[s]ome loss of (formal) freedom of contract on the one side has to be accepted for the overall gain, i.e. for the much higher gain of material freedom of contract on the other side.'[15]

Although traditional and modern contract law significantly differ from each other in the way they treat weaker parties, both share the same normative basis underlying the national private law systems—the focus on the individual and justice between

---

[11] Collins 1999, p. 49.

[12] See Colombi Ciacchi 2010.

[13] For example, the conduct of business rules for investment firms, such as the duty to act in the client's best interest or the duty to know one's customer, which now form part of the EU and national regulatory frameworks for investment services, have largely originated within the general private laws, in particular, contract laws, of the Member States. On this in more detail, see Cherednychenko 2009, pp. 929 et seq.

[14] See, for example, Hondius 1999; Lurger 2011, pp. 376 et seq.; Lurger 2011.

[15] Grundmann 2011, p. 506.

the parties. National private law, in particular contract law, has been conceived as that part of law which secures a sphere of positive freedom for private parties and provides a special legal framework which enables the parties to enjoy such freedom. To ensure that the exercise of the positive freedom is not subject to extensive government controls in the public interest, private law is constructed as a system of rights or entitlements, such as freedom of contract. This traditional idea of private law implies that private law discourse aims to dispense corrective justice between private parties focusing on the criteria originating in the relationship between the parties and not on the attainment of external political, social or economic goals.[16] Even though particularly during the last half century or more private law discourse in many legal systems has to a greater or lesser extent been influenced by policy considerations following the rise of economic and social regulation,[17] the basic ethical-societal conception of private law as the law which should *primarily* focus on the relationship between the two private parties has remained present in modern contract law.[18] This normative premise has been reflected *both* in the formal and substantive notions of freedom of contract in national contract laws.

12.2.2 EU Contract Law: Freedom of Contract Regulated in the Name of the Internal Market

The EU challenges implicitly the traditional understanding of private law as it has evolved in national legal systems. It has been widely noted that the *acquis communautaire* in the field of private law is primarily concerned with creating the internal market and is therefore regulatory in nature.[19] The main question posed by the European legislator has been not how to ensure justice between market participants but rather how to make the internal market function better. In this context, contract law has been viewed as an instrument for achieving market integration. As such it is not addressed to persons with independent interests as ends in themselves but rather to market functionaries, such as consumers and traders, who are considered to be instrumental to market building.[20] Alongside the central objective of establishing the European internal market, the collective objectives of European integration include, *inter alia*, the protection of consumers. At the same time, the

---

[16] On this, see Bydlinki 1996, pp. 92 et seq.

[17] On this development, see Collins 1999.

[18] Cf. Schmid 2011, p. 21, who speaks in this context about the weak version of corrective justice which has remained present throughout the evolutionary path of private law. According to it, if one were to hypothetically ignore the regulatory dimension of a particular private law norm beyond the relationships between the two private parties, the application of the norm should lead to the outcome which respects the minimum requirements of justice between the parties. See also Cherednychenko 2007, pp. 49 et seq.

[19] See, for example, Micklitz 2005, 2009; Schmid 2005; Collins 2009.

[20] On this in more detail, see Micklitz 2015b. Cf. Hesselink 2007; Bartl 2015.

adoption of EU measures aimed at protecting this category of private parties is not driven by interpersonal justice-related concerns given the weaker bargaining position of consumers viz-à-viz traders in the first place. In fact, such measures are primarily justified by the considerations of ensuring access of consumers to the internal market.[21] After all, without consumers and consumer protection, the completion of the internal market would be impossible.

The strong internal market rationale underpinning EU contract law has major implications for the concept of freedom of contract reflected in EU secondary legislation in this field. The European model of freedom of contract can be described as that of the freedom of contract regulated in the name of the establishment and smooth functioning of the internal market. On the one hand, EU contract law enables freedom of contract by actively promoting market access for consumers. The enabling side of the marketised freedom of contract in this sense manifests itself most strikingly in the EU regulation of services of general economic interest, such as electricity, gas, telecommunication, and transport. The obvious concern of the EU legislature in this area has been that these particular services remain accessible to everybody, including most vulnerable consumers, following the replacement of public monopolies with a broad variety of private suppliers operating in a competitive market. In this context, Directive 2009/72 concerning common rules for the Internal Market in electricity,[22] for example, obliges Member States to ensure that all household customers enjoy 'universal service', i.e. 'the right to be supplied with electricity of a specified quality within their territory at reasonable, easily and clearly comparable, transparent and non-discriminatory prices'.[23] In addition, the same directive requires that Member States ensure that there are adequate safeguards to protect vulnerable customers.[24] In this context, Member States must define the concept of vulnerable customers. Such a concept 'may refer to energy poverty and, *inter alia*, to the prohibition of disconnection of electricity to such customers in critical times'.

Another interesting example of the enabling side of the internal market-oriented freedom of contract in EU contract law can be found in the area of financial services. Directive 2014/92/EU on the comparability of fees related to payment accounts, payment accounts switching and access to payment accounts with basic features obliges Member States to ensure that all consumers legally resident in the EU have access to payment accounts with basic features.[25] Such a payment account should at least enable consumers to place funds, withdraw cash, and execute and

---

[21] Cf. Micklitz 2011, who argues that EU contract law is governed by the model of 'access justice' ('*Zugangsgerechtigkeit*'). The idea behind this model of justice is that EU law is supposed to provide for a legal framework which would ensure that consumers, including those particularly vulnerable, have a realistic chance of access to the market.

[22] Directive 2009/72, *OJEU* 2009 L 211/65.

[23] Directive 2009/72, Article 3(3).

[24] Directive 2009/72, Article 3(7).

[25] Directive 2014/92/EU, *OJEU* 2014 L257/214, Article 16.

receive payment transactions.[26] Member States should ensure that all or a sufficient number of credit institutions established in their territory offer payment accounts with basic features and that they do so free of charge or for a reasonable fee.[27] The consumer right to a basic bank account introduced by Directive 2014/92/EU positively promotes financial inclusion and equality in the access to payment services by ensuring access to payment accounts with basic features 'irrespective of the consumers' financial circumstances, such as their employment status, level of income, credit history or personal bankruptcy'.[28]

On the other hand, EU contract law also limits the marketised freedom of contract through mandatory protective standards. In consumer law, these include, for example, withdrawal rights, various information obligations, unfair contract terms controls, and remedies for non-conforming goods. In the area of financial services law, the post-crisis era witnessed a shift from consumer protection through information, or 'soft' paternalism to consumer protection through financial product bans and other major restrictions on financial contracting, or 'hard' paternalism.[29] For example, under the Markets in Financial Instruments Directive II and the Markets in Financial Instruments Regulation (MiFIR),[30] national financial supervisory authorities may prohibit, suspend or restrict the marketing or sale of investment products in or from its Member State where significant investor protection concerns arise, or a threat is posed to the orderly functioning and integrity of financial markets or to the stability of the whole or part of the financial system within at least one Member State.[31] Moreover, the MiFIR empowers the European Securities and Markets Authority (ESMA) to intervene in national markets by temporarily prohibiting or restricting the marketing or sale of investment products in similar circumstances.[32] It also gives ESMA coordination powers with regard to product intervention by national supervisory authorities.[33]

Enabling and restricting freedom of contract thus go hand-in-hand in EU contract law.[34] Freedom of contract is regulated with a view to promoting the internal market. Moreover, in some areas affected by EU contract law, such as financial

---

[26] Directive 2014/92/EU, Article 17(1).

[27] Directive 2014/92/EU, Articles 16 and 18, respectively.

[28] Directive 2014/92/EU, rec 35.

[29] On this in more detail, see Cherednychenko 2014b.

[30] Directive 2014/65/EU, *OJEU* 2014 L 173/349 (MiFID II) and Regulation (EU) No. 600/2014, *OJEU* 2014 L 173/84 (MiFIR).

[31] MiFIR, Article 42 and MiFID II, Article 69(2)(s) in conjunction with MiFIR, Article 42.

[32] MiFIR, Article 40. This power of ESMA relates to the general clause in ESMA's founding Regulation, which empowers ESMA to temporarily prohibit or restrict certain financial activities in the cases specified in relevant EU legislation or in the case of an emergency situation (Regulation (EU) No. 1095/2010, *OJEU* 2010 L 331/84, Article 9(5)).

[33] MiFIR, Article 43.

[34] Cf. Micklitz 2015a, b, p. 30.

services, the exercise of freedom of contract by private parties is also subject to public supervision by administrative agencies. In fact, the rise of public supervision over private relationships and public enforcement of contract-related rules in many areas of private law has led to the development of EU supervision private law as part of EU regulatory private law.[35] European supervision private law is made up of regulatory contract-related conduct of business rules for financial institutions that are cast as supervision standards and are enforced by public authorities through administrative law means; while such rules form part of a specific supervisory framework that is not concerned with private relationships in the first place, nevertheless, in essence, they have a direct bearing upon such relationships. The financial product intervention powers of ESMA and national financial supervisory authorities mentioned above are just one notable example.

How does this European model of the freedom of contract regulated in the name of the internal market which is embodied in EU contract law relate to the national concepts of freedom of contract described above? By enabling and restricting freedom of contract through protective standards, the marketised freedom of contract in EU contract law clearly reaches far beyond the concept of formal freedom of contract that lies at the foundations of traditional national contract laws. Whilst formal freedom of contract leaves it to the individual to find ways to gain access to the market and stops short of ensuring real freedom of contract for those individuals who have gained such access, the internal market-oriented freedom of contract in EU contract law tends to ensure that weaker parties have a fair chance to participate in the single market. In so doing, however, the marketised freedom of contract in EU contract law cannot be equated with the substantive freedom of contract as it has developed in the national legal systems. Although EU contract law does afford some protections to consumers that could help the latter in maximizing their freedom of contract, it views consumer protection not as an end in itself but as a means for completing the internal market. Therefore, the logic of internal market-oriented freedom of contract and the logic of substantive freedom of contract may not only mutually reinforce each other but at times also clash with each other. An example of the conflict between the two philosophies is provided by the full harmonisation EU measures in the field of contract law, such as the Consumer Credit Directive,[36] that generally preclude Member States from maintaining or adopting stricter rules than those contained therein, over-emphasizing market integration over consumer protection.

[35] On this development in more detail, see Cherednychenko 2014a.

[36] Directive 2008/48/EC, *OJEU* 2008 L 133/66.

12.3 Freedom of Contract in EU Free Movement Law

12.3.1 The Effect of Fundamental Freedoms in Private Law Relationships

Apart from secondary EU legislation, the sphere of freedom of contract is also affected by EU free movement law. It is undisputed today that fundamental freedoms can have far-reaching implications for the relationships between private parties. Whilst it goes beyond the scope of this contribution to provide an exhaustive overview of case law on this subject, two ways in which fundamental freedoms can affect private law relationships deserve special mention in this context.[37]

Firstly, the application of fundamental freedoms in the realm of contract law can be triggered by the acts of the Member States' public authorities with relevance to contracts. Thus, the case law of the CJEU concerning free movements often involves contractual disputes in which a private party from one Member State seeks access to the market of another Member State which is barred by national regulation.[38] The latter may, for instance, prohibit the conclusion of contracts for certain forms of service or make it conditional upon compliance with certain requirements. The issue before the CJEU in such disputes is normally whether a contract-related restriction imposed by a national public authority on the exercise of a fundamental freedom can be justified on the grounds of public policy, public security or public health. These cases formally involve the acts of public authorities and hence the vertical effect of fundamental freedoms between citizens and EU Member States. In practical terms, however, they are also about the indirect horizontal effect of free movement rights between the private parties affected by such acts.

In addition, the exercise of fundamental freedoms can be affected by private parties. The acts of a private party in one Member State can pose obstacles to the exercise of free movement rights by a private party in another Member State, prompting the latter to seek judicial protection. Two concepts have been adopted by the CJEU to respond to this type of situations: 'direct horizontal effect' and 'positive obligations'. The direct horizontal effect of fundamental freedoms implies that private parties are bound by such freedoms in the same way as the Member States and hence can directly invoke them in a dispute between each other. In private law terms this implies that a contract which is contrary to a fundamental freedom van be declared void and or an obligation to pay damages can arise. Over the years, the CJEU has progressively expanded the reach of direct horizontal effect with respect to fundamental freedoms. Whilst the direct horizontal effect was initially limited to the free movement of persons, the freedom to provide services, and the freedom of

---

[37] For an overview, see, for example, Davies 2012, 2013; Schepel 2012.

[38] See, for example, Case C-36/02, *Omega*, ECLI:EU:C:2004:614.

establishment, in the *Fra.bo* case, it was possibly even extended to the free movement of goods.[39]

Given the far-reaching effects of free movement rights in private law relationships, how do these economic freedoms influence the sphere of freedom of contract when providing (financial) services? Does EU free movement law reinforce the notions of freedom of contract underpinning the national legal systems or support the idea of regulated freedom of contract embodied in EU secondary legislation? Alternatively, does it impose its own conception of freedom of contract? As we will see in the following, the case law of the CJEU reveals an uneasy relationship between fundamental freedoms and freedom of contract.

12.3.2 Fundamental Freedoms: Protecting Unregulated Freedom of Contract with an Interstate Element

At first sight, the application of fundamental freedoms to Member State restrictions on free movement can easily be understood in terms of promoting freedom of contract.[40] Indeed, such restrictions interfere with the contractual choices and preferences of private parties and thus constitute state intervention into the domain of freedom of contract. However, a closer look at the application of free movement rights to the acts of public authorities in the contractual sphere reveals that fundamental freedoms protect private initiative and freedom of contract with an *interstate element*, i.e. in relation to cross-border contract or domestic contracts to which one party is foreign.[41] The freedom of contract protected by fundamental freedoms cannot therefore be equated with any national concept of freedom of contract.

A typical situation that may trigger the application of fundamental freedoms to Member State measures affecting the cross-border provision of services is illustrated by the *Omega* case. The German police authority issued an order against the German company Omega forbidding it from exploiting a 'killing game'. For manufacturing this game Omega had co-operated with the British Company Pulsar Advanced Games Systems Ltd. Omega challenged the compatibility of the prohibition order issued against it with the fundamental freedom to provide services. Although the *Omega* case arose in the administrative law context, restrictions on the

[39] Case C-171/11, *Fra.bo*, ECLI:EU:C:2012:453. On the free movement of persons, see for example, Case C-415/93, *Bosman*, ECLI:EU:C:1995:463; Case C-281/98, *Angonese*, ECLI:EU:C:2000:296; on the freedom to provide services, see for example, Case 36/74, *Walrave*, ECLI:EU:C:1974:140; Case C 341/05, *Laval*, ECLI:EU:C:2007:809; on the freedom of establishment see for example Case C-309/99, *Wouters*, ECLI:EU:C:2002:98; Case C-438/05, *Viking*, ECLI:EU:C:2007:772.

[40] See Davies 2013, p. 55.

[41] Cf. Davies 2012, p. 810.

conclusion of interstate service contracts may also be imposed in the contract law context.

Consider the following hypothetical example. In the absence of specific EU secondary legislation to this effect, a financial supervisory authority of one Member State issues a prohibition to bring a certain highly risky consumer credit product manufactured in another Member State on the market within its jurisdiction. The product is banned because it is designed for particularly vulnerable consumers with limited financial resources, while in 90% of the cases the purchase of that product is likely to result in loan default. Such a scenario is not unrealistic given that in the wake of the recent financial crisis some national financial regulators were granted powers to ban dangerous credit products under the newly introduced product intervention regimes.[42] The UK Financial Conduct Authority, for example, has already used such powers to prohibit the so-called 'non-income verified mortgages' that were marketed by lenders as products where evidence of income would not be required.[43] What is notable about our example is that the credit product ban restricts the free movement of services guaranteed by Article 56 of the TFEU and, unless justified on public policy grounds, could be struck down by the CJEU as being contrary to EU law.

As this example shows, the freedom to provide services fosters unregulated freedom of contract in the cross-border context. As such, it may have de-regulatory effects on national laws, supporting the formal understanding of freedom of contract and undermining the efforts aimed at promoting the idea of substantive freedom of contract. What is more, the concept of unregulated freedom of contract underpinning the application of the free movement of services to state measures may be out of touch with the model of regulated freedom of contract enshrined in EU secondary legislation in the field of contract law. Like EU free movement law, EU contract law is also strongly oriented towards the establishment of the internal market. However, in contrast to EU free movement law, it does impose significant restrictions on freedom of contract that generally apply in both cross-border and purely domestic situations. In fact, as has already been mentioned above, the EU financial regulation adopted post-crisis granted the product intervention powers to national and European financial supervisory authorities in a number of areas. Apart from investment products, these include, *inter alia*, mortgages and payment accounts.[44]

The application of fundamental freedoms to the acts of private parties reflects a similar model to that of their application to the acts of public authorities. The primary good protected by the direct horizontal effect of free movements is the unregulated freedom of contract with an interstate element. The CJEU has extended

[42] On this in more detail, see Cherednychenko 2014b, pp. 416 et seq.

[43] Financial Services Authority, Mortgage Market Review: Responsible Lending, Chapter 3, para 3.3; Chapter 2.

[44] See European Banking Authority, Guidelines on product oversight and governance arrangements for retail banking products, Final Report, EBA/GL/2015/18, p. 11.

the scope of the free movements to horizontal relationships based on the principle of effectiveness ('*effet utile*') of EU law. The (in)famous judgement of the CJEU in *Laval* provides a striking illustration of the Court's conceptualisation of freedom of contract in the context of the free movement of services.

Laval was a Latvian company that posted Latvian workers to Sweden to work on building sites operated by a Swedish construction company. The Latvian workers earned 40% less than their Swedish counterparts. Swedish trade unions undertook collective action in order to force Laval to sign a collective agreement guaranteeing certain levels of pay to the posted workers but it refused. Having reiterated the *Viking* principles, the CJEU held that this restriction on the freedom to provide services could not be justified because it went far beyond what was allowed by Directive 96/71 on the employment of posted workers. The following considerations of the Court are particularly notable in the present context:

> [C]ompliance with Article 49 EC [now Article 56 TFEU; OOC] is also required in the case of rules which are not public in nature but which are designed to regulate, collectively, the provision of services. The abolition, as between Member States, of obstacles to the freedom to provide services would be compromised if the abolition of State barriers could be neutralised by obstacles resulting from the exercise of their legal autonomy by associations or organisations not governed by public law […] In the case in the main proceedings, it must be pointed out that the right of trade unions of a Member State to take collective action by which undertakings established in other Member States may be forced to sign the collective agreement for the building sector — certain terms of which depart from the legislative provisions and establish more favourable terms and conditions of employment as regards the matters referred to in Article 3(1), first subparagraph, (a) to (g) of Directive 96/71 and others relate to matters not referred to in that provision — is liable to make it less attractive, or more difficult, for such undertakings to carry out construction work in Sweden, and therefore constitutes a restriction on the freedom to provide services within the meaning of Article 49 EC.[45]

The CJEU's reasoning makes it clear that the direct horizontal effect of the free movement of services enables private parties to conclude interstate service contracts in the internal market without being hindered therein by other private parties exercising their legal autonomy under the national law of a particular Member State. The concept of unregulated freedom of contract with an interstate element that underpins the direct application of the freedom to provide services to the acts of private parties is thus in fundamental conflict with the classical idea of freedom of contract grounded in the ethical-societal conception of national private laws as the laws that primarily focus on the individual and justice between the parties.

The question that arises in this context is how far the direct horizontal effect of the freedom to provide services actually extends in the domain of freedom of contract protected by the national private laws of the Member States. For example, would it be contrary to EU free movement law if a bank established in one Member

---

[45] Case C 341/05, *Laval*, ECLI:EU:C:2007:809, paras 98–99. See also Case 36/74, *Walrave*, ECLI:EU:C:1974:140, paras 17 and 18; Case C-415/93, *Bosman*, ECLI:EU:C:1995:463, paras 83 and 84; Case C-309/99, *Wouters*, ECLI:EU:C:2001:390, para 120.

State refused mortgages to consumers wishing to buy properties in other Member States or, more generally, to consumers from other Member States?

At present, the case law of the CJEU does not provide an unequivocal answer to this question. So far the Court has not applied the freedom to provide services directly to discriminatory conduct of a private party providing services to the general public. However, it granted direct horizontal effect in a similar context to the free movement of workers in *Angonese*.[46] In this case, a private banking undertaking required that prospective employees should provide a certificate to be issued by the public authorities of Bolzano in order to prove their linguistic knowledge. The Court held that Article 39 EC (now Article 45 TFEU) 'precludes an employer from requiring persons applying to take part in a recruitment competition to provide evidence of their linguistic knowledge exclusively by means of one particular diploma issued only in one particular province of a Member State'.[47]

Moreover, in his conclusion in *Viking,* Advocate General Maduro argued that 'the rules on free movement apply directly to any private action that is capable of effectively restricting others from exercising their right of freedom of movement'.[48] According to Schepel, this statement provides a good summary of the law as it stands, given that all attempts to limit the reach of the direct horizontal effect so far have been undermined by the CJEU.[49]

It is not excluded, therefore, that the direct horizontal effect of the freedom to provide services potentially encompasses not only third party interventions, like that of trade unions in *Laval*, hindering the conclusion of service contracts between two other parties, but also discriminatory conduct of (financial) service providers, like that of banks, viz-à-viz potential customers. It remains to be seen whether the CJEU will go that far. In any case, it is clear that the extension of direct horizontal effect to such a sensitive area would imply a profound encroachment upon freedom of contract in the national legal systems.

12.3.3 Fundamental Rights: A Different Dimension to the Concept of Freedom of Contract in Free Movement Law?

The above analysis has shown that the unregulated freedom of contract with an interstate element promoted by the vertical and horizontal effect of fundamental freedoms may significantly interfere with the classical idea of freedom of contract enshrined in the national contract laws of the Member States. In particular, the

[46] Case C-281/98, *Angonese*, ECLI:EU:C:2000:296.

[47] Case C-281/98, *Angonese*, ECLI:EU:C:2000:296, para 46.

[48] Opinion of Advocate General Maduro in Case C-438/05, *Viking*, ECLI:EU:C:2007:292, para 43.

[49] Schepel 2013, pp. 1213–1214.

application of free movement rights to national restrictions on the conclusion of (financial) service contracts could impair the realization of the idea of substantive freedom of contract. Moreover, at times it may be out of touch with the concept of regulated freedom of contract reflected in EU secondary legislation in the field of contract law. Recourse to traditional justification grounds for limiting free movement rights, such as public policy, public security or public health, alone may not be enough to prompt a move away from the strong market rationale in free movement law. This holds particularly true when it comes to the direct application of fundamental freedoms to the acts of private parties. Despite the CJEU's famous pronouncement in *Bosman* that 'there is nothing to preclude individuals from relying on justifications on grounds of public policy, public security or public health',[50] it is highly doubtful that individuals will be able to do so with some degree of success. The promotion of unregulated freedom of contract with an interstate element may therefore come at a heavy price for personal freedom.

At the same time, it has been increasingly recognized that the restrictions on economic freedoms can be justified with a view to protecting fundamental rights.[51] Given the growing relevance of fundamental rights in the context of free movement law, the question arises whether recourse to the EUCFR could make a difference in terms of strengthening the relative importance of the well-established concepts of freedom of contract in the national legal systems and EU contract law. In particular, what notion of freedom of contract is protected by the freedom to conduct a business that was initially recognized as a general principle of Community law and is now enshrined in Article 16 EUCFR? Can resort to this and other fundamental rights lead to a reorientation of a profoundly functional understanding of freedom of contract in free movement law aimed at maximising the effectiveness of economic freedoms?

A good starting point for this investigation is to have a look at the interpretation of the freedom to conduct a business provided by the CJEU in its recent case law. According to the Court in *Sky Österreich*:

> The protection afforded by Article 16 of the Charter covers the freedom to exercise an economic or commercial activity, the freedom of contract and free competition, as is apparent from the explanations relating to that article, which, in accordance with the third subparagraph of Article 6(1) TEU and Article 52(7) of the Charter, have to be taken into consideration for the interpretation of the Charter. […] In addition, the freedom of contract includes, in particular, the freedom to choose with whom to do business […], and the freedom to determine the price of a service […].[52]

The Court's reasoning appears to suggest that the freedom of contract protected by Article 16 EUCFR largely corresponds to the traditional conception of freedom of contract adopted in the national contract laws of the Member States. Notably, the

[50] Case C-415/93, *Bosman*, ECLI:EU:C:1995:463, para 85.

[51] See, for example, Cherednychenko 2006; Morijn 2006; De Vries 2013; Schepel 2013.

[52] Case 283/11, *Sky Österreich*, ECLI:EU:C:2013:28, paras 42–43. See also Case 426/11, *Alemo-Herron*, ECLI:EU:C:2013:521, para 32.

Court explicitly recognizes that the freedom to choose with whom to do business and the freedom to determine the price of a service fall within the scope of the freedom to conduct a business. In this way, the conventional understanding of freedom of contract as a manifestation of party autonomy in national legal systems seems to be elevated to the status of an EU fundamental right that could serve as a legitimate aim for limiting the reach of free movement rights in the contract law domain. If this understanding of the Court's interpretation of Article 16 EUCFR is correct, the bank from one Member State could invoke this fundamental right as a defence against the claim of a private individual from another Member State arising from the bank's refusal to conclude a mortgage contract with him or her contrary to the free movement of services enshrined in Article 56 TFEU.

In light of the CJEU's pronouncements in *Viking* and *Laval*, the success of this defence, however, will depend on the outcome of a 'balancing test' to be conducted by the Court in which it will consider whether the exercise of the fundamental right can justify a restriction on the exercise of the fundamental freedom. As the CJEU's controversial judgement in *Laval* shows, the fundamental rights considerations may not always outweigh the freedom to provide services under the justification regime. As is well-known, in that case the Court ruled that the freedom to provide services precludes a trade union acting in the exercise of its fundamental right to take collective action to force a provider of services established in another Member State to sign a collective agreement. The inclusion of the freedom of contract as a fundamental right in the category of 'legitimate interests' capable of justifying restrictions on the fundamental freedom to provide services thus does not guarantee its prevalence in each case. Particularly in such sensitive horizontal cases, a more comprehensive 'double' proportionality test, as developed by Advocate General in her opinion in *Commission* v. *Germany*,[53] could offer a better solution than a simple 'balancing test'.[54] The essence of the 'double' proportionality is that the restriction of free movement rights *and* the restriction of fundamental rights are legitimate as long as they pass the proportionality test:

> A fair balance between fundamental rights and fundamental freedoms is ensured in the case of a conflict only when the restriction by a fundamental right on a fundamental freedom is not permitted to go beyond what is appropriate, necessary and reasonable to realise that fundamental right. Conversely, however, nor may the restriction on a fundamental right by a fundamental freedom go beyond what is appropriate, necessary and reasonable to realise the fundamental freedom.[55]

Whilst resort to the freedom to conduct a business in free movement law has the potential to promote a traditional national concept of freedom of contract

---

[53] Opinion of Advocate General Trstenjak in Case C-271/08, *Commission v. Germany*, ECLI:EU:C:2010:183.

[54] Cf. Opinion of Advocate General Trstenjak, in Case C-171/11, *Fra.bo*, ECLI:EU:C:2012:176, where she suggests extending the application of the 'double' proportionality test to horizontal situations.

[55] Opinion of Advocate General Trstenjak in C-271/08, *Commission v. Germany*, ECLI:EU:C:2010:183, para 190.

understood in a more formal sense,[56] recourse to other fundamental rights may provide support for the idea of substantive freedom of contract. In fact, the *Omega* case provides support for this assumption. As the CJEU's judgement in this case shows, the obligation of the EU and Member State public authorities to interpret and apply public policy exceptions to the free movement of services guaranteed by Article 56 of the TFEU in the light of EU fundamental rights may enable the Member States to justify their derogations from this economic freedom and thus defend the idea of substantive freedom of contract.

In order to illustrate this point, let me further develop the hypothetical case involving the consumer credit product ban introduced in the previous section. As mentioned above, let us assume that this ban restricts the free movement of services guaranteed by Article 56 of the TFEU. In order to justify this restriction, however, the financial supervisory authority argues that bringing the given credit product on the consumer market in its Member State would be contrary to the principle of consumer protection enshrined in Article 38 of the EUCFR. Interpreting and applying the public policy exception in the light of this principle could then lead to the conclusion that the prohibition of the financial product in question cannot be regarded as a measure that unjustifiably undermines the freedom to provide services.[57]

Thus, in light of the judgment of the CJEU in *Omega*, it seems plausible to argue that the obligations of the EU and Member State public authorities to interpret and apply EU law in the light of the EUCFR have some potential to reinforce the idea of substantive freedom of contract at national level. In this way, recourse to the EUCFR could also bring free movement law closer to the concept of regulated freedom of contract embodied in EU contract law, particularly in the area of financial services. It remains to be seen, however, to what extent this potential will be realized. In any case, the possibility of invoking the EUCFR in order to justify the national prohibitions of certain consumer credit products does not mean that such bans will always be upheld by the CJEU. Whilst the Court recognizes that the protection of EU fundamental rights is a legitimate interest which, in principle, justifies a restriction on the freedom to provide services on public policy grounds, it also requires that measures which restrict this freedom are necessary for the protection of the interests which they are intended to guarantee and that those objectives cannot be attained by less restrictive measures.[58] Moreover, it can be questioned to what extent this test is particularly well suited for the protection of fundamental rights given the supremacy of market concerns over non-market values implied therein.[59] The above mentioned 'double proportionality' test might be better equipped to serve this purpose. At the same time, it should be noted that judicial activism in the area of financial product intervention involves significant

[56] Cf. Case 426/11, *Alemo-Herron*, ECLI:EU:C:2013:521.

[57] Cf. Schwintowski 2015.

[58] See, for example, Case C-36/02, *Omega*, ECLI:EU:C:2004:614, para 36.

[59] Cf. Morijn 2006.

risks, given the difficulties involved in regulating consumer financial products, and consumer markets more generally, and the lack of experience as to how to address this complexity on the basis of broadly formulated fundamental freedoms and rights.[60]

12.4 Concluding Remarks

In this contribution, I have sought to determine the reach of EU free movement in the contractual sphere, with a particular focus on (financial) services. Building upon the concept of 'formal' freedom of contract and that of 'substantive' freedom of contract in the national contract laws of the Member States, as well as the notion of the freedom of contract regulated in the name of the internal market in EU secondary legislation, I have explored the conceptualisation of freedom of contract in free movement law. Particular attention in this context has been given to the interplay between fundamental economic freedoms and EU fundamental rights.

The analysis has revealed an uneasy relationship between the national concepts of formal and substantive freedom of contract and the idea of unregulated freedom of contract with an interstate element promoted by the vertical and horizontal application of the economic freedom to provide services. Moreover, a manifestly functional conception of freedom of contract pursued by the CJEU in free movement law with a view to maximising the *effet utile* of economic freedoms may be out of touch with the model of regulated freedom of contract enshrined in EU secondary legislation.

Resort to fundamental rights, in particular the freedom to conduct a business and the principle of consumer protection enshrined, respectively, in Article 16 EUCFR and Article 38 EUCFR, has some potential to strengthen the relative importance of national concepts of freedom of contract in free movement law, leading to a more balanced approach to the application of economic freedoms. A balanced approach would recognize that freedom of contract in Europe has many faces and that there is a need for a harmonious coexistence of different ideas behind freedom of contract within a multi-level EU legal order.

However, the extent to which the fundamental right's potential to prompt a move away from a highly instrumentalist view of freedom of contract in free movement law will be realised largely depends on the CJEU's approach to balancing fundamental freedoms and fundamental rights against each other. In particular, the 'double' proportionality test whereby both the restriction of economic freedoms and the restriction of fundamental rights are legitimate as long as they pass the proportionality test deserves further exploration.

---

[60] On this, see, for example, Moloney 2010, pp. 142 et seq.

References

Bartl M (2015) Internal Market Rationality, Private Law and the Direction of the Union: Resuscitating the Market as the Object of the Political. European Law Journal 21:572–598
Bydlinki F (1996) System und Prinzipien des Privatrechts. Springer, Vienna/New York
Cherednychenko OO (2006) EU Fundamental Rights, EC Freedoms and Private Law. European Review of Private Law 14:23–61
Cherednychenko OO (2007) Fundamental Rights, Contract Law and the Protection of the Weaker Party: A Comparative Analysis of the Constitutionalisation of Contract Law, with Emphasis on Risky Financial Transactions. Sellier, Munich
Cherednychenko OO (2009) European Securities Regulation, Private Law and the Investment Firm-Client Relationship. European Review of Private Law 17:925–952
Cherednychenko OO (2014a) Public Supervision over Private Relationships: Towards European Supervision Private Law. European Review of Private Law 22:37–67
Cherednychenko OO (2014b) Freedom of Contract in the Post-Crisis Era: Quo Vadis? European Review of Contract Law 10:390–421
Cherednychenko OO, Reich N (2015) The Constitutionalization of European Private Law: Gateways, Constraints, and Challenges. European Review of Private Law 23:797–827
Collins H (1999) Regulating Contracts. Oxford University Press, Oxford
Collins H (2009) Governance Implications for the European Union of the Changing Character of Private Law. In: Cafaggi F, Muir-Watt H (eds) Making of European Private Law: Governance Design. Edward Elgar, Cheltenham/Northampton, pp 269–288
Colombi Ciacchi A (2010) Party Autonomy as a Fundamental Right in the European Union. European Review of Contract Law 6:303–318
Davies G (2012) Freedom of Movement, Horizontal Effect, and Freedom of Contract. European Review of Private Law 20:805–827
Davies G (2013) Freedom of Contract and the Horizontal Effect of Free Movement Law. In: Leczykiewicz D, Weatherill S (eds) The Involvement of EU Law in Private Law Relationships. Hart Publishing, Oxford, pp 53–69
de Vries SA (2013) Balancing Fundamental Rights with Economic Freedoms According to the European Court of Justice. Utrecht Law Review 9:169–192
Grundmann S (2011) The Future of Contract Law. European Review of Contract Law 7:490–527
Hartkamp A (2010) The Effect of the EC Treaty in Private Law: On Direct and Indirect Horizontal Effects of Primary Community Law. European Review of Private Law 18:527–548
Hesselink M (2007) European Contract Law: A Matter of Consumer Protection, Citizenship, or Justice? European Review of Private Law 15:323–348
Hondius E (1999) Bescherming van de zwakkere als nieuw paradigma in het privaatrecht. In: Hartlief T, Stolker CJJM (eds) Contractvrijheid. Kluwer, Deventer, pp 387–393
Kennedy D (2006) Three Globalizations of Law and Legal Thought: 1850–2000. In: Trubek DM, Santos A (eds) The New Law and Economic Development: A Critical Appraisal. Cambridge University Press, Cambridge, pp 19–73
Leczykiewicz D, Weatherill S (2013) Private Law Relationships and EU Law. In: Leczykiewicz D, Weatherill S (eds) The Involvement of EU Law in Private Law Relationships. Hart Publishing, Oxford, pp 1–8
Lurger B (2011) Grundfragen der Vereinheitlichung des Verstragsrechts in der Europäischen Union. Springer, Vienna
Lurger B (2011) The 'Social' Side of Contract Law and the New Principle of Regard and Fairness. In: Hartkamp AS, Hesselink MW, Hondius EH, Mak C, du Perron CE (eds) Towards a European Civil Code. Kluwer Law International, Nijmegen, pp 353–386
Mak C (2016) Free Movement and Contract Law. In: Twigg-Flesner C (ed) Research Handbook on EU Consumer and Contract Law. Edward Elgar, Cheltenham/Northampton, pp 182–196
Micklitz H-W (2005) The Concept of Competitive Contract Law. Penn State International Law Review 23:549–585

Micklitz H-W (2009) The Visible Hand of European Regulatory Private Law. The Transformation of European Private Law from Autonomy to Functionalism in Competition and Regulation. Yearbook of European Law 28:3–59
Micklitz H-W (2011) Introduction – Social Justice and Access Justice in Private Law. In: Micklitz H-W (ed) The Many Concepts of Social Justice in European Private Law. Edward Elgar, Cheltenham/Northampton, pp 3–57
Micklitz H-W (2015a) On the Intellectual History of Freedom of Contract and Regulation. Penn State Journal of Law & International Affairs 4:1–32
Micklitz H-W (2015b) The Constitutional Transformation of Private Law Pillars through the ECJ. Unpublished paper presented at the annual conference of the Society of European Contract Law (SECOLA) on 'The Charter and European Contract Law', Oxford, 25–26 June 2015 (on file with the author)
Moloney N (2010) How to Protect Investors: Lessons from the EC and the UK. Cambridge University Press, Cambridge
Morijn J (2006) Balancing Fundamental Rights and Common Market Freedoms in Union Law: Schmidberger and Omega in the Light of the European Constitution. European Law Journal 12:15–40
Rutgers J W (2009) The European Economic Constitution, Freedom of Contract and the DCFR. European Review of Contract Law 5:95–108
Schepel H (2012) Constitutionalising the Market, Marketising the Constitution, and to Tell the Difference: On the Horizontal Application of the Free Movement Provisions in EU Law. European Law Journal 18:177–200
Schepel S (2013) Freedom of Contract in EU Free Movement Law: Balancing Rights and Principles in European Public and Private Law. European Review of Private Law 21:1211–1230
Schmid C U (2005) The Instrumentalist Conception of the Acquis Communautaire in Consumer Law and its Implications on a European Contract Law Code. European Review of Contract Law 1:211–227
Schmid C U (2011) The Thesis of the Instrumentalisation of Private Law by the EU in a Nutshell. In: Joerges C, Ralli T (eds) European Constitutionalism without Private Law. Private Law without Democracy. Joseph Beuys/Bono, Oslo, pp 7–35
Schwintowski H-P (2015) Standardisation – Prior or Instead of Information – A Fundamental Criticism of the European Information Model for Financial and Insurance Products. In: Purnhagen K, Rott P (eds) Varieties of European Economic Law and Regulation: Liber Amicorum for Hans Micklitz. Springer, New York/Heidelberg/Dordrecht, pp 549–567
Weatherill S (2013) The Elusive Character of Private Autonomy in EU Law. In: Leczykiewicz D, Weatherill S (eds) The Involvement of EU Law in Private Law Relationships. Hart Publishing, Oxford, pp 9–27
Weber M (1992) Economy and Society. University of California Press, Berkeley/Los Angeles

Chapter 13
The Charter of Fundamental Rights and the Reach of Free Movement Law

Filippo Fontanelli and Amedeo Arena

Abstract This chapter discusses two underrated and connected aspects that determine the applicability of the Charter in the area of the market freedoms. First, the Charter can be a decisive standard of review for domestic measures only when they are covered by EU law but are not precluded by it. In this respect, the distinction between non-preclusion and non-application of EU law is overlooked in the case law and in the scholarship. Second, because the applications of EU law and the Charter are aligned, the latter suffers from the uncertainties of the former. This chapter concludes that the entry into force of the Charter has exposed the blurred contours of the application of EU law, in particular in the area of the market freedoms.

Keywords Market freedoms · Federalising effect · Charter of Fundamental Rights of the EU · Court of Justice · Application of EU law · Article 51 of the Charter · Jurisdiction of the Court of Justice

Contents

13.1 Introduction 294
13.2 Non-Covered Measures and the Application of EU Law 295
13.3 Non-Precluded Measures 299

The work is the outcome of both authors' collaboration. Amedeo Arena drafted Sects. 13.1–13.3, Filippo Fontanelli drafted Sects. 13.4–13.7.

F. Fontanelli (✉)
University of Edinburgh, Edinburgh, UK
e-mail: filippo.fontanelli@ed.ac.uk

A. Arena
Università degli Studi di Napoli "Federico II", Naples, Italy
e-mail: a.arena@unina.it

M. Andenas et al. (eds.), *The Reach of Free Movement*,
DOI 10.1007/978-94-6265-195-1_13

13.4 The Blurred Line Between Non-Preclusion and Non-Application ... 301
13.5 The Scope of Application of EU Law in the Common Market ... 304
13.6 An Unintended Federalising Effect ... 308
13.7 Conclusions ... 310
References ... 312

13.1 Introduction

The Charter of Fundamental Rights of the European Union (the Charter) does not apply to State measures when no other rule of EU law applies to them, including the rules on free movement. The Twitter version of this chapter, therefore, would read '*The Charter neither restricts nor enlarges the application to domestic measures of EU law rules, including the rules on the market freedoms*'. Nevertheless, it is worth observing how this symbiotic relation between the Charter and EU law—the *Fransson*-equivalence, as it were—works out in practice.[1] The claim we make is obvious, but its importance is underrated: When the scope of application of EU law has imprecise boundaries, so has the Charter, and this happens frequently when the EU law at stake is the law of the internal market. Whereas the uncertainty mostly resolves itself (domestic measures are either prohibited by EU law or are not, regardless of whether they are allowed or just not contemplated), in certain cases it has consequential effects: these are the cases of non-preclusion.

One of the central points of this chapter is the underrated importance of non-precluded measures. More precisely, it is argued that State measures that are not precluded by EU law are the springboard of the federalising effects of the Charter. It is important to delineate the category of non-precluded measures accurately, before expanding on its implications.[2] To assess the impact of the Charter on the four freedoms, it is indispensable to observe the application of EU law to domestic measures at large. This is intentional: as it is explained below, the application of the Charter and the application of EU law go hand in hand. This alignment carries within a simplification (the Charter's application overlaps with the application of EU law) and a complication (the scope of application of EU law is uncertain).

The question of State acts' compliance with EU law is normally fashioned as a binary determination. Either a State act breaches EU law, and is therefore unlawful, or it does not, and is therefore lawful. For instance, Article 34 TFEU prohibits national measures which restrict the imports of goods from other Member States.

---

[1] The *Fransson* equivalence dictates that the scope of application of EU law and the Charter to State measures is the same, *ratione materiae*. Whereas (then) President Skouris praised the *Fransson*-equivalence, it arguably creates more problems than it solves. See, respectively, Skouris 2013 and Fontanelli 2013.

[2] The importance of non-precluded measures under the Charter is discussed in Fontanelli 2014.

These measures are therefore unlawful: domestic courts are required to set them aside.[3] Conversely, Article 34 TFEU does not preclude quantitative restrictions on imports justified on grounds of public security, nor does it prohibit measures that do not entail a quantitative restriction.[4] These measures are therefore lawful, as a matter of EU law, and will apply.

However, the dichotomy is somewhat simplistic because it obfuscates a further distinction. A prohibition of door-step-selling of jewellery, which does not restrict cross-border trade in goods, is simply *not covered* by Article 34 TFEU.[5] On the contrary, a ban on equipment increasing the power of mopeds which seeks to protect human health is covered, but *not precluded*, by the same provision.[6] The former measure lies outside the scope of EU law altogether, whilst the latter falls within the scope of EU law, but does not breach it. The two categories of non-covered and non-precluded measure deserve separate treatment.

This chapter observes, in succession, the received knowledge regarding State measures that fall outside the scope of EU law (Sect. 13.2) and State measures that fall under EU law, but are not precluded by it (Sect. 13.3). It then maps the blurred division between such categories (Sect. 13.4), to identify the problems that, in turn, affect the reach of market freedoms and the Charter at once (Sect. 13.5). One of the striking effects of this theoretical blur is that, ultimately, State authorities might choose to follow the Charter just out of precaution (Sect. 13.6).

Our main conclusion is that this theoretical uncertainty is lamentable, and that one of the unintended effects of the Charter's growing application is that the Court of Justice of the EU (the Court) has gradually come under an enormous pressure to address the long-ignored problem of the precise application of EU law to domestic measures.

13.2 Non-Covered Measures and the Application of EU Law

Non-covered measures are those measures that do not breach EU law because they do not fall under its reach in the first place. Their identification implicates knowing the contours of the application of EU law. However, whether EU law applies to a specific State measure is a question that often cannot be answered with certainty.

Obviously, the scope of application of EU is a function of the extent of the EU's competences. However, whether the EU has competence over certain matters is a poor predictor of whether a certain matter of domestic law will fall under EU law. First, the exact boundaries of the competences listed in Articles 3–6 TFEU are

[3] TFEU, Article 34.

[4] TFEU, Article 36.

[5] Case C-441/04, *A-Punkt Schmuckhandels*, ECLI:EU:C:2006:141.

[6] Case C-142/09, *Lahousse and Lavichy*, ECLI:EU:C:2010:694.

difficult to draw *in abstracto*.[7] The 'internal market', in particular, is more a goal than a specific subject matter. Second, a measure may fall within an area where the EU has a non-exclusive competence to enact legislation, but has not yet done so. In such scenario, unless the national measure is in breach of obligations laid down in the Treaties, the *existence* of EU competences does not warrant the inference that the measure falls within the scope of EU law.[8] Third, and conversely, the *absence* of EU competences in the area regulated by the national measure is no guarantee that such a measure lies beyond the reach of EU law. While in principle Member States are free to legislate in areas where the Treaties have not conferred competences upon the Union, they still cannot exercise those competences in a manner inconsistent with EU law.[9]

The latter scenario arises regularly in the operation of the market freedoms. Market freedoms are constructed negatively: Member States are required not to breach them, but do not point specifically to any course of action. Whereas Union legislation promotes positive integration of the internal market through the approximation of domestic laws, the market freedoms as protected in the Treaties reflect a model of negative integration. Under the Treaty provisions on the four freedoms, States are not asked to adopt specific conduct, but are enjoined from raising trade obstacles, irrespective of what matter they might be regulating. The principle of conferral, which delineates the outer limits of EU competence, cannot restrain the reach of the EU market freedoms *ratione materiae*.

To determine whether a certain domestic measure falls under the TFEU free movement provisions, the Court established, among others, a test that does not rely on the attribution of competences but on the factual matrix of the situation at hand.[10] This is the test of 'purely internal situations'. It relates to the practical

---

[7] For instance, legal commentators have highlighted the difficulty in determining the exact boundaries of the EU exclusive competence in the area of the 'establish[ment] of the competition rules necessary for the functioning of the internal market' as per Article 3(1)(b) TFEU. See, for instance, Dashwood 2004, p. 371 (arguing that such definition is inaccurate); Mastroianni 2005, p. 398 (noting that the above definition adopts the pre-Lisbon teleological approach to the vertical division of powers); Schütze 2008, p. 717 (arguing that the drafters have fallen victim to an 'ontological fallacy' insofar as the category of 'rules necessary for the functioning of the internal market' does 'not, by definition, require the exclusion of all national action within their scope').

[8] See Case C-198/13, *Julian Hernández and Others*, ECLI:EU:C:2014:2055, para 36 ('the mere fact that a national measure comes within an area in which the European Union has powers cannot bring it within the scope of EU law'). See also Joined Cases C-483/09 and C-1/10, *Gueye and Salmerón Sánchez*, ECLI:EU:C:2011:583, paras 55, 69 and 70; and Case C-370/12, *Pringle*, ECLI:EU:C:2012:756, paras 104–105, 180–181.

[9] See Case C-348/96, *Calfa*, ECLI:EU:C:1999:6, para 17 ('Although in principle criminal legislation is a matter for which the Member States are responsible, the Court has consistently held that Community law sets certain limits to their power, and such legislation may not restrict the fundamental freedoms guaranteed by Community law'). See also Case 186/87, *Cowan*, ECLI:EU:C:1989:47, para 19; Case 203/80, *Casati*, ECLI:EU:C:1981:261 para 27.

[10] That test is firmly grounded in the wording of several TFEU provisions in the area of internal market: Articles 30 and 34 TFEU prohibit custom duties and quantitative restrictions in trade 'between Member States'; Article 45(1) TFEU, concerning the free movement of workers,

coordinates of the case (the conduct, the nationality of the persons affected, the location of the interests involved). It is not a sophisticated legal test but it is founded on a plausible assumption: when there is no trans-border element to a factual scenario, it can be presumed that EU law does not apply to it.[11] The same remarks apply, in essence, to the exercise of citizenship rights—a field where the 'purely internal situation' test has often been the only relatively reliable device to police the interplay between EU and domestic law.

Cases like *Rottman*, *Viking*, *Wittgenstein* and *Pfleger* illustrate very well the grasp of EU market freedoms and citizenship rights over matters where the Treaties did not confer any competence on the EU.[12] These cases arose in the application of rules governing the withdrawal of German citizenship, the UK regime of strike rights, the Austrian rules prohibiting the use of nobility titles, and Austrian criminal law punishing the use of unlicensed gambling machines. All these measures have at least one crucial aspect in common: they govern matters that, according to the principle of conferral, should rest with the Member States. Nonetheless, all these measures had an impact on the exercise of a market freedom or an EU citizenship right. As a result, these measures *fell under the scope of EU law* and some of them were ultimately *in breach thereof* (in *Wittgenstein*, the restriction to Article 21 TEFU rights was deemed proportionate). In all these cases the existence of a trans-border element (Mr. Rottman's previous Austrian citizenship, the trans-border operation of the Finnish ferry company, Ms. Wittgenstein's dealings with a non-Austrian administration, criminal prosecution of Czech individuals in Austrian courts) was a better predictor of the application of EU law than the principle of conferral. As Advocate General Spuznar put it, '… it is precisely when they are

(Footnote 10 continued)

expressly refers to 'nationality'; Article 49 TFEU, prohibiting restrictions on establishment 'by citizens of a Member States in the territory of another Member State'; Article 56 TFEU, in turn, prohibits restrictions on the freedom to provide services 'in respect of national of Member States who are established in a Member State other than that of the person for whom the services are intended'; finally, Article 69 TFEU prohibits restrictions on the movement of capital 'between Member States, as well as between Member States and third countries'.

[11] See Arena 2011, p. 207 (noting that the Court's 'traditional' approach to purely internal situations implies that the existence of a cross-border element in the case's factual matrix entails the presumption that the national measure has an impact on cross-border trade). See also Tryfonidou 2009, p. 200 ('Under this approach … if the goods that are involved in the facts have remained confined within the territory of one and the same Member Sate, the situation immediately qualifies as purely internal and this signifies the end of the enquiry as to a possible violation of Article 28 EC').

[12] Case C-135/08, *Rottmann*, ECLI:EU:C:2010:104; Case C-438/05, *Viking*, ECLI:EU:C:2007:772; Case C-208/09, *Sayn-Wittgenstein*, ECLI:EU:C:2010:806; Case C-390/12, *Pfleger and Others*, ECLI:EU:C:2014:281.

exercising their powers that the Member States must take care to ensure that EU law is not deprived of its effectiveness.'[13]

It might be tempting, then, to seek guidance as to the scope of EU law by looking at the boundaries of the jurisdiction of the Court of Justice in the context of the preliminary ruling procedure.[14] Indeed, the Court has repeatedly held that its task is not to give advisory opinions 'on general or hypothetical questions'[15] and, in particular, that it may refuse to provide a preliminary ruling if 'the interpretation of European Union law sought bears no relation to the actual facts of the main action'.[16]

However, that approach is theoretically flawed because, in the context of the preliminary ruling procedure, the Court's task is to rule on the interpretation (or validity) of EU law, not to its applicability in the main proceedings. It is thus no wonder that, according to settled case law, the Court leaves it to the referring court to determine 'both the need for a preliminary ruling in order to enable it to deliver judgment and the relevance of the questions which it submits to the Court.'[17]

Moreover, such a 'jurisdictional' criterion may yield false positives, i.e. situations where the Court provides a preliminary ruling although the situation at hand lies beyond the scope of EU law. In the context of the internal market the Court has on several occasions provided preliminary rulings on a provision of EU law that did not apply to the main proceedings, because they concerned purely internal situations. For instance, in *Dzodzi* the Court ruled on the interpretation of EU provisions that were 'made applicable' in the main proceedings by way of a reference contained in national provisions. The Court considered that it was 'manifestly in the interest of the Community legal order that, in order to forestall future differences of interpretation, every Community provision should be given a uniform interpretation irrespective of the circumstances in which it is to be applied'.[18] Likewise, in *Guimont*, the Court provided guidance on Article 34 TFEU even if the main proceedings concerned a purely internal situation, holding that a preliminary ruling can be useful when national law requires that a national producer enjoy the same rights as those enjoyed under EU law by a producer of another Member State in the same situation.[19]

By the same token, the criterion in question may yield false negatives, i.e. situations where the Court declines its jurisdiction to give a preliminary ruling in circumstances falling within the scope of EU law. For instance, the Court may

---

[13] Opinion in Case C-165/14, *Rendón Marín*, ECLI:EU:C:2016:675, para 113.

[14] See Case C-281/15, *Sahyouni*, ECLI:EU:C:2016:343, para 23 'It follows therefrom that neither the provisions of Regulation No. 1259/2010, referred to by the referring court, nor those of Regulation No. 2201/2003, nor any other legal act of the European Union applies to the dispute in the main proceedings'.

[15] Case C-212/04, *Adeneler and Others*, ECLI:EU:C:2006:443, para 42.

[16] Case C-238/05, *Asnef–Equifax*, ECLI:EU:C:2006:734, para 17.

[17] See for instance Case C-571/10, *Kamberaj*, ECLI:EU:C:2012:233, para 40.

[18] Cases C-297/88 and C-197/89, *Dzodzi*, ECLI:EU:C:1990:360, para 37.

[19] Case C-448/98, *Guimont*, ECLI:EU:C:2000:663, para 23.

refuse to answer a preliminary question if the referring court fails to define the factual and legislative context of the questions: in *Z.Ś. and Others,* the Court ruled that the request for a preliminary ruling on the interpretation of Article 8 of Regulation no. 561/2006 on road transport was inadmissible because the referring court did not specify what paragraph was the subject of its question and how the interpretation sought was necessary to resolve the dispute in the main proceedings.[20]

13.3 Non-Precluded Measures

Non-precluded measures are Member State measures which fall under the scope of EU law, but are in line the with the applicable EU provisions. These can occur in a number of situations, which are not mutually exclusive. A few examples can be mentioned, some of which are fairly obvious.

At the outset, the internal market fundamental freedoms envisage a number of express and implied derogations. National measures in accordance with those derogations are not precluded by EU law, but fall within its scope. Article 52(1) TFEU, for instance, provides that the right of establishment is no bar to national provisions granting special treatment for foreign nationals on grounds of public policy, public security or public health.[21] Moreover, the Court recognised a number of overriding reasons relating to the public interest that can serve as a justification for the introduction of indistinctly applicable restrictions at the national level.[22] By the same token, the Court acknowledged that Member States can take measures to prevent the abuse of the free movement provisions set out in the TFEU.[23]

---

[20] Case C-325/15, *Z.Ś. and Others*, ECLI:EU:C:2016:107, paras 32–33.

[21] See also the express derogations laid down in Article 36, 45(3), 62, and 65 TFEU.

[22] For a non-exhaustive list, see Case C-288/89, *Gouda*, ECLI:EU:C:1991:323, para 14: 'the overriding reasons relating to the public interest which the Court has already recognized include professional rules intended to protect recipients of the service (Joined Cases 110/78 and 111/78, *Van Wesemael*, ECLI:EU:C:1979:8, para 28); protection of intellectual property (Case 62/79, *Coditel*, ECLI:EU:C:1980:84); the protection of workers (Case 279/80, *Webb*, ECLI:EU:C:1981:314, para 19; Joined Cases 62/81 and 63/81, *Seco v EVI*, ECLI:EU:C:1982:34, para 14; Case 113/89, *Rush Portuguesa*, ECLI:EU:C:1990:142, para 18); consumer protection (Case 220/83, *Commission v France*, ECLI:EU:C:1986:461, para 20; Case 252/83, *Commission v Denmark*, ECLI:EU:C:1986:462, para 20; Case 205/84, *Commission v Germany*, ECLI:EU:C:1986:463, para 30; Case 206/84, *Commission v Ireland*, ECLI:EU:C:1986:464, para 20; *Commission v Italy*, cited above, para 20; and *Commission v Greece*, cited above, para 21), the conservation of the national historic and artistic heritage (*Commission v Italy*, cited above, para 20); turning to account the archaeological, historical and artistic heritage of a country and the widest possible dissemination of knowledge of the artistic and cultural heritage of a country (*Commission v France*, cited above, para 17, and *Commission v Greece*, cited above, para 21).'

[23] See, e.g., Case 33/74, *Van Binsbergen*, ECLI:EU:C:1974:131, para 13; Case C-196/04, *Cadbury Schweppes*, ECLI:EU:C:2006:544, para 35; Case C-212/97, *Centros*, ECLI:EU:C:1999:126, para 24.

Furthermore, positive integration provisions laid down in EU legislation may also envisage areas of permissible national action falling within the scope of EU law. First, EU legislation may require the adoption of certain measures at the national level. Directives are an obvious example, although also certain provisions laid down in regulations may envisage implementation at the national level.[24] In *SGS Belgium*, for instance, the Court ruled that States, by setting administrative penalties on the economic operators identified in Regulation No. 2988/95 to protect EU's financial interests, were implementing that Regulation.[25]

Second, EU legislation may, within its scope of application, expressly authorise certain categories of national measures.[26] A case in point is that of minimum harmonisation clauses, enabling Member States to enact 'stricter or more detailed' requirements, relative to the 'floor' set by the EU legislature, as long as they do not exceed the 'ceiling' set by EU primary law.[27] Another example is that of EU legislation affording Member States different options: under the old version of the 'Dublin' regulation, for instance, Member States could process an asylum request instead of returning the applicant back to the Member State of entry.[28] Similarly, under the Audiovisual Media Services Directive, each Member State can decide either to prohibit product placement or to authorise it subject to a number of requirements set out in that directive.[29]

Third, EU legislation may harmonise a certain matter only partially, thus enabling Member States to regulate other aspects of the same matter.[30] For instance, in *De Agostini*, the Court ruled that although the Television Without Frontiers Directive had harmonized national provisions on television advertising and sponsorship, it had done so 'only partially'.[31] Accordingly, it could not be regarded as 'excluding completely and automatically the application of rules other than those specifically concerning the broadcasting and distribution of programmes', nor as

---

[24] Case C-403/98, *Monte Arcosu*, ECLI:EU:C:2001:6, para 26 ('although [...] the provisions of [...] regulations generally have immediate effect in the national legal systems without its being necessary for the national authorities to adopt measures of application, some of their provisions may none the less necessitate, for their implementation, the adoption of measures of application by the Member States.').

[25] Case C-367/09, *SGS Belgium and Others*, ECLI:EU:C:2010:648, paras 34–35.

[26] See, generally, Arena 2016.

[27] See, generally, De Cecco 2006; Rott 2003.

[28] Council Regulation (EC) No. 343/2003 of 18 February 2003 establishing the criteria and mechanisms for determining the Member State responsible for examining an asylum application lodged in one of the Member States by a third-country national. See Joined Cases C-411/10 and C-493/10 *N.S. and others* EU:C:2011:865.

[29] Article 11 of Directive 2010/13/EU of the European Parliament and of the Council of 10 March 2010 on the coordination of certain provisions laid down by law, regulation or administrative action in Member States concerning the provision of audiovisual media services (Audiovisual Media Services Directive).

[30] See Schütze 2009, p. 195: 'Where European law does not harmonize all aspects within a policy area, Community terminology speaks of partial harmonization'.

[31] Joined cases C-34/95, C-35/95, and C-36/95, *De Agostini*, ECLI:EU:C:1997:344, para 32.

precluding 'the application of national rules with the general aim of consumer protection', such as the Swedish ban on misleading advertising that applied also, but not only, to television advertising.[32] This category of rules probes the blurry line between non-preclusion and non-application: whereas a matter is regulated by EU law, some specific aspects of it are not. In the practice, it might be difficult to argue conclusively that national measures relating to the latter specific issues are allowed by EU law, instead of them being irrelevant for EU law. Sometimes, the characterisation is a matter of convention or, worse, convenience. Some cases will be discussed below, to show the ambiguity of this category of rules.

13.4 The Blurred Line Between Non-Preclusion and Non-Application

It is now necessary to explain why the difference between non-preclusion and non-application is fundamental. It might be argued that the difference does not really come with a practical consequence: whether a domestic measure is not covered or not prohibited by EU law, it will simply be lawful under EU law. The case law of the Court of Justice, indeed, has often reflected this nonchalant approach to the issue.

For instance, the blurring is visible in the decisions of the Court regarding non-discriminatory measures regulating the opening hours of shops. In line with the *Keck* doctrine, the Court has regularly found that rules on shops' opening times are selling arrangements (as opposed to product requirements) and therefore do not breach Article 34 TFEU.[33] In *Turnhout*, a 2014 case, the Court confidently noted that, as observed 'on a number of occasions', Articles 34–36 TFEU '*do not apply* to national rules concerning the closure of shops' which are indistinctly applicable.[34] To take but one example, consider how the Court addressed the same kind of measures in *B&Q*, a case of 1992:

> …the legislation at issue pursued an aim *which was justified* under Community law. National rules restricting the opening of shops on Sundays reflected certain choices relating to particular national or regional socio-cultural characteristics. It was for the Member States to make those choices *in compliance with the requirements of Community law*, in particular the principle of proportionality.[35]

It is clear in this case that the Court, which confirmed the measure's compliance with EU law requirements, hinted at non-preclusion, rather than non-application. However, the conclusion in the same case, which abruptly used the language of

[32] Ibid., paras 33–34 and 38.

[33] Joined Cases C-267/91 and C-268/91, *Keck and Mithouard*, ECLI:EU:C:1993:905.

[34] Case C-483/12, *Pelckmans Turnhout*, ECLI:EU:C:2014:304, para 24, emphasis added.

[35] Case C-169/91, *Stoke-on-Trent*, ECLI:EU:C:1992:519, para 11.

non-application, reveals that, in essence, the Court used non-application and non-preclusion interchangeably:

> …Article [34 TFEU] is to be interpreted as meaning that the prohibition which it lays down *does not apply* to national legislation prohibiting retailers from opening their premises on Sundays.[36]

Indeed, in these cases the distinction would not come with a practical difference, and the Court's conceptual oscillation is without consequence. However, there is at least one vital distinction which should call for a more rigorous separation between non-precluded and non-covered State measures: general principles of EU law and the Charter only apply to non-precluded measures.[37]

Let's observe *Karner*, another case referring to a selling arrangement (a rule on advertising, prohibiting certain misleading statements made to sell goods bought at judicial auctions) which falls in time roughly halfway (2004) between *B&Q* and *Turnhout*. In this case, the Court took pains '*first of all, to determine whether* [the domestic measure] *falls within the scope of application of Article* [34 TFEU]'.[38] After recalling the *Keck* doctrine on selling arrangements, the Court noted that the measure was not discriminatory and therefore was '*not caught by the prohibition in Article* [34 TFEU]'.[39] This was, in other words, a measure which fell under EU law but was not precluded (unlike the selling arrangements in *Turnhout*, which escaped EU regulation altogether). The Court, then, proceeded to review the measure's compliance with Article 10 of the European Convention on Human Rights (freedom to impart information). The domestic measure was indeed considered to constitute an interference, albeit proportionate and justifiable, with the corresponding general principle of EU law.

Like general principles, the Charter applies only to State measures that implement EU law.[40] In other words, a State measure can be reviewed against the Charter only if it falls under the scope of EU law. When a measure does not fall under EU law, the Charter is irrelevant. When a measure is prohibited by EU law, the Charter has no added value in the review of EU-legality: the measure must be disapplied regardless of whether it respects the Charter or not. Consequently, the Charter only matters as a standard of review when it applies to—and prohibits—non-precluded measures. In essence, the added value of the Charter as a binding source is the possibility that it sanctions the illegality of State measures that are governed, but not precluded, by EU law.[41]

---

[36] Ibid., para 17.

[37] See for instance the orders in Case C-328/15, *Târşia*, ECLI:EU:C:2016:273; Case C-520/15, *Aiudapds*, ECLI:EU:C:2016:124.

[38] See Case C-71/02, *Karner*, ECLI:EU:C:2004:181, para 35.

[39] Ibid., para 43.

[40] Article 51(1) of the Charter.

[41] Of course, the Charter also applies to the acts of EU institution, and has already proved to be an important touchstone of their legality. See for instance Joined Cases C-293/12 and C-594/12,

The *Fransson* case provides a good illustration of the application of the Charter to non-precluded measures.[42] The Swedish measure (providing for the criminal prosecution of tax wrongdoing) was found to implement EU law, because it sought to discourage and punish tax evasion, including VAT evasion, in line with Article 325 TFEU. Therefore, the Swedish measure fell under the scope of EU law and did not raise issues of compliance with the implemented norms. However, the application of EU law triggered the application of the Charter too. As a result, the Charter could be used as an additional standard of review of the domestic measure. Whereas in that case the Court found no obvious breach of the Charter,[43] it is only a matter of time before a non-precluded measure is declared EU-illegal for breach of the Charter. Two cases can be described, briefly, in which this this scenario almost came into being. One deals with market freedoms, the other with the rights of EU citizens. In neither case the Court sanctioned the EU-illegality of a non-precluded norm for a breach of the Charter—this scenario has never materialised so far. Nonetheless, a short discussion of the legal and factual matrix of these disputes will show that this outcome should not be ruled out: future cases might warrant it and expose the doctrinal intricacies that underpin it.

The first case is *Sky Italia*.[44] Italian law regulates the broadcasting of advertising, setting different limits for free-tv and pay-tv operators. Pay-tv channels are granted a lower quota of advertising broadcast time. The measure was challenged by Sky in domestic courts, for constituting an obstacle to the cross-border provision of services. The Court, asked for a preliminary ruling, confirmed that the Italian measure fell under the scope of application of Article 56 TFEU, as it could indeed result in a market barrier. Nevertheless, the Court accepted Italy's explanation that the regulation of advertising was necessary to protect consumers against invasive advertising practices. In essence, the measure fell under EU law, but was not precluded by it. Since EU law applied, the Charter applied too, and the issue of these measures' compliance with the Charter was raised. Sky argued that the limitation on advertising was in breach of the Charter's right of freedom of information and freedom of expression: the rules constrained the company's right to freely determine their broadcasting programming. The Court dismissed the claim without even looking into it, referring to the evidentiary shortcomings of Sky's position. It noticed that the file did not contain a sufficient explanation of how the domestic rule on competition could harm media pluralism.[45] The claim, therefore, failed on the evidence but was plausible on the law. The Court conveniently stopped short of

(Footnote 41 continued)

Digital Rights Ireland, ECLI:EU:C:2014:238; Case C-236/09, Association Belge and Others, *ECLI:EU:C:2011:100; Case C-362/14,* Schrems, *ECLI:EU:C:2015:650.*

[42] Case C-617/10, *Åkerberg Fransson* ECLI:EU:C:2013:105.

[43] Namely, it concluded that the cumulating of criminal and administrative sanctions did not necessarily breach the principle of *ne bis in idem* protected in Article 50 of the Charter.

[44] Case C-234/12, *Sky Italia*, ECLI:EU:C:2013:496.

[45] Ibid., paras 23–24.

entering the review on the merits of the autonomous Charter-based claim, even if the basic matrix of the case (certain tv broadcasters were subject to discriminatory constraints) might have sufficed for the Court to instruct the domestic court about the possible breach of Article 11(2) of the Charter.

A more recent example is the case *Commission v. UK*.[46] In infringement proceedings, the Commission argued that the UK breached EU law by making child benefits for EU citizens conditional upon a requirement of lawful residence. More precisely, the Commission argued that the UK was in breach of Regulation 883/2004, since the concept of 'habitual residence' therein—an element which States can use to allocate benefits—is a matter of fact and cannot be equated to the right to residence under Directive 2004/38 (where residence can be made conditional to economic activity).[47] The Court conceded to the Commission that the requirement of lawful residence is indirectly discriminatory. However, it noted that justifications are available, when they pursue a legitimate interest and are proportionate and necessary:

> …it is clear from the Court's case-law that the need to protect the finances of the host Member State justifies in principle the possibility of checking whether residence is lawful when a social benefit is granted in particular to persons from other Member States who are not economically active, as such grant could have consequences for the overall level of assistance which may be accorded by that State.[48]

Therefore, the UK measure was non-precluded by EU law. Whereas the Commission's claim did not concern any possible breach of the Charter, UK judges might review the measure upon application, and set it aside each time it entails an unjustified restriction of Charter's rights. For instance, there might be cases where, in fact, the State's failure to pay child benefit might cause a severe harm to the applicant's right to private and family life.[49] In those circumstances, which are difficult to anticipate but can arise in the practice, the Charter will cause the disapplication of otherwise EU-compliant measures.

Neither case discussed above resulted eventually in a national measure being struck down for breach of the Charter (despite compliance with EU law at large). This scenario has not yet occurred in the practice, but there is no reason why it should not occur. These cases were helpful because only for circumstantial reasons (Sky's under-substantiated claim under the Charter; the Commission's lack of interest in Charter-based review) did the Charter not matter to the outcome. With slightly changed circumstances, cases can arise when non-precluded measures are declared incompatible with the Charter, showing the added value of the latter source in a way that has so far been dormant.

---

[46] Case C-308/14, *Commission v United Kingdom*, ECLI:EU:C:2016:436.

[47] Regulation (EC) No. 883/2004 of 29 April 2004 on the coordination of social security systems, Article 1, let j.

[48] C-308/14, *Commission v United Kingdom*, ECLI:EU:C:2016:436, para 80.

[49] See Article 7 of the Charter.

13.5 The Scope of Application of EU Law in the Common Market

The expansive force of EU law, and of the Charter with it, is evident in the field of the fundamental freedoms. Any measure capable of raising an obstacle to free movement is subject to EU law. Consider the *Pfleger* case, intimated above: Austrian law forbids the use of gambling machines without a license. This was considered an obstacle to the freedom of provision of services, the measure hence fell under EU law. Automatically, the Charter's provisions protecting property and business rights applied too.[50]

To be true, cases like this make the added relevance of the Charter hard to discern. The measure falling under Article 56 TFEU, the applicable Charter standards on freedom of business and right to property were essentially redundant (that is, the same test for breach would refer to either Article 56 TFEU or Articles 15–17 of the Charter). However, it is worth noting how a putatively internal matter, i.e. the establishment of criminal conduct and the applicable sanctions, was attracted under the umbrella of EU law, even without breaching it.

At this point, it is easy to understand a basic issue: if the difference between non-application and non-preclusion is blurry, it follows by necessity that that the difference between application and non-application of EU law is equally blurry. This difficulty can be observed in some recent opinions of the Advocate Generals of the Court.

One case in point is *C*.[51] The preliminary reference questioned the compatibility with EU law of the Finnish regime of additional taxes on retirement pensions. The relevant standard was the prohibition of discrimination on grounds of age. Advocate General Kokott, before turning to the application of the non-discrimination principle, examined whether the measure fell under the scope of EU law at all:

> 62. According to the judgment in *Pfleger*, situations governed by EU law also include those in which national legislation is such as to restrict the fundamental freedoms guaranteed by the Treaty. A Member State can justify such a restriction only if, at the same time, it observes the fundamental rights provided for in the Charter.
>
> 63. In the present case, the taxation of the taxpayer's retirement pension might constitute a restriction of a fundamental freedom and thus fall within the scope of the Charter. After all, the pension received by the taxpayer in 2013 derives at least in part from an activity which he previously carried on in a Member State other than the Republic of Finland. To that extent, the fact that that pension is taxed in Finland may constitute a restriction of the taxpayer's freedom of movement as a worker.[52]

[50] See Articles 15–17 of the Charter.

[51] Case C-122/15, *C*, ECLI:EU:C:2016:391.

[52] Ibid., footnotes omitted.

These reflections, which incidentally noted that the situation at hand is not purely internal, seemed to point to a finding of application of EU law: the tax might indeed constitute a restriction of a market freedom.

However, the Advocate General noted that in the *specific* case at issue the Finnish measure did not, in practice, create any restriction to the freedom of movement of workers.[53] She concluded therefore that the measure does not fall under the scope of EU law at all (which is different from saying it is not precluded by it, as the build-up seemed to suggest).[54] This conclusion clearly treats breaches of the fundamental freedom and the application of EU law co-terminous. When there is no breach of the fundamental freedom, EU law does not apply (nor does the Charter). Only when a breach arises, the whole system of EU law *cum* Charter comes into play. This idea is convenient because it simplifies the set of possibilities, apparently ruling out the possibility of non-preclusion: when application and breach go hand in hand, there is no place for application without breach.

The scrapping of the non-preclusion scenario might be, after all, the Columbus' egg in the field of market freedoms. Because in this area the application of EU law depends on the negative effects of domestic measures (rather than the attribution of competences), there is no such thing as a non-precluded measure: if a measure does not breach a fundamental freedom it is virtually irrelevant under the applicable Treaty provisions.

This simplification, however, does not appear to enjoy consensus. Consider the wording of another recent Opinion of Advocate General Wathelet,[55] concerning a citizenship case:[56]

> If a Treaty provision *does not preclude* a Member State from refusing a right of residence subject to compliance with certain conditions, *it follows by definition that the situation in question falls within the scope of that provision*. If that were not the case, the Court would have to decline jurisdiction to answer the question referred.[57]

The main proceedings concerned a *Zambrano*-like dispute. A Pakistani woman who had been married to a German citizen and resided with him in the UK wished to remain there after he moved to Pakistan. She had two kids, who were German citizens. The question was whether she had a right to reside in the UK, whether derived from the ex-husband or the children.[58]

---

[53] Ibid., paras 65–66.

[54] The judgment of the Court did not address the claim under Article 45 TFEU and only found that Directive 2000/78, the framework directive on non-discrimination on the workplace, did not apply to the circumstances of the case.

[55] Case C-115/15, *NA*, ECLI:EU:C:2016:487.

[56] As explained above, citizenship rights and market freedoms share their negative normative value, and sit uneasily with the non-preclusion category. This is why cases on citizenship and cases on fundamental freedoms, for the purpose of this chapter, can be studied together.

[57] Ibid., para 122 (emphasis added).

[58] Interestingly, the case was almost hypothetical, as she had been granted residence by the UK under the ECHR.

In the passage quoted above, Wathelet clearly described the category of non-precluded measures, which are covered by EU law precisely because they are not prohibited by the Treaties. It can be appreciated how, within a few months, Wathelet and Kokott came to apparently opposite conclusions regarding the possibility that measures that do not breach fundamental freedoms or citizenship rights be nevertheless covered by EU law. Advocate General Spuznar had already expressed his view regarding whether EU law applies to measures engaging with (but not necessarily precluded by) Articles 20 in his Opinion to *Rendón Marín*,

> …as citizens of the Union, those children have the right to move and reside freely throughout the territory of the European Union and any restriction of that right *falls within the ambit of EU law*.[59]

It is nevertheless possible to re-characterise Spuznar's dictum and Wathelet's opinion in *SA*, reading them as a mere rephrasing of the *ERT* doctrine (measures that derogate from EU law fall under its scope).[60] It would be possible to reconcile the views of Kokott, Spuznar and Wathelet in this light. Whereas only measures that *actually* restrict fundamental freedoms or citizenship rights fall under the scope of EU law, there will be some restrictive measures which are justified under EU law. These will be allowed measures (not simply non-precluded) and will fall under EU law, whereas all non-restrictive measures will lie outside its scope. This construction would be consistent with Kokott's view (no *actual* restriction means no application of EU law) and with Spuznar and Wathelet's (an *actual* restriction means that EU law applies, but the restriction might be allowed by EU law).

Similar uncertainties affect national measures concerning areas subject to harmonisation at the EU level. The Court has consistently held that Member States' stricter measures adopted pursuant to minimum harmonisation clauses must comply with other provisions of EU law, notably those concerning fundamental rights.[61] Yet, in *Hernandez* the Court took the view that Article 11 of Directive 2008/94, stating that Member States had the option to introduce laws more favourable to employees than those laid down in that directive, did not grant Member States 'an option of legislating by virtue of EU law', but merely recognised a 'power which the Member States enjoy under national law'.[62] Hence, national measures providing additional protection could not 'be regarded as implementing EU law within the

---

[59] Opinion in Case C-165/14, *Rendón Marín*, EU:C:2016:75, para 120, emphasis added.

[60] Case C-260/89, *ERT v DEP*, ECLI:EU:C:1991:254. On this case, see Cruz Villalón 2010.

[61] See, e.g., Case C-389/96, *Aher-Waggon*, ECLI:EU:C:1998:357, para 16: 'it is necessary to consider whether a Member State which, like the Federal Republic of Germany, has introduced stricter noise limits has, in exercising that power, infringed other provisions of Community law, in particular Article 30 of the Treaty'; Case C-6/98, *ARD*, ECLI:EU:C:1999:532, para 42: 'the attainment of the objective of Directive 89/552 […] is not affected in any way if Member States impose stricter rules on advertising […] on condition, however, that those rules are compatible with other relevant provisions of Community law'.

[62] Case C-198/13, *Julian Hernández and Others*, ECLI:EU:C:2014:2055, para 44.

meaning of Article 51(1) of the Charter' and, accordingly, 'be examined in the light of the guarantees of the Charter'.[63]

By the same token, in *Safe Interenvios*, the Court took the view that, in providing that the Member States may adopt 'stricter provisions' in the field covered by the Money Laundering Directive, Article 5 of that directive did not grant the Member States 'a power or obligation to legislate by virtue of EU law', but simply recognised a 'power which the Member States enjoy under national law to provide for such stricter provisions outside the framework of the regime established by the directive'.[64] Yet, the Court added that that power had to be exercised 'in compliance with EU law, in particular the fundamental freedoms guaranteed by the Treaties' and noted that, since national stricter provisions could restrict the provision of money transfer management services, they could only be regarded as permissible 'if they are compatible with the fundamental rights the observance of which is ensured by the Court' and protected by the Charter.[65] In sum, although the Charter was held inapplicable due to the lack of an implementation link between EU legislation and the relevant national provisions, the latter's impact on cross-border trade put EU law and fundamental rights back into play.

13.6 An Unintended Federalising Effect

Whereas the Charter only applies to domestic measures implementing EU law, it is possible to observe, or at least speculate over, its spill-over onto non-EU matters. In *Fransson*, it was made clear that a measure could find under the scope of EU law objectively, that is, irrespective of whether it was passed with the intention of implementing EU law.[66]

The unintended implementation of EU law, combined with the attraction mechanism described above (EU law attracts under its scope any measure that breaches it), makes it very hard to know *a priori* whether a specific measure will ever engage with EU law, and possibly enter into conflict with the Charter.

A case in point it the dispute *WebmindLicenses*.[67] At stake was the practice of Hungarian authorities, which transmitted information obtained secretly in pending criminal proceedings to the authorities in charge of the parallel tax assessment. In the main proceedings, the case was made that the use of this evidence in the tax proceedings breached the principles on procedural fairness protected under Articles 41, 47 and 48 of the Charter, in particular the right to defense, and the right to

[63] Ibid., para 48.

[64] Case C-235/14, *Safe Interenvios*, ECLI:EU:C:2016:154, para 79.

[65] Ibid., paras 99, 109.

[66] The *Fransson* case in this respect is paradigmatic, as it concerns Swedish measures passed before Sweden's accession to the EU.

[67] Case C-419/14, *WebMindLicenses*, ECLI:EU:C:2015:832.

privacy in Articles 7 and 8 of the Charter. In ascertaining first the applicability of EU law, the Advocate General Wathelet was very swift: tax assessment proceedings concern, in part, crimes involving VAT. In line with the *Fransson* judgment, domestic measures regulating VAT collection fall under scope of EU law. As a result, the domestic measures and practice at stake in *WebmindLicenses* are likewise covered by EU, and Article 51 of the Charter is triggered as a consequence. The Court agreed, and introduced the review of the measures at stake against the Charter with a paragraph that encapsulates the subject of this chapter:

> It follows that EU law does not *preclude* the tax authorities from being able in the context of an administrative procedure, in order to establish the existence of an abusive practice concerning VAT, to use evidence obtained in the context of a parallel criminal procedure that has not yet been concluded, *provided that the rights guaranteed by EU law, especially by the Charter, are observed.*[68]

It is fair to assume that the State rules on the collection and use of evidence in criminal and tax proceedings, and on the exchange of information between the respective authorities, were drafted without the intention to implement EU law, nor the awareness that EU law could be engaged unintendedly. Advocate General Wathelet's finding leads to the conclusion that these rules, which were never intended to relate to EU law, must comply with the Charter or might be set aside in specific circumstances, when the domestic courts find that a breach of the Charter occurred. The consequences of this scenario are disruptive: when decisive evidence was obtained illegally or the individual could not challenge it in fair proceedings, the ensuing decision must he held null and void. The same result follows when the domestic courts are unable to perform this check of Charter-compliance:

> [domestic courts] must disregard that evidence and annul that decision if, as a result, the latter has no basis. That evidence must also be disregarded if the national court is not empowered to check that it was obtained in the context of the criminal procedure in accordance with EU law or cannot at least satisfy itself, on the basis of a review already carried out by a criminal court in an *inter partes* procedure, that it was obtained in accordance with EU law.[69]

The only wise option available to a rational legislator to avoid these unexpected challenges, it seems, is to ensure already at the drafting stage that all pieces of legislation comply with the Charter, irrespective of any expected link with the implementation of EU law. This concern should also affect the action of executive and police authorities.

In other words, it is to be expected that State authorities, which cannot predict all the factual and legal scenarios that might entail a link between EU law and domestic legislation, comply with the EU Charter as a matter of convenience, rather than obligation. This was for instance the choice of the Swedish legislator, after *Fransson*. Whereas the Court's judgment identified the implementation of EU law only with respect only with the VAT-portion of the domestic tax assessment

---

[68] Ibid., para 68 (emphasis added).

[69] Ibid., para 98.

proceedings, it was much easier to reform the whole system (VAT and non-VAT) to achieve compliance with EU law. Indeed, the Supreme Court applied the principles stated in *Fransson* and found that domestic law breached EU obligations. It also established a new principle whereby individuals who received a tax surcharge and were prosecuted as a result of the same tax offence were entitled to a new trial.[70] Clearly, the reform did encompass both EU-related and non-EU-related tax assessments, and thus resulted in a voluntary (but inevitable) Charterisation of this field of Swedish law.

This instance is not surprising and is possibly a common occurrence. A rational lawmaker might indulge in voluntary federalisation, subscribing to the Charter's obligations even when it is not supposed to, for at least two reasons: to anticipate EU-related problem that are difficult to predict in theory and to maintain uniformity in the law, where a change relating only to the EU-related details would cause unnecessary fragmentation.

13.7 Conclusions

Any inquiry into the scope of application of the Charter to Member States inevitably opens a can of doctrinal worms. The reasons are obvious: in *Fransson* and some following cases, the Court trumpeted the perfect alignment between the Charter's application and the application of EU law. Knowing when the Charter applies to State measures would therefore require knowing when EU law applies to them—a Sisyphean task if there is one, especially in the field of market freedoms and citizenship rights.

As explained above, there is no reliable test to exclude a given domestic situation from the application of the Treaty rules on the fundamental freedoms. The most used indicators, that is, the principle of conferral and the 'purely internal situation' test, are imperfect and can yield false negatives. This is a problem in itself, which has so far been studied predominantly thinking of *preclusive* situations. When EU law has a prohibitive force, it should be known in advance to which domestic measures it applies.

Less attention has been paid to the non-preclusion scenario, but more troubles are well under way. The applicability of the Charter in non-preclusion cases creates another scenario of great legal uncertainty. Measures that raise no issue of compliance with (other rules of) EU law might in fact be prohibited under the Charter. The Court gives domestic judges little guidance to make this determination, and for law-makers and State authorities at large it is virtually impossible to anticipate with certainty whether their measures and acts will ever be scrutinised under the Charter.

A possible outcome of this state of affairs is that States behave pragmatically, and 'incorporate' the 'federal' Charter among the touchstones of lawfulness for all

[70] On the reception of *Fransson* in Swedish law, see Nergelius 2016, pp. 97–98.

their acts. However, this unintended federalisation of the Charter, which derives from the impossibility to determine with precision its scope of application, goes against the spirit of the several safeguards contained in Article 51(2) of the Charter and Article 6(1) TEU ('the Charter does not extend the scope of application of EU law').[71] States find themselves in a double-bind: if they do not over-comply with the Charter they might face unexpected Charter-based review of their acts. In any event, the trade-off between autonomy and compliance is one that should not be required by reason of conceptual sloppiness: it is the Court's responsibility to bring clarity in this area of law.

Whereas the really hard cases might lie at the borderline between non-application and non-preclusion, the state of uncertainty reaches further. National courts are confused by the Chinese boxes of the interlocking scopes of application of fundamental rights and EU law. See for instance how a Dutch judge phrased a question for preliminary ruling.[72] The question refers to the compliance with EU law of a concession regarding the tax deduction of studying costs, which might raise issues of discrimination on grounds of age. After asking the Court whether Directive 2000/78 would apply to the domestic measure (i.e., whether EU law applies at all), the judge asked:

> [If the Directive does not apply, m]*ust the principle of non-discrimination on the grounds of age, as a general principle of EU law, be applied* to a tax concession on the basis of which training expenditure is only deductible under certain circumstances, *even when that concession falls outside the material scope of Directive 2000/78/EC and when that arrangement does not implement EU law?*[73]

The phrasing is striking because the judge lists in the question the exact reasons why the answer is no: if the measure fall outside the scope of the Directive and does not implement EU law otherwise, EU fundamental principles (whether as general principles or as Charter provisions) cannot apply.

One can only wonder whether this incredible confusion is the result of the much maligned reasoning of the Court in *Mangold/Kücükdeveci*.[74] One thing is certain: fundamental rights and the Charter are routinely treated, whether deliberately (see the choice of the Swedish authorities after *Fransson*) or mistakenly (see the preliminary question above) as a federal source of law that applies to Member States

---

[71] Please note that this "spontaneous harmonisation" effect is not restricted to the Charter, but extends to other areas of EU law. For instance, the prospect of creating reverse discrimination against their nationals induced Member States to amend or repeal their laws as a whole, whereas EU law only required to disapply them *vis-à-vis* nationals of other Member States. A case in point is the Italian legislation on pasta products, which the ECJ only declared inapplicable to producers from other Member States (Case 407/85, *Drei Glocken*, ECLI:EU:C:1988:401, para 25), but was eventually struck down as a whole by the Italian Constitutional Court in Judgment no. 443 of 1997.

[72] Case C-548/15 *de Lange.*

[73] Emphasis added.

[74] Respectively, Case C-144/04, *Mangold*, ECLI:EU:C:2005:709; Case C-555/07, *Kücükdeveci*, ECLI:EU:C:2010:21.

without restrictions *ratione materiae*. The combined effect of this trend with the inherently expansive application of the four freedoms will certainly continue to challenge the tolerance of Member States.

References

Arena A (2011) I limiti della competenza pregiudiziale della Corte di giustizia in presenza di situazioni puramente interne: la sentenza Sbarigia. Diritto dell'Unione Europea 1:201–222

Arena A (2016) Exercise of EU Competences and Pre-emption of Member States' Powers in the Internal and the External Sphere: Towards 'Grand Unification'? Yearbook of European Law 35:28–105

Cruz Villalón P (2010) 'All the guidance', ERT and Wachauf. In: Poiares Maduro M, Azoulai L (eds) The Past and Future of EU Law. The Classics of EU Law Revisited on the 50th Anniversary of the Rome Treaty. Hart, Oxford, pp. 162–169

Dashwood A (2004) The relationship between the Member States and the European Union/European Community. Common Market Law Review 41:355–381

De Cecco F (2006) Room to move? Minimum harmonization and fundamental rights. Common Market Law Review 43:9–30

Fontanelli F (2013) Implementation of European Union Law by Member States under Article 51 (1) of the Charter of Fundamental Rights. Columbia Journal of European Law 20:193–247

Fontanelli F (2014) Implementation of EU Law through Domestic Measures after Fransson: the Court of Justice Buys Time and 'Non-preclusion' Troubles Loom Large. European Law Review 5:682–700

Mastroianni R (2005) Le competenze dell'Unione. Il Diritto dell'Unione Europea 390–409

Nergelius J (2016) The Nordic States and the European Convention on Human Rights. In: Arnold R (ed) The Convergence of the Fundamental Rights Protection in Europe. Springer, Dordrecht, pp. 85–98

Rott P (2003) Minimum harmonisation for the completion of the internal market? The example of consumer sales law. Common Market Law Review 40:1107–1130

Schütze R (2008) Lisbon and the Federal Order of Competences: A Prospective Analysis. European Law Review 33:709–722

Schütze R (2009) From Dual to Cooperative Federalism: the Changing Structure of European Law. Oxford University Press, Oxford

Skouris V (2013) Développements Récents de la Protection des Droits Fondamentaux dans l'Union Européenne: Les Arrêts Melloni et Åkerberg Fransson. Il Diritto dell'Unione Europea 2:229–243

Tryfonidou A (2009) The Outer Limits of Article 28 EC: Purely Internal Situations and the Development of the Court's Approach through the Years. In: Barnard C, Odudu O (eds) The Outer Limits of European Union Law. Hart Publishing, Oxford/Portland, Oregon, pp. 197–224

Part IV
Looking Abroad

Chapter 14
Creating a National Market in the United States Through the Dormant Commerce Clause?

Eszter Belteki

Abstract To compare the development of the internal market in the EU, the creation of the national market in the United States of America provides an excellent starting point. However, in order to fully comprehend the evolution of the latter, this chapter will demonstrate through a historical analysis, how such a market could materialise without an express provision about this in the Constitution of the United States of America. This will involve the examination of the drafting and early interpretation of the commerce clause in the first part. The second part will analyse the main decisions of the Supreme Court in which the negative or dormant commerce clause developed, focusing on the extent to which limitation placed on the states under this clause assisted in the creation of the national market. The last part will demonstrate that even though there is a strict scrutiny of state laws under the modern interpretation of the commerce clause, a worrying new trend seems to have emerged in recent Supreme Court decisions that allows for discriminatory laws to be imposed by the states against other states and their nationals.

Keywords Dormant commerce clause · National market · United States · US Constitution

Contents

14.1 Introduction 316
14.2 Interstate Commerce After the American Revolution 317
 14.2.1 Interstate Commerce 317
 14.2.2 Interstate Commerce Before the Constitutional Convention 319
 14.2.3 Interstate Commerce and the Constitutional Convention 321
 14.2.4 Ratification of the Constitution and the Federalist—Anti-Federalist Debate.... 326

E. Belteki (✉)
Durham Law School, Durham University, Palatine Centre, Stockton Road, Durham DH1 3LE, UK
e-mail: eszter.belteki@gmail.com

M. Andenas et al. (eds.), *The Reach of Free Movement*,
DOI 10.1007/978-94-6265-195-1_14

14.3 The Development of the Dormant Commerce Clause 329
14.3.1 The First Answer: Dual Federalism 330
14.3.2 The Concurrent Authority Approach 333
14.3.3 The Novel National—Local Test 335
14.3.4 A Narrower Definition of Commerce 338
14.3.5 The Direct-Indirect Burden Test 340
14.4 The Modern Approach to the Dormant Commerce Clause 342
14.4.1 The First Tier Test: The Anti-Discrimination Principle 343
14.4.2 The *Pike* Balancing Test 349
14.4.3 The New Trend: Increasing the Powers of the States to Regulate Interstate Commerce 354
14.5 Conclusion 359
References 363

14.1 Introduction

Whilst the United States of America often provides a point of comparison with the European Union for its regulation of the national market,[1] it is important to highlight that the Constitution of the United States of America does not include a provision for the creation of a national market. The only provision of the Constitution alluding to this is the commerce clause, which states that '[Congress shall have power …] To regulate commerce with foreign nations, and among the several states, and with the Indian tribes.'[2] This chapter will, however, demonstrate that even though no express provision about the creation of a national market exists in the Constitution, such may be identified as one of the purposes for the adoption and the subsequent application of the commerce clause.

Firstly, the reasons for the adoption of the commerce clause will be examined. The chapter will explore how the economic situation of the states and their commercial relationship with each other were implemental in the drafting and adoption of the Constitution. Particular attention will also be placed on the text of the commerce clause as well as the definitions of the various terms of the clause before and during the adoption of the Constitution.

In the second part, the chapter will analyse the most influential decisions of the Supreme Court about the negative aspects of the commerce clause. It will discuss how the interpretation of the commerce clause developed this negative side that focuses on the extent to which the rights of the states are limited to regulate in the same area as Congress. On the other hand, an emphasis is also going to be placed upon whether the ideology of the creation of a national market was present in the main judgments of the Supreme Court.

In the last part, the chapter will focus on the modern interpretation of the negative or dormant commerce clause and will demonstrate the development of the

[1] See for instance Schütze 2009 or Barnard 2009.

[2] Constitution of the United States, Article I, Section 8, third clause.

current two-tier test. It will also argue that even though there is a strict scrutiny of state laws under the modern test, a new trend of cases that may be characterised into four separate groups seems to be emerging in the Supreme Court.

14.2 Interstate Commerce After the American Revolution

14.2.1 Interstate Commerce

Instead of a reference to a national market, the commerce clause of the Constitution of the United States of America on its face grants Congress with the authority to 'regulate […] commerce among the states'.[3] In order to fully understand the meaning of this expression, the interpretation of 'commerce' and 'among the states' in the era after the American Revolution, and particularly during the eighteenth century, will have to be analysed separately.

14.2.1.1 'Commerce'

One is to face quite a challenging task when looking for the definition of commerce in the eighteenth century. As with many terms included in the Constitution, no uniform interpretation of commerce can be identified at the time of its drafting and adoption. The various understandings of commerce, as illustrated by various commentators, can be categorised into three different groups based on the extent of the definition.

The first group of commentators claim that 'commerce' referred to a broader range of activities in the eighteenth century than the economic activity as it is understood nowadays.[4] Commerce, it is argued, was understood as 'intercourse' with sound 'social connotations', which effectively meant that an 'interaction and exchange between persons' could be classified as 'commerce' in that period, including all economic and non-economic activity related to commerce.[5] Such meanings of commerce can be identified in a dictionary written in the same age as the Constitution that defined commerce as "intercourse; exchange of one thing for another" and a "common or familiar intercourse", along with various other textual references from the era.[6] A wider understanding of commerce was also utilised by the economists of the era, such as Tench Coxe or Adam Smith, who claimed that 'commerce' included not only 'trading goods but also manufacturing, mining, grazing, agriculture, fisheries, banking, insurance, and corporations.'[7] Nelson and

[3] Constitution of the United States, Article I, Section 8.

[4] Balkin 2010, p. 5 and Amar 2005, p. 107.

[5] Balkin 2010, p. 5 and Amar 2005, p. 107.

[6] Balkin 2010, p. 15 and Amar 2005, p. 107.

[7] Nelson and Pushaw 1999, pp. 15–16 and 20.

Pushaw further argued that commerce at the time could be identified with any 'gainful activity.'[8]

A second group of scholars argued that at the time of the adoption of the Constitution commerce encompassed a somewhat narrower extent of activities. These activities were still, however, a wider definition of commerce than it is generally understood nowadays and included the three main economic activities of the states: 'manufacturing, agriculture and commerce.'[9] For instance, Tushnet argues, that commerce was used in this sense in various 'newspapers and legislative debates' in the era.[10] Others also demonstrated through the definitions of commerce in various English dictionaries at the time that commerce included not only the general 'buying and selling of goods,' but also the activities that produced these goods, such as manufacture and agriculture.[11]

A third group of commentators, on the other hand, argued that the meaning of commerce at the era of founding was merely understood as the activities that would normally be regarded as 'trade' or an 'exchange of merchandise between different places.'[12] Merchandise, according to Barnett, was understood as 'what [was] produced by agriculture and manufacturing.'[13] Cooke even supports a narrower understanding of commerce by claiming that it was essentially 'transportation [...] of persons or property.'[14] He thus identified interstate commerce as such transportation 'between points in different States.'[15] It is key to highlight, however, that if commerce is to include only transportation and the trade of merchandise, the production of such cannot be held to be included in the definition of commerce.[16]

It will be demonstrated below that this debate between these three different understandings of commerce has occupied a fundamental position in the interpretation of the commerce clause. However, another element of the commerce clause, the 'among the states' expression, would also become crucial in the interpretation of the clause.

14.2.1.2 'Among the States'

The meaning of 'among' at the time of the adoption of the Constitution and immediately preceding it is claimed to have been understood as 'the mingling of' or

[8] Nelson and Pushaw 1999, pp. 13–20.

[9] Tushnet 2009, p. 162.

[10] Tushnet 2009, p. 162.

[11] Nelson and Pushaw 1999, p. 15.

[12] Noyes 1906, p. 255; Nelson and Pushaw 1999, p. 17 and Pushaw 2012, p. 1710.

[13] Barnett 2002, p. 1284. Nelson and Pushaw, however, claimed that these activities would be classified as 'merchandize' during this era. See Nelson and Pushaw 1999, p. 17.

[14] Cooke 1910, p. 299.

[15] Cooke 1910, p. 299.

[16] Noyes 1906, pp. 256–257 and Barnett 2002, p. 1248.

'associated with.'[17] The meaning of 'among the states' may therefore be interpreted as including activities that involved more than one state. This could thus also imply a certain out-of-state element, usually the import or export of an article of commerce from or to another state. Due to the development of the states during this era, interstate commerce was, however, less common than the more practical and easily accessible commerce within the boundaries of a state.[18]

14.2.2 Interstate Commerce Before the Constitutional Convention

Having secured their independence resulted not only in the political, but the economic independence of the previous colonies, which position, unsurprisingly, created a new challenge for them.

One of the responses of Britain to this newly gained independence of the old colonies was the imposition of various measures restricting the ability of the latter to engage in trade with Britain and 'its colonies in the West Indies'.[19] The states, therefore, in order to strengthen their own economic performance, turned to concentrate on the development of their local economies and commerce.[20] The manufacture and agricultural production mainly focused on serving those 'in the immediate vicinity' and for producing goods for home-consumption.[21] The interstate commerce that existed before and at the time of the adoption of the Constitution thus seems to have been limited and consisted mostly in the transportation of goods between states by means of 'vessels, […] stage coaches, wagons and pack-horses.'[22] However, many legislators in the states at the time believed that the out-of-state flow of commerce could have harmed their economy, which effectively resulted in many states enacting laws that clearly placed the economic actors situated within their states in a more favourable position over those operating out of the state boundaries.[23]

The situation did not change with the adoption of the Articles of Confederation either. The draft Articles proposed by Dickinson contained a measure prohibiting discrimination of out-of-state citizens, especially 'in matters of trade' and these citizens were also to be granted the same 'Rights, Liberties, Priviledges [sic] Exemptions & Immunities in Trade, Navigation & Commerce' as those living in a

---

17 Nelson and Pushaw 1999, p. 43.

18 Maggs 1998, p. 1198.

19 Friedman and Deacon 2011, p. 1887 and LeBoeuf 1994, pp. 595–596.

20 Eule 1982, p. 430 and Williams 2005, p. 162.

21 Noyes 1906, p. 254.

22 Noyes 1906, p. 254.

23 Eule 1982, p. 430 and Williams 2005, p. 162.

state.[24] The Committee in charge of the drafting of the Articles, however, disagreed with these proposals and transformed these into affirmative powers possessed by Congress, whereby it could impose 'duties and imposts on foreign commerce.'[25] It thus became apparent that whilst Congress was given several powers under this document, the various states remained reluctant to grant the power to Congress to address the restrictive measures of Britain by using a collective national voice and to regulate interstate trade.[26] The measures enacted by states discriminating against each other through duties imposed on interstate trade within the Confederation thus remained.[27]

With the economy gradually weakening, the adoption of local protectionist measures, such as discriminatory trade duties, undeniably escalated in states with a dominant position in a particular area of trade.[28] In the meantime, the states with a less influential position adopted measures that allowed the free flow of commerce into and out of their states.[29] One such instance was the establishment of free ports in Connecticut, Delaware and New Jersey, whilst in New York a law enacted in 1785 imposed the same duties on goods imported from Connecticut, New Jersey, Rhode Island and Pennsylvania as those from Britain.[30] This measure effectively resulted in a trade war between the above states.[31]

Whilst these conflicts may have resulted in harm to the economies of various states, they also prompted a debate about the solution of these conflicts in the newly created union of states. One such solution was proposed by the reformists of the era, such as Madison, who claimed that Congress should be given powers to enact 'a uniform trade policy' in order to repair the 'leak' in the 'vessel' of the Confederacy.[32] This statement could thus be argued to be in support of the ideal of creating a uniform system of interstate commerce to protect the interest of the nation as a whole. This reformist idea, however, would have required to grant powers to Congress that had clearly belonged to the states previously and this ideology, unsurprisingly, was not welcomed by all states.[33] To discuss the various options available to solve these problems, an interstate conference was called in

[24] Denning 2005, p. 78.

[25] Denning 2005, p. 79.

[26] Friedman and Deacon 2011, p. 1887.

[27] Noyes 1906, pp. 253–254.

[28] Noyes 1906, p. 254; Friedman and Deacon 2011, p. 1888; Brogan 1999, p. 193 and Nelson and Pushaw 1999, p. 24. For a description of these measures in Virginia, New York, Connecticut, Massachusetts. Rhode Island and South Carolina see Denning 2005, pp. 60–66.

[29] Friedman and Deacon 2011, p. 1888.

[30] Friedman and Deacon 2011, p. 1888 and LeBoeuf 1994, p. 597.

[31] Eule 1982, p. 430; Friedman and Deacon 2011, p. 1889; Tribe 2000, vol. 1, p. 1044 and *H P Hood & Sons, Inc v Du Mond, Commissioner of Agriculture and Markets* (1949) 336 YS 525, p. 533.

[32] Friedman and Deacon 2011, p. 1888 and Denning 2005, p. 55.

[33] Denning 2005, p. 52.

Annapolis, which ultimately resulted in the call for the Constitutional Convention in Philadelphia to alter the Articles of Confederation.[34]

14.2.3 Interstate Commerce and the Constitutional Convention

The delegates to the Constitutional Convention arrived in the times of this 'economic chaos,'[35] which was dominated by discriminatory commercial measures between the states within the union. Understandably, many of the delegates therefore aimed to devise a solution to this problem and indeed several proposals were presented to the Convention that aimed at tackling this particular issue.

The new ideal by the reformists claiming that Congress should be granted with powers to enact uniform trade policies had already been present in the proposals submitted to the Convention. Whilst the proposals of Hamilton and Randolph did not explicitly mention commerce, these suggested a more open-ended interpretation of the powers of the 'Legislature of the United States.'[36] Hamilton even argued for the 'Legislature' to be able 'to pass all laws […] which they shall judge necessary to the common defence and general welfare of the Union.'[37] Randolph also suggested to impose some limitations on the power of the 'Legislature,' but he did not propose such an open-ended and seemingly limitless power as Hamilton.[38] He imagined that the legislature would enact laws in cases where 'the separate states are incompetent, or in which the harmony of the United States may be interrupted by the exercise of individual Legislation […].'[39] It could thus be argued that both Hamilton and Randolph recognised that the creation of a uniform system was necessary in certain areas of law to ensure that the newly devised federal system would work effectively. Therefore, if the creation of a uniform system of interstate commerce was beneficial for the nation as a whole, they both seemed to be in favour of the creation of such a system. If one is to follow this wide interpretation of grant of power to Congress, it may be established that they might have been in favour of allowing Congress to regulate activities that were included in the wider understanding of commerce at the time.

Moreover, the reformist plans presented by Pinckney and Paterson proposed to provide a solution expressly to the problems present in the area of interstate commerce. Pinckney proposed for Congress to have 'the exclusive power, of regulating the trade of the several states as well with foreign nations as with each

---

[34] Friedman and Deacon 2011, p. 1891; Amar 2005, p. 254 and Brogan 1999, p. 194.

[35] McGinley 1992, p. 412.

[36] Abel 1940, p. 433.

[37] Abel 1940, p. 433.

[38] Abel 1940, p. 433.

[39] Abel 1940, p. 433 and Amar 2005, p. 108.

other—of levying duties upon imports and exports.'[40] The proposal of Paterson, similarly to that of Pinckney, argued for Congress to be able 'to pass acts for the regulation of trade as well with foreign nations as with each other.'[41] The solution presented to the Convention through these plans was seemingly the transfer of regulatory authority to Congress in the area of interstate commerce and the consequent creation of a uniform system of interstate commerce. It is essential to highlight, however, that most of the proposals that specifically addressed this area did not refer to interstate 'commerce,' but 'trade.'[42] It may therefore be argued that the group of delegates who called for a uniform regulation in the area of interstate commerce, understood commerce to encompass the activities of trade only, which was the narrowest interpretation of commerce at the time.

Nonetheless, one may also find references to 'commerce' in the opening speeches at the Convention by the delegates. For instance, Randolph claimed that a transfer of regulatory power over commerce to the federal government would boost not only 'trade, but also "navigation," "agriculture," "manufactures," and "great national works."'[43] Pinckney, when referring to the 'commercial interests' of the United States identified those as "trade," "fisheries," and crops such as "[w]heat," "tob [acco]," and "[r]ice & [i]ndigo."'[44] It may thus be argued that a second group of Framers supported the creation of a uniform system of interstate commerce, adopting a wider understanding of 'commerce', which included activities other than trade.[45]

Another question, however, arose from this transfer of power to Congress as it did not clarify whether the states were intended to be limited in their actions in the area of interstate commerce. It will therefore first be examined whether the Framers of the Constitution intended an exclusive power to be granted to Congress in this area. It will then be explored whether it was the intention of the Framers to limit the states in this area if such power was granted to Congress.

14.2.3.1 Exclusive Grant of Power to Congress

Whilst creating a novel federalist system, the Framers also created a new nation that was to become an 'indestructible union composed of indestructible states.'[46] Such a system, however, required certain areas that were of concern to the federal nation to be addressed uniformly by the federal government.[47] Interstate commerce emerged

---

[40] Abel 1940, p. 434.

[41] Abel 1940, p. 434.

[42] Abel 1940, p. 434.

[43] Pushaw 2012, p. 1719.

[44] Pushaw 2012, p. 1719.

[45] Nelson and Pushaw 1999, p. 41.

[46] Sedler 2009, p. 1490.

[47] Balkin 2010, p. 12.

as one such area during the debates at the Convention. In an era governed by protectionist and discriminatory commercial measures imposed by the various states, the 'nearly universal'[48] solution that developed during the debates was the creation of a 'centrally regulated'[49] 'uniform system'[50] regulating interstate commerce.

The support that this solution received from the delegates firstly demonstrated that almost all of them recognised that there was a fundamental hindrance to the regulatory power over interstate commerce in the then existing system under the Articles of Confederation.[51] As in that system the states were the ones who had power to regulate commerce with other states, the Congress of the Confederation was unable to respond to any discriminatory regulatory measures that affected more than one state or interstate commerce as a whole. Secondly, this common understanding, however, also served as an indicator that the delegates might not have considered it necessary to state the 'obvious' reasons for the creation of this uniform system.[52] Various commentators have, however, subsequently attempted to identify these 'obvious' reasons as the guarantee of the 'interstate commercial harmony'[53] and also the strengthening of the 'national unity.'[54]

The method of creating this uniform system of interstate commerce also indicated that the Framers were in general agreement about the solution to the problem of regulating this area: they unanimously adopted Article 1, Section 8 of the Constitution of the United States, which granted regulatory power over this area to Congress.[55] The so-called commerce clause, the third clause of this section, as subsequently ratified, states that '[Congress shall have power …] To regulate commerce with foreign nations, and among the several states, and with the Indian tribes.'

Whereas it was clear that Congress was granted regulatory powers over the area of interstate commerce, it was, however, still unclear whether this grant of power was an exclusive grant of power to Congress and whether this resulted in states losing their regulatory authority over the same area. The delegates were faced with the above fundamental question even before discussing the regulation of interstate commerce or the supremacy clause.[56] The majority of the delegates, in effect, seemed to have supported the idea that when state acts would regulate an area

---

[48] Abel 1940, p. 443.

[49] Larsen 2004, p. 845.

[50] Eule 1982, p. 435. See also McGinley 1992, pp. 412–413 and Denning 2008, p. 481.

[51] Abel 1940, p. 446.

[52] Abel 1940, p. 446 and *H P Hood & Sons, Inc v Du Mond, Commissioner of Agriculture and Markets* (1949), p. 534.

[53] Denning 2008, p. 481.

[54] Eule 1982, p. 435. See also Abel 1940, pp. 443–444.

[55] Williams 2008, p. 423.

[56] Article VI, para 2 of the Constitution of the United States states: 'This Constitution, and the Laws of the United States which shall be made in pursuance thereof; and all treaties made, or which shall be made, under the authority of the United States, shall be the supreme law of the land;

where the regulatory power had been granted to the federal government in the Constitution, the state acts could be held unconstitutional.[57] This, they claimed, would ensure that the state and federal laws would be 'complementary' to each other.[58]

Some delegates, nevertheless, considered that the opportunity may arise where state and federal laws may overlap and it would subsequently have to be decided which laws were to prevail. For such instances, Randolph proposed that the federal government should have rights to annul state laws contrary to 'the articles of the Union',[59] which position was extended to include 'any treaties subsisting under the authority of the union.'[60] Even though defeated conclusively, Pinckney even proposed for this provision to be broadened to include 'all laws which to them [the federal government] shall appear improper.'[61] Various other statements of the delegates at the Convention, as highlighted by Abel, also demonstrate that the delegates widely supported the ideal that when the federal government was entrusted with the powers over one area, that was to exclude the states from regulating in the same subject matter.[62]

It may thus be deduced from the above examination that Congress was granted with exclusive regulatory powers over the area of interstate commerce. On the other hand, it still has to be examined how this affected the regulatory powers of the states in the area that previously belonged to them: whether these would be withdrawn or whether they were still allowed to regulate certain areas of interstate commerce.

14.2.3.2 Limitations on State Powers

As highlighted by Abel, the regulation of interstate commerce was discussed on nine occasions during the Convention.[63] Even though this seems to be a limited opportunity to discuss whether the solution to the discriminatory state commercial measures was the deprivation of the states of their legislative rights in this area, this question, in effect, constituted one of the key subjects addressed by the delegates. As Abel identified it, the commerce clause, according to the uniform position of the delegates, was to become a preventative national measure against the discriminatory

(Footnote 56 continued)

and the judges in every state shall be bound thereby, anything in the constitution or laws of any state to the contrary notwithstanding.'

[57] Abel 1940, pp. 483–485.

[58] Abel 1940, pp. 483–485.

[59] Abel 1940, p. 485.

[60] Abel 1940, pp. 485–486.

[61] Abel 1940, p. 486.

[62] Abel 1940, p. 488. Abel also highlighted, for instance, statements of Butler, Lansing, King and Sherman in support of this ideology. See Abel 1940, pp. 486–488.

[63] Abel 1940, p. 470.

and protectionist state regulations.[64] Conversely, the delegates did not seem to adopt a uniform measure as a means to achieve this goal.

One group of delegates were supporting the standpoint that the states should be allowed to retain those powers over commerce that concerned activities that were 'purely local in character.'[65] Sherman, for instance, argued that the states would 'never give up all power over trade,'[66] which view also seems to have been supported by Bedford, who argued that the states, at least, should retain their 'independent power to encourage local industries by bounties and similar devices.'[67]

The opposing view, that states should be deprived of all their powers over commerce seems to have been indirectly supported by another group of delegates. For example, Madison—supported by others, such as Langdon and Pinckney—argued in the last days of the Convention that he "was more and more convinced that the regulation of Commerce was in its nature indivisible and ought to be wholly under one authority."[68] Moreover, this position of Madison can also be identified in a letter included in the Records of the Federal Convention that stated that there was a general consensus between the delegates of the Convention that claimed that the states were incompetent to regulate in the areas of foreign and interstate commerce because of the discriminatory measures that the states imposed in these areas.[69] It is the view of several commentators that the majority of the delegates supported the ideology of the latter group and the position that by granting Congress the authority to regulate interstate commerce, states were effectively deprived of their powers to regulate the same area.[70] It will thus have to be investigated further whether this remained the position after the Constitution was sent for ratification to the states.

14.2.4 *Ratification of the Constitution and the Federalist—Anti-Federalist Debate*

14.2.4.1 Ratification Debates

It is essential to highlight that during the period of the ratification debates in some states, the ratification of the Constitution also resulted in the repeal of some of the discriminatory measures enacted by the states.

---

[64] Abel 1940, pp. 470–472.

[65] Nelson and Pushaw 1999, p. 44.

[66] Abel 1940, p. 490. Note the referral to 'trade' and not 'commerce.'

[67] Abel 1940, pp. 490–491 and Nelson and Pushaw 1999, p. 44.

[68] Farrand 1937, vol. 2, p. 625 and Abel 1940, p. 492.

[69] Boykin 2012, p. 94.

[70] Abel 1940, p. 493; Williams 2008, pp. 423–424; McGinley 1992, p. 413; Larsen 2004, p. 846 and Denning 2008, p. 486.

For instance, in Virginia, the import duties imposed on 'liquor, wine, flour, sugar and coffee' by An Act for ascertaining certain Taxes and Duties, and for establishing a permanent Revenue from 1781 was repealed before the state ratified the Constitution.[71] The revocation of this act was called for by those engaged in the trade of these, who argued that this import duty was "inconsistent with the spirit of the Union."[72] Furthermore, supporters of the ideal of the protection of national interest are also identifiable. In North Carolina, for example, Davie highlighted that 'the general objects of the Union' were "to promote the commerce, agriculture and manufactures, of America."[73]

The main discussions about the regulatory powers of Congress and the states over the area of interstate commerce at the time of the ratification debates can be found mostly in the discussions of those who belonged to the one of the two main political groupings at the time.

14.2.4.2 The Federalist—Anti-Federalist Debate

The adoption of the novel federal constitution, unsurprisingly, resulted in significant political debates that also influenced certain constitutional ideas. After the drafting of the Constitution two main political ideologies emerged, which also influenced the ratification debates of the proposed Constitution.

14.2.4.3 The Federalists

Those supporting the adoption of the Constitution came to form the political group of 'The Federalists', who argued for a powerful federal government to become the supervisor of state and local governments.[74]

Interstate commerce was viewed by the Federalists as a reasonably important fundamental keystone of the novel federalist system. Hamilton emphasised on various occasions in the Federalist Papers that commerce had been a motive for numerous wars up until the creation of the United States.[75] After having obtained their independence from Britain, Hamilton also recognised that the various states had attempted unsuccessfully to address the restrictive measures of Britain separately.[76] He further identified that the states became even more disunited by

---

[71] Denning 2005, pp. 60–61.

[72] Denning 2005, p. 61.

[73] Barnett 2001, p. 121.

[74] Eileen Hunt Botting, 'Protofeminist Responses to the Federalist-Antifederalist Debate', The Federalist Papers (Yale University Press 2009) 533.

[75] Hamilton and Madison 2009, No. 6, p. 26 and No. 7, pp. 33–34.

[76] Hamilton and Madison 2009, No. 22, pp. 107–108.

engaging in a commercial war, thereby restricting interstate commerce.[77] He claimed that this war resulted from the common situation where neighbouring states 'are natural enemies of each other' based on a 'secret jealousy' towards each other.[78] He thus argued that in the 'commercial republic' of the United States of America, the peaceful method to terminate this situation is for the states to organise themselves in a 'confederate republic,'[79] where the commercial interests of the states, including those of manufacture and agriculture, would be represented by a united government.[80] Accordingly, Hamilton claimed that it had become a widely adopted position that for the advancement of trade and 'the relationship between the Northern and Southern economies', the regulation of interstate commerce should be placed in the hands of 'a federal superintenden[t].'[81] Madison was also in support of the 'new power'[82] that the Constitution created in the area of commerce as he considered one of the functions of the newly created union to act as the 'guardian of commerce.'[83]

It accordingly appears that the Federalists were strongly espousing the ideal that the regulation of interstate commerce should be placed in the hands of Congress. The viewpoint of Madison and Hamilton, on the other hand, seem to have diverged on whether this resulted in the transfer of power from the states to the federal government in this area.

According to Hamilton, there were three ways in which the 'sovereignty' of the states in certain areas could be 'exclusively delegated to the United States.'[84] Firstly, where delegation occurred through 'express terms' in the Constitution, secondly, where the federal government was given express authority in an area and the states were forbidden from regulating 'the like' area.[85] The third instance, he claimed, was where the federal government was given powers in an area and the exercise of 'a similar authority in the States would be absolutely and totally contradictory and repugnant.'[86] He enumerated the commerce clause under the first category, where Congress was granted with the powers of 'exclusive legislation' over the area of interstate commerce.[87] On the other hand, he did not necessarily regard the grant of this exclusive authority a limitation on the states in the same area. He thus argued that when it was the intention of the Framers to deprive the

---

[77] Hamilton and Madison 2009, No. 32, pp. 155–156.

[78] Hamilton and Madison 2009, No. 6, p. 31.

[79] Hamilton and Madison 2009, No. 6, p. 28.

[80] Hamilton and Madison 2009, No. 11, p. 54 and No. 12, pp. 73–74 and Nelson and Pushaw 1999, p. 41.

[81] Hamilton and Madison 2009, No. 11 54 and No. 22 107; Nelson and Pushaw 1999, p. 41.

[82] Hamilton and Madison 2009, No. 45, p. 238.

[83] Hamilton and Madison 2009, No. 14, p. 67.

[84] Hamilton and Madison 2009, No. 32, pp. 155–156.

[85] Hamilton and Madison 2009, No. 32, p. 156.

[86] Hamilton and Madison 2009, No. 32, p. 156.

[87] Hamilton and Madison 2009, No. 32, p. 156.

states of their powers in an area, where they were considered to be the improper guardians of the same powers, a 'negative clause' was drafted by the Framers.[88] It may therefore be asserted that Hamilton did not support the ideal that states should be deprived of their powers in total to regulate interstate commerce as no 'negative clause' can be found in the Constitution that would expressly state the above.[89]

Madison was, however, in support of a different method to attain the uniform regulation of interstate commerce. He claimed that the commerce clause was, in fact, intended as a 'negative and preventive' measure to eliminate the discriminatory protectionist laws enacted by the states.[90] It may thus be argued that he claimed that the commerce clause also served as a limitation on state authority in the area of interstate commerce.[91]

It consequently appears that the Federalists have adopted a wider understanding of the term 'commerce,' which included the areas of manufacture and agriculture. They further understood the part 'among the States' of the commerce clause to refer to activities 'between the states.'[92] They also appeared to be in support of the viewpoint that to provide a solution to the discriminatory protectionist measures imposed by the states after the Revolution, the power over interstate commerce had to be transferred to the federal government. On the other hand, they seem to have disagreed about the means to achieve such a system and have argued for different means to attain the same end.

14.2.4.4 The Anti-Federalists

The opposing political group that had an influence over the ratification debates of the Constitution was 'The Anti-Federalists,' who were fundamentally opposed to the adoption of the Constitution and aimed to call a second convention.[93] One of their main criticisms of the proposed Constitution was that it created a federal government that possessed powers too great without allocating adequately wide powers to the states.

The extent and severity of the problems posed by the discriminatory measures can be clearly derived from the fact that disagreements were surprisingly almost non-existent between the Federalists and the Anti-Federalists in the area of interstate commerce.[94] Those who were so strongly opposed to the idea of a centralised power in the hands of the federal government also considered it necessary for the

---

[88] Hamilton and Madison 2009, No. 32, p. 158.

[89] Hamilton and Madison 2009, No. 32, p. 158.

[90] Letter of February 13, 1829, to J.C. Cabell, Farrand 1937, vol. 3, p. 478—as referred to from Abel 1940, p. 469. See also Tribe 2000, pp. 1044–45 and Konar-Steenberg 2009, p. 962.

[91] Eule 1982, p. 431 and McGinley 1992, p. 413.

[92] Nelson and Pushaw 1999, pp. 44–46.

[93] Brant 1965, p. 39.

[94] Nelson and Pushaw 1999, p. 36 and Friedman and Deacon 2011, p. 1894.

federal government to be entrusted with the creation of a uniform system of interstate commerce.

Nonetheless, the method of obtaining this uniform system was still unclear: Congress was granted the exclusive authority to regulate interstate commerce, but it was still not determined what was to happen to measures enacted by the states in the same area.

14.3 The Development of the Dormant Commerce Clause

The search for a solution to the above question has been ongoing since the adoption of the Constitution. The commerce clause has thus unsurprisingly become one of the most litigated areas of the federal Constitution, with disagreements about its meaning continuing up to date.

Whilst searching for the above solution, the interpretation of the commerce clause has also developed a double—an affirmative and a negative—understanding. This dual understanding of the commerce clause developed around the two main questions posed previously. The affirmative understanding involves the authority of Congress and the limitations of these powers of Congress. The negative aspect examines the commerce clause from the angle about which the Constitution remained silent: whether the grant of power to Congress limits the authority of the states to regulate in this area. This dual understanding of the commerce clause thus resulted in crucial questions about the regulation of this system: not only about the extent of the limitations of the powers of the states that inevitably restricts the powers of the federal government, but about the situation vice versa as well.

In the following, the chapter will investigate the interpretation of the commerce clause through the main judgments of the Supreme Court in this area and how these provided a solution to the two main fundamental questions that originate from the interpretation of the commerce clause. It will also place a special emphasis on the development of the definition of interstate commerce by analysing the understanding of 'commerce' and 'among the states,' where possible, in the judgments.

14.3.1 The First Answer: Dual Federalism

The first main case of the Supreme Court that required the interpretation of the commerce clause was *Gibbons v Ogden*,[95] which concerned the operation of steamboats in the interstate route between New York and Elizabethtown.[96] Gibbons operated his steamboats with a licence granted under federal laws on this route,

[95] *Gibbons v Ogden* (1824) 22 US 1.

[96] *Gibbons v Ogden* (1824) 22 US 1, pp. 2–4.

which had been stopped from navigating the waters of New York.[97] Ogden, when filing for the injunction to request the above, claimed that Gibbons violated the license requirement imposed by the state of New York for intrastate navigation that had created exclusive rights for him to navigate the waters of New York from 1808 until 1838.[98] Gibbons, in response claimed that the New York law was contrary to —among others—the commerce clause of the federal Constitution.[99]

Before declaring whether this state law contravened the federal commerce clause, Chief Justice Marshall attempted to provide a decision in the case by firstly defining interstate commerce. He thus first held that commerce was to be defined widely and should be identified as 'commercial intercourse'.[100] This 'organic conception of commerce,' he held, clearly included navigation.[101] He subsequently adopted the view that 'commerce among the states' was to be understood as 'intercourse' that was to do 'with the states,' that 'intermingled with' the states and that 'concern[ed] more States than one.'[102] This viewpoint seems to be in direct support of the first ideology about the wide definition of commerce in the times of the adoption of the Constitution. On the other hand, if one is to follow the ideology that the Framers of the Constitution only wished for the economic areas of commerce to be included in the commerce clause, it may be argued that Chief Justice Marshall, in effect, extended the definition of commerce to areas that might not have been intended to be included in the Constitution by the Framers.[103]

After having established that the regulation of interstate navigation falls under the commerce clause, Chief Justice Marshall established—adopting the approach of Federalists—that Congress had been given exclusive powers to regulate interstate commerce.[104] He consequently held—following the approach advocated for by Madison—that while Congress was granted with exclusive powers over interstate commerce, states were still able to exercise their regulatory power in areas that concerned 'their own purely internal affairs, whether of trading or police.'[105] Such subject matters, in the opinion of Chief Justice Marshall, included 'inspection laws, quarantine laws, health laws of every description, as well as laws for regulating the internal commerce of a State, and those which respect turnpike roads, [and] ferries.'[106]

---

[97] *Gibbons v Ogden* (1824) 22 US 1, pp. 2–4.

[98] *Gibbons v Ogden* (1824) 22 US 1, pp. 4–8.

[99] *Gibbons v Ogden* (1824) 22 US 1, pp. 186.

[100] *Gibbons v Ogden* (1824) 22 US 1, pp. 189–190 and 193–194.

[101] Frankfurter 1964, p. 42. Barnett also highlighted that the future Chief Justice Marshall also advocated for the same interpretation of commerce during the ratifying convention in Virginia. See Barnett 2001, p. 123.

[102] *Gibbons v Ogden* (1824) 22 US 1, pp. 189–190 and 193–194.

[103] Tushnet 2009, pp. 162–163.

[104] *Gibbons v Ogden* (1824) 22 US 1, pp. 199–200 and Corwin 1933, p. 484.

[105] *Gibbons v Ogden* (1824) 22 US 1, pp. 209–210.

[106] *Gibbons v Ogden* (1824) 22 US 1, pp. 209–210.

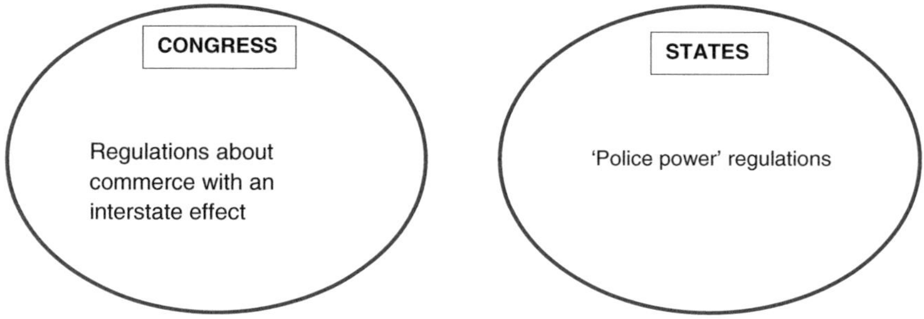

Fig. 14.1 Distribution of powers between Congress and States in the field of commerce as a result of *Gibbons v Ogden* (*Source*: Eszter Belteki)

Thus, it may be argued, states were still able to regulate commerce, but only those activities that concerned the so-called 'police power[s]' of the state.[107] A particular characteristic of these activities was that they could still be held constitutional even if they had 'considerable influence on commerce' as the power to regulate these belonged to the states and not the federal government.[108] The above approach adopted by Chief Justice Marshall demonstrated the initial support for the ideal of the 'dual federalist' system of the United States.[109] Adopting this ideology, it may be argued that two separate spheres of regulatory power exist in the area of commerce based on the subject matter of the regulation. Correspondingly, the regulatory power over interstate commerce was granted to Congress and that over intrastate commerce—or as Chief Justice Marshall characterised these as 'police powers'—was still possessed by the states (Fig. 14.1).

An implication of this model addresses the negative understanding of the commerce clause. If Congress was to have exclusive powers over interstate commerce, the states, adopting the Madisonian approach,[110] were implied not to possess any regulatory power in this area. This provides the Supreme Court with the ability to hold state regulations unconstitutional under the commerce clause in this dual federalist model. As soon as a federal statute existed that regulated the area of commerce in question, state laws would further become 'invalidated' under the supremacy clause.[111] A further aspect of this approach is that it would be the Supreme Court who would be able to determine the limits of the powers of the states in regulating interstate commerce and as a consequence would possess the power to extend or limit their regulatory powers.[112]

---

[107] Corwin 1933, p. 480.

[108] Chemerinsky 2013, p. 462.

[109] Corwin 1933, p. 481.

[110] Letter of February 13, 1829, to J.C. Cabell, Farrand 1937, vol. 3, p. 478—as referred to from Abel 1940, p. 469. See also Tribe 2000, pp. 1044–45 and Konar-Steenberg 2009, p. 962.

[111] Denning 2015, para 6.02.

[112] Frankfurter 1964, p. 18.

Furthermore, many ensuing cases involved the interpretation of the commerce clause from this negative understanding. One such case was *Willson v Black Bird Creek,*[113] where Chief Justice Marshall characterised this negative understanding as the 'dormant' aspect of the commerce clause.[114] This case concerned a Delaware law that allowed for the building of a dam on Black Bird Creek that was argued to be unconstitutional under the 'dormant state' of the commerce clause as it 'interfered with interstate navigation'.[115] Chief Justice Marshall subsequently held that the state law in question was not unconstitutional, as it was merely the exercise of the police powers of the state, which resulted in the improvement of 'the health of the local inhabitants', the regulatory power over which clearly belonged to the state.[116]

Whilst the above cases did not result in the adoption of the expression 'dormant commerce clause' for the negative aspects of the commerce clause immediately, as the successor of Chief Justice Marshall did not agree with the formulation of this dual federalist approach to the commerce clause, the majority of constitutional scholars and Supreme Court judges originate the term dormant commerce clause from the decision in *Gibbons v Ogden.*[117] Moreover, most of the succeeding challenges under the commerce clause argued in front of the Supreme Court for an extensive time concerned the interpretation of this negative aspect. The successor of Chief Justice Marshall, Chief Justice Taney, was thus entrusted with the task of engaging in the further interpretation of this aspect of the commerce clause.

14.3.2 The Concurrent Authority Approach

Whilst Chief Justice Marshall adopted the view that the states did not possess powers to regulate interstate commerce as that power had been exclusively granted to Congress under the commerce clause, this standpoint appeared to be unacceptable for his successor, Chief Justice Taney. He, instead, formulated a novel position, which claimed that the regulatory powers of the states under the commerce clause were not limited in all instances. Following his approach, the states had regulatory powers over interstate commerce when Congress had not legislated in the same area that the states had done so. This approach would consequently result

[113] *Willson v Black Bird Creek Marsh Co* (1829) 27 US (2 Pet) 245.

[114] *Willson v Black Bird Creek Marsh Co* (1829) 27 US (2 Pet) 245, 252, Frankfurter 1964, p. 28 and Friedman and Deacon 2011, p. 1920.

[115] Felmly 2003, p. 472.

[116] Chapin 1991, p. 165.

[117] *Gibbons v Ogden* (1824) 22 US 1. See also Felmly 2003, p. 472 about the debates when this doctrine was 'formally adopted.'

in the Supreme Court being deprived of its tasks as understood by Chief Justice Marshall of determining the limits of the powers of the states in such instances.[118] Chief Justice Taney thus established an ideology—strongly in opposition to the ideology developed by Chief Justice Marshall—of 'concurrent authority' over interstate commerce between Congress and the states in *The Licence Cases*.[119]

Following this approach, the states were able to exercise regulatory powers that would have been held unconstitutional under the dual federalist theory. The 'concurrent authority' approach recognised that the states had before and since the adoption of the Constitution had been enacting legislations that had regulated the area of interstate commerce and refused to invalidate these laws based on the distinction established by *Gibbons v Ogden*[120] between commerce and police powers, since Chief Justice Taney claimed that the above characterisation based on the subject matter of the regulation was 'untenable.'[121] Under the dual federalist approach states would not have been recognised as holding any regulatory powers over interstate commerce, as that was claimed to be an area the regulation of which had been exclusively granted to Congress.

The concurrent authority approach, on the other hand, claimed that the states were allowed to regulate the same areas as Congress in the limited instances where Congress was silent, i.e. it had not legislated, in the subject matter in question. This viewpoint also seemingly rejects the ideology that the grant of regulatory powers to Congress under the commerce clause was exclusive if states could still regulate the same area. Accordingly, it may be argued that the states were allowed to retain their regulatory authority over a wider area of commerce than under the previous approach.

An additional way through which Chief Justice Taney wished to achieve the restrictions of the powers of Congress was the restrained interpretation of the definition of commerce. For instance, he argued that the 'intercourse of persons' could still be regulated by the states, since such acts did not constitute commerce in *The Passenger Cases*.[122]

This novel standpoint also addressed the question whether the commerce clause posed a limitation on the regulatory powers of the states in interstate commerce. Chief Justice Taney claimed that such a limitation might only exist when Congress had enacted a legislation about the same subject matter that the states had done so.[123] It is interesting to highlight that this determination adopted the approach previously developed by Chief Justice Marshall, whose decision in *Gibbons v*

---

[118] Denning 2008, p. 432; Lang 2012, p. 79 and McGinley 1992, p. 413.

[119] *The Licence Cases* (1847) 46 US 504, p. 579, Denning 2008, p. 434 and Friedman and Deacon 2011, p. 1930.

[120] *Gibbons v Ogden* (1824) 22 US 1.

[121] Frankfurter 1964, p. 51; Denning 2008, p. 432.

[122] The Passenger Cases (1849) 7 How 283, pp. 474 and 493 as referred to from Frankfurter 1964, p. 59.

[123] Frankfurter 1964, p. 50.

Ogden[124] Chief Justice Taney was so strongly opposed to.[125] What was important, still, according to him, was the subject matter of the regulation. On the other hand, he did not adopt the approach completely as in *The Licence Cases*[126] he held that a state regulation could only be held unconstitutional under the commerce clause if the subject matter of both the state and federal regulations was a 'truly national concern.'[127] Unsurprisingly, he failed to identify what regulations would constitute a 'truly national concern' in the four later commerce clause cases presented to the Supreme Court while he served as its Chief Justice.[128] On the other hand, it would seem that with acknowledging that certain subject matters were of 'truly national concern',[129] he, in effect, recognised that a uniform national system was required to regulate such matters.

It may consequently be established that the model of the dual federalist approach seemed to have been partly rejected by the Supreme Court with the inception of the concurrent authority approach. Traces of the dual federalist approach could still be identified in the concurrent authority approach as, for instance, the characterisation of a regulation based on its subject matter was still utilised by the Court.[130] Another trace of the dual federalist approach present in this novel approach was that Congress and the states still possessed exclusive regulatory powers. Congress regulated subject matters of 'truly national concern'[131] that it assumed the exclusive regulatory power over when it enacted federal law about these. Until that point, the regulatory power over the subject matter of the regulation was an exclusive one of the states.

The concurrent authority approach, however, also created a novel problem as it became obvious that in certain subject matters, both Congress and the states would want to regulate. It therefore posed a challenge to decide which of them possessed regulatory powers over the subject matter in question, with a test that lacked clear definition.

14.3.3 The Novel National—Local Test

The change that determined the method the Supreme Court applied in the interpretation of the commerce clause for the subsequent decades arrived in a case once again about navigation laws. In *Cooley v Board of Wardens of the Port of*

---

124 *Gibbons v Ogden* (1824) 22 US 1.

125 McGinley 1992, p. 413.

126 *The Licence Cases* (1847) 46 US 504.

127 McGinley 1992, p. 413.

128 Friedman and Deacon 2011, p. 1930 and Denning 2008, p. 432.

129 McGinley 1992, p. 413.

130 Tribe 2000, pp. 1046–1047.

131 McGinley 1992, p. 413.

Philadelphia[132] Cooley, the owner of two vessels was required to pay a fine for contravening a state pilotage law of Pennsylvania, which regulation, he argued, was invalid under the commerce clause.[133]

In delivering the unanimous opinion of the court, Justice Curtis firstly held that it was 'settled' that the understanding of commerce encompassed navigation.[134] He consequently argued that the regulation of pilots "offering and rendering their services, of the responsibilities which shall rest upon them, of the powers they shall possess, of the compensation they may demand, and of the penalties by which their rights and duties may be enforced" amounted to regulation about navigation and thus of commerce.[135] It may thus become apparent that in the area of navigation, Justice Curtis adopted the approach that argued for the wider understanding of commerce.

He subsequently claimed that it had not been addressed by the Court clearly beforehand whether Congress had been given exclusive authority to regulate interstate commerce that deprived states of all their authority.[136] He thus formulated the viewpoint that this was not the case and the grant of power to Congress under the commerce clause did not 'expressly exclude the States from exercising an authority over its subject-matter.'[137] He subsequently argued that the states were still allowed to regulate the areas in interstate commerce that were 'imperatively demanding […] diversity' and could therefore only be adequately addressed by 'local' state regulation.[138] Consequently, Congress was to regulate only those 'national' areas of interstate commerce that required 'exclusive legislation by Congress.'[139]

This novel approach of 'selective exclusiveness'[140] seemingly rejects the interpretation of the commerce clause under the dual federalist approach as formulated by Chief Justice Marshall. Whilst he argued that both Congress and the

---

[132] *Aaron B Cooley v The Board of Wardens of the Port of Philadelphia, to the use of the Society for the Relief of distressed Pilots, their Widows and Children* (1851) 53 US (12 How) 299.

[133] *Aaron B Cooley v The Board of Wardens of the Port of Philadelphia, to the use of the Society for the Relief of distressed Pilots, their Widows and Children* (1851) 53 US (12 How) 299, pp. 300–301.

[134] *Aaron B Cooley v The Board of Wardens of the Port of Philadelphia, to the use of the Society for the Relief of distressed Pilots, their Widows and Children* (1851) 53 US (12 How) 299, p. 315.

[135] *Aaron B Cooley v The Board of Wardens of the Port of Philadelphia, to the use of the Society for the Relief of distressed Pilots, their Widows and Children* (1851) 53 US (12 How) 299, p. 316.

[136] *Aaron B Cooley v The Board of Wardens of the Port of Philadelphia, to the use of the Society for the Relief of distressed Pilots, their Widows and Children* (1851) 53 US (12 How) 299, p. 318.

[137] Ibid.; Friedman and Deacon 2011, p. 1924.

[138] *Aaron B Cooley v The Board of Wardens of the Port of Philadelphia, to the use of the Society for the Relief of distressed Pilots, their Widows and Children* (1851) 53 US (12 How) 299, Tribe 2000, pp. 1048–1049 and McGinley 1992, p. 414.

[139] *Aaron B Cooley v The Board of Wardens of the Port of Philadelphia, to the use of the Society for the Relief of distressed Pilots, their Widows and Children* (1851) 53 US (12 How) 299, Tribe 2000, pp. 1048–1049.

[140] Schütze 2009, p. 91.

states had exclusive powers to regulate the areas that they possessed based on a distinction characterised by the subject matter of the regulation, the selective exclusiveness approach made this dependant on the 'nature' of the subject matter. If it concerned a subject matter of 'local' nature that required diverse application by the different states, the exclusive power to regulate remained with the states. If the regulation, however, concerned a subject matter that was of 'national' nature, requiring a uniform regulation by Congress, the exclusive powers of regulating this area were granted to Congress. On the other hand, as highlighted, this test still retained the characteristics of the dual federalist approach by claiming that both Congress and the states still possessed exclusive powers over the different areas of interstate commerce. It may thus be argued that this approach was not a complete rejection of the dual federalist approach, but an alteration of it.

This selective exclusiveness standpoint thus addressed both the fundamental questions that originate from the commerce clause. Firstly, it claimed that Congress was granted exclusive powers; however, the extent of these was limited to areas of interstate commerce that were of 'national' nature. It also addressed the second question, arguing that the powers of the states were limited in the areas of interstate commerce as they could not regulate areas of 'national' concern. On the other hand, they had powers to regulate areas of interstate commerce of 'local' concern, which Congress could not interfere with.

Another key characteristic of this approach is that it fails to clearly identify what matters of 'local' and 'national' nature were (see Fig. 14.2).[141] To determine the above, Justice Curtis in this case used a more technical approach, similar to the one adopted by Chief Justice Taney previously: he held that what should be examined is whether a federal regulation had been enacted about a similar subject matter.[142] This, he held, would show how Congress regarded the nature of the subject matter. It may thus be argued that three situations could arise based on this approach:

(1) If Congress had enacted a regulation claiming that it was to regulate the subject matter, that was of 'national' nature;
(2) if Congress had enacted a regulation claiming that it is for the states to regulate a certain area, that was of 'local' nature and
(3) if Congress had not legislated in the area, it was to be held of 'local' nature .[143]

This part of his judgment, in effect, blended the previously adopted approaches to the interpretation of the commerce clause. The first category was already present under the dual federalist approach and the third category was an alteration of the concurrent authority approach.

---

[141] Felmly 2003, p. 473.

[142] *Aaron B Cooley v The Board of Wardens of the Port of Philadelphia, to the use of the Society for the Relief of distressed Pilots, their Widows and Children* (1851) 53 US (12 How) 299, pp. 317–318 and 323–324.

[143] Schütze 2009, p. 91 and Lang 2012, pp. 80–81.

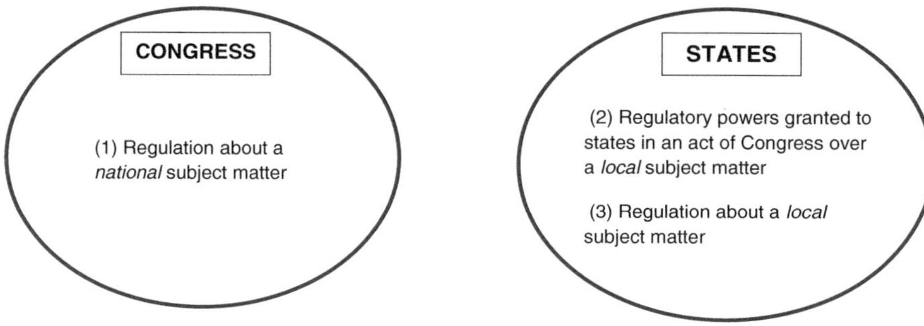

Fig. 14.2 Distribution of powers between Congress and States in the field of commerce as a result of the application of the selective exclusiveness approach (*Source*: Eszter Belteki)

The novel approach was, in fact, the second category, which allowed Congress to transfer its exclusive authority to the states in an area that it was assigned to regulate. This interpretation would have not existed under the dual federalist approach and it may also be argued that this approach developed due to the recognition by Congress that states should possess regulatory powers over certain matters that might have been delegated to Congress in the Constitution. On the other hand, if Congress is able to delegate its exclusive powers to the states, would it not be acting unconstitutionally as these powers had been granted exclusively for them for a uniform interpretation to be applied to interstate commerce? Or would Congress simply be exercising its powers as it was 'necessary and proper' under Article I, Section 8? These questions, however, remained unanswered in this case.

Justice Curtis subsequently found that the Act of Congress in question belonged to the second category as it was, in effect, a grant of power to states to regulate 'all pilots in the bays, inlets, rivers, harbors, and ports of the United States' until Congress withdrew this authority.[144] He thus held that the regulation of Pennsylvania was not invalid under the commerce clause as its 'nature' had previously been declared by an act of Congress to be an area of 'local' concern, which could 'be the best provided for' by state regulation.[145]

A characteristic of this novel approach that may be emphasised is that Justice Curtis, similarly to the previous decisions, recognised that certain areas of interstate commerce that were of national nature required a uniform regulatory system. The new national-local test that he devised also, firstly, provided a novel approach for determining the limits of the regulatory powers of both Congress and the state in areas of interstate commerce. It also constituted a reconciliation attempt of the previous interpretations of the commerce clause: it retained characteristics of the

[144] *Aaron B Cooley v The Board of Wardens of the Port of Philadelphia, to the use of the Society for the Relief of distressed Pilots, their Widows and Children* (1851) 53 US (12 How) 299.

[145] *Aaron B Cooley v The Board of Wardens of the Port of Philadelphia, to the use of the Society for the Relief of distressed Pilots, their Widows and Children* (1851) 53 US (12 How) 299, p. 319.

dual federalist and concurrent authority approaches.[146] A 'new era' thus commenced where the Supreme Court by utilising this new test could make the 'indefiniteness' of the commerce clause 'in some way manageable.'[147] This new era, however, also required the Supreme Court to take into consideration the two fundamental questions that arose after the adoption of the Constitution and especially the commerce clause.

14.3.4 A Narrower Definition of Commerce

A main feature of the cases following *Cooley v Board of Wardens of the Port of Philadelphia*[148] was the interpretation of the understanding of commerce and how this affected the extent of the regulatory powers of Congress and the states. Whilst in *Cooley v Board of Wardens of the Port of Philadelphia*[149] it was claimed that the definition of commerce encompassed navigation, the concept of commerce as a whole was not clearly defined by Justice Curtis. This enabled the Supreme Court to create novel, more restrictive interpretations of the concept of commerce.

Kidd v Pearson[150] was such an instance. The interpretation of the definition of commerce adopted in this case stated that manufacture was inherently different from commerce. Therefore, any state law regulating manufacture could not be held unconstitutional under the commerce clause, since that area was not classed as commerce.[151] Whilst devising this interpretation Justice Lamar adopted the test formulated by Chief Justice Marshall, which claimed that the determinant in the test whether the states had regulatory powers over an area of interstate commerce was the subject matter. On the other hand, he argued that it had to be determined whether the subject matter of the regulation could be classified as commerce, which had to be determined based on its 'functions.'[152] He consequently held that manufacture could not be categorised as commerce since its function, he argued, was 'the fashioning of raw materials into a change of form for use.'[153] He distinguished this from thc functions of commerce, which he held, involved 'the buying and selling and the transportation incidental thereto.'[154]

---

[146] Tribe 2000, p. 1047 and McGinley 1992, p. 414.

[147] Denning 2008, p. 436.

[148] *Aaron B Cooley v The Board of Wardens of the Port of Philadelphia, to the use of the Society for the Relief of distressed Pilots, their Widows and Children* (1851) 53 US (12 How) 299.

[149] *Aaron B Cooley v The Board of Wardens of the Port of Philadelphia, to the use of the Society for the Relief of distressed Pilots, their Widows and Children* (1851) 53 US (12 How) 299.

[150] *Kidd v Pearson* (1888) 128 US 1.

[151] Williams 2007, p. 1867.

[152] Williams 2007, p. 1867.

[153] *Kidd v Pearson* (1888) 128 US 1, p. 20.

[154] *Kidd v Pearson* (1888) 128 US 1, p. 20.

Justice Lamar, further adopting the narrowest interpretation of the definition of commerce, which was classed under the third group in the beginning of this chapter, argued that the definition of commerce did not only exclude manufacture but 'agriculture, horticulture, stockraising, domestic fisheries, mining—in short every branch of human industry' could not be classified as commerce either.[155] Accordingly, if the state law was to regulate any of these activities, it did not regulate commerce and, thus, could not be held unconstitutional under the commerce clause.[156]

By restricting the definition of commerce, Justice Lamar also seems to have restricted the regulatory powers of Congress in interstate commerce, as it could no longer legislate in areas that it might have been allowed to do so under the previous decisions. Correspondingly, this restriction also resulted in the increase of the activities that the states were allowed to regulate. This regulatory power of the states further expanded in various following cases and was held to include activities such as 'ginning,' 'the manufacture of oleomargarine' or mining.[157] Moreover, the nature of the subject matter was no longer significant once it was established that the function of the subject matter was the production of an article of commerce.

It may thus also be argued that this position not only adopted a restricted definition of commerce, but, at the same time, also created a transformed interpretation of the dual federalist approach to the commerce clause. Under this new approach, the regulatory powers of the states not only increased, but they were also allowed to exercise their regulatory powers in areas that could have been held to belong exclusively to Congress under the previous approaches. Analogously, Congress was still able to exercise its exclusive regulatory powers over interstate commerce, but only over activities that were included in the narrow definition of commerce and that were interstate in nature. In order to determine what this concept included, Justice Lamar firstly identified commerce as 'the buying and selling and the transportation incidental' to the production of an article of commerce.[158] He subsequently devised a test for the interpretation of when the powers of Congress over interstate commerce commenced. He held that such regulatory powers of Congress began to take effect from the time when the article of commerce was 'shipped, or entered with a common carrier for transportation to another State, or have been started upon such transportation in a continuous route or journey.'[159]

It thus seemed that even though initially the commerce clause granted regulatory powers over a wide range of activities to Congress, the extent of these activities commenced to be restricted by the Supreme Court. Furthermore, these restrictions

[155] Davis 1907, p. 215.

[156] For the application of this standpoint see for instance *Morgan's Louisiana & TR & SS Co v Louisiana Board of Health* (1886) 118 US 455, *Pound v Turck* (1877) 95 US (5 Otto) 459 or *Hannibal & St J R Co v Husen* (1878) 95 US (5 Otto) 465, as referred to from Denning (2015) para 6.04.

[157] Williams 2007, p. 1868.

[158] Williams 2007, p. 1868.

[159] *Kidd v Pearson* (1888) 128 US 1, p. 25.

also became apparent in the interpretation of the definition of the 'commerce' and 'among the states' components of the commerce clause. As a result, the powers of the states therefore seemed to increase, while the powers of Congress commenced to be restricted by the Supreme Court.

14.3.5 The Direct-Indirect Burden Test

Following the creation of the novel federalist system, not only the political and constitutional landscape, but the economy of the United States had been transforming as well.[160] For instance, with the creation of interstate railways, it was becoming less problematic to produce 'goods that could be advertised and sold nationwide.'[161] With such developments in interstate transportation, commerce—in its widest definition—commenced to transform. Whilst at the time of the adoption of the Constitution producing articles of commerce for the interstate or national market was not common, such interstate production, transportation and trade became more regular.

This changing economic climate, however, required a uniform system of interstate commerce even more than in 1787, where the flow of commerce would not be restricted by discriminatory measures imposed by states on out-of-state commerce. On the other hand, following the national-local test of *Cooley,*[162] the complete elimination of discriminatory measures would have required the Supreme Court to hold all areas of interstate commerce of 'national' nature. This would have required the extension of the regulatory powers of Congress and the reduction of the areas the regulatory powers over which were still held to belong to the states. Based on the developments in technology, many cases from this era were inevitably brought as challenges of regulations of activities related to the novel railways.

The first group of cases in this era that asked for the invalidation of state regulations under the negative aspect of the commerce clause were those that applied the test devised in *Cooley.*[163] In *Smith v Alabama*[164] the Supreme Court found the state regulation that required train operators to 'be licensed by a state board of examiners' to be of local concern and thus constitutional under the negative aspect of the commerce clause.[165] Conversely, in *Wabash, St Louis & Pacific*

[160] Denning 2008, p. 437.

[161] Denning 2008, p. 438.

[162] *Aaron B Cooley v The Board of Wardens of the Port of Philadelphia, to the use of the Society for the Relief of distressed Pilots, their Widows and Children* (1851) 53 US (12 How) 299, pp. 317–319.

[163] *Aaron B Cooley v The Board of Wardens of the Port of Philadelphia, to the use of the Society for the Relief of distressed Pilots, their Widows and Children* (1851) 53 US (12 How) 299, pp. 317–319.

[164] *Smith v Alabama* (1888) 124 US 465.

[165] Chemerinsky 2013, p. 464.

Railway Co v Illinois[166] the application of the national-local test resulted in holding the state regulation about 'the intrastate rates' that railway operators could charge for out-of-state articles of commerce unconstitutional under the negative aspect of the commerce clause.[167] Therefore, while these cases extended the regulatory powers of the states in some areas, contravening the ideal that uniform legislation was required by Congress exclusively in all areas of interstate commerce, they also reduced the regulatory powers of the states in certain areas.

The second group of cases of this era devised a novel test the focus of which was placed on the interpretation of what constituted commerce 'among the states' contrary to that of 'commerce.' However, the novel test adopted an approach that instead of the nature of the subject matter of the regulation examined its effects.

This method thus determined that if the state regulation was 'only indirectly, incidentally, and remotely' affecting interstate commerce, it was not unconstitutional under the negative commerce clause.[168] Acts with such effect were held to be, for instance, the restriction of 'train speed within city limits' and the requirements to have a specific number of 'brakemen on freight trains of over 25 cars' in the area of railway regulations.[169] Moreover, a similar test was also utilised when holding states laws about the quarantine of cattle or state blue sky laws constitutional.[170] Consequently, under this approach the regulations that posed such a 'substantial' burden on interstate commerce that they were deemed to be a 'direct burden,' were held to be invalid under the negative aspect of the commerce clause as the regulatory powers over such activities belonged exclusively to Congress.[171] Such direct burden was found in *Seaboard Air Line Railway v Blackwell*,[172] where under the state regulation an interstate train would have been required to come to a halt '124 times within 123 miles.'[173]

Whereas it may seem that the Supreme Court upheld the distinction between the two distinct and exclusive regulatory powers over interstate commerce, during this period the limits of these powers became highly blurred. Whilst applying the *Cooley*[174] test utilised the nature of the subject matter of the regulation, with the direct-indirect test the subject matter of the regulation became less relevant, and it was the effects of the regulation that had to be examined. Such an examination relied on 'subjective, and eminently manipulable distinctions' and effectively

---

[166] *Wabash, St. Louis and Pacific Railway Company v Illinois* (1886) 118 US 557.

[167] Tribe 2000, p. 1048 and Chemerinsky 2013, p. 464.

[168] Tribe 2000, p. 1049; Denning 2008, pp. 438–439 and Cushman 2000, pp. 1111–1114.

[169] Tribe 2000, p. 1049. See the cases *Accord, Erb v Morasch* (1900) 177 US 584; *Chicago, Rock Island & Pacific Railway Company v Arkansas* (1911) 219 US 453.

[170] Cushman 2000, pp. 1116–1117.

[171] Tribe 2000, p. 1049.

[172] *Seaboard Air Line Railway v Blackwell* (1917) 244 US 310.

[173] Tribe 2000, p. 1049.

[174] *Aaron B Cooley v The Board of Wardens of the Port of Philadelphia, to the use of the Society for the Relief of distressed Pilots, their Widows and Children* (1851) 53 US (12 How) 299.

resulted in regulations about the same subject matter by the states being held in one case constitutional and unconstitutional in another.[175]

It may be argued that the lack of a clear definition of a concept, such as 'commerce,' may prove beneficial in situations where it serves for the harmonisation of the laws with the advancements of society and the economy.[176] On the other hand, the approach of the Supreme Court to the negative aspects of the commerce clause in 1927 could be summarised as 'the states [...] [were allowed to] regulate interstate commerce, but not too much.'[177] The contradictory judgments about the same subject matter and the above statement clearly demonstrate that the lack of a clear standard had created high legal uncertainty, increasing the need for a reform in this area.

14.4 The Modern Approach to the Dormant Commerce Clause

It became apparent for the Supreme Court towards the middle of the twentieth century that the direct-indirect approach it previously adopted in dormant commerce clause cases would be unsuitable for the challenges argued in front of the modern Supreme Court.[178] An important element that contributed toward this change was the various opinions of Chief Justice Stone, who was the main critic of the direct-indirect test.[179] Therefore, expectedly, a new approach emerged in this era about the interpretation of the negative aspect of the commerce clause, which effectively transformed into the current modern approach.[180]

A challenge to a state regulation under the dormant commerce clause will have to satisfy a novel 'two-tiered standard' in order to be held unconstitutional:[181] it will have to be deemed non-discriminatory under the first anti-discrimination tier and will, secondly, also have to satisfy a novel balancing test. In the following, the development of each of these tiers will be considered separately.

---

[175] Williams 2007, pp. 1869 and 1872. Two such subject matters of these cases were the taxation of out-of-state goods and racial segregation on modes of transportation, see ibid., 1874–1876.

[176] Justice Holmes, for instance, in *Towne v Eisner* (1918) 245 US 418, 438. stated: 'a word is not a crystal, transparent and unchanged; it is the skin of a living thought and may vary greatly in color and content according to the circumstances and the time in which it is used.'

[177] Powell 1928, p. 491.

[178] Felmly 2003, p. 475 and Regan 1986, p. 1094.

[179] Regan 1986, p. 1094. See *DiSanto v Pennsylvania* (1927) 273 US 34; *Southern Pacific Co v Arizona ex rel Sullivan, Attorney General* (1945) 325 US 761.

[180] McGinley 1992, p. 414.

[181] Day 2003, pp. 46–47; Friedman and Deacon 2011, p. 1926; Felmly 2003, p. 47 and Larsen 2004, p. 850.

14.4.1 *The First Tier Test: The Anti-Discrimination Principle*

Modern cases addressing the dormant commerce clause, somewhat surprisingly, do not concentrate on the interpretation of either 'commerce' or 'among the states.' These cases have developed a novel test that focuses on an entirely different approach to the commerce clause: discrimination in the area of commerce between the states.

Even though it has been argued above that discriminatory and protectionist measures constituted one of the reasons that led to the call for the creation of a uniform system for the regulation of interstate commerce, what these measures can be identified as has been failed to take centre-stage in decisions about the interpretation of the commerce clause until after the New Deal.[182] On the other hand, state regulations challenged under the dormant commerce clause, now have to be first examined based on their discriminatory nature. If a regulation is found to be discriminatory under this tier, it is subsequently held unconstitutional under the dormant commerce clause doctrine, without it having to be examined further under the second tier.

As with many times before in the case of commerce, for the purposes of the dormant commerce clause analysis, the Supreme Court has opted for the adoption of a 'fairly broad' interpretation of 'discrimination,'[183] which is now defined as 'any disparity in the treatment of in-state and out-of-state interests—whether business, users, or products.'[184] Such unequal treatment is commonly identified in constitutional law in three manners in a state regulation, which classification has also been adopted in cases discussing the dormant commerce clause.[185]

14.4.1.1 Facial Discrimination: Per Se Invalid

Firstly, a state regulation may be 'facially discriminatory' by discriminating 'on its face.'[186] Such a regulation was identified in *Dean Milk Co v City of Madison,*[187] where the state law in question required the milk sold locally to have been processed within five miles of the city.[188] Even though this law was silent on the out-of-state interests, it was still found to be facially discriminatory and thus

---

[182] Larsen 2004, p. 844.

[183] Tribe 2000, p. 1059. Larsen also highlighted that the definition of discrimination 'remarkabl [y]' differs for the dormant commerce clause from the other constitutional doctrine. Larsen 2004, pp. 844 and 854.

[184] Tribe 2000, p. 1059; Larsen 2004, p. 853 and Denning 2008, p. 496.

[185] Larsen 2004, p. 854.

[186] Larsen 2004, p. 854.

[187] *Dean Milk Co v City of Madison* (1951) 340 US 349.

[188] Tribe 2000, p. 1083 and Larsen 2004, p. 863.

unconstitutional as it was held to have imposed different burdens on in- and out-of-state interests.[189] The state law in question was also examined further under the second tier test, which will be analysed later.

This requirement for the examination of facially discriminatory laws under the second tier test was, however, held to be unnecessary following the decision in *Philadelphia v New Jersey*.[190] This case concerned a state regulation that prohibited the importation of out-of-state waste claiming that the state did not have enough space to allocate to such waste. Furthermore, New Jersey claimed that 'the improper disposal' of the out-of-state waste would pose high risks to 'the public health, safety, and welfare.'[191] The state regulation was held to be facially discriminatory, as the only reason for the prohibition of the importation of out-of-state waste was its origin.[192] The Supreme Court in this decision held that a state regulation that is facially discriminatory is prohibited under the dormant commerce clause, unless 'there is some reason, apart from the[ir] origin [of articles of commerce], to treat them differently.'[193]

Baldwin v G A F Seelig Inc[194] also involved a state regulation about dairy, asking for a minimum price to be paid for 'milk purchases,' which, in effect, resulted in an advantageous position for in-state milk producers.[195] The Supreme Court held that the state law was invalid under the dormant commerce clause, as it added extra costs on out-of-state dairy farmers, and was therefore also discriminatory in effect.[196] Another state regulation that was held to be unconstitutional based on its facially discriminatory nature was identified in *Chemical Waste Management, Inc v Hunt*,[197] in which the regulation in question imposed an additional fee expressly on 'hazardous waste' originating out-of-state disposed of in the state of Alabama.[198]

In *Maine v Taylor*,[199] the Supreme Court, however, created an exception to this general rule. They held a facially discriminatory state law prohibiting the importation of baitfish from other states constitutional, reasoning that allowing such imports would contaminate the rivers of the state with 'parasites and alien fish

---

[189] Despite the act showing clear discriminatory characteristics, it was, surprisingly, still examined under the second tier test of the modern approach. See Larsen 2004, p. 863.

[190] *Philadelphia v New Jersey* (1978) 437 US 617.

[191] Slattery 2008, p. 1269 and Thompson 2004, p. 226.

[192] Petragnani 1994, p. 1218.

[193] *Philadelphia v New Jersey* (1978) 437 US 617, 626–627 and Farber 1986, p. 397.

[194] *Baldwin, Commissioner of Agriculture & Markets, et al. v GAF Seelig Inc* (1949) 294 US 511, 523.

[195] Collins 1988, p. 97.

[196] Collins 1988, p. 97.

[197] *Chemical Waste Management, Inc v Hunt* (1992) 504 US 334.

[198] Larsen 2004, p. 862 and Tribe 2000, pp. 1065–1066.

[199] *Maine v Taylor* (1986) 477 US 131.

species.'[200] To justify the departure from the per se rule of invalidity they examined the state law in question under the second-tier test, which will be analysed later.

14.4.1.2 Discrimination in Effect

The second type of state regulation that may not be upheld is when the regulation is found to be 'discriminatory in effect.'[201] Such discriminatory effect was identified recently when two separate regulations enacted by Massachusetts were 'operating together' in *West Lynn Creamery, Inc v Healy*,[202] which were held to have created a disparate treatment of in- and out-of-state interests.[203] The two acts in questions created a system where a monthly premium was paid by 'every dealer in milk products' to a fund that subsequently distributed these to in-state dairy dealers.[204] The Supreme Court, however, held the state law invalid under the dormant commerce clause and argued that this was because its discriminatory effects "artificially encourag[ed] in-state production even when the same goods could be produced at lower cost in other States."[205] In reaching this decision, the Supreme Court also argued that the examination of the state law under the first tier had to occur on a "case-by-case analysis of purposes and effects" of the laws.[206]

The discriminatory effect may, however, be present in solely one state regulation on its own, such as in *C & A Carbone, Inc v Town of Clarkstown*.[207] The state regulation in this case required the waste of the city of Clarkstown 'to be processed at the local transfer station prior to leaving town', which in its effects deprived waste haulers from the opportunity to choose a different place to process their waste other than the state appointed private station.[208] This deprivation of free choice was thus held to be disparate treatment of the out-of-state actors of interstate commerce, resulting in "a protectionist effect", consequently making the act unconstitutional.[209]

14.4.1.3 Purposeful Discrimination

Thirdly, a state regulation may show signs of 'purposeful discrimination' when the purpose behind the statute is to create an unequal treatment for in- and out-of-state

---

[200] *Maine v Taylor* (1986) 477 US 131 as referred to from Mank 2009, p. 11.
[201] Larsen 2004, p. 854.
[202] *West Lynn Creamery, Inc v Healy* (1994) 512 US 186.
[203] Larsen 2004, pp. 855–856.
[204] Larsen 2004, p. 855.
[205] Konar-Steenberg 2009, p. 968.
[206] Drahozal 1999, p. 244.
[207] *C & A Carbone, Inc v Town of Clarkstown* (1994) 511 US 383.
[208] Larsen 2004, p. 856.
[209] Larsen 2004, p. 856.

interests.[210] As finding such a purpose requires the examination of 'motives, objectives and end of the legislative body', this type of discrimination is discovered less commonly than the other two types of discrimination.[211] A fundamental decision where the test to identify such discrimination was developed was *Kassel v Consolidated Freightways Corp*,[212] which concerned a regulation enacted by Iowa banning double-tractor trailers longer than sixty-five feet from their roads.[213] Firstly, the Court analysed whether the 'safety objectives' of the act were valid, but found these 'illusory.'[214] It subsequently investigated whether the act 'disproportionately burdened out-of-state interests,' and held that it indeed did so.[215] It lastly examined various statements of the governor of Iowa and found that his support was based on protectionist and discriminatory reasons to benefit the interests of the citizens of Iowa over those coming out of the state.[216]

It may also be argued that in order for a state regulation to be held invalid under the first tier test of the modern approach it will also have to satisfy another component, identified by McGreal.[217] He argued that it will also have to be established that the actors concerned by the state regulation in- and out-of-state are, in fact, 'compet[ing] with one another.'[218] For instance, in *Parker v Brown*,[219] this component was not satisfied as the producers of raisins were held not to be in competition with the 'distributors and consumers', and thus the state regulation was held not to be discriminatory.[220]

It may therefore be argued that if discrimination of any of the above three types is identified in the state regulation, it will be held invalid under the first tier test of the dormant commerce clause, and will not have to be examined under the second tier test of the modern approach. On the other hand, it will be demonstrated below that this approach has not always been followed by the Supreme Court.

14.4.1.4 A Uniform National Market

The emergence of this scrutiny of a state regulation from a discriminatory or protectionist perspective has also re-initiated the debate whether it was the intention of the Framers to create an area of free trade within the United States with the

[210] Larsen 2004, p. 854.
[211] Larsen 2004, p. 859.
[212] *Kassel v Consolidated Freightways Corp* (1981) 450 US 662.
[213] Larsen 2004, p. 859.
[214] Larsen 2004, p. 859.
[215] Larsen 2004, p. 860.
[216] Larsen 2004, p. 860. See also Tribe 2000, pp. 1072–1073.
[217] McGreal 1998, p. 1195.
[218] McGreal 1998, p. 1195. This position was also previously identified by Regan 1986, p. 1096.
[219] *Parker v Brown* (1943) 317 US 341.
[220] Regan 1986, p. 1096.

adoption of the commerce clause. As one may expect, no uniform approach has been accepted about this ideology, but two fundamentally contrasting positions may be identified in the judgments of the Supreme Court and in the academic commentaries.

Political Justifications

The first position, embraced by Tribe, Regan, Kitch and Balkin, argues that the purpose of the commerce clause was—based on the 'political theory of union'[221]—aimed at the promotion of the 'national connection and social cohesion.'[222] Thus a discriminatory or protectionist measure, following this viewpoint, should be held invalid if it posed a threat—as Hamilton stated during the Constitutional Convention—to the 'general welfare of the Union.'[223] This threat may be identified in hostile and retaliatory measures by states against each other.[224]

Another political justification for the development of the dormant commerce clause can be identified in *McCulloch v Maryland*,[225] where it was held by Justice Stone that when a law enacted by a state placed substantial burdens on out-of-state interests, that had to be reviewed by the judiciary, as the interests of those out-of-state could not be adequately represented in the state legislation.[226] The same justification reappeared in the subsequent case of *H P Hood & Sons v Du Mond*,[227] in which the Supreme Court argued that as out-of-state interests are not represented politically within a state, it is for the Justices to guarantee that these are also taken into consideration and are not harmed by any actions of the state.[228] This approach can also be identified in the early case of *McCulloch v Maryland*,[229] where it was held by Justice Stone that when a law enacted by a state placed substantial burdens on out-of-state interests, that had to be reviewed by the judiciary as the interests of those out-of-state could not be adequately represented in the state legislation.[230]

[221] Tribe 2000, p. 1057.

[222] Balkin 2010, p. 17 and Regan 1986, p. 1114—also making a reference to Kitch.

[223] Abel 1940, p. 433.

[224] Baker and Konar-Steenberg 2006, p. 30.

[225] *McCulloch v Maryland* (1819) 17 US (4 Wheat) 316.

[226] *McCulloch v Maryland* (1819) 17 US (4 Wheat) 316, pp. 429–430.

[227] *H P Hood & Sons, Inc v Du Mond, Commissioner of Agriculture and Markets* (1949) 336 US 525.

[228] Farber 1986, p. 396 and Chemerinsky 2013, p. 460.

[229] *McCulloch v Maryland* 17 US (4 Wheat) 316 (1819).

[230] *McCulloch v Maryland* 17 US (4 Wheat) 316 (1819), pp. 429–430.

Economic Justifications

The other position claims that the purpose of the adoption of the commerce clause was the creation of an area of free trade or a common market.[231] Such was the standpoint adopted in *Commonwealth Edison Co v Montana*,[232] where it was expressly held by the Supreme Court that the creation of such a market was 'the very purpose of the commerce clause.'[233] Justice Cardozo famously characterised this approach as 'the peoples of the several states must sink or swim together' in *Baldwin v G A F Seelig Inc.*[234] The same approach also seems to have been adopted in *H P Hood & Sons v Du Mond*,[235] where it was held that the 'economic unit' of the United States of America 'is the Nation.'[236] This unit was held not only to serve to advance the ideal of the free market for 'every framer and every craftsman,' but also to protect consumers from exploitation through the free competition that is offered within the nation.[237]

According to Justice Jackson, to ensure that the above was maintained 'home embargoes […] customs duties or regulations' were meant to be abolished since the drafting of the Constitution.[238] This approach can also be identified in *Philadelphia v New Jersey*,[239] in which case it was held that facially discriminatory measures represented 'the evils of economic isolation' that could have a negative effect on the national area of free trade.[240] By holding that the 'states are not separable economic units' the Supreme Court also seemed to have adopted the above approach.[241]

Another justification for the development of the first tier test can be identified in the claims of those who called for the elimination of protectionist measures and thus, indirectly, argued for a free national market. Such was the approach of Justice Scalia in *New Energy Co of Indiana v Limbach*,[242] who held that the discriminatory measure could only be held valid if it was found not to relate to 'economic protectionism.'[243]

---

[231] Farber 1986, p. 396 and Regan 1986, p. 1092.

[232] *Commonwealth Edison Co v Montana* (1981) 101 SCt 2946.

[233] O'Fallon 1982, p. 416.

[234] *Baldwin, Commissioner of Agriculture & Markets, et al. v GAF Seelig Inc* (1949) 294 US 511.

[235] *H P Hood & Sons, Inc v Du Mond, Commissioner of Agriculture and Markets* (1949) 336 US 525.

[236] McGreal 1998, p. 1222.

[237] Tribe 2000, p. 1058.

[238] *H P Hood & Sons, Inc v Du Mond, Commissioner of Agriculture and Markets* (1949) 336 US 525, 539.

[239] *Philadelphia v New Jersey* (1978) 437 US 617.

[240] *Philadelphia v New Jersey* (1978) 437 US 617, p. 624 and Felmly 2003, p. 478.

[241] *Philadelphia v New Jersey* (1978) 437 US 617 and Lang 2012, p. 81.

[242] *New Energy Co of Indiana v Limbach* (1988) 486 US 269.

[243] *New Energy Co of Indiana v Limbach* (1988) 486 US 269, p. 274.

Whilst not expressly stated in the Constitution, the adoption of the ideal of a national market within the United States, as rightly argued by Williams, may be the preferable justification constitutionally, not only for the anti-discrimination principle, but for the dormant commerce clause as a whole.[244] In reaching this conclusion, he effectively blended the above two contrasting opinions into the second one. He thus argued that an area of free trade within the Union firstly 'promote[s] political union,' which in effect makes the first position of political theory part of the second standpoint of the common market.[245] He also claimed that an area of free trade would 'reduce the likelihood of interstate retaliation.'[246] Such retaliatory actions were not only demonstrated to have occurred before the Constitutional Convention, but it has also been established above that these trade wars had played a fundamental role in the demand for the creation of a uniform regulation of interstate commerce. It may also be argued that discriminatory or protectionist measures could be classified as such actions, and thus the creation of a national market may provide a preventative measure against these. Williams argued that, thirdly, a national market would 'foster economic wealth', which also seems to form part of both the above contrasting standpoints.[247]

14.4.2 The Pike *Balancing Test*

If a state regulation is found to be non-discriminatory, it will still have to satisfy the second tier of the modern approach test to be upheld as a valid exercise of the regulatory powers of a state under the dormant commerce clause.

This second tier test originated from the ideology developed by Justice Stone in three cases about the specifications of modes of transportation. He first presented his understanding of the dormant commerce clause in his dissenting opinion in *DiSanto v Pennsylvania*.[248] In this dissenting opinion he rejected the then applied direct-indirect test for being 'too mechanical, too uncertain in its application and too remote from actualities, to be of value.'[249] He thus proposed that a state regulation should be firstly examined taking into account 'all the facts and circumstances, such as the nature of the regulation, its function, the character of the business involved and the actual effect on the flow of commerce.'[250]

He argued that a state law should subsequently only be upheld under the dormant commerce clause if, firstly, 'the interests' concerned in the state regulation are

---

[244] Williams 2008, p. 426.

[245] Williams 2008, p. 426.

[246] Williams 2008, p. 426.

[247] Williams 2008, p. 426.

[248] *DiSanto v Pennsylvania* (1927) 273 US 34 as referred to from Denning 2008, pp. 443–444.

[249] Denning 2008, p. 444.

[250] Denning 2008, p. 444.

'peculiarly local' and, secondly, if the regulation is held not to encroach upon the 'national interest in maintaining the freedom of commerce across state lines.'[251] This approach therefore seemed to adopt the previous national-local test, but in an amended form. Justice Stone claimed that it should be the interests in the regulation and not the subject matter or the nature of the activities regulated that determine whether a violation of the dormant commerce clause occurred. Moreover, this approach arguably adopted the viewpoint demonstrated above that the commerce clause was created to ensure a uniform national market.

The above method of Justice Stone was adopted soon after a decade in *South Carolina State Highway Department v Barnwell Brothers*.[252] The state regulation concerned in this case was a seemingly non-discriminatory restriction imposed on 'the size and weight of trucks' using the state roads, which was upheld until Congress legislated in the area.[253] On the other hand, Justice Stone argued that even if a state regulation is held to be non-discriminatory, and provided that there is no federal regulation about the same subject matter, the courts had to assess the regulation from two aspects.[254] They first had to examine 'whether the state legislature … has acted within its province' and, secondly, they had to establish 'whether the means of regulation chosen are reasonably adapted to the end sought.'[255] Regarding the first aspect, Justice Stone held that a non-discriminatory measure about the size and weight of trucks could be imposed by the states if it was "a safety measure and […] a means of securing the economical use of its highways."[256] Under the second aspect, even though it was established that the state law was a means to attain the "safe and economical use of [the] highways", it was still held that it imposed an undue burden on interstate commerce, and was thus held invalid under the dormant commerce clause.[257]

In *Southern Pacific Co v Arizona*,[258] Justice Stone, then Chief Justice of the Supreme Court, was finally provided with the opportunity to apply the test he previously developed. This case concerned a statute enacted by Arizona about the length requirements for 'passenger and freight trains', substantially distinct from the same requirements in the neighbouring states.[259] Chief Justice Stone, however, decided to refine his previous approach and stated that it first had to be assessed whether the subject matter of the regulation was of 'local' concern 'in character and

[251] Denning 2008, p. 444.

[252] *South Carolina State Highway Department v Barnwell Brothers* 303 US 177 (1938), as referred to from Denning 2008, p. 445.

[253] Denning 2008, p. 445.

[254] Denning 2008, p. 445.

[255] Denning 2008, p. 445 and Dowling 1940, p. 9.

[256] Twyman 1995, p. 391.

[257] Twyman 1995, pp. 391–392.

[258] *Southern Pacific Co v Arizona* 625 US 761 (1945), as referred to from Denning 2008, p. 446.

[259] Denning 2008, p. 446.

effect.'[260] In order to be upheld as a valid law, the state regulation in question also had to be demonstrated to have an 'impact on the national commerce' that 'does not seriously interfere with its operation.'[261] This seems to support the ideology that the creation of the national market was supported by Chief Justice Stone, since he also recognised that certain activities would have an impact on the national market that was worth protecting from harmful impacts. He consequently found the state law unconstitutional under the dormant commerce clause, as he held that it, in effect, interfered with the operation of interstate commerce. He held that the claims of the state that the requirements imposed by the state would be advantageous for interstate commerce were unfounded as it was actually identified during the trial court decision that these requirements 'would actually raise the accident rate.'[262]

The above methods devised by Chief Justice Stone formed the basis of the current second tier test of claims under the dormant commerce clause. This new test was formulated in *Pike v Bruce Church Inc*,[263] which concerned, once again, however in a different subject matter, a state regulation enacted by Arizona. The state law in question required the cantaloupes cultivated and marketed in Arizona to comply with packaging approved by the state.[264] This requirement was argued to have been created by the state of Arizona out of "the fear that some growers were shipping inferior or deceptively packaged produce, with the result that the reputation of Arizona growers generally was being tarnished and their financial return concomitantly reduced."[265] Bruce Church Inc, a cultivator of cantaloupes, however, packed and processed their cantaloupes in California, which was argued to have contravened the Arizona state law.[266] When that law was challenged under the dormant commerce clause, Justice Stewart devised the way the examination of the law was to be performed if it was found to be non-discriminatory under the now first tier enquiry. He held that it first had to be determined whether 'the statute regulates even-handedly to effectuate a legitimate local public interest.'[267] He subsequently held that in the case in question, 'protecting and enhancing the reputations of the growers were "surely legitimate state interests".'[268] The Court, however, also highlighted that this legitimate interest transformed into 'enhanc[ing] their reputation [of the State] through the reflected good will of the company's superior produce.'[269]

260 Denning 2008, p. 446.
261 Denning 2008, p. 446.
262 Twyman 1995, pp. 392–393.
263 *Pike v Bruce Church Inc* (1970) 397 US 137.
264 Zelinsky 2010, 414.
265 Day 2003, p. 50.
266 Day 2003, p. 50.
267 O'Fallon 1982, p. 407.
268 Day 2003, p. 50.
269 *Pike v Bruce Church Inc* (1970) 397 US 137.

If a legitimate interest is found in the state regulation, the Court will have to perform a balancing enquiry to assess the extent of the effects of the regulation on interstate commerce. If this effect is found to be 'only incidental,' the regulation will be upheld, however, a 'clearly excessive' effect will result in the invalidation of the state law.[270] When determining the above, the Court takes into consideration two aspects: 'the nature of the local interest involved' and whether this interest 'could be promoted as well with a lesser impact on interstate activities.'[271] This clearly seems to support the ideal that the protection of the national market took priority over state regulations in areas of 'local' concern.

It is to be highlighted that this balancing test will place a high judicial scrutiny on the state regulation, which at this point will have passed a strict examination under the first tier test. What the second-tier test focuses on is not the interpretation of the definition of 'commerce' or 'among the states,' but the extent of the regulatory powers of the states. How the states exercise such a power is placed under examination by analysing the burdens and the effects of the regulations as a whole on the national market. It would therefore seem that under the modern approach to the dormant commerce clause, the powers of the states have decreased substantially, as their regulations will be scrutinised from several aspects under a two-tier test, if they are found to be non-discriminatory.

14.4.2.1 Discriminatory Laws Investigated Under the Balancing Test

Even though many of the cases mentioned during the analysis of the first-tier test found that state laws were discriminatory and thus invalid, in many of them the Supreme Court still engaged in the examination of the state law under the second-tier test.

Even though *Pike v Bruce Church Inc*[272] had not been decided at this point, origins of the subsequent balancing test can be found in *Dean Milk Co v City of Madison,*[273] where the Supreme Court found that the state law aimed to regulate the commerce of milk to pursue a legitimate local public interest, which was the 'protection of the health and safety of state citizens' is a legitimate local purpose.[274] However, the state wished to achieve this by protecting 'the economic welfare' of the state industry through prohibiting the sale of milk produced out-of-state completely.[275] Regulation through these measures, the Supreme Court held, was not even-handed as other measures were available to attain the same goal that were

[270] *Pike v Bruce Church Inc* (1970) 397 US 137.

[271] McGinley 1992, p. 146; O'Fallon 1982, p. 407 and Denning 2008, p. 447.

[272] *Pike v Bruce Church Inc* (1970) 397 US 137.

[273] *Dean Milk Co v City of Madison* (1951) 340 US 349.

[274] Gerhart 2011, p. 373.

[275] Gerhart 2011, p. 373.

non-discriminatory, such as the wider inspection of the milk originating from out-of-state.[276]

Even though the per se rule of invalidity had been established and *Pike v Bruce Church Inc*[277] had already been decided by then, the state law imposing high fees on out-of-state hazardous waste in *Chemical Waste Management, Inc v Hunt*[278] was still examined under the *Pike* test and was found unconstitutional under the dormant commerce clause. The Supreme Court arrived at this decision by holding that there were other non-discriminatory means to attain the legitimate local interest end of limiting the amount of hazardous waste within the state that the state sought.[279]

Whilst the decision in *Maine v Taylor*[280] seemed to have departed from the first-tier test of holding a discriminatory state regulation invalid if it was discriminatory, as it passed the second-tier test, it was upheld as a constitutional exercise of the regulatory powers of the state under the dormant commerce clause. According to the Supreme Court the legitimate local purpose of the protection of the baitfish could only be attained by enacting the discriminatory measure and no other non-discriminatory measures were available for the state.[281] Thus, the state could actually impose a discriminatory measure that affected interstate commerce. This decision, in effect, arguably also became an area where the regulatory powers of the states over interstate commerce could be extended to: the protection of local wildlife, unique to the area. It could, however, also be highlighted that since baitfish was a unique animal in that particular state out of the whole nation, the discriminatory measure in effect allowed for the protection of the national market as a whole.

Whereas it has been demonstrated above that under the modern approach to the dormant commerce clause, a state regulation will have to satisfy the highly strict two-tier test, separate lines of cases also emerged that utilised this approach to extend the regulatory powers of the states in the area of interstate commerce.

14.4.3 The New Trend: Increasing the Powers of the States to Regulate Interstate Commerce

Whilst the modern approach to the dormant commerce clause has been utilised to restrict the activities that states are allowed to regulate, it has also resulted in the extension of the areas that the states are allowed to regulate. It is, however, fundamental to highlight, that under the modern approach—contrary to the dual federalist approach—the decision whether a state regulation violates the dormant

[276] Gerhart 2011, p. 373.

[277] *Pike v Bruce Church Inc* (1970) 397 US 137.

[278] *Chemical Waste Management, Inc v Hunt* (1992) 504 US 334.

[279] Cantrell 2009, p. 159.

[280] *Maine v Taylor* (1986) 477 US 131.

[281] Gerhart 2011, p. 374.

commerce clause will not be made based on its subject matter, but on a case-by-case basis, scrutinising the state law from several distinct aspects. Hence, it may be argued that the characterisation of the regulatory powers of Congress and the states over interstate commerce as 'mutually exclusive' is not only blurred, but is no longer adequate.[282]

Furthermore, a new trend seems to have emerged in the Supreme Court, whereby it is possible to identify four main categories of cases where it is highly likely that a decision whether a state regulation is valid under the dormant commerce clause, will be made in favour of the state. Whilst these categories have been limited in number, since Justice Scalia—one of the key opponents to the ideal of a dormant commerce clause—has been a Justice of the Supreme Court, their number has been extended by two to the total of four.

14.4.3.1 The Market Participant State

The first category of these cases includes states laws that regulate the activities of the states when that is acting as a participant in the market and not its regulator.[283]

This extension of regulatory power originates from the decision in *Hughes v Alexandria Scrap*,[284] which case concerned a 'scheme' established by a law enacted by Maryland that allowed the state to purchase 'crushed automobile hulks from in-state scrap processors at a premium price.'[285] The Supreme Court held that this law could not be challenged under the dormant commerce clause as Maryland simply acted in its capacity as a market participant, specifically, 'as a purchaser' and 'was not interfering with the natural functioning of an interstate market.'[286] Whilst this decision seemingly extended the powers of the states into wider areas of interstate commerce, the Supreme Court has not refrained from applying it in subsequent cases.[287]

Conversely, the Court having recognised that this extension of powers may 'undermine the national common market,' it has placed two limitations on this expansion of powers.[288] The first limitation may be invoked where a state regulation has a "substantial regulatory effect outside of a particular market," where it has been held to act as the market participant.[289] This limitation was devised in *South-Central Timber Development v Wunnicke*,[290] where Alaska intended to

[282] Williams 2007, p. 1851 and O'Fallon 1982, p. 396.
[283] Williams and Denning 2009, p. 294.
[284] *Hughes v Alexandria Scrap Corp* 426 US 794 (1976).
[285] Tribe 2000, p. 1088.
[286] Tribe 2000, p. 1088.
[287] One such case was *Reeves, Inc v Stake* 447 US 429 (1980) and see also Tribe 2000, p. 1089.
[288] Williams and Denning 2009, p. 295.
[289] Williams and Denning 2009, p. 295.
[290] *South-Central Timber Development v Wunnicke* 467 US 82 (1984).

regulate the 'timber-processing market,' when it was only held to be a participant of the 'timber-sale market.'[291] It was clear for the Supreme Court that the purpose of the regulation was 'to benefit the local timber-processing industry,' and the requirement of the state law of local processing of timber was consequently held invalid under the dormant commerce clause for the above reason.[292]

The second restriction was set on the taxes imposed by the states on businesses that are not parties to transactions with the state.[293] Such was the case in *New Energy v Limbach*[294] where a tax credit was offered as an incentive for the 'sales of ethanol produced in the state.'[295] Whilst Ohio argued that it should have been identified as the market participant when it offered this tax credit, the Supreme Court disagreed, and held that 'the state was neither purchasing nor selling ethanol', but was merely performing a 'governmental activity' of calculating taxes.[296]

It may thus be argued that despite the two restrictions, a state may enact a valid discriminatory state regulation in the area of interstate commerce if it can demonstrate that it acts as the 'market participant' in the area of commerce in question under the first group of cases of the new trend.

14.4.3.2 Manufacture as Opposed to Commerce

Another way the powers of the states have been extended under this new trend as recently as April 2013 occurred in *McBurney v Young*,[297] in which case the Supreme Court seems to have extended the manufacture exception under the dormant commerce clause, as devised by *Kidd v Pearson*,[298] to state records. In this case the Freedom of Information Act of Virginia was challenged by Mark J McBurney and Roger W Hurlbert under the dormant commerce clause.[299] Hurlbert argued that the state regulation that only allowed access to public records for citizens of the state was a violation of the dormant commerce clause, since it prevented him, a citizen of another state, from conducting the inter-state business of procuring the 'real estate tax records' from Virginia.[300]

The Supreme Court rejected his argument for various reasons. Justice Alito first held that the state law did not perform any regulatory function and did not 'burden'

---

[291] Williams and Denning 2009, p. 295.
[292] Williams and Denning 2009, p. 295.
[293] Williams and Denning 2009, p. 296.
[294] *New Energy Co of Indiana v Limbach* (1988) 486 US 269.
[295] Williams and Denning 2009, p. 296.
[296] Williams and Denning 2009, p. 296 and Tribe 2000, p. 1093.
[297] *McBurney v Young* (2013) 569 US.
[298] *Kidd v Pearson* (1888) 128 US 1.
[299] *McBurney v Young* (2013) 569 US.
[300] *McBurney v Young* (2013) 569 US.

interstate commerce.[301] He argued that in previous cases where the state laws were invalidated under the dormant commerce clause, it could be demonstrated that the regulation was a hindrance on 'the natural functioning of the interstate market' in two ways: either by the regulation imposing a ban or by the state enacting a 'burdensome regulation.'[302] As Justice Alito could not demonstrate that the state regulation performed any of the above two, he argued that it effectively created the 'benefit' of creating and providing 'to its own citizens copies [...] of state records.'[303]

Even though he consequently asserted that the case was 'not governed by the dormant commerce clause,' he still devoted a part of his judgment to assessing whether the act would be invalid under the dormant commerce clause.[304] He then held that as Virginia was the 'sole manufacturer' of the state records, it could adopt such 'protectionist' measures as it 'reflect[ed] the essential and patently unobjectionable purpose of state government—to serve the citizens of the State.'[305]

The decision of the Supreme Court in this case seems surprising as it seems to return to the approach where the powers of the states were extended based on the subject matter of the regulation. It will have to be seen whether this return to the previous interpretation will be utilised in the future by the Supreme Court and how it will fit into the modern approach to the dormant commerce clause.

14.4.3.3 Congressional Authorisation

Another way for the states to be able to regulate an area that may have an effect on interstate commerce is by doing so under specific authorisation from Congress. Such was the case in *Prudential Insurance v Benjamin*,[306] where a tax imposed merely on out-of-state insurance companies operating within South Carolina was held valid under the dormant commerce clause, as it had been authorised specifically by the McCarran-Ferguson Act of Congress.[307] Several other acts have been enacted by Congress that have authorised states to regulate areas that may affect interstate commerce, such as allowing the prohibition of the 'importation of alcoholic beverages manufactured in other states or nations' under the Wilson Act.[308] These acts have also justified state actions that discriminate against out-of-state interests, such as banking regulations or discriminatory state taxes.[309]

---

[301] *McBurney v Young* (2013) 569 US.

[302] *McBurney v Young* (2013) 569 US, p. 13.

[303] *McBurney v Young* (2013) 569 US, pp. 13–14.

[304] *McBurney v Young* (2013) 569 US, p. 13.

[305] *McBurney v Young* (2013) 569 US, p. 14.

[306] *Prudential Insurance Co v Benjamin* 328 US 408 (1946).

[307] Williams 2005, p. 157.

[308] Wilson Act 27 USC § 121 (2000) and Williams 2005, p. 155.

[309] Williams 2005, pp. 155–156.

Therefore, a state is able to enact discriminatory laws in an area of commerce, provided that such action has been previously authorised by Congress, which seems to, however, directly contradict the intention of the Framers.[310] As it has been demonstrated above, the Framers seemed to have agreed on the need for the creation of a uniform system for the regulation of interstate commerce that was to be regulated by Congress. On the other hand, by the delegation of its authority to the states, it may be argued that Congress is effectively acting contrary to its powers under the commerce clause.

14.4.3.4 Traditional State Functions

A novel way that expanded the regulatory powers of the states in the area of interstate commerce was created in 2007 through the decision delivered in *United Haulers Association v Oneida-Herkimer Solid Waste Management Authority.*[311] This case concerned a state law enacted by the State of New York that 'forced haulers' 'to bring waste to facilities owned and operated by a state-created public benefit corporation.'[312]

Whilst Chief Justice Roberts in delivering the opinion of the Court adopted the modern approach to assess whether the state law was violating the dormant commerce clause, he effectively created an exception to the first tier test.

This exception was created when he held that discrimination could only be present between 'similar entities' following the decision in *General Motors v Tracy.*[313] Chief Justice Roberts interpreted this standpoint by claiming that discrimination could only be present between 'private entities' and not between states, who are responsible for the protection of 'the health, safety and welfare' of their citizens.[314] He subsequently argued that the state law in question regulated 'waste disposal,' which was "both typically and traditionally" a function that rested with the states, as also recognised by Congress.[315] Thus, he failed to examine whether the state law discriminated between the state entity and the private entities that are operating in the same area. On the other hand, he held that the state law was non-discriminatory because it did not treat the in- and out-of-state private entities

[310] Williams 2005, p. 155.

[311] *United Haulers Association, Inc, et al. v Oneida-Herkimer Solid Waste Management Authority et al.* (2007) 550 US.

[312] *United Haulers Association, Inc, et al. v Oneida-Herkimer Solid Waste Management Authority et al.* (2007) 550 US (Chief Justice Roberts), p. 1.

[313] *General Motors Corp v Tracy* 519 US 278, 298 (1997).

[314] *United Haulers Association, Inc, et al. v Oneida-Herkimer Solid Waste Management Authority et al.* (2007) 550 US (Chief Justice Roberts), p. 10.

[315] *United Haulers Association, Inc, et al. v Oneida-Herkimer Solid Waste Management Authority et al.* (2007) 550 US, p. 12.

differently.[316] Whilst it is indisputable that Chief Justice Roberts claimed that he investigated the state law in question under the anti-discrimination principle, it is argued that with his interpretation of the test, he effectively created immunity for state monopolies from dormant commerce clause challenges. Whether this was the intention of the Framers is highly arguable, if the viewpoint is adopted that they intended to create a uniform national market.

As Chief Justice Roberts found that the state law in question satisfied the first tier test of the modern approach, he then set out to examine it under the second tier test. He, however, found it 'unnecessary' to determine whether the state law imposed an 'incidental burden on interstate commerce' as he held the public benefits of the state law would outweigh any such burden in the balancing enquiry.[317] The Court also subsequently acknowledged that the state law in question effectively amounted to a policy adopted by New York, which ousted "competition with regulation or monopoly control."[318] On the other hand, Chief Justice Roberts found no powers vested in the Supreme Court in the Constitution to decide whether this policy of creating monopolies is contrary to the commerce clause.[319] It would thus seem that the Supreme Court had not been persuaded by the arguments that the commerce clause was to create a uniform national market. If such approach had been adopted by the Supreme Court, it is argued, the creation of a monopoly would have been found to clearly burden interstate commerce. Consequently, if a state law has been enacted in an area that may pose a burden on interstate commerce, it will escape scrutiny under the dormant commerce clause, if the area is a traditional function of the states, and where an entity operated by the state enjoys a monopoly in the area in question.

This decision, however, also attracted a wide range of criticism from commentators for two reasons. Firstly, the facts of the case were highly similar to those of *C & A Carbone, Inc v Town of Clarkstown*,[320] however, the Court distinguished this case from the latter on the basis that the latter enacted regulation favouring a 'private' entity, whilst in this case the operator in question was a 'public' entity.[321] Secondly, the Court with the determination of traditional public functions of state government effectively resurrected a principle that had previously been held 'unworkable' in cases decided under the affirmative commerce clause following *Garcia v San Antonio Metropolitan*.[322]

---

[316] *United Haulers Association, Inc, et al. v Oneida-Herkimer Solid Waste Management Authority et al. (2007)* 550 US, p. 13.

[317] *United Haulers Association, Inc, et al. v Oneida-Herkimer Solid Waste Management Authority et al.* (2007) 550 US, pp. 14–15.

[318] *United Haulers Association, Inc, et al. v Oneida-Herkimer Solid Waste Management Authority et al.* (2007) 550 US, p. 12.

[319] *United Haulers Association, Inc, et al. v Oneida-Herkimer Solid Waste Management Authority et al.* (2007) 550 US, pp. 12–13.

[320] *C & A Carbone, Inc v Town of Clarkstown* (1994) 511 US 383.

[321] Coenen 2010, p. 544 and Denning (n. 49) 649.

[322] *Garcia v San Antonio Metropolitan Transit Authority* (1985) 469 US 528 and Denning 2008, p. 471 for a further discussion on the topic.

Despite the wide criticism of the above case, the approach of the Supreme Court has not changed in this area as the same exception was applied in the subsequent case of *Department of Revenue v Davis*.[323] This case effectively extended the above exemption to apply to state laws that regulate 'the issuance of bonds to raise revenue for public projects.'[324] Justice Souter held that such activity fell under the 'traditional' function of state governments, as it served to protect 'the health, safety and welfare of' the citizens of the state.[325] It is thus of high probability that this exemption will be extended in future cases to activities that were previously held to be discriminatory, if the same activity is provided by the state. On the other hand, this has not only resulted in the broadening of the regulatory powers of the states, but may also provide an incentive for states to enter into areas, where they have not been previously present, when they are seeking to limit out-of-state actors from that area.

14.5 Conclusion

This chapter has demonstrated that despite an express provision in the Constitution, since the drafting of the Constitution an ideology may be identified that supports the creation of a uniform national market.

First, the chapter placed an emphasis on how the concept of commerce and interstate commerce has developed since the drafting of the Constitution with the passage of time. It has demonstrated that commentators have been unable to identify a clearly uniform definition of commerce at the time of the Constitutional Convention, which has had a fundamental effect on the development of the dormant commerce clause. Whilst Chief Justice Marshall in the first case about the commerce clause adopted the definition of 'intercourse'[326] as commerce and also attempted to define the concept 'among the states', whether his interpretation of the commerce clause would be adopted nowadays is highly unlikely.

It has been argued above that one of the main reasons for the calling of the Constitutional Convention was the commercial warfare that the states engaged in against each other. It has been established that the Constitutional Convention therefore aimed to solve this problem by creating a uniform regulation of interstate commerce. It has, however, also been highlighted that the Constitution failed to unequivocally assert whether this amounted to an exclusive grant of power to Congress and whether it was intended to limit the regulatory powers of the states in the area of interstate commerce. The importance of the creation of this system has

[323] *Department of Revenue v Davis* (2008) 553 US.

[324] Williams and Denning 2009, p. 260.

[325] *Department of Revenue v Davis* (2008) 553 US (Justice Souter), p. 11 and Coenen 2010, p. 560.

[326] *Gibbons v Ogden* (1824) 22 US 1, pp. 189–190 and 193–194.

been also highlighted by demonstrating that the usual debate between the Federalist and Anti-Federalist was almost non-existent in this area. It has, however, been demonstrated that it was a debate between two main advocates of the Federalists, who disagreed over the above two fundamental questions left unanswered by the express text of the Constitution.

The development of the commerce clause has subsequently been discussed from a historical viewpoint. Firstly, the decision in *Gibbons v Ogden*[327] was analysed and it was discussed how Chief Justice Marshall devised the dual federalist interpretation of the commerce clause. It was also mentioned that one of the characteristics of this interpretation was that state regulations could be held unconstitutional if they regulated areas the regulatory power over which belonged to Congress exclusively.

The novel concurrent authority approach of Chief Justice Taney was subsequently examined and it was argued that even though he expressly rejected the previous dual federalist interpretation of the dormant commerce clause, certain characteristics of the latter approach were still traceable in his novel approach. It was also highlighted that Chief Justice Taney recognised that certain subject matters were of 'truly national concern'[328] that may be utilised to demonstrate that he was supporting the ideology of creating a uniform national market in certain areas of interstate commerce.

The novel national-local test originating from *Cooley v Board of Wardens of the Port of Philadelphia*[329] was then argued to fall within the dual federalist interpretation of the dormant commerce clause, but also to have adopted certain aspects of the concurrent authority approach. It was also claimed that a new area was created in this decision that allowed Congress to transfer its exclusive authority to the states in the area of interstate commerce. Moreover, it was argued that similarly to Chief Justice Taney, Justice Curtis also recognised that certain subject matters were of national concern that needed to be addressed in a uniform manner nationally.

The reasons for the exclusion of manufacture from the definition of commerce was subsequently analysed through the decision in *Kidd v Pearson.*[330] This resulted in a brief period of regression to a decision based on the subject matter of the regulation, which consequently also led to the ideal of a national market being placed in the background.

On the other hand, the ideology returned with the direct-indirect test, where if a state regulation placed a direct burden on the interstate commerce, it could not be upheld. This approach, however, proved quite ineffective in cases decided about the dormant commerce clause and a modern two-tier test was developed soon

[327] *Gibbons v Ogden* (1824) 22 US 1.

[328] McGinley 1992, p. 413.

[329] *Aaron B Cooley v The Board of Wardens of the Port of Philadelphia, to the use of the Society for the Relief of distressed Pilots, their Widows and Children* (1851) 53 US (12 How) 299.

[330] *Kidd v Pearson* (1888) 128 US 1.

afterwards. Both tiers of the test have been analysed respectively and it was also demonstrated that a state regulation will be subject to a high level of judicial scrutiny under the modern test. Special emphasis has also been placed on the development of the first anti-discrimination tier and how that may be closely related to the ideology of the creation of the national market.

It has, however, also been established that whereas it may seem that the powers of the states consequently became quite limited under the strict judicial scrutiny, a new trend can be identified, where the regulatory powers of the states were in fact extended and not limited. After discussing the decisions of the Supreme Court under this new trend under four different groups, it would seem that the ideal of a uniform national market has again been pushed to the background.

In conclusion, it is argued that the change in the definition of commerce and the development of the dormant commerce clause doctrine effectively resulted in the gradual return to the position, where states are restricted in their regulatory powers under the commerce clause, but are still allowed to enact certain discriminatory measures. This standpoint, however, seems remarkably similar to the one that ultimately called for the re-drafting of the Articles of Confederation, where the main problem was the lack of the authority of Congress to address the discriminatory state measures in a uniform manner. It assuredly seems that the four areas where the powers of the states have been increased may also result in the federal government being deprived of the opportunity to assert its authority over all areas of interstate commerce under the dormant commerce clause. Consequently, under this position it may be argued that both of the fundamental questions posed after the adoption of the commerce clause have been answered. Congress was not granted exclusive authority to regulate all areas of interstate commerce and states were not automatically limited from regulating in the area of interstate commerce.

As it is highly unlikely that a Constitutional Convention would be called nowadays, it is argued that the Justices of the Supreme Court have been interpreting the commerce clause from a standpoint that aimed to adapt to the developments and changes in each era of the decisions. Whether our times require the return to discriminatory and protectionist measures by the states and limited regulatory powers possessed by Congress, especially when our markets have become globally interconnected—as demonstrated in recent global financial crises—is profoundly questionable.

Table of Cases

Aaron B Cooley, Plaintiff in Error, v The Board of Wardens of the Port of Philadelphia, to the use of the Society for the Relief of distressed Pilots, their Widows and Children, Defendants (1851) 53 US (12 How) 299

Accord, Erb v Morasch (1900) 177 US 584

Baldwin, Commissioner of Agriculture & (and) Markets, et al. v G A F Seelig, Inc (1949) 294 US 511

C & A Carbone, Inc v Town of Clarkstown (1994) 511 US 383

Chemical Waste Management, Inc v Hunt (1992) 504 US 334
Chicago, Rock Island & Pacific Railway Company v Arkansas (1911) 219 US 453
Commonwealth Edison Co v Montana (1981) 101 SCt 2946
Dean Milk Co v City of Madison (1951) 340 US 349
Department of Revenue v Davis (2008) 553 US
DiSanto v Pennsylvania (1927) 273 US 34
Garcia v San Antonio Metropolitan Transit Authority (1985) 469 US 528
Gibbons v Ogden (1824) 22 US 1
Hannibal & St J R Co v Husen (1878) 95 US (5 Otto) 465
H P Hood & (and) Sons, Inc v Du Mond, Commissioner of Agriculture and Markets (1949) 336 US 525
Kassel v Consolidated Freightways Corp (1981) 450 US 662
Kidd v Pearson (1888) 128 US 1
Maine v Taylor (1986) 477 US 131
McBurney v Young (2013) 569 US
McCulloch v Maryland (1819) 17 US (4 Wheat) 316
Morgan's Louisiana & TR & SS Co v Louisiana Board of Health (1886) 118 US 455
New Energy Co of Indiana v Limbach (1988) 486 US 269
Parker v Brown (1943) 317 US 341
Philadelphia v New Jersey (1978) 437 US 617
Pike v Bruce Church Inc (1970) 397 US 137
Pound v Turck (1877) 95 US (5 Otto) 459
Seaboard Air Line Railway v Blackwell (1917) 244 US 310
Smith v Alabama (1888) 124 US 465
Southern Pacific Co v Arizona ex rel Sullivan, Attorney General (1945) 325 US 761
The Licence Cases (1847) 46 US 504
The Passenger Cases (1849) 48 US 283
Towne v Eisner (1918) 245 US 418
United Haulers Association, Inc, et al. v Oneida-Herkimer Solid Waste Management Authority et al. (2007) 550 US
Wabash, St Louis and Pacific Railway Company v Illinois (1886) 118 US 557
West Lynn Creamery, Inc v Healy (1994) 512 US 186
Willson v Black-Bird Creek Marsh Co (1829) 27 US (2 Pet) 245

Acknowledgements The research leading to this chapter has received funding from the European Research Council under the European Union's Seventh Framework Programme (FP/2007-2013)—ERC Grant Agreement n. 312304. The author wishes to thank Professor Robert Schütze and the participants of 'The Constitutional Implications of Free Movement' conference for their helpful comments on this chapter.

References

Abel AS (1940) The Commerce Clause in the Constitutional Convention and in Contemporary Comment. Minnesota Law Review 25:432–494

Amar AR (2005) America's Constitution: A Biography. Random House

Baker J, Konar-Steenberg M (2006) "Drawn from Local Knowledge… And Conformed to Local Wants": Zoning and Incremental Reform of Dormant Commerce Clause Doctrine. Loyola University Chicago Law Journal 38:1–42

Balkin JM (2010) Commerce. Michigan Law Review 109:1–51

Barnard C (2009) Restricting Restrictions: Lessons for the EU from the US? Cambridge Law Journal 68:575–606

Barnett RE (2001) The Original Meaning of the Commerce Clause. The University of Chicago Law Review 68:101–147

Barnett RE (2002) Is the Rehnquist Court an Activist Court - The Commerce Clause Cases. University of Colorado Law Review 73:1275–1290

Botting EH (2009) Protofeminist Responses to the Federalist-Antifederalist Debate. In: Hamilton A, Jay J, Madison J (1787–1788) The Federalist Papers (Ian Shapiro edn). Yale University Press

Boykin S (2012) The Commerce Clause, American Democracy, and the Affordable Care Act. The Georgetown Journal of Law & Public Policy 10:89–114

Brant I (1965) The Bill of Rights: Its Origin and Meaning. Bobbs-Merrill

Brogan H (1999) The Penguin History of the United States of America. Penguin Group

Cantrell WJ (2009) Cleaning Up the Mess: United Haulers, the Dormant Commerce Clause and Transaction Costs Economics. Columbia Journal of Environmental Law 34:149–190

Chapin R (1991) Chadha, Garcia and the Dormant Commerce Clause Limitation on State Authority to Regulate. The Urban Lawyer 23:163–187

Chemerinsky E (2013) Constitutional Law. Wolters-Kluwer

Coenen DT (2010) Where United Haulers Might Take Us: The Future of the State-Self-Promotion Exception to the Dormant Commerce Clause Rule. Iowa Law Review 95:541–629

Collins R (1988) Economic Union as a Constitutional Value. New York University Law Review 63:43–129

Cooke FH (1910) The Pseudo-Doctrine of the Exclusiveness of the Power of Congress to Regulate Commerce. Yale Law Journal 20:297–308

Corwin ES (1933) Congress's Power to Prohibit Commerce a Crucial Constitutional Issue. Corrnell Law Quarterly 18:477–506

Cushman B (2000) Formalism and Realism in Commerce Clause Jurisprudence. The University of Chicago Law Review 97:1089–1150

Davis JW (1907) The Growth of the Commerce Clause. The American Lawyer 15:213–218

Day D (2003) Revisiting Pike: The Origins of the Nondiscrimination Tier of the Dormant Commerce Clause Doctrine. Hamline Law Review 27:45–61

Denning BP (2005) Confederation-Era Discrimination against Interstate Commerce and the Legitimacy of the Dormant Commerce Clause Doctrine. Kentucky Law Journal 94:37–99

Denning BP (2008) Reconstructing The Dormant Commerce Clause Doctrine. William and Mary Law Review 50:417–516

Denning BP (2015) Bittker on Regulation Interstate & Foreign Commerce. Aspen Publishers

Dowling NT (1940) Interstate Commerce and State Power. Virginia Law Review 27:1–28

Drahozal CR (1999) Preserving the American Common Market: State and Local Governments in the United States Supreme Court. Supreme Court Economic Review 7:233–283

Eule JN (1982) Laying the Dormant Commerce Clause to Rest. Yale Law Journal 91:425–485

Farber DA (1986) State Regulation and the Dormant Commerce Clause. Const Comment 3:395–414

Farrand M (ed) (1937) The Records of the Federal Convention of 1787. Yale University Press

Felmly PC (2003) Beyond the Reach of States: The Dormant Commerce Clause, Extraterritorial State Regulation, and the Concerns of Federalism. Maine Law Review 55:467–515

Frankfurter F (1964) The Commerce Clause Under Marshall, Taney and Waite. Quadrangle Books
Friedman B, Deacon DT (2011) A Course Unbroken: The Constitutional Legitimacy of the Dormant Commerce Clause. Virginia Law Review 97:1877–1938
Gerhart AQ (2011) Dormant Commerce Clause Implications of Pennsylvania Dairy Regulations. Penn State Environmental Law Review 19:361–382
Hamilton A, Jay J, Madison J (2009) The Federalist Papers (Ian Shapiro edn). Yale University Press
Konar-Steenberg M (2009) One Nation or One Market? Liberals, Conservatives, and the Misunderstanding of HP Hood & Sons v Dumond. University of Pennsylvania Journal of Constitutional Law 11:957–983
Lang A (2012) The Marshall Doctrine, The Taney Doctrine and Calhounian Federalism. The Dartmouth Law Journal 10:76–93
Larsen JL (2004) Discrimination in the Dormant Commerce Clause. South Dakota Law Review 49:844–866
LeBoeuf J (1994) The Economics of Federalism and the Proper Scope of the Federal Commerce Power. San Diego Law Review 31:555–616
Maggs GE (1998) Translating Federalism: A Textualist Reaction. The George Washington Law Review 66:1198–1205
Mank B (2009) The Supreme Court's New Public-Private Distinction under the Dormant Commerce Clause: Avoiding the Traditional versus Nontraditional Classification Trap. Hastings Constitutional Law Quarterly 37:1–64
McGinley PC (1992) Trashing the Constitution: Judicial Activism, the Dormant Commerce Clause, and the Federalism Mantra. Oregon Law Review 71:409–456
McGreal PE (1998) The Flawed Economics of the Dormant Commerce Clause. William and Mary Law Review 39:1191–1287
Nelson GS, Pushaw RJ (1999) Rethinking the Commerce Clause: Applying First Principles to Uphold Federal Commercial Regulations but Preserve State Control Over Social Issues. Iowa Law Review 85:1–173
Noyes WC (1906) Development of the Commerce Clause of the Constitution. Yale Law Journal 16:253–258
O'Fallon JM (1982) The Commerce Clause: A Theoretical Comment. Oregon Law Review 61:395–420
Petragnani AM (1994) The Dormant Commerce Clause on Its Last Leg. Albany Law Review 57:1215–1253
Powell TR (1928) Current Conflicts between the Commerce Clause and State Police Power 1922–1927. Minnesota Law Review 12:470 - 491
Pushaw RJ (2012) Obamacare and the Original Meaning of the Commerce Clause: Identifying Historical Limits on Congress's Powers. University of Illinois Law Review 2012:1703–1754
Regan DH (1986) The Supreme Court and State Protectionism: Making Sense of the Dormant Commerce Clause. Michigan Law Review 84:1091–1287
Schütze R (2009) From Dual to Cooperative Federalism: The Changing Structure of European Law. Oxford University Press
Sedler RA (2009) The Constitution and the American Federal System. Wayne Law Review 55:1487–1544
Slattery TJ (2008) The Dormant Commerce Clause: Adopting a New Standard and a Return to Principle. William and Mary Bill of Rights Journal 17:1243–1280
Thompson AD (2004) Public Health, Environmental Protection, and the Dormant Commerce Clause: Maintaining State Sovereignty in the Federalist Structure. Case Western Reserve Law Review 55:213–241
Tribe LH (2000) American Constitutional Law. Foundation Press
Tushnet M (2009) The Constitution of the United States of America: A Contextual Analysis. Hart Publishing
Twyman WFJ (1995) Beyond Purpose: Addressing State Discrimination in Interstate Commerce. South Carolina Law Review 46:381–447

Williams NR (2005) Why Congress May Not "Overrule" the Dormant Commerce Clause. UCLA Law Review 53:153–238
Williams NR (2007) The Commerce Clause and the Myth of Dual Federalism. UCLA Law Review 54:1847–1929
Williams NR (2008) The Foundations of the American Common Market. Notre Dame Law Review 84:409–469
Williams NR, Denning BP (2009) The "New Protectionism" and the American Common Market. Notre Dame Law Review 85:247–312

Chapter 15
Beyond Parallel Powers. EU Treaty-Making Power Post-Lisbon

Mads Andenas and Luca Pantaleo

Abstract This chapter examines the competence divide between the EU and the Member States in the field of the common commercial policy, and its relation to the internal division of competence relating to the common market. It considers that in light of the novelties introduced by the Treaty of Lisbon and the developments that have occurred in recent case law and practice, there seems to be an emerging trend pointing to a conceptual and practical separation of EU external and internal powers—which would mark a departure from the so-called principle of parallel powers. As is well known, the latter requires that EU internal competences be mirrored by corresponding parallel external competences. However, it is argued that it does not impose a parallel in the other direction, bringing the authors to the conclusion that the EU has the power to conclude an agreement even in areas where the corresponding internal powers belong to the Member States. The competence of the latter would not be infringed or encroached upon by the conclusion of such an agreement to the extent that the Member States retain the power to implement the agreement at the internal level. This chapter demonstrates that this trend has clearly emerged in the framework of the common commercial policy but it may in principle also apply to other EU external powers.

Keywords EU law · Common commercial policy · EU external competence · Parallel powers · International trade

M. Andenas (✉)
Department of Private Law, University of Oslo, St. Olavs plass, PO Box 6706, 0130 Oslo, Norway
e-mail: mads.andenas@jus.uio.no

L. Pantaleo
Faculty of Public Management, Law and Safety, The Hague University of Applied Sciences, Johanna Westerdijkplein 75, 2521 EN The Hague, The Netherlands
e-mail: l.pantaleo@hhs.nl

M. Andenas et al. (eds.), *The Reach of Free Movement*,
DOI 10.1007/978-94-6265-195-1_15

Contents

15.1 Introduction 368
15.2 The Division of Competence Between the EU and Its Member States from Opinion 1/94 to the Coming into Force of the Treaty of Lisbon 370
15.3 The Scope and Limits of Article 207 TFEU 374
15.4 Article 207(6) and the Principle of Parallelism Between Internal and External Powers 380
15.5 Possible Systemic Explanations for a Departure from Parallel Powers 385
15.6 International Agreements in the Field of Transport 389
15.7 Conclusions 394
References 395

15.1 Introduction

The European Union essentially has four fundamental external powers: namely trade, development cooperation, association of third countries and organisations, and foreign and security policy. Among these powers, only the Common Commercial Policy (CCP) is expressly qualified as exclusive by the Treaties. As we shall see in the following pages, the CCP has always been the key element of EU's external powers, for it represents the external projection of the very essence of the Union: the common market. It therefore comes as no surprise that any, explicit or implicit, desired or fortuitous, evolution of the CCP and of its scope end up reviving the attention of scholarship. This is exactly what has happened in relation to the amendments to the CCP introduced by the Treaty of Lisbon. At the time of writing, that is to say precisely seven years after the coming into force of the Reform Treaty, the new CCP has already inspired what has rapidly become an abundant body of literature.[1] This revived interest is all the more justified if one considers that the Reform Treaty, as is perhaps natural, has brought along some major innovations. Not least amongst these is the creation of a new EU competence concerning foreign direct investment which has given rise to so much controversy in the last few years.[2] This article does not aim to assess in a comprehensive manner all the legal implications of the new CCP. Instead, in the next few pages, we will focus on the interaction between external and internal powers of the EU. In order to do this, we will take the CCP both as a case study and as the starting point for our analysis. We will not go into much detail as regards other external powers. Space and consistency make an all-encompassing examination impossible. Briefly then, the new CCP provision (Article 207 TFEU) appears to have eliminated shared competence

[1] To name but a few scholarly works, see Bungenberg and Herrmann 2013; Villalta Puig 2011; Bungenberg 2010; Cremona 2010; Dimopoulos 2010; Andenas 2016.

[2] See, among many, Dimopoulos 2011; Bungenberg et al. 2011, 2013; Bischoff 2011; Villalta Puig 2012; Natov 2013.

in respect of both GATS and TRIPs, in particular by bringing under EU exclusive competence the so-called sensitive sectors of trade in services[3] and commercial aspects of intellectual property. Since the whole GATT came within the Union's exclusive competence as early as 1994,[4] it has been maintained that, as EU law currently stands, all WTO Agreements fall within EU exclusive competence. Hahn and Danieli have argued that participation of the Member States in the conclusion of a hypothetical new Final Act would not be necessary unless such Act would be extended to matters not covered in the Doha Development Round.[5] Although EU practice has already abundantly shown that the choice to conclude mixed agreements is not always based on legal grounds. Often enough, the nature and the form of an agreement is dictated by complex political compromises.[6]

Though we agree, by and large, with Hahn and Danieli's argument, nevertheless we will show that there exists a certain degree of ambiguity in Article 207 TFEU. When coupled with the Member States' determination to preserve the pre-Lisbon's *status quo*,[7] there seems to be sufficient room for diverging interpretations of the reach and scope of the CCP provision and, more generally, its relation to the internal division of competence. The question is not simply one of internal interest as to the allocation of powers between the EU and its Member States. Rather, it is one of general constitutional and international value. The point is not simply to decide whether and to what extent a certain competence lies with the EU, the Member States or both. Rather the point is whether or not, as EU law currently stands, the Union's trade policy and powers—the CCP—correspond to the international conception of trade. In other words, whether or not the CCP encompasses all aspects of *international trade as it emerges from international law*, irrespective of the internal allocation of competence for the purposes of the common market.

The article will be organised as follows. First, we will summarise the historical evolution of the division of competence between the Union and its Member States in the field of the CCP, as it has emerged from the different versions of the Treaties and from some landmark ECJ decisions. Second, we will analyse the post-Lisbon developments, in an attempt to assess the impact of such developments on the current allocation of competence. Finally, we will try to present some general

---

[3] These sectors are cultural and audiovisual services, along with social, education and health services. See Article 207(4), subparagraph 3(a) and (b).

[4] Opinion 1/94, *Competence of the Community to conclude international agreements concerning services and the protection of intellectual property*, ECLI:EU:C:1994:384.

[5] Hahn and Danieli 2013, p. 62.

[6] Maresceau 2010, p. 16.

[7] This is clearly demonstrated by the position taken by some Member States (and to a certain extent by the Council) in two post-Lisbon judgments that will be thoroughly analysed below, namely *Daiichi Sankyo* and *Conditional Access Services*. As delightfully noted by a prominent scholar, the Member States went so far as arguing that "Article 207 did not say what it evidently said". See Kuijper 2016a, p. 3. Along the same lines but in the context of the debate concerning the TTIP, see Kuijper 2016b, pp. 99–101 and footnotes.

conclusions concerning the constitutional relation between internal powers—i.e. law-making power—and external powers—i.e. treaty-making power, which may be applicable beyond the boundaries of the CCP.

15.2 The Division of Competence Between the EU and Its Member States from Opinion 1/94 to the Coming into Force of the Treaty of Lisbon

When, in the late 1980s, the Contracting Parties of GATT 1947 decided it was time to reform the system and switch to a more institutionalised multilateral trade organisation, the (then) European Economic Community (EEC) was not yet formally a party to GATT, though all its Member States were. However, the EEC had been a *de facto* party to GATT for many years. Following the end of the transitional period of the common market, the EEC took on broad powers, at the internal level, in areas covered by GATT 1947. Therefore, as early as 1970, and despite not being formally party to the agreement, the Commission announced to Third States the EEC's intention to comply with GATT 1947, 'as a customs union and as an economic union in accordance with the letter and the spirit of the General Agreement in the same way as all other contracting parties'.[8] The other Contracting Parties of GATT 1947 accepted the Community's preparedness to assume all obligations arising from that agreement[9] and even the ECJ, in the landmark *International Fruit Company* ruling,[10] endorsed the EEC's informal, *de facto* membership.[11] As regards the allocation of competence, there was no clear division between the EEC and the Member States, but it was widely accepted that GATT came within shared competence, as demonstrated by the fact that agreements negotiated in the context of GATT 'were concluded either as "Community agreements" by the EEC alone or as "mixed agreements" by the EEC together with the individual EEC States'.[12]

This situation changed in 1994 on the occasion of the conclusion of the Final Act of the Uruguay Round that established the WTO. Although the Commission had been appointed as the sole negotiator of the WTO Agreements,[13] the division of

[8] Minutes of Meeting held on 12 and 13 February 1970, GATT doc. C/M/61, available at http://www.wto.org/gatt_docs/c.htm, pp. 6 et seq.

[9] Ibid.

[10] Joined Cases 21/72–24/72, *International Fruit Company*, ECLI:EU:C:1972:115, para 18, where the Court held that 'in so far as under the EEC Treaty the Community has assumed the powers previously exercised by Member States in the area governed by the General Agreement, the provisions of that agreement have the effect of binding the Community'.

[11] In particular, the EEC participated 'like a GATT contracting party *sui generis* in all GATT bodies except the Budget Committee'. See Petersmann 1986, pp. 36–37, emphasis in the original.

[12] Ibid.

[13] However, the Commission was assisted by a committee of representatives of Member State governments, who were meaningfully nicknamed 'the mothers-in-law'. See Burgeois 1995, p. 763.

competence remained an unresolved issue. This uncertainty proved to be a continuous source of tension between the Commission and the Member States, which eventually led the former to request an Opinion from the ECJ just a few days before the signature of the Final Act.[14] *Opinion 1/94* was in turn handed down only a few days before the conclusion of the Final Act and the deposit of Community and Member States' respective instruments of ratification.[15] The Commission maintained that all WTO Agreements fell within Community exclusive competence either under the CCP or under the implied powers doctrine.[16] However, the ECJ did not agree with this view. In that landmark, yet widely criticised Opinion, the Court granted exclusive competence to the Community on the basis of the CCP provision (then Article 113 EEC) as regards trade in all goods, but found that both GATS and TRIPs fell within shared competence.

As for GATS, the ECJ held that the Community only had competence concerning one of the four modes of supply of services established by the agreement in question—i.e. cross-frontier supplies. In particular, the Court found that the other three modes all entailed the movement of natural and legal persons. Exclusive competence under the CCP could not therefore apply to them on account of the existence of specific chapters of the Treaty concerning the free movement of persons.[17] The ECJ also set out what would later become the transport exception. In particular, it argued that transport services were also to be excluded from Article 113 EEC, as demonstrated by the existence of a specific title of the Treaty devoted to transport services distinct from the title concerning the CCP and by the Court's previous case law concerning transport agreements.[18]

The ECJ came to the same conclusions as regards TRIPs, yet from a different angle. Instead of grounding the exclusion of the CCP provision on other rules or chapters of the Treaty, the Court resorted to a purely teleological argument, which is reminiscent of the 'centre of gravity test'.[19] In particular, it noted that only those parts of the agreement which were closely linked with international trade could be considered as coming within the CCP. This was the case for TRIPs rules concerning counterfeited goods.[20] All other provisions of TRIPs fell outside the CCP, for their primary purpose was not the regulation of international trade—which would have pulled them into the realm of the CCP—but the harmonisation of intellectual property rights protection. Therefore, they also fell within shared competence.

---

[14] The Commission filed its request on 6 April 1994, while the Final Act was signed on 15 April 1994.

[15] The Opinion was delivered on 15 November 1994, while the ratifications were deposited jointly on 30 December 1994, that is only 2 days before the coming into force of the WTO Agreements.

[16] For a comprehensive overview of the implied powers doctrine, see Eeckhout 2011, pp. 70 et seq.

[17] Opinion 1/94, *cit.*, paras 43 et seq.

[18] Ibid., paras 48–50. Transport issues will be further analysed below.

[19] See below.

[20] Ibid., paras 54 et seq.

The Court not only rejected the idea that the exclusive nature of Community competence could be based on former Article 113 EC, which contained explicit reference neither to services nor to intellectual property,[21] but it also rejected the idea that the competence in question could be inferred from the implied powers doctrine, as suggested by the Commission. According to the Court, it could not be argued that Community competence extended to all aspects covered by GATS and TRIPs by virtue of such a doctrine. The ECJ refused to endorse the idea that Member States' external competence had been entirely pre-empted on the basis of Treaty provisions conferring internal powers to the Community or by the existence of internal legislative acts in relevant fields.

The ECJ's stand in *Opinion 1/94* was quite strict. For this reason, it has been widely criticised. Both the scope of the CCP and the implied powers doctrine were interpreted in a particularly narrow way, which led scholarship to label the decision in question as expressive of accentuated judicial self-restraint. *Opinion 1/94* has been variously described as a missed opportunity, a severe setback or as the expression of a strain of 'legal minimalism'.[22] After all, as noted by a prominent scholar, 'what [was] considered to be trade in the whole world [was] neither trade *nor* commerce for the purposes of the EC'[23] and was not considered to be part of the Community's trade policy powers.

Opinion 1/94 was probably decisively—hence negatively—influenced by the delicate political juncture of that time and by the unusual time pressure under which the ECJ was placed by the Commission's last-minute request.[24] The main drawback of the decision was that the demarcation-line between Community and Member State competence was particularly imprecise and therefore liable to give rise to potentially endless discussions, especially in regards to TRIPs.[25] On account of the absence of any explicit allocation of competence between the Community and its Member States—and with the exception of counterfeited goods which clearly came within the CCP, the assessment of which obligations stemming from TRIPs fell within Community competence was left completely to the Court's interpretation.

Community competence in respect of GATS was in fact—more or less—clearly delimitated by the Treaty, if only in a negative sense: what did not come within the scope of other specific chapters of the Treaty could, reasoning *a contrario*, be included in the CCP. This *argumentum a contrario*, however, did not apply to TRIPs. In relation to the latter, the ECJ adopted a case-by-case assessment, which has been referred to as the *Dior* test: in order to ascertain whether or not a certain

[21] The provision in question stated that 'the common commercial policy shall be based on uniform principles, particularly in regard to changes in tariff rates, the conclusion of tariff and trade agreements, the achievement of uniformity in measures of liberalization, export policy and measures to protect trade such as those to be taken in case in case of dumping and subsidies'.

[22] See Hilf 1995, p. 258; Maunu 1995, p. 123. The expression 'legal minimalism' was first employed by Koopmans 1986, p. 931.

[23] Pescatore 1999, p. 393, emphasis in the original.

[24] Hilf 1995, pp. 245–249.

[25] Ibid., at 257 et seq.

provision of TRIPs fell within Community competence, it was necessary to assess whether or not the Community had already approved harmonising measures in the area covered by the provision in question.[26] If the answer was negative, the respective competence still lay with the Member States, and vice versa.[27] At first sight, this approach may appear relatively straightforward. However, if one looks further, the picture changes considerably. According to this decision, the allocation of competence between the Community and its Member States concerning TRIPs was indefinite by definition, for it depended on the ever-changing reach of internal legislation. Although the solution proffered by the ECJ was probably justified by historical and political reasons, it was unsatisfactory from a legal point of view. By 'judging the whole matter according to the allocation of competence, real or imaginary, for the purpose of the internal market',[28] the Court was regrettably ignoring the evolution of international trade law as it emerged from the Uruguay Round, which encompassed not only trade in goods, but also trade in services, intellectual property, and, to some extent, foreign investment.[29] For our purposes, it is worth noting that the ECJ's reasoning was based on the assumption that internal and external competences were closely interrelated. More precisely, the existence and scope of one—external competence—was entirely dependent on the existence and scope of the other—internal competence—and vice versa. In short, one sort of power necessarily presupposed the other, in line with the ECJ's well-established implied powers doctrine.

The allocation of competence between the EU and the Member States in the field of the CCP went through a major evolution in the 2000s. To begin with, the Treaty of Nice revised the provision concerning the CCP—then re-numbered Article 133 EC—in order to confer explicit competence in relation to trade in services and intellectual property (Article 133(5) EC). Based on this development, the ECJ held that Community exclusive competence concerning GATS had extended to all four modes of supply of services, with two caveats. First, shared competence was retained in connection with agreements relating to trade in cultural and audiovisual services, educational services, and social and human health services, which were labelled 'sensitive sectors'. Second, the exception concerning transport services, which in the meantime had been codified by the framers in Article 133(6) EC, was reiterated.[30] However, the Treaty of Nice did not affect the situation concerning TRIPs. The Court has therefore continued to employ the case-by-case assessment developed in *Dior* until recent times.[31]

---

[26] Holdgaard 2008, pp. 1244 et seq.

[27] See Case C-300/98 & C-392/98, *Dior and Others*, ECLI:EU:C:2000:688, para 49. Also Case C-53/96, *Hermès International*, ECLI:EU:C:1998:292, paras 24 et seq.

[28] Pescatore 1999, p. 399.

[29] Gaja and Adinolfi 2012, pp. 223 et seq.

[30] See Opinion 1/08, *General Agreement on Trade in Services (GATS)*, ECLI:EU:C:2009:739, paras 119 et seq.

[31] Case C-431/05, *Merck Genéricos*, ECLI:EU:C:2007:496, para 34.

The second major development coincided with the coming into force of the Treaty of Lisbon. Article 207 TFEU (former Article 133 EC) will be analysed in depth in the following section. Suffice it to say that the principal novelty of the provision in question was that trade in goods, in services and in commercial aspects of intellectual property are purportedly no longer subject to separate rules. These three forms of trade are now all merged in a single provision (Article 207(1) TFEU), although different decision-making procedures may apply depending on the subject matter. In the next few pages, we will consider how and to what extent such innovation is likely to affect the division of competence between the EU and its Member States in the field of the CCP.

15.3 The Scope and Limits of Article 207 TFEU

The most remarkable achievement of the Treaty of Lisbon with regard to the CCP was without a doubt, as mentioned above, the merging of trade in goods, services and intellectual property into a single category. However, the amendments made by the Reform Treaty extended beyond such accomplishment. Another useful innovation was the elimination of any reference whatsoever to shared competence. While Article 133 EC had explicitly classified agreements relating to the sensitive sectors as falling within shared competence, in Article 207 TFEU all references to shared competence disappeared. Trade agreements on services and intellectual property were equated with other trade agreements, save for the requirement of unanimous voting in the Council (in certain cases). Since agreements concerning trade in goods have been under the Union's exclusive competence since *Opinion 1/94* and agreements concerning all other forms of trade are now placed on an equal footing, it seemed safe to conclude that Article 207 TFEU has pulled all agreements hitherto mentioned into the realm of exclusive competence.[32]

The Court was requested to interpret Article 207 TFEU in the *Daiichi Sankyo* case.[33] A question arose in a Greek court concerning the reach of a national patent relating to a pharmaceutical product, which required that the court interpret certain provisions of the TRIPs Agreement governing the field of pharmaceutical patents. The Greek court needed to know whether the provisions in question came within Union or Member State competence. The referring court therefore asked the ECJ: 'Does Article 27 of the TRIPs Agreement setting out the framework for patent protection fall within a field for which the Member States continue to have primary competence and, if so, can the Member States themselves accord direct effect to that provision, and can the national court apply it directly subject to the requirements laid down by national law?'[34] The Greek court clearly had in mind the *Dior* test.

---

[32] Müller-Graff 2008, p. 191; Dimopoulos 2008, p. 107; Cremona 2006, p. 30.

[33] Case C-414/11, *Daiichi Sankyo*, ECLI:EU:C:2013:520.

[34] Ibid., para 32 n. 1.

In the pre-Lisbon era, where TRIPs fell within shared competence, it would have been necessary to determine whether or not the EU had already legislated in the area covered by the TRIPs provision in question. Only the existence of such legislation would have pulled the field into the Union's competence. Otherwise, the corresponding competence still lay with Member States.

The *Dior* test was deemed to be applicable not only by the referring court, but also by Cruz Villalón AG, supported—perhaps unsurprisingly—by all the Member State governments who intervened in the proceedings.[35] Cruz Villalón AG evoked the existence of a strict interrelation between internal and external competence, arguing that a systemic interpretation of Article 207 TFEU made immediately apparent that 'intellectual property is a shared competence and must remain so'.[36] The inclusion of the whole TRIPs agreement within the Union's exclusive competence would have the effect of bringing the substantive core of industrial property law into the realm of EU law, thus deactivating—internal—shared competence. Cruz Villalón AG therefore maintained that the rule established in *Dior* and subsequent case law continued to be valid, in general, and was applicable to Article 27 TRIPs, in particular.[37] However, in an attempt to safeguard the *effet utile* of Article 207 TFEU, Cruz Villalón AG admitted that the innovations contained in the Treaty of Lisbon were aimed at preparing a sort of smooth transition from shared to exclusive competence, at least in the long run.[38]

The Court, however, took a completely different view. To begin with, it emphasized the fact that Article 207 TFEU differed considerably from its predecessor, Article 133 EC, and even more considerably from the provision that was in force when the WTO Agreements were concluded—i.e. Article 113 EEC. This made it clear that the EU's intention had been to depart from *Opinion 1/94* and subsequent case law. The Court held that the assessment concerning the allocation of competence between the Union and its Member States had to be interpreted in light of the innovations brought about by the Treaty of Lisbon. The ECJ therefore acknowledged that TRIPs fell within exclusive competence and it did so in very broad terms. Among other things, it stated that 'the context of those rules is the liberalisation of international trade, *not the harmonisation of the laws of the Member States* of the European Union'.[39] In this way, the ECJ emphasised the international dimension of TRIPs, by referring to it as being an integral part of the WTO system, more specifically of the cross-sector retaliation system established therein. In other words, the Court seemed to say that TRIPs was an instrument of

[35] The following parties took part in the proceedings: the Commission, Greece, Germany, France, Italy, the Netherlands, Portugal, Finland, Sweden, and the United Kingdom.

[36] Opinion of A.G. Cruz Villalón in Case C-414/11, *Daiichi Sankyo*, ECLI:EU:C:2013:49, para 59. True, the protection of intellectual property rights in Member States is still, by and large, national. For an overview concerning the establishment of a common European legal framework in this field, see Geiger 2013.

[37] Ibid., paras 60–62.

[38] Ibid., paras 64–79.

[39] *Daiichi Sankyo*, para 60. Emphasis added.

international trade and had to be understood as such for the purpose of the CCP. It could not be artificially severed from its context based exclusively on considerations pertaining to the internal division of competence, as both the referring court and Cruz Villalón AG had suggested. The external dimension—namely, the liberalisation of trade—was conceptually separate from the internal dimension—namely, the harmonisation of Member States' laws. This is particularly meaningful in a field such as intellectual property, where harmonisation has progressed quite slowly and has taken place mostly through enhanced cooperation.[40]

In light of this judgment, one may argue that the intention of the Lisbon legislature was to create an unambiguous, single allocation of competence, which could potentially encompass all aspects of external trade *as emerging from international trade law* and go beyond the somewhat artificial fragmentation resulting from the internal division of powers as codified by former Article 133 EC. In other words, the framers might have wanted to bring to a close what Bungenberg referred to as an 'unreadable, unsystematic and complex system of competence rules',[41] resulting from the previous version of the Treaty, read in conjunction with the ECJ's case law.

The ECJ's interpretation of Article 207 TFEU in *Daiichi Sankyo* seemed squarely in line with the foregoing view. Indeed, the Court's own comparison with former Article 133 EC helps clarify the interpretation of Article 207 TFEU it sought to impose. The comparative approach is not a new interpretive tool for the ECJ. The court has often taken into consideration the different versions of the Treaty in shaping its understanding of primary law reforms. In particular, the Court employed precisely this approach in dealing with Article 207 TFEU's predecessor. As noted by Cremona, the ECJ's general approach to Article 133 EC has shown a certain caution—if not a veritable self-restraint—insofar as the Court seemed to regard that provision 'as a reflection of the outcome of Opinion 1/94 and the Member States' response to that—in other words, as a rather specific compromise'.[42] From this perspective, one may argue that the ECJ's broad construction of Article 207 TFEU proposed in *Daiichi Sankyo* could suggest that the Court is amenable to regard the provision in question, with its allegedly radical switch to exclusivity, more as a major breakthrough from the previous dynamics, than as a sort of gradual step towards a smooth transition from the *status quo ante*. In other words, the Court might be willing to endorse a proactive interpretation of Lisbon's innovations concerning the CCP, in order to favour EU's unitary action and reduce the Member States' role in respect of international trade issues.

Just a few weeks after *Daiichi Sankyo* was handed down, the ECJ issued another ruling which seemed to point in the same direction. In *Conditional Access Services*, the Court was confronted with a request for annulment brought by the Commission against the Council's decision to ratify the European Convention on the legal

[40] Ankersmit 2014, p. 207.

[41] Bungenberg 2010, p. 131.

[42] Cremona 2010, p. 684.

protection of services based on, or consisting of, conditional access. The Council chose the harmonisation provision as the legal basis of its decision, namely Article 114 TFEU, along with Article 218 TFEU. However, the Commission argued that the Convention was primarily aimed at regulating trade between the Union and third countries, and not between the Member States. Hence, the correct legal basis was Article 207(4) TFEU, which deals with international trade, and not Article 114 TFEU, which deals with the internal market.[43] It is noteworthy that Member State laws had already been harmonised at the internal level by Directive 98/84/EC, which laid down a very similar legal protection for EU market actors providing these sorts of services in the common market.

The ECJ applied the aforementioned centre of gravity test, a tool often employed by the Court when it has to determine which is the correct legal basis for a certain EU measure. Briefly, the centre of gravity test is derived from the principle of conferral and it serves this very purpose. Since the EU can only adopt legislation if and to the extent that a corresponding power is conferred on it by the Treaties, EU measures have to be grounded in a specific legal provision granting the EU power to act in that area. Therefore, the ECJ has always required that the choice of legal basis be grounded in objective factors that are open to judicial review. The most common objective factor is the aim of the measure. EU institutions must identify the goal pursued by a certain measure and choose the legal basis accordingly. Hence, for example, if the aim of a measure is the liberalisation of international trade, the correct legal basis is clearly Article 207 TFEU. If, on the contrary, the objective pursued by a measure is the functioning of the common market, the legal basis is indeed Article 114 TFEU. Things may not always be so simple. Often, an EU measure pursues multiple objectives. However, according to established ECJ case law, that circumstance alone does not necessarily require the use of multiple legal bases. To borrow from the Court's own words, if a measure 'has a twofold component and if one of those is identifiable as the main or predominant purpose or component, whereas the other is merely incidental, that measure must be based on a single legal basis, namely that required by the main or predominant purpose or component'.[44] In *Conditional Access Services*, the ECJ was called upon to determine, first, whether the contested decision pursued a single or a twofold purpose. And, in the latter scenario, whether its primary purpose was the promotion of international trade, or the harmonisation of legislation, or both on an equal footing.

The Council, supported by several Member States, put forward a number of arguments suggesting that the contested decision could not be considered a CCP measure and that the Convention in question was only indirectly, if at all, linked with the promotion of trade with third countries. After all, it imposed an obligation on the parties to lay down common definitions for unlawful activities and to introduce a common system of sanctions and remedies. In addition, as pointed out

---

[43] The views expressed by the parties are summarised in the judgment. Case C-137/12, *Commission v Council*, ECLI:EU:C:2013:675, paras 35–50.

[44] Ibid., para 53.

by France, Poland and Sweden, some provisions of the Convention, unlike Directive 98/84/EC, were of a criminal nature. This circumstance alone, they argued, was sufficient to rule out the possibility of grounding the adoption of the Convention on Article 207 TFEU.[45] The arguments made by the Council and the intervening Member States, not unlike those put forward by Cruz Villalón AG in *Daiichi Sankyo*, were all based on an implicit, but clear, premise. These arguments all seemed to assume that drawing the Convention in question within the boundaries of the CCP, which is an EU (external) exclusive competence, would have encroached upon the exercise of Member States' (internal) shared competence in the field of the common market.[46]

The ECJ followed, by and large, the Commission's position. It stated that the Convention in question fell within the scope of the CCP and that, in turn, the correct legal basis was the one invoked by the Commission, namely Article 207 TFEU. Briefly, the Court came to this conclusion on the basis of two main arguments. First, it maintained that the common system of definitions and sanctions was to be understood as a means of achieving the primary objective of the Convention—which was the promotion of trade with third countries—and not as a separate objective in and of itself.[47] Second, the ECJ refused to ground the choice of legal basis exclusively on the criminal nature of the sanctions envisaged by the Convention. It did so for two reasons. First, the ECJ stated that, based on the wording of the Convention, the sanctions need not necessarily be criminal in nature. Second, even if the sanctions *were* necessarily criminal, the Court declared that the 'argument does not explain why Article 114 TFEU would be the correct legal basis in the circumstances'.[48]

We will come back to the argument relating to the criminal nature of certain implementing measures of a given international treaty in the following section of this article. For now, we will limit our comment on this ruling to a few basic considerations. To begin with, it is noteworthy that the nature of the Convention in question changes, as a consequence of the judgment, from mixed to exclusive. If the legal basis of the decision ratifying the Convention is Article 207 TFEU, Member State participation is no longer justified under Union law. More precisely: Member State participation is unlawful without the authorisation of the Union, as it would constitute a breach of EU exclusive competence. This is, in and of itself, quite a major consequence of *Conditional Access Services*.[49] In addition, this judgment

[45] Ibid., paras 40–48.

[46] This also seems to be the opinion of Ankersmit 2014, pp. 202–203.

[47] *Commission v. Council*, paras 70–71.

[48] Ibid., para 72.

[49] As a result of the judgment the Convention in question has indeed been adopted by the Union based exclusively on Article 207 TFEU. See Council Decision (EU) 2015/1293 of 20 July 2015 on the conclusion, on behalf of the European Union, of the European Convention on the legal protection of services based on, or consisting of, conditional access. Particularly meaningful is the declaration annexed to the decision where it is stated that the Union "expresses its concern regarding the application of Article 9 and Article 10(3) of the Convention, following the accession

seems to reinforce an impression that had already emerged in *Daiichi Sankyo*, namely that EU external powers are increasingly uncoupled from its internal powers and that their exercise is gaining more and more autonomy from the exercise of corresponding internal implementing powers for the purposes of the common market, regardless of the extent to which the latter is affected by a given international agreement concluded by the EU.

There are two possible objections to this reading of *Conditional Access Services*. First, it may be argued that the ECJ came to these conclusions only because the internal market had already been harmonised by Directive 98/84/EC. And certainly, if this directive had not existed, it would have been much harder to maintain that the Convention did not imply harmonisation of Member States' laws. It is undeniable that Directive 98/84/EC played an important role in the ECJ's reasoning. If anything, it made its life much easier. After all, the Court relied heavily on the existence of the directive to demonstrate that harmonisation was not the objective—or, at least, the predominant objective—of the Convention. However, this fact alone does not prove that the ECJ would have come to a different conclusion if the common market in the field of conditional access services had yet to be harmonised at the time of conclusion of the Convention. To this end, it is worth mentioning the position of Kokott AG, who addressed this issue directly in her Opinion. More specifically, she seemed to endorse the vision of a possible separation of the use of external powers and of internal powers. In an important passage, where she assessed the interpretation of Article 207(6) TFEU—which is allegedly, as we will see in the next section, the provision codifying the principle of parallelism—she stated:

> Article 207 TFEU can serve *a fortiori* as the legal basis for measures which do not lead to harmonisation of legislative provisions of the Member States within the Union (internal harmonisation) but, as in this case, contribute, in respect of external relations, to the approximation of the legislative provisions in the Union and in third countries (external harmonisation). The object of many modern trade agreements is precisely this kind of harmonisation: those agreements provide for the creation of uniform legal standards – if appropriate in the form of minimum standards – for certain products, activities or sectors with a view to facilitating cross-border trade.[50]

We will further analyse Article 207(6) in the next section. Without going into too much detail, suffice it to say that the conceptual separation between internal and

---

(Footnote 49 continued)

of the Union thereto, on the basis of its exclusive competence". The provisions mentioned in the declaration are those relating to the voting rights within the Convention and to the amendment procedure. The question is truly a matter of concern in light of the fact that some Member States of the EU have ratified the Convention before the Union. Among these Member States, some (but not all) have denounced the Convention a few months after the judgment was handed down. The status of signatures and ratifications can be consulted on the website of the Council of Europe at the following address: https://www.coe.int/en/web/conventions/full-list/-/conventions/treaty/178.

[50] Opinion of A.G. Kokott in Case C-137/12, *Commission v. Council*, ECLI:EU:C:2013:441, para 67.

external harmonisation, suggested by Kokott AG, seems to confirm the idea that external powers are no longer entirely dependent on the exercise of internal powers for the purposes of the common market. Whilst in fact, the two dimensions are indeed inextricably interrelated, as a matter of law, things might be different. As we shall see in the next section, it is worth underlining the fact that Kokott AG took a completely different position in a pre-Lisbon case which raised similar issues.

There is another objection to this reading of *Conditional Access Services*. It could be argued that this ruling merely represents yet another application of the centre of gravity test and that, as such, it is a mere doctrinal sophism to derive from it such far-reaching consequences. It is certainly true that the ECJ limited itself to the essential conclusions. The Court stated that the right legal basis was Article 207 TFEU because the primary objective of the Convention in question was the liberalisation of trade with third countries. It did not go so far as Kokott AG, nor did it go so far as the argument we make here. However, one has to read this judgment, as any other judgment, in the broader context in which it is placed. The Treaty of Lisbon has certainly widened EU external powers in the field of the CCP. It is certain too, as we shall see in the next section, that it has altered the relation between internal and external powers, as demonstrated by the amendments to Article 207(6) TFEU. There are several hints at the uncoupling of EU treaty-making powers from EU legislative powers. Our argument is that the ECJ in its recent case law is doing nothing other than confirming this existing trend.

There may, however, still be room for a few caveats in the process of detaching EU internal and external powers in the field of the CCP. In the next section, we shall examine these caveats. First, we will address Article 207(6) TFEU. This provision, although amended with respect to its predecessor, still contains a rather unclear reference to parallel powers. Second, we will turn to the examination of international agreements in the field of transport, which are the object of Article 207 (5) TFEU. We will try to demonstrate that these provisions do not contradict the substance of our main argument.

15.4 Article 207(6) and the Principle of Parallelism Between Internal and External Powers

In order to address the question of parallel powers, we shall first take a step back and reconsider *Daiichi Sankyo*. When it comes to intellectual property, the Treaty of Lisbon has reiterated the ambiguous language of its predecessor. What is defined as 'trade-related aspects of intellectual property' at the international level becomes 'commercial aspects of intellectual property' at the Union level. The two expressions are not entirely equal. Hence doubts arise over whether or not they are supposed to have different meanings.

In fairness, several scholars have argued that the meaning of 'commercial aspects of intellectual property' should be determined by reference to TRIPs.[51] A trade-related aspect of intellectual property according to the WTO Agreements should, as such, fall within the scope of the corresponding EU law provision. However, it is worth noting that the opposite view still enjoys institutional support, as demonstrated by Cruz Villalón AG's recent affirmations in *Daiichi Sankyo*: 'it should be beyond dispute that the concept of "commercial aspects of intellectual property" within the meaning of Article 207(1) TFEU must be an autonomous concept of European Union law' and should not be 'determined, in a more or less stable or consistent way, by the agreements to which the European Union is a party'.[52] Although Cruz Villalón AG did not mention Article 207(6) TFEU to support his argument, his position seems to rely on the idea that EU external competence should mirror its internal powers, and vice versa. The same position was submitted by the Council and the intervening Member States. They argued that 'commercial aspects of intellectual property' should be 'understood as being an entirely determinable part of the rules governing that subject-matter'.[53] They referred to Article 207(6) TFEU as a basis for excluding EU external competence where the EU lacked corresponding internal powers.

This question brings us to the issue of parallel powers. Former Article 133(6) EC established an explicit parallel between EU internal and external competences insofar as it stated that an 'agreement *may not be concluded* by the Council if it includes provisions which would go beyond the Community's internal powers'.[54] Although the ECJ never ruled on this question, it was widely accepted that the provision under consideration was intended to exclude external powers whenever the Community lacked corresponding internal powers.[55] Interestingly enough, the issue was examined in-depth by Kokott AG in a case—introduced and eventually withdrawn by the Commission—concerning the ratification of Vietnam's accession to the WTO (hereinafter: *Vietnam* case).[56]

Perhaps unsurprisingly, the Commission and the Council disagreed over the question of whether accession should have been approved by the Community alone, as submitted by the former, or required the simultaneous approval of the individual Member States, as submitted by the latter and a significant number of the Member

---

[51] Dimopoulos 2008, p. 108; Markus Krajewski 2005, pp. 110–111; Cremona 2006, p. 30.

[52] Opinion, *cit.*, *supra*, note 34, para 58.

[53] Ibid., para 45.

[54] Emphasis added. It should be noted that the reference to the Council is a drafting mistake, since the agreements in question are indeed concluded by the Council, but clearly on behalf of the Union. It was the latter that could not conclude agreements in such situations.

[55] Hermann 2002, p. 22.

[56] The Commission's decision to withdraw the case was probably justified by the fact that the Treaty of Lisbon had come into force in the meantime. However, the Court's understanding of former Article 133(6) would not have been completely devoid of significance, since it could have served as guidance for the interpretation of the similar, yet not identical provision introduced by the Treaty of Lisbon (i.e. Article 207(6)).

State governments.[57] In particular, the Council argued that the Member States' ratification was necessary, among other reasons, on account of the principle of parallel powers as codified by Article 133(6) EC. For insofar as the Community did not have internal implementing powers, the Council argued, it lacked the competence to conclude an international agreement in that area. This was the case, in particular, for some of the market-access rules applying to hospital services and medical care, and for Article 61 TRIPs, concerning criminal sanctions relating to counterfeited goods and copyright piracy. In both cases, the Community treaty-making power was to be excluded precisely for want of corresponding internal law-making powers.[58]

Two circumstances warrant mention at this point. First of all, as Community law stood at that time, agreements concerning sensitive sectors were still listed as coming within shared competence. Therefore, the Member States' ratification of Vietnam's accession could perhaps have been admitted on that ground. Second, as far as TRIPs was concerned, the existence and the nature of Community competence, at the time of the *Vietnam* case, would normally have been determined through the application of the *Dior* test. The Council's argument intended to show that the ECJ's case law concerning the WTO Agreements, and in particular TRIPs, did not apply where the Community lacked implementing powers at the internal level. This seems fairly logical. It was not possible to apply the *Dior* test, which was aimed at assessing the extent and coverage of Community internal legislation, where such legislation could not exist. The Council's position was, by and large, upheld by Kokott AG. As Community law stood at that time, she acknowledged that the Community had no powers in respect of the issues referred to by the Council and therefore they fell outside Community external competence as per Article 133(6) EC. However, since the Commission withdrew its application, the ECJ did not confirm or reject this position.[59]

As already mentioned above, the Council and the intervening Member State governments more or less reiterated the argument made in *Vietnam* in both *Daiichi Sankyo* and *Conditional Access Services*. We pointed out above that the arguments used by these parties in those judgments were based on a common premise: namely, that the exercise of EU external powers should not encroach upon Member States' internal shared powers. Is there any difference between *Vietnam* and the

---

[57] That is to say Germany, Spain, France, Finland, the United Kingdom, Greece and the Czech Republic.

[58] See the position maintained by the Council and the intervening Member States governments as summarised by the Opinion of A.G. Kokott in Case C-13/07, *Commission v. Council*, ECLI:EU:C:2009:190, paras 152 et seq.

[59] It seems worth noting that the post-Lisbon practice concerning the ratification of third countries accession to the WTO has changed. The relevant decisions are now based on Article 207(4) TFEU rather than Article 207(6) TFEU, however in conjunction with Articles 91 and 100 TFEU relating to transport. See, among others, Proposal for a Council Decision establishing the position to be taken by the European Union within the General Council of the World Trade Organization on the accession of the Republic of Seychelles to the WTO, COM/2014/0664 final.

post-Lisbon cases? There is: the difference is precisely, and no less than, the coming into force of the Treaty of Lisbon. Article 207(6) TFEU is without a doubt reminiscent, but by no means identical to Article 133(6) EC. While the latter clearly excluded the conclusion of an agreement by the Community if its provisions went beyond the Community's internal powers, thus establishing an explicit parallelism, the former is somewhat more nuanced. It stipulates as follows:

> The exercise of the competences conferred by this Article in the field of the common commercial policy *shall not affect the delimitation of competences between the Union and the Member States*, and shall not lead to harmonisation of legislative or regulatory provisions of the Member States in so far as the Treaties exclude such harmonisation.[60]

While the second section duplicates the same exemption relating to prohibition of harmonisation, the first section of the provision in question, in our understanding, avoids establishing any clear parallelism between internal and external powers. *Not being affected* is not exactly the same thing as *being paralleled*. As noted by Eeckhout, 'the opening phrase of Article 207(6) appears to do no more than confirm the principle of conferral'.[61] Does the provision in question require the existence of parallel powers in the same manner as Article 133(6) EC, thus excluding external competence where internal action is ruled out by the Treaty?

If one applies Kokott AG's reasoning in *Vietnam* or Cruz Villalón AG's similar stand in *Daiichi Sankyo*, the answer could very well be affirmative. A number of scholars have also taken a stand in favour of this view. On the one hand, Dimopoulos has argued that, since the 'principle of parallelism constitutes one of the cornerstones of external competence', the EU is only empowered to conclude an agreement 'to the extent that it is competent to legislate in [the same] area of the internal market'.[62] On the other hand, Weiß comes to a more nuanced conclusion, since he maintains that the conclusion of an agreement in the field of the CCP shall only be ruled out if it leads 'to a harmonisation which the Treaty excludes'.[63] As we shall see in the next section, there is no doubt that EU external action cannot lead to harmonisation in areas where such harmonisation is prohibited. However, what the Treaty does not say is that the conclusion of an agreement in a field where the EU has no corresponding law-making powers would inevitably be at variance with Article 207 TFEU, that it would necessarily lead to a breach of the prohibition of harmonisation. We argue that this view sits best with the spirit of Lisbon's innovations and, most importantly, with more recent developments.

In *Daiichi Sankyo*, where exclusive competence of the Union was acknowledged in very broad terms, the ECJ made no reference to Article 207(6). True, the Court did not affirm that the TRIPs Agreement as a whole, as opposed to just the provision which was the main focus of its judgment (i.e. Article 27 TRIPs), came within exclusive competence as a result of Lisbon's amendments. However, given

[60] Emphasis added.

[61] Eeckhout 2011, p. 61.

[62] Dimopoulos 2008, pp. 118–119.

[63] Weiß 2013, p. 39.

the circumstances of the case, one can perhaps assume that if the ECJ had wanted to set an exception to Union exclusivity on the basis of Article 207(6) TFEU, it would have been a good opportunity to do so. In other words, the Court's silence on this point, coupled with the broad language used to recognize the Union's exclusivity, should not be understood as a regrettable omission, but as an implicit rejection of the principle of parallel powers.

This reasoning does not appear to be limited to intellectual property. It may well extend to services and, eventually, beyond the boundaries of the CCP. EU exclusivity is not new as regards the four modes of supply of services established by GATS, as the ECJ had already stated in *Opinion 1/08*. However, if one took the view of Cruz Villalón AG and of the intervening Member State governments, it would have been possible to argue that, since the Union has only ancillary internal competence for health, culture and education, the purpose of Article 207(4)(a) and (b) TFEU is not to transfer agreements regarding the sensitive sectors from the area of shared competence to the Union's exclusive competence, thus equating these services with non-sensitive sectors' services. Pursuant to the principle of parallel powers, that transfer would be incompatible with the limited EU internal powers in such sectors. However, the position taken by the Court in *Conditional Access Services*, and further strengthened by Kokott AG's Opinion, should be sufficient to exclude any such parallelism between internal and external competence in the field of services.[64]

We have already pointed out that the Council and the intervening Member States claimed that the exclusive competence of the EU in *Conditional Access Services* was excluded, among other things, on the basis of Article 207(6) TFEU. We have also seen that Kokott AG explicitly rejected such an exclusion, on the basis of an interpretation of Article 207(6) TFEU that was substantially different from her interpretation of Article 133(6) EC in *Vietnam*. She argued that the competence to conclude an international agreement is only excluded on account of Article 207(6) where harmonisation of Member States' legislation is explicitly ruled out by the Treaties.[65] This is fairly reasonable, but also significantly different from what she had stated in *Vietnam*. While in *Vietnam* she seemed to suggest a strict parallelism between external and internal competence, in *Conditional Access Services* she argued that the exclusion of external competence could only be based on an explicit prohibition of internal harmonisation. The ECJ completely sidestepped an assessment of the provision at hand, but confirmed that the Union enjoyed exclusive competence to conclude the Convention in question, despite the fact that the latter contained some provisions which could trigger Member States' internal competence, not least over criminal sanctions.

If our understanding is correct, Article 207(6) TFEU ought to be interpreted as allowing the EU to conclude an international agreement *even* in areas where it has little or no implementing powers at the internal level, that is, irrespective of the

[64] See *contra* Villalta Puig 2011, p. 297.

[65] Opinion, paras 63–69.

internal distribution of powers in the same area. Consequently, EU external powers in certain areas would be broader than, and independent from, the EU's s internal competence for the purposes of the common market. In the next section of this article, we will present some more general arguments to justify such a conclusion. We will also consider whether, and to what extent, this might be applied to areas of EU law other than the CCP.

15.5 Possible Systemic Explanations for a Departure from Parallel Powers

In the previous pages, we have tried to demonstrate that there is an emerging trend pointing to the uncoupling of EU treaty-making powers from EU law-making powers. Based on a combined reading of the reformed CCP provision and of the ECJ's post-Lisbon case law interpreting that provision, we have argued that the conclusion of an agreement by the EU does not necessarily require the existence, at the internal level, of parallel implementing powers. Even if implementing powers belong to the Member States, and not to the EU, the conclusion of such agreements would not necessarily encroach on Member States' internal competence.

As a matter of principle, the fact that EU external powers are broader than EU internal powers is not too problematic. First of all, as noted by Gaja and Adinolfi, Article 3(2) TFEU is based on the premise that 'EU exclusive competence to conclude international agreements is broader than EU exclusive competence to adopt normative acts'.[66] Secondly, Krajewski, who was arguably the first scholar—and perhaps the only scholar so far—to propose a similar interpretation of Article 207 TFEU, rightly pointed out that this situation is common practice in federal systems,[67] as well as in regional, non-federal states. We are aware that the comparison between the Union and a state is always dangerous. However, one cannot help but noticing that both federal states and regional states have exclusive treaty-making powers, without necessarily holding corresponding law-making powers. This does not affect their ability to enter into international agreements. International practice plainly accepts this state of play, since the two dimensions are strictly separated. It is true that the line of reasoning applicable to states cannot apply directly to international organisations. The former must deal with their internal offshoots, which are by no means subjects of international law; the same does not hold true for EU Member States. In addition, regional or federal states generally possess quite effective tools for making sure that their international obligations are respected and not undermined by internal institutional dynamics.

[66] Gaja and Adinolfi 2012, p. 219. The passage was translated from Italian into English by one of the authors.

[67] Krajewski 2012, pp. 306–307.

This means the risk of a clash between the state and its offshoots is lower. It does not eliminate it altogether, however, as the *LaGrand* case clearly demonstrates.[68] The same scenario can be applied to the European Union. If, say, the EU breaches an international agreement—a Union agreement—due to a lack of implementation —or erroneous implementation—by one or more of its Member States, who hold implementing power, the EU will be held responsible at the international level, much as the United States was held responsible in the *LaGrand* case. Not to mention that the EU legal order seems to possess sufficient legal instruments to reduce the risk of a clash with its Member States, amongst which the principle of loyal cooperation,[69] as well as the infringement procedure.

The only limit to such a construal of EU treaty-making power, at least in the field of the CCP, lies in Article 207(6) TFEU, and more specifically its second part. According to this provision, the EU cannot conclude an international agreement if it would lead to harmonisation ruled out by the Treaties. There are a number of fields in which harmonisation is expressly excluded. To name but a few: the integration of immigrants (Article 79(4) TFEU), education and vocational training (Articles 165(4) and 166(4) TFEU), culture (Article 167(5) TFEU), health (Article 168(5) TFEU), administrative cooperation (Article 197(2) TFEU), and so forth. This limitation should, however, be understood as an exception and, as such, should be construed strictly, in accordance with the ECJ's well-established case law on the interpretation of provisions of an exceptional nature.[70] We argue that Article 207(6) would not be infringed by the mere conclusion of an agreement whose implementation covers an area in which harmonisation is prohibited. Rather, that provision would be infringed if, and only if, the agreement in question contained obligations that go so far as to leave Member States with little or no implementing powers—i.e., no margin of appreciation—or require implementation to be carried out at the EU level. As long as the EU does not take action, that is to say it does not adopt internal acts aimed at approximating Member States' laws in order to

[68] This case concerned Karl-Heinz and Walter Bernhard LaGrand, two German citizens convicted of murder and sentenced to death in the United States. In violation of the Vienna Convention on Consular Relations, the LaGrands were not granted the right to consular assistance from their State of nationality by Arizona State courts. The LaGrands were executed by Arizona authorities despite Germany having initiated proceedings before the International Court of Justice and obtained a provisional order requiring the United States to delay the execution pending resolution of the dispute. See *LaGrand (Germany* v. *United States of America), Judgment, I.C.J. Reports 2001*, p. 466.

[69] This is also the opinion of Krajewski 2012, pp. 305–306. On the duty of loyal cooperation, see the thoughtful analysis of Hillion 2010, pp. 87–115.

[70] We are referring here to the well-known ECJ case law relating to the exceptions to the functioning of the common market, such as the prohibition of quantitative restrictions between Member States in accordance with Article 36 TFEU. It is impossible to provide a detailed analysis of this topic. The case law is exemplified by the landmark Case 120/78, *Rewe-Zentral (Cassis de Dijon)*, ECLI:EU:C:1979:42, paras 8 et seq.; Case 286/86, *Deserbais*, ECLI:EU:C:1988:434. A thoughtful examination can be found in de Búrca and Craig 2008, p. 677.

implement the international agreement in question, Article 207(6) cannot be violated.

It could be argued that if Member States are forced to take action to implement a Union agreement falling within an area in which harmonisation is excluded, this is equivalent to harmonisation—at least indirectly. In this case, Member States' internal competence would be encroached upon by the exercise of EU treaty-making power and, as a consequence, the principle of conferral would be infringed. This objection is not very convincing however. The reverse argument is actually stronger. Preventing the EU from exercising an—explicitly conferred—external competence in order *not* to encroach upon Member States' internal competence would be tantamount to encroaching upon EU external competence. For example, it would be a violation of EU external powers if the EU were prevented from concluding an international agreement whose primary aim was to promote international trade—as in *Conditional Access Services*—because it also contains obligations falling within an area in which harmonisation is prohibited or in which the Member States retain extensive (exclusive) powers, as in the case of criminal sanctions with a trade linkage. Indeed, this would be a genuine violation of the principle of conferral. The Member States are involved in the decision-making process of the Union. As it has been rightly pointed out, sometimes the political structure of a federal or regional state can, in and of itself, be a sufficient guarantee of the autonomy and of the prerogatives of the constituents.[71] This reasoning can be applied to an international organisation such as the EU. The Member States are sufficiently protected through their—decisive—role, via the Council, in approving Union agreements.

These institutional dynamics can already be observed in recent practice. Larik has rightly pointed out that a remarkable post-Lisbon development is that

> [r]egardless of whether the Member States could or could not be forced out of international organizations or agreements, some seem to leave voluntarily once the EU arrives [...] But this does not mean a loss of power altogether. They simply retreat into the EU's internal space and exercise their – significant – decision-making powers in the Council and bodies such as the Trade Committee.[72]

Obviously, this is not to say that, just because the Member States sit in the Council or in other bodies, the EU can exercise its treaty-making powers irrespective of the distribution of powers set out by the Treaties. It simply means that the Member States have enough tools at their disposal to prevent a breach of their prerogatives—many more than the EU has. The exercise of an explicitly conferred external competence cannot be hindered based on considerations relating to the Member States' residual internal powers. The external and internal dimensions can, and ought to be, separated.

This point brings us to another decision handed down by the ECJ. The Commission sought annulment once again of the Council decision ratifying the

---

[71] Gutierrez-Fons 2014, p. 92.

[72] See Larik 2015, p. 795.

Partnership and Cooperation Agreement with the Philippines (hereinafter: *the Philippines* case). The decision had multiple legal groundings. Specifically, the Council relied on Article 207 TFEU (CCP), Article 209 TFEU (development cooperation policy, hereinafter: DCP), Articles 79(3) (readmission of third country nationals), 91 and 100 (transport), and 191(4) (environment). The Commission did not question the use of a double external competence, namely Articles 207 and 209 TFEU. It only contested the supplementary use of multiple internal legal bases. Using the well-established centre of gravity case law, the Commission argued, briefly, that the trade and the development cooperation parts of the agreement were equally relevant objectives. As a consequence, the use of a double legal basis—and, therefore, of a double external competence—was fully justified. However, the fact that the agreement in question laid down quite extensive obligations in the fields of transport, illegal immigration, and the environment did not suffice, so the Commission argued, to change the nature of the agreement, which remained a—trade and—development cooperation agreement.[73]

The arguments of the Council, supported by all intervening Member States,[74] were quite straightforward. In short, the Council maintained that the agreements set out clear legal commitments in the mentioned fields. Such obligations exceeded the boundaries of DCP and, in order to be implemented, required action to be taken on the basis of provisions of the Treaties other than the CCP and the DCP.[75] This line of reasoning did not persuade the ECJ. In principle, the Court did no more than apply the centre of gravity test. It assessed whether the obligations laid down by the agreement were 'so extensive that they constitute distinct objectives that are neither secondary nor indirect in relation to the objectives of development cooperation'.[76] The Court found that this was not the case. As already pointed out, this principle is not new, and it has been applied previously to other development cooperation agreements. The Philippines agreement was a special case though. As noted by the ECJ, the word 'development' did not even appear in the title.[77] The obligations set out therein were actually quite extensive, especially in relation to migration issues. It is in analysing these issues that the Court made quite a meaningful statement. According to the ECJ, it could not be argued that the Philippines agreement 'prescribes in concrete terms the manner in which cooperation concerning readmission of nationals of the contracting parties is to be implemented'.[78] This argument fits squarely with the idea that the conclusion of an international agreement is one thing—i.e., the exercise of EU treaty-making power—while its implementation is another. Implementation may still

[73] The Commission's argument is summarised in the judgment. Case C-377/12, *Commission v Council*, ECLI:EU:C:2014:1903, paras 16–23.

[74] Intervening Member States were the Czech Republic, Germany, Ireland, Greece, Austria and the United Kingdom.

[75] Ibid., paras 24–33.

[76] Ibid., para 48.

[77] Ibid., para 45.

[78] Ibid., para 58.

be carried out in accordance with the—internal—division of powers, even if the EU has no (internal) power at all in the corresponding field.

One more thing should not go unmentioned. First of all, it should be noted that, if roles were reversed, the separation between the external and internal dimensions would not be considered a massive problem. There are countless examples of situations in which the Member States act at the international level in areas where the corresponding internal powers belong to the EU. Sometimes this is a consequence of the traditional State-centred structure of international law.[79] Other times, however, it is a deliberate choice by the EU legal system. The most striking example is the international representation of the Economic and Monetary Union (EMU), which is currently carried out by the Member States sitting in international organisations, such as the International Monetary Fund (IMF). As is well known, this is an area of EU exclusive internal competence, where the Member States of the Eurozone have no residual internal power whatsoever. According to the *ERTA* principle, now codified in Article 216(1) TFEU, this should imply that the parallel exclusive external power also belongs to the Union.[80] Article 219(4) TFEU, however, provides that '[w]ithout prejudice to Union competence and Union agreements as regards economic and monetary union, Member States may negotiate in international bodies and conclude international agreements'. From a legal viewpoint, this provision amounts to the authorisation required by Article 2(1) TFEU for the Member States to act in areas of EU exclusive competence. For our purposes, however, it could amount to the proverbial final piece of the puzzle.

15.6 International Agreements in the Field of Transport

In light of the foregoing, it seems that there is one residual area in which EU treaty-making power might still be inextricably related to the internal division of powers, namely transport. For Article 207(5) TFEU reiterates the reference to the special rules concerning the common transport policy (CTP).

What today stands as the transport exception is, in essence, an ECJ creation, which was eventually codified in a Treaty provision. In order to contextualize that exception, it is worth reviewing the origins of EU external competence in the field of transport. First and foremost, one cannot help but notice what appears to be a striking contradiction. At the internal level, transport has always been (along with agriculture) a commercial activity to which the Treaties have given special

[79] For example, many international organisations, whose field of activity falls within areas of EU —sometimes exclusive—competence, only allow membership of States, and not of other international organisations. To mention only the most important one, this is the case of the United Nations and its myriad specialised agencies, such as ICAO.

[80] Case 22/70, *Commission v. Council (ERTA)*, ECLI:EU:C:1971:32.

treatment.[81] It touches on some delicate interests in respect of which several Member States have been reluctant to accept the Union's interference. For many years, the Member States sitting in the Council have simply failed to agree even on basic compromises when it came to measures concerning transport, so that the CPT gained the unflattering title of 'saddest chapter in the history of European integration'.[82] Although the CPT has been largely developed in more recent years and perhaps no longer deserves such labelling, the internal impasse has been accompanied by surprising external vitality. As noted by Stevens, 'much of the jurisprudence, which establishes the external competence of the Commission to negotiate with third countries and international organisations on behalf of the EU as a whole, arises from cases involving transport policy'.[83] Herein lies the contradiction we referred to above. Effectively, the ECJ has handed down most of its initial—and as such groundbreaking—implied powers decisions in the field of external competence in connection with transport matters, despite the Union's difficulties implementing its policy internally.

The foundational stone of such jurisprudence is indeed the aforementioned *ERTA* judgment, which is named after the European Agreement concerning the work of crews of vehicles engaged in international road transport. The agreement in question was signed in 1962, but never entered into force, and negotiations for a revision were opened in 1967. At that time, the Community had already adopted internal harmonising measures in the same field.[84] Although no external competence was conferred on the Community by the Treaty, the ECJ acknowledged the existence of—exclusive—competence wherever the Community had adopted internal measures which could be affected by Member States' international action.[85] This ruling was confirmed and extended in *Opinion 1/76*,[86] which also involved transport. Starting from the *ERTA* principle, the Court added that, even when there was no prior internal legislation involved, the Community external power could be inferred from the Treaty provisions establishing the corresponding internal power, inasmuch as the conclusion of an international agreement was necessary for the attainment of a specific Treaty objective.[87] The case at hand concerned the establishment of a legal framework governing navigation on the Rhine and Moselle rivers. Therefore, the exercise of an external competence was necessary to involve Switzerland, the only third country having access to the Rhine.

---

[81] Greaves 1999/2000, pp. 261 et seq.

[82] Erdmenger 1983, p. 89.

[83] Stevens 2004, p. 221.

[84] See Regulation (EEC) No. 543/69 of the Council of 25 March 1969 on the harmonisation of certain social legislation relating to road transport.

[85] *ERTA*, *cit.*, paras 81–91.

[86] Opinion 1/76, *Draft Agreement establishing a European laying-up fund for inland waterway vessels*, ECLI:EU:C:1977:63.

[87] Eeckhout 2011, p. 78.

It should be mentioned here that, around the same time, the EU exclusive competence on the CCP was taking form on a parallel, yet separate, track.[88] The consequence of this autonomous development was that agreements concerning transport were not included in the CCP, even where those agreements had considerable links with trade. This situation did not escape the Commission's notice and it did try to bridge the gap between the two policies in the early 1990s. The very first attempt of this sort coincided with the Commission's submission of a proposal for a Council decision 'instituting a consultation and authorization procedure for the commercial relations of the member states with third countries in the field of aviation'.[89] The reference to 'commercial relations' was indeed no accident.[90] Though these events eventually led, some years later, to yet another historic ruling in the cases collectively known as the *Open Skies* cases,[91] the ECJ cut the ground from under the Commission's feet in *Opinion 1/94*. In that decision, the Court shaped what is currently known as the transport exception. First and foremost, it rejected the argument that agreements in the field of transport could be considered part of the CCP, even where the agreements were economic in nature. This was so because of the existence of a specific Treaty chapter devoted to transport. The ECJ mentioned its own case law—*ERTA* and the likes—as proof thereof.[92] In this way, the potential link between exclusive competence under the CCP and agreements concerning transport was severed. The Court also ruled that exclusive competence could only be grounded on the implied powers doctrine as formulated in *ERTA* and *Opinion 1/76*.

As we have already observed, the allocation of competence resulting from *Opinion 1/94* was set in stone by the Treaty of Nice. However, it is worth noting a curiosity concerning transport. Article 133 EC stated that international agreements in that field 'shall continue to be governed by the provisions of Title V and Article 300'. To many observers, the expression 'shall continue' immediately appeared awkward, since it is unusual 'to stipulate that something remains as it was'.[93]

[88] See, in particular, Opinion 1/75, *Understanding on a Local Cost Standard*, ECLI:EU:C:1975:145; Opinion 1/78, *International Agreement on Natural Rubber*, ECLI:EU:C:1979:224.

[89] Stevens 2004, p. 229.

[90] Ibid.

[91] Those cases concerned the conclusion of bilateral air transport agreements between several EU Member States and the USA aimed at modifying already existing agreements on the same subject matter, with a view to further liberalizing civil aviation between the Parties. The Commission successfully challenged the conclusion of those agreements in several identical infringement procedures, in which the Court expressly acknowledged that the competence to enter into those agreements lay with the Community. Member States competence, as the Court argued, had in fact been pre-empted by the approval of Community measures establishing the internal market in air transport. The factual and legal background to the cases is summarized in the judgments. See, *ex plurimis*, Case C-467/98, *Commission v. Denmark*, ECLI:EU:C:2002:625, paras 3–29. For a critical comment see Franklin 2005, pp. 96 et seq.

[92] Opinion, *cit.*, paras 48–50.

[93] Hermann 2002, p. 22.

In order to safeguard the division of competence resulting from the ECJ's previous case law, the use of another expression, such as 'are governed', would have been more than enough and perhaps also more technically appropriate. The Treaty of Lisbon did in fact abandon the odd language. Therefore, it might be assumed that if the framers of Nice felt the need to resort to a particular expression *exclusively* for agreements concerning transport, it was because they intended to put emphasis on this aspect.

Such emphasis was indeed acknowledged by the ECJ in *Opinion 1/08*,[94] in which it analysed the scope of Article 133(6) EC at length, against the rest of the CCP provision. The case concerned the conclusion, consequent to the Community enlargements of 1995 and 2004, of agreements modifying the Schedules of Specific Commitments of the Community and its Member States under GATS. As usual, the Commission claimed that those agreements fell within the Community's exclusive competence, while the Council and several intervening Member States invoked shared competence. In order to maintain the inclusion of transport agreements in the CCP, the Commission had submitted, *inter alia*, the same argument as in *Opinion 1/94*. But this time, the Parliament also supported the move. According to the Commission and the Parliament, Article 133(6) EC should be deemed applicable only in agreements which were exclusively, or at the very least predominantly, devoted to transport and not when, as in the case at hand, the object was 'trade in services in general, transport services for their part being only ancillary or secondary within the agreements'.[95]

The ECJ explicitly rejected this argument, stating that it 'would make no sense to specify in the middle of a provision relating to the common commercial policy that agreements in the field of transport *which are not related to trade in transport services* fall within the transport policy and not the common commercial policy'.[96] The Court then turned to the interpretation of the expression 'shall continue', acknowledging its intensifying nature: as the ECJ put it, that language reflected 'the intention that a form of status quo ante should be preserved in that field'.[97] In this way, the possible link between international trade and transport services was eradicated, in favour of a more internally-oriented construction.

One can indeed be critical of the reasons that led the ECJ to abruptly and categorically exclude agreements concerning transport from the scope of the CCP. The reasons given were not necessarily consistent, at least from a legal perspective.[98] Govaere has rightly pointed out that this exclusion was 'most likely to be explained by the fact that the introduction by the CJEU of the doctrine of

---

[94] Opinion 1/08, *General Agreement on Trade in Services (GATS)*, ECLI:EU:C:2009:739.

[95] Ibid., para 155.

[96] Ibid., para 158 (emphasis added).

[97] Ibid., para 159.

[98] See in particular the critical considerations of Jacques H. J. Bourgeois, *op. cit.*, 776 et seq.

implied powers [...] was precisely based on the transport chapter of the Treaty'.[99] However, what initially followed—perhaps understandably—from the ECJ's need to justify its own case law, later on unfortunately became an isolated anomaly in the broader context of the CCP.

Does this state of affairs still make sense in the new, overarching post-Lisbon conception of CCP? We believe that, as a matter of principle and logic, there is no conceivable rationale for excluding transport, and only transport, from the Union's exclusive competence concerning the CCP. There is no serious logical reason, for example, to exclude from the CCP international agreements that are solely or predominantly economic in nature, i.e. their object and purpose is to promote international trade in all its forms, just because they may affect, directly or indirectly, the CPT. To borrow from the Court's own language used in *Daiichi Sankyo*, international agreements 'with a specific link to international trade' should logically be included in the CCP. The whole post-Lisbon case law, characterised by a clear-cut application of the centre of gravity test and by the emerging idea that EU external powers are more and more independent from the internal division of competence, seems to point in this direction.

Needless to say, the Court has not yet had the opportunity to interpret Article 207(5) TFEU. In principle, the provision in question could be interpreted as referring solely to agreements exclusively devoted to transport, and not to trade agreements that are likely to indirectly or directly affect transport. In our view, such an interpretation would not be incompatible with the Treaty and, above all, would sit well with the very spirit of the reform brought about by the Treaty of Lisbon. As we have already observed, the Treaty of Lisbon clearly aimed to bring the CCP into line with a WTO-oriented conception of external trade, in order to create a parallel between the CCP and international trade as it emerges from international practice. The inclusion of agreements concerning transport services would be part and parcel of that reforming spirit. The case law analysed in the previous pages seemed to confirm the ECJ's willingness to endorse such a spirit, paving the way for the detachment of EU treaty-making powers from EU law-making powers.

This is not to say, however, that the Court will go so far as to affirm that the new CCP includes transport agreements 'with a specific link to international trade'. On the contrary, the ECJ might want to indulge, as it did in *Opinion 1/08*, the Member States' desire to preserve a *status quo*. In this sense, what we have labelled the transport exception may prove to be a sort of refuge, in which the Member States have locked away their participation in the WTO, and in any other trade agreement, in order to forestall the risk that one day the Union might claim exclusive competence over the whole range of WTO obligations and trade law in general. These are, however, more political considerations, which are not for us to discuss. In the previous pages, we have tried to demonstrate that a strict parallelism between internal and external powers is neither necessary, nor is it required by the Treaties. We shall refrain from engaging in political statements and abide by our role as lawyers.

---

[99] Govaere 2011, pp. 149–150.

15.7 Conclusions

As the title of this chapter suggests, the basic argument presented above can be summarised as follows. In light of the novelties introduced by the Treaty of Lisbon and the developments which have occurred in the case law and practice, there seems to be an emerging trend towards a conceptual and practical separation of EU external and internal powers—in other words, of EU treaty-making and law-making powers. This trend has clearly emerged in the framework of the CCP. This is perhaps natural, as EU trade policy is traditionally the most proactive of EU foreign policies. However, the same dynamics may apply to other EU external powers, such as development cooperation, as showed by the *Philippines* case.

To put it differently, we argue that the principle of parallel powers only works in one direction. The principle requires that EU internal competences be mirrored by corresponding parallel external competences. However, it does not impose a parallel in the other direction. This position may well entail that the EU has the power to conclude an agreement even in areas where the corresponding internal powers belong to the Member States. The competence of the latter would not be infringed or encroached upon by the conclusion of such an agreement to the extent that the Member States retain the power, at the very least, to implement the agreement at the internal level. It is worth noting that this does not imply a breach of the principle of conferral. That principle would be infringed in the case of a so-called reverse *ERTA* effect, as codified by Article 216 TFEU—in other words, if the EU could derive implied internal powers from express external powers.

Post Scriptum

Pending the publication of this chapter Sharpston AG has delivered her Opinion concerning the EU-Singapore Free Trade Agreement (EUSFTA).[100] As is well known, on 16 October 2015 the Commission has requested an Opinion of the ECJ under Article 218(11) TFEU on the allocation of competences between the European Union and the Member States as regards the conclusion of EUSFTA.

The AG's Opinion provides a thoughtful and well-reasoned analysis of EU external competences in the field of the CCP. For the purpose of this chapter, it is not, however, necessary to examine it in full detail. Suffice it to say that the lengthy Opinion authoritatively confirmed the foundation of our main argument—namely, that EU treaty-making power post-Lisbon in the field of the CCP is fundamentally detached from EU internal law-making power. In particular, Sharpston AG argued at para 109 that Article 207(6) TFEU should not be interpreted as meaning that "the exercise of the European Union's competence over the common commercial policy depends on whether the European Union enjoys internal competence on some other basis and/or has exercised that competence". Even more clearly, she further added

[100] Avis 2/15, *Opinion on the Conclusion of the Free Trade Agreement between the European Union and the Republic of Singapore*, Opinion of Advocate General Sharpston delivered on 21 December 2016, ECLI:EU:C:2016:992.

that "insisting on parallelism between the external aspect of the common commercial policy and the internal aspect of other EU policies finds no support in other parts of Article 207 TFEU." It is true that her interpretation of what we referred to as the transport exception is perhaps broader than the one proffered above. It is also true that her narrow interpretation of EU external competence over portfolio investment might be reminiscent, at least indirectly, of the principle of parallel powers inasmuch as it excluded the existence of such competence on account of the lack of EU secondary legislation in the field.[101] However, this may be seen as a consequence of the Commission's own submissions on this issue. More specifically, the Commission argued that EU competence over portfolio investment is based on the so-called implied powers doctrine codified by Article 3(2) TFEU. The common rules referred to in the provision in question would be, according to the Commission, the Treaty provisions on free movement of capital, Articles 63 and 64 TFEU. Sharpston AG disagreed.

In its Opinion of 16 May 2017, the ECJ sidestepped the question of parallel powers and avoided dwelling on the interpretation of Article 207(6) TFEU, merely citing its text in para. 164. As far as transport is concerned, it has essentially confirmed its well-established case law, according to which commitments contained in EU FTAs that relate to transport, services "do not fall within the common commercial policy" (para. 168) but can nonetheless be covered by EU exclusivity insofar as the conditions referred to in Article 3(2) TFEU are met.

References

Andenas M (2016) The European Union as a Global Model for Trade and Investment. Social Science Research Network. ISSN 1556-5068

Ankersmit L (2014) The Scope of the Common Commercial Policy after Lisbon: The Daiichi Sankyo and Conditional Access Services Grand Chamber Judgments. Legal Issues of Economic Integration 41:193–210

Bischoff JA (2011) Just a Little Bit of Mixity? The EU's Role in the Field of International Investment Protection Law. Common Market Law Review 8:1527–1569

Bungenberg M (2010) Going Global? The EU Common Commercial Policy after Lisbon. In: Herrmann C, Terhechte JP (eds) European Yearbook of International Economic Law. Springer, Berlin/Heidelberg, pp 123–152

Bungenberg M, Griebel J, Hindelang S (eds) (2011) International Investment Law and EU Law. Springer, Berlin/Heidelberg

Bungenberg M, Herrmann C (eds) (2013) European Yearbook of International Economic Law – Common Commercial Policy after Lisbon, Special Issue. Springer, Berlin/Heidelberg

Bungenberg M, Reinisch A, Tietje C (eds) (2013) EU and Investment Agreements: Open Questions and Remaining Challenges. Hart Publishing, Oxford

Burgeois J (1995) The EC in the WTO and Advisory Opinion 1/94: An Echternach Procession. Common Market Law Review 32:763–787

---

[101] See ibid., paras 346–361.

Cremona M (2006) A Constitutional Basis for Effective External Action? An Assessment of the Provisions on EU External Action in the Constitutional Treaty. EUI Working Paper Law

Cremona M (2010) Balancing Union and Member States Interests: Opinion 1/2008, Choice of Legal Base and the Common Commercial Policy under The Treaty of Lisbon. European Law Review 35:678–694

de Búrca G, Craig P (2008) EU Law: Text, Cases and Materials. Oxford University Press, Oxford

Dimopoulos A (2008) The Common Commercial Policy after Lisbon: Establishing Parallelism between Internal and External Economic Relations? Croatian Yearbook of European Law and Policy 4:101–129

Dimopoulos A (2010) The effects of the Lisbon Treaty on the principles and objectives of the Common Commercial Policy. European Foreign Affairs Review 15:153–170

Dimopoulos A (2011) EU Foreign Investment Law. Oxford University Press, Oxford

Eeckhout P (2011) EU External Relations Law. Oxford University Press, Oxford

Erdmenger J (1983) The European Community Transport Policy: Towards a Common Transport Policy. Gower, Aldershot

Franklin C (2005) Flexibility vs. Legal Certainty: Article 307 EC and Other Issues in the Aftermath of the Open Skies Cases. European Foreign Affairs Review 10:79–115

Gaja G, Adinolfi A (2012) Introduzione al diritto dell'Unione europea. Laterza, Bari

Geiger C (2013) Constructing European intellectual property: Achievements and new perspectives. Edward Elgar, Cheltenham

Govaere I (2011) EU Common Commercial Policy throwing off the Shackles of "Mixity"'. In: Govaere I, Quick R, Bronckers M, Burgeois J (eds) Trade and competition law in the EU and beyond. Edward Elgar, Cheltenham, pp 144–158

Greaves R (1999/2000) EC Transport Law and Policy: A Status Report. Cambridge Yearbook of European Legal Studies 2:261–284

Gutierrez-Fons J (2014) Transatlantic Adjudication Techniques: The Commerce Clause and the EU's Internal Market Harmonisation Clause in Perspective. In: Fahey E, Curtin D (eds) A Transatlantic Community of Law. Cambridge University Press, Cambridge, pp 69–101

Hahn M, Danieli L (2013) You'll Never Walk Alone: The European Union and Its Member States in the WTO. In: Bungenberg M, Herrmann C (eds) European Yearbook of International Economic Law – Common Commercial Policy after Lisbon, Special Issue. Springer, Berlin/Heidelberg, pp 49–63

Hermann CW (2002) Common Commercial Policy after Nice: Sisyphus Would Have Done a Better Job. Common Market Law Review 39:7–29

Hilf M (1995) The ECJ's Opinion 1/94 on the WTO – No surprise, but wise? European Journal International Law 6:245–259

Hillion C (2010) Mixity and Coherence in EU External Relations: The Significance of the Duty of Cooperation. In: Hillion C, Koutrakos P (eds) Mixed Agreements Revisited. Hart Publishing, Oxford, pp 87–115

Holdgaard R (2008) Case C-431/05, Merck Genéricos – Produtos Farmacêuticos Lda v. Merck & Co. Inc. (M & Co.) and Merck Sharp & Dohme Lda (MSL), Judgment of the Court of Justice (Grand Chamber) of 11 September 2007, [2007] ECR I-7001. Common Market Law Review 45:1233–1250

Koopmans T (1986) The Role of Law in the Next Stage of European Integration. International Comparative Law Quarterly 35:925–931

Krajewski M (2005) External Trade Law and the Constitution Treaty: Towards a Federal and More Democratic Common Commercial Policy? CMLR 42:91–127

Krajewski M (2012), The Reform of the Common Commercial Policy. In: Biondi A, Eeckhout P, Ripley S (eds) EU Law after Lisbon, Oxford University Press, Oxford, pp 292–311

Kuijper PJ (2016a) Litigation on External Relations Powers after Lisbon: The Member States Reject Their Own Treaty. Legal Issues of Economic Integration 43:1–13

Kuijper PJ (2016b) Some Final Questions and Conclusions. In: Pantaleo L, Douma W, Takacs T (eds) Tiptoeing to TTIP: What Kind of Agreement for What Kind of Partnership? CLEER Papers, pp 93–101

Larik J (2015) No Mixed Feelings: The Post-Lisbon Common Commercial Policy in Daiichi Sankyo and Commission v. Council (Conditional Access Convention). Common Market Law Review 52:779–799

Maresceau M (2010) A Typology of Mixed Bilateral Agreements. In: Hillion C, Koutrakos P (eds) Mixed Agreements Revisited. Hart Publishing, Oxford, pp 11–29

Maunu A (1995) The implied external competence of the European Community after the ECJ Opinion 1/94, towards coherence or diversity? Legal Issues of Economic Integration 22:115–128

Müller-Graff PC (2008) The Common Commercial Policy Enhanced by the Reform Treaty of Lisbon? In: Dashwood A, Maresceau M (eds) Law and Practice of EU External Relations: Salient Features of a Changing Landscape. Cambridge University Press, Cambridge, pp 188–201

Natov N (2013) The EU and Foreign Investment: Some Questions after the new Regulation. Czech Yearbook of International Law 4:69–89

Pescatore P (1999) Opinion 1/94 on 'Conclusion' of the WTO Agreement: Is There an Escape from a Programmed Disaster? Common Market Law Review 36:387–405

Petersmann EU (1986) The EEC as a GATT Member – Legal Conflicts between GATT law and European Community Law. In: Hilf M, Jacobs F, Petersmann EU (eds) The European Community and GATT. Kluwer, Deventer, pp 23–89

Stevens H (2004) Transport Policy in the European Union. Palgrave Macmillan, Basingstoke

Villalta Puig G (2011) The Common Commercial Policy after Lisbon: An Analysis of the Reforms. European Law Review 36:289–301

Villalta Puig G (2012) Trade and Investment Relations between the European Union and Australia: for a Bilateral Economic Integration Agreement. European Foreign Affairs Review 17:213–239

Weiß W (2013) Common Commercial Policy in the European Constitutional Area: EU External Trade Competence and the Lisbon Decision of the German Federal Constitutional Court. In: Bungenberg M, Herrmann C (eds) European Yearbook of International Economic Law. Common Commercial Policy, Special Issue. Springer, Berlin/Heidelberg

Table of Cases

Court of Justice of the European Union: Numerical Order

26/62, *Van Gend en Loos*, ECLI:EU:C:1963:1
6/64, *Costa v ENEL*, ECLI:EU:C:1964:66
56/64 & 58/64, *Consten and Grundig*, ECLI:EU:C:1966:19
29/69, *Stauder*, ECLI:EU:C:1969:57
11/70, *Internationale Handelsgesellschaft*, ECLI:EU:C:1970:114
22/70, *Commission v. Council (ERTA)*, ECLI:EU:C:1971:32
21/72–24/72, *International Fruit Company*, ECLI:EU:C:1972:115
4/73, *Nold*, ECLI:EU:C:1974:51
2/74, *Reyners*, ECLI:EU:C: 1974:68
8/74, *Dassonville*, ECLI:EU:C:1974:82
33/74, *van Binsbergen*, ECLI:EU:C:1974:131
36/74, *Walrave*, ECLI:EU:C:1974:140
32/75, *Cristini*, ECLI:EU:C:1975:120
48/75, *Royer*, ECLI:EU:C:1976:57
104/75, *de Peijper*, ECLI:EU:C:1976:67
26/76, *Metro SB-Großmärkte*, ECLI:EU:C:1977:167
63/76, *Inzirillo*, ECLI:EU:C:1976:192
71/76, *Thieffry*, ECLI:EU:C:1977:65
110/78 & 111/78, *van Wesemael*, ECLI:EU:C:1979:8
120/78, *Rewe-Zentral (Cassis de Dijon)*, ECLI:EU:C:1979:42
132/78, *Denkavit Loire*, ECLI:EU:C:1979:139
138/78, *Stölting*, ECLI:EU:C:1979:46
175/78, *Saunders*, ECLI:EU:C:1979:88
15/79, *Groenveld*, ECLI:EU:C:1979:253
44/79, *Hauer*, ECLI:EU:C:1979:290
62/79, *Coditel*, ECLI:EU:C:1980:84
788/79, *Gilli and Andres*, ECLI:EU:C:1980:171
130/80, *Kelderman*, ECLI:EU:C:1981:49

M. Andenas et al. (eds.), *The Reach of Free Movement*,
DOI 10.1007/978-94-6265-195-1

203/80, *Casati*, ECLI:EU:C:1981:261
279/80, *Webb*, ECLI:EU:C:1981:314
53/81, *Levin*, ECLI:EU:C:1982:105
62/81 & 63/81, *Seco v EVI*, ECLI:EU:C:1982:34
115/81 & 116/81, *Adoui and Cornuaille*, ECLI:EU:C:1982:183
249/81, *Commission v Ireland (Buy Irish)*, ECLI:EU:C:1982:402
40/82, *Commission v United Kingdom*, ECLI:EU:C:1984:33
152/82, *Forcheri*, ECLI:EU:C:1983:205
177/82, *van de Haar*, ECLI:EU:C:1984:144
72/83, *Campus Oil*, ECLI:EU:C:1984:256
220/83, *Commission v France*, ECLI:EU:C:1986:461
252/83, *Commission v Denmark*, ECLI:EU:C:1986:462
261/83, *Castelli*, ECLI:EU:C:1984:280
293/83, *Gravier*, ECLI:EU:C:1985:69
44/84, *Hurd v Jones*, ECLI:EU:C:1986:2
60/84, *Cinéthèque*, ECLI:EU:C:1985:329
94/84, *Deak*, ECLI:EU:C:1985:264
157/84, *Frascogna*, ECLI:EU:C:1985:243
178/84, *Commission v Germany*, ECLI:EU:C:1987:126
197/84, *Steinhauser*, ECLI:EU:C:1985:260
205/84, *Commission v Germany*, ECLI:EU:C:1986:463
206/84, *Commission v Ireland*, ECLI:EU:C:1986:464
216/84, *Commission v France (Milk Substitutes)*, ECLI:EU:C:1988:81
221/85, *Commission v Belgium*, ECLI:EU:C:1987:81
407/85, *Drei Glocken*, ECLI:EU:C:1988:401
24/86, *Blaizot*, ECLI:EU:C:1988:43
98/86, *Mathot*, ECLI:EU:C:1987:89
118/86, *Nertsvoederfabriek*, ECLI:EU:C:1987:424
222/86, *Heylens*, ECLI:EU:C:1987:442
286/86, *Deserbais*, ECLI:EU:C:1988:434
30/87, *Bodson*, ECLI:EU:C:1988:225
186/87, *Cowan*, ECLI:EU:C:1989:47
344/87, *Bettray*, ECLI:EU:C:1989:226
C-69/88, *Krantz*, ECLI:EU:C:1994:296
C-145/88, *Torfaen Borough Council*, ECLI:EU:C:1989:593
C-297/88 & C-197/89, *Dzodzi*, ECLI:EU:C:1990:360
C-331/88, *Fedesa and Others*, ECLI:EU:C:1990:391
C-49/89, *Corsica Ferries France*, ECLI:EU:C:1989:649
C-113/89, *Rush Portuguesa*, ECLI:EU:C:1990:142
C-154/89, *Commission v France*, ECLI:EU:C:1991:76
C-180/89, *Commission v Italy*, ECLI:EU:C:1991:78
C-198/89, *Commission v Greece*, ECLI:EU:C:1991:79
C-260/89, *ERT v DEP*, ECLI:EU:C:1991:254
C-288/89, *Gouda*, ECLI:EU:C:1991:323
C-1/90 & C-176/90, *SAE*, ECLI:EU:C:1991:327

C-2/90, *Commission v Belgium (Walloon waste)*, ECLI:EU:C:1992:310
C-76/90, *Säger*, ECLI:EU:C:1991:331
C-204/90, *Bachmann*, ECLI:EU:C:1992:35
C-256/90, *Mignini*, ECLI:EU:C:1992:173
C-112/91, *Werner*, ECLI:EU:C:1993:27
C-159/91 & C-160/91, *Poucet and Pistre*, ECLI:EU:C:1993:63
C-168/91, *Konstantinidis*, ECLI:EU:C:1993:115
C-169/91, *Stoke-on-Trent*, ECLI:EU:C:1992:519
C-267/91 & C-268/91, *Keck and Mithouard*, ECLI:EU:C:1993:905
C-320/91, *Corbeau*, ECLI:EU:C:1993:198
C-92/92 & C-326/92, *Phil Collins*, ECLI:EU:C:1993:847
C-275/92, *Schindler*, ECLI:EU:C:1994:119
C-292/92, *Hünermund and Others*, ECLI:EU:C:1993:932
C-364/92, *SAT Fluggesellschaft v Eurocontrol*, ECLI:EU:C:1994:7
C-379/92, *Peralta*, ECLI:EU:C:1994:296
C-391/92, *Commission* v *Greece*, ECLI:EU:C:1995:199
C-393/92, *Gemeente Almelo*, ECLI:EU:C:1994:171
C-46/93 & C-48/93, *Brasserie du Pêcheur and Factortame*, ECLI:EU:C:1996:79
C-131/93, *Commission v Germany*, ECLI:EU:C:1994:290
C-133/93, *Crispoltoni II*, ECLI:EU:C:1994:364
C-363/93, C-407/93–C-411/93, *Lancry*, ECLI:EU:C:1994:315
C-384/93, *Alpine Investments*, ECLI:EU:C:1995:126
C-412/93, *Lecler-Siplec*, ECLI:EU:C:1995:26
C-415/93, *Bosman*, ECLI:EU:C:1995:463
C-418/93, *Semeraro Casa Uno*, ECLI:EU:C:1996:242
C-29/94–C-35/94, *Aubertin and Others*, ECLI:EU:C:1995:39
C-55/94, *Gebhard*, ECLI:EU:C:1995:411
C-134/94, *Esso Española*, ECLI:EU:C:1995:414
C-163/94, C-165/94 & C-250/94, *Sanz de Lera*, ECLI:EU:C:1995:451
C-18/95, *Terhoeve*, ECLI:EU:C:1999:22
C-34/95–C-36/95, *de Agostini*, ECLI:EU:C:1997:344
C-43/95, *Data-Delecta*, ECLI:EU:C:1996:357
C-70/95, *Sodemare SA*, ECLI:EU:C:1997:301
C-250/95, *Futura Participations and Singer*, ECLI:EU:C:1997:239
C-343/95, *Calì & Figli (SEPG)*, ECLI:EU:C:1997:160
C-368/95, *Bauer Verlag*, ECLI:EU:C:1997:325
C-398/95, *SETTG v Ypourgos Erasias*, ECLI:EU:C:1997:282
T-175/95, *BASF*, ECLI:EU:T:1999:99
C-14/96, *Paul Denuit*, ECLI:EU:C:1997:260
C-50/96, *Schröder*, ECLI:EU:C:2000:72
C-51/96 & C-191/97, *Deliège*, ECLI:EU:C:2000:199
C-53/96, *Hermès International*, ECLI:EU:C:1998:292
C-67/96, *Albany*, ECLI:EU:C:1999:430
C-85/96, *Martínez Sala*, ECLI:EU:C:1998:217

C-118/96, *Safir*, ECLI:EU:C:1998:170
C-158/96, *Köhll*, ECLI:EU:C:1998:171
C-184/96, *Commission v France*, ECLI:EU:C:1998:495
C-264/96, *ICI v United Kingdom*, ECLI:EU:C:1998:370
C-266/96, *Corsica Ferries France*, ECLI:EU:C:1998:306
C-274/96, *Bickel and Franz*, ECLI:EU:C:1998:563
C-348/96, *Calfa*, ECLI:EU:C:1999:6
C-369/96 & C-376/96, *Arblade and Others*, ECLI:EU:C:1999:575
C-389/96, *Aher-Waggon*, ECLI:EU:C:1998:357
C-416/96, *Eddline El-Yassini*, ECLI:EU:C:1999:107
C-67/97, *Bluhme*, ECLI:EU:C:1998:584
C-114/97, *Commission v Spain*, ECLI:EU:C:1998:519
C-115/97–C-117/97, *Brentjens*, ECLI:EU:C:1999:434
C-124/97, *Läärä*, ECLI:EU:C:1999:435
C-212/97, *Centros*, ECLI:EU:C:1999:126
C-219/97, *Drijvende*, ECLI:EU:C:1999:437
C-292/97, *Karlsson*, ECLI:EU:C:2000:202
C-302/97, *Konle*, ECLI:EU:C:1999:271
C-378/97, *Wijsenbeek*, ECLI:EU:C:1999:439
C-412/97, *ED*, ECLI:EU:C:1999:324
C-6/98, *ARD*, ECLI:EU:C:1999:532
C-44/98, *BASF*, ECLI:EU:C:1999:440
C-49/98, C-50/98, C-52/98, C-54/98, & C-68/98–C-71/98, *Finalarte and Others*, ECLI:EU:C:2001:564
C-58/98, *Corsten*, ECLI:EU:C:2000:527
C-67/98, *Zenatti*, ECLI:EU:C:1999:514
C-165/98, *Mazzoleni*, ECLI:EU:C:2001:162
C-169/98, *Commission v France*, ECLI:EU:C:2000:85
C-190/98, *Graf*, ECLI:EU:C:2000:49
C-224/98, *D'Hoop*, ECLI:EU:C:2002:432
C-254/98, *TK Heimdienst*, ECLI:EU:C:2000:12
C-281/98, *Angonese*, ECLI:EU:C:2000:296
C-300/98 & C-392/98, *Dior and Others*, ECLI:EU:C:2000:688
C-318/98, *Fornasar and Others*, ECLI:EU:C:2000:337
C-355/98, *Commission v Belgium (Private Security)*, ECLI:EU:C:2000:113
C-403/98, *Monte Arcosu*, ECLI:EU:C:2001:6
C-405/98, *Gourmet International Products*, ECLI:EU:C:2001:135
C-448/98, *Guimont*, ECLI:EU:C:2000:663
C-467/98, *Commission v. Denmark*, ECLI:EU:C:2002:625
C-473/98, *Toolex*, ECLI:EU:C:2000:379
C-157/99, *Smits and Peerbooms*, ECLI:EU:C:2001:404
C-164/99, *Portugaia Construçoes*, ECLI:EU:C:2002:40
C-283/99, *Commission v Italy (Private Security)*, ECLI:EU:C:2001:307
C-309/99, *Wouters*, ECLI:EU:C:2002:98
C-324/99, *Daimler Chrysler*, ECLI:EU:C:2001:682

C-385/99, *Müller-Fauré*, ECLI:EU:C:2003:270
C-390/99, *Canal Satélite Digital*, ECLI:EU:C:2002:394
C-459/99, *MRAX*, ECLI:EU:C:2002:461
C-475/99, *Ambulanz Glöckner*, ECLI:EU:C:2001:577
C-515/99, C-519/99–C-524/99 & C-526/99–C-540/99, *Reisch and Others*, ECLI:EU:C:2002:135
C-50/00, *Pequeños Agricultores*, ECLI:EU:C:2002:462
C-60/00, *Carpenter*, ECLI:EU:C:2002:434
C-101/00, *Tulliasiamies*, ECLI:EU:C:2002:505
C-112/00, *Schmidberger*, ECLI:EU:C:2003:333
C-136/00, *Danner*, ECLI:EU:C:2002:558
C-137/00, *Milk Marque*, ECLI:EU:C:2003:429
C-150/00, *Commission v. Austria ('Vitamins')*, ECLI:EU:C:2004:237
C-218/00, *Cisal*, ECLI:EU:C:2002:36
C-280/00, *Altmark*, ECLI:EU:C:2003:415
C-324/00, *Lankhorst-Hohorst*, ECLI:EU:C:2002:749
C-355/00, *Freskot AE*, ECLI:EU:C:2003:298
C-388/00 & C-429/00, *Radiosistemi*, ECLI:EU:C:2002:390
C-416/00, *Morellato*, ECLI:EU:C:2003:475
C-98/01, *Commission v United Kingdom*, ECLI:EU:C:2003:273
C-167/01, *Inspire Art*, ECLI:EU:C:2003:512
C-192/01, *Commission v Denmark*, ECLI:EU:C:2003:492
C-243/01, *Gambelli*, ECLI:EU:C:2003:597
C-285/01, *Burbaud*, ECLI:EU:C:2003:432
C-322/01, *DocMorris*, ECLI:EU:C:2003:664
C-383/01, *Den Danske Bilimportører*, ECLI:EU:C:2003:352
C-387/01, *Weigel*, ECLI:EU:C:2004:256
C-422/01, *Skandia*, ECLI:EU:C:2003:380
C-463/01, *Commission v Germany (Mineral Water)*, ECLI:EU:C:2004:797
C-491/01, *British American Tobacco*, ECLI:EU:C:2002:741
T-177/01, *Jégo-Quéré*, ECLI:EU:T:2002:112
C-12/02, *Grilli*, ECLI:EU:C:2003:538
C-36/02, *Omega*, ECLI:EU:C:2004:614
C-42/02, *Lindman*, ECLI:EU:C:2003:613
C-71/02, *Karner*, ECLI:EU:C:2004:181
C-171/02, *Commission v Portugal (Private Securities)*, ECLI:EU:C:2004:270
C-138/02, *Collins*, ECLI:EU:C:2004:172
C-148/02, *Garcia Avello*, ECLI:EU:C:2003:539
C-200/02, *Zhu and Chen*, ECLI:EU:C:2004:639
C-224/02, *Pusa*, ECLI:EU:C:2004:273
C-255/02, *Halifax*, ECLI:EU:C:2006:121
C-262/02, *Commission v France (Alcoholic Beverages Advertisement)*, ECLI:EU:C:2004:431
C-386/02, *Baldinger*, ECLI:EU:C:2004:535
C-442/02, *CaixaBank France*, ECLI:EU:C:2004:586

C-20/03, *Burmanjer and Others*, ECLI:EU:C:2005:307
C-26/03, *Stadt Halle and RPL Lochau*, ECLI:EU:C:2005:5
C-72/03, *Carbonati Apuani*, ECLI:EU:C:2004:506
C-134/03, *Viacom II*, ECLI:EU:C:2005:94
C-152/03, *Ritter-Coulais*, ECLI:EU:C:2006:123
C-189/03, *Commission v Netherlands (Private Security firms)*, ECLI:EU:C:2004:597
C-209/03, *Bidar*, ECLI:EU:C:2005:169
C-267/03, *Lindberg*, ECLI:EU:C:2005:246
C-446/03, *Marks & Spencer*, ECLI:EU:C:2005:763
C-458/03, *Parking Brixen*, ECLI:EU:C:2005:605
C-514/03, *Commission v Spain (Private Security)*, ECLI:EU:C:2006:63
C-540/03, *Parliament v Council*, ECLI:EU:C:2006:429
C-94/04 & C-202/04, *Cipolla*, ECLI:EU:C:2006:758
C-109/04, *Kranemann*, ECLI:EU:C:2005:187
C-144/04, *Mangold*, ECLI:EU:C:2005:709
C-158/04 & C-159/04, *Alfa Vita Vassilopoulos*, ECLI:EU:C:2006:562
C-170/04, *Rosengren and Others*, ECLI:EU:C:2007:313
C-196/04, *Cadbury Schweppes*, ECLI:EU:C:2006:544
C-212/04, *Adeneler and Others*, ECLI:EU:C:2006:443
C-338/04, C-359/04 & C-360/04, *Placanica and Others*, ECLI:EU:C:2007:133
C-366/04, *Schwarz*, ECLI:EU:C:2005:719
C-372/04, *Watts*, ECLI:EU:C:2006:325
C-410/04, *ANAV*, ECLI:EU:C:2006:237
C-434/04, *Ahokainen and Leppik*, ECLI:EU:C:2006:609
C-441/04, *A-Punkt Schmuckhandel*, ECLI:EU:C:2006:141
C-470/04, *N*, ECLI:EU:C:2006:525
C-519/04 P, *Meca-Medina and Majcen*, ECLI:EU:C:2006:492
C-65/05, *Commission v Greece (Online Games)*, ECLI:EU:C:2006:673
C-76/05, *Schwarz*, ECLI:EU:C:2007:492
C-101/05, *A*, ECLI:EU:C:2007:804
C-110/05, *Commission v Italy (Italian Trailers)*, ECLI:EU:C:2009:66
C-112/05, *Commission v Germany*, ECLI:EU:C:2007:623
C-134/05, *Commission v Italy ('Extrajudicial Debt Recovery')*, ECLI:EU:C:2007:435
C-142/05, *Mickelsson and Roos*, ECLI:EU:C:2009:336
C-238/05, *Asnef–Equifax*, ECLI:EU:C:2006:734
C-254/05, *Commission v Belgium*, ECLI:EU:C:2007:319
C-295/05, *Asociación Nacional de Empresas Forestales (Asemfo)*, ECLI:EU:C:2007:227
C-297/05, *Commission v Netherlands*, ECLI:EU:C:2007:531
C-298/05, *Columbus Container Services*, ECLI:EU:C:2007:754
C-319/05, *Commission v Germany*, ECLI:EU:C:2007:678
C-341/05, *Laval un Partneri*, ECLI:EU:C:2007:809
C-393/05, *Commission v Austria (Ecological Labelling)*, ECLI:EU:C:2007:722

C-404/05, *Commission v Germany (Ecological Labelling)*, ECLI:EU:C:2007:723
C-431/05, *Merck Genéricos*, ECLI:EU:C:2007:496
C-432/05, *Unibet*, ECLI:EU:C:2007:163
C-433/05, *Sandström*, ECLI:EU:C:2010:184
C-438/05, *Viking*, ECLI:EU:C:2007:772
C-465/05, *Commission v. Italy ('Private Security Services')*, ECLI:EU:C:2007:781
C-143/06, *Ludwigs-Apotheke*, ECLI:EU:C:2007:656
C-147/06 & C-148/06, *SECAP and Santorso*, ECLI:EU:C:2008:277
C-194/06, *Orange European Smallcap Fund*, ECLI:EU:C:2008:289
C-212/06, *Walloon (Flemish Care Insurance Scheme)*, ECLI:EU:C:2008:178
C-244/06, *Dynamic Medien*, ECLI:EU:C:2008:85
C-265/06, *Commission v Portugal (Tinted Windows)*, ECLI:EU:C:2008:210
C-319/06, *Commission v Luxembourg ('Posted Workers')*, ECLI:EU:C:2008:350
C-346/06, *Rüffert*, ECLI:EU:C2008:189
C-500/06, *Corporación Dermoestética*, ECLI:EU:C:2008:421
C-518/06, *Commission v Italy (Car Insurance)*, ECLI:EU:C:2008:477
C-524/06, *Huber*, ECLI:EU:C:2008:724
C-527/06, *Renneberg*, ECLI:EU:C:2008:566
C-13/07, *Commission v. Council*, ECLI:EU:C:2010:327
C-42/07, *Liga Portuguesa*, ECLI:EU:C:2009:519
C-88/07, *Commission v Spain*, ECLI:EU:C:2009:123
C-141/07, *Commission v Germany*, ECLI:EU:C:2008:492
C-164/07, *Wood*, ECLI:EU:C:2008:321
C-169/07, *Hartlauer*, ECLI:EU:C:2009:141
C-171/07 & C-171/07, *Apothekerkammer des Saarlandes*, ECLI:EU:C:2009:316
C-205/07, *Gysbrechts and Santurel*, ECLI:EU:C:2008:730
C-221/07, *Zablocka-Weyhermüller*, ECLI:EU:C:2008:681
C-316/07, C-358/07–C-360/07 & C-409/07–C-410/07, *Stoß*, ECLI:EU:C:2010:504
C-324/07, *Coditel Brabant*, ECLI:EU:C:2008:621
C-350/07, *Kattner Stahlbau*, ECLI:EU:C:2009:127
C-481/07 P, *SELEX*, ECLI:EU:C:2009:461
C-531/07, *Fachverband*, ECLI:EU:C:2009:276
C-544/07, *Rüffler*, ECLI:EU:C:2009:258
C-555/07, *Kücükdeveci*, ECLI:EU:C:2010:21
C-570/07 & C-571/07, *Blanco Pérez and Chao Gómez*, ECLI:EU:C:2010:300
C-73/08, *Bressol*, ECLI:EU:C:2010:181
C-100/08, *Commission v. Belgium ('Wild Birds')*, ECLI:EU:C:2009:537
C-103/08, *Gottwald*, ECLI:EU:C:2009:597
C-135/08, *Rottmann*, ECLI:EU:C:2010:104
C-153/08, *Commission v Spain (Gambling Tax)*, ECLI:EU:C:2009:618

C-160/08, *Commission v Germany (Ambulance Services)*, ECLI:EU:C:2010:230
C-219/08, *Commission v Belgium (Posted Workers)*, ECLI:EU:C:2009:599
C-258/08, *Ladbrokes Betting & Gaming*, ECLI:EU:C:2010:308
C-271/08, *Commission v Germany*, ECLI:EU:C:2010:426
C-333/08, *Commission v France ('Positive List')*, ECLI:EU:C:2010:44
C-400/08, *Commission v Spain*, ECLI:EU:C:2011:172
C-447/08 & C-448/08, *Sjøberg and Gerdin*, ECLI:EU:C:2010:415
C-515/08, *Dos Santos Palhota*, ECLI:EU:C:2010:589
C-565/08, *Commission v. Italy ('Lawyers' Fees')*, ECLI:EU:C:2011:188
C-28/09, *Commission v Austria*, ECLI:EU:C:2011:854
C 34/09, *Ruiz Zambrano*, ECLI:EU:C:2011:124
C-108/09, *Ker-Optika*, ECLI:EU:C:2010:725
C-137/09, *Josemans*, ECLI:EU:C:2010:744
C-142/09, *Lahousse and Lavichy*, ECLI:EU:C:2010:694
C-208/09, *Sayn-Wittgenstein*, ECLI:EU:C:2010:806
C-236/09, *Association Belge and Others*, ECLI:EU:C:2011:100
C-291/09, *Guarnieri & Cie*, ECLI:EU:C:2011:217
C-347/09, *Dickinger and Ömer*, ECLI:EU:C:2011:582
C-367/09, *SGS Belgium and Others*, ECLI:EU:C:2010:648
C-421/09, *Humanplasma*, ECLI:EU:C:2010:760
C-434/09, *McCarthy*, ECLI:EU:C:2011:277
C-483/09 & C-1/10, *Gueye and Salmerón Sánchez*, ECLI:EU:C:2011:583
C-72/10 & C-77/10, *Costa and Cifone*, ECLI:EU:C:2012:80
C-293/10 *Stark v DAS*, ECLI:EU:C:2011:355
C-385/10, *Elenca*, ECLI:EU:C:2012:634
C-443/10, *Bonnarde*, ECLI:EU:C:2011:641
C-456/10, *ANETT*, ECLI:EU:C:2012:241
C-484/10, *Ascafor*, ECLI:EU:C:2012:113
C-571/10, *Kamberaj*, ECLI:EU:C:2012:233
C-617/10, *Åkerberg Fransson*, ECLI:EU:C:2013:105
C-40/11, *Iida*, ECLI:EU:C:2012:691
C-150/11, *Commission v Belgium*, ECLI:EU:C:2012:539
C-171/11, *Fra.bo SpA*, ECLI:EU:C:2012:453
C-197/11 & C-203/11, *Libertao*, ECLI:EU:C:2013:288
C-256/11, *Dereci and Others*, ECLI:EU:C:2011:734
C-283/11, *Sky Österreich*, ECLI:EU:C:2013:28
C-379/11, *Caves Krier Frères*, ECLI:EU:C:2012:798
C-414/11, *Daiichi Sankyo*, ECLI:EU:C:2013:520
C-426/11, *Alemo-Herron*, ECLI:EU:C:2013:521
C-61/12, *Commission v Lithuania*, ECLI:EU:C:2014:172
C-86/12, *Alokpa and Moudoulou*, ECLI:EU:C:2013:645
C-87/12, *Ymeraga and Ymeraga-Tafarshiku*, ECLI:EU:C:2013:291
C-137/12, *Commission v Council*, ECLI:EU:C:2013:675
C-234/12, *Sky Italia*, ECLI:EU:C:2013:496

C-293/12 & C-594/12, *Digital Rights Ireland*, ECLI:EU:C:2014:238
C-370/12, *Pringle*, ECLI:EU:C:2012:756
C-377/12, *Commission v Council*, ECLI:EU:C:2014:1903
C-378/12, *Onuekwere*, ECLI:EU:C:2014:13
C-390/12, *Pfleger and Others*, ECLI:EU:C:2014:281
C-400/12, *M.G.*, ECLI:EU:C:2014:9
C-428/12, *Commission v Spain*, ECLI:EU:C:2014:218
C-481/12, *UAB Juvelta*, ECLI:EU:C:2014:11
C-483/12, *Pelckmans Turnhout*, ECLI:EU:C:2014:304
C-573/12, *Ålands Vindkraft*, ECLI:EU:C:2014:2037
C-87/13, *X*, ECLI:EU:C:2014:2459
C-198/13, *Julian Hernández and Others*, ECLI:EU:C:2014:2055
C-333/13, *Dano*, ECLI:EU:C:2014:2358
C-417/13, *Öbb Personenverkehr and Others*, ECLI:EU:C:2015:38
C-423/13, *Vilniaus Energija*, ECLI:EU:C:2014:2186
C-463/13, *Stanley International Betting and Others*, ECLI:EU:C:2015:25
C-512/13, *Sopora*, ECLI:EU:C:2015:108
C-530/13, *Schmitzer*, ECLI:EU:C:2014:2359
C-98/14, *Berlington Hungary and Others*, ECLI:EU:2015:386
C-165/14, *Rendón Marín*, ECLI:EU:C:2016:675
C-198/14, *Visnapuu*, ECLI:EU:C:2015:751
C-235/14, *Safe Interenvios*, ECLI:EU:C:2016:154
C-308/14, *Commission v United Kingdom*, ECLI:EU:C:2016:436
C-333/14, *Scotch Whisky Association*, ECLI:EU:C:2015:845
C-354/14, *SC Capoda Import-Export*, ECLI:EU:C:2015:658
C-362/14, *Schrems*, ECLI:EU:C:2015:650
C-374/14, *Attikis*, ECLI:EU:C:2015:582
C-375/14, *Laezza*, ECLI:EU:C:2016:60
C-419/14, *WebMindLicenses*, ECLI:EU:C:2015:832
C-547/14, *Philip Morris Brands and Others*, ECLI:EU:C:2016:325
C-115/15, *NA*, ECLI:EU:C:2016:487
C-122/15, *C*, ECLI:EU:C:2016:391
C-281/15, *Sahyouni*, ECLI:EU:C:2016:343
C-325/15, *Z.Ś. and Others*, ECLI:EU:C:2016:107
C-328/15, *Târşia*, ECLI:EU:C:2016:273
C-520/15, *Aiudapds*, ECLI:EU:C:2016:124

Court of Justice of the European Union: Alphabetical Order

A

A, ECLI:EU:C:2007:804 (C-101/05)
Adeneler and Others, ECLI:EU:C:2006:443(C-212/04)
Adoui and Cornuaille, ECLI:EU:C:1982:183 (115/81 & 116/81)
Aher-Waggon, ECLI:EU:C:1998:357 (C-389/96)
Ahokainen and Leppik, ECLI:EU:C:2006:609 (C-434/04)
Aiudapds, ECLI:EU:C:2016:124 (C-520/15)
Åkerberg Fransson, ECLI:EU:C:2013:105 (C-617/10)
Ålands Vindkraft, ECLI:EU:C:2014:2037 (C-573/12)
Albany, ECLI:EU:C:1999:430 (C-67/96)
Alemo-Herron, ECLI:EU:C:2013:521 (C-426/11)
Alfa Vita Vassilopoulos, ECLI:EU:C:2006:562 (C-158/04 & C-159/04)
Alokpa and Moudoulou, ECLI:EU:C:2013:645 (C-86/12)
Alpine Investments, ECLI:EU:C:1995:126 (C-384/93)
Altmark, ECLI:EU:C:2003:415 (C-280/00)
Ambulanz Glöckner, ECLI:EU:C:2001:577 (C-475/99)
ANAV, ECLI:EU:C:2006:237 (C-410/04)
ANETT, ECLI:EU:C:2012:241 (C-456/10)
Angonese, ECLI:EU:C:2000:296 (C-281/98)
Apothekerkammer des Saarlandes, ECLI:EU:C:2009:316 (C-171/07 & C-171/07)
A-Punkt Schmuckhandel, ECLI:EU:C:2006:141 (C-441/04)
Arblade and Others, ECLI:EU:C:1999:575 (C-369/96 & C-376/96)
ARD, ECLI:EU:C:1999:532 (C-6/98)
Ascafor, ECLI:EU:C:2012:113 (C-484/10)
Asnef–Equifax, ECLI:EU:C:2006:734 (C-238/05)
Asociación Nacional de Empresas Forestales (Asemfo), ECLI:EU:C:2007:227 (C-295/05)
Association Belge and Others, ECLI:EU:C:2011:100 (C-236/09)
Attikis, ECLI:EU:C:2015:582 (C-374/14)
Aubertin and Others, ECLI:EU:C:1995:39 (C-29/94–C-35/94)

B

Bachmann, ECLI:EU:C:1992:35 (C-204/90)
Baldinger, ECLI:EU:C:2004:535 (C-386/02)
BASF, ECLI:EU:C:1999:440 (C-44/98)
BASF, ECLI:EU:T:1999:99 (T-175/95)
Bauer Verlag, ECLI:EU:C:1997:325 (C-368/95)
Berlington Hungary and Others, ECLI:EU:2015:386 (C-98/14)
Bettray, ECLI:EU:C:1989:226 (344/87)

Bickel and Franz, ECLI:EU:C:1998:563 (C-274/96)
Bidar, ECLI:EU:C:2005:169 (C-209/03)
Blaizot, ECLI:EU:C:1988:43 (24/86)
Blanco Pérez and Chao Gómez, ECLI:EU:C:2010:300 (C-570/07 & C-571/07)
Bluhme, ECLI:EU:C:1998:584 (C-67/97)
Bodson, ECLI:EU:C:1988:225 (30/87)
Bonnarde, ECLI:EU:C:2011:641 (C-443/10)
Bosman, ECLI:EU:C:1995:463 (C-415/93)
Brasserie du Pêcheur and Factortame, ECLI:EU:C:1996:79 (C-46/93 & C-48/93)
Brentjens, ECLI:EU:C:1999:434 (C-115/97–C-117/97)
Bressol, ECLI:EU:C:2010:181 (C-73/08)
British American Tobacco, ECLI:EU:C:2002:741(C-491/01)
Burbaud, ECLI:EU:C:2003:432 (C-285/01)
Burmanjer and Others, ECLI:EU:C:2005:307 (C-20/03)

C

C, ECLI:EU:C:2016:391 (C-122/15)
Cadbury Schweppes, ECLI:EU:C:2006:544 (C-196/04)
CaixaBank France, ECLI:EU:C:2004:586 (C-442/02)
Calfa, ECLI:EU:C:1999:6 (C-348/96)
Calì & Figli (SEPG), ECLI:EU:C:1997:160 (C-343/95)
Campus Oil, ECLI:EU:C:1984:256 (72/83)
Canal Satélite Digital, ECLI:EU:C:2002:394 (C-390/99)
Carbonati Apuani, ECLI:EU:C:2004:506 (C-72/03)
Carpenter, ECLI:EU:C:2002:434 (C-60/00)
Casati, ECLI:EU:C:1981:261 (203/80)
Castelli, ECLI:EU:C:1984:280 (261/83)
Caves Krier Frères, ECLI:EU:C:2012:798 (C-379/11)
Centros, ECLI:EU:C:1999:126 (C-212/97)
Cinéthèque, ECLI:EU:C:1985:329 (60/84)
Cipolla, ECLI:EU:C:2006:758 (C-94/04 & C-202/04)
Cisal, ECLI:EU:C:2002:36 (C-218/00)
Coditel, ECLI:EU:C:1980:84 (62/79)
Coditel Brabant, ECLI:EU:C:2008:621 (C-324/07)
Collins, ECLI:EU:C:2004:172 (C-138/02)
Columbus Container Services, ECLI:EU:C:2007:754 (C-298/05)
Commission v. Austria ('Vitamins'), ECLI:EU:C:2004:237 (C-150/00)
Commission v Austria (Ecological Labelling), ECLI:EU:C:2007:722 (C-393/05)
Commission v Austria, ECLI:EU:C:2011:854 (C-28/09)
Commission v Belgium, ECLI:EU:C:1987:81 (221/85)
Commission v Belgium (Walloon waste), ECLI:EU:C:1992:310 (C-2/90)
Commission v Belgium (Private Security), ECLI:EU:C:2000:113 (C-355/98)
Commission v Belgium, ECLI:EU:C:2007:319 (C-254/05)
Commission v. Belgium ('Wild Birds'), ECLI:EU:C:2009:537 (C-100/08)

Commission v Belgium (Posted Workers), ECLI:EU:C:2009:599 (C-219/08)
Commission v Belgium, ECLI:EU:C:2012:539 (C-150/11)
Commission v. Council (ERTA), ECLI:EU:C:1971:32 (22/70)
Commission v. Council, ECLI:EU:C:2010:327 (C-13/07)
Commission v Council, ECLI:EU:C:2013:675 (C-137/12)
Commission v Council, ECLI:EU:C:2014:1903 (C-377/12)
Commission v Denmark, ECLI:EU:C:1986:462 (252/83)
Commission v Denmark, ECLI:EU:C:2003:492 (C-192/01)
Commission v France, ECLI:EU:C:1986:461 (220/83)
Commission v France (Milk Substitutes), ECLI:EU:C:1988:81 (216/84)
Commission v France, ECLI:EU:C:1991:76 (C-154/89)
Commission v France, ECLI:EU:C:1998:495 (C-184/96)
Commission v France, ECLI:EU:C:2000:85 (C-169/98)
Commission v France (Alcoholic Beverages Advertisement), ECLI:EU:C:2004:431 (C-262/02)
Commission v France ('Positive List'), ECLI:EU:C:2010:44 (C-333/08)
Commission v Germany, ECLI:EU:C:1986:463 (205/84)
Commission v Germany, ECLI:EU:C:1987:126 (178/84)
Commission v Germany, ECLI:EU:C:1994:290 (C-131/93)
Commission v Germany (Mineral Water), ECLI:EU:C:2004:797 (C-463/01)
Commission v Germany, ECLI:EU:C:2007:623 (C-112/05)
Commission v Germany, ECLI:EU:C:2007:678 (C-319/05)
Commission v Germany (Ecological Labelling), ECLI:EU:C:2007:723 (C-404/05)
Commission v Germany, ECLI:EU:C:2008:492 (C-141/07)
Commission v Germany (Ambulance Services), ECLI:EU:C:2010:230 (C-160/08)
Commission v Germany, ECLI:EU:C:2010:426 (C-271/08)
Commission v Greece, ECLI:EU:C:1991:79 (C-198/89)
Commission v Greece, ECLI:EU:C:1995:199 (C-391/92)
Commission v Greece (Online Games), ECLI:EU:C:2006:673 (C-65/05)
Commission v Ireland (Buy Irish), ECLI:EU:C:1982:402 (249/81)
Commission v Ireland, ECLI:EU:C:1986:464 (206/84)
Commission v Italy, ECLI:EU:C:1991:78 (C-180/89)
Commission v Italy (Private Security), ECLI:EU:C:2001:307 (C-283/99)
Commission v Italy ('Extrajudicial Debt Recovery'), ECLI:EU:C:2007:435 (C-134/05)
Commission v. Italy ('Private Security Services'), ECLI:EU:C:2007:781 (C-465/05)
Commission v Italy (Car Insurance), ECLI:EU:C:2008:477 (C-518/06)
Commission v Italy (Italian Trailers), ECLI:EU:C:2009:66 (C-110/05)
Commission v. Italy ('Lawyers' Fees'), ECLI:EU:C:2011:188 (C-565/08)
Commission v Lithuania, ECLI:EU:C:2014:172 (C-61/12)
Commission v Luxembourg ('Posted Workers'), ECLI:EU:C:2008:350 (C-319/06)

Commission v Netherlands (Private Security firms), ECLI:EU:C:2004:597 (C-189/03)
Commission v Netherlands, ECLI:EU:C:2007:531 (C-297/05)
Commission v Portugal (Private Securities), ECLI:EU:C:2004:270 (C-171/02)
Commission v Portugal (Tinted Windows), ECLI:EU:C:2008:210 (C-265/06)
Commission v Spain, ECLI:EU:C:1998:519 (C-114/97)
Commission v Spain (Private Security), ECLI:EU:C:2006:63 (C-514/03)
Commission v Spain, ECLI:EU:C:2009:123 (C-88/07)
Commission v Spain (Gambling Tax), ECLI:EU:C:2009:618 (C-153/08)
Commission v Spain, ECLI:EU:C:2011:172 (C-400/08)
Commission v Spain, ECLI:EU:C:2014:218 (C-428/12)
Commission v United Kingdom, ECLI:EU:C:1984:33 (40/82)
Commission v United Kingdom, ECLI:EU:C:2003:273 (C-98/01)
Commission v United Kingdom, ECLI:EU:C:2016:436 (C-308/14)
Consten and Grundig, ECLI:EU:C:1966:19 (56/64 & 58/64)
Corbeau, ECLI:EU:C:1993:198 (C-320/91)
Corporación Dermoestética, ECLI:EU:C:2008:421 (C-500/06)
Corsica Ferries France, ECLI:EU:C:1989:649 (C-49/89)
Corsica Ferries France, ECLI:EU:C:1998:306 (C-266/96)
Corsten, ECLI:EU:C:2000:527 (C-58/98)
Costa v ENEL, ECLI:EU:C:1964:66 (6/64)
Costa and Cifone, ECLI:EU:C:2012:80 (C-72/10 & C-77/10)
Cowan, ECLI:EU:C:1989:47 (186/87)
Crispoltoni II, ECLI:EU:C:1994:364 (C-133/93)
Cristini, ECLI:EU:C:1975:120 (32/75)

D

Daiichi Sankyo, ECLI:EU:C:2013:520 (C-414/11)
Daimler Chrysler, ECLI:EU:C:2001:682 (C-324/99)
Danner, ECLI:EU:C:2002:558 (C-136/00)
Dano, ECLI:EU:C:2014:2358 (C-333/13)
Dassonville, ECLI:EU:C:1974:82 (8/74)
Data-Delecta, ECLI:EU:C:1996:357 (C-43/95)
de Agostini, ECLI:EU:C:1997:344 (C-34/95–C-36/95)
de Peijper, ECLI:EU:C:1976:67 (104/75)
Deak, ECLI:EU:C:1985:264 (94/84)
Deliège, ECLI:EU:C:2000:199 (C-51/96 & C-191/97)
Den Danske Bilimportører, ECLI:EU:C:2003:352 (C-383/01)
Denkavit Loire, ECLI:EU:C:1979:139 (132/78)
Dereci and Others, ECLI:EU:C:2011:734 (C-256/11)
Deserbais, ECLI:EU:C:1988:434 (286/86)
D'Hoop, ECLI:EU:C:2002:432 (C-224/98)
Dickinger and Ömer, ECLI:EU:C:2011:582 (C-347/09)
Digital Rights Ireland, ECLI:EU:C:2014:238 (C-293/12 & C-594/12)
Dior and Others, ECLI:EU:C:2000:688 (C-300/98 & C-392/98)

DocMorris, ECLI:EU:C:2003:664 (C-322/01)
Dos Santos Palhota, ECLI:EU:C:2010:589 (C-515/08)
Drei Glocken, ECLI:EU:C:1988:401 (407/85)
Drijvende, ECLI:EU:C:1999:437 (C-219/97)
Dynamic Medien, ECLI:EU:C:2008:85 (C-244/06)
Dzodzi, ECLI:EU:C:1990:360 (C-297/88 & C-197/89)

E

ED, ECLI:EU:C:1999:324 (C-412/97)
Eddline El-Yassini, ECLI:EU:C:1999:107 (C-416/96)
Elenca, ECLI:EU:C:2012:634 (C-385/10)
ERT v DEP, ECLI:EU:C:1991:254 (C-260/89)
Esso Española, ECLI:EU:C:1995:414 (C-134/94)

F

Fachverband, ECLI:EU:C:2009:276 (C-531/07)
Fedesa and Others, ECLI:EU:C:1990:391 (C-331/88)
Finalarte and Others, ECLI:EU:C:2001:564 (C-49/98, C-50/98, C-52/98, C-54/98, & C-68/98–C-71/98)
Forcheri, ECLI:EU:C:1983:205 (152/82)
Fornasar and Others, ECLI:EU:C:2000:337 (C-318/98)
Fra.bo SpA, ECLI:EU:C:2012:453 (C-171/11)
Frascogna, ECLI:EU:C:1985:243 (157/84)
Freskot AE, ECLI:EU:C:2003:298 (C-355/00)
Futura Participations and Singer, ECLI:EU:C:1997:239 (C-250/95)

G

Gambelli, ECLI:EU:C:2003:597 (C-243/01)
Garcia Avello, ECLI:EU:C:2003:539 (C-148/02)
Gebhard, ECLI:EU:C:1995:411 (C-55/94)
Gemeente Almelo, ECLI:EU:C:1994:171 (C-393/92)
Gilli and Andres, ECLI:EU:C:1980:171 (788/79)
Gottwald, ECLI:EU:C:2009:597 (C-103/08)
Gouda, ECLI:EU:C:1991:323 (C-288/89)
Gourmet International Products, ECLI:EU:C:2001:135 (C-405/98)
Graf, ECLI:EU:C:2000:49 (C-190/98)
Gravier, ECLI:EU:C:1985:69 (293/83)
Grilli, ECLI:EU:C:2003:538 (C-12/02)
Groenveld, ECLI:EU:C:1979:253 (15/79)
Guarnieri & Cie, ECLI:EU:C:2011:217 (C-291/09)
Gueye and Salmerón Sánchez, ECLI:EU:C:2011:583 (C-483/09 & C-1/10)
Guimont, ECLI:EU:C:2000:663 (C-448/98)
Gysbrechts and Santurel, ECLI:EU:C:2008:730 (C-205/07)

H

Halifax, ECLI:EU:C:2006:121 (C-255/02)
Hartlauer, ECLI:EU:C:2009:141 (C-169/07)
Hauer, ECLI:EU:C:1979:290 (44/79)
Hermès International, ECLI:EU:C:1998:292 (C-53/96)
Heylens, ECLI:EU:C:1987:442 (222/86)
Huber, ECLI:EU:C:2008:724 (C-524/06)
Humanplasma, ECLI:EU:C:2010:760 (C-421/09)
Hünermund and Others, ECLI:EU:C:1993:932 (C-292/92)
Hurd v Jones, ECLI:EU:C:1986:2 (44/84)

I

ICI v United Kingdom, ECLI:EU:C:1998:370 (C-264/96)
Iida, ECLI:EU:C:2012:691 (C-40/11)
Inspire Art, ECLI:EU:C:2003:512 (C-167/01)
International Fruit Company, ECLI:EU:C:1972:115 (21/72–24/72)
Internationale Handelsgesellschaft, ECLI:EU:C:1970:114 (11/70)
Inzirillo, ECLI:EU:C:1976:192 (63/76)

J

Jégo-Quéré, ECLI:EU:T:2002:112 (T-177/01)
Josemans, ECLI:EU:C:2010:744 (C-137/09)
Julian Hernández and Others, ECLI:EU:C:2014:2055 (C-198/13)

K

Kamberaj, ECLI:EU:C:2012:233 (C-571/10)
Karlsson, ECLI:EU:C:2000:202 (C-292/97)
Karner, ECLI:EU:C:2004:181 (C-71/02)
Kattner Stahlbau, ECLI:EU:C:2009:127 (C-350/07)
Keck and Mithouard, ECLI:EU:C:1993:905 (C-267/91 & C-268/91)
Kelderman, ECLI:EU:C:1981:49 (130/80)
Ker-Optika, ECLI:EU:C:2010:725 (C-108/09)
Köhll, ECLI:EU:C:1998:171 (C-158/96)
Konle, ECLI:EU:C:1999:271 (C-302/97)
Konstantinidis, ECLI:EU:C:1993:115 (C-168/91)
Krantz, ECLI:EU:C:1994:296 (C-69/88)
Kranemann, ECLI:EU:C:2005:187 (C-109/04)
Kücükdeveci, ECLI:EU:C:2010:21 (C-555/07)

L

Läärä, ECLI:EU:C:1999:435 (C-124/97)
Ladbrokes Betting & Gaming, ECLI:EU:C:2010:308 (C-258/08)
Laezza, ECLI:EU:C:2016:60 (C-375/14)
Lahousse and Lavichy, ECLI:EU:C:2010:694 (C-142/09)

Lancry, ECLI:EU:C:1994:315 (C-363/93, C-407/93–C-411/93)
Lankhorst-Hohorst, ECLI:EU:C:2002:749 (C-324/00)
Laval un Partneri, ECLI:EU:C:2007:809 (C-341/05)
Lecler-Siplec, ECLI:EU:C:1995:26 (C-412/93)
Levin, ECLI:EU:C:1982:105 (53/81)
Libertao, ECLI:EU:C:2013:288 (C-197/11 & C-203/11)
Liga Portuguesa, ECLI:EU:C:2009:519 (C-42/07)
Lindberg, ECLI:EU:C:2005:246 (C-267/03)
Lindman, ECLI:EU:C:2003:613 (C-42/02)
Ludwigs-Apotheke, ECLI:EU:C:2007:656 (C-143/06)

M

Mangold, ECLI:EU:C:2005:709 (C-144/04)
Marks & Spencer, ECLI:EU:C:2005:763 (C-446/03)
Martínez Sala, ECLI:EU:C:1998:217 (C-85/96)
Mathot, ECLI:EU:C:1987:89 (98/86)
Mazzoleni, ECLI:EU:C:2001:162 (C-165/98)
McCarthy, ECLI:EU:C:2011:277 (C-434/09)
Meca-Medina and Majcen, ECLI:EU:C:2006:492 (C-519/04 P)
Merck Genéricos, ECLI:EU:C:2007:496 (C-431/05)
Metro SB-Großmärkte, ECLI:EU:C:1977:167 (26/76)
M.G., ECLI:EU:C:2014:9 (C-400/12)
Mickelsson and Roos, ECLI:EU:C:2009:336 (C-142/05)
Mignini, ECLI:EU:C:1992:173 (C-256/90)
Milk Marque, ECLI:EU:C:2003:429 (C-137/00)
Monte Arcosu, ECLI:EU:C:2001:6 (C-403/98)
Morellato, ECLI:EU:C:2003:475 (C-416/00)
MRAX, ECLI:EU:C:2002:461 (C-459/99)
Müller-Fauré, ECLI:EU:C:2003:270 (C-385/99)

N

N, ECLI:EU:C:2006:525 (C-470/04)
NA, ECLI:EU:C:2016:487 (C-115/15)
Nertsvoederfabriek, ECLI:EU:C:1987:424 (118/86)
Nold, ECLI:EU:C:1974:51 (4/73)

O

Öbb Personenverkehr and Others, ECLI:EU:C:2015:38 (C-417/13)
Omega, ECLI:EU:C:2004:614 (C-36/02)
Onuekwere, ECLI:EU:C:2014:13 (C-378/12)
Orange European Smallcap Fund, ECLI:EU:C:2008:289 (C-194/06)

P

Parking Brixen, ECLI:EU:C:2005:605 (C-458/03)
Parliament v Council of the European Union, ECLI:EU:C:2006:429 (C-540/03)

Paul Denuit, ECLI:EU:C:1997:260 (C-14/96)
Pelckmans Turnhout, ECLI:EU:C:2014:304 (C-483/12)
Pequeños Agricultores, ECLI:EU:C:2002:462 (C-50/00)
Peralta, ECLI:EU:C:1994:296 (C-379/92)
Pfleger and Others, ECLI:EU:C:2014:281 (C-390/12)
Phil Collins, ECLI:EU:C:1993:847 (C-92/92 & C-326/92)
Philip Morris Brands and Others, ECLI:EU:C:2016:325 (C-547/14)
Placanica and Others, ECLI:EU:C:2007:133 (C-338/04, C-359/04 & C-360/04)
Portugaia Construçoes, ECLI:EU:C:2002:40 (C-164/99)
Poucet and Pistre, ECLI:EU:C:1993:63 (C-159/91 & C-160/91)
Pringle, ECLI:EU:C:2012:756 (C-370/12)
Pusa, ECLI:EU:C:2004:273 (C-224/02)

R

Radiosistemi, ECLI:EU:C:2002:390 (C-388/00 & C-429/00)
Reisch and Others, ECLI:EU:C:2002:135 (C-515/99, C-519/99–C-524/99 & C-526/99–C-540/99)
Rendón Marín, ECLI:EU:C:2016:675 (C-165/14)
Renneberg, ECLI:EU:C:2008:566 (C-527/06)
Rewe-Zentral (Cassis de Dijon), ECLI:EU:C:1979:42 (120/78)
Reyners, ECLI:EU:C: 1974:68 (2/74)
Ritter-Coulais, ECLI:EU:C:2006:123 (C-152/03)
Rosengren and Others, ECLI:EU:C:2007:313 (C-170/04)
Rottmann, ECLI:EU:C:2010:104 (C-135/08)
Royer, ECLI:EU:C:1976:57 (48/75)
Rüffert, ECLI:EU:C2008:189 (C-346/06)
Rüffler, ECLI:EU:C:2009:258 (C-544/07)
Ruiz Zambrano, ECLI:EU:C:2011:124 (C 34/09)
Rush Portuguesa, ECLI:EU:C:1990:142 (C-113/89)

S

SAE, ECLI:EU:C:1991:327 (C-1/90 & C-176/90)
Safe Interenvios, ECLI:EU:C:2016:154 (C-235/14)
Safir, ECLI:EU:C:1998:170 (C-118/96)
Säger, ECLI:EU:C:1991:331 (C-76/90)
Sahyouni, ECLI:EU:C:2016:343 (C-281/15)
Sandström, ECLI:EU:C:2010:184 (C-433/05)
Sanz de Lera, ECLI:EU:C:1995:451 (C-163/94, C-165/94 & C-250/94)
SAT Fluggesellschaft v Eurocontrol, ECLI:EU:C:1994:7 (C-364/92)
Saunders, ECLI:EU:C:1979:88 (175/78)
Sayn-Wittgenstein, ECLI:EU:C:2010:806 (C-208/09)
SC Capoda Import-Export, ECLI:EU:C:2015:658 (C-354/14)
Schindler, ECLI:EU:C:1994:119 (C-275/92)
Schmidberger, ECLI:EU:C:2003:333 (C-112/00)
Schmitzer, ECLI:EU:C:2014:2359 (C-530/13)

Schrems, ECLI:EU:C:2015:650 (C-362/14)
Schröder, ECLI:EU:C:2000:72 (C-50/96)
Schwarz, ECLI:EU:C:2005:719 (C-366/04)
Schwarz, ECLI:EU:C:2007:492 (C-76/05)
Scotch Whisky Association, ECLI:EU:C:2015:845 (C-333/14)
SECAP and Santorso, ECLI:EU:C:2008:277 (C-147/06 & C-148/06)
Seco v EVI, ECLI:EU:C:1982:34 (62/81 & 63/81)
Semeraro Casa Uno, ECLI:EU:C:1996:242 (C-418/93)
SELEX, ECLI:EU:C:2009:461 (C-481/07 P)
SETTG v Ypourgos Erasias, ECLI:EU:C:1997:282 (C-398/95)
SGS Belgium and Others, ECLI:EU:C:2010:648 (C-367/09)
Sjøberg and Gerdin, ECLI:EU:C:2010:415 (C-447/08 & C-448/08)
Skandia, ECLI:EU:C:2003:380 (C-422/01)
Sky Italia, ECLI:EU:C:2013:496 (C-234/12)
Sky Österreich, ECLI:EU:C:2013:28 (C-283/11)
Sodemare SA, ECLI:EU:C:1997:301 (C-70/95)
Sopora, ECLI:EU:C:2015:108 (C-512/13)
Smits and Peerbooms, ECLI:EU:C:2001:404 (C-157/99)
Stadt Halle and RPL Lochau, ECLI:EU:C:2005:5 (C-26/03)
Stanley International Betting and Others, ECLI:EU:C:2015:25 (C-463/13)
Stark v DAS, ECLI:EU:C:2011:355 (C-293/10)
Stauder, ECLI:EU:C:1969:57 (29/69)
Steinhauser, ECLI:EU:C:1985:260 (197/84)
Stoke-on-Trent, ECLI:EU:C:1992:519 (C-169/91)
Stölting, ECLI:EU:C:1979:46 (138/78)
Stoß, ECLI:EU:C:2010:504 (C-316/07, C-358/07–C-360/07 & C-409/07–C-410/07)

T

Târşia, ECLI:EU:C:2016:273 (C-328/15)
Terhoeve, ECLI:EU:C:1999:22 (C-18/95)
Thieffry, ECLI:EU:C:1977:65 (71/76)
TK Heimdienst, ECLI:EU:C:2000:12 (C-254/98)
Toolex, ECLI:EU:C:2000:379 (C-473/98)
Torfaen Borough Council, ECLI:EU:C:1989:593 (C-145/88)
Tulliasiamies, ECLI:EU:C:2002:505 (C-101/00)

U

UAB Juvelta, ECLI:EU:C:2014:11 (C-481/12)
Unibet, ECLI:EU:C:2007:163 (C-432/05)

V

van Binsbergen, ECLI:EU:C:1974:131 (33/74)
van de Haar, ECLI:EU:C:1984:144 (177/82)
Van Gend en Loos, ECLI:EU:C:1963:1 (26/62)

van Wesemael, ECLI:EU:C:1979:8 (110/78 & 111/78)
Viacom II, ECLI:EU:C:2005:94 (C-134/03)
Viking, ECLI:EU:C:2007:772 (C-438/05)
Vilniaus Energija, ECLI:EU:C:2014:2186 (C-423/13)
Visnapuu, ECLI:EU:C:2015:751 (C-198/14)

W

Walloon (*Flemish Care Insurance Scheme*), ECLI:EU:C:2008:178 (C-212/06)
Walrave, ECLI:EU:C:1974:140 (36/74)
Watts, ECLI:EU:C:2006:325 (C-372/04)
Webb, ECLI:EU:C:1981:314 (279/80)
WebMindLicenses, ECLI:EU:C:2015:832 (C-419/14)
Weigel, ECLI:EU:C:2004:256 (C-387/01)
Werner, ECLI:EU:C:1993:27 (C-112/91)
Wijsenbeek, ECLI:EU:C:1999:439 (C-378/97)
Wood, ECLI:EU:C:2008:321 (C-164/07)
Wouters, ECLI:EU:C:2002:98 (C-309/99)

X

X, ECLI:EU:C:2014:2459 (C-87/13)

Y

Ymeraga and Ymeraga-Tafarshiku, ECLI:EU:C:2013:291 (C-87/12)

Z

Zablocka-Weyhermüller, ECLI:EU:C:2008:681 (C-221/07)
Zenatti, ECLI:EU:C:1999:514 (C-67/98)
Zhu and Chen, ECLI:EU:C:2004:639 (C-200/02)
Z.Ś. and Others, ECLI:EU:C:2016:107 (C-325/15)

International Court of Justice

LaGrand (Germany v. *United States of America), Judgment,* I.C.J. Reports 2001

Regional Courts

European Court of Human Rights

Goodwin v. *UK* [2002] 35 EHRR 18
Rees v United Kingdom (1987) 9 EHRR 56

National Courts

Denmark

Ugeskrift for Retsvæsen 2011.539 H

United Kingdom

Countryside Alliance and others v. HM Attorney General [2006] EWCA Civ 817
R (on the application of Robertson) v. Wakefield MDC [2002] QB 1052, 170

United States of America

Aaron B Cooley, Plaintiff in Error, v The Board of Wardens of the Port of Philadelphia, to the use of the Society for the Relief of distressed Pilots, their Widows and Children, Defendants (1851) 53 US (12 How) 299
Accord, Erb v Morasch (1900) 177 US 584
Baldwin, Commissioner of Agriculture & (and) Markets, et al v G A F Seelig, Inc (1949) 294 US 511
C & A Carbone, Inc v Town of Clarkstown (1994) 511 US 383
Chemical Waste Management, Inc v Hunt (1992) 504 US 334
Chicago, Rock Island & Pacific Railway Company v Arkansas (1911) 219 US 453
Commonwealth Edison Co v Montana (1981) 101 SCt 2946
Dean Milk Co v City of Madison (1951) 340 US 349
Department of Revenue v Davis (2008) 553 US
DiSanto v Pennsylvania (1927) 273 US 34
Garcia v San Antonio Metropolitan Transit Authority (1985) 469 US 528
Gibbons v Ogden (1824) 22 US 1
Hannibal & St J R Co v Husen (1878) 95 US (5 Otto) 465
H P Hood & (and) Sons, Inc v Du Mond, Commissioner of Agriculture and Markets (1949) 336 US 525
Kassel v Consolidated Freightways Corp (1981) 450 US 662
Kidd v Pearson (1888) 128 US 1

Maine v Taylor (1986) 477 US 131
McBurney v Young (2013) 569 US
McCulloch v Maryland (1819) 17 US (4 Wheat) 316
Morgan's Louisiana & TR & SS Co v Louisiana Board of Health (1886) 118 US 455
New Energy Co of Indiana v Limbach (1988) 486 US 269
Parker v Brown (1943) 317 US 341
Philadelphia v New Jersey (1978) 437 US 617
Pike v Bruce Church Inc (1970) 397 US 137
Pound v Turck (1877) 95 US (5 Otto) 459
Seaboard Air Line Railway v Blackwell (1917) 244 US 310
Smith v Alabama (1888) 124 US 465
Southern Pacific Co v Arizona ex rel Sullivan, Attorney General (1945) 325 US 761
The Licence Cases (1847) 46 US 504
The Passenger Cases (1849) 48 US 283
Towne v Eisner (1918) 245 US 418
United Haulers Association, Inc, et al v Oneida-Herkimer Solid Waste Management Authority et al (2007) 550 US
Wabash, St Louis and Pacific Railway Company v Illinois (1886) 118 US 557
West Lynn Creamery, Inc v Healy (1994) 512 US 186
Willson v Black-Bird Creek Marsh Co (1829) 27 US (2 Pet) 245

MIX
Papier aus verantwortungsvollen Quellen
Paper from responsible sources
FSC® C105338

If you have any concerns about our products,
you can contact us on
ProductSafety@springernature.com

In case Publisher is established outside the EU,
the EU authorized representative is:
Springer Nature Customer Service Center GmbH
Europaplatz 3, 69115 Heidelberg, Germany

Printed by Libri Plureos GmbH
in Hamburg, Germany